Cases and Readings

for use with

Cost Management

Second Edition

Edward J. Blocher
University of North Carolina

Kung H. Chen
University of Nebraska

Thomas W. Lin
University of Southern California

 **McGraw-Hill**
Irwin

Boston   Burr Ridge, IL   Dubuque, IA   Madison, WI   New York   San Francisco   St. Louis
Bangkok   Bogotá   Caracas   Kuala Lumpur   Lisbon   London   Madrid   Mexico City
Milan   Montreal   New Delhi   Santiago   Seoul   Singapore   Sydney   Taipei   Toronto

McGraw-Hill Higher Education

A Division of The McGraw·Hill Companies

Cases and Readings for use with
COST MANAGEMENT: A STRATEGIC EMPHASIS
Edward J. Blocher, Kung H. Chen, Thomas W. Lin

Published by McGraw-Hill/Irwin, an imprint of the McGraw-Hill Companies, Inc., 1221 Avenue of
the Americas, New York, NY 10020. Copyright © 2002, 1999 by the McGraw-Hill Companies, Inc.
All rights reserved.

1 2 3 4 5 6 7 8 9 0 CUS/CUS 0 9 8 7 6 5 4 3 2 1

ISBN 0-07-249883-8

www.mhhe.com

Preface

To extend the teaching materials of *Cost Management: A Strategic Emphasis*, this casebook provides additional cases and articles for each chapter. The cases and articles are an important part of the text and have the same teaching objectives. The problem material in the text includes short cases and exercises, while this casebook provides longer cases and articles to facilitate more extensive discussion and analysis.

We feel that cases serve a very important role in the cost management course. We know of many faculty who use cases from a variety of sources to supplement the text they are using. We have provided these materials in this book for easier access, greater convenience, and lower overall cost to the instructor and student.

Using cases has two important benefits. First, the use of a case requires the student to develop analytical skills by organizing the unstructured information in the case, devising appropriate analyses, and drawing appropriate conclusions. Second, the cases permit a more thorough strategic analysis of a given firm than would be possible with a problem or exercise. With a richer amount of information about the case firm and its environment, the student can more effectively apply the concepts of strategy and competitive advantage explained in chapter 2: Strategic Analysis and Strategic Cost Management.

Each of the cases can be used as an exercise in competitive analysis to set the stage for the decision problem in the case, whatever that might be. A firm facing a lease-or-buy decision will want to assess the strategic, competitive situation of the firm before making the decision. Similarly, a firm considering the outsourcing of a department or activity will want to begin the analysis with an assessment of the strategic issues facing the firm, and then to make the outsourcing decision with these issues in mind. In this way, the cases can be used to effectively put each decision problem in a strategic context. Rather than to make a cost calculation and then "consider the qualitative factors," which can be done with problems and exercises, the case more readily allows an approach in which the strategic issues are considered first and are an integral part of the solution of the case.

One or two articles are included for each chapter to provide an opportunity for more in-depth coverage. We have included discussion questions for each article. Some of the articles are examples of how actual firms have implemented the cost management methods explained in the chapter. These stories show some of the implementation issues that arise in practical situations. Other articles report the results of surveys, which provides a perspective for how the cost management methods are used in practice. Others have a technical focus, and provide an opportunity to look more closely at the methods explained in the chapter and on the effects of using the methods.

We hope you will find these cases and readings helpful. We welcome feedback from students and instructors.

Edward J. Blocher
Kung H. Chen
Thomas W. Lin

Acknowledgments

The following materials have been reprinted with permission from the **Institute of Management Accountants** (© Copyright by Institute of Management Accountants, Montvale, NJ):

Management Accounting

Mike Anastas, "The Changing World of Management Accounting and Financial Management," October 1997. (Reading 1-1)

Jack Bailes, James Nielsen, Stephen Lawton, "How Forest Product Companies Analyze Capital Budgets," October 1998. (Reading 11-1)

Chee W. Chow, Kamal M. Haddad, James E. Williamson, "Applying the Balanced Scorecard to Small Companies," August 1997. (Reading 2-2)

Steve Coburn, Hugh Grove, Tom Cook, "How ABC was Used in Capital Budgeting," May 1997. (Reading 11-2)

Stephen Crow, Eugene Sauls, "Setting the Regent Transfer Price," December 1994. (Reading 19-1)

Nick Fera, "Using Shareholder Value to Evaluate Strategic Choice," November 1997. (Reading 20-1)

David R. Fordhan, S. Brooks Marshall, "Tools for Dealing with Uncertainty," September 1997. (Reading 8-1)

Robert S. Kaplan, Dan Weiss, Eyal Desheh, "Transfer Pricing with ABC," May 1997. (Reading 19-3)

Gerald H. Lander, Mohamed E. Bayou, "Does ROI Apply to Robotic Factories?". (Reading 19-2)

Peter J. Leitner, "Beyond the Numbers," May 1998. (Reading 20-2)

Kenneth A. Merchant, "How Challenging Should Profit Budget Targets Be?" (Reading 9-2)

Adel M. Novin, "How to Find the Right Bases and Rates," March 1992. (Reading 7-1)

George Schmelze, Rolf Geier, Thomas El Buttross, "Target Costing at ITT Automotive," December 1996. (Reading 5-1)

Bonnie P. Stivers, Teresa Joyce Covin, Nancy Green Hall, Steve W. Smalt, "How Nonfinancial Performance Measures are Used," February 1998. (Reading 2-1)

Dan W. Swenson, "Managing Costs Through Complexity Reduction at Carrier Corporation," April 1998. (Reading 3-1)

Robert N. West, Amy N. Snyder, "How to Set Up a Budgeting and Planning System," January 1997. (Reading 9-1)

Management Accounting Quarterly

Charles D. Bailey, "Estimation of Production Costs and Labor Hours Using a Free Excel Add-In," Summer 2000. (Reading 7-2)

William J. Cenker, Robert Bloom, "The Leasing Conundrum," Spring 2000. (Reading 10-1)

Anthony J. Hayzen, James M. Reeve, "Examining the Relationships in Productivity Accounting," Summer 2000. (Reading 17-2)

David Johnsen, Parvez Sopariwala, "Standard Costing is Alive and Well at Parker Brass," Winter 2000. (Reading 15-1)

Harper A. Roehm, Larry Weinstein, Joseph F. Castellano, "Management Control Systems: How SPC Enhances Budgeting and Standard Costing," Fall 2000. (Reading 15-2)

Kennard T. Wing, "Using Enhanced Cost Models in Variance Analysis for Better Control and Decision Making," Winter 2000. (Reading 16-1)

Strategic Finance

Terrell L. Carter, Ali Ml Sedghat, Thomas D. Williams, "How ABC Changed the Post Office," February 1998. (Reading 4-1)

C.S. Kulesza, Keith Russell, Gary H. Siegel, "Counting More, Counting Less," September 1999. (Reading 1-2)

Gregory T. Lucier, Sridhar Seshadri, "GE Takes Six Sigma Beyond the Bottom Line," May 2001. (Reading 6-1)

Joseph A. Ness, Michael J. Schroeck, Rick A. Letendre, Willmar J. Douglas, "The Role of ABM in Measuring Customer Value: Parts I and II," March and April 2001. (Reading 17-3)

Jon Scheumann, "Why Isn't the Controller Having More Impact?" April 1999. (Reading 1-3)

Richard H. Snyder, "How I Reengineered a Small Business," May 1999. (Reading 12-1)

Nancy Thurley Hill, Kevin T. Stevens, "Structuring Compensation to Achieve Better Financial Results," March 2001. (Reading 20-3)

Ann Triplett, Jon Scheumann, "Managing Shared Services with ABM," February 2000. (Reading 14-2)

Cases from Management Accounting in Practice

Volume 1 (1985): The Pump Division (Case 7-2)

Volume 2 (1986): The Atlantic City Casino (Case 2-1), Analysis of the Accounting Function (Case 18-1) Polymer Products Company (Case 19-1)

Volume 4 (1987): Industrial Chemical Company (Case 18-2)

Volume 5 (1989): The Rossford Plant (Case 13-2), Tektronics, Inc. (Case 4-3), The United L/N Plant (Case 13-3)

Volume 6 (1992): Superior Valve Company (Case 10-4)

Volume 7 (1992): Toll Revenue Sharing (Case 14-1)

Volume 8 (1992): California Illini Manufacturing (Case 5-1)

Volumes 10/11 (1997): East River Manufacturing (Case 12-3), Kenco Engineering (Case 13-1), Standard Soap Corporation (Case 12-2)

Volume 12 (1998): Brookwood Medical Center, prepared by Thomas L. Albright and Robin Cooper (Case 14-1), MosCo Inc. (Case 4-2), Precision System Inc. (Case 6-1)

Volume 14 (1998): OutSource, Inc., prepared by Paul A. Dierks (Case 20-3)

Volume 15 (2000): Mercedes-Benz All Activity Vehicle (AAV) (Case 5-4)

The following materials have been reprinted with permission from the **American Accounting Association**:

Accounting Horizons

Wilton L. Accola, "Assessing Risk and Uncertainty in New Technology Investments," September 1994. (Reading 11-3).

Carole B. Cheatham, Leo R. Cheatham, "Redesigning Cost Systems: Is Standard Costing Obsolete?" December 1996. (Reading 15-3)

Robert S. Kaplan, David P. Norton, "Transforming the Balanced Scorecard from Performance Measurement to Strategic Management: Part 1," March 2001. (Reading 18-1)

Robert E. Malcolm, "Overhead Control Implications of Activity Costing," December 1991. (Reading 16-3)

Issues in Accounting Education

Ramji Balakrishnan, Utpal Bhattacharya, "Ace Company (B): The Option Value of Waiting and Capital Budgeting," Fall 1997. (Case 11-5)

Robert Capettini, C.W. Chow, J.E. Williamson, "Instructional Case: The Proper Use of Feedback Information," Spring 1992. (Case 16-2)

Chee W. Chow, "Instructional Case: Vincent's Cappuccino Express – A Teaching Case to Help Students Master Basic Cost Terms and Concepts Through Interactive Learning," Spring 1995. (Case 3-1)

Chee W. Chow, Yuhchang, Dennis F. Togo, "Ace Company: A Case for Incorporating Competitive Consideration into Teaching of Capital Budgeting," Fall 1995. (Case 11-2)

Dean Crawford, Eleanor G. Henry, "Budgeting and Performance Evaluation at the Berkshire Toy Company," May 2000. (Case 16-1)

Vijay Govindarajan, John K. Shank, "Profit Variance Analysis: A Strategic Focus," Fall 1989. (Reading 17-1)

Julie H. Hertenstein, "Component Technologies, Inc.: Adding Flexconnex Capacity," May 2000. (Case 11-4)

Alison Hubbard Ashton, Robert H. Ashton, Laureen Maines, "Instructional Case: General Medical Center -- Evaluation of Diagnostic Imaging Equipment," November 1998. (Case 11-5)

Jack M. Ruhl, Jerry G. Kreuze, "Startup, Inc.: Linking Financial Accounting, Managerial Accounting, and Strategic Management," Fall 1997. (Case 2-3).

George J. Staubus, "The Case of the Almost Identical Twins," Spring 1993. (Case 11-1)

Additional Acknowledgements:

Robert N. Anthony, "Baldwin Bicycle Case." Reprinted with permission. (Case 10-3)

Edward J. Blocher, Kevin Fox, "Cost Volume Profit Analysis and Strategy: The ALLTEL Pavilion." Reprinted with permission. (Case 8-4)

Robert J. Bowlby, "How Boeing Tracks Costs A to Z," *The Financial Executive*. Reprinted with permission. (Reading 13-1)

Jean C. Cooper, James D. Suver, "Variance Analysis Refines Overhead Cost Control," *Healthcare Financial Management*. Reprinted with permission. (Reading 16-2)

David A. Kunz, Keith A. Russell, "Midwest Petro-Chemical Company," Institute of Management Accountants, 1996. Used with permission. (Case 20-1)

Thomas W. Lin, Kenneth A. Merchant, "China Huaneng Group." Reprinted with permission. (Case 20-5)

Joseph San Miguel, "Target Costing" (Case 5-3), "Emerson Electric Company" (Case 9-1), "Dallas Consulting Group" (Case 17-1). Reprinted with permission.

Dennis P. Tishlias, "Reasonable Joint Cost Allocations in Nonprofits," *The Journal of Accountancy*. Reprinted with permission. (Reading 14-1)

Table of Contents

Chapter 1	**Cost Management: An Overview**	**1-1**
Case 1-1	Critical Success Factors	1-2
Case 1-2	Contemporary Management Techniques	1-3
Case 1-3	Pricing	1-4
Case 1-4	Selected Ethics Cases	1-5
	The Changing World of Management Accounting and Financial Management	1-6
	Counting More, Counting Less	1-10
	Why Isn't The Controller Having More Impact	1-16
Chapter 2	**Strategic Analysis and Strategic Cost Management**	**2-1**
Case 2-1	Atlantic City Casino (Value Chain Analysis)	2-2
Case 2-2	Strategic Analysis	2-5
Case 2-3	Business Strategy	2-6
Case 2-4	Strategic Analysis	2-10
	How Nonfinancial Performance Measures are Used	2-11
	Applying the Balanced Scorecard to Small Companies	2-16
Chapter 3	**Basic Cost Concepts**	**3-1**
Case 3-1	Strategy, CSFs, Cost Objects, and Performance Measures	3-2
Case 3-2	Cost Drivers and Strategy	3-3
	Managing Costs Through Complexity Reduction at Carrier Corporation	3-4
Chapter 4	**Activity-Based Costing and Management**	**4-1**
Case 4-1	Blue Ridge Manufacturing (Activity-Based Costing for Marketing Channels)	4-2
Case 4-2	MosCo, Inc. (Activity-Based Management)	4-7
Case 4-3	Tektronix (Activity-Based Costing for Production Process Changes)	4-29
	How ABC Changed the Post Office	4-33

Chapter 5	**Target Costing, Theory of Constraints, and Life Cycle Costing**	**5-1**
Case 5-1	California-Illini Manufacturing (The Theory of Constraints)	5-2
Case 5-2	Blue Ridge Manufacturing (B)..	5-8
Case 5-3	Target Costing	5-9
Case 5-4	Mercedes-Benz All Activity Vehicle (AAV)..	5-10
	Target Costing at ITT Automotive	5-15
Chapter 6	**Total Quality Management**	**6-1**
Case 6-1	Precision Systems, Inc..	6-2
	GE Takes Six Sigma Beyond the Bottom Line	6-7
Chapter 7	**Cost Estimation**..	**7-1**
Case 7-1	The High-Low Method and Regression Analysis..	7-2
Case 7-2	The Pump Division (Cost Estimation)	7-3
Case 7-3	Laurent Products (Cost Estimation, Activity-Based Costing).................................	7-5
Case 7-4	Custom Photography (Regression Analysis)...	7-9
	Applying Overhead: How to Find the Right Bases and Rates	7-10
	Estimation of Production Costs and Labor Hours Using a Free Excel Add-In	7-14
Chapter 8	**Cost-Volume-Profit Analysis**	**8-1**
Case 8-1	Cost-Volume-Profit Analysis and Strategy...	8-2
Case 8-2	Cost-Volume-Profit Analysis and Cost Estimation...	8-3
Case 8-3	Cost-Volume-Profit Analysis and Strategy...	8-4
Case 8-4	Cost-Volume-Profit Analysis and Strategy: The ALLTEL Pavilion........................	8-6
Case 8-5	Sensitivity Analysis; Regression Analysis..	8-16
	Tools for Dealing with Uncertainty	8-17
Chapter 9	**Strategy and the Master Budget**..	**9-1**
Case 9-1	Emerson Electric company	9-2
	How to Set Up a Budgeting and Planning System	9-16
	How Challenging Should Profit Budget Targets Be?..	9-23

Chapter 10 **Decision Making with Relevant Costs and Strategic Analysis** 10-1

Case 10-1   Decision Making Under Uncertainty 10-2
Case 10-2   Profitability Analysis 10-4
Case 10-3   Baldwin Bicycle Company 10-6
Case 10-4   The Superior Valve Division 10-10
Case 10-5   OmniSports Inc. 10-14

            The Leasing Conundrum 10-16

Chapter 11 **Capital Budgeting** 11-1

Case 11-1   The Case of the Almost Identical Twins 11-3
Case 11-2   ACE Company (A) 11-5
Case 11-3   Ace Company (B) 11-7
Case 11-4   Component Technologies, Inc.: Adding Flexconnex Capacity 11-10
Case 11-5   General Medical Center 11-15

            How Forest Product Companies Analyze Capital Budgets 11-24
            How ABC Was Used in Capital Budgeting 11-29
            Assessing Risk and Uncertainty in New Technology Investments 11-37

Chapter 12 **Job Costing** 12-1

Case 12-1   Constructo Inc. (Under or Over-Applied Overhead) 12-2
Case 12-2   Standard Soap Corp. (Traditional Job Costing Versus ABC Job Costing) 12-4
Case 12-3   East River Manufacturing (A) (Problems of Traditional Job Costing) 12-18

            How I Reengineered A Small Business 12-29

Chapter 13 **Process Costing** 13-1

Case 13-1   Kenco Engineering Corp. (A) (A Hybrid Job and Process Costing) 13-2
Case 13-2   The Rossford Plant (Two Production Processes with the Traditional Volume-
            Based Costing System) 13-8
Case 13-3   The United L/N Plant (Scraps and Defects) 13-14

            How Boeing Tracks Costs, A to Z 13-17

Chapter 14	**Cost Allocation: Service Departments and Joint Product Costs**	14-1
Case 14-1	Southwestern Bell Telephone (Revenue Allocation)	14-2
Case 14-2	Brookwood Medical Center (Cost Allocation)	14-5
	Reasonable Joint Cost Allocations in Nonprofits	14-12
	Managing Shared Services with ABM	14-16
Chapter 15	**The Flexible Budget And Standard Costing: Direct Materials And Direct Labor**	15-1
Case 15-1	Hoof and Fin Restaurants	15-3
	Standard Costing Is Alive And Well At Parker Brass	15-6
	Management Control systems: How SPC enhances Budgeting and Standard Costing	15-14
	Redesigning Cost Systems: Is Standard Costing Obsolete?	15-20
Chapter 16	**Standard Costing: Factory Overhead**	16-1
Case 16-1	Berkshire Toy Company	16-3
Case 16-2	The Mesa Corporation	16-14
	Using Enhanced Cost Models in Variance Analysis for Better Control and Decision Making	16-19
	Variance Analysis Refines Overhead Cost Control	16-27
	Overhead Control Implications of Activity Costing	16-33
Chapter 17	**Managing Marketing Effectiveness And Productivity**	17-1
Case 17-1	Dallas Consulting Group	17-3
	Profit Variance Analysis: A Strategic Focus	17-5
	Examining the Relationships in Productivity Accounting	17-17
	The Role of ABM in Measuring Customer Value	17-25

Chapter 18   **Management Control and Strategic Performance Measurement**............   18-1

Case 18-1   Analysis of the Accounting Function..   18-2
Case 18-2   Industrial Chemicals Company (Control of Research and Development)............   18-4
Case 18-3   Absorption Versus Variable Costing and Ethical Issues.......................................   18-7
Case 18-4   Strategic Performance Measurement   18-9
Case 18-5   Strategic Performance Measurement: Employee Benefits...................................   18-10
Case 18-6   Strategic Performance Measurement: Regression Analysis   18-11

              Transforming the Balanced Scorecard from Performance Measurement to   18-12
                 Strategic Management: Part 1 ....

Chapter 19   **Strategic Investment Units and Transfer Pricing**   19-1

Case 19-1   Investment SBUs; Strategy; International Issues   19-3
Case 19-2   Transfer Pricing; Strategy   19-6
Case 19-3   Better Life Products, Inc. (Transfer Pricing)...   19-7
Case 19-4   Transfer Pricing (Foreign Sales Corporations); Use of the Web   19-9

              Setting the Right Transfer Price...   19-10
              Does ROI Apply to Robotic Factories?   19-17
              Transfer Pricing with ABC...   19-22

Chapter 20   **Management Compensation and Business Valuation**   20-1

Case 20-1   Midwest Petro-Chemical Company (Evaluating a Firm).....................................   20-3
Case 20-2   Evaluating a Firm   20-10
Case 20-3   OutSource, Inc. (Economic Value Added)   20-11
Case 20-4   Columbia/HCA Healthcare Corp. (Business Valuation).......................................   20-18
Case 20-5   China Huaneng Group   20-25

              Using Shareholder Value to Evaluate Strategic Choices   20-37
              Beyond the Numbers   20-43
              Structuring Compensation to Achieve Better Financial Results   20-50

Chapter 1
Cost Management: An Overview
Cases

1-1   Critical Success Factors
1-2   Contemporary Management Techniques
1-3   Pricing
1-4   Selected Ethics Cases

Readings

"The Changing World of Management Accounting and Financial Management"
This article discusses the findings of Project Millennium, a qualitative market research project conducted for the Institute of Management Accountants. The project involved focus group studies of management accountants, consultants, and business executives to identify the role of management accounting and of the management accountant of the future.

Discussion Questions:
1. What are the key findings of the Millennium Project?
2. What are the implications of these findings for the education and training of management accountants?

"Counting More, Counting Less"
This article is a survey to update the 1995 Practice Analysis of Management Accounting. The highlights of the survey include an improved image of management accounting, a continued focus to forward-looking, strategic types of tasks, and more of a shift to business partnership in contrast to financial reporting only.

Discussion Questions:
1. What are the key findings of the Practice Analysis of Management Accounting?
2. What are the implications of these findings for the education and training of management accountants?

"Why Isn't The Controller Having More Impact"
In this article, a management consultant points out some of the obstacles management accountants face in becoming business partners. The author includes some suggestions of speeding the process of becoming a business partner.

Discussion Question:
What are the obstacles to the controller/management accountant becoming a business partner. What suggestions does the author offer?

Cost Management: An Overview

1-1. Critical Success Factors

Kirsten Malon has found a way to profitably exploit her computer know-how. She has started a firm that offers consulting services for computer and software repair and analysis. Most of her customers have purchased computers or software systems with little vendor support and need help in installing and using the systems effectively. Kirsten has expanded her business recently to include 25 technicians besides herself, and her client base has grown to over 1,900. Many of these clients are on a retainer arrangement (a fixed fee per month which guarantees access to a certain number of hours of technician time) to stabilize her cash flow. With the success of the business, Kirsten is now thinking about beginning a related business which would publish books and newsletters on computer and software issues.

REQUIRED:

What are the critical success factors likely to be for Kirsten's business, now and into the future? What cost management information is she likely to need: management planning and decision making, management and operational control, or product and service costing, and why?

1-2. Contemporary Management Techniques

DeLight Inc., is a large manufacturer of lighting fixtures for both wholesalers and electrical contractors. An important aspect of the business with electrical contractors is Delight's ability to develop product leadership through innovation, quality, and service. In contrast, in the wholesale business, Delight competes primarily on the basis of lowest price. De-Light has prospered in the recent five years because of its careful attention to developing and maintaining a sustainable competitive advantage in each of its markets.

REQUIRED:

Which of the ten types of contemporary management techniques does DeLight probably use? Explain your answer.

1-3.   Ethics, Pricing

AeroSpace Inc. is a manufacturer of airplane parts and engines for a variety of military as well as civilian aircraft. Though there are many commercial customers for most of the company's products, the U.S. government is the only buyer of the firm's rocket engines. Because AeroSpace is the sole provider of the engines, the government buys the engines at a price equal to cost plus a percent markup.

The cost system in place at AeroSpace is under review by top management, with the objective of developing a system which will provide more accurate and more timely cost management information.

At the current phase of the study of the cost system, it is now apparent that the new system, while more accurate and timely, will result in lower costs being assigned to the rocket engines and higher costs being assigned to the firm's other products. Apparently, the current (less accurate) cost system has over- costed the engines and under-costed the other products. On hearing of this, top management has decided to scrap the plans for the new cost system, because the rocket engine business with the government is a significant part of AeroSpace's business, and the reduced cost will reduce the price and thus the profits for this part of AeroSpace's business.

REQUIRED:

As a staff cost analyst on the cost review project, how do you see your responsibility when you hear of the decision of top management to cancel the plans for the new cost system?

1-4. Selected Ethics Cases

After his first two years at Bronson Beverages (BB), a publicly held wholesaler of beers and wines, Jim Best has advanced to a senior cost analyst position with a very good salary.

REQUIRED:

For each of the following situations Jim will face in the coming year, indicate how you see his responsibility, and how he should respond.

1. Jim learns that a significant portion of the firm's beer inventory has passed its shelf life and by local ordinance and company policy, should be destroyed. Because of concern about the effect on profits and his bonus, the chief operating officer decides that the beer should be sold anyway.

2. As part of his regular duties, Jim reviews BB's financial statements for inconsistencies and errors. While reviewing the recent report, Jim notices that non-trade accounts receivable (note: non-trade receivables arise from non-operating events, such as a loan to an employee, customer, etc; trade receivables arise from sales on credit) have increased sharply over the prior year. Upon inquiry, Jim finds out that the firm is lending money to one of its customers so that it can make purchases from BB. Jim knows that in his state, beer and wine purchases must be paid for in cash, by state law. Jim wonders if the treatment of the loan as a non-trade receivable is OK, or if it should be classified as a trade receivable?

3. Jim learns that BB has just been granted the franchise to sell a popular new line of custom-brewed beers. The franchise will improve BB's sales and profits substantially, and should mean a significant boost to BB's share price. Jim knows that, until the news of the franchise is made public, he is restricted by the SEC from using this insider information to trade in BB's shares and make unfair profits as a result. That evening, Jim and his wife have dinner with some friends, and one of them says she has heard there are some good things going on at BB, and asks Jim to comment. What should Jim say?

4. Jim is analyzing the sales and cost of sales in specialty wines when he discovers that one of the firm's customers has greatly increased purchases in this, the last month of the firm's fiscal year. Jim goes to talk to the salesperson for this customer to offer his congratulations. The salesperson says that he has simply shipped in advance the customer's order for the following month, so that it would appear on the current year's financial report. This tactic would help the salesperson meet his sales target and would also improve BB's sales and profits for the current year. The salesperson says there is a small chance that the customer will reject the shipment and send it back, but then says, "We will worry about that if it happens."

5. Working late one night, Jim notices that one of the top marketing executives has come into the office and is removing a box full of office supplies. He says in a joking manner to Jim as he leaves, "BB won't miss this stuff, and I really need it for my other business."

THE CHANGING WORLD OF MANAGEMENT ACCOUNTING AND FINANCIAL MANAGEMENT

By Mike Anastas

Imagine that you have just entered a time capsule that transports you to your office as it will look in the year 2007. The controller is video conferencing with the company's director of operations in Central Europe. They are discussing various cost management strategies based on information they see on their computer screens.

As you observe the sparsely populated offices, you notice several video conferences taking place among on-site staff and managers working at home or in other far-flung locations. Participants are discussing the successful use of electronic data interchange and straight-through processing and are making decisions based on sales and production activity information that is updated instantly on their PCs.

You already know or have witnessed how much management accounting and financial management have changed in the last 10 years, but you couldn't have predicted all the changes you see in your office of the future. Every executive is conducting business on the Internet, accessing instant snapshots of accounting and financial data on their laptop computers as they manipulate various business scenarios and send results around the globe as only the most progressive companies do now. Also, electronic data interchange will be the standard rather than the exception, and straight-through processing will create strategic alliances between vendors and customers at every level of production.

These are among the images and predictions from Project Millennium, a qualitative market research project we conducted for the Institute of Management Accountants earlier this year (see sidebar). Participants in the research envision major changes in the responsibilities of accounting and financial managers as well as the work they do and the equipment they use. They also predict that there will be fewer management accountants, but they will be at more senior levels in the corporation. And they will share more in decision making for their companies along with other members of their cross-functional teams.

Some participants in Project Millennium tagged the management accountant and financial manager of the future an "internal consultant," someone with the curiosity and flexibility to change and motivate others to change. These internal consultants will add value by helping their organizations find ways to stay profitable and keep ahead of the competition.

Management accountants and financial managers of the future will be expected to have command of the latest information technology software as well as an overall understanding of the business. To be successful, they will be proficient in communicating ideas through written form and verbal presentations. Performance reviews in the future will be based on the ability to analyze information and situations and make decisions that drive the business rather than the ability to measure the business. The key will be their ability to stay ahead of change.

FEWER BUT MORE SENIOR PEOPLE

IMA members and other lenders in the industry predict a trend for more chief executive officers (CEOs) and chief operating officers (COOs) to be recruited from the ranks of management accountants and financial managers because of an increasing emphasis on financial management and the need for people who can decipher financial data and present the results as strategic information. In fact, the most notable shift in the profession is away from analysis of the past toward strategic thinking about the future. "There are some who are predicting the disappearance of the financial function in corporations over time...but the upper-echelon people are getting much more heavily involved in the strategic direction of the organization. [It is hoped] it will be more analytical with a higher level of work product and less detail on record keeping."

Information technology is pushing management accountants and financial managers up the ladder as they become advisors or internal consultants to other managers in the company who have access to software to manage costs and budgets. As the end user takes responsibility for the task, the accountant becomes responsible for the system and process, but not for the final report. "Ten years from now, there may be fewer people in finance because the people in line management and the business units will possess the knowledge about costs and budgeting. They will be enabled by technology and decision analysis tools, along with a few management accountants and financial managers."

INTERNAL CONSULTANTS AND STRATEGISTS

Changes brought about by information technology, which freed management accountants and financial managers from tracking past performance, have put them in the enviable position of becoming "internal consultants" who create strategies and recommendations to guide management decisions. "Management accountants can be the bridge between functions and they can be key players because they have that overview that many others do not have." "The finance and accounting department is really the information center...to understanding where the organization is coming from and where it is going."

Senior accounting and finance professionals are in a central position to keep their companies on track. "The financial managers of the future will be looking at every aspect of a company's operations. They will be at the right hand of their CEO and COO to monitor the resources of the company, the people, the products, ideas and innovations, to make sure the company is focused and stays on the right track."

But to be effective internal consultants, financial professionals must master special consulting skills, especially communications and interpersonal relations. "Your interpersonal skills are going to have to be better than ever." "All the skills related to communication—speaking, listening, sending, receiving—will be paramount." "The ability to communicate, both verbally and in writing, and leadership skills will differentiate between the extremely successful management accountants and others."

ABOUT PROJECT MILLENIUM

"Project MILLENNIUM: Customers and Future Markets...Looking Ahead to 2007..." was designed to help the IMA predict major changes and skills required for professionals in management accounting and financial management. Focus group discussions among IMA members and executives who employ IMA members were held in New York, Chicago, San Francisco, Dallas, Cleveland, Philadelphia, Tampa, and Atlanta between December 1996 and February 1997. Individual interviews were conducted among industry experts, consultants, and visionaries in information technology as well as officers of the IMA, major corporations, and other professional organizations. Some of their quotes illustrate this article.

What are some of the other predictions? Companies will continue to place a premium on those individuals who have a broad overview of business and who can use case studies as a basis for solving problems. "There's going to be more demand for people who can learn from case studies that show how to increase ongoing earnings per share."

Also, as organizations downsize and run on leaner staffs, there is a growing appreciation for individuals who propose new ideas and suggest taking risks. One IMA member in San Francisco calls these employees "intrepreneurs." "An 'intrepreneur' is someone who works for a company and is able and willing to take risks there, to gamble for the greater good."

And management accountants and financial managers have to start thinking in new ways. "Accountants tend to be pretty good at productivity and administration. In 2007 we will need people who are also good in creative entrepreneurial ideas and teamwork."

DECISION-MAKING TEAM MEMBER

Today more companies are relying on cross-functional teams to run their operations, and by 2007 nearly every company will be run by such strategic teams. Decision making often involves interaction with a variety of executives within an organization, and participation of accounting and finance people is essential because of their skills and disciplines. "The management accountant of 10 years from now will be more of a team player, an integral partner in operations...respected more for business acumen and decision-making...helping to lend order and structure to making the right business decisions." Professionals who are responsible for accounting will have migrated to be more information-based strategic business advisors...The accountant has to be one of the people around the table when strategic decisions are made."

Being effective as one of the decision-makers around the table means having an overview of the total business picture—beyond cost and budgets. "Management accountants with broad business perspectives will be a necessity...as integrators of all the business activities, things that are already happening, such as performance management, balanced scorecards, process improvement, ABC, ABM...because of our knowledge and role as the common denominator for business."

Management accountants and financial managers seem to welcome this new view of themselves. "We're no longer the bean counters. We're making decisions..." "We do a lot less book-keeping and lot more analysis and making decisions." "You don't just bring information to the table anymore, you're making decisions at the table."

In addition, the future of management accounting and financial management includes the adoption of new theories and approaches, such as strategic cost management, that require new ways of thinking. "Strategic cost management means controlling the costs of our suppliers, especially in heavy manufacturing. Not just to minimize costs but to maximize creativity, to get a better product or more functionality. The whole firm would be focused on how we can reduce costs and strengthen our position."

This shift in thinking not only will affect management accountants and financial managers who already are involved in the profession, but it will place new requirements on students preparing to enter the arena. Ideally, those coming into the field in the future will be well rounded and interested in more than fundamental skills. "Every student should have a more broad-based education...to be a more dynamic contributor to the team."

INITIATING AND IMPLEMENTING NEW TECHNOLOGY

Management accountants and financial managers will continue to be the primary consumers of new information technology in most organizations. Accounting was among the first functions to be automated with early spreadsheet programs. Consequently, accounting and finance managers generally are more well prepared than others to seek and evaluate new software. They connect the end user to the technology that accesses information. "The big success factor is realizing that accountants are informational managers." Mastery of technology is seen as essential for the future. "If you don't stay current with the technology, your career is in jeopardy."

The shift from looking backward to looking forward has been facilitated by new software. "The relevancy of historical information will decline as the importance

of immediate information and projections increases. And technology is the primary driver of that." "With electronic commerce and technology...it's conceivable that in 10 years you will no longer have accounts receivable and accountants payable departments. We'd be out of that business."

Some large, multinational corporations still operate MS-DOS systems on networks, but the average organization is operating Windows-based PCs connected by corporate intranets and the Internet, which facilitates electronic data interchange and straight-through processing. These new methods of data exchange make the role of management accountants and financial managers even more critical. "With your PCs we can run circles around the mainframe that was controlled by the Data Processing Department."

But the downside is that corporate accountants often complain they are being asked to produce more information with fewer people. As data go online for every manager to see on a PC, there is a demand for instant information. That means management accountants must produce more financial analyses, not just masses of data, so leaders can build strategies and make decisions based on more precise information. "Many more companies will be using Online Analytical Processing (OLAP) to go beyond the general ledger and to slice and dice the data in all kinds of ways, such as detailed customer and sales analysis."

And management accountants and financial managers will be using sophisticated information technology to create predictive data that forecast demand, production, sales, costs, and reported earnings. For example, "We will be converting activity-based costs systems from feedback to 'feed-forward' systems so you can estimate as you implement strategies like commonality and minimum component counts."

STAYING AHEAD OF CHANGE

Most visionaries in accounting and finance believe the rate of change will accelerate as we move into the next century. Changes in management accounting and finance will require changes in the way individuals approach their work. "Employers will not be content with accountants who view themselves mainly as scorekeepers...they want people who can influence the score, not simply report the score. It's going to require a different mindset...a shift in the way we view our positions."

The shift from record keeping to strategizing and forecasting demands that individuals develop special skills to be effective. "The management accountant has to be more of a change agent and a sales person rather than just a reporter—someone who can sell the idea of what to do with the information."

By the year 2007, most organizations will be sourcing and selling around the world. "...A lot of our suppliers and customers are going to be overseas, and we better get prepared for it." "There are very few businesses out there not touched by the international dimension some way."

But many individuals feel ill-prepared to deal with the global market. "If I were starting out today, I would learn about global markets and learn a foreign language...the kinds of things you'll really be able to use on a day-to-day basis."

Another significant change in the next 10 years will be greater diversity in the accounting and finance departments. "People coming from every field you can imagine...there's much greater diversity in the workforce..."

And most companies will be using the new media and forms of communication now being used by large multinational organizations. "There will be less business face-to-face, more by e-mail and teleconferencing. Communications will have to be more effective and precise." "The Internet will play an important role in the way we educate ourselves."

One IMA member in Cleveland summed up her philosophy about change, and it seems to apply to everyone in the profession who wants to be successful and add value to their organizations. "Learning is a lifetime proposition. We should go to school to 'learn how to learn,' to adapt and to change, not stand still..."

COUNTING MORE, COUNTING LESS

Transformations in the Management Accounting Profession

By Keith A. Russell, CMA; Gary H. Siegel, CPA; and C.S. "Bud" Kulesza, CMA, CFMA

From bean counter, corporate cop, and financial historian to valued business partner, the role of management accountants in many firms in the last decade has evolved into the center of strategic activity. Escalating change in an increasingly competitive international business environment has provided management accountants with the opportunity to reinvent the profession and increase their value to the organization.

These changes are among the major findings of the largest continuing analysis of the management accounting and finance profession. The 1999 Practice Analysis of Management Accounting, titled *Counting More, Counting Less: Transformations in the Management Accounting Profession,* provides a snapshot of the current state of the management accounting profession in the U.S., how the profession has changed, and where the profession is headed. The key events leading to this latest report are described in the sidebar, "Why Research Was Needed."

HIGHLIGHTS OF THE 1999 PRACTICE ANALYSIS

The 1999 Practice Analysis focuses a lens on the accounting function and offers insight into the broad changes under way in American firms in the new information economy. The 1995 Practice Analysis described a profession in transition. The 1999 Practice Analysis documents the transformation of corporate accountants from financial historians to business partners. Increasing numbers of management accountants spend most of their time as internal consultants or business analysts. Many have moved from the accounting department to be physically located in the operating departments they service. They work on cross-functional teams and are actively involved in decision making.

As firms adopted a customer focus as the key component to their quality improvement programs, management accountants focused on serving their "internal customers." Accepting the adage, "the customer is always right," management accountants work closely with their "customers" to provide the right information and help use the information to make better decisions.

The 1999 Practice Analysis results reflect the current state of the management accounting profession in the U.S. and indicate where the profession is heading.

IMPROVED IMAGE

When compared to the baseline measures of the 1995 Practice Analysis, the 1999 results show ongoing and escalating change in the work performed by management accountants, in their role in the organization, and in the value they bring to decision making. Clear winners in the technological revolution that fostered the new information economy, management accountants are in increased demand within their organizations for their advice, expertise, and involvement. About 70% of the respondents in all size firms say that compared to five years ago people outside the finance function believe that management accountants bring more value to the company.

COMMUNICATION WITH NONACCOUNTANTS INCREASING

In 1995, 48% of management accountants worked on cross-functional teams. In 1999, that has increased to 56%. Management accountants spend more time communicating with people in their firm than five years ago. Universally, respondents agree that good interpersonal skills are essential for success.

SHIFTS IN WORK LOCATION

Traditionally, accountants worked in accounting departments that were physically removed from the operating departments of their companies. In 1999, however, 20% of all respondents report that at least half the management accountants in their company have moved out of the centrally located accounting area and are located with the operating departments they serve as part of the business team. In larger companies, 45% of respondents indicate that at least half are now located with the operating departments they service.

HOW MANAGEMENT ACCOUNTANTS DEFINE THEMSELVES

When asked which term they used to describe their work, 39% of respondents said finance, 33% said accounting, and 28% use a different term. Finance appears to be a more inclusive and acceptable term for describing all the varied activities the respondents perform. The most common reasons given for using the term finance have to do with the positive connotations associated with finance and the negative connotations connected with accounting. Interestingly, none of the respondents used the term "management accountant" to describe themselves.

- Finance is forward-looking, while accounting looks backward.
- Finance is more all-inclusive.
- Accounting refers to debits and credits.
- Accountants are "number crunchers."

Skills needed for success. The 1995 Practice Analysis includes a database with information about 162 knowledge, skills, and abilities (KSAs) necessary for success in the accounting profession. The 1999 Practice Analysis respondents were asked to describe, for the benefit of undergraduate accounting majors, the most important KSAs necessary for success. They are:

- Communication (oral, written, and presentation) skills.
- Ability to work on a team.
- Analytical skills.
- Solid understanding of accounting.
- An understanding of how a business functions.

Respondents also were asked to identify the most important new KSAs they learned over the past five years. See Table 1 for their answers. It shouldn't be surprising that computer skills topped the list.

QUALITY OF LIFE

Due to the increased demand for their services, finance function personnel work long hours. As a result, there is increasing concern on the part of respondents about the balance between work and personal life. Two comments from the survey reflect this concern:

"In the last couple of years especially, we have just been burning people out. They've been working incredible hours trying to get information out faster than they've ever gotten information out before."

"I think one of the real issues is work/life balance. I don't think you find work/life balance in most finance jobs ... Frankly, I think people are feeling that they are running and they are giving up family life. We are recognizing it; we are concerned."

THE PACE OF CHANGE

Change in the profession is ongoing and accelerating. The overwhelming majority of respondents interviewed stated that the rate of change in their organizational role has been more rapid over the 1995-99 period than the 1990-95 period.

Not one respondent expects the rate of change to decrease! In fact, respondents expect the rate of change to increase over the next three years. Management accountants say that change is driven by technology, the need for more rapid information, globalization, and the increasingly competitive environment. Management accountants aren't just managing change: They are initiating change.

WHERE THE PROFESSION IS GOING

Financial professionals report a shift over the past five years from traditional accounting work activities to newer, more value-added activities. Compared to five years ago, respondents spend more time performing the following work activities:

- Internal consulting.
- Long-term, strategic planning.
- Computer systems and operations.
- Managing the accounting/finance function.
- Process improvement.
- Performing financial and economic analysis.

Looking ahead three years, they expect to spend more time on the same work activities. Compared with five years ago, respondents say that they spend less time performing the following work activities:

- Accounting systems and financial reporting.
- Consolidations.
- Managing the accounting/finance function.
- Accounting policy.
- Short-term budgeting process.
- Project accounting.
- Compliance reporting.
- Cost accounting systems.
- Tax compliance.

Looking ahead three years, they expect to spend less time on these same critical work activities. Interestingly, these are traditional accounting work activities. Respondents were asked to identify the single most critical work activity for their firm's success in 1999. See Table 2 for their responses.

Long-term strategic planning, process improvement, and customer and product profitability were recently introduced to the profession. Indeed, these functions weren't part of the traditional accounting vocabulary 10 years ago.

CHANGES IN THE ROLE OF THE FINANCE FUNCTION

Many respondents believe the changes taking place in their work are driven by changes in the finance function. Leading changes include:

- Partner/consultant in management decisions.
- Finance is more involved with other aspects of business.
- More planning/strategy.
- More computerized technology.
- More involved in team building/decision making.
- More involved in evaluating company efficiency.

Management accountants also believe the current trend toward business partnering will continue. Changes expected over the next three years are:

- Less reporting of information; more planning and analysis.
- More computerized/technology/software.
- More partnering and consulting in management decisions.
- More involvement with operations.
- More analysis of profitability and performance evaluation.

IMPLICATIONS AND RECOMMENDATIONS FOR ACCOUNTING EDUCATORS

The two most critical work activities for the success of respondents' companies in 1999 are strategic planning and process improvement; neither is taught in most accounting curricula. To better meet the needs of their students and corporate customers, college and university educators should obtain a better understanding of the work performed in modern firms. The insights gained from the 1999 Practice Analysis should be used to address needed curriculum changes.

FOR CORPORATIONS

Corporations should become more involved in the academic community through advisory boards, participation in job fairs, faculty internships, guest speaker activities, plant visits, etc. This involvement will help ensure that the changes occurring in corporate America are shared with the academic community. Such interaction is necessary to enable students and faculty to remain abreast of the changes taking place in the profession and to identify the KSAs needed for success.

FOR PROFESSIONAL ASSOCIATIONS

Professional associations need to maintain their leadership role of identifying, supporting, and perpetuating the positive changes taking place in the profession. Specifically, they should:

- Continue the development of CPE courses and benchmarks for finance function organizations.
- Continue to encourage and support the interaction between accounting educators and practitioners.
- Compare professional certification examinations contents and specifications with the results of this research.
- Develop a universally accepted title for the new organizational role of management accountants.
- Inform accounting educators about the changes that occurred in the profession and where the profession is headed.
- Work closely with accounting educators to develop changes in the accounting curriculum consistent with the future of the profession.

BEYOND STRATEGIC PARTNERING

In a November 1990 article in Management Accounting, Gerald Ross, managing director of Change Lab, Toronto, Canada, predicted the changes under way for management accountants. Ross stated that the 1990 management accountant was using traditional tools at the operational level. He felt that to survive and flourish in the new technological world, management accountants would need to begin using more sophisticated tools and move from the operational level into the strategic level in their firms.

Events over the past decade have proven Ross to be prescient. Where does the profession go from here? The 1999 Practice Analysis predicts that management accountants go beyond business partnering and broaden their role to strategic partnering. Management accountants will become more involved in running the business. They will become more proactive.

Clearly, change will be the constant into the new millennium for finance function professionals.

IMA, in an ongoing effort to meet member needs, formed an alliance with the Financial Executives Institute (FEI) to complete a research project to determine the skills corporate executives expected from entry-level accountants and the skills entry-level accountants brought to the job. *What Corporate America Wants in Entry-Level Accountants* (IMA, 1994) revealed a significant gap between corporate expectations and entry-level skills. The gap had developed because the curricula of many accounting and business programs weren't focused on the changes occurring in corporate accounting or on the needs of the corporations that hired accounting and business graduates. (This gap was later confirmed by the AACSB in *A Report of the AACSB Faculty Leadership Task Force,* 1995-96).

The obvious question raised by *What Corporate America Wants* was, "What knowledge, skills, and abilities (KSAs) were necessary for entry-level professionals?"

To answer this question, the IMA completed its first study of work, *The Practice Analysis of Management Accounting* (IMA, 1995). This study documented in unprecedented detail the work activities performed in U.S. companies and the KSAs necessary for competent performance of those work activities. Respondents for the study were drawn from membership rosters of the AICPA, IMA, FEI, and IIA and included management accountants at all organizational levels, entry-level to CFO. Many colleges and universities used the Practice Analysis database to revise curricula, and businesses used it to develop skill-based training.

The 1995 Practice Analysis also revealed the emerging contours of the new management accountant: one who was working on cross-functional teams and becoming more heavily involved in strategic planning and business decision making. Less time was being spent in traditional roles because technology automated many time-consuming tasks. Instead, management accountants were spending increasing amounts of time in new roles as an internal consultant, analyst, and valued business partner.

In 1999, IMA heard from members that change in the profession was accelerating. Accordingly, the Institute, with participation and cooperation from the AICPA, undertook the 1999 Practice Analysis to focus on change in the profession. The Gary Siegel Organization completed the research on this follow-up research study as well as the two earlier studies. *Focus on the Horizon: CPA Vision Project* (AICPA, 1998), identified forces that were impacting, and provided visioning for, their members.

Using information provided from respondents drawn from members of the IMA and AICPA, researchers set out to determine:

1. How the work of management accountants and their role in their companies have changed over the past five years, and

2. How the work will change in the next three years.

Table 1.
MOST IMPORTANT KSAs
ACQUIRED OVER THE PAST 5 YEARS

	Number	Percent
Computer skills/technology/networks	146	49.70%
Accounting software	60	20.40%
Teaching/speaking/communication	44	15.00%
Project management/leadership	40	13.60%
New laws/accounting rules/SEC requirements	33	11.20%
Interpersonal skills	28	9.50%
Learn about operations, i.e., HR/marketing	25	8.50%
Evaluation of profitability/financial analysis	22	7.50%
Other	20	6.80%
Process evaluation skills in own or other business	19	6.50%
Auditing/tax laws	18	6.10%
Internet skills	16	5.40%
Long-range planning	16	5.40%
Mergers and acquisitions	15	5.10%
New degree/certificate	9	3.10%
Cash management	7	2.40%
Risk management	4	1.40%
TOTAL CASES	294	100.00%

Table 2.
SINGLE MOST CRITICAL
WORK ACTIVITY IN 1999

	Number	Percent
Long-term, strategic planning	75	25.30%
Process improvement	30	10.10%
Customer and product profitability	27	9.10%
Accounting systems and financial reporting	16	5.40%
Short-term budgeting process	15	5.10%
Mergers, acquisitions, and divestments	15	5.10%
Perform financial and economic analysis	14	4.70%
External financing	14	4.70%
Computer systems and operations	13	4.40%
Performance evaluation	9	3.00%
Project accounting	7	2.40%
Internal consulting	7	2.40%
Tax planning and strategy	7	2.40%
Capital budgeting	6	2.00%
Cost accounting systems	5	1.70%
Quality systems and control	5	1.70%
Risk management	5	1.70%
Investment of funds	5	1.70%
Credit and collection	4	1.30%
Educating the organization	4	1.30%
Managing the accounting/finance function	4	1.30%
Compliance reporting for government or regulatory agencies	3	1.00%

Resource management	3	1.00%
Consolidations	1	0.30%
Internal auditing	1	0.30%
Tax compliance	1	0.30%
Human resources and personnel	1	0.30%

WHY ISN'T THE CONTROLLER HAVING MORE IMPACT:

The Choice For Controllers Is Clear: Become A Business Partner Or Become Irrelevant

By Jon Scheumann

Why don't corporations catch more bad decisions in the planning stage and correct them before they grow into costly mistakes? Sometimes, bad decisions slip by because the person with the right skills isn't on the management planning team. And often the person with the right skills is the controller. Yet, in many companies, the controller is left out of the planning process or is brought in after the key decisions already have been made.

The same skills that enable controllers to lay out financial plans and institute controls can become the tools to predict the future consequences of corporate decisions. With these tools, controllers can show management why a seemingly attractive acquisition is likely to prove indigestible or why a seemingly lucrative contract is likely to create an accounting nightmare.

Because of their ability to help management make sound strategic and tactical decisions, an increasing number of controllers are taking their place at the planning table as business partners. A recent study by Gunn Partners finds that by the year 2002, controllers expect to be spending about 30% more time on business partnership than they are now and about 20% less time on traditional controller functions.

CHANGES WILL BE SLOW

Our Gunn Partners study sees the likelihood of a much slower and more difficult transition to business partner than most controllers anticipate. The study cites a number of obstacles.

- Corporate controllers are failing to prove to top management and operating managers that they belong at the planning table.
- There are no traditional paths or training programs for becoming a business partner, and too few controllers are taking the initiative to use available resources, such as peers who have made the transition.

- Most controllers still are placing primary emphasis on fulfilling their traditional functions, leaving little time for the kinds of strategic initiatives that would encourage management to accept them as business partners.
- Many controllers aren't ready to make the changes required to become business partners. For instance, our study finds that most controllers hope to reduce the amount of time they spend managing people over the next few years. Yet, controllers who have succeeded in becoming business partners stress the need to devote much more time to people issues.

While the overall indication is that the road to business partnership may be much rockier than most controllers realize, we did find that one group of controllers is already well along in the transition. These are the controllers who report to the head of a business unit as opposed to those who report to the CFO or a corporate controller. Controllers who report to the head of a business unit said that activities related to business partnership comprise more than 50% of their most significant activities—as opposed to just 25% for controllers reporting to the CFO and 27% for those reporting to the corporate controller.

The study clearly shows that at this time the actions of most controllers aren't aligned with their goal of becoming business partners. Controllers are still focused on managing the finance function and aren't doing as much as they could to help the business compete in the marketplace. There's a gap between their goal and the actions they're taking to get there.

SHORTEN THE PATH

As controllers, what actions can you take? Here are a few:

- Learn the competencies you need to become a business partner and discover where you can get them. If there are no traditional programs, find other routes such as learning from peers who have made the transition.

- Improve the efficiency of your traditional controller functions so they take less time and leave you more time for business partnering.
- Work at proving to management that the role of the modern controller is shifting toward business partner and that it makes sense to place less emphasis on controllership and more on partnership.
- Recognize that to become a successful business partner you must spend more time, not less, guiding and coaching people. Then figure out what you have to do to reshape this human element—and get started.

Until the goal of becoming a business partner becomes more than wishful thinking, corporations won't realize the full benefits of the controller's valuable capabilities and perspective, shareholders will gain less value from their investment, and controllers will become increasingly frustrated and discouraged. It's in everyone's interest for controllers to make this transition. Management should encourage it—the controllers should fight to make it happen.

Chapter 2
Strategic Analysis and Strategic Cost Management
Cases

2-1   Atlantic City Casino (Value Chain Analysis)
2-2   Strategic Analysis
2-3   Business Strategy
2-4   Strategic Analysis

Readings

"How Nonfinancial Performance Measures are Used"

This article presents the findings of a survey of top executives regarding the use of nonfinancial information in evaluating the performance of managers and the firms they work for. The results are given for both United States and Canadian respondents, to provide an opportunity to compare the two. The discussion is particularly relevant for firms using the balanced scorecard, because of its focus on nonfinancial as well as financial information.

Discussion Questions:
1. Do the results of the survey support the use of the balanced scorecard as described in the chapter?
2. How would you tie together the five categories of nonfinancial information mentioned in the article with the four groups of critical success factors in the balanced scorecard?
3. Identify the differences in response between the United States and Canadian respondents, and explain the significance of these differences.

"Applying the Balanced Scorecard to Small Companies"

This article reports the findings of a case study of four small firms to identify the potential use of the balanced scorecard in these firms and to determine the differences in the use of the scorecard across industries. The industries include a food ingredients company, a commercial bank, a biotechnology firm, and an electronics firm.

Discussion Questions:
1. Did these four firms adopt the balanced scorecard? Why or why not?
2. For each of the firms, examine the scorecard presented in the article and use it to determine what you think is likely to be or should be the competitive strategy of the firm. Does it seem that the balanced scorecard is consistent with the nature of the firm's business and strategy?
3. How do the scorecards differ across firms? Can you explain why?

Food   bank   biotech   electronics

1)

Cases

2-1.   Atlantic City Casino

Several years ago the management of a large hotel chain, Hotel Corporation of American (HCA) purchased a casino in Las Vegas. Pleased with the results HCA constructed another casino in Atlantic City shortly after casino gaming was legalized in that city. At the time the proposal in this case arose (see below) there were 9 other casinos operating and 2 additional casinos under construction.

The casino is an independent operating unit within the hotel chain. For example, all financial and accounting services are provided in-house. The casino has been profitable since the day it opened. However, the level of profits has not been satisfactory. Corporate management is well aware that HCA would have been better off if the huge sums involved in the construction of the casino had been invested in certificates of deposit.

THE PROPOSAL

Management of the Atlantic City Casino has employed several consulting services to study the market and the casino's position in the market. Consumer surveys have shown that the casino is viewed as an average casino, with no distinguishing characteristics. Coupled with its location (several blocks from where most of the casinos are located) this perception of blandness seems to explain the casino's relatively small walk-in trade (most visitors to Atlantic City visit more than one casino; people staying at one casino who visit a second are considered walk-ins at the second casino).

A proposal has been made to expand the casino and hotel (state law prescribes a fixed number of hotel rooms per square feet of casino space). As part of this expansion, the proposal includes the construction of a theme entertainment center. The center would be separate from, but attached to, the casino. The showpiece of the center would be a large Ferris wheel designed to look like a giant wheel of fortune. It would be visible from a large portion of the boardwalk. Additionally, the area would include a unique water slide, bumper cars, a space capsule ride and a fun house. Throughout the area would be a number of small souvenir and snack shops, push carts, tent shows and midway-type games to provide an old-fashioned style carnival atmosphere. An admission fee would be charged to enter the theme center and most of the rides and entertainment would be included in the admission fee. Management expects to be able to use free admission tickets to the center as a promotional item. There would be easy access from the center to the casino floor. It is anticipated that a large number of the visitors to the center would also visit the casino.

Although management is impressed by the plan and has already had detailed architectural plans prepared for the expansion, they are cautious. When the casino was first built, everyone was enthusiastic about the casino's potential, but the results have been disappointing. Management wants a thorough study made of the financial prospects for this expansion before committing funds to it.

Detailed financial data for every casino in Atlantic City are public information and are routinely exchanged. Thus, data such as that given in Tables A and B are readily available.

REQUIRED:

1. Complete a value chain analysis. Describe your understanding of the competitive position of the Atlantic City Casino. Identify areas for potential cost reduction and/or value added for customers.

2. Should HCA make the investment in the theme entertainment center? Why?

3. HCA is considering a balanced scorecard for the Atlantic City Casino. For each of the four areas within the balanced scorecard, list two or three examples of measurable critical success factors which should be included.

(IMA adapted)

TABLE A Selected Annual Financial Data (000s omitted)				
	Revenues			
Property	Casino	Rooms	Food and Beverage	Net Income
Atlantic City Casino	$220,183	$14,862	$36,833	$23,921
Competitors				
1	254,753	17,604	36,457	40,979
2	224,077	14,836	34,493	18,834
3	237,700	15,787	35,168	47,146
4	158,602	9,897	18,788	1,574
5	210,848	13,870	35,265	64,765
6	251,675	17,665	33,867	17,904
7	147,037	10,191	35,020	(9,075)
8	121,581	13,469	21,863	2,246
9*	123,947	12,157	22,643	(1,176)
* In operation in 19X4 for only 6.5 months				

TABLE B
Selected Statistics

Property	Casino Space (square feet)	Number of Rooms	Number of Restaurants
Atlantic City Casino	50,850	521	7
Competitors			
1	59,857	727	9
2	59,296	645	9
3	59,439	512	9
4	49,639	501	14
5	52,083	750	7
6	40,814	504	8
7	50,516	500	5
8	34,408	504	6
9	60,000	612	8

2-2.   Strategic Analysis

Sovera Enterprises, an expanding conglomerate, was founded 35 years ago by Emil Sovera. The company's policy has been to acquire businesses that show significant profit potential; if a business fails to attain projected profits, it is usually sold. Currently, the company consists of eight businesses acquired throughout the years; three of those businesses are described here.

LaBue Videodiscs produces a line of videodisc players. The sale of videodisc players has not met expectations, but LaBue's management believes that the company will succeed in being the first to develop a moderately priced videodisc recorder/player. Market research predicts that the first company to develop this product will be a star.

Ulysses Travel Agencies also showed potential, and the travel industry is growing. However, Ulysses' market share has declined for the last two years even though Sovera has contributed a lot of money to Ulysses' operations. The travel agencies located in the Midwestern and eastern sections of the country have been the biggest drain on resources.

Reddy Self-Storage was one of the first self-storage companies to open. For the last three years, Reddy has maintained a large market share while growth in the self-storage market has slowed considerably.

Ron Ebert, chairman of Sovera, prepared the agenda for the company's annual planning meeting where the present businesses were evaluated and strategies for future acquisitions were formulated. The following statements of strategy for each of the subsidiary companies discussed were formulated on the basis of the master plan:

LaBue Videodiscs. Sovera's discretionary resources are to be employed to support the growth of this business. The future officers of Sovera are to be developed here.

Ulysses Travel Agencies. An orderly disposal of the least profitable locations is the initial objective. Once the disposals are complete, an acceptable profit and growth strategy for the remaining locations will be formulated.

Reddy Self-Storage. The strategy for this company is to maintain efficient operations and maximize the generation of cash for use in the further development of Sovera's other businesses.

These strategy statements were part of the strategic plan presented to Sovera's board of directors. The directors' only debate was whether Sovera should sell the entire Ulysses organization rather than parts of it. However, the board approved all three statements as presented and circulated them to managers throughout the three units as the corporation's "new marching orders."

REQUIRED:

1. Identify at least four general characteristics that differentiate the three businesses described above, and explain how these characteristics influenced the formulation of a different strategy for each business.
2. Discuss the likely effects of the three strategy statements on the behavior of top management and middle management of each of the three businesses.
   (CMA adapted)

2-3. Strategic Analysis[1]

Terry Merton, CPA, hardly noticed the bright sunshine as she drove down the freeway in late October, 20X0 on her way to her job as controller for a small manufacturing company in her hometown of Brightside, California. She was contemplating the prospect of starting an accounting and tax practice. Although quite satisfied with her present employment, she was very excited about the possibility of owning her own business. Prior to her present position, Terry had worked for four years in the small business division of a Big 5 public accounting firm's Brightside office and had dreamed of opening her own practice. Terry had decided that 20X1 is the year her dream will become a reality.

Arriving at her office early, Terry began to think about the possible market segments she might serve and the types of tax and accounting problems these potential clients might have. For instance, Terry might simply establish a tax practice which would focus on serving individuals who typically require only simple return preparation. Serving this target market segment would mean preparing simple tax returns, such as form 1040 and other schedules commonly completed for individuals along with the 1040.

On the other hand, Terry could establish both a tax and accounting practice. This would mean she would serve both individuals and small businesses, although her primary target market would be small businesses. Pursuing this alternative would mean that she would render tax services for individuals, small businesses, estates, trusts and pension plans. Further, she would provide compilation, review and audit services for small businesses, as well as advice on designing accounting information systems. Terry knew that her first step would be to identify the market segment she wished to serve. To be successful, she would have to serve the selected target market very well.

Once she identified her target market segment, Terry could then make a decision about her competitive strategy -- whether to implement a cost leadership of differentiation strategy.

Pursuing a cost leadership strategy meant that she would attract clients by keeping her prices (and her costs) low. At the same time, Terry would still be attentive to providing quality service on a timely basis. She would compete on the basis of price and monitor costs to be sure they were kept low.

Pursuing the differentiation strategy meant providing services which are considered to be unique. Differentiating her product probably meant that Terry would provide above-average service and develop a more personal relationship with clients. With the differentiation strategy, Terry would be able to charge above-average prices for the services provided to clients and would not have to be as attentive to cost control as she would under the cost leadership strategy.

In considering which strategy to pursue, Terry thought about a nationally known provider of tax preparation services for individuals, which had offices located throughout the U.S. This national firm used television, radio and billboard advertising to present 17 reasons why taxpayers should do business with their firm. Terry was certain that the national firm had a costly centralized administrative structure. The firm's tax preparers were typically not CPA's, but were graduates of a training program conducted by the firm. Terry felt that this nationally-known firm was pursuing a differentiation strategy, since it emphasized the 17 reasons but did not emphasize low price.

If Terry selected the individual tax market, she could employ the cost leadership strategy. The limited tax expertise required would allow Terry to remain at her present employment. She would hire Jim Wallace, an experienced semi-retired preparer of uncomplicated tax returns. Terry would locate her tax practice in a storefront in a nearby shopping mall. Rent was very low there, and there was a high volume of pedestrian traffic past the location. Given this heavy pedestrian traffic, Terry reasoned that she

---

[1] Prepared by Jack M. Ruhl and Jerry G. Kreuze, © American Accounting Association, 1997. Used with permission.

would incur little advertising cost. Terry expected that her costs could be kept low compared with the nationally-known firm for two reasons: (1) she would provide minimal training for Jim and (2) she would have minimal administrative and advertising costs.

Now, Terry thought about the small business market. Here, Terry thought about using the differentiation strategy. With the differentiation strategy, the services she would provide would be significantly different from the services provided by competitors. Terry would differentiate herself along a number of dimensions, many of which related to her extensive experience with the Brightside business community. First from her experience working in a Big 5 firm's small business division, Terry is acquainted with all the bankers in town. She knows how to prepare financial presentations for clients seeking loans in such a way that the loan applications are almost always approved. She also is familiar with virtually all the small business rental property in town, and can direct clients to the most reasonably priced locations. Finally, she is thoroughly familiar with the operation of a small business and can provide extremely useful insights to small business owners. Terry would provide small businesses with many reasons to patronize her new firm. If the small business strategy is pursued, Terry will leave her $40,000/year controller position to become the principal employee of Startup, Inc.

Terry would like to finance her new business start-up costs entirely from her personal savings. This is not possible, however, since she just recently purchased a new automobile for cash, which left her with a savings account balance of only $2,400. She will need a business loan to cover start-up costs including the purchase of a computer and software. Prior to contacting Bill Andersen, the loan officer a t a nearby bank, Terry prepares some preliminary profit estimates. Terry's estimates of the revenues and costs associated with each strategy for the first year of operation, 20X1, are presented in exhibit 1.

Terry projects revenues of $67,500 (450 Clients at $150/client) and $91,350 (203 clients at $450/client) under the cost leadership and differentiation strategies, respectively (see exhibit 1). Supplies average $10 per client and constitute the only variable costs for Startup, Inc. The fixed expenses vary between the strategies in several respects:

1. If she pursues the small business strategy, Terry will incur significantly higher liability insurance costs each year than she would under the cost leadership strategy. This is due to the fact that she has much more liability exposure since she will be doing attest work (reviews and audits).
2. Annual computer software costs will be greater under the small business strategy. This is because each year Terry will purchase specialized CD-ROM tax preparation disks needed to properly prepare the estate and trust returns. Additional software is also needed if she wishes to advise clients with regard to pensions.
3. If she pursues the small business strategy, Terry will incur additional expense for club membership dues and entertainment expenses compared with the cost leadership strategy. This is due to the fact that Terry knows that she can develop the estate and trust work through social contacts with bankers and attorneys.
4. Under the individual tax strategy, Terry will continue in her present employment position. She will hire Jim Wallace for $500/week. Although not a CPA, Jim is approaching retirement at the public accounting firm where Terry had been employed. Jim would be happy to work part-time at Startup, Inc. Terry is impressed with Jim's qualifications and is confident he could prepare uncomplicated tax returns. The differentiation strategy, however, will entail more complicated tax return preparations, which are beyond Jim's capabilities. Under the small business strategy, Terry would resign from her controller position and work full-time for Startup, Inc., drawing a salary of $600 per week.
5. Terry's home has a very large attached apartment which she presently leases to two college students at a rent of $500 per month. The students' lease expires on December 31, 20X0. Under the small business strategy, she will not renew the lease. Instead, she will set up the offices of Startup, Inc. in the apartment. Under the cost leadership provider strategy, the students would continue to occupy the

apartment, since space in a nearby strip mall will be leased for Startup's offices. The strip mall space would provide needed pedestrian traffic and high visibility for Startup, Inc., and avoid traffic congestion in Terry's residential neighborhood.

6. Anticipating the complexity of clients under the small business strategy and considering the fact that she has been out of public accounting for three years, Terry estimates $8,000 in annual training costs. Minimal training costs are projected with the individual tax strategy since Jim Wallace already possesses the necessary experience, and the level of tax expertise required is minimal.

OBTAINING A BUSINESS LOAN

Terry faxed the financial projections in Exhibit 1 to Bill Andersen in early November 20X0. As a loan officer, Bill must follow a set of specific guidelines in making his loan approval decisions. If Bill approves too many loans which ultimately are "bad," he will be dismissed from his job. For all loan applications, he must be able to justify after-the-fact his decision to the bank's board of directors, based largely on the loan applicant's financial statements. In assessing the credit worthiness of Terry's loan application, Bill plans to use operating income before depreciation and working capital as surrogates for cash-paying ability. Terry will offer her nearly new automobile as collateral. The bank's policy is to approve loans only if the annual payments are less than the beginning working capital balance and the projected before depreciation operating income for the next 12 months. The bank has also instituted a policy to have all loans due and payable on demand at the end of any calendar year if the payee is not in compliance with the original loan requirements.

Bill's bank has a maximum loan period for startup companies of five years. At an interest rate of ten percent per annum, Startup, Inc. qualifies for an $8,000 maximum loan requiring a $2,110 annual payment. Consequently Startup's December 31 working capital balance and annual operating income (before depreciation expense) must not fall below $2,110, or the bank loan becomes due and payable.

REQUIRED:

1. From Bill Andersen's perspective, which practice strategy is better? Why?

2. From a managerial and strategic planning perspective, which practice strategy should Terry pursue? Why?

EXHIBIT 1
Startup, Inc.
Projected Income Statements Under Two Competitive Strategies
For the Twelve Months Ended December 31, 20X1

		Strategies for Practice	
		Cost Leadership	Differentiation
Revenues	(450 clients at $150)	$67,500	
	(203 clients at $450)		$91,350
Variable Expenses			
	Supplies ($10 per client)	4,500	2,030
Contribution Margin		63,000	89,320
Fixed Expenses:			
	Depreciation—Computer	1,600	1,600
	Software	500	4,000
	Liability Insurance	2,400	11,680
	Rental—Furniture	5,660	5,660
	Club Membership & Entertainment	—	1,200
	Preparer Salary	26,000	31,200
	Secretarial Salary	16,000	16,000
	Advertising	200	1,180
	Rent—office	8,400	—
	Training	—	8,000
	Total Fixed Expenses	60,760	80,520
Operating Income		$ 2,240	$ 8,800

2-4. Strategy, International

Barry McDonald, CFO for Recreational Products, Inc (RPI), is convinced it would be profitable for his firm to invest in a manufacturing operation in Singapore. RPI makes a variety of recreational products, including sporting goods, sportware, and camping equipment. RPI is known as a very high quality producer, with features and prices greater than most in the industry. One of the largest divisions in RPI is the boating division, which makes a variety of sailboats and fishing boats from 16 feet up to large sailboats of 40+ feet in length. These boats are now manufactured in two US plants. Barry's idea is to utilize the available low cost labor, materials resources and the favorable business climate in Singapore to build a manufacturing plant there for producing the larger sailboats. The finished boats would be sold to existing customers (boat dealers) in the United States and Canada, and a new effort would be made to sell some of the product in Asia and Australia. Barry forecasts sales of US$50 million, cost of sales (manufacturing in the Singapore plant) of $34 million, and other expenses of approximately $10 million. The government of Singapore would provide a tax holiday for the project, but the return of profits to the United States would be taxed in the US at the US rate of 34%.

Barry's research showed that the cost of the plant in Singapore would be $20 million. Funds for the investment could come from the firm's own resources at a cost of approximately 12%, or through a subsidized loan from the government of Singapore at a 5% rate. With these figures and other estimates, Barry figured the after-tax cash flow of the plant would be a positive $4 million per year for the next 15 years, the expected life of the plant.

REQUIRED:

1. What does RPI's competitive position appear to be for the entire firm, and for the boating division? What are some of the likely critical success factors for the boating division?
2. Does Barry's plan for the Singapore plant fit the strategic competitive position you developed in (1) above?
3. What do you think are some of the key international issues that are relevant for Barry's proposal?

HOW NON-FINANCIAL PERFORMANCE MEASURES ARE USED

By Bonnie P. Stivers, CPA; Teresa Joyce Covin; Nancy Green Hall, and Steven W. Samlt, CPA

CERTIFICATE OF MERIT

Most executives agree that there is no magic formula —or one right measure—for evaluating business performance. Therefore, in an effort to capture the essence of business performance, many companies are creating new performance measurement systems that include a broad range of financial and non-financial measures.

Although we know much about the use of financial measures in companies, our knowledge of these new, non-financial performance measures is limited. To determine the scope of current practice, we surveyed top executives in U. S. Fortune 500 firms and in Canadian Post 300 companies. The study was sponsored by the Michael J. Coles College of Business at Kennesaw State University and funded by the Canadian Institute of Chartered Accountants. Study results indicate that top executives in both countries believe that non-financial measures are important. But the study also identifies two serious drawbacks: (1) Although non-financial factors are viewed as important, they may not be measured, and (2) Even when non-financial factors are measured, they may not be used. (For a description of the study design and survey sample, see sidebar.)

THE STUDY OF NON-FINANCIAL PERFORMANCE MEASURES

Although much is being written about non-financial performance measures, very little is known about actual current practices. The objective of this study was to provide a comprehensive picture of the process of non-financial measurement. Specifically, the study examined the degree to which top executives in Fortune 500 and Post 300 firms identify particular non-financial performances factors as important, whether firms are measuring important non-financial factors, and whether or not companies actually are using non-financial performance factor information in their planning processes.

The questionnaire asked study participants to indicate, using a five-point scale, the importance of each of 21 non-financial performance factors in setting company goals. For discussion purposes, we have grouped the factors into five general categories: customer service, market performance, innovation, goal achievement, and employee involvement.

The five categories of non-financial performance measures are illustrated in Figure 1. For each individual performance measure, the figure shows of the 253 firms in the total sample: (1) number of firms identifying the factor as important, (2) number of firms actually measuring the factor, and (3) number of firms actually using the factor in the planning process.

An individual factor was identified as highly important if it received a rating of four or greater on the five-point scale of importance. Results of the study indicate that customer service factors are perceived to be the most important measures. Of the 253 responding firms, 235 (92.9%) rated "customer satisfaction" and "delivery performance/customer service" as highly important. "Product/process quality" was rated as highly important by 206 (81.4%) of the responding firms and "service quality" by 205 (81.0%) of the 253 firms (Figure 1).

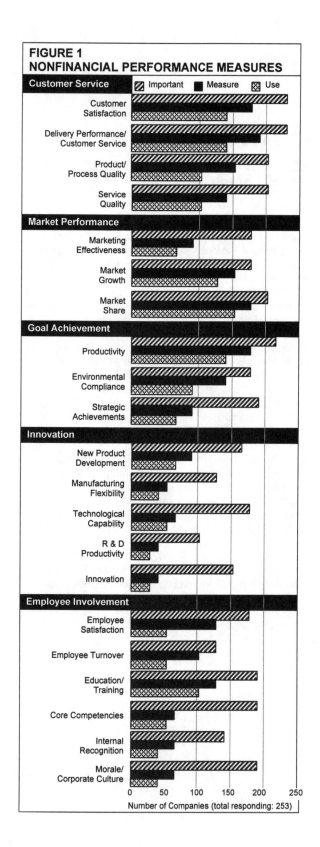

FIGURE 1
NONFINANCIAL PERFORMANCE MEASURES

Legend: Important, Measure, Use

Customer Service
- Customer Satisfaction
- Delivery Performance/ Customer Service
- Product/ Process Quality
- Service Quality

Market Performance
- Marketing Effectiveness
- Market Growth
- Market Share

Goal Achievement
- Productivity
- Environmental Compliance
- Strategic Achievements

Innovation
- New Product Development
- Manufacturing Flexibility
- Technological Capability
- R & D Productivity
- Innovation

Employee Involvement
- Employee Satisfaction
- Employee Turnover
- Education/ Training
- Core Competencies
- Internal Recognition
- Morale/ Corporate Culture

Number of Companies (total responding: 253)
0   50   100   150   200   250

Market performance and goal performance and goal achievement also are perceived to be highly important categories. "Market share" in the market performance category was rated highly important by 200 (70.1%) of the responding firms, and "productivity" in the goal achievement category was rated highly important by 211 (83.4%) of the firms (Figure 1).

Factors in the innovation and employee involvement categories were perceived to be less important in goal setting. Looking at the individual measures, we see that "R&D productivity" in the innovation category was rated as highly important by only 112 (44.3%) of the 253 firms, and "employee turnover" in the employee involvement category was rated as highly important by only 122 (48.2%) of the 253 firms.

The results of the study have important implications for those in the position of designing effective performance measurement systems. The first step is to get the right mix of key factors. If we were to develop a "hit" list of critical, non-financial factors to include in any performance measurement system by listening to Kaplan[1], Drucker[2], and Reichheld[3], we would include the following: market standing, innovation, productivity, customer service, and employee involvement. Although the responding executives in this study did identify market share, productivity, and customer service as highly important factors, they perceived innovation and employee involvement measures to be less important. This is clearly an area of concern if we believe what many business experts are saying about the increasing importance of innovation and human capital. It may well be that in the coming decade, intellectual capital will impact the bottom line more than booked, tangible assets. If this is the case, performance measurement systems must include leading indicators that tap human capital. This is one way managers will be able to manage and control knowledge.

THE IMPORTANCE-MEASUREMENT GAP

Our results show a substantial importance-measurement gap. That is, many companies that view non-financial performance factors as important are not capturing data on these factors. As one would expect, the importance-measurement gap is greatest for factors that are perceived to be unmeasurable or at best difficult to measure. For example, in the employee involvement category, although 192 (75.9%) companies rated "morale and corporate culture" as highly important, only 72 (37.5%) are measuring this factor. There is a similar finding for "core competencies"—192 companies (75.9%) rated the factor as highly important, but only 69 (35.9%) are measuring this factor.

It is interesting to note that just as the categories of innovation and employee involvement received lower overall ratings of importance, responding firms indicated these two categories also have a low incidence of measurement. In particular, the non-financial performance factor least likely to be measured is "innovation." Although 160 firms (63.2%) rated the factor as highly important, only 35 firms (21.8%) are measuring this factor.

On the other hand, a number of other factors have a high rate of measurement. In the market performance category, 200 companies (79.1%) rated "market share" as highly important, and 182 firms (91.0%) are measuring this factor. "Market growth" was rated as highly important by 181 firms (71.5%), and 154 firms (85.1%) are measuring this factor. In the customer service category, "customer satisfaction" and "delivery performance/customer service" have measurement rates of 79.5% and 83.8%, respectively. In goal achievement, "productivity" has a measurement rate of 82.9%

After a firm identifies the right mix of factors to include in the performance measurement system, it is critical that these factors get measured and reported. "What gets measured gets done" implies that the organization becomes what it measures. If you cannot measure something, you cannot control it, and control is essential. The results of this study show a substantial importance-measurement gap for a number of highly important factors, particularly in the categories of innovation and employee involvement. Many of these factors may be perceived to be unmeasurable or difficult to measure. However, the fact is that precise data collection may not be possible; a collection effort that provides even crude data can prove valuable. "What matters...is not the absolute magnitude in any area but the trend...that the measurements will give...no matter how crude and approximate the individual readings are by themselves."[4] Companies may have to experiment with measuring and interpreting different factors. The objective is to provide action-oriented information to managers—not to report balance sheet figures.

THE MEASUREMENT-USE GAP

The final step in the performance measurement process is the use of measurements in developing and monitoring strategic plans. In this study, we found evidence that a large number of businesses are collecting data that are not being used to inform managers in the planning process. We call this the measurement-use gap. Of course, the underlying assumption is that if companies are collecting the data

on important factors, they intend to use the data to make business decisions. To illustrate the measurement-use gap, look at "delivery performance/customer service" in the customer service category (Figure 1). While 197 (83.8%) of 235 study participants (who rated it highly important) indicated that their companies measure this factor, only 140 (71.1%) of 197 indicated that their firms actually use this information for planning purposes. In practical terms, this means that 28.9% of the firms are collecting information that serves no useful purpose in the planning process.

The measurement-use gap appears to be most pronounced in the category of employee involvement. Measures such as "employee satisfaction," "employee turnover," "internal recognition," and "morale and corporate culture" are not used in the planning process by more than 40% of the firms that collect data on these factors.

Study results show that the measurement-use gap is the smallest in the market performance category. For "market growth," 132 (85.7%) of 154 responding firms measuring the factor are using the factor. Results are similar for "market share" in that 161 (88.5%) of 182 responding firms measuring the factor report that they are also using the data. These are measures that have been around for a while; hence, managers are able to interpret the data and translate the information into action items.

The measurement-use gap appears to be moderate for the factors in the categories of customer service, innovation, and goal achievement. Roughly 25% of the companies who measure these factors do not use the results in their planning process.

The underlying assumption is valid—if companies collect data on important performance factors, they intend to use the data to make business decisions. Why would companies identify factors as important, collect measurements on these factors, and then not use the information in the planning process? Certainly, in the case of the employee involvement category, the measures are "softer" than in categories such as market performance. The measurements may be more difficult to understand, and, for this reason, managers may have trouble in translating the information into action items. If, for whatever reason, a firm finds that it is using resources to collect data but fails to use the resulting information, this is an inefficient use of resources that must be checked. Either the information is not relevant, in which case the factor should be deleted from the performance measurement system, or, if the information is perceived to be critical and managers do not know how to use it, every effort must be made to understand the significance of the information.

COMPARING U.S. AND CANADIAN RESPONSES

We also wanted to examine the extent to which perceptions of the importance, measurement, and use of non-financial performance measures were similar across U.S. and Canadian firms.

Both U.S. and Canadian respondents indicate that customer service and market performance categories are most important in setting company goals and that the other categories examined are at least moderately important. The only statistically significant difference between U.S. and Canadian firms is in their perception of the importance of the innovation category. U.S. respondents indicate that these measures are more important in the goal-setting process. U.S. and Canadian firms also show similar patterns in the measurement and use of non-financial performance factors.

For both U.S. and Canadian firms, market performance, customer service, and goal achievement are shown to be the most used and measured non-financial performance categories. However, consistent with U.S. firms' belief concerning the importance of the innovation category, the U.S. firms represented in this sample indicate that they are significantly more likely to both measure and use factors in the innovation category. Although there are several possible explanations for differences between U.S. and Canadian firms as they relate to innovation, it is likely that differences are due, at least in part, to competitive influences. Previous research has shown that competitive pressure often serves as a catalyst for innovation and forces firms to adopt creative internal structures to be responsive to changing markets.[5]

GETTING PAST THREE RED FLAGS TO A DYNAMIC SYSTEM

The performance measurement process involves: (1) the identification of important financial and non-financial factors, (2) measurement of these factors, and (3) use of factors in developing and monitoring strategic plans. The results of this study, based on responses from the top executives of Fortune 500 and Post 300 firms, provide a comprehensive picture of the process of non-financial performance measurement—and show that U.S. and Canadian firms face similar challenges. We believe that study results highlight three red flags.

First, measures of innovation and employee involvement were not perceived to be as important as customer service and market standing—this is a concern. If we believe the business experts who are telling us that human capital and other intangible

HOW THE SURVEY WAS DESIGNED

Questionnaires were mailed to the top executives of Fortune 500 firms in the United States and Post 300 firms in Canada. The names and addresses of study participants were compiled from two databases: Compact Disclosure and CANCORP Canadian Financials. One hundred and two of the Fortune 500 U.S. firms and 151 of the Post 300 Canadian firms responding to the mail survey, providing an overall response rate of 31.625%. This response rate is significantly higher than might be expected given previous research on survey response rates for companies of this size.[1] Involvement by the Canadian Institute of Chartered Accountants may account for this higher than usual response rate; previous research has shown that endorsement by a well-known external party yields significantly higher response rates.[2] Respondents were chairmen of the board (70), chief executive officers (85), and chief financial officers (98). Based on 1993 Compact Disclosure and CANCORP Canadian Financials data, the average number of individuals employed by responding U.S. firms was 23,835, and the average number of employees in the Canadian responding firms was 7,689.

[1]Dennis H. Tootelian and Ralph M. Gaedeke, Fortune 500 List Revisited 12 Years Later: Still an Endangered Species for Academic Research?" *Journal of Business Research*, Vol. 15, No. 4, August 1987, pp. 359-363.

[2]Linda Rochford, "Surveying a Targeted Population Segment: The Effects of Endorsement on Mail Questionnaire Response Rate," Journal of Marketing Theory & Practice, Vol. 3, Spring 1995, pp. 86-97.

assets classed as intellectual capital are becoming the basis of competitive advantage and wealth creation, then it is imperative that measures of innovation and employee involvement be included in the performance measurement systems—that is, identified, measured, and used to design and monitor strategic plans. Although results show that U.S. firms view measures of innovation as more important in the goal setting process and are more likely to measure and use innovation factors, both U.S. and Canadian firms show substantial importance-measurement and measurement-use gaps.

Second, study results indicate a strong importance-measurement gap for certain factors. That is, although top executives believe that certain non-financial factors are highly important, a large number of firms are not capturing data on these measures. It is clear that some factors are more difficult to measure than others. But, even crude measurements on critical factors can provide valuable input to the control framework. To close the importance-measurement gap, companies may need to experiment with different measurement methodologies.

Third, results of the study suggest a substantial measurement-use gap. That is, a large number of companies are collecting data that are not being used by managers in the planning process. The reasons underlying the measurement-use gap should be investigated. If the firms are collecting data that are not useful, these factors should be deleted from the performance measurement system. If the data are on factors that are perceived to be critical, however, it may be that managers need help in learning how to use the information in the strategic planning process.

To develop a successful performance measurement system, managers must clearly understand the interests of the stakeholders (customers, employees, and investors), the strategic objectives of the company, and every aspect of the company's business processes. Only then can they be assured that the performance measurement system includes the right factors, both financial and non-financial. Long-term commitment to the system is required to assure that the factors are measured, understood, and used. The result can be a performance measurement system that is clearly linked to strategy, is dynamic, and is action-oriented.

---

[1] Robert S. Kaplan and David P. Norton, "The Balanced Scorecard—Measures that Drive Performance," *Harvard Business Review*, January-February, 1992, pp. 71-79; Norton (1993); "Putting the Balanced Scorecard to Work," *Harvard Business Review*, September-October, 1993, pp. 134-147; "Using the Balanced Scorecard as a Strategic Management System," *Harvard Business Review,* January-February 1996, pp. 75-85.

[2] Peter F. Drucker, *Managing for the Future*, New York: Truman Talley Books/Dutton, 1992: *Post-Capitalist Society*, Harper Business, New York, 1993: "The Age of Social Transformation," *The Atlantic Monthly*, November 1994, pp. 53-80.

[3] Frederick F. Reichheld, *The Loyalty Effect*, Harvard Business School Press, Boston, 1996.

[4] Drucker, *Managing for the Future*.

[5] Robert Simmons, *Levers of Control: How Managers Use Innovative Control Systems to Drive Strategic Renewal,* Harvard Business School Press, Boston, 1995.

APPLYING THE BALANCED SCORECARD TO SMALL COMPANIES

Companies are designing their performance goals—and keeping score—based on their unique needs and perceived critical success factors.

By Chee W. Chow, Kamal M. Haddad, and James E. Williamson, CPA

On October 30, 1996, Pacific Inland Bank of Anaheim, Calif., announced that it had changed its vision and strategy to such an extent that it was also changing its name to Security First Bank in a complete restructuring to transform it into "a true community bank, one that serves small businesses, professionals, and consumers."[1]

The restructuring at Security First is only one example of how American companies are making major changes in responding to an increasingly competitive global economy. Indeed, the need for fundamental change is so strong that some leading authorities from academia and industry have called for a complete rethinking and reengineering of Corporate America. For example, in their book, *Reengineering the Corporation*,[2] authors Hammer and Champy emphasize that it no longer is enough to do traditional tasks better. Rather, the realities of the current competitive environment require that the old "individual-based task-oriented" management concept be discarded completely and replaced with a "team-based process-oriented" management concept.

The current emphasis on restructuring has created a new problem for management because traditional measures of financial performance no longer are adequate to fully assess how the newly restructured organization is doing. Not only will successful restructuring require innovation in the way organizations view and measure performance, but developing, implementing, and evaluating such measures may be the greatest challenge that companies will have to face. In fact, a recent survey has found that "80% of large American companies want to change their performance measurement systems."[3] The "Balanced Scorecard" may be just what organizations need to help them restructure successfully to meet the demands of the 21st Century.

WHAT IS THE BALANCED SCORECARD?

Essentially, the Balanced Scorecard is a set of financial and nonfinancial measures relating to a company's critical success factors. What is innovative about the concept is that the components of the scorecard are designed in an integrative fashion such that they reinforce each other in indicating both the current and future prospects of the company. More than others, Kaplan and Norton probably deserve much of the credit for elucidating and increasing the awareness of this concept.[4]

When Kaplan and Norton introduced the concept of the Balanced Scorecard they were looking for ways to concentrate corporate focus on performance measurement innovation. This focus was considered necessary because traditional management reporting systems have been found to be not much help in measuring performance in the new manufacturing environment. While these backward-looking "task" or "cost object" oriented measurement systems generated financial results for numerous organizational units—including results by entity, lines of business, cost centers, and profit centers—they failed to supply the information necessary to pull strong future performance out of the organization.

Today's managers know that yesterday's accounting results tell little about what actually can help grow market share and profits—things like employee development and turnover, innovative services that enhance customer values, the quality of vendor services, and benefits from advancements in research and development. A key advantage of the Balanced Scorecard is that it puts strategy, structure, and vision at the center of management's focus.

Another advantage is that because the Balanced Scorecard emphasizes an integrated combination of traditional and nontraditional performance measures, it keeps management focused on the entire business process and helps ensure that actual current operating performance is in line with long-term strategy and customer values. In so doing, the Balanced Scorecard helps maintain a balance

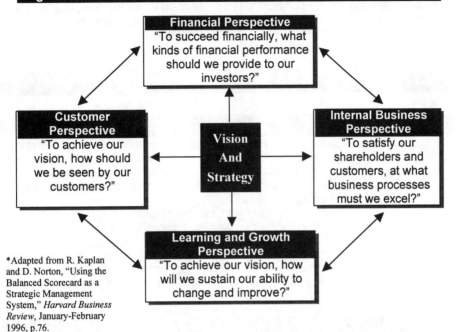

Figure 1. TRANSLATING STRATEGY INTO OPERATIONAL TERMS*

Financial Perspective
"To succeed financially, what kinds of financial performance should we provide to our investors?"

Customer Perspective
"To achieve our vision, how should we be seen by our customers?"

Vision And Strategy

Internal Business Perspective
"To satisfy our shareholders and customers, at what business processes must we excel?"

Learning and Growth Perspective
"To achieve our vision, how will we sustain our ability to change and improve?"

*Adapted from R. Kaplan and D. Norton, "Using the Balanced Scorecard as a Strategic Management System," *Harvard Business Review*, January-February 1996, p.76.

between building long-range competitive abilities and recognizing investors' attention to financial reports. To this extent the Balanced Scorecard does retain traditional financial measures. But these financial measures are viewed in the larger context of the company's competitive strategies for creating "future value through investment in customers, suppliers, employees, processes, technology, and innovation."[5]

Because of the way the Balanced Scorecard aids in successful restructuring by linking together all subunits and members in a concerted effort to enhance the overall goals and objectives of the organization, many leading-edge companies have begun to adopt this new approach. For example, in late 1989, Bank of Montreal's "corporate performance was heading downhill fast." Chairman and Chief Executive Officer Mathew Barrett and his team, deciding that "a successful turn-around strategy had to include a new approach to performance measurement," used the Balanced Scorecard to help solve the company's problems. A partial list of other adopters includes KPMG Peat Marwick, Tenneco, Allstate, AT&T, and Elf Atochem.[6]

MAJOR COMPONENTS OF A BALANCED SCORECARD

A well designed Balanced Scorecard combines financial measures of past performance with measures of the firm's' drivers of future performance. The specific objectives and measures of an organization's Balanced Scorecard are derived from the firm's vision and strategy. As such, the relevance perspectives and their relative importance can be expected to vary among firms. There is some agreement, however, that the framework for a Balanced Scorecard will include at least four major perspectives: financial, customer, internal business process, and learning and growth (Figure 1).

The financial perspective serves as the focus for the objects and measures in the other scorecard perspectives. This perspective reflects the concern in for-profit enterprises that every action should be part of a network of cause-and-effect relationships that culminate in improving short- and long-run financial performance. In the process of identifying goals and measures, different financial metrics may be appropriate for different units within the organization, linking that unit's financial objectives to the overall business unit strategy.

But how is a company to achieve its financial goals? Current wisdom is that every company needs to pay attention to the needs and desires of its customers because customers pay for the company's costs and provide for its profit. Companies need to identify the customer and market segments in which they choose to compete. This customer perspective allows companies to align their measures of customer values (i.e., satisfaction, loyalty, retention, acquisition, and profitability) with targeted customers and market segments.

Table 1.	RESPONSE FROM AN ELECTRONICS FIRM
Goals	**Measures**
Customer Perspective	
Quality	Own quality relative to industry standards; number of defects; first pass yields; delivered product quality; number of visits to customers to calibrate quality; number of returns; number and quality of customers.
Price	Own price relative to competitive market price; sales volume; customer willingness to pay.
Delivery	Actual versus planned; number of ontime deliveries; number of days early/late; current backlog; aging of past due orders.
Shipments	Sales growth; number of customers that make up 90% of shipments; % military sales; number of new-to-us part numbers shipped.
New products	Number of new products to support new semiconductors; rate of technology improvements; % of sales from products introduced in last two years.
Support	Response time; customer satisfaction surveys.
Internal Capabilities	
Efficiency of manufacturing process	Cycle time; lead time; manufacturing overhead cost/quarter; rate of increase in use of automation each quarter; days' sales in WIP; yield.
New product introduction	Rate of new product introduction/quarter
New product success	New products quarterly sales; number of orders.
Sales penetration	Actual sales versus plan; increases in number of $1 million customers each quarter.
New businesses	Number of new businesses each year.
Innovation	
Technology leadership	Product performance compared to competition; number of new products with patented technology in them; annual rate of increase in number of new products per engineer.
Cost leadership	Manufacturing overhead per quarter as a percent of sales; rate of decrease in cost of quality per quarter.
Market leadership	Market share in all major markets; number of systems developed to meet customer requests and requirements.
Research and development	Number of new products; number of patents.
Financial Perspective	
Sales	Annual growth in sales and profits.
Cost of sales	Extent it remains flat or decreases each year.
Profitability	Return on total capital employed.
Prosperity	Cash flows.
Employees and Community Perspective	
Competitive salaries and benefits	Salaries compared to norm in local area.
Opportunity	Individual contribution, personal satisfaction in job; opportunity to share in company financial success.
Citizenship	Company contributions to community and the institutions that generate the environment; extent to which employees are encouraged to contribute to the community.

Another component of the scorecard focuses on those internal business processes that will deliver the objectives that the financial and customer perspectives have established for customers and shareholders. This component expands the focus beyond improving existing operating processes to defining a complete internal process value chain that includes identifying current and future customer needs and developing solutions for those needs. This perspective will be unique to each company as it identifies the complete chain of processes that add to the value customers receive from its products and services.

Based on the objectives established in the financial, customer, and internal business process perspectives, a company needs to identify objectives and measures to drive continuous organizational learning and growth. The objectives in the learning and growth perspective should be the drivers of successful outcomes in the first three perspectives.

Because the Balanced Scorecard expands the company's set of objectives beyond traditional financial measures, managers will be able to measure how their business units create value for current and future customers. The Balanced Scorecard also helps to measure the need to enhance internal capabilities and the firm's investment in people, systems, and those procedures necessary to improve future performance. In other words, the Balanced Scorecard is an attempt to capture the essence of the organization's critical value-creating activities. The Balanced Scorecard also aids in communicating the company's goals and rewarding those employees whose efforts enhance those goals. Because of the financial perspective, the Balanced Scorecard retains an interest in short-term performance but, at the same time, clearly reveals those drivers leading to long-term financial and competitive performance.

FITTING THE BALANCED SCORECARD TO THE ORGANIZATION

Developing a Balanced Scorecard involves a process of custom designing a strategic management measurement system for a specific organization. The process is begun by making a preliminary assessment of the overall business strategy of the organization. The focus is on integration of the entire business process but not overly emphasizing the individual tasks. Once the overall business process is identified, along with its goals and objectives, it should be possible to identify and rank the measures believed to capture the essence of the organization's progress toward those goals and objectives.

To date, reported applications of the Balanced Scorecard mostly have been confined to large, international companies. These companies tend to face more turbulent and competitive environments, have more dispersed and varied products and processes that they to coordinate and monitor, and also have more resources for undertaking change initiatives. In comparison, small or local companies may have different needs such that what works for large companies may be ineffective or unnecessary for them. To gain some insights into the potential applicability of the Balanced Scorecard in small or local companies, we undertook a dialogue with four such companies operating in Southern California whose size ranged from 100 to 1,200 employees. This dialogue with a top-level manager, either the CEO or a senior vice president from each company, was loosely structured in the form of a question and response survey asking to what extent the company had considered developing a Balanced Scorecard to fir its particular needs. Each company was asked to identify up to five major components, along with the goals and associated performance measures, that might form the basis for an effective Balanced Scorecard for it.

Another objective of our study was to explore how the Balanced Scorecard might vary across industries, so we looked at four companies from different industries: electronics manufacturing, food ingredients, banking, and biotechnology. The Balanced Scorecards suggested by these companies are shown in Tables 1-4. Because of space limitations, however, we will discuss only the responses from the electronics firm, as shown in Table 1, in any detail.

We also asked each of the top managers to what extent their company had implemented a performance monitoring system similar to the Balanced Scorecard and if they thought such a system could be beneficial to their company. Only one of the responding companies said it had totally implemented such a system, with the other companies reporting that their current implementation status ranged from 3 to 7 on a scale of 1 to 10. All responding companies, however, said they thought such a system would be extremely beneficial, with the lowest score being 8 on a scale of 1 to 10, and half of the companies gave the value of the concept a perfect 10 rating.

The electronics firm selected the customer perspective, emphasizing the goals of quality, price,

Table 2. RESPONSE FROM A FOOD INGREDIENTS COMPANY

Goals	Measures
Financial Perspective	
Capture an increasing share of industry growth.	Company growth versus industry growth.
Secure the base business while remaining the preferred supplier to our customers.	Volume trend by line of business; revenue trend by line of business; gross margin.
Expand aggressively in global markets.	Ratio of North American sales to international sales.
Commercialize a continuous stream of profitable new ingredients and services.	Percent of sales from products launched within the past five years; gross profit from new products.
Customer Perspective	
Become the lowest-cost supplier.	Total cost of using our products and services relative to total cost of using competitive products and services.
Tailor products and services to meet local needs.	Cross-sell ratio.
Expand those products and services that meet customers' needs better than competitors.	Percent of products in R&D pipeline that are being test-marketed by out customers (percent of pipeline value).
Customer satisfaction.	Customer surveys.
Internal Perspective	
Maintain lowest cost base in the industry.	Our total costs relative to number one competitor; inventory turns; plant utilization.
Maintain consistent predictable production processes.	First pass success rate.
Continue to improve distribution efficiency.	Percent of perfect orders.
Build capability to screen and identify profitable products and services.	Change in pipeline economic value (risk-adjusted decision tree approach similar to option pricing methodology).
Integrate acquisitions and alliances efficiently.	Revenues per salary dollar.
Learning and Growth Perspective	
Link the overall strategy to the reward and recognition system.	Net income per dollar of variable pay.
Foster a culture that supports innovation and growth.	Annual preparedness assessment; quarterly reports (done by VP-MGR).
Develop those competencies critical to the overall critical gaps to be filled.	Percent competency deployment matrix filled.

delivery, and development of new products as of primary importance. This selection probably is typical of the contemporary world view that customers and their values must come first if the company is going to maintain long-term financial stability and growth.

The second component selected is internal capabilities. But analysis of the goals and measures attached to this component indicates that customer values and market penetration are still on the minds of the company's management. There definitely is a linkage here that the management clearly recognizes.

Third, the company values innovation which, again, clearly reflects the linkage with customer values and market penetration. In this area, we also see that they are very concerned with quality, the cost of quality, and its cause and effect on competitive market prices.

Fourth, the company indicates, but with little discussion, that there is a need to provide shareholders some relatively short-run traditional financial results. That the company places this component fourth is an indication that it sees customer values, product development and innovation, and market penetration as drivers of financial performance.

Finally, the company management's explicit identification of an employee perspective reflects its belief that a well-paid and satisfied workforce is key to attaining the company's overall goals and objectives.

DIFFERENT GOALS AND SCORECARDS

As we mentioned earlier, an important consideration in applying the Balanced Scorecard approach is to recognize that each organization is unique and, therefore, requires a different set of goals, objectives, and strategies to attain its mission. This fact is evident when we look at the items selected by some of the other companies for their scorecard.

A company in the food ingredients industry (Table 2) says it is first interested in the financial perspective but then proceeds to identify many goals and measures in the other perspectives that will enhance the financial goals along with the goals of perspective.

The responses from a commercial bank are illustrated in Table 3. An interesting observation about this scorecard is that it sets out a separate community perspective. This viewpoint probably reflects the traditional community role that bank managers think may be expected of them.

Finally, a biotechnology firm in its Balanced Scorecard (Table 4) selected the customer perspective as of primary importance. The financial perspective comes after customers and technological leadership. Thus, across the four types of companies considered there is a clear indication that management is designing the goals and measures to fit the company's unique needs and perceived role. Further, these responses suggest that the Balanced Scorecard can be an effective management tool for small companies as well.

FOUR NEW MANAGEMENT PROCESSES

Kaplan and Norton show how the Balanced Scorecard will let managers introduce "four new management processes that, separately and in combination, contribute to linking long-term strategic objectives with short-term actions."[7] Figure 2 shows how the integration of the four processes lead to the Balanced Scorecard.

The first process—translating the vision—helps managers build a consensus of opinion about the organization's vision and strategy. Because it is very important to translate vision and strategy into operational terms that employees can understand and use to guide actions at their local level, the vision and

strategy statements must be expressed as an agreed-upon integrated set of objectives and measures that describe the long-term drivers of success.

The second process—communicating and linking—helps management tie overall objectives and strategies to department and individual objectives. This process replaces the traditional way departments are evaluated by financial performance and individual incentives. The advantages of this new approach is the way it ensures that all levels of the organization are made aware of and understand the company's long-term strategy. The scorecard also ensures that individual and departmental objectives are in agreement with the long-term strategy.

The third process—business planning—helps organizations integrate their business and financial plans. Kaplan and Norton explain that most organizations today are trying to implement a variety of change programs that are competing with each other for time, energy, and resources.[8] This competition can be so intense and inner focused that it is difficult to integrate these diverse initiatives to achieve the firm's overall strategic goals. The Balanced Scorecard can be used to set goals that provide a basis for allocating resources and setting priorities. The scorecard also can aid in eliminating some initiatives and selecting others that are more effective for moving the organization toward its long-term strategic objectives.

The fourth process—feedback and learning—helps management direct the organization toward strategic learning. This process is different from traditional feedback and review models that focus on whether the company, departments, or individuals have met their budgeted financial objectives. An advantage of the Balanced Scorecard approach over traditional models is that it focuses management's attention on managing results from the perspective of customers, internal business processes, and learning and growth. This real-time learning perspective can increase organizations' nimbleness in modifying strategies in response to changing circumstances.

THE PERSONAL SCORECARD

Because achieving a company's goals requires a concerted effort on the part of everyone, there is a need to translate the goals and objectives down to the individual level. Translating the company scorecard into specific goals and measures at the individual level is important for motivating and focusing the individuals and teams performing the work. There is no reason why all the individual scorecards should be identical because each member may have a unique role in the

Table 3. RESPONSE FROM A COMMERCIAL BANK

Goals	Measures
Shareholders — Financial Perspective	
Return on assets of 1% or more and return on equity of 15% or more.	Net interest margin; noninterest income; noninterest expense.
Efficiency ratio of 68% or less.	Overhead expenses.
Growth in assets of 15% or more.	Asset growth.
Loan losses of .5% or less.	Number of problem loans; early detection rate.
Loan delinquencies over 30 days of 2% or less.	Number of bad loan underwriting; number of loan delinquencies.
Customer Perspective	
Personalized quality service	Number of complaints; amount spent on training; number of rewards and recognitions; customer satisfaction.
Competitive products	Sales volume; number of customers; number of products offered a year; extent products are "user friendly" compared to competition; degree of use of technology (where appropriate).
Pricing	Cost of doing business; own price relative to competition; extent service is better than competition.
Customer satisfaction	Customer surveys.
Employee Perspective	
Competitive wages and benefits.	Annual market review.
Participation in success of the organization.	Bonuses based on corporate and personal performance; sales incentives; recognition.
Enhanced job skills.	Training/schooling; coaching.
Objective evaluation of performance.	Performance standards; job descriptions.
Enhance upward career movement.	Number of promotions from within; posting of most open positions.
Community Perspective	
Support worthwhile community activities.	Extent of employee participation; extent of financial support.
Act as good corporate citizens.	Extent employees are encouraged to vote; extent of support and activities that foster this attitude.

organization. The goals and needs of any organization are many and varied, and skills, talents, and interests also vary across individuals. To attain the greatest success as a whole requires organizations to exploit these individual differences and to seek and create synergies among its members. Thus, unlike a golf team, where the team score is simply the sum of individual team members' scores, most organizations are more like a football team, where the team outcome depends on coordination and cooperation in addition to specialization among team members. Accordingly, while the individual personal scorecards need to be consistent with the organization's overall strategies, goals, and measures, there also needs to be flexibility in accommodating individual strengths and weaknesses.

A question that remains is whether an organization's compensation system should be linked to its Balance Scorecard measures. Some companies believe that tying financial reward to performance is a powerfully motivating incentive and have done so.[9] If an organization is considering using such a linkage in its compensation scheme, however, it is important to realize that there also are risks involved with this approach. Does the organization have the right measures on the scorecard? Does the organization have valid and reliable data for the selected measures of performance? Are there undesirable consequences that could arise from actions aimed at achieving the

Table 4. RESPONSE FROM A BIOTECHNOLOGY FIRM

Goals	Measures
Customer Perspective (How can we improve customer perceptions and relationships?)	
New products	Percent of sales from new products.
Early purchase of seasonal products	Percent of sales recorded by early purchase date.
Accurate invoices	Percent error-free invoices.
Early payment	Percent of customers who pay early.
Product quality	Product performance vs. industry quality standards.
Customer satisfaction	Customer satisfaction surveys.
Internal Business Perspective (Efficiency; how can we be more cost-effective?)	
Low-cost producer	Unit cost vs. competitors.
Reduce inventory	Inventory as percent of sales.
New products	Number of actual introductions vs. target.
Innovation Perspective (How can we establish and maintain technological leadership?)	
New active ingredients	Number of new ingredients identified by internal discovery program.
Proprietary positions	Number of patents that create exclusive marketing rights.
Financial Perspective (How do we build shareowner value?)	
Growth	Percent increase in top line revenue.
Profitability	Return on equity; earnings per share.
Industry leadership	Market share.

established targets? Those types of questions need to be explored before an organization adopts an incentive strategy based on achieving certain targeted goals.

We do know that if the current trend of shifting emphasis from individual achievement to cooperation and teamwork continues, companies will need to reexamine their short-term formula-based incentive compensation systems. Moreover, when companies adopt the Balanced Scorecard approach, they move to a longer-term viewpoint and may need to set incentive rewards more subjectively. According to Kaplan and Norton, the longer-term subjective evaluation process appears to have the advantage of being less susceptible to the game playing and distortions associated with explicit, formula-based rules.[10] There is little doubt that the Balanced Scorecard has a role to play in incentive compensation systems. Exactly what that role will be will become clear as companies experiment with various ways to link rewards to scorecard measures.

IMPLEMENTING THE BALANCED SCORECARD

If the experience of other companies is any guide,[11] the design and implementation process for installing a Balanced Scorecard may take two years or more. A typical schedule may contain all or some of the following component stages.

Stage 1. A strategic planning retreat involving all levels of management is held to identify strategic issues and discuss possible solutions. A major purpose of this meeting is to achieve a consensus among the individual members concerning the company's overall vision and strategic goals and objectives. This step should lead to identifying the critical perspectives in the company's Balanced Scorecard.

Stage 2. A strategic planning committee is formed to formulate objectives for each previously identified perspective in the firm's Balanced Scorecard.

Stage 3. Using the Balanced Scorecard as a communication tool, the strategic planning committee seeks comments on and acceptance of the company's Balanced Scorecard from all members of the organization.

Stage 4. Based on feedback from the dialogue with the individual members, the strategic planning committee revises the company's Balanced Scorecard.

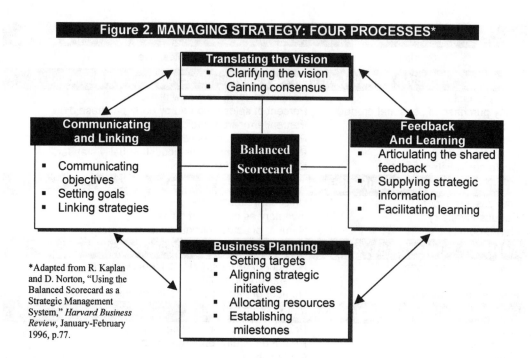

Figure 2. MANAGING STRATEGY: FOUR PROCESSES*

Translating the Vision
- Clarifying the vision
- Gaining consensus

Communicating and Linking
- Communicating objectives
- Setting goals
- Linking strategies

Balanced Scorecard

Feedback And Learning
- Articulating the shared feedback
- Supplying strategic information
- Facilitating learning

Business Planning
- Setting targets
- Aligning strategic initiatives
- Allocating resources
- Establishing milestones

*Adapted from R. Kaplan and D. Norton, "Using the Balanced Scorecard as a Strategic Management System," *Harvard Business Review*, January-February 1996, p.77.

Stage 5. The revised balanced Scorecard is communicated to the individual members. Thereupon, each individual member is required to develop a personal Balanced Scorecard that supports the company's overall goals and objectives described in its Balanced Scorecard.

Stage 6. The strategic planning committee reviews the individual Balanced Scorecards and may revise not only the personal scorecards but also the company's Balanced Scorecard.

Stage 7. Based on final Balanced Scorecards, management formulates a five-year strategic plan for the overall organization. The first-year plan is expanded into the annual operating plan for the following year.

Stage 8. Individual and company progress is reviewed quarterly to identify areas that need immediate attention and additional work.

Stage 9. Based on the individual personal Balanced Scorecards, the company's personnel committee in conjunction with each individual's supervisor evaluates each member's performance for the past year and makes recommendations relating to retention promotion, salary increases, or other rewards.

Stage 10. The strategic planning committee revises the company's Balanced Scorecard and the five-year strategic plan based on external and internal scanning of the company's current condition and changes in the economic environment.

Because the process is so lengthy, managers should lose no time in evaluating the Balanced Scorecard concept to see if they want to implement it or other methods that will promote and support change to better measurement and reward systems.

A SCORECARD FOR THE 21ST CENTURY

Maybe it is time to try something new. The Balanced Scorecard appears to be an exciting new idea that may help firms restructure to survive in difficult times. The scorecard also appears to be a concept that helps management direct its attention to those goals and objectives and the measures that drive the company toward achieving those goals and objectives that will allow the company to reengineer or restructure to meet the needs of the 21st Century.

The Balanced Scorecard is not so structured that it can serve all organizations uniformly. But, instead, its strength really lies in providing for management the ability to design a unique scorecard that specifically firs the needs of that company, subunit, or individual employee.

Perhaps most important, while the Balanced Scorecard is relatively new on the performance measurement scene, its perceived advantages at this time indicate that it may be with us for quite awhile.

Chee W. Chow, Ph.D., is Vern Odmark Professor of Accountancy, San Diego State University, San Diego, Calif. Kamal M. Haddad, Ph.D., is professor of finance, San Diego State University, and James E. Williamson, Ph.D., CPA, is director of the School of Accounting, San Diego State University. He is a member of the San Diego Chapter, through which he submitted this article. He may be contacted at (619) 594-6021 or e-mail jameswilliamson@sdsu.edu.

[1] James Granelli, "Troubled Bank Tries Fresh Start," *Los Angeles Times*, October 31, 1996, pp. D1, D4

[2] Michael Hammer and James Champy, *Reengineering the Corporation*, Harper Business, New York, N.Y., 1993.

[3] Bill Birchard, "Making it Go," *CFO*, October 1995, pp. 42-51.

[4] Robert Kaplan and David Norton, "The Balanced Scorecard—Measures That Drive Performance," *Harvard Business Review*, January-February 1992, pp. 71-79.

[5] Robert S. Kaplan and David P. Norton, *Translating Strategy Into Action: The Balanced Scorecard,* Harvard Business School Press, Boston, Mass., 1996, p.7.

[6] Birchard, pp. 49-51.

[7] Robert Kaplan and David Norton, "Using the Balanced Scorecard as a Strategic Management System," *Harvard Business Review*, January-February 1996, p. 75.

[8] Kaplan and Norton, p. 75.

[9] Kaplan and Norton, p. 81.

[10] Kaplan and Norton, p. 82.

[11] Kaplan and Norton, p. 78-79.

Chapter 3
Basic Cost Concepts

Cases

3-1   Strategy, CSFs, Cost Objects, and Performance Measures
3-2   Cost Drivers and Strategy

Readings

"Managing Costs Through Complexity Reduction at Carrier Corporation"
This article, based on the experience of Carrier Corporation, a United Technologies company, and one of the world's largest manufacturers of heating and air conditioning products, explains how product complexity is a key driver of total costs. The article also explains how product complexity can be measured and some techniques for reducing complexity.

Discussion Questions:
1. Why does product complexity lead to increased costs?
2. Explain 3-4 useful measures of product complexity.
3. Identify and explain 2-3 techniques for reducing product complexity and cost.

3-1. Strategy, CSFs, Cost Objects, and Performance Measures[1]

Three years ago, Vincent Chow completed his degree in accounting. The economy was in a depressed state at the time, and Vincent managed to get an offer of only $20,000 per year as a bookkeeper. In addition to its relatively low pay, this job had limited advancement potential.

Since Vincent was an enterprising and ambitious young man, he declined this offer and started a business of his own. He was convinced that because of changing lifestyles, a drive-through coffee establishment would be profitable. He was able to obtain backing from his parents to open such an establishment close to the industrial park area in town. Vincent named his business The Cappuccino Express and decided to sell only two type types of coffee; cappuccino and decaffeinated.

As Vincent had expected, the Cappuccino Express was very well received. Within three years, Vincent had added another outlet north of town. He left the day-to-day management of each site to a manager and focused his own attention on overseeing the entire enterprise. He also hired an assistant to do the record keeping and to perform selected other shores.

REQUIRED:

1. What is the competitive strategy of Vincent's business – cost leadership, differentiation, or focus?
2. What are the critical success factors of The Cappuccino Express? Which of these are controllable by Vincent?
3. What major tasks does Vincent have to undertake in managing The Cappuccino Express?
4. What are the costs of operating The Cappuccino Express? Choose a cost object and classify each of these costs as direct or indirect, fixed or variable, controllable or uncontrollable, product cost or period cost, or opportunity cost.
5. Vincent would like to monitor the performance of each site manager. What measure, or measures, should he use?
6. If you had suggested more than one measure, which of these should Vincent select if he could use only one?

---

[1] Prepared by Chee W. Chow, © American Accounting Association, 1997. Used with permission.

3-2.   Cost Drivers, Strategy.

Joe Costanzo is owner of a growing chain of grocery stores in the Richmond, Virginia and the Washington, D.C. area. Joe's stores specialize in organic and other specialty foods and other specialty products, which have attracted a strong following. As his business matures, Joe is now more interested in understanding how he can better manage the profitability of his stores. In particular, he is interested in understanding what drives the costs in his business.

REQUIRED:

As a potential consultant to Joe, develop a proposal for a consulting engagement which would focus on the profitability and cost driver issues Joe is concerned about. The proposal should address which types of cost drivers should be studied and why. Also, the proposal should identify what are likely to be the important cost drivers in this business.

MANAGING COSTS THROUGH COMPLEXITY REDUCTION AT CARRIER CORPORATION

By Dan W. Swenson, CMA

Carrier, a United Technologies' Company, is the world's largest manufacturer of air conditioning and heating products. Competition is intense, however, and among its six largest competitors, Carrier is the only one that is not Japanese owned. The director of cost improvement for Carrier's worldwide operations notes that Carrier's customers demand "a wide range of products that have unquestionable quality and include state-of-the-art features. Further, they expect these products to be delivered when needed, at a competitive price."

As the industry leader, Carrier strives to maintain its dominant position through innovative product design (product differentiation), high-quality low-cost manufacturing (zero defects and cost leadership), and time-based competition. (See Figure 1.) To achieve these objectives, Carrier implemented a series of improvement initiatives, including just-in-time, product and process standardization, strategic out-sourcing, supply chain management, target costing, and performance measurement. Complexity reduction is a common goal among each of these initiatives.

While Carrier's manufacturing environment was changing dramatically at the plant level, its parent company, United Technologies, continued to emphasize financial reporting and control at the corporate level and placed relatively little emphasis on developing modern cost management systems for its manufacturing plants. Therefore, the manufacturing plants lacked the cost management information that was needed to support the above improvement initiatives adequately, and profitability suffered. "The intense competition, coupled with ever increasing customer demands, have made it difficult to maintain adequate profit margins on many products. Accordingly, NAO's (Carrier's North American Operations) profitability had dropped significantly below historical levels."

Carrier needed what it describes as a set of "enablers" to support the development of cost effective product designs and manufacturing processes. Activity-based cost management was selected as the enabler, or tool, that provides the necessary financial and activity information. Following its implementation, ABCM has been used by Carrier to quantify the benefits of redesigning plant layouts, using common parts, outsourcing, strengthening supplier and customer relationships, and developing alternative product designs. In some cases, even though management knows intuitively how to improve its operations, until the improvements are quantified they are not acted upon.

COMPLEXITY REDUCTION PROGRAM

Carrier embarked upon its complexity reduction program to reduce the amount of complexity in both the design and manufacture of its products. In many ways the term complexity is analogous to variety. A company's complexity increases as the breadth of its product line expands, as each product uses more unique components, and as more process options are available to manufacture the product. The costs associated with this complexity fall as manufacturing processes are simplified and standardized and as companies offer fewer product options. At Carrier, a strategy to reduce complexity is the common thread that runs through each of its improvement initiatives (see Figure 1). Excessive product and process complexity drives costs up, increases lead time, and makes quality more difficult to control. According to Gonsalves and Eiler,[1] "Complexity factors are the biggest single driver of cost. They are also the single biggest inhibitors of throughput."

To measure its progress at reducing complexity costs, Carrier classifies manufacturing costs as being either unit-related, batch-related, product-sustaining, or structural. Unit-related costs fluctuate with the number of units produced. Direct material and direct labor are examples of unit-related costs. Batch-related costs vary according to the number of batches produced, and examples include material handling and first-part inspection costs. Product-sustaining costs change based on the number of different types of products produced. Designing new products and maintaining part numbers in the information system are examples of product-sustaining costs. Finally, structural costs tend to be fixed and are not related to the number of units, batches, or products produced.[2]

For most companies, batch and product-sustaining costs are closely associated with manufacturing complexity. These costs increase as product lines expand, as more component parts are developed, and as batch production is utilized. For measurement and control purposes, Carrier classifies all batch and product-sustaining costs as "costs of complexity." Furthermore, Carrier has developed financial and nonfinancial performance measures to benchmark its progress at removing complexity from its value chain. Financial performance measures include complexity costs as a percentage of overhead, complexity costs as a percentage of total product costs, and complexity costs as a percent of revenue. Nonfinancial performance measures include the number of common components and manufacturing process options available (which it tries to minimize) and the extent to which certified suppliers and strategic outsourcing are used (which it tries to encourage). Complexity reduction targets are in place for Carrier's current product line, and they also are used during the development of new products. Some of its complexity measures are illustrated in Table 1.[3]

Carrier's complexity reduction process has evolved into a formal, systematic program with corporate-wide visibility. The cost of complexity (COC) programs are administered at the plant level by COC teams. COC teams are formed by recruiting mid-level managers from each functional area including manufacturing, engineering, accounting, and materials management. Once a team is formed, it documents its goals, objectives, and deliverables. It then agrees to a methodology for financially evaluating complexity costs and potential cost reduction opportunities. The team also develops a process to target products and processes for standardization (a primary means of complexity reduction). The COC teams receive top management support from a steering committee that oversees and monitors the success of the COC program. Carrier considers this program to be one of its critical success factors.

STEPS TO COMPLEXITY REDUCTION

The complexity reduction process begins when someone (the originator) proposes an idea for complexity reduction, completes a Complexity Reduction Form, and marks up the product's prints, specification sheets, and other applicable documents. The originator also can use the Complexity Reduction Form to suggest changes in parts, processes, or procedures. For example, the originator might see an opportunity to eliminate the use of single-application unique parts and replace them with common parts that have multiple applications. Originators also might propose process cost reductions, such as replacing a batch process with a point-of-use process.

The Complexity Reduction Form is forwarded to the plant coordinator who records the proposal in the Complexity Reduction Log. The coordinator also records a description of the proposal, the date it was received, its status, and potential outcomes.

The proposal then moves on to one of the area coordinators who evaluates its feasibility and uses an activity-based costing methodology to perform a financial analysis. (See Table 2.)

If the area coordinator rejects the complexity reduction proposal, he or she will provide the originator with a written explanation of reasons for the rejection within two weeks of receiving the proposal. (The originator can appeal a negative decision by resubmitting his or her proposal to the steering committee that oversees the COC program.)

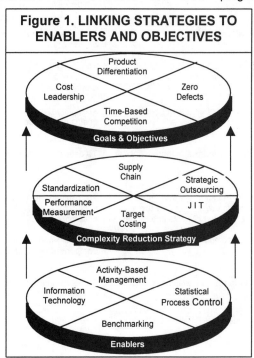

Figure 1. LINKING STRATEGIES TO ENABLERS AND OBJECTIVES

Table 1. SUGGESTED COMPLEXITY MEASURES

Measures	Purpose	Objective	Benchmark
% of components that are standard—parts that are readily available and can be purchased in very short lead times (off the shelf).	To determine if we are taking advantage of opportunities to purchase components at low prices due to market pressures on suppliers.	To generate cost reductions by using standard components for noncore competency parts.	To be determined.
% of components that are unique—used in less than 50% of the models.	To determine the degree we use common components in our products.	To promote the use of common components.	To be determined.
% of purchased parts that are certified.	To determine the confidence level we have in our suppliers.	To encourage actions to eliminate incoming inspection of material.	100%.
# of suppliers by commodity code.	To determine progress made in establishing long-term strategic relationships with suppliers.	To promote actions to reduce the number of suppliers and development of long-term supplier relationships.	To be determined.
% of suppliers up on EDI.	To determine percent of supplier base that we use EDI technology to obtain material for production requirements.	To use EDI technology to reduce lead times and manufacturing material coordination cost.	To be determined.
Number of processes in plant (assembly 1,2 press, coil, paint, weld, etc.).	To determine degree of vertical integration.	To encourage focus on just a few key capabilities in each plant.	To be determined.
Number of process types (number of machines, i.e., brake presses, turrets).	To determine degree of process proliferation.	To reduce process-sustaining cost.	To be determined.
Capacity utilization by process type.	To identify the degree of excess capacity by process type.	To obtain the benefits of process rationalization.	80-85% utilization on a two-shift basis.
Complexity cost batch cost + product sustaining cost.	To highlight the overhead cost associated with manufacturing complexity.	To establish targets and plans for reducing these costs. To track progress against plans.	To be determined.
Complexity cost % batch + product cost/total overhead.	To highlight the percent of overhead cost associated with manufacturing complexity.	To establish targets and plans for reducing these costs. To track progress against plans.	To be determined.
Complexity cost as a % of cost of completed production.	To highlight the percent complexity cost is of total product cost. To demonstrate impact of capacity utilization.	To encourage actions to increase capacity utilization of resources.	To be determined.
Complexity cost as a % of revenue.	To highlight the percent complexity cost is of revenue.	To ensure an adequate return is obtained in complexity cost.	To be determined.
Commonality index # of models/total # part.	To determine the degree modularity is used.	To encourage use of modularity in product designs.	To be determined.
Proliferation index/total # of different components used divided by the average # of components in a model.	To highlight the attention given to design for manufacturability and assembly.	To encourage the use of common components.	To be determined.
Total # of components.	To highlight the total number of components managed in the operation.	To encourage design for manufacturability and assembly actions to reduce the number of components.	To be determined.
% of components that are purchased.	To determine degree of vertical integration.	To encourage more strategic outsourcing.	To be determined.

Table 2. STANDARDIZATION SAVING WORKSHEET — ABC BURDEN ANALYSIS

Nonstandardized *

Part Number	Unit Volume	WIP	Prime Costs		ABC Burden			
			Material	Labor	Unit	Batch	Product-Sustaining Cost	Structural
40RM500061	10,000		80.11	16.50	17.7665	2.1080	2.8693	2.4638
40RM500071	500		80.11	20.90	22.4731	4.5135	3.9245	3.0897
40RM500081	250		80.11	20.90	22.4731	6.4042	4.3440	3.1927
TOTAL EXTENSION BY VOLUME	10,750		$861,182.50	$180,675.00	$184,519.83	$24,937.80	$31,741.25	$26,981.03

Standardized

Part Number	Unit Volume	WIP	Prime Costs		ABC Burden			
			Material	Labor	Unit	Batch	Product-Sustaining Cost	Structural
40RM500061	10,750							
TOTAL EXTENSION BY VOLUME	10,750		$861,182.50	$177,375.00	$190,989.88	$22,633.05	$30,829.93	$26,981.03
Savings			$0.00	$3,300.00	$3,529.95	$2,304.75	$911.32	$0.00
Total Savings			$10,046.03					

* Note that in this example the nonstandardized costs represent the current costs (using ABC) for making the three component parts. The proposal is to eliminate the three components and replace them with one common component. This analysis illustrates how the proposed change would produce savings of $10,046 due to reductions in labor, unit, batch, and product-sustaining costs.

If the area coordinator approves the complexity reduction proposal, it is prioritized and scheduled for implementation by the production engineering coordinator.

Once the project is under way, its progress is monitored through a Complexity Reduction Project Status Report. This report identifies the responsible individuals, the planned implementation dates, and projected cost savings.

The Complexity Reduction Log and Project Status Reports are maintained in an online computer network. All projects are updated at least once a month. Hard copies of the log and status reports also are posted monthly on the plant bulletin boards.

LINKAGE TO OTHER INITIATIVES

Carrier implemented ABCM to support its complexity reduction programs.[4] The financial analysis in the previous example illustrates how ABCM information is used to compare the costs and benefits of changing to a standardized part. In addition to the cost/benefit analysis for complexity reduction proposals, ABCM also is used to support other improvment initiatives as illustrated at Carrier's McMinville manufacturing plant.

Just-in-time. The McMinville plant began its complexity reduction journey by simplifying and streamlining manufacturing processes. Just-in-time (JIT) production methods were adopted, and modular work cells were set up for equipment in the factory. These changes were supported by an activity analysis that pointed to material handling as a major cost driver. Furthermore, ABCM was used to calculate the financial benefits of reducing cycle times, raw material, work-in-process inventories, and storage space requirements. After implementing JIT, savings occurred through reduced material handling costs, lower inventory investments, and by avoiding a physical expansion of the plant (even though new products were transferred to McMinville from other Carrier factories).

In the early stages of the complexity reduction program, management realized that production workers were an untapped resource for productivity improvement ideas. Therefore, these workers were placed on work cell teams, and each team became responsible for workflow, quality, and throughput. Prior to these changes, the production supervisors spent most of their time troubleshooting problems and expediting work orders. These problems currently are being handled by the line worker teams, and the supervisors now have enough time to plan their workloads and monitor the financial results of their work cells.

Standardization. Standardizing parts and manufacturing processes is another way in which the McMinville plant has achieved complexity reduction. The standardization process is divided into two different programs—one targets new product designs, and the other one targets existing products. The objective for both programs is to encourage the use of common components and manufacturing processes. For example, the plant has a preferred parts list for new products to minimize the proliferation of new component parts and thus control product-sustaining costs.

McMinville also has financial incentives (lower product costs) to reduce the number of components used in existing products. The plant currently maintains 280 different circuit breakers and 580 different fasteners to support its product lines. Its goal is to eliminate well over 50% of the circuit breakers and fasteners by promoting the use of common components. Maintaining an extensive parts list causes complexity whether the parts are components or finished goods. The high costs of unique components now are reflected in McMinville's product costs.

As a specific example of complexity reduction, product and process complexity was reduced at the McMinville plant when it developed common sizes for some of the sheet metal components that go into subassemblies. Each subassembly has a minimum size requirement for its sheet metal components. Therefore, if a sheet metal component will be used for multiple subassembly sizes, it must be cut large enough to fit the largest subassembly. The decision

maker is now confronted with a cost-benefit tradeoff—he or she must balance the savings associated with using common components against the scrap produced by trimming the oversized sheet metal components to fit small subassemblies. The power of ABCM is its ability to compare the savings from lower batch-related and product sustaining costs with the additional cost of producing sheet metal scrap.

If common components are not practical, the next best alternative to reduce complexity is to use common manufacturing processes. In fact, some manufacturing processes become more cost effective when flexible, but expensive, computerized equipment is replaced with inexpensive dedicated equipment. The McMinville plant used dedicated equipment to achieve fewer and less expensive changeovers, to lower work-in-process, and to reduce cycle times. For this manufacturing process, JIT sparked the interest in dedicated equipment, but ABCM supported the financial analysis that justified the changes. Change occurs much more quickly at McMinville when the financial impact is highly visible.

Strategic outsourcing. As McMinville's complexity reduction program evolved, management considered many change proposals to reduce complexity and improve productivity. One such proposal was to outsource the sheet metal painting operation. Intuitively, managers at the plant were confident that outsourcing the painting operation would be cost effective and improve productivity. At a higher level, however, management would not approve the change. These managers relied upon a traditional

Figure 2. NEED TO REDUCE COMPLEXITY

Drivers

External benchmarks correlate excess complexity with financial underperformance.

Competition intensifying due to: new competitors, existing competitors, restructuring and refocusing systems, and operations.

Financial targets raised creating a current shortfall in profits.

Carrier Today

Many activities under way to understand and reduce complexity

- Eliminated product lines,
- Moved subassemblies to point of use,
- Consolidated like platforms,
- Created press cells,
- Outsourced paint/converted to pre-painted materials,
- Outsourced product lines,
- Greater understanding of how complexity affects cost, and
- Organization-wide desire to tackle complexity issues.

Costs remain too high

- Complexity still overwhelming,
- Excess capacity in noncore processes,
- Mismatch between product and manufacturing process design.

Objective

Reshape Carrier and build its future by cost effectively focusing on core products, components, and processes to deliver necessary variety.

---

financial analysis that only considered the cost of direct materials, direct labor, and an overhead allocation. Using this analysis, outsourcing the painting operation appeared to have a negative payback.

Once ABCM data were available, however, an analysis produced results that were quite different from the traditional financial analysis. ABCM quantified the cost of many support activities that had not been considered previously, such as material handling, inspection, inventory holding, and environmental costs. After including the cost of these activities, managers at the plant found the cost of in-house painting to be considerably higher than the cost of outsourcing the painting operation. Furthermore, by purchasing pre-painted sheet metal, quality improved and in-plant cycle time fell by five days. In the final analysis, outsourcing the painting operation proved to be very cost effective, and it also supported the goals of JIT and complexity reduction.

Supply chain management. To further improve its competitiveness, Carrier has been strengthening its supplier relationships. Actions taken by its suppliers greatly influence the price, quality, and delivery speed of Carrier's products. For example, the McMinville plant has developed a partnership with a supplier of nonproduction service parts. This supplier now staffs McMinville's service parts warehouse and is fully responsible for purchasing, stocking, and scheduling service parts. McMinville's ABCM model illustrates how the supplier can source service parts and actually run the warehouse more cost effectively than McMinville can with its own employees.

The McMinville plant currently is considering a partnership with a supplier of copper tubing. This supplier would be responsible for managing the copper tubing portion of McMinville's raw materials warehouse. Through this partnership, the copper tubing supplier would exploit certain of its core competencies. It has detailed knowledge of material flow from its own plants, where the tubing is formed, to its customers. Many of the copper tubing suppliers also have the latest technology for copper tubing fabrication. Therefore, the partnership might be expanded to include some fabrication of copper tubing parts. (The vendor may choose to perform some operations at its own facility and others at McMinville.) As the vendor becomes directly involved in McMinville's production process, it can (or might be required to) propose improvement programs. These improvements might be in product functionality, the production process, or quality. And, finally, vendor management of this activity also will reduce cycle time. Once again, ABCM helps Carrier make better decisions by considering the entire cost of an activity and not just the "out-of-pocket" costs such as the cost of the raw materials.

Target costing. In the current competitive marketplace, customers often dictate the price they will pay for a given set of product features. Therefore, Carrier has eliminated "cost plus" pricing for its products and now uses a target costing approach. The target costing process begins when Carrier estimates the price customers will pay for a new product offering (the target selling price). After subtracting a desired profit margin from the target selling price, a target cost is established. The new product's target cost then is compared with its estimated cost. (Cost estimates are based on the new product's initial design and current manufacturing processes.) If the product's estimated cost is higher than its target cost, engineers will attempt to either design costs out of the product or improve the manufacturing process. In the end, if the target cost cannot be met, the product will not go into production.

Both the complexity reduction program and ABCM are linked to target costing at Carrier. These initiatives encourage engineers to control costs by designing products that use common components and standard manufacturing processes. Gone are the days when engineers prided themselves in developing unique, elegant parts.[5] When the new products do require new component designs, the engineers try to use existing manufacturing processes to build the components. To facilitate this new directive, product designers are now part of an engineering team that includes manufacturing engineers. The team uses a "design for manufacturability" philosophy in which the design team works with manufacturing to introduce product designs that use cost effective manufacturing processes.

Performance measures. An activity dictionary with common process definitions supports performance measurement among the Carrier plants. Managers at the plants use the dictionary to develop internal benchmarks for activity-based process costs. The managers also share information to learn from the low-cost producers. At the McMinville plant, the first line production supervisors also receive monthly reports with financial (labor, material usage, and scrap) and nonfinancial (production schedule targets) information. The supervisors are accountable for budgeted process costs in their areas, and the results influence their performance evaluation.

At the product level, Carrier uses ABCM to support product mix decisions. Its product mix at each site is based on a product profitability analysis. For example, unprofitable products are either dropped or moved to another Carrier location, and profitable products are emphasized. Essentially, this system encourages competition among the plants—the most efficient plants win bids for new products and take over production contracts from less efficient plants.

Even though the McMinville plant appropriately has dropped some product lines and added others, it has taken some missteps along the way. Some products that appeared to be unprofitable mistakenly were dropped (existing products) or avoided (new business). This scenario occurred because management did not conduct the following analysis:

- Before rejecting an unprofitable product, management should make every effort to remove costs from the product's design or production process.
- When the plant has excess capacity in the short run and sales revenue more than covers variable cost, new products should be considered for production (and existing products should not necessarily be dropped).

STAYING COMPETITIVE WITH HARD DATA

Carrier's complexity reduction program along with its other improvement initiatives have combined to produce quantifiable results (Figure 2). But more work needs to be done for Carrier to maintain its competitive edge. In the current competitive environment, Carrier is striving to better understand cost behavior and the steps it can take to maintain its position as the world's largest manufacturer of air conditioning and heating products. Even though Carrier's management believes that product and process complexity hurts profitability, it needs hard financial data. ABCM provides the information managers need to make difficult decisions.

Dan Swenson, CMA, Ph.D., is assistant professor of accounting, College of Business and Economics, University of Idaho, Moscow, Idaho. He submitted this article through the Washington Tri-Cities Chapter, of which he is a member. He can be reached at (208) 885-7367.

The support of the American Productivity and Quality Center (APQC), the Consortium for Advanced Manufacturing-International (CAM-I), the sponsor companies, and the other members of the research team (Richard Brown, John Campi, George Foster, Larry Maisel, and John Miller) is gratefully acknowledged.

[1]F.A. Gonsalves and R. G. Eiler, "Managing Complexity Through Performance Measurement," MANAGEMENT ACCOUNTING, August 1996, p. 35.

[2]For an in-depth discussion of this classification scheme, see Robin Cooper, "Cost Classification in Unit-Based and Activity-Based Manufacturing Cost Systems," *Journal of Cost Management,* Fall 1990, pp. 1-14.

[3]In their article, "Managing complexity Through Performance Measurement," Gonsalves and Eiler provide additional examples of complexity performance measures.

[4]As part of the ABCM best practices study, sponsored by the APQC and CAM-I, the research team searched for characteristics that were common among the best practice companies. One finding was that each of the 15 best practice companies had linked ABCM to another improvement initiative. Total quality management (TQM). Just-in-time (JIT) manufacturing, and business process reengineering (IBPR) were some of the other initiatives that were linked to ABCM. This linkage provides direction for the ABCM implementation and a ready application for the ABCM information once it becomes available.

[5]A new product at the McMinville plant recently required three design attempts before its target cost was achieved. It was obtained only after the design team brought the part count down from 160 to 60 parts.

Chapter 4
Activity-Based Costing and Management
Cases

4-1   Blue Ridge Manufacturing (Activity-Based Costing for Marketing Channels)
4-2   MosCo, Inc. (Activity-Based Management)
4-3   Tektronix (Activity-Based Costing for Production Process Changes)

Readings
"How ABC Changed the Post Office"

The article describes the activity-based cost study and market strategy study conducted for the United States Post Office by Coopers & Lybrand. The specific focus of the analysis was the cost/benefit of including credit and debit card transactions in post offices. The ABC study projected costs for the credit/debit card program and found significant savings for adoption. The Post Service Board of Governors approved the plan in October 1994.

Discussion Questions:
1. What are the unit, batch, and product level activities at the Post Office, and what are the cost drivers for each?
2. What does the ABC model show about the relative costs of the different payment options: cash, check, credit card, and debit card?
3. What are the limitations of the ABC analysis done of the Post Office as described in the article?

Cases

4-1. Blue Ridge Manufacturing

BACKGROUND:

Blue Ridge Manufacturing is one of a dozen companies that produces and sells towels for the U.S. "sports towel" market. A "sports towel" is a towel that has the promotion of an event or a logo printed on it. They're called sports towels because their most popular use is for distribution in connection with major sporting events such as the Super Bowl, NCAA Final Four, Augusta National Golf Tournament and the U.S. Open Tennis Tournament. Towels with college, NBA and NFL team logos, and promotions for commercial products such as soft drinks, beer, fast food chains, etc., are also big sellers.

The firm designs, knits, prints and embroiders towels. The firm knits all the towels it sells and tracks costs for towel production separately from the cost to customize the towels. Seventy-five percent of its orders include logo design, while the balance are print only and require the payment of a license fee for the logo used. However, about 15% of its orders include embroidery. Towels are made in three sizes: regular (18" x 30"), hand (12" x 20") and mid-range (15"x 24"). The normal production cycle for an order of white towels is three days. If a customer wants a colored towel, the basic white towel made by Blue Ridge is sent to a dyeing firm, which extends the production cycle of an order by three days. Also, occasionally, customers order towels in sizes other than the three standard sizes. These towels are called "special".

The firm now produces a "medium" quality towel. They have had some difficulty with the "staying power" of the material printed on these towels, which is attributed to the towel quality, the ink and the printing process. Customers have complained that the ink "lays on the surface" and it cracks and peels off.

Blue Ridge recently made a break-through in developing an ink that soaks into the towel, won't wash out and is non-toxic. A big advantage of this ink is that it avoids EPA disposal requirements because is can be "washed down the drain". Due to these characteristics of its new ink, Blue Ridge is considering upgrading the quality of the basic towel it produces because it will "take" the ink better, both the towel and the ink will last longer and the product will sell at a higher price. If it takes this step, the company will evaluate expanding its marketing and sales area with the objective of "going national".

CUSTOMERS:

Except for a few non-regional chains, Blue Ridge's sales are predominantly in the southeastern states. The company sells its products to 986 different customers. These customers differ primarily in the volume of their purchases, so management classifies each customer in one of three groups: large (8 customers), medium (154 customers) and small (824 customers). Large customers are primarily national chains, small customers are single store operations (including pro shops at golf courses) and medium-sized customers are small chains, large single stores or licensing agents for professional sports teams and manufacturers of consumer products. Table 1 gives the product and customer size statistics for 2001.

Blue Ridge has a different approach to customers in each of its three categories. A small group of in-house sales people sell directly to buyers in the large customer category. Independent manufacturer representatives, on commission, call on the license holder or the manager of a store in the medium customer category. Ads placed in regional and national magazines and newspapers target customers primarily in the small-customer segment, who call or mail in their orders.

Blue Ridge does not give discounts and it ships all order free on board (FOB) point of origin, i.e., customers pay their freight costs.

MANUFACTURING:

Blue Ridge has a modern knitting and printing plant in the foothills of North Carolina's Blue Ridge Mountains. Upgrading the facilities over recent years was accompanied by the introduction of an activity-based costing (ABC) system to determine product costs. The cost accounting system is fairly sophisticated and management has confidence in the accuracy of the manufacturing cost figures for each product line. Table 2 shows the firm's unit costs for various items.

Company management is committed to adopting advanced manufacturing techniques such as benchmarking and just-in-time (JIT). The corporate culture necessary for the success of such techniques is evolving and worker empowerment is already a major program. In addition, workers are allowed several hours away from regular work assignments each week for training programs conferring on budgets and work improvements and applying the ABC system.

PERFORMANCE:

The company is profitable. However, management has become concerned about the profitability of the customers in its three customer-size categories—large, medium and small. Different customers demand different levels of support. Management has no basis for identifying customers that generate high profits or to drop those that do not generate enough revenues to cover the expenses to support them. Under the previous accounting system, it wasn't possible to determine the costs of supporting individual customers.

With the introduction of ABC, it now may be possible to determine customer profitability. Table 3 shows how the administrative and selling costs are assigned and re-assigned between various functions within the selling and marketing areas and to sub-activities in the selling and marketing areas. Table 4 provides a list of selling and marketing activities and the activity base to use in assigning costs to each.

REQUIRED:

The managers of Blue Ridge Manufacturing have hired your consulting firm to advise them on the potential of using strategic cost analysis in assessing the profitability of their customer accounts.
Your analysis should include:

1. What is Blue Ridge's competitive strategy?
2. What type of cost system does Blue Ridge use, and is it consistent with their strategy?
3. Develop a spreadsheet analysis which can be used to assess the profitability of the three customer groups of Blue Ridge—large, medium and small customer account sizes. Use the information in Tables 1-4 to trace and allocate the costs necessary for the analysis.

TABLE 1
BLUE RIDGE MANUFACTURING
Sales Information

Product and Customer Size Statistics		Sales in Units by Customer Account Size			
		Large	Medium	Small	Total
Towel:	Regular	27,250	16,600	10,550	54,400
	Mid-Size	36,640	18,552	10,308	65,500
	Hand	35,880	19,966	95,954	151,800
	Special	480	3,426	594	4,500
Number of Units Sold		100,250	58,544	117,406	276,200
Number of Units Embroidered		5,959	6,490	29,394	41,842
Number of Units Dyed		20,536	9,935	12,328	42,798
Sales Volume Revenue		$308,762	$183,744	$318,024	$810,530
Number of Orders Received		133	845	5,130	6,108
Number of Shipments Made		147	923	5,431	6,501
Number of Invoices Sent		112	754	4,737	5,603
Accounts with Balance >60 Days		1	11	122	134

TABLE 2
BLUE RIDGE MANUFACTURING
Unit Cost Information

Line 1 Direct Manufacturing Costs Per Unit

		Quantity	Sales Price	Material	Labor	Overhead	Unit Cost
Towels:	Regular	54,400	$3.60	$0.60	$0.37	$0.22	$1.19
	Mid-Size	65,500	3.20	0.50	0.33	0.20	1.03
	Hand	151,800	2.55	0.39	0.31	0.19	0.89
	Special	4,500	4.00	0.67	0.48	0.29	1.44

Line 2 Direct Costs of Customizing Per Unit

	Quantity	Cost	Material	Labor	Overhead	Total
Inking (based on passes)	552,400	—	$0.0030	$0.0045	$0.0742	$0.0817
Dyeing	42,798	$0.11	—	—	0.0000	0.1100
Embroidery	41,842	—	0.0026	0.1750	1.0994	1.2770

Direct Labor Wage Rate: $9.00 (Including Fringes)
Inking requires one pass for each color used; average two colors per towel (i.e., 2 per unit), and is used on all towels.

TABLE 3
BLUE RIDGE MANUFACTURING
Selling and Administrative Costs and Activities

Costs Incurred in Each Function (Shipping, Sales, Marketing)

Directly Assigned To:

	Total	Shipping	Sales	Marketing	Other	Total Assigned	Unassigned
Administration	$170,000	$ 17,000	$ 37,400	$20,400	$56,100	$130,900	$39,100*
Selling	155,000	15,500	117,800	9,300	12,400	155,000	
	$325,000	$ 32,500	$155,200	$29,700	$68,500	$285,900	$39,100

Each function is used for the Following Activities — Percentage of:

Selling and Administrative Activities:	Shipping	Sales	Marketing	Other
Entering Purchase Orders		55		10
Commissions		10		
Shipping Activities	65			15
Invoicing				20
Cost to Make Sales Calls		30		10
Checking Credit				10
Samples, Catalog Info.	5		10	
Special Handling Charges	5			5
Distribution Management	10		10	
Marketing, by Customer Type		5		
Advertising/Promotion			30	
Marketing	15		50	5
Administrative Office Support				20
Licenses, Fees				5
	100	100	100	100

* Note that $39,100 of the SG&A cost was not directly assigned. This amount represents the facility-sustaining activity cost.

TABLE 4
BLUE RIDGE MANUFACTURING
Activities and Cost drivers

Cost Drivers for Allocating Costs of Activities to Customer Groups (Large, Medium, Small)

Activity	Cost Driver
Entering Purchase Orders	Number of Orders
Commissions	Sales Dollars with Medium Customers
Shipping Activities	Number of Shipments
Invoicing	Number of Invoices
Cost to Make Sales Calls	Sales Dollars with Large Customers
Checking Credit	Percent Accounts >60 Days
Samples, Catalog Info.	Sales Dollars
Special Handling Charges	Management Estimate[1]
Distribution Management	Sales Dollars
Marketing, by Customer Type	Sales Dollars
Advertising/Promotion	Management Estimate[2]
Marketing	Number of Units Sold[3]
Administrative Office Support	Number of Units Sold[4]
Licenses, Fees	Sales Dollars with Medium Customers

[1]20% to medium-sized customers; 80% to small-sized customers.
[2]25% to medium-sized customers; 75% to small-sized customers.
[3]Excluding Specials
[4]Excluding Specials

4-2. MosCo, Inc.

The evening before the annual two-year budget review, Cosmos "Chip" Offtiol, MosCo's director of operations, was confident. While he waited for the latest financial estimates, he thought of the plan he and his staff had methodically prepared, which successfully addressed all the crises this new business unit was facing: developing competitive transfer pricing on an aging product, developing and marketing new products to external customers against an established market leader, reducing manufacturing costs, improving manufacturing utilization, and improving its slim levels of profitability.

When Jonathan Janus, MosCo's controller, solemnly delivered the requested pro forma income statements, Offtiol's mood changed dramatically. Instead of sustained profit, Offtiol was shocked to see significant projected operating losses. He wondered why his extensive planning had not improved MosCo's 1995 and 1996 financial results. With less than 24 hours before he was to offer senior management a viable business plan, he felt abandoned and hopeless.

BACKGROUND

MosCo, a semiconductor design and manufacturing company, is a wholly owned subsidiary of Computer Systems, Inc. (CSI), a leading manufacturer of client/server systems, workstations, and personal computers. During 1993 and 1994, MosCo manufactured and sold to CSI a single product, the x100, a 100 MHz, 10 nanosecond microprocessor. The x100 is a .75 micron device packaged in a 339 pin-grid array (PGA) and is used in CSI's servers and workstations. MosCo has sold CSI 150,000 units of the x100 in each of the past two years.

Although MosCo sells entirely to its corporate parent, the company was required to establish competitive prices for its devices by Q394. Previously, the x100 had been sold to CSI at full cost. Establishing competitive prices was but one of many changes CSI required MosCo to make. In 1995, CSI planned to change all its major business units into profit centers. CSI management felt each business unit needed flexibility and independence to react to rapidly changing market conditions. CSI believed that if its business units were profit centers, they would be more accountable for their own financial success. Their strategies and annual performance would be more visible and measurable as well. This change meant they could sell their devices to external customers using available manufacturing capacity. MosCo could also recover the large development costs for future products and control their destiny.

MosCo established the competitive market selling price of the x100 at $850, based on industry price/performance comparisons. CSI approved of this market-based method of establishing transfer prices, which ensured that CSI could purchase internally at a competitive price while placing the burden of cost management appropriately on MosCo. Jonathan Janus, MosCo's controller, prepared revised financial statements applying the $850 transfer price to MosCo's 1993 and 1994 shipments (see Exhibit 1). Gordon Scott, MosCo's vice president and general manager, was pleased to see MosCo had generated profits of $4.9M and $1.9M for 1993 and 1994, respectively, on annual revenues of $127.M, after applying the newly established transfer price. The profit decline in 1994 reflected the establishment and staffing of MosCo's new marketing department. This department was created to identify and open external market opportunities for new products currently under development.

As FY95 approaches, MosCo management is faced with a number of pressures and unknowns. CSI is under severe competitive pressures in their server and workstation product lines and is already demanding a price reduction on the x100. They also insist MosCo remain profitable. Carlotta Price, head of MosCo's new marketing department, determined from industry studies that the price/performance for microprocessors halves every 18 months (Moore's law). To remain competitive, merchant semiconductor companies consistently were offering some combination of price reductions and/or performance improvements, so that their products' price/performance (price per unit of speed) halved every 1.5 years. Thus, for the x100 and for every CPU MosCo developed and manufactured, Price believed the market would require similarly timed price/performance offerings. Price knew any price reductions would require offsetting cost reductions if MosCo was to remain profitable and wondered what the manufacturing organization was thinking.

As product development was no longer working on any x100 performance improvements, Price computed required price reductions on the x100 following the industry model. The x100 would continue at the $850 price through Q195, then drop to $637.50 at the start of Q295, drop to $425.00 at the start of Q196, and to $318.75 at the start of Q496. Price was troubled by these prices as she knew CSI was requesting 150,000 units in FY95 but only 75,000 in FY96. CSI indicated it expected a customer shift away from workstations and into CSI's new personal computer line. (Appendix I presents an overview of the semiconductor manufacturing process typically found in a microprocessor supplier such as MosCo. Appendix II presents an overview of the product costing process used by MosCo.)

Product cost for the x100 had remained constant during FY93 and FY94 at approximately $665 (see Exhibit 2). Price computed cost reductions of approximately $166.25 per year (to $498.75 in FY95 and $332.50 in 1996) would be necessary to maintain the x100's current gross margin of ~22%. She wondered if manufacturing could achieve a cost reduction that steep.

Concurrent with the x100 pricing activities, P. J. Watt, head of product development, sent an urgent request to Scott, Price, Janus, and Offtiol for $3M in funding. This funding would accelerate the completion of an integer-only microprocessor, the x50 and the follow-on CPU, the x75. The x50, a new product already under development, could be completed with $IM of the additional funding and made available for volume shipment by the beginning of FY95. The remaining $2M would be spent during FY95 and FY96 to complete development and ready the x75 for volume shipment by the beginning of FY97.

The x50 is a 50 MHz, 20 nanosecond CPU, manufactured like the x100, using the present .75 micron technology. But unlike the x100, the x5O does not have a floating-point processor. The elimination of the floating-point processor reduces the size and power requirements of the CPU. The x50 and x75 can be packaged in a 168 pin-grid array (PGA) that costs $15, that is, $35 less than the 339 PGA used by the x100. However, the testing parameters of the x50 and x75 are significantly different than for the x100 and require a Bonn tester, which MosCo does not currently own. This $2M tester, if purchased, will add $1 .2M in annual depreciation and other direct operating costs and $800K in incremental annual support costs to the present level of manufacturing spending.

The x50 and x75 are targeted as entry devices for CSI' s personal computer business. NoTel is the market leader in .75 micron integer-only microprocessors. Their N50 CPU (also 50 MHz, 20 nanoseconds) sells for $500. The N50 has just been announced with volume shipments to coincide with the beginning of MosCo' s FY95. MosCo' s new marketing department estimates the demand for the x50 from CSI and potential new external customers could easily exceed 1,000 units per year. To break into this market, Price recommended heavy market promotion and a price/performance two times the competition's. Estimates for unit sales potential from advertising are 100,000 for the first $1,000, up to 500,000 for the second $1,000, and over 1M for a third million-dollar advertising expenditure.

With the increased pricing pressures from both CSI and the external marketplace, product cost reduction became critical. This fact, coupled with the request from product development for additional funding, had Gordon Scott very concerned. He knew it was important to bring out the x50 and x75 quickly, but the pricing pressures for their market entrance and the pricing pressures from CSI on the x100 seemed almost impossible to meet and still achieve a profit in FY95 and 96. He knew, however, if he didn't maintain a profitable operation, his tenure would be short.

Reduced product costs leading to competitive manufacturing appeared to be the critical factor necessary to sustain MosCo's slim profit levels. Scott asked Offtiol, the director of operations, to formulate a series of recommendations for developing and manufacturing an expanded CPU product line in FY95 and FY96. He asked that the recommendations be completed by the annual two-year budget review, scheduled to commence in a month. Scott knew that soon after MosCo's budget review he would have to present a credible business plan to CSI management. He worried how he could develop a viable plan in light of the obstacles.

THE OFFTIOL PLAN

Offtiol started his preparation by reviewing the detailed x100 product cost (see Exhibits 2, 3, and 4). He immediately assembled a team comprising Janus from Finance, T. Q. Marcel from Quality, and Beeb Ruby from Training. The team, led by Marcellus deStepper, manager of wafer fabrication, conducted a cost review by activity. Offtiol, like Scott, believed significant cost reductions would be necessary to maintain profitability. He had recently taken an executive development course in activity-based costing and knew it was a proven method for better understanding cost structures and cost drivers and highlighting nonvalue-added work. Offtiol was excited, given the size of the assignment and his belief there were both cost reduction opportunities in manufacturing and necessary improvements in the current standard cost system. He felt the current standard cost system did not properly capture the complexity of MosCo's production process. He felt an ABC analysis could provide the insight necessary to reduce the x100 product cost by the $166 marketing had requested.

The team mapped the processes of the entire operation and then reassigned costs to the newly defined activities (see Exhibits 5a-c). The direct manufacturing operation was now better delineated by equipment use (see Exhibit 5b). The manufacturing support organizations were also better understood. Their key activities were costed, then each was aligned to the manufacturing operation it supported (see Exhibit 5c). MosCo's ABC team reset the x100 product cost in line with the tine practical capacity of the manufacturing process. The team saw capacity utilization as a major driver of product cost. The old product costing methodology was based on the planned utilization of each manufacturing process with underutilized manufacturing costs absorbed into product costs.

The revised x100 product cost (see Exhibits 6 and 7) was pleasing but not totally surprising to Offtiol. It confirmed his belief in the inaccuracies of the old costing method. The new x100 product cost of $437.50 was $227.61 lower than the $665.11 original cost shown by the old system. It did not make sense to charge the x100 for the costs of resources it did not consume. Offtiol felt he could commit immediately to Price's 1995 product cost reduction request of $166.

To achieve the 1996 product cost goal of $332.50, Offtiol and his team looked further into the activity-based costing results. The study clearly showed that wafer fabrication was the largest area of manufacturing cost. Offtiol, with the help of Janus, computed that if the x100 wafer cost was reduced from the 1995 level of $3,000/wafer to $1,866/wafer, the x100 total product cost would be lowered by $105, achieving the desired $332.50. To obtain a wafer cost of $1,866, spending reductions of ~$25.5M or 38% in wafer fabrication would have to be achieved (see Chart I). Offtiol again asked deStepper to review the fabrication area for further cost reduction opportunities. He asked deStepper to formulate a plan that could reduce direct wafer fabrication spending by ~$25.5M (from $67.4M to $41.9M).

DeStepper returned in two weeks with an alternative plan (see Chart II). His team found nominal spending opportunities by: (1) reducing monitor wafer usage, (2) redesigning wafer lot handling procedures, and (3) better placement of inspection stations. DeStepper's most significant discovery was the 64% increase in capacity attained by increasing equipment uptime (the time equipment is not undergoing repair or preventive maintenance). Higher uptime, however, required an annual investment of ~$1.8M in additional equipment engineers. While this investment would increase wafer fabrication spending to ~$69.2M, wafer fabrication capacity would increase from 26,000 to ~42,700 in annual wafer starts. The increased capacity actually decreased the cost/wafer to $1,845, which was $21 lower than Offtiol had requested.

Offtiol dismissed DeStepper's alternative plan outright. "Spending needed to decrease, not *increase!*" Offtiol exclaimed and reiterated his request to reduce fabrication spending by 38%. Offtiol then focused his team's cost reduction efforts on packaging costs, another major cost component of the x100. (MosCo had spent close to $8.8M annually on chip packages). He asked MosCo's purchasing manager,

---

Chart I
X100 1996 target product cost analysis
(x100 gross die / wafer = 50)

Manufacturing Area	Cost/ Wafer	Cost/ Die	Cum. Cost/ Die
Desired wafer cost	$1,866.00	$37.32	$37.32
Yielded raw wafer cost	$50.00	$1.00	$38.32
Probe cost/wafer	$500.00	$10.00	$48.32
Probe yield		25.0%	$193.28
339 PGA package cost		$50.00	$243.28
Assembly cost		$8.00	$251.28
Assembly yield		90.0%	$279.20
Test cost		$40.00	$319.20
Test yield		96.0%	$332.50

Current fabrication spending:	$67,392,000
Desired level of spending: (22,464 annual wafer production @$ 1,866)	$41,917,824
Required spending reduction:	$25,474,176
	38%

Chart II
DeStepper Alternate Capacity and Spending Plan

	Current Level	Proposed Level
Total wafer start capacity	26,000	42,707
Engineering wafer starts	1,040	1,040
Production wafer starts	24,960	41,667
Fabrication line yield	90%	90%
Annual wafer completions	22,464	37,500
Annual spending level	$67,392,000	$67,392,000
DeStepper's added spending		$1,797,120
Proposed spending level		$69,189,120
Cost/wafer	$3,000	$1,845

Nomial, to pressure MosCo's 339 PGA supplier to lower their $50 price. Nomial told Offtiol she had already made this request and was reminded by the vendor that the 339 PGA was a unique design, used by only MosCo for the x100. With order volumes declining by 50% in a year, Nomial said it would be difficult to keep the $50 package price from increasing.

The final area of review was the x50 proposal. Offtiol and the team reviewed its product cost, necessary manufacturing process, and spending requirements (see Exhibits 8 and 9). Offtiol compared the x50 product cost (computed assuming all production capacity was used to manufacture the x50) with the product cost of the x100 and noted a few significant cost differences. The reduced size of the x50 (no floating point processor) increased the number of dies able to be placed on each wafer, thus reducing the fabrication cost/die 67% from the x100 ($61.00 for the x100; $20.33 for the x50). The increase in the number of dies on each wafer increased the probe time, however, and increased the probe cost per wafer by 25% ($500 for the x100, $625 for the x50). He was pleased with the doubling of assembly capacity resulting from the smaller package required by the x50 (202,500 annual assembly starts for the x100; 405,000 for the x50). The increase in assembly throughput reduced the x50 assembly costs by 50%. Offtiol was pleasantly surprised at the x50's lower test costs. Even though the x50 required a new tester, the lower annual operating costs versus the x100, along with the reduced testing time (from the elimination of the floating point unit), resulted in a per unit test cost of only $5 versus $40 for the x100.

With the x50's cost structure now soundly understood, Offtiol could better appreciate the high but achievable profit margins of the x50. The margins ranged from 75% during Q1-Q395 to ~67% in Q495 when the marketing-required price reduction took effect (see Chart III). If deStepper could achieve the $1,866 wafer cost by the start of 1996 (see Exhibits 10 and 11), the x50 could obtain a very respectable margin of ~59% in the second half of 1996 at the required price of $125. Using the capacity available in 1995 and 1996 to produce 50,000 and 215,000 units, respectively, easily convinced Offtiol to fund the x50 development effort and purchase the new tester. While the product specifications for the x75 were not yet available, he also agreed to fund its development effort. He felt the x75 would achieve the same product margins the x50 demonstrated.

Just as Offtiol was completing his x50 product development meeting, Nomial called and suggested outsourcing and then disinvesting MosCo' s assembly operations. She had found an assembly house that could assemble the x50 in its required 168 PGA for $5 per device (in volume levels of 500,000) with equivalent yields to those MosCo projected. Offtiol thought this idea had merit until he compared the $5 external assembly cost/device to the internal cost estimate of $4. He quickly concluded outsourcing would only increase the overall product cost and therefore was not a viable option.

	Chart III		
	Q195-Q395	Q495-Q296	Q396 & Q496
Price	$250.00	$187.50	$125.00
Cost	$62.50	$62.50	$51.02
Margin $	$187.50	$125.00	$73.98
Margin %	75.0%	66.7%	59.2%

A week before the budget review, Offtiol asked Janus to prepare new pro forma income statements for FY94, FY95, and FY96. He wanted to reflect all his cost reduction targets and product-funding levels. He was curious to see the levels of profit he would generate in 1995 and 96 from: (1) the revised x100 product cost, (2) the 1996 cost reduction targets in wafer fabrication and their effect on the x100 and x50, (3) the funding of the x50 and x75, (4) the purchase of the Bonn tester the x50 required, (5) the utilization of 1995 and 1996 capacity for manufacturing the x50, (6) the additional advertising expense necessary to promote the x50 fully in the marketplace, and (7) the selling of the x100 and x50 using the marketing department pricing model. Offtiol was confident his decisions would prove sound and keep MosCo profitable in 1995 and 1996.

Now, after a second review of Janus's pro forma income statements (see Exhibits 12a-c), Offtiol had become very anxious. He had to present a viable set of recommendations to MosCo's senior management the following day. He thought he and his team had explored and included all viable options in Janus's statements. Finally, Offtiol concluded the cause of the projected FY95 and FY96 losses was the overly aggressive pricing model. He decided he would present Janus's projections, highlight the losses in spite of the cost reductions reflected, and suggest keeping the x100 price at $850 for all of 1995 and at $637.50 for all of 1996. The $23.9M increase in FY95 revenue would turn the ~$(15.2M) loss into an $8.7M profit. But the $17.9M increase in FY96 revenue would only improve the loss of ~$(40.5M) to ~$(22.6M). Offtiol was convinced Scott would also agree Price's pricing model was too aggressive. He was certain Scott would approve a revised x100 price and be receptive to a higher price for the x50, which could offset the remaining projected 1996 loss. Offtiol felt it would take a combination of his cost reduction efforts and higher prices to maintain MosCo's profitability and thus demonstrate to CSI MosCo's ability to transform itself into a competitive business unit.
(IMA Case)

REQUIRED:

In reviewing Offtiol's assessments and conclusions, has he proposed the optimal recommendations?
Specifically:
1.   What caused the 1995 x100 product cost to drop by $227 after reflecting the ABC review and the new costing approach? Did spending decrease or just shift for each of the wafer fabrication, probe, assembly, test, and process development?
2.   What are the drivers of manufacturing cost? Of product cost?
3.   Was it practical or plausible to reduce direct wafer fabrication by 38% or $25.5M?
4.   Should Offtiol have looked at areas other than wafer fabrication to identify further cost reductions? If so, where?
5.   Why is there still underutilized manufacturing capacity when the x50 is being manufactured?
6.   Is the pricing model in fact too aggressive? Should Offtiol propose increasing the prices of the x100 and x50?
7.   What pricing advantages does Mosco's competitor, Notel, have, knowing their N50 (see Exhibit 10) has 33% more die/wafer than the x50? (Assume the same wafer, probe, assembly, and test costs and yields as the x50.)

APPENDIX I

OVERVIEW OF THE SEMICONDUCTOR MANUFACTURING PROCESS

Semiconductor devices are made from silicon, which is material refined from quartz. Silicon is used because it can be altered easily to promote or deter electrical signals. Electronic switches, or transistors, that control electrical signals can be formed on the surface of a silicon crystal by the precisely controlled addition of certain elements designed in microscopically small patterns.

Silicon is first melted to remove impurities and grown into long crystals (ingots), which vary in size from .5 inches to 16 inches in diameter (typical sizes in use today are 6, 8 and 12 inch). The purified silicon is sliced into wafers on which integrated circuits will be patterned. As the size of an integrated circuit is extremely small, hundreds, even thousands, of circuits can be formed on a wafer at the same time.

Integrated circuits (typically referred to as "chips" or "dies") are an array of transistors made up of various connected layers, designed to perform specific operations. Each layer is a specific circuit pattern, (approximately 20 are used in present processes). A glass plate (called a reticle) is used to pattern each layer on the wafer during the fabrication process.

FABRICATION

In the fabrication process, blank wafers are first insulated with a film of oxide, then coated with a soft, light-sensitive plastic called photoresist. The wafers are masked by a reticle and flooded with ultraviolet light, exposing the reticle's specific circuit pattern on the unmasked portion of the wafer. Exposed photoresist hardens into the proper circuit layer outline. Acids and solvents are used to strip away unexposed photoresist and oxide, baring the circuit pattern to be etched by either chemicals or superhot gases. More photoresist is placed on the wafer, masked, and stripped, then implanted with chemical impurities, or dopants, that form negative and positive conducting zones. Repeating these steps builds the necessary layers required for the integrated circuit design to be completed on the wafer.

PROBE

In the probe process, an electrical performance test of the functions of each of the completed integrated circuits is performed while each die is still on the wafer. The nonfunctioning dies are marked with ink; the functioning dies are left unmarked and moved to assembly.

ASSEMBLY

In the assembly process, each die is cut from the wafer with a diamond saw. The good dies are placed in the cavity of a ceramic package. The bonding pads from the dies are connected by very thin aluminum wires into the leads of the package, creating the necessary electrical connection from the chip to the package. The package is then sealed, with a metal lid placed over the exposed dies in the package.

TEST

Once the device is completely packaged, it is tested to ensure all electrical specifications of the integrated circuit are met.

The completed, packaged semiconductor device is now ready to be soldered to a printed circuit board, which in turn will be installed into a computer system.

APPENDIX II
OVERVIEW OF THE PRODUCT COSTING PROCESS

Semiconductor product costing is a multiple-step process in which manufacturing costs measure value added to raw material as it is processed. Value-added typically is defined as production or capacity throughput divided by spending. The cost system collects, accumulates, and yields material and manufacturing costs through each stage of production.

- First, the costs of raw materials used and the unit costs of each stage of manufacturing are established.

- Next, raw wafer and wafer production costs are converted to die costs. In wafer fabrication and probe, manufactured material is in wafer form. As such, the unit costs of the raw wafer and manufacturing in these stages are captured initially as cost/wafer. In assembly, where the wafer is cut into dies, the unit of measure also changes to dies. Thus, to complete the costing of the final product, which is in die form, cost/wafer must be converted to cost/die.
- Finally, the unit die costs are accumulated in the sequence of the manufacturing process and yielded at each stage. Yield refers to the production units successfully manufactured in each stage. The semiconductor manufacturing process typically loses much of its production due to misprocessing or nonfunctioning dies. Yielding the accumulated unit cost at each manufacturing stage applies the cost of lost production units to the cost of good production units.

At MosCo, the unit production cost of each major manufacturing stage (wafer, fabrication, probe, assembly, test) has been determined by applying that stage's annual spending to the annual volume of production (see Exhibits 2 and 3) or capacity (see Exhibits 6 and 7).

Exhibits 3 and 7 highlight the computation of unit cost at each stage of manufacturing. In wafer fabrication and probe, the production unit is a wafer. Unit cost through these two stages is computed as wafer cost. In assembly and test, the wafer has been diced to remove the dies. The good dies continue through assembly; the nonfunctioning dies are discarded. Unit cost through these two manufacturing stages is computed as die cost.

At each stage of production, production loss (or yield) is experienced. Yield loss is typically greatest during probe, when each die on the wafer is first tested to determine if it is functioning as designed. At probe, the effectiveness and quality of the wafer fabrication process, through which the multiple circuit layers have been placed on the wafer, is revealed. In wafer fabrication, the wafers used solely for engineering testing (to insure equipment is properly calibrated, and not used for production) are also eliminated (treated similar to production yield loss) in the calculation of wafer cost.

Exhibits 2 and 6 highlight the computation of product cost. The unit cost of each manufacturing stage is listed. For the raw wafer, wafer fabrication, and probe, the unit cost (wafer) is converted to die cost. The material cost is reflected at the manufacturing stage at which it is introduced. To determine a final or complete product cost, the cost per die is accumulated through each manufacturing stage and yielded for the production loss experienced in that stage. Yielding the accumulated die cost has the effect of placing the total cost of manufacturing on the good production units (or expected good production units if the total production capacity costing method is used).

Exhibit 2 highlights the accumulation of costs the x100 incurs during manufacturing. The cost and application of raw material can be seen at the start of wafer fabrication and assembly. Wafer to die conversion, based on the x100's specification of 50 die on each wafer, is used to compute the equivalent die cost from the raw wafer, and at wafer fabrication and probe. Finally, the treatment of production loss (yield) can be seen throughout the costing process, as the accumulated cost at each stage of production is increased by the planned or expected yield at that stage, resulting in an accumulated cost that reflects the total cost of production applied to the good dies produced or expected after each stage.

Exhibit 1.

MosCo, Inc.
Income Statement

	1993	1994
Revenue		
X100: 150,000 @$850	$127,500,000	$127,500,000
Cost of sales		
Wafers: (16,595 @$45)	$746,775	$746,775
Packages: (175,000 @$50)	$8,750,000	$8,750,000
Mfg. spending	$91,112,000	$91,112,000
Total cost of sales	$100,608,775	$101,608,775
Gross margin ($)	$26,891,225	$26,891,225
Gross margin (%)	21%	21%
Process development	$14,000,000	$14,000,000
Product development	$5,000,000	$5,000,000
Marketing & administration	$3,000,000	$6,000,000
Operating profit	$4,891,225	$1,891,225

Exhibit 2.

MosCo, Inc.
Fy94 Product Cost Worksheet
x100
GROSS DIE / WAFER: 50

Description	Cost / Wafer	Cost / Die	Cum Cost / Die
Yielded raw wafer	$50.00	$1.00	$1.00
Wafer Production cost	$5,245.15	$104.90	$105.90
Probe production cost	$785.71	$15.71	$121.62
Probe yield		25%	$486.47
339 PGA package cost		$50.00	$536.47
Assembly production cost		$9.26	$545.73
Assembly yield		90%	$606.36
Test production cost		$32.14	$638.51
Test yield		96%	$665.11
Total x100 product cost			$665.11

4-15

Exhibit 3

MosCo, Inc.
FY94 USED CAPACITY AND PROCESS COSTS WORKSHEET
x100

Operation	Per year	Mfg. Spending	Cost/Unit
Planned wafer capacity	16,595		
Engineering test wafers	1,040		
Planned wafer starts	15,555		
Wafer fabrication yield	90%		
Planned wafer production	13,999.50	$73,429,500	$5,245.16
Planned probed wafer starts	14,000	$11,000,000	$785.71
Gross die/wafer (x100 = 50)	50		
Total gross die thru probe	700,000		
Probe yield for x100	25%		
x100 probed die output	175,000		
Planned assembly starts	175,000	$1,620,000	$9.26
x100 assembly yield	90%		
Planned assembly completions	157,500		
Planned test starts	157,500	$5,062,500	$32.14
x100 test yield	96%		
Planned test output	151,200		
Total manufacturing spending		$91,112,000	

4-16

Exhibit 4.

MosCo, Inc.
FY94 Spending Summary By Organization

Organization	Manufacturing				Research & Develop		SG&A	TOTAL
	Fabrication	Probe	Assembly	Test	Prod Devp	Proc Devp	MKT & ADM	
Direct Mfg	$57,000,000	$11,000,000	$1,620,000	$5,062,500				$74,682,500
Res & Devp					$2,000,000	$9,000,000		$11,000,000
Mkt & Admin							$5,000,000	$5,000,000
Support Org's								
Facilities	$5,500,000				$1,000,000	$3,000,000	$500,000	$10,000,000
Yield Eng	$2,000,000							$2,000,000
Cimt	$4,000,000				$2,000,000	$2,000,000	$500,000	$8,500,000
Qual & Rel	$3,537,500							$3,537,500
Purchasing	$1,392,000							$1,392,000
Tot Support	$16,429,500				$3,000,000	$5,000,000	$1,000,000	$25,429,500
Tot Spending	$73,429,500	$11,000,000	$1,620,000	$5,062,500	$5,000,000	$14,000,000	$6,000,000	$116,112,000

Fabrication	$73,429,500
Probe	$11,000,000
Assembly	$1,620,000
Test	$5,062,500
Tot Mfg Spending	$91,112,000

4-17

Exhibit 5a.

MosCo, Inc.
Fy94 Activity-Based Spending Summary by Organization

Activity	Manufacturing				Research & Develop		Sg&A	Total
	Fabrication	Probe	Assembly	Test	Prod Devp	Proc Devp	Mkt & Adm	
Direct mfg (see Exhibit 5b)	$57,000,000	$11,000,000	$1,620,000	$5,062,500				$74,682,500
Res & devp					$2,000,000	$9,000,000		$11,000,000
Mkt & admin								
Marketing							$3,000,000	$3,000,000
Administration							$1,000,000	$1,000,000
Finance/Hr							$1,000,000	$1,000,000
Total							$5,000,000	$5,000,000
Total support (see Exhibit 5c)	$10,392,000	$2,000,000		$3,037,500	$3,000,000	$6,000,000	$1,000,000	$25,429,500
Total spending	$67,392,000	$13,000,000	$1,620,000	$8,100,000	$5,000,000	$15,000,000	$6,000,000	$116,112,000

Fabrication	$67,392,000
Probe	$13,000,000
Assembly	$1,620,000
Test	$8,100,000
Tot Mfg Spending	$90,112,000

Exhibit 5b.

MosCo, Inc.
FY94 Direct Manufacturing Activity-Based Spending Summary

Activity	Manufacturing				Research & Develop		Sg&A	Total
	Fabrication	Probe	Assembly	Test	Prod Devp	Proc Devp	Mkt & Adm	
Equipment Capacity: Driven by Equipment Installation								
Depreciation	$30,000,000	$3,500,000	$520,000	$1,400,000				$35,420,000
Utility costs	$5,000,000	$1,000,000	$50,000	$500,000				$6,550,000
Property/site	$5,000,000	$500,000	$50,000	$100,000				$5,650,000
Total	$40,000,000	$5,000,000	$620,000	$2,000,000				$47,620,000
Equipment capacity: driven by Equipment Uptime								
Equip engn'rs	$8,000,000	$2,000,000		$1,762,500				$11,762,500
Monitor wafer	$1,000,000							$1,000,000
Op'n supplies	$1,000,000	$1,000,000	$100,000	$300,000				$2,400,000
Total	$10,000,000	$3,000,000	$100,000	$2,062,500				$15,162,500
Equipment capacity: driven by production								
Direct labor	$5,000,000	$2,000,000	$800,000	$700,000				$8,500,000
Monitor wafer	$1,000,000							$1,000,000
Op'n supplies	$1,000,000	$1,000,000	$100,000	$300,000				$2,400,000
Total	$7,000,000	$3,000,000	$900,000	$1,000,000				$11,900,000
Tot dir mfg	$57,000,000	$11,000,000	$1,620,000	$5,062,500				$74,682,500

Tot dir mfg: (new Bonn tester) | $1,215,000

Exhibit 5c.

MosCo, Inc.
FY94 Support Group Activity-Based Spending Summary

Activity	Manufacturing				Research & Develop		Sg&A	Total
	Fabrication	Probe	Assembly	Test	Prod Devp	Proc Devp	Mkt & Adm	
Facilities:								
D/I Water	$1,000,000							$1,500,000
Site support	$500,000			$100,000	$500,000	$500,000	$500,000	$2,100,000
Utilities	$3,000,000			$400,000	$500,000	$2,000,000		$5,900,000
Chemicals	$500,000							$500,000
Total	$5,000,000			$500,000	$1,000,000	$3,000,000	$500,000	$10,000,000
Yield eng: yield improvement:		$2,000,000						$2,000,000
Cimt:								
Shop floor system	$1,000,000			$1,000,000				$2,000,000
Networks	$500,000			$500,000	$1,000,000	$500,000	$250,000	$2,750,000
Field svc	$500,000			$500,000	$500,000		$250,000	$1,750,000
System devp					$500,000	$500,000		$1,000,000
Equip connection						$1,000,000		$1,000,000
Total	$2,000,000			$2,000,000	$2,000,000	$2,000,000	$500,000	$8,500,000
Quality:								
Doc control	$1,000,000							$1,000,000
Fail analysis	$500,000			$100,000		$250,000		$850,000
Equip calibrate	$500,000			$437,500		$750,000		$1,687,500
Total	$2,000,000			$537,500		$1,000,000		$3,537,500
Purchasing	$1,392,000							$1,392,000
Total sup spend	$10,392,000	$2,000,000		$3,037,500	$3,000,000	$6,000,000	$1,000,000	$25,429,500
Total sup spend: (new Bonn tester)				$810,000				

Exhibit 6

MosCo, Inc.
Fy94 Revised Product Cost Worksheet
x100
GROSS DIE / WAFER: 50

DESCRIPTION	COST/WAFER	COST/DIE	CUM COST/DIE
Yielded raw wafer	$50.00	$1.00	$1.00
Wafer production cost	$3,000.00	$60.00	$61.00
Probe production cost	$500.00	$10.00	$71.00
Probe yeld		25%	$284.00
339 PGA package cost		$50.00	$334.00
Assembly production cost		$8.00	$342.00
Assembly yield		90%	$380.00
Test production cost		$40.00	$420.00
Test yield		96%	$437.50
TOTAL x100 PRODUCT COST			$437.50

Exhibit 7.

MosCo, Inc.
FY94 USED CAPACITY AND PROCESS COSTS WORKSHEET
x100

OPERATION	PER YEAR	MFG. SPENDING	COST/UNIT
Planned wafer capacity	26,000		
Engineering test wafers	1,040		
Planned wafer starts	24,960		
Water fabrication yield	90%		
Planned wafer production	22,464	$67,392,000	$3,000.00
Planned probed wafer starts	26,000	$13,000,000	$500.00
Gross die/wafer (x10 = 50)	50		
Total gross die through probe	1,300,000		
Probe yield for x100	25%		
x100 probed die output	325,000		
Planned assembly starts	202,500	$1,620,000	$8.00
x100 assembly yield	90%		
Planned assembly completions	182,250		
Planned test starts	202,500	$8,100,000	$40.00
x100 test yield	96%		
Planned test output	194,400		
TOTAL MANUFACTURING SPENDING		$90,112,000	

Exhibit 8.

MosCo, Inc.
FY95 PRODUCT COST WORKSHEET
x50
GROSS DIE / WAFER: 150

DESCRIPTION	COST/WAFER	COST/DIE	CUM COST/DIE
Yielded raw wafer	$50.00	$0.33	$0.33
Wafer production cost	$3,000.00	$20.00	$20.33
Probe production cost	$625.00	$4.17	$24.50
Probe yield		70%	$35.00
168 PGA package cost		$15.00	$50.00
Assembly production cost		$4.00	$54.00
Assembly yield		96%	$56.25
Test production cost		$5.00	$61.25
Test yield		98%	$62.50
TOTAL x50 PRODUCT COST			$62.50

Exhibit 9.

MosCo, Inc.
FY95 PROJECTED CAPACITY AND PROCESS COSTS WORKSHEET
x50

OPERATION	PER YEAR	MFG. SPENDING	COST/UNIT
Planned wafer capacity	26,000		
Engineering test wafers	1,040		
Planned wafer starts	24,960		
Wafer fabrication yield	90%		
Planned wafer production	22,464	$67,392,000	$3,000.00
Planned probed wafer starts	20,800	$13,000,000	$625.00
Gross die/wafer (x50 = 150)	150		
Total gross die through probe	3,120,000		
Probe yield for x50	70%		
x50 probed die output	2,187,400		
Planned assembly starts	405,000	$1,620,000	$4.00
x50 assembly yield	90%		
Planned assembly completions	364,500		
Planned test starts	405,000	$2,025,000	$5.00
x50 test yield	96%		
Planned test output	388,800		
TOTAL MANUFACTURING SPENDING		$84,037,000	

4-22

Exhibit 10

MosCo, Inc.
FY96 REVISED PRODUCT COST WORKSHEET
(reflecting requested wafer fabrication spending reduction)
x50
GROSS DIE / WAFER: 150

DESCRIPTION	COST/WAFER	COST/DIE	CUM COST/DIE
Yielded raw wafer	$50.00	$0.33	$0.33
Wafer production cost	$1,866.00	$12.44	$12.77
Probe production cost	$625.00	$4.17	$16.94
Probe yield		70%	$24.20
168 PGA package cost		$15.00	$39.20
Assembly production cost		$4.00	$43.20
Assembly yield		96%	$45.00
Test production cost		$5.00	$50.00
Test yield		98%	$51.02
TOTAL x50 PRODUCT COST			$51.02

Exhibit. 11

MosCo, Inc.
FY96 PROJECTED CAPACITY AND PROCESS COSTS WORKSHEET
(reflecting requested wafer fabrication spending reduction)
x50

OPERATION	PER YEAR	MFG. SPENDING	COST/UNIT
Planned wafer capacity	26,000		
Engineering test wafers	1,040		
Planned wafer starts	24,960		
Wafer fabrication yield	90%		
Planned wafer production	22,464	$41,917,824	$1,866.00
Planned probed wafer starts	20,800	$13,000,000	$625.00
Gross die/wafer (x50 = 150)	150%		
Total gross die through probe	3,120,000		
Probe yield for x50	70%		
x50 probed die output	2,184,000		
Planned assembly starts	405,000	$1,620,000	$4.00
x50 assembly yield	90%		
Planned assembly completions	364,500		$1,866.00
Planned test starts	405,000	$2,025,000	$5.00
x50 test yield	96%		
Planned test output	388,800		
TOTAL MANUFACTURING SPENDING		$58,562,824	

Exhibit 12a.

MosCo, Inc.
"OFFTIOL" PRO FORMA INCOME STATEMENT

	1994 REVISED	1955 RECOM'D	1996 RECOM'D
REVENUE:	$127,500,000	$115,312,500	$63,476,562
COST OF SALES:			
raw material costs	$9,496,775	$10,348,010	$8,282,255
production costs	$90,112,000	$59,063,500	$27,788,853
total product cost	$99,608,775	$69,411,510	$36,071,108
product gross margin	$27,891,225	$45,900,990	$27,405,454
%	21.9%	39.8%	43.2%
underutilized costs	$0	$33,073,500	$38,873,971
total cost of sales	$99,608,775	$102,485,010	$74,945,079
GROSS MARGIN:	$27,891,225	$12,827,490	($11,468,516)
%	21.9%	11.1%	-18.1%
PROCESS DEVELOPMENT:	$15,000,000	$15,000,000	$15,000,000
PRODUCT DEVELOPMENT:	$6,000,000	$6,000,000	$6,000,000
MARKETING & ADMINISTRATION:	$6,000,000	$7,000,000	$8,000,000
OPERATING PROFIT / (LOSS):	$891,225	($15,172,510)	($40,468,516)

4-24

Exhibit 12b.

MosCo, Inc.
FY95 "OFFTIOL" PRO FORMA INCOME STATEMENT WORKSHEET

	x100	x50	FY95
REVENUE:			
Q1: (37,500 @$850)	$31,875,000		
Q2-Q4: (112,500 @$637.50)	$71,718,750		
Q1-Q3 (37,500 @$250)		$9,375,000	
Q4: (12,500 @$187.50)		$2,343,750	
	$103,593,750	$11,718,750	$115,312,500
RAW MATERIAL COSTS:			
Wafers: (16,595 @$45)	$746,775		
(583 @$45)		$26,235	
Packages: (175,000 @$50)	$8,750,000		
(55,000 @$15)		$825,000	
	$9,496,775	$851,235	$10,348,010
PRODUCTION COSTS:			
Fabrication: (14,000 @$3,000)	$42,000,000		
(524 @$3,000)		$1,572,000	
Probe:(14,000 @$500)	$7,000,000		
(524 @$625)		$327,500	
Assembly: (175,000 @8)	$1,400,000		
(55,000 @$4)		$220,000	
Test: (157,000@$40)	$6,280,000		
(52,800 @$5)		$264,000	
	$56,680,000	$2,383,500	$59,063,500
UNDERUTILIZED COSTS:			
Fabrication: ($67,392,000-($42,000,000+$1,572,000))			$23,820,000
Probe: ($13,000,000-($7,000,000+$327,500))			$5,672,500
Assembly: ($1,620,000-($1,400,000+$220,000))			$0
Test: ($8,100,000-$6,280,000)+($2,025,000-$264,000)			$3,581,000
			$33,073,500

4-25

Exhibit 12c.

MosCo, Inc.
FY96 "OFFrIOL "PRO FORMA INCOME STATEMENT WORKSHEET

	x100	x50	FY95
REVENUE:			
QI-Q3: (56,250 $425)	$23,906,250		
Q4: (18,750 @$318.75)	$5,976,562		
Q1-Q2: (107,500 @$187.50)		$20,156,250	
Q3-Q4: (107,500 @$125)		$13,437,500	
	$29,882,812	$33,593,750	$63,476,562
RAW MATERIAL COSTS:			
Wafers: (7,991 @$45)	$359,595		
(2,448 @$45)		$110,160	
Packages: (86,875 @$50)	$4,343,750		
(231,250 @$15)		$3,468,750	
	$4,703,345	$3,578,910	$8,282,255
PRODUCTION COSTS:			
Fabrication: (6,950 @$1,866)	$12,968,700		
(2,203 @$1,866)		$4,110,798	
Probe: (6,950 @$500)	$3,475,000		
(2,203 @$625)		$1,376,875	
Assembly: (86,875 @$8)	$695,000		
(231,250 @$4)		$925,000	
Test: (78,187 @$40)	$3,127,480		
(222,000 @$5)		$1,110,000	
	$20,266,180	$7,522,673	$27,788,853

		FY95
UNDERUTILIZED COSTS:		
Fabrication: ($41,917,824-($12,968,700+$4,110,798))		$24,838,326
Probe: ($13,000,000-($3,475,000 +$1,376,875))		$8,148,125
Assembly: ($1,620,000-($695,000+$925,000))		$0
Test: ($8,100,000-$3,127,480)+($2,025,000-$1,110,000)		$5,887,520
		$38,873,971

Exhibit 13.

MosCo, Inc.
PRODUCT SPECIFICATIONS

	x100	x50	N50
FUNCTION:	CPU/CISC	CPU/CISC	CPU/CISC
TECHNOLOGY:	CMOS .75U	CMOS .75U	CMOS .75U
FREQUENCY:	100 mhz	50 mhz	50 mhz
SELLING PRICES			
actual: 1994 Q1:			
1994 Q2:	$850.00		
1994 Q3:			
1994 Q4:			
proposed 1995 Q1:			
1995 Q2	$637.50	$250.00	$500.00
1995 Q3			
1995 Q4	$187.50		$375.00
1996 Q1	$425.00		
1996 Q2			
1996 Q3	$125.00		$250.00
1996 Q4	$318.75		

	x100	x50	N50
RAW WAFER COST:	$45	$45	$45
WAFER PRODUCTION COST:	$3,000	$3,000	
PROBE COST/WAFER:	$500	$625	
GROS DIE/WAFER:	50	150	200
GOOD DIE THRU TEST (EQS):	10.8	98.8	141.1
PROBE YIELD:	25%	70%	75%
PACKAGE TYPE:	339 PGA	168PGA	168 PGA
PACKAGE COST:	$50	$15	$15
ASSEMBLY COST:	$8	$4	
ASSEMBLY YIELD:	90%	96%	
TEST COST:	$40	$5	
TEST YIELD:	96%	98%	

Exhibit 14.

MosCo, Inc.
FY95 & FY96 CAPACITY AVAILABLE

(W) wafers / (D) die	TOTAL CAPACITY AVAILABLE	x100 CAPACITY USED FY 95 (150,000)	FY 96 (75,000)	AVAILABLE CAPACITY FOR x50 FY 95	FY 96	MAXIMUM USED BY x50 FY 95	FY 96	AVAILABLE CAPACITY FY 95	FY 96
FAB STARTS	26,000 (w)	16,595	7,991						
ENGINEERING STARTS	1,040 (w)	1,040	1,040						
PRODUCTION STARTS	24,960 (w)	15,555	7,723	9,405	17,237	582	2,447	8,823	14,790
PRODUCTION COMPLETES	22,464 (w)	14,000	6,950	9,464	15,514	524	2,202	7,940	13,312
x100 PROBE STARTS	26,000 (w)	14,000	6,950	12,000	19,050				
x50 PROBE STARTS	20,800 (w)			9,600	15,240	524	2,202	9,076	13,038
339 PGA ASSEMBLY STARTS	202,500 (d)	175,000	86,875	27,500	115,625				
339 PGA ASSEMBLY COMPLETES	188,250 (d)	157,500	78,187						
168 PGA ASSEMBLY STARTS	405,000 (d)			55,000	231,250	55,000	231,250	0	0
168 PGA ASSEMBLY COMPLETES	388,800 (d)			52,800	222,000	52,800	222,000	0	0
x100 TEST STARTS	202,500 (d)	157,500	78,187					45,000	124,313
x100 TEST COMPLETES	194,400 (d)	151,200	75,060					43,200	119,340
x50 TEST STARTS	405,000 (d)			405,000	405,000	52,800	222,000	352,200	183,000
x50 TEST COMPLETES	396,900 (d)			396,900	396,900	51,744	217,560	345,156	179,340

4-3. Tektronix

BACKGROUND

Tektronix, Inc. headquartered in Portland, Oregon, is a world leader in the production of electronic test and measurement instruments. The company's principal product since its founding in 1946 has been the oscilloscope (scope), an instrument that measures and graphically displays electronic signals. The two divisions of the Portables Group produce and market high and medium-performance portable scopes.

Tektronix experienced almost uninterrupted growth through the 1970s based on a successful strategy of providing technical excellence in the scope market and continually improving its products in terms of both functionality and performance for the dollar. In the early 1980s, however, the lower priced end of the division's medium-performance line of scopes was challenged by an aggressive low-price strategy of several Japanese competitors. Moving in from the low-price, low-performance market segment in which Tektronix had decided not to compete, these companies set prices 25 percent below the U.S. firm's prevailing prices. Rather than moving up the scale to more highly differentiated products, the group management decided to block the move.

The first step was to reduce the prices of higher-performance, higher-cost scopes to the prices of the competitors' scopes of lower performance. This short-term strategy resulted in reported losses for those instruments. The second step was to put in place a new management team whose objective was to turn the business around. These managers concluded that, contrary to conventional wisdom, the Portables Group divisions could compete successfully with foreign competition on a cost basis. To do so, the divisions would have to reduce costs and increase customer value by increasing operational efficiency.

PRODUCTION PROCESS CHANGES

The production process in the Portables Group divisions consisted of many functional islands, including etched circuit board (ECB) insertion, ECB assembly, ECB testing, ECB repair, final assembly, test, thermal cycle, test/QC, cabinet fitting, finishing, boxing for shipment, and shipment. The new management team consolidated these functionally-oriented activities into integrated production lines in open work spaces that allow visual control of the entire production area. Parts inventory areas were also placed parallel to production lines so that at each work station operators would be able to pull their own parts. This in essence created an early warning system that nearly eliminated line stoppages due to stockouts.

Additional steps that were taken in the early to mid 1980s to solve managerial and technical problems include implementation of just-in-time (JIT) delivery and scheduling techniques and total quality control (TQC), movement of manufacturing support departments into the production area, and implementation of people involvement (PI) techniques to move responsibility for problem solving down to the operating level of the divisions. The results of these changes were impressive: substantial reductions in cycle time, direct labor hours per unit, and inventory, and increases in output dollars per person per day and operating income. The cost accounting group had dutifully measured these improvements, but had not effectively supported the strategic direction of the divisions.

COST ACCOUNTING SYSTEM

DIRECT MATERIALS AND DIRECT LABOR

The total manufacturing cost of the newest portable scopes produced with the latest technologies has 75% direct materials, 3% direct labor, and 22% factory overhead. In most cases, direct materials and direct labor are easily traced to specific products for costing purposes. Prior to the mid 1980s, however, the divisions' attempts to control direct labor had been a resource drain that actually *decreased* productivity.

There were approximately twenty-five production cost centers in the Portable Instruments Plant. Very detailed labor efficiency reports were prepared monthly for each cost center and each major step in the production process. In addition, an efficiency rating for each individual employee was computed daily. Employees reported the quantity of units produced and the time required to produce them, often overestimating the quantity produced to show improved efficiency against continually updated standards. The poor quality of collected data resulted in semi-annual inventory-downs when physical and book quantities were compared.

"The inadequacy of our efficiency reporting system became clear when we analyzed one of our new JIT production lines," commented Michael Wright, Financial Systems Application Manager. "On a JIT manufacturing line, once the excess inventory has been flushed out, it is essentially impossible for any person to work faster or slower than the line moves. However, if one person on the line is having a problem, it immediately becomes apparent because the product flow on the line stops. Corrective action is then taken, and the line is started up again.

"On that line, the system told us that the efficiency of each of the workers was decreasing. However, stepping back from the detail of the situation allowed us to look at the overall picture. We found that the costs incurred on the line were going down and its product output was going up. Obviously, it was becoming more, not less, efficient."

The quantity of direct labor data collected and processed also was a problem. Production employees often spent twenty minutes per day completing required reports when they could have been producing output. Additionally, the accounting staff was processing 35,000 labor transactions per month to account for what amounted to 3 percent of total manufacturing cost.

"Transactions cost money," observed John Jonez, Group Cost Accounting Manager, "and lots of transactions cost lots of money."

In response to these problems, the group accounting staff greatly simplified its procedures. It abandoned the measurement of labor performance for each operation, and greatly reduced the number of variances reported. The number of monthly labor transactions fell to less than 70, allowing the staff to spend more time on factory overhead allocation and other pressing issues.

FACTORY OVERHEAD

The product costing system allocated all factory overhead costs to products based on standard direct labor hours. A separate rate was computed for each manufacturing cost center. This system led to rapidly increasing rates: the direct labor content of the group's products had been continually decreasing for years, while factory overhead costs were increasing in absolute terms.

"Because the costing system correlated overhead to labor, our engineers concluded that the way to reduce overhead costs was to reduce labor," commented Jonez. "The focus of cost reduction programs therefore had been the elimination of direct labor. However, most of this effort was misdirected, because there was almost no correlation between overhead cost incurrence and direct labor hours worked. Our system penalized products with proportionately higher direct labor, but it wasn't those products that caused overhead costs. We proved that. We attacked direct labor and it went down, but at the same time overhead went up.

"We therefore knew that we needed a new way to allocate overhead. More fundamentally, we needed a way for the cost accounting system to support the manufacturing strategy of our group. The objective was clear-to provide management with accounting information that would be useful in identifying cost reduction opportunities in its operating decisions as well as provide a basis for effective reporting of accomplishments."

APPROACH TO METHOD CHANGE

INITIAL STEPS

The first step taken by Wright and Jonez in developing a new overhead allocation method was to establish a set of desirable characteristics for the method. They decided that it must accurately assign costs to products, thus providing better support for management decisions than the old method. It must support the JIT manufacturing strategy of the Portables Group. It also must be intuitively logical and easily understandable by management. And finally, it must provide information that is accessible by decision makers.

The next step was to interview the engineering and manufacturing managers who were the primary users of product cost information. These users were asked, "What is it that makes your job more difficult? What is it that makes certain products more difficult to manufacture? What causes the production line to slow down? What is it that causes overhead?" The answers to these questions were remarkably consistent-there were too many unique part numbers in the system. This finding revealed a major flaw in the ability of the direct labor-based costing method to communicate information critical for cost-related decisions. Manufacturing managers realized there were substantial cost reduction opportunities through the standardization of component parts, but there was no direct method to communicate this idea to design and cost-reduction engineers who made part selection decisions.

Although difficult to quantity, some costs are associated with just carrying a part number in the database. Each part number must be originally set up in the system, built into the structure of a bill of materials, and maintained until it is no longer used. Moreover, each part must be planned, scheduled, negotiated with vendors, purchased, received, stored, moved, and paid for. Having two parts similar enough that one could be used for both applications requires unnecessary duplication of these activities, and therefore unnecessary costs.

Standardizing parts results in several indirect benefits. Fewer unique part numbers usually means fewer vendors and greater quality of delivered parts. It also means smoother JIT production, fewer shutdowns of manufacturing lines, and greater field reliability. These observations led to a preliminary consensus on the need to develop a product costing method that would quantify and communicate the value of parts standardization.

COST ANALYSIS

"To confirm our assessment," stated Jonez, "we segmented the total manufacturing overhead cost pool. The costs of all cost centers comprising the pool were categorized as either materials-related or conversion-related based upon rules developed in conjunction with operating managers.(See Table 1)

"Material-related costs pertain to procurement, scheduling, receiving, incoming inspection, stockroom personnel, cost-reduction engineering, and information systems. Conversion-related costs are associated with direct labor, manufacturing supervision, and process-related engineering. Application of the rules resulted in an approximately 55/45 split between materials overhead (MOH) and conversion overhead (COH). This finding further confirmed the inadequacy of the existing method, which applied all overhead based on direct labor."

The accounting analysts decided to focus their initial efforts on the MOH pool. To improve their understanding of the composition of the pool and thus assist them in developing a method for its allocation, Wright and Jonez consulted operating managers and further segmented it into:

1. Costs due to the value of parts,

2. Costs due to the absolute number of parts used,

3. Costs due to the maintenance and handling of each different part number and

4. Costs due to each use of a different part number.

The managers believed that the majority of MOH costs were of type (3). The costs due to the value of parts (1) and the frequency of the use of parts (2 and 4) categories were considered quite small by comparison.

The analysts therefore concluded that the material-related costs of the Portables Group would decrease if a smaller number of different part numbers were used in its products. This cost reduction would result from two factors. First, greater volume discounts would be realized by purchasing larger volumes of fewer unique parts. Second, material overhead costs would be lower. "It was the latter point that we wanted our new allocation method to focus on," commented Wright.

"Our goal," continued Jonez, "was to increase customer value by reducing overhead costs. Our strategy was parts standardization. We needed a tactic to operationalize the strategy."
(IMA Case)

REQUIRED:

1. Using assumed numbers, develop a cost allocation method for materials overhead (MOH) to quantify and communicate the strategy of parts standardization.

2. Explain how use of your method would support the strategy.

3. Is any method which applies the entire MOH cost pool on the basis of one cost driver sufficiently accurate for product decisions in the highly competitive portable scope markets? Explain.

4. Are MOH product costing rates developed for management reporting appropriate for inventory valuation for external reporting? Why or why not?

Table 1
Rules for Overhead Segmentation by Cost Center Classification

1) *Production.* The overhead costs of any cost center containing direct labor employees are assigned 100 percent to the COH pool.

2) *Group/Division/Product Group Support.* The total costs of any manufacturing staff cost center are assigned 50 percent to the COH pool and 50 percent to the MOH pool.

3) *Group/Division/Product Group Support.* The total costs of any manufacturing support cost center (e.g., Material Management of Information Systems) are assigned 100 percent to the MOH pool.

4) *Manufacturing Cost-Reduction Engineering.* The total costs of any cost reduction engineering cost center are assigned 100 percent to the MOH pool.

5) *Manufacturing Process-Related Engineering.* The total costs of any process-related engineering cost center are assigned 100 percent to the COH pool.

HOW ABC CHANGED THE POST OFFICE

To meet its competition, the U.S. Postal Service had to change and offer customers credit/debit card service.

By Terrell L. Carter; Ali M. Sedghat, CMA; and Thomas D. Williams

The U.S. Postal Service is a unique federal entity in several respects. First, the USPS is unique in that it is open to private sector competition. Competition includes companies such as Federal Express, United Parcel Service, Mail Boxes Etc., and a host of other similar companies. Few other government agencies or departments operate in a similar business environment.

Retailers as well as USPS competitors have long accepted credit cards as payment options for goods and services. Moreover, new technologies are beginning to lead to a "cashless" world. Customers are seeking convenience and value, while businesses are striving for increased sales and guaranteed payment. Given the competitive forces facing the USPS and the rapid pace at which new technologies are becoming available, USPS management realized that it had to use innovative business methods to maintain and increase its market share against its competition and provide increased value to its customers while ensuring cost effectiveness.

Based on this evaluation of its position in the marketplace, the USPS engaged Coopers & Lybrand (C&L) to conduct activity-based cost studies of its key revenue collection processes and market strategy study for a national credit card and debit card program. To obtain an understanding of the cash, check, and credit/debit card activities, C&L reviewed USPS data and procedure manuals, interviewed USPS headquarters staff, and conducted telephone surveys of front window supervisors and district office accounting personnel. Using an activity-based cost modeling approach, C&L defined the cash and check process in terms of the activities that link together to make the processes. C&L also identified unit, batch, and product sustaining activities; resources for each of the activities; and the transaction volumes for each activity. Unit activity was the acceptance and processing of a payment by item. Batch activities involved close-out at the end of the day, consolidation, and supervisory review. Product activities included maintenance charges for bank accounts and deposit reconciliation (cash and checks) and terminal maintenance and training (credit and debit cards).

After building the cash and check cost models, C&L defined activity-based costs for the credit and debit card activities similarly. The components of the cash, check, and credit/debit card activities are shown in Table 1. The activity cost models for the cash and check

---

TABLE 1
ANALYSIS OF ACTIVITIES

Cash Process Activities	Credit/Debit Card Activities	Check Process Activities
1. Receive cash	1. Process card transactions.	1. Receive checks
2. Deposit cash	2. Close out point-of-sale (POS) terminal.	2. Deposit checks
3. Maintain bank accounts (including cash concentration and funds mobilization).	3. Reconcile credit and debit card receipts.	3. Maintain bank accounts (including cash concentration and funds mobilization).
4. Reconcile bank accounts.	4. Process chargebacks.	4. Reconcile bank accounts.
	5. Maintain POS and telecommunications equipment.	

TABLE 2A
ACTIVITY-BASED COST MODEL FOR CASH PROCESSES

Unit Activities	Driver	Cost per Driver	Driver Quantities	Annual Cost
Accept cash	Number of cash transactions	$0.49	921,881,239	$451,173,288
Processing of cash by bank	Number of cash transactions	0.02	921,881,239	19,974,271
Batch Activities				
Close-out and supervisor review of clerk	Number of close-outs	5.79	28,029,443	162,255,662
Consolidation and deposit of unit's receipts	Number of deposits	16.16	9,902,381	160,016,636
Review and transfer funds-time	Number of accounts	1,884.47	7,490	14,114,698
Product Activities				
Maintenance charges for bank accounts	Number of accounts	114.32	7,490	856,286
Reconciling bank accounts	Number of accounts	1,935.94	7,490	14,500,182
	TOTAL COST			**$822,891,023**

TABLE 2B.
ACTIVITY-BASED COST MODEL FOR CHECK PROCESSES

Unit Activities	Driver	Cost per Driver	Driver Quantities	Annual Cost
Accept checks	Number of checks	$0.98	120,173,780	$117,627,298
Processing of checks by bank	Number of checks	0.06	120,173,780	7,335,089
Processing of returned checks	Number of bad checks	25.16	143,436	3,608,400
Batch Activities				
Close-out and supervisor review of clerk	Number of close-outs	2.67	28,029,443	74,887,229
Consolidation and deposit of unit's receipts	Number of deposits	2.07	9,902,381	20,505,861
Review and transfer funds-time	Number of accounts	25.16	7,490	1,873,980
Product Activities				
Maintenance charges for bank accounts	Number of accounts	14.91	7,490	111,641
Reconciling bank accounts	Number of accounts	251.80	7,490	1,185,971
	TOTAL COST			**$227,135,469**

activities are shown in Table 2. The activity-based cost models for the credit card and debit card activities are shown in Table 3. C&L also conducted product pricing and profitability analyses of the credit/debit card test program.

In analyzing data from Phase 1 of the USPS credit card and debit card test market plan and the organizational costs associated with serving USPS customers through its 28,728 post office, 9,059 stations and branches, and 1,605 community postal units, C&L identified the following issues affecting costs, product pricing, competitiveness, and customer value.[1]

1. USPS provides a limited assortment of payment options relative to the competition:

- Cash and check payments are predominant USPS payment options,

- Competitors provide credit card payment options, and

- Most USPS transactions must occur at a post office

2. USPS generates a large volume of low-value cash transactions:

- The majority of transactions are $20 or less, and

- Transactions on a per-dollar basis are expensive to process.

3. USPS' check receipts processing is costly:

TABLE 3A
ACTIVITY-BASED COST MODEL FOR CREDIT CARD PROCESSES

Unit Activities	Driver	Cost per Driver	Driver Quantities	Annual Cost
Process credit card	Number of credit transactions	$0.80	357,796	$287,217
Payment of credit card fee	$ size of transactions	0.01	18,512,365	252,474
Processing chargebacks	Number of chargebacks	23.87	120	2,865
Batch Activities				
Close-out terminal	Number of close-outs	1.30	160,596	208,581
Reconciling daily receipts—district	Number of stations	65.84	1,500	98,767
Process from 1908	Number of 1908s	9.04	2,884	26,072
Product Activities				
Maintain equipment	Number of terminals	275.60	1,875	516,754
Training	Number of districts	22,311.84	5	111,559
	TOTAL COST			**$1,504,289**

TABLE 3B
ACTIVITY-BASED COST MODEL FOR DEBIT CARD PROCESSES

Unit Activities	Driver	Cost per Driver	Driver Quantities	Annual Cost
Process debit card	Number of debit transactions	$0.86	35,262	$30,260
Batch Activities				
Close-out terminal	Number of close-outs	0.12	160,596	19,746
Reconciling daily receipts—district	Number of stations	6.24	1,500	9,359
Process from 1908	Number of 1908s	0.86	2,884	2,470
Product Activities				
Maintain equipment	Number of terminals	26.11	1,875	48,965
Training	Number of districts	2,114.16	5	10,571
	TOTAL COST			**$121,371**

- Extra steps are required,

- Additional bank charges are incurred, and

- $3-$4 million is lost to bed checks.

4. Policies and procedures are not consistent.

5. Based on independent surveys, cash, check, and credit/debit card processes are not uniform.

PROJECTED COST MODEL FOR USPS

The ABC study also revealed hidden and indirect costs for each of the payment activities. Combining all of the costs resulted in the breakdown shown in Table 4. C&L

pointed out that "total incremental costs for a national credit/debit card program are immaterial in relation to total USPS payment processing costs that exceed $1 billion per year, based on the activity-based cost study data collected through the February/March 1994 time frame."[2] The cost data showed that the net benefit of

TABLE 4
PROCESSING COSTS

Activity Processing of		Cost Per Dollar Processed	
Cash	$20	$.045	$.048
Checks	$51	$.038	$.040
Credit Cards	$52	$.081	$.027
Debit Cards	$49	$.071	$.015

accepting credit and debit cards would be negative through 1997. Projections showed that from 1998 through 2000, the net benefits of card acceptance would be $5.2 million, $15.6 million, and $28.8 million, respectively (see Table 5).

In summarizing these findings, C&L reported that, "Credit and debit card processing costs are relatively high at the moment due to the normal impact of process start-up, low initial volume and high initial implementation costs. However, as volumes continue to grow, projected credit and debit card costs can become competitive with current cash and check processing costs."[3] C&L also reported that "credit and debit card processing costs for retail window transactions becomes cost effective once total card revenue exceeds 3%-4% of total revenues from retail transactions. As card volume continues to displace cash and check transactions, card costs become even more advantageous."[4]

TABLE 5
PROJECTED COST MODEL

Base Line	1994	1995	1996	1997	1998	1999	2000
Cash	822,856,044	879,004,435	938,710,365	1,003,001,968	1,071,923,013	1,145,819,941	1,225,066,230
Check	227,789,177	242,987,911	259,731,645	277,371,596	296,274	316,534,152	338,252,449
Total Cost	1,050,645,221	1,121,992,346	1,198,442,010	1,280,373,564	1,368,197,371	1,462,354,093	1,563,318,679
Card Program							
Cash	822,856,044	867,786,033	899,084,296	933,386,322	967,692,345	1,001,794,407	1,035,444,902
Check	227,789,177	238,356,354	250,021,816	259,526,699	269,039,899	278,505,217	287,864,197
Credit	1,511,405	18,948,017	46,924,315	69,641,084	96,614,272	127,254,140	161,39,635
Debit	125,709	3,112,999	13,839,778	21,074,881	29,567,163	39,187,991	49,833,387
Total Cost	1,052,282,335	1,128,203,403	1,209,870,205	1,283,628,986	1,362,913,679	1,446,741,755	1,534,482,121
Net Benefit (Cost)	(1,637,114)	(6,211,057)	(11,428,195)	(3,255,422)	5,283,692	15,612,238	28,836,558

COST PER DOLLAR

Base Line	1994	1995	1996	1997	1998	1999	2000
Cash	0.045	0.042	0.044	0.043	0.042	0.042	0.042
Check	0.037	0.035	0.036	0.036	0.036	0.035	0.035
Card Program							
Cash	0.045	0.042	0.045	0.045	0.045	0.046	0.047
Check	0.037	0.036	0.037	0.038	0.038	0.039	0.039
Credit	0.082	0.035	0.033	0.029	0.028	0.027	0.027
Debit	0.073	0.023	0.021	0.017	0.016	0.015	0.015

Note: The 1994 Model Totals were higher than actual Phase 1 Cost Models due to the incremental start-up costs of the national program. C&L stressed that data for this model would be subject to change as new data and information become available and for the model to continue to be useful, it would have to be updated on a periodic basis to reflect ongoing program management modification.

COOPERS & LYBRAND'S RECOMMENDATION

Based on its analysis of the market test, a Gallup survey, and market trends, C&L recommended that the USPS use a three-phase strategy toimplement a national policy of accepting both credit and debit cards: Phase I—Market Test (which was already completed); Phase II—Mobilize and Market; Phase III—Modify.

Mobilize and market. This two-step phase began with an aggressive mobilization effort to implement nationwide acceptance of credit and debit cards for selected USPS products and services at retail windows beginning with larger offices. The potential benefits were identified as increased customer satisfaction, increased sales, and improved processing efficiency. The second step was an aggressive targeted marketing campaign designed to increase credit card usage at USPS retail windows. "Studies indicate that a targeted marketing campaign can have significant impact on consumer use

4-36

of debit and credit cards. A recent study concluded that the value of increased sales more than covered the additional expense of advertising."[5] The potential benefits identified were increased credit/debit card volume, increased total sales, and reduced transaction costs.

Modify. This phase entailed implementing improved credit/debit card processing technology and procedures to increase the benefits and continue to reduce the costs of the national card program. C&L recommended installing online point-of-sale terminals and consolidating all card authorization and transaction processing. The national implementation would use standalone card verification terminals, and this phase would replace them with integrated equipment. The potential benefits identified would be improved processing efficiency, reduced processing costs, reduced transaction errors and rejects, and improved management information.

TABLE 6

Through March 1997	Total Number of Transactions	Total Dollar Transactions	Average Ticket	Total Chargebacks*
Credit Cards	26,494,680	$1,276,263,936	$48	$61,723
Debit Cards	2,251,720	$ 118,529,332	$53	n/a

*Chargebacks are charges that customers dispute, which, after investigating, the card companies reverse. This becomes an expense to the merchant

---

THE BOARD APPROVES CARDS

Senior postal management decided on the basis of the C&L analysis and a decision analysis report (DAR) prepared by USPS Finance to propose to the USPS Board of Governors ("Board") that credit and debit cards be accepted nationally at USPS retail windows. Management recommended an aggressive two-year implementation. By the end of the second year, 33,000 post offices would be equipped with 50,000 card terminals and trained USPS personnel.[6] The DAR provided the following breakdown:

Expense investment (50,000 card terminals)	$25,893,000
Installation expense	3,825,000
Total investment (fiscal years 1995 and 1996)	$29,718,000
Operating costs in first full year (FY 97)	$30,327,000

Customer service initiative with no claimed ROI

Potential cost savings and revenue enhancements not included.

It is important to note the last two points. The program, while virtually ensuring an ROI and cost savings, was not being proposed for the financial benefits. Instead, as USPS CFO Michael J. Riley said in his presentation to the Board, "It is important to note that this is a customer service initiative which does not attempt to claim a return on investment. This is in spite of the fact that many retailers report savings from processing less currency and checks, as well as increased revenue from offering this growing retail payment option. We base our DAR on increased customer satisfaction."[7] In October 1994, the Board unanimously approved the proposal without any modifications.

THE ROLL-OUT

The next stop after Board approval was to get a contract in place for a credit card processor and a vendor to supply the 50,000 card terminals. A contract was competitively awarded the following spring to NationsBank with NaBanco, a national card processor, as its subcontractor.[8] NaBanco also would supply the terminals under a contract it had with a manufacturer in Atlanta, Microbilt, Inc. In April 1995, the roll-out began.

Since April 1995, the program has broadened in scope to include phone and mail orders for stamps including philately and vending machines. Because of demand, the contract recently was modified to increase the number of card terminals shipped to more than 67,000. From a customer service perspective, credit and debit card acceptance has been a runaway success, and even with such an aggressive implementation schedule it has been difficult to satisfy demand.

This project has been a very successful customer-driven initiative. Since the roll-out began, there have been more than 300 positive news articles covering this program. Not only do customers enjoy the convenience and flexibility of not having to carry as much cash, but USPS retail window clerks, who feel safer because there is less cash in their drawers, benefit as well. USPS clerks also like card acceptance because card transactions are more accurate than counting cash, so their liability is minimized.[9]

The USPS benefits because it gets funds the next day from card transactions at a very competitive discount rate. The payment infrastructure created by card acceptance has helped the USPS launch new products and market tests more quickly. Starting credit card acceptance later benefited the Postal Service because it could add debit card acceptance at the same time with one roll-out rather than two. The USPS is now the nation's largest debit card acceptor. The program has been highly successful in all of its aims, as these important statistics show (see Table 6). See Figure 1 for the growth trends in transaction and dollar-volume.

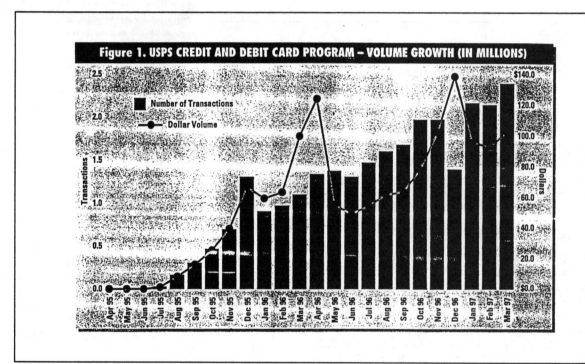

Figure 1. USPS CREDIT AND DEBIT CARD PROGRAM – VOLUME GROWTH (IN MILLIONS)

AS EASY AS ABC: MAXIMIZING VALUE

The popularity of activity-based costing and activity-based management is growing. In the private sector, hundreds of companies have adopted activity-based costing and management approaches to cost finding and cost accounting. These range from manufacturers such as John Deere to service firms such as American Express. Many have gone a step further and adopted activity-based management approaches.

Now, local and national public sector organizations are beginning to apply activity-based costing and activity-based management to the task of reinventing government. These organizations range from the road maintenance department in Indianapolis to enormous federal agencies such as the USPS as described here.

Earlier attempts at improving government operations have been largely unsuccessful. Activity-based costing and activity-based management approaches are allowing these government organizations to discover and take advantage of four elements missing from earlier performance improvement attempts. They include:

- Financial and performance information systems that enable and encourage managers to make strategic process improvements that maximize value to customers and taxpayers.
- A management and organizational structure built around processes or how the work gets done in an organization.
- A strategy for managing the human aspects of changing from a static bureaucracy to a dynamic, improvement-driven organization.
- A common financial and managerial language for different parts of an organization and all of a government's agencies.

Activity-based costing approaches are ever evolving. Nearly every organization applying these approaches discovers new uses. They go far beyond ABC's original purpose of calculating accurate product costs, all the way to activity-based management, a comprehensive management approach. The case of the USPS's national credit card and debit card program provides an excellent example of how effective activity-based approaches can be in facilitating strategic process improvements that maximize value to customers while ensuring economic viability and cost effectiveness..

Terrell L. Carter is assistant treasurer, payment technologies, for the United States Postal Service. A 28-year career employee., Terry holds a B.S. degree in Computer Information Systems from Strayer College, Washington, D.C. and is an executive MBA fellow at Loyola College in Maryland. He is a member of the Treasury Management Association. He can be reached at (202) 268-2330.

Ali M. Sedaghat, CMA, DBA, KPMG Faculty Alumni Fellow, is an associate of accounting at Loyola College in Maryland. He earned his B.A. degree from Abadan Institute of Technology and MBA and DBA degrees from The George Washington University. He is a member of IMA's Baltimore Chapter, through which this article was submitted.

Thomas D. Williams is the financial management officer for the National Institute of Allergy and Infectious Diseases at the National Institutes of Health. A 15-year career employee of the federal government, Tom has extensive experience in domestic and international governmental budgeting, accounting, finance, and management. Tom is also an executive MBA fellow at Loyola College in Maryland.

Authors acknowledge valuable contributions by Julie Jack, Julie Moore, and Matthew Wong.

[1] "United States Postal Service Credit/Debit Card Strategy—Final Report," Coopers & Lybrand L.L.P., Washington, D.C., April 19, 1994, p. 8.

[2] Ibid., page 37.

[3] Ibid., page 3.

[4] Ibid., page 12.

[5] Ibid., page 31.

[6] 6,000 "contract" stations would not be included in the two-year implementation.

[7] "Credit-Debit Card Acceptance at the Retail Window," presentation to the Board of Governors, October 3, 1994.

[8] NaBanco is now First Data Merchant Services (FDMS).

[9] USPS window clerks must compensate the USPS for shortages, so errors in cash handling are costly to them.

Chapter 5
Target Costing, Theory of Constraints, and Life Cycle Costing

Cases

5-1   California-Illini Manufacturing (The Theory of Constraints)
5-2   Blue Ridge Manufacturing (B)
5-3   Target Costing
5-4   Mercedes-Benz All Activity Vehicle (AAV)

Readings

"Target Costing at ITT Automotive"
This article provides a good example of an actual application of target costing. The example is of the production and sale of brake systems, an intensely competitive industry. The article explains how value engineering is used. Two important concepts of the article are (1) target costing is a moving target, and as prices fall in the industry, target costs and manufacturing costs are required to fall as well, and (2) target costing is a bottom-up, team-oriented process that requires cross-functional teams. Also, the article explains how ITT uses "tracking sheets" to manage the life cycle costs of the product.

Discussion Questions:
1. How are prices set at ITT Automotive?
2. How does ITT Automotive obtain information about a competitor's costs?
3. What are the target costing tools used at ITT Automotive?
4. How is the tracking sheet used in ITT Automotive's target costing system?

Cases

5-1. California-Illini Manufacturing

The California-Illini Manufacturing Company's (CI) plant operates in the rural central valley of California. It is family-owned and run. CI's plant manager, a grandson of the founder, went to school with many of the employees. Despite this family atmosphere, CI is the largest producer of plain and hard-faced replacement tillage tools in the United States. It averages annual sales of $13 million. Farmers use tillage tools to cultivate the land. Hard-facing, the application of brazed chromium carbide to leading edges, increases a tool's durability.

THE PRODUCTION PROCESS

Historically, CI grew from the founders' original blacksmith shop, and today the production process is still relatively simple. The plant manager described the process as "You simply take a piece of metal. And then you bang, heat, and shape it until it's a finished product. It really isn't a sophisticated process. We just do it better than anyone else." The production process is like a flow following a routing from one cost center to another in a sequence of move, wait, setup, and runtime for each process. Work-in-process inventories in the move and wait stage litter the plant. Economic lot size rules determine the size of each batch while production schedules push jobs onto the floor.

THE COST SYSTEM: MEASURING PERFORMANCE

CI uses standard unit costs to measure performance and profit potential. In this cost system, each materials and labor input is given a standard usage, and production managers are evaluated on their ability to meet or improve upon these standards. Differences from the standard were called "variances." For example, if a certain manufacturing operation required at standard 5 minutes, the operator would be expected to complete a lot of 100 parts in 500 minutes. If actually 550 minutes were required, there would be a 50 minute unfavorable variance. Also, using the operator's wage rate, the cost of the variance could be calculated.

CI'S IMPROVEMENT STRATEGY

The depressed market in the mid-1980s caused a 1986 net loss of close to $1.8 million. Inventory turns were down to one and a half, and cash flow was poor. Facing these conditions, management adopted a new strategy stressing improvements in accounting performance and reduction of inventories. Their strategies for improvement included: increasing productivity, cost cutting (overhead control), improving technology, and increasing prices.

1. **Productivity**. Productivity improvements centered on direct labor productivity measures. Output per direct labor hour was the crucial factor. Accordingly, improving efficiency, by definition, consisted of keeping direct labor busy producing as much product as possible during regular working hours. Actions supporting this strategy were 1) reducing idle manhours between jobs, 2) increasing batch sizes to maximize runtime, and 3) reducing setup times.

   The operational control system measured the "earned labor hours" for each department daily. While the plant manager only received these reports weekly, he was still aware of the daily figures. Budget reports, including variances, while processed monthly, were often two to three weeks late! Thus, they had little direct impact on day-to-day decisions. However, the plant manager knew what the accounting reports should be like from his daily earned labor hours information.

The short-term results of these efforts were impressive because plant efficiency measures rose about 15%. There were, however, some negative, unanticipated side effects in work-in-process levels, scheduling, and overtime.

First, work-in-process levels increased. In order to improve efficiency measures, departments kept processing large lots regardless of current demand. Once a machine had been set up, to economically justify large batches, the rationale was to provide for both current and future inventory needs. Consequently, finished goods grew from two to six-months' supply.

Second, the large batch sizes made scheduling difficult. They reduced plant flexibility by keeping machines on single jobs for long periods. Therefore, it was difficult to adjust for normal production problems and still maintain the production schedule. Machines were not readily available for special situations and expediting.

Finally, these large batches, while increasing productivity, created the need for overtime to maintain the schedule. Overtime in the finishing department, for example, increased by 15-20%, thus raising operating expenses. The larger lots reduced the variety of products produced each production period. This increased the lead time for custom orders could get stuck behind jobs with long runtimes. Overtime, then, became necessary to expedite out-of-stock orders. These factors combined with low sales volumes to create losses and more cash flow problems.

2. **Overhead.** Overhead improvement focused on two strategies. The first was direct cost reduction. The second concentrated on reducing unit costs by increasing volume. The higher volumes allowed overhead to be absorbed over more units. However, because CI's cost structure had large fixed obligations (like union contracted pension fund contribution), potential overhead savings were minimal.

The results of these strategies were unimpressive. The union didn't make many concessions, and few overhead savings occurred. Production volumes did increase, but the plant was producing to cover overhead rather than to satisfy immediate demand. Management hoped that increasing sales would eventually take care of the excess production. Unfortunately, this didn't happen. By 1989 inventories were 24% higher than in 1986. And, once again, there were cash flow and earnings problems.

3. **Technology.** CI considered the technology focus to be particularly troublesome. Concentrating on reducing unit costs through technology improvement often blocked out other aspects of the decision. Management's assumptions were that the savings from each decision flowed directly to the bottom line. However for CI this myopic view of unit costs encouraged mistakes.

Management's use of robots provided a vivid example of the problems. Robots were investigated as a means of decreasing the unit costs for the application knife. The anhydrous ammonia applicator knife was popular worldwide, to revitalize the soil with ammonia fertilizer after each harvest. Although CI led the industry in product quality, it was a high-cost producer. The primary reason was determined to be hand welding, using expensive piece rates, with manual electric arc welders.

After a unit-cost analysis, the savings in labor and applied overhead seemed to justify the introduction of welding robots (Tables 1,2,3). Subsequent price reductions increased sales from 20,000 to more than 60,000 units in the first. At the new, lower, price the company seemed to still realize savings of $1.25 per unit.

Unfortunately, these savings were illusory. During the second year, other manufacturers became price competitive and sales volume dropped to 40,000 units; however, management still believed the robots saved the company money. At a 10% discount rate the three-year net present value was $63,730. A major problem was that labor savings disappeared as manual welders found work in other areas of the plant. In fact, the robots required additional new hires and caused increases in utilities and maintenance costs. New operating expenses were greater than the increased throughput. Thus, management was misled by its focus on standard unit costs.

4. **Selling Prices.** Unfortunately, the market for the firm's products was very competitive. Due to such macroeconomic factors as government programs and foreign grain production, the domestic market was shrinking. Internationally, CI's high unit costs made foreign markets difficult to enter. Consequently, management perceived the marketplace to be mostly out of their control. Their main focus was on improving plant performance. Nonetheless, CI still tried to increase the sales volume in domestic markets and to find new foreign markets. As for the foreign markets they experienced some success and some failures.

In an attempt to find new international markets, the company successfully set up a working relationship with a John Deere distributor in Mexico and, unsuccessfully pursued a contract in Saudi Arabia. This failure was very revealing because Saudi Arabian soils were made to order for CI's product. The Saudi's cultivation process was particularly abrasive for tillage tools. Because of frequent breakdowns, crews with replacement parts had to constantly follow the field workers. But with CI's parts this practice wasn't necessary. Consequently, the Saudis were very enthusiastic about the company's products. Unfortunately, CI did not believe the 10% profit margins to be large enough. CI rejected the Saudi Arabia offer. This happened while at the same time the plant was having difficulty with operating expenses, overhead, and inventories. Thus, the accounting cost standards influenced market decisions as well as leading to questionable, limited improvements in manufacturing. All was not harmonious among management as well.

During this time, marketing and production meetings were frequent. Marketing pointed out that while quality was good, prices were too high and lead times were too inaccurate. On the other hand, production complained that marketing was constantly messing up their production schedules.

Using this combination of efficiency improvement, overhead reduction, unit-cost reductions and sales margins, management proceeded, over an 18-month period, to reduce domestic volume by 11.5% and to turn away significant foreign opportunities. Overall, decisions to improve the performance of the company using standard cost measurement failed. By February 1989, operating expenses were 20% greater than the disastrous 1986 figures. During the same period, inventories increased by 24%, and net profits continued to deteriorate.

At year-end CI hired a new Production Control/Inventory Control (PCIC) manager. However, the plant manager was suspicious when the PCIC manager came to him with revised schedules. The PCIC manager suggested processing job lots of 100 to 150 part rather than the current 6,000. The plant manager questioned the PCIC manager's ability. "Clearly he isn't very knowledgeable. How can we make any money running only small lots? The setup costs will kill us!

Finally the PCIC manager gave the plant manager a copy of The Goal by E. Goldratt and J. Cox. After reading the first few pages, the plant manager recognized many similarities between his plant and the one described in this book.

REQUIRED:

1. What is the firm's competitive strategy? Does the strategy seem appropriate?

2. What motivated the cost reduction strategy? Did the cost reduction strategy work? Why?

3. How did CI's standard cost system affect the cost reduction strategy?

4. What is the role of work-in-process in the cost reduction strategy?

5. Is the new Production control/Inventory Control (PCIC) manager on the right track with the smaller lot sizes?

6. What steps is the PCIC likely to take now?

7. What type of cost system should be used at CI?

(IMA adapted)

TABLE 1
IMPACT OF ROBOTICS ON STANDARD COST
ANHYDROUS AMMONIA KNIVES

Department	Material: Before	After	Labor: Before	After	Overhead: Before	After	Total: Before	After
Cold Shear	$2.000	$2.000	$0.068	$0.068	$0.238	$0.238	$2.306	$2.306
Hot Forge			$0.127	$0.127	$0.445	$0.445	$0.572	$0.572
Heat Treat			$0.025	$0.025	$0.088	$0.088	$0.113	$0.113
Shot Blast			$0.025	$0.025	$0.088	$0.088	$0.113	$0.113
Arc Weld	$6.500	$6.500	$1.380	$0.250	$4.830	$0.875	$12.710	$7.625
Paint/Pack			$0.076	$0.076	$0.266	$0.266	$0.342	$0.342
Total	$8.500	$8.500	$1.701	$0.571	$5.954	$1.999	$16.155	$11.070
Selling Price							$18.150	$14.310
Gross Margin							12.353%	29.274%
Unit Profit							$1.995	$3.241
Note – OH/DL = 3.5/1								

TABLE 2
IMPACT OF ROBOTICS ON STANDARD COST
ANHYDROUS AMMONIA KNIVES

Year	Unit Savings	Unit Sales	+(–) Profits	Present Value (10%)
1	$1.245	6,000	$ 74,700	$ 67,909
2	$1.245	4,000	49,800	41,157
3	$1.245	4,000	49,800	37,415
Total			$174,300	$146,482
Initial investment				$ (60,000)
Net present value				$ 86,482

5-6

TABLE 3
IMPACT OF ROBOTICS ON STANDARD COST
ANHYDROUS AMMONIA KNIVES

Actual Results:

Year	Net Additional: Labor	Maintenance	Utilities	Total Additional: Expenses	Net Additional: Throughput	+(-) Profits	Present Value (10%)
1	$52,000	$2,000	$4,000	$ 58,000	$155,600	$97,600	$88,727
2	$92,000	$2,000	$4,000	$ 98,000	$ 39,400	($58,600)	($48,430)
3	$92,000	$2,000	$4,000	$ 98,000	$ 39,400	($58,600)	($44,027)
Total				$254,000	$234,400	($19,600)	($3,730)
Initial Investment							($60,000)
Net Present Value							($63,730)

5-2. Blue Ridge Manufacturing (B)

Note: For the background information on this case, see Case 4-1. Case (B) is a continuation of Case 4-1

UPDATE OF RECENT DEVELOPMENTS

Blue Ridge Manufacturing (BRM) has found that the new non-toxic ink has stimulated sales substantially, so the firm has extended its markets both nationally and internationally. It has upgraded the quality of all its products and developed new products including bathrobes and bath towels for upscale hotels and resorts, bed and breakfasts, and some corporate clients. The majority of the new products also involve imprinting a logo or some form of embroidery.

At the same time BRM has been expanding its product line, significant new competition has developed, especially from non-U.S.-based manufacturers, particularly in Asian counties. These new competitors have caused BRM to lower its prices in some markets, and has reduced BRM's market share in many markets.

An important aspect of the new products for hotels and resorts is that these products sometimes involve a significant amount of design work. In contrast to BRM's other products which have logos and design that are standardized by license agreement, the hotel products fall into two categories. First, there are some well-established hotels and resorts that have a global logo and for which the design effort is negligible. The customer's logo or design is well specified and easy to work with in the production of the bathrobes, towels or other products. Second, there are some hotels and resorts that are not a part of a large chain, which may not have a well-designed logo for their towels and bathrobes. These customers require a significant amount of extra work in helping the customer develop a design that is workable for the desired products. The extra work can be as much as 18-26 hours per order, but is more often less than 10 hours. The bathrobes require more design time, roughly 2-16 hours per order, while the towels usually require 1-6 hours per order, when the additional design work is necessary. From recent months' results, it appears that the new products will become a significant part of BRM's overall business, especially the customers from smaller hotels and resorts that need design help. In view of the success of the new products, BRM is thinking of putting in place a product development team, a permanent activity within the firm, which would search out new product ideas and develop new products on an on-going basis.

REQUIRED:

1. What is BRM's strategy now that it has developed the new products and become a global competitor? Has the strategy changed?

2. How should BRM adapt to the new competitive environment?

5-3. Target Costing[3]

Morrow Company is a large manufacturer of auto parts for the auto manufacturers and parts distributors. Morrow has plants throughout the world, but most are located in North America. Morrow is known for the quality of its parts and for the reliability of its operations. Customers receive their orders in a timely manner and there are no errors in the shipment or billing of these orders. For these reasons, Morrow has been able to prosper in a business that is very competitive, with competitors such as Delphi, Visteon and others.

Morrow just received an order for 100 auto parts from National Motors Corp., a major auto manufacturer. National proposed a $1,500 selling price per part. Morrow usually earned 20% operating margin as a percent of sales. Morrow recently decided to use target costing in pricing its products. An examination of the production costs by the engineers and accountants showed that this part was assigned a "standard" full cost of $1,425 per part (this includes $1,000 production, $200 marketing, and $225 general & administration costs per part). A Value Assessment Group (VAG) undertook a cost reduction program for this part. Two production areas that were investigated were the defective unit rate and the tooling costs. The $1,000 production costs included a normal defective cost of $85 per part. Group leaders suggested that production changes could reduce defective cost to $25 per part.

Forty-five different tools were used to make the auto part. The group discovered that the number of tools could be reduced to 30 and less expensive tools could be used on this part to meet National's product specifications. These changes saved an additional $105 of production cost per part. By studying other problem areas, the group found that general & administration costs could be reduced by $50 per unit through use of electronic data interchange with suppliers and just-in-time inventory management.

In addition, Morrow's sales manager told the Group that National might be willing to pay a higher selling price because of Morrow's quality reputation and reliability. He believed National's proposed price was a starting point for negotiations. Of course, National had made the same offer to some of Morrow's competitors.

REQUIRED:

1. What should be Morrow's target cost per auto part? Explain.

2. As a result of the Value Engineering Group's efforts, determine Morrow's estimated cost for the auto part. Will Morrow meet the target cost for the part? Do you recommend that Morrow take on the National offer? Explain your reasons.

---

[3] Joseph San Miguel. Used with permission.

5-4. Mercedes-Benz All Activity Vehicle (AAV)[4]

During the recession beginning in the early 1990s, Mercedes-Benz (MB) struggled with product development, cost efficiency, material purchasing and problems in adapting to changing markets. In 1993, these problems caused the worst sales slump in decades, and the luxury carmaker lost money for the first time in its history. Since then, MB has streamlined the core business, reduced parts and system complexity, and established simultaneous engineering programs with suppliers.

In their search for additional market share, new segments, and new niches, MB started developing a range of new products. New product introductions included the C-class in 1993, the E-class in 1995, the new sportster SLK in 1996, and the A-class and M-class All Activity Vehicle (AAV) in 1997. Perhaps the largest and most radical of MB's new projects was the AAV. In April 1993, MB announced it would build its first passenger vehicle-manufacturing facility in the United States. The decision emphasized the company's globalization strategy and desire to move closer to its customers and markets.

Mercedes-Benz United States International used function groups with representatives from every area of the company (marketing, development, engineering, purchasing, production, and controlling) to design the vehicle and production systems. A modular construction process was used to produce the AAV. First-tier suppliers provided systems, rather than individual parts or components, for production of approximately 65,000 vehicles annually.

THE AAV PROJECT PHASES

The AAV has moved from concept to production in a relatively short period of time. The first phase, the concept phase, was initiated in 1992. The concept phase resulted in a feasibility study that was approved by the board. Following board approval, the project realization phase began in 1993, with production commencing in 1997. Key elements of the various phases are described below.

CONCEPT PHASE, 1992-1993

Team members compared the existing production line with various market segments to discover opportunities for new vehicle introductions. The analysis revealed opportunities in the rapidly expanding sports utility vehicle market that was dominated by Jeep, Ford, and GM. Market research was conducted to estimate potential worldwide sales opportunities for a high-end AAV with the characteristics of a Mercedes-Benz. A rough cost estimate was developed that included materials, labor, overhead, and one-time development and project costs. Projected cash flows were analyzed over a 10-year period using net present value (NPV) analysis to acquire project approval from the board of directors. The sensitivity of the NPV was analyzed by calculating "what-if" scenarios involving risks and opportunities. For example, risk factors included monetary exchange rate fluctuations, different sales levels due to consumer substitution of the AAV for another MB product, and product and manufacturing cost that differed from projections.

Based on the economic feasibility study of the concept phase, the board approved the project and initiated a search for potential manufacturing locations. Sites located in Germany, other European countries, and the United States were evaluated. Consistent with the company's globalization strategy, the decisive factor that brought the plant to the United States was the desire to be close to the major market for sports utility vehicles.

---

[4] Prepared by Thomas L. Albright, © Institute of Management Accountants, 2000. Used with permission.

PROJECT REALIZATION PHASE, 1993-1996

Regular customer clinics were held to view the prototype and to explain the new vehicle concept. These clinics produced important information about how the proposed vehicle would be received by potential customers and the press. Customers were asked to rank the importance of various characteristics including safety, comfort, economy, and styling. Engineers organized in function groups designed systems to deliver these essential characteristics. However, MB would not lower its internal standards for components, even if initial customer expectations might be lower than the MB standard. For example, many automotive experts believed the superior handling of MB products resulted from manufacturing the best automobile chassis in the world. Thus, each class within the MB line met strict standards for handling, even though these standards might exceed customer expectations for some classes. MB did not use target costing to produce the lowest-price vehicle in an automotive class. The company's strategic objective was to deliver products that were slightly more expensive than competitive models. However, the additional cost would have to translate into greater perceived value on the part of the customer.

Throughout the project realization phase, the vehicle (and vehicle target cost) remained alive because of changing dynamics. For example, the market moved toward the luxury end of the spectrum while the AAV was under development. In addition, crash test results were incorporated into the evolving AAV design. For these reasons, MB found it beneficial to place the design and testing team members in close physical proximity to other functions within the project to promote fast communication and decision making. Sometimes new technical features, such as side air bags, were developed by MB. The decision to include the new feature on all MB lines was made at the corporate level because experience had shown that customers' reactions to a vehicle class can affect the entire brand.

PRODUCTION PHASE, 1997

The project was monitored by annual updates of the NPV analysis. In addition, a three-year plan (including income statements) was prepared annually and reported to the headquarters in Germany. Monthly departmental meetings were held to discuss actual cost performance compared with standards developed during the cost estimation process. Thus, the accounting system served as a control mechanism to ensure that actual production costs would conform to target (or standard) costs.

TARGET COSTING AND THE AAV

The process of achieving target cost for the AAV began with an estimate of the existing cost for each function group. Next, components of each function group were identified, with their associated costs. Cost reduction targets were set by comparing the estimated existing cost with the target cost for each function group. These function groups included the following: doors, sidewall and roof, electrical system, bumpers, powertrain, seats, heating system, cockpit, and front end. Next, cost reduction targets were established for each component. As part of the competitive benchmark process, MB bought and tore down competitors' vehicles to help understand their costs and manufacturing processes.

The AAV manufacturing process relied on high value-added systems suppliers. For example, the entire cockpit was purchased as a unit from a systems supplier. Thus, systems suppliers were part of the development process from the beginning of the project. MB expected suppliers to meet established cost targets. To enhance function group effectiveness, suppliers were brought into the discussion at an early stage in the process. Decisions had to be made quickly in the early stages of development.

The target costing process was led by cost planners who were engineers, not accountants. Because the cost planners were engineers with manufacturing and design experience, they could make reasonable estimates of costs that suppliers would incur in providing various systems. Also, MB owned much of the tooling, such as dies to form sheet metal, used by suppliers to produce components. Tooling costs are a substantial part of the one-time costs in the project phase.

INDEX DEVELOPMENT TO SUPPORT TARGET COSTING ACTIVITIES I[5]

During the concept development phase, MB team members used various indexes to help them determine critical performance, design, and cost relationships for the AAV. To construct the indexes, various forms of information were gathered from customers, suppliers, and their own design team. Though the actual number of categories used by MB was much greater, Table 1 illustrates the calculations used to quantify customer responses to the AAV concept. For example, values shown in the importance column resulted from asking a sample of potential customers whether they consider each category extremely important when considering the purchase of a new MB product. Respondents could respond affirmatively to all categories that applied.

Table 1. Relative Importance Ranking by Category

Category	Importance	Relative Percentage
Safety	32	41%
Comfort	25	32
Economy	15	18
Styling	7	9
Total	79	100

To gain a better understanding of the various sources of costs, function groups were identified together with target cost estimates. (MB also organizes teams called function groups whose role is to develop specifications and cost projections.) As shown in Table 2, the relative target cost percentage of each function group was computed.

Table 2. Target Cost and Percentage by Function Group

Function Group	Target Cost	Percentage of Total
Chasis	$x,xxx	20%
Transmission	$x,xxx	25
Air conditioner	$x,xxx	5
Electrical System	$x,xxx	7
Other function groups	$x,xxx	43
Total	$xx,xxx	100%

---

[5] All numbers have been altered for proprietary reasons; however, the tables illustrate the actual process used in the development of the AAV.

Table 3 summarizes how each function group contributes to the consumer requirements identified in Table 1. For example, safety was identified by potential customers as an important characteristic of the AAV; some function groups contributed more to the safety category than others. MB engineers determined chassis quality was an important element of safety (50% of the total function group contribution).

Table 3. Function Group Contribution to Customer Requirements

Function Group/Category	Safety	Comfort	Economy	Styling
Chassis	50%	30%	10%	10%
Transmission	20	20	30	
Air conditioner		20		5
Electrical system	5		20	
Other systems	25	30	40	85
Total	100%	100%	100%	100%

Table 4 combines the category weighting percentages from Table 1 with the function group contribution from Table 3. The result is an importance index that measures the relative importance of each function group across all categories. For example, potential customers weighted the categories of safety, comfort, economy, and styling as .41, .32, .18, and .09, respectively. The rows in Table 4 represent the contribution of each function group to the various categories. The importance index for the chassis is calculated by multiplying each row value by its corresponding category value, and summing the results ((.50 x .41) + (.30 x .32) + (.10 x .18) + (.10 x .09) = .33.

Table 4. Importance Index of Various Function Groups

Function Group/ Category	Safety .41	Comfort .32	Economy .18	Styling .09	Importance Index
Chassis	.50	.30	.10	.10	.33
Transmission	.20	.20			.20
Air conditioner		.20	.05	.05	.07
Electrical system	.05				.06
Other systems	.25	.40	.85	.85	.35
Total	1.00	1.00	1.00	1.00	

As shown in Table 5, the target cost index is calculated by dividing the importance index by the target cost percentage by function group. Managers at MB used indexes such as these during the concept design phase to understand the relationship of the importance of a function group to the target cost of a function group. Indexes less than one may indicate a cost in excess of the perceived value of the function group.

Thus, opportunities for cost reduction, consistent with customer demands, may be identified and managed during the early stages of product development. Choices made during the project realization phase were largely irreversible during the production phase because approximately 80% of the production cost of the AAV was for materials and systems provided by external suppliers.

The AAV project used a streamlined management structure to facilitate efficient and rapid development. The streamlined MB organization produced an entirely new vehicle from concept to production in four years. Using the target costing process as a key management element, MB manufactured the first production AAV in 1997.

Table 5. Target Cost Index

Function Group/Index	(A) Importance Index	(B) % of Target Cost	(C) A/B Target Cost Index
Chassis	.33	.20	1.65
Transmission	.20	.25	.80
Air conditioner	.07	.05	1.40
Electrical Systems	.06	.07	.86
Other systems	.35	.43	.81
Total		1.00	

Questions for Discussion:

1. What is the competitive environment faced by MB?
2. How has MB reacted to the changing world market for luxury automobiles?
3. Using Cooper's cost, quality, and functionality chart, discuss the factors on which MB competes with other automobile producers such as Jeep, Ford, and GM.[6]
4. How does the AAV project link with MB strategy in terms of market coverage?
5. Explain the process of developing a component importance index. How can such an index guide managers in making cost reduction decisions?
6. How does MB approach cost reduction to achieve target costs?
7. How do suppliers factor into the target costing process? Why are they so critically important to the success of the MB AAV?
8. What role does the accounting department play in the target costing process?

---

[6] Robin Cooper, When Lean Enterprises Collide, Boston: Harvard Business School Press, 1995

TARGET COSTING AT ITT AUTOMOTIVE

By George Schmelze, CPA; Rolf Geir; and Thomas E. Buttross, CMA

Intense competition and pressure from customers to reduce prices has forced many companies to reduce their costs to survive. These companies have found that most costs are committed once production begins, and, therefore, the costs must be reduced earlier in the product life cycle, particularly while the product is in the planning and design stages. Target costing is a proven, effective method of reducing production costs throughout the product life cycle, without reducing quality or functionality and without increasing the time it takes to design and develop a product. At ITT Automotive, the brakes area has been using target costing for three to four years, and it provides an excellent model that other areas of the company are beginning to emulate.

Target costing is a proactive, strategic cost management philosophy that is price-driven, customer-focused, design-centered, and cross-functional.[1] Unlike traditional cost control systems, which do not control costs until production has commenced, the target costing philosophy requires that aggressive cost management occur in the product planning stage, the product design stage, and the production stage. By designing lower costs into the product, companies realize the best sources of cost savings—before the product reaches the production stage. These cost savings cannot be realized, however, with traditional costing systems, such as standard costing systems and activity-based costing systems.[2]

Target costing transcends the functional areas of a company. For target costing to be successful, integration is needed in the form of cross-functional teams comprising engineering, product design, production, purchasing, sales, finance, cost accounting, cost targeting, and, in many cases, customers and suppliers. Upper-level management support is crucial to the success of target costing because resources need to be allocated to the target costing area, and the cross-functional teams must be empowered to make many critical decisions.

Target costing differs from traditional "cost-plus" costing. Rather than the selling price being a function of estimated costs, the target cost is a function of the selling price and a desired profit. Furthermore, with target costing, the target cost is determined before the product is designed. The target costing equation is as follows:

Target Price – Target Profit = Target Cost

Various factors are considered when computing the future selling price of the proposed product including functionality of the product, projected sales volumes, and quality. For example, management strategy may call for a price that maintains or increases market share.

Due to intense competition, many companies have little flexibility when setting a price. When market conditions are extremely competitive, the price may be driven by the market. In other cases, the target cost of the downstream company is the target price of the upstream company. Where selling price and profit margin are fixed by competitive pressures and management policies, respectively, reducing the firm's production costs may be the only source of increased earnings.

Once the target cost is computed, it must be assigned to final assembly, subassemblies, and components before design can begin. After the product is designed, estimated costs of production are compared with target costs. If the estimated costs are higher than the target costs, value engineering is employed to help the company achieve its target. Value engineering is a process in which the cross-functional team attempts to reduce costs during the design and preproduction stages without compromising quality and functionality by determining the optimal processes, materials, and machinery needed for production.

Estimated costs are compared with the targets throughout the product life cycle. Once the product reaches production, however, cost maintenance (as opposed to cost reduction) generally becomes the objective.

TARGET COSTING AT ITT AUTOMOTIVE

To illustrate the process of target costing, let's look at the target costing practices at ITT Automotive. ITT Automotive, one of the world's largest suppliers of auto parts, produced sales of $4.8 billion in 1994, which represented an increase of more than 34% compared to 1993. In 1995, sales were approximately $5.7 billion. Products produced include brake systems and components, wiper handling systems and components, fluid handling systems and components, structural systems and components, electric motors, switches, and lamps. More than 35,000 employees work for the company, with the vast majority of these employees located in the United States and Germany.

The brakes area has used target costing extensively for the last few years because of an extremely competitive environment. For example, the price of anti-lock brake systems, which currently sell for about $200, is expected to drop to $100 by the year 2000. Furthermore, the functionality of the product is expected to increase.

ESTABLISHING THE TARGET PRICE AND TARGET MARGIN

At ITT Automotive, price is generally set externally, either by competitive pressure or by the customer's target costing system. For example, the price that Mercedes-Benz offers ITT Automotive for an anti-lock brake system (ABS) is Mercedes-Benz's target cost.

The first step in the process occurs when ITT Automotive receives an invitation to bid from the customer. Due to the competitive nature of this industry, ITT Automotive cannot use "cost-plus" pricing when setting the price. The price that the company generally will quote is a price that already has been set by market conditions. An analysis then is performed to determine if the product fits ITT Automotive's strategic goals and if the volume can be produced. Financial information including internal rate of return (IRR) and return on investment (ROI) also are calculated to ensure that ITT Automotive can earn a proper return. If productivity increases (reductions in price) are expected by the customer, the analysis must include an explanation concerning how the productivity increases will be achieved.

To determine whether the price is feasible, a permanent cost targeting group made up of

employees with backgrounds in engineering, cost accounting, and sales receives the quote. Keeping in mind that the product being quoted will not be produced for several years, the ITT Automotive cost targeting group makes a determination concerning whether enough value engineering can be accomplished before the product is produced in order to meet the quoted price. Other factors considered by the cost targeting team when determining the feasibility of a price include previous quotes issued, economic factors such as anticipated inflation and interest rates, competitor pricing, and cost structure.

Because ITT Automotive does not produce automobiles, it does not have information concerning prices (and costs) of competitors' component parts. Information from a tear-down analysis of a competitor's product, however, may provide ITT Automotive with information that is useful in determining a competitor's costs and, by adding a reasonable margin, the competitor's price. Tear-down analysis, sometimes referred to as reverse engineering, is an analytical process in which a company will examine in detail a competitor's product. During tear-down analysis, a competitor's product is torn apart by engineers, component by component. An indication of the competitor's design, estimated cost structure, quality, functionality, and possible processes used to build the product are garnered from this process. From this analysis, ITT Automotive may be able to improve designs or processes in order to reduce cost without losing functionality (or to increase functionality and quality without increasing costs). The information garnered from this study is recorded on a standardized document that compares each competitor's product with ITT Automotive's product. This information is useful for price setting because the tear-down analysis provides information concerning the estimated cost structure of the competitor.

Price setting is an iterative process. The cost targeting team will try to find ways to reduce costs in order to accept a bid without comprising ITT Automotive's expected return. For example, the cost targeting team may consult with the design engineers who may suggest that some new process or technology will be available when the produce is produced that will reduce the cost of the product.

ASSIGNING THE TARGET COST.

The target cost is the target price minus the target margin. Finding the target cost is a relatively straightforward calculation; the difficulty for most companies is reaching the target cost in order to meet the company's profit objectives. The target cost should include all costs related to the new product. At ITT Automotive, target costs include direct materials, direct labor, tooling costs, depreciation, promotion, service, and working capital.

Once the target cost has been computed, specific targets are assigned first to final assemblies, then to subassemblies, and then finally to individual components. This work is performed by individuals in the permanent cost targeting group. Although the setting of the targets is a cross-functional procedure, the ITT Automotive team believes that it is critical for someone who is independent to first set the targets. Once the targets are set initially in cost targeting, feedback is given to the cost targeting area from various members of the cross-functional team, including purchasing and production, concerning targets that are considered unreasonable. This step allows the cross-functional team to be involved in the target-setting process without bogging down the process.

Individual targets are set for each component that is purchased, along with targets for burden and labor. The target costs are tracked throughout the product's life cycle, beginning with the design of the product, continuing when tooling is released, and not concluding until the product is discontinued.

In many situations, the price that ITT Automotive will receive for the product will become lower each year. Thus, the target costs will have to be lower each year to provide the company with the same return from year to year. Eventually the margin will become too small, and new products will have to be developed. Figure 1 shows a typical target costing situation, where cost targets are lower each year fueled by productivity increases. The targets are met by using cross-functional teams, setting early cost targets, engaging in value engineering (including tear-down analysis of competitor products and concurrent engineering and production), and forming partnerships with suppliers.

Then these targets are compared with quotes (or estimated costs for items such as depreciation). If the targets are not met, costs are reduced through value engineering and value analysis.

SOME TARGET COSTING TOOLS USED AT ITT AUTOMOTIVE

Achieving the target cost requires companies to take a disciplined approach toward value improvement. Value improvement occurs when functionality and quality are held constant while costs are reduced or when quality and functionality are increased while price is held constant,[3] At ITT Automotive, achieving the target cost is accomplished through several techniques including the use of cross-

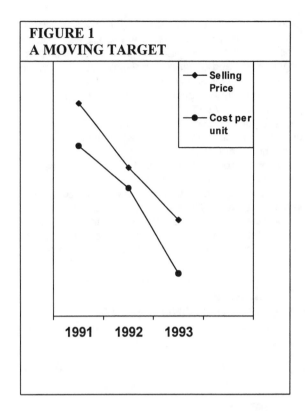

**FIGURE 1
A MOVING TARGET**

functional teams, setting early cost targets, value engineering, and forming partnerships with suppliers.

The target costing process, however, does not end in the early stages of the product life cycle. Once the product reaches production, cost maintenance is practiced through profit improvement planning and value analysis. These techniques help individuals in all of the functional areas take ownership for meeting cost targets throughout the product's life cycle.

One byproduct of the use of cross functional teams is increased understanding of processes and product design by members of the cross-functional team. Members of the cross-functional team at ITT Automotive must have knowledge of processes and design to contribute in a meaningful way to the target costing process. For example, purchasing personnel must have a working knowledge of how the product is designed to make optimal decisions concerning the purchase of components and parts. Similarly, the cost targeting personnel must have a basic understanding of the prices of component parts and subassemblies in order to make decisions concerning the allocation of target costs.

Value engineering is another important component of target costing at ITT Automotive. The objective of value engineering is to reduce costs without reducing functionality or quality without increasing costs before the product reaches the production line. During value engineering, the cross-functional team will try to determine optimal processes, materials, and equipment for designing, engineering, and producing the product.[4] The value engineering philosophy recognizes that decisions made early in the design process affect price and product costs. At ITT Automotive, members of the cross-functional team are empowered to find the most optimal processes, materials used, tooling and capital investment requirements and to decide whether to make or outsource the product. Tear-down analysis also is performed during value engineering.

Target costing should result in improved relationships with suppliers. At ITT Automotive, key suppliers are considered an integral part of the target costing team. This arrangement allows the suppliers to take "ownership" of the target costing process.

These suppliers should be consulted early in the product life cycle, and they should play a significant role in product design and development.

Occasionally, a supplier may have a difficult time in meeting the target cost. In cases where the supplier is having this type of problem, ITT Automotive will ask for a detailed analysis of the supplier's cost to help the supplier reduce costs. This analysis is extremely detailed and provides the starting point for ITT Automotive to suggest some "value analysis" that will help the supplier reduce its costs.

Cost tracking sheets are used in the cost targeting area to keep track of the "targets" and to compare the targets with actual costs. At ITT Automotive, these sheets are used to assign the target cost from the final product to final assemblies, subassemblies, and components. Each tracking sheet becomes more

---

FIGURE 2
COST TRACKING SHEETS

ABS System

Description	Design Stage		Tool Stage		Production Stage	
	Target	Quote	Target	Quote	Target	Quote
Control Unit	a	a + 1	a	a + 5	a	a − 1
Motor etc.	x	x	x	x	x	x
Production Cost	x	x	x	x	x	x
Other	x	x	x	x	x	x
Total Cost	x	x	x	x	x	X

Control Unit-Final Assembly

Description	Design Stage		Tool Stage		Production Stage	
	Target	Quote	Target	Quote	Target	Quote
Bracket	X	X	X	X	X	x
ECU	X	x	x	x	x	x
Piston Assembly	b	b + 2	b	b + 1	b	b − .1

Piston Assembly-Subassembly

Description	Design Stage		Tool Stage		Production Stage	
	Target	Quote	Target	Quote	Target	Quote
O-ring	x	x	x	x	x	x
Valve	x	x	x	x	x	x
Spring	x	x	x	x	x	x

Cost tracking sheets are prepared for the final product, final assemblies, and sub-assemblies, the latter includes tracking of individual components

specific until, finally, the individual components are tracked.

The tracking sheets track the cost of the product throughout the product life cycle: at the design stage (DS), when the tooling is in place (TS), and finally, when the product reaches production (PS). Setting early targets helps ITT Automotive investigate and try to remedy problem situations. For example, if the Quote of a certain supplier is higher than the target, the cross-functional team may decide to visit the supplier to determine why there is a difference between the target and the quote. Figure 2 shows a hypothetical example of this process. Investment in capital equipment, which can be quite substantial, also is tracked through the use of cost tracking sheets.

ITT Automotive periodically conducts meetings with the cross-functional team to hold them responsible for the targets that were set and to develop, through brainstorming, ways to further reduce costs. At these "profit improvement planning" meetings, a "checklist" of problems are discussed among the cross-functional team. Before the meeting, each member of the team is handed a document detailing each of the problem areas, the person(s) responsible for eliminating the problem, comments on why the problem is occurring, and a suggested completion date for solving the problem. During the meeting, the person responsible for the area where the problem is occurring will discuss the steps that are being taken to solve the problem and receive suggestions from members of the cross-functional team.

Value analysis at ITT Automotive is used on products that are not yielding an adequate return. The results of value analysis may not be as great as the results from value engineering because value analysis is performed during the production stage—after ITT Automotive is locked into a good portion of its costs. The results from value analysis, however, can be dramatic.

Readers interested in more information about target costing can look forward to the research monograph, *Target Costing and Value Engineering* by Robin Cooper and Regine Slagmulder, to be published by the IMA Foundation for Applied Research, Inc., in early 1997. It is the first in a series of five books by Cooper on Japanese cost management practices. CAM-1 (Consortium for Advanced Manufacturing-International) recently issued *Target Costing: The New Frontier in Strategic Cost Management*, which provides practical insights on how to use target costing for profit planning and cost management. It can be ordered (C1/$50) by calling (800) 638-4427, ext. 278, or faxing (201) 573-9507.

TARGET COSTING MARKET SHARE

ITT Automotive uses target costing to maintain its profitability and increase its market share during these extremely competitive times in the automotive industry. Although the process is difficult at times, and costly resources are needed to have an effective target costing system, companies such as ITT Automotive have found the investment critical to meeting their corporate objectives successfully.

Target costing basically is a bottom-up, team-oriented philosophy. It is a very structured method of setting and achieving goals. For target costing to be successful, setting up cross-functional teams is not enough. Most important, there must be senior management support for the process. Senior management must allocate the necessary resources to the project and must empower the cross-functional teams to make critical decisions. Other requirements include setting early cost targets, performing competitive analysis and value engineering, forming partnerships with suppliers, and applying pressure to everyone in the value chain to reduce costs.

George Schmelzle, CPA, is an assistant professor of accountancy at the University of Detroit, Mercy. He was a faculty intern at ITT Automotive in the summer of 1995. He is a member of the Detroit Chapter of the IMA, through which this article was submitted. He can be reached at (312) 993-3327.

Rolf Geier heads the target costing/value analysis team in the brakes department at ITT Automotive. Additional credits are given to Gerd Klostermann. He is head of the target costing/value analysis team in Europe with worldwide responsibilities.

Thomas E. Buttross, CMA, is an assistant professor of accountancy at Indiana University, Kokomo. He is a member of the Detroit Chapter of IMA. He can be reached at (317) 455-9471.

1. *Target Costing—The New Frontier in Strategic Cost Management,* The Consortium for Advanced Manufacturing-International (CAM-1), Bedford, Tex., 1995.

2. Activity-based costing can provide valuable input for the target costing product design stage. Product designers can use cost tables that include actual cost data from the ABC system as well as pro forma amounts for processes not currently used by the company. See Takeo Yoshikawa, John Innes, and Falconer Mitchell, "Cost Tables: A Foundation of Japanese Cost Management," *Journal of Cost Management*, Fall 1990, Vol. 4, No. 3, pp. 30-36.
3. The personal computer is a good example of the latter. Although the price of computers has remained constant the past few years, functionality has increased dramatically.
4. *Implementing Target Costing—Management Accounting Guideline #28*, a joint research project of the Society of Management Accountants of Canada, the Institute of Management Accountants, and the Consortium for Advanced Manufacturing-International, 1995.

Chapter 6
Total Quality Management

Cases

6-1   Precision Systems, Inc.

Readings

"GE Takes Six Sigma Beyond the Bottom Line"

Reports on the success of GE Medical Systems Inc.'s Six Sigma effort. The
article describes the training programs for employees in statistical process control
and services and information offered by the Web site of the company to support
the quality improvement efforts of more than 300,000 employees world-wide.

Discussion Questions:
1. What is a Six Sigma approach?
2. Describe the processes that GE used to implement its Six Sigma program.
3. What are black belts? What roles do black belts play in GE's Six Sigma
    program?

Cases

6-1. Precision Systems, Inc.

Suresh S. Kalagnanam, *University of Saskatchewan*, Ella Mae Matsumura, *University of Wisconsin-Madison*

Precision Systems, Inc. (PSD) has been in business for more than 25 years and has generally reported a positive net income. The company manufactures and sells high-technology instruments (systems). Each product line at PSI has only a handful of standard products, but configuration changes and add-ons can be accommodated as long as they are not radically different from the standard systems.

Faced with rising competition and increasing customer demand for quality, PSI adopted total quality management (TQM) in 1989. Many employees received training, and several quality initiatives were launched. Like most businesses, PSI concentrated on improvements in the manufacturing function and achieved significant improvements. However, little was done in other departments.

In early 1992, PSI decided to extend TQM to its order entry department, which handles the critical functions of preparing quotes for potential customers and processing orders. Order processing is the first process in the chain of operations after the order is received from a customer. High-quality output from the order entry department improves quality later in the process and allows PSI to deliver higher-quality systems both faster and cheaper, thus meeting the goals of timely delivery and lower cost.

As a first step, PSI commissioned a cost of quality (COQ) study in its order entry department. The study had two objectives:

- To develop a system for identifying order entry errors,
- To determine how much an order entry error costs.

PSI'S ORDER ENTRY DEPARTMENT

PSI's domestic order entry department is responsible for preparing quotations for potential customers and taking actual sales orders. PSI's sales representatives forward requests for quotations to the order entry department, though actual orders for systems are received directly from customers. Orders for parts are also received directly from customers. Service-related orders (for parts or repairs), however, are generally placed by service representatives. When PSI undertook the COQ study, the order entry department consisted of nine employees and two supervisors, who reported to the order entry manager. Three of the nine employees dealt exclusively with taking parts orders, while the other six were responsible for system orders. Before August 1992, the other six were split equally into two groups: One was responsible for preparing quotations, and the other was responsible for taking orders.

The final outputs of the order entry department are the quote and the order acknowledgment or "green sheet." The manufacturing department and the stockroom use the green sheet for further processing of the order.

The order entry department's major suppliers are: (1) sales or service representatives; (2) the final customers who provide them with the basic information to process further; and (3) technical information and marketing departments, which provide configuration guides, price masters, and similar documents (some in printed form and others on-line) as supplementary information. Sometimes there are discrepancies in the information available to order entry staff and sales representatives with respect to price, part number, or configuration. These discrepancies often cause communication gaps between the order entry staff, sales representatives, and manufacturing.

An order entry staff member provided the following example of lack of communication between a sales representative and manufacturing with respect to one order.

> If the sales reps have spoken to the customer and determined that our standard configuration is not what they require, they may leave a part off the order. [In one such instance] I got a call from manufacturing saying when this system is configured like this, it must have this part added.... It is basically a no charge part and so I added it (change order #1) and called the sales rep and said to him, "Manufacturing told me to add it." The sales rep. called back and said, "No [the customer] doesn't need that part, they are going to be using another option ... so they don't need this." Then I did another change order (#2) to take it off because the sales rep said they don't need it. Then manufacturing called me back and said "We really need [to add that part] (change order #3). If the sales rep. does not want it then we will have to do an engineering special and it is going to be another 45 days lead time...." So, the sales rep and manufacturing not having direct communication required me to do three change orders on that order; two of them were probably unnecessary.

A typical sequence of events might begin with a sales representative meeting with a customer to discuss the type of system desired. The sales representative then fills out a paper form and faxes it or phones it in to an order entry employee, who might make several subsequent phone calls to the sales representative, the potential customer, or the manufacturing department to prepare the quote properly. These phone calls deal with such questions as exchangeability of parts, part numbers, current prices for parts, or allowable sales discounts. Order entry staff then keys in the configuration of the desired system, including part numbers, and informs the sales representative of the quoted price. Each quote is assigned a quotation number. To smooth production, manufacturing often produces systems with standard configurations in anticipation of obtaining orders from recent quotes for systems. The systems usually involve adding on special features to the standard configuration. Production in advance of orders sometimes results in duplication in manufacturing, however, because customers often fail to put their quotation numbers on their orders. When order entry receives an order, the information on the order is reentered into the computer to produce an order acknowledgment. When the order acknowledgment is sent to the invoicing department, the information is reviewed again to generate an invoice to send to the customer.

Many departments in PSI use information directly from the order entry department (these are the internal customers of order entry). The users include manufacturing, service (repair), stockroom, invoicing, and sales administration. The sales administration department prepares commission payments and tracks sales performance. The shipping, customer support (technical support), and collections departments (also internal customers) indirectly use order entry information. After a system is shipped, related paperwork is sent to customer support to maintain a service-installed database in anticipation of technical support questions that may arise. Customer support is also responsible for installations of systems. A good order acknowledgment (i.e., one with no errors of any kind) can greatly reduce errors downstream within the process and prevent later nonvalue-added costs.

Exhibit 1-1. Examples of Failures

1. Incomplete information on purchase order.
2. Transposition of prices on purchase order.
3. More than one part number on order acknowledgment when only one is required.
4. Incorrect business unit code (used for tracking product line profitability) on the order acknowledgment.
5. Freight terms missing on the purchase order.
6. Incorrect part number on order acknowledgment.
7. Incorrect shipping or billing address on the order acknowledgment.
8. Credit approval missing (all new customers have a credit approval before an order is processed).
9. Missing part number on order acknowledgment.
10. Customer number terminated on the computer's database (an order cannot be processed if customer number is missing).
11. Incorrect sales tax calculation on the order acknowledgment.
12. Part number mismatch on purchase order.

COST OF QUALITY

Quality costs arise because poor quality may—or does—exist. For PSI's order entry department, poor quality or nonconforming "products" refer to poor information for further processing of an order or quotation (see Exhibit 1-1 for examples). Costs of poor quality here pertain to the time spent by the order entry staff and concerned employees in other departments (providers of information, such as sales or technical information) to rectify the errors.

CLASS I FAILURES

Class I failure costs are incurred when nonconforming products (incorrect quotes or orders) are identified as nonconforming before they leave the order entry department. The incorrect quotes or orders may be identified by order entry staff or supervisors during inspection of the document. An important cause of Class I failures is lack of communication. Sample data collected from the order entry staff show that they encountered more than 10 different types of problems during order processing (see Exhibit 1-1 for examples). Analysis of the sample data suggests that, on average, it takes 2.3 hours (including waiting time) to rectify errors on quotes and 2.7 working days for corrections on orders. In determining costs, the COQ study accounted only for the time it actually takes to solve the problem (i.e., excluding waiting time). Waiting time was excluded because employees use this time to perform other activities or work on other orders. The total Class I failure costs, which include only salary and fringe benefits for the time it takes to correct errors, amount to more than 4% of order entry's annual budget for salaries and fringe benefits (see Exhibit 1-2).

CLASS II FAILURES

Class II failure costs are incurred when nonconforming materials are transferred out of the order entry department. For PSI's order entry department, "nonconforming" refers to an incorrect order acknowledgment as specified by its users within PSI. The impact of order entry errors on final *(external)* customers is low because order acknowledgments are inspected in several departments, so most errors are corrected before the invoice (which contains some information available on the order acknowledgment) is sent to the final customer. Corrections of the order entry errors does not guarantee that the customer receives a good quality system, but order entry's initial errors do not then affect the final customer. Mistakes that affect the final customer can be made by employees in other departments (e.g., manufacturing or shipping).

Exhibit 1-2. Estimated Annual Failure Costs (as a percentage of order entry's annual salary and fringe benefits budget)

	Order Entry	Other Department	Total Costs
Class I Failure Costs			
Quotations	1.1%	0.4%	1.5%
Orders	0.9%	1.7%	2.6%
Total Class I Failure	2.0%	2.1%	4.1%
Class II Failure Costs			
Order acknowledgments	2.6%	4.4%	7.0%
Change orders	2.6%	—	2.6%
Final customers	0.02%	0.1%	0.1%
Return authorizations	1.9%	—	1.9%
Total Class II Failure	7.12%	4.5%	11.6%
Total Failure Costs	9.1%	6.6%	15.7%

Sample data collected from PSI's users of order entry department information show that more than 20 types of errors can be found on the order acknowledgment (see Exhibit 1-1 for examples). The cost of correcting these errors (salary and fringe benefits of order entry person and a concerned person from another PSI department) accounts for approximately 7% of order entry's annual budget for salaries and fringe benefits (see Exhibit 1-2).

In addition to the time spent on correcting the errors, the order entry staff must prepare a change order for several of the Class II failures. Moreover, a change order is required for several other reasons not necessarily controllable by order entry. Examples include: (1) changes in ship-to or bill-to address by customers or sales representatives, (2) canceled orders, and (3) changes in invoicing instructions. Regardless of the reason for a change order, the order entry department incurs some cost. The sample data suggest that for every 100 new orders, order entry prepares 71 change orders; this activity accounts for 2.6% of order entry's annual budget for salaries and fringe benefits (see Exhibit 1-2).

Although order entry's errors do not significantly affect final customers, customers who find errors on their invoices often use the errors as an excuse to delay payments. Correcting these errors involves the joint efforts of the order entry, collections, and invoicing departments; these costs account for about 0.12% of order entry's annual budget (see Exhibit 1-2).

The order entry staff also spends considerable time handling return authorizations when final customers send their shipment back to PSI. Interestingly, more than 17% of the goods are returned because of defective shipments, and more than 49% fall into the following two categories: (1) ordered in error and (2) 30-day return rights. An in-depth analysis of the latter categories suggests that a majority of these returns can be traced to sales or service errors. The order entry department incurs costs to process these return authorizations, which account for more than 1.9% of the annual budget (see Exhibit 1-2). The total Class I and Class II failure costs account for 15.7% of the order entry department's annual budget for salaries and fringe benefits. Although PSI users of order entry information were aware that problems in their departments were sometimes caused by errors in order entry, they provided little feedback to order entry about the existence or impact of the errors.

CHANGES IN PSI'S ORDER ENTRY DEPARTMENT

In October 1992, preliminary results of the study were presented to three key persons who had initiated the study: the order entry manager, the vice president of manufacturing, and the vice president of service and quality. In March 1993, the final results were presented to PSI's executive council, the top decision-making body. Between October 1992 and March 1993, PSI began working toward obtaining the International Organization for Standardization's ISO 9002 registration for order entry and manufacturing practices, which it received in June 1993.

The effort to obtain the ISO 9002 registration suggests that PSI gave considerable importance to order entry and invested significant effort toward improving the order entry process. Nevertheless, as stated by the order entry manager, the changes would not have been so vigorously pursued if cost information had not been presented. COQ information functioned as a catalyst to accelerate the improvement effort. In actually making changes to the process, however, information pertaining to the different types of errors was more useful than the cost information.

REQUIRED QUESTIONS

1. Describe the role that assigning costs to order entry errors played in quality improvement efforts at Precision Systems, Inc.
2. Prepare a diagram illustrating the flow of activities between the order entry department and its suppliers, internal customers (those within PSI), and external customers (those external to PSI).
3. Classify the failure items in Exhibit 1-1 into internal failure (identified as defective before delivery to internal or external customers) and external failure (nonconforming "products" delivered to internal or external customers) with respect to the order entry department. For each external failure item, identify which of order entry's internal customers (i.e., other departments within PSI that use information from the order acknowledgment) will be affected.
4. For the order entry process, how would you identify internal failures and external failures? Who would be involved in documenting these failures and their associated costs? Which individuals or departments should be involved in making improvements to the order entry process?
5. What costs, in addition to salary and fringe benefits, would you include in computing the cost of correcting errors?
6. Provide examples of incremental and breakthrough improvements that could be made in the order entry process. In particular, identify prevention activities that can be undertaken to reduce the number of errors. Describe how you would prioritize your suggestions for improvement.
7. What nonfinancial quality indicators might be useful for the order entry department? How frequently should data be collected or information be reported? Can you make statements about the usefulness of cost-of-quality information in comparison to nonfinancial indicators of quality?

GE TAKES SIX SIGMA BEYOND THE BOTTOM LINE

*By GREGORY T. LUCIER AND SRIDHAR
SESHADRI*

Imagine working for a company where every employee is required to go through two weeks of intensive training in statistical process control. Then at the end of this training, participants are required to demonstrate proficiency by completing two projects that directly improve either company or customer performance.

On top of that, the company's website provides 24/7 access to the tools and methodology required to support the quality improvement efforts of more than 300,000 employees world-wide. The site is constantly and consistently measuring and quantifying thousands upon thousands of active projects.

Has your satellite TV system somehow mingled the contents of the business channel with a late-night science fiction film? No. You're experiencing GE's Six Sigma quality program, one that has netted the corporation such amazing results that now GE's customers are clamoring for help.

GETTING STARTED

Roll back to 1981, when Jack Welch first took the helm at GE and began to transform (or reshape) the company from a $25 billion bureaucratic quagmire into a well-run and highly respected $100 billion giant. Welch understood the "command and control" management approach had run its course and spent the next 20 years resolutely pursuing other options, borrowing best practices, and implementing winning strategies.

Through the remainder of the '80s, GE employed corporate-wide streamlining to get the fat out of its organization while maintaining the muscle. In 1989, as the tumult began to settle, Welch realized the need to empower employees and give them a greater level of participation in the decision-making process. Despite a decade of change, the level of hierarchy and top-down communication had remained an impediment. To solve this, Welch launched an initiative known as Work-Out™, which is designed to facilitate focused decision making, resolve issues, and improve processes. A Work-Out session is generally led by those closest to a process or issue, with the goal toward finding workable solutions and developing action plans. Work-Out can be used to eliminate unnecessary steps and streamline tasks or to remove barriers between different departments or reporting levels. Built into this process are mechanisms for ensuring management buy-in and follow-through.

Some Work-Out session examples are:

- Improving back-office processing with new financial systems,
- Improving internal paperwork flow, and
- Streamlining approval processes.

By the mid-'90s it was time to shake things up again, this time with a focus on quality. Not because GE wasn't performing well, but because feedback from employees convinced the CEO that, despite top- and bottom-line growth, quality wasn't where it should be.

Welch decided Six Sigma was the way to go. He had learned about Six Sigma from Larry Bossidy, a former GE executive who left to take the helm at Allied Signal, a company then implementing the program. Bossidy introduced Welch to Mikel Harry of the Six Sigma Academy and to this breakthrough strategy for statistical process control. Jack Welch had always maintained that GE must look outside itself to identify and adopt best practices wherever they could be found. So in the spring of 1995, Welch asked Bossidy to share his unique Six Sigma philosophy with GE's executive council.

They were impressed. Welch set targets out past five years and proclaimed Six Sigma the largest, most significant initiative ever undertaken at GE. Since that

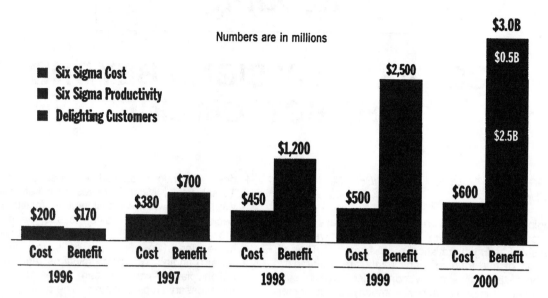

Figure 1: GE's Results from Six Sigma

Numbers are in millions

- Six Sigma Cost
- Six Sigma Productivity
- Delighting Customers

	1996	1997	1998	1999	2000
Cost	$200	$380	$450	$500	$600
Benefit	$170	$700	$1,200	$2,500	$3.0B ($2.5B / $0.5B)

proclamation, Six Sigma has been implemented aggressively and has become deeply ingrained in the corporation's culture. The company has deployed the methodology more extensively than any other to date, and maintaining its vitality continues to be a top priority. Throughout GE, there's a commonly echoed phrase...Six Sigma is "The Way We Work." Acquiring and using Six Sigma skills is considered a core competency for leadership roles, and each year new "stretch" goals and projects are established.

In terms of bottom-line impact, payback, ROI, benefit—whatever you want to call it—GE has achieved it. During the first five years of the program, the company increased annual productivity gains by over 266% and improved operating margins from 14.4% to 18.4% (see Figure 1). The bottom line was enhanced tremendously, and stock-holders were rewarded handsomely and consistently.

Six Sigma wasn't invented by GE (Motorola initiated a version of Six Sigma in the late 1980s). But the results the corporation has achieved from its implementation have attracted attention from several fronts, especially a large segment of the international business community and GE's customers. In response, GE decided to offer customers high-level instruction in Six Sigma. For example, last year our group, GE Medical Systems, began taking Six Sigma to healthcare customers. That first effort resulted in over $94 million in benefits after touching only a fraction of the market. And as recognition grows, so will the numbers.

A CLOSER LOOK AT THE SIX SIGMA APPROACH

The name Six Sigma is derived from a statistical heritage and focus on measuring product or process defects. Sigma is the Greek letter assigned to represent standard deviation. Achieving a Six Sigma level of quality equates to nearly error-free performance—where a given process produces only 3.4 defects out of a million opportunities.

Here are some perspectives on levels of Sigma:

SIGMA	DEFECTS PER MILLION OPPORTUNITIES
2	308,537
3	66,807
4	6,210
5	233
6	3.4

Most organizations would probably rate their current quality at between Three and Four Sigma. When Jack Welch challenged GE to become a Six Sigma organization in four years, he was in effect calling for a reduction in defect levels of 84% per year. At stake was an estimated $8-$10 billion in costs consumed by lower levels of quality.

Figure 2: D M A I C

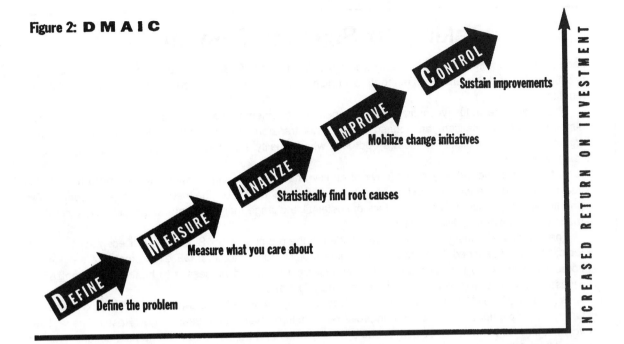

While the measure of quality is the cornerstone of the Six Sigma approach, it's the methodology and tools driving process change that translate to the difference between a simple quality campaign slogan and a rigorous management philosophy based on science. At the heart of the Six Sigma approach is a method summarized by the acronym DMAIC (see Figure 2).

Define. The GE process starts here. Teams work to clearly define problems related to the business or critical to customer satisfaction. CTQ (Critical to Quality) factors essential for customer satisfaction are correlated with the overall business process at issue. Project charters are established, required resources are identified, and leadership approvals are obtained to maximize project outcomes.

In preparation for this phase, employee training includes a review of process mapping techniques and orientation to online tools available to support teams.

Measure. The next stage is to establish base-level measures of defects inherent in the existing process. Customer expectations are defined to determine "out of specification" conditions. Training for this phase consists of basic probability and statistics, statistical analysis software, and measurement analysis.

While this heavy bombardment of statistics causes many participants to run for cover, GE makes it easier for employees to learn. It partners experienced Six Sigma practitioners with employees going through the training for the first time, which

helps beginners overcome the challenge of mastering the concepts. And the use of automated tools minimizes the time required for complex calculations.

Analyze. In this phase, teams explore underlying reasons for defects. They use statistical analysis to examine potential variables affecting the outcome and seek to identify the most significant root causes. Then they develop a prioritized list of factors influencing the desired outcome.

Tools used for this phase include multivariate analysis, test for normality, ANOVA, correlation, and regression. Again, these tools aren't for those who have difficulty balancing a checkbook, but most participants succeed with help from their mentors.

Improve. During this phase, teams seek the optimal solution and develop and test a plan of action for implementing and confirming the solution. The process is modified and the outcome measured to determine whether the revised method produces results within customer expectations.

Additional statistical methods covering design of experiments and multiple linear regression are reviewed with trainees to support the final analysis of the problem and to test the proposed solutions.

Control. To ensure changes stick, ongoing measures are implemented to keep the problem from recurring. Control charting techniques are used as the basis for developing the ongoing measures.

The concept of control—taking concrete steps to make sure improvements don't unravel over time—

Taking Six Sigma to Customers

Once we had proof that the system really works, we decided to take Six Sigma beyond internal projects. Our group, GE Medical Systems, is offering its expertise to customers to enhance value and provide additional benefits.

The healthcare industry continues to experience monumental changes and tough challenges. Lower reimbursement, competition, and consolidation have transformed organizations from a 1980s' model—targeting quality at all costs—to today's approach where quality and efficiency must be the driving forces in the delivery of care.

In the 1990s, the industry saw a bevy of quality and reengineering consultants attempt to remedy the situation, but such efforts at cost cutting were quickly cancelled by the need to rehire personnel. Old operational habits also died hard for a lack of sustainable change management that should have included—among other elements—skills transfer.

The healthcare industry has quickly responded to the promise of Six Sigma. As of December 2000, GE Medical Systems reported 1,149 active Six Sigma projects for customers. GE even created a service unit expressly dedicated to providing Six Sigma management tools and processes to healthcare organizations requesting more extensive assistance in improving performance.

Is it working? Yes. Commonwealth Health Corporation, a 478-bed medical center in Kentucky, began its journey to implement a Six Sigma improvement culture over three years ago. Results have been overwhelming as the medical center reports a reinvigorated and transformed management culture. Within a mere 18 months, errors in one ordering process were reduced over 90%, overall operating expenses had been reduced by $800,000, and employee survey results had improved by 20%. These results were from a single division within the organization. Now the medical center has realized improvements in excess of $1.5 million and is expanding the program to other areas.

One of the main reasons the program is working is because customers determine project scope, acquire on-site training and tools, and verify the benefits they have received. During last year alone, 466 customer projects were completed that resulted in $91.2 million in customer benefits. Because it relies on rigorous statistical methods and puts control mechanisms in place, Six Sigma actually connects the dots among quality, cost, process, people, and accountability.

Some customers are using GE'S Six Sigma program to achieve even higher measures of success. As part of their Star Initiative, a system-wide performance improvement effort, Virtua Health of Marlton, N.J., saw the Six Sigma program as an opportunity to vault their system to the next level of clinical quality, patient satisfaction, and financial performance. Walter Ettinger, M.D., executive vice president at Virtua, credits the partnership with GE and the use of the Six Sigma program as helping to make vital changes in the organization. "The Six Sigma program has provided everyone in the organization with a common language and toolbox for achieving our objectives. The methodology is sound, and we have begun to get buy-in from our medical staff, who are very results oriented and turned off by initiatives du jour. Our goal is to use Six Sigma to create an outstanding experience for our patients, which is the first priority of our Trustees."

has been missing from other process improvement initiatives. It's this phase of Six Sigma that leads to long-term payoffs—both in quality and monetary terms.

IMPLEMENTING THE PROGRAM

Training for GE employees takes about 10 classroom days spread over four sessions and 90 calendar days. Action teams are created in each class to attack an existing business problem. As each aspect of Six

Variations on a Theme

There are a couple of variations to the DMAIC process we mentioned. One involves the opportunity-to create a Six Sigma process where there are existing processes in place. In this case, participants use a variation of DMAIC called Design for Six Sigma (DFSS).

Here's an example of an actual DFSS project that author Sridhar Seshadri completed in working to-ward his Green Belt certification. In this project, one of GE'S businesses developed and implemented an entire business plan to provide professional services ranging from project management, systems integration, and consulting services regarding installation of complex medical imaging systems.

Prior to this project, GE. typically installed such equipment with value-added services almost being an afterthought. The DFSS team—operating under the notion that the "whole solution" included hardware, software, and professional services—went through a formal DEFINE and MEASURE phase where customer requirements and analyses of the market were rigorously scrutinized.

The team then developed a business plan using a statistical modeling tool called Crystal Ball. The "stakeholders," including business leaders and other participants essential to making the project work, reviewed the business plan. Finally, the process was test-run at a few customer sites, then formalized and implemented.

So how is this different from a traditional rollout of a new project? First, DFSS applies a level of rigor not consistently seen in traditional business plans— consistent being the key word. Second, since Six Sigma is "institutionalized," everyone involved immediately understood the details of the project and could provide meaningful feedback and advice. Third, with project tracking the team was able to review similar projects across all of GE and learn from them. This set of services first implemented in the fall of 1999 is now routinely offered in over 90% of customer projects.

Sigma is taught, the team immediately applies the concepts to the chosen problem.

There's a progression of competency levels beginning with Green Belts—and all employees from clerical staff up are required to reach this level of proficiency. Green Belts must complete the required training and two projects to achieve certification. They must also complete one additional project and eight hours of post-certification training each year. While Green Belts are trained in Six Sigma, they hold non-Six Sigma positions within the company. New employees are expected to obtain Green Belt certification within the first year of employment.

All other "Belts" are 100% Six Sigma assignments and are selected from the top performers in our talent pipeline:

- Black Belts act as technical and cultural change agents for quality. They are leaders of small teams implementing/executing the Six Sigma methodology in business-related projects, and they coach Green Belts on their projects. Today there are more than 4,500 Black Belts within GE.

- Master Black Belts teach, mentor, and develop Six Sigma tools and are full-time teachers of the Six Sigma process. Today there are over 800 Master Black Belts within GE.

- Champions back and promote the Six Sigma initiative and work with executives to help drive initiatives into daily operations and business metrics.

The mentoring structure behind Six Sigma training and the full-time dedication of the Black Belts and Master Black Belts have provided the momentum necessary to complete thousands of projects at GE.

THE PAYBACK

To evaluate the payback of the significant commitment during the initial five-year implementation, we can look at individual projects and the cumulative results of thousands of projects.

One division recently reduced its annual expense for teleconferencing by $1.5 million encompassing a total of 19 million minutes. Another team cut customer order processing time in half. As a rule of thumb, GE managers expect that each project will save between $50,000 and $150,000.

When talking about the payback associated with Six Sigma, think about popcorn. One kernel popping by itself (or one project completed) won't make much of a difference. But if you keep the heat on and thousands of kernels pop, you've multiplied the results exponentially. GE has kept the heat on now for five years, and the results are in. The following is a summary of some key performance measures at GE.

	SIX SIGMA BEGINS: 1995	FIVE YEARS LATER 2000
Annual Productivity Gain	1.5%	4.0%
Operating Margin	14.4%	18.4%
Inventory Turns	5.8%	9.2%

By internal calculations, the benefits of Six Sigma exceeded $2 billion in 2000. Certainly a four-to-one pay-back in quality and the associated savings resulting from reduced cycle times and defects would interest many considering similar options for their organizations.

The lesson we learned at GE is that there is definitely a payback. Complete dedication to the program and enterprise-wide implementation is attainable and rewarding in terms of quality, productivity, and the bottom line.

Greg Lucier is president and CEO of GE Medical Systems Information Technologies. With more than 15 years of technology management experience, he joined GE in 1995 as a manager of business development and later that year was named president and general manager of GE Transportation Systems, GE-Harris Railway Electronics. In 1999 he became vice president and general manager of global services at GE Medical Systems. He was promoted to his current position in August 2000. You can reach Greg at Greg.Lucier@med.ge.com.

Sridhar Seshadri is vice president and general manager of Healthcare Solutions with GE Medical Information Systems Information Technologies. He has held this position since July 2000. Before joining GE Medical Systems in 1998 as business manager, IT Services, he served as lead engineer, imaging systems, with the University of Pennsylvania's Radiology Department and launched the Medical

Informatics Group, responsible for developing Picture Archiving and Communication Systems. You can reach Sridhar at Sridhar.Seshadri@med.ge.com.

Both authors hold Green Belts.

Chapter 7
Cost Estimation

Cases

7-1   The High-Low Method and Regression Analysis
7-2   The Pump Division (Cost Estimation)
7-3   Laurent Products (Cost Estimation, Activity-Based Costing)
7-4   Custom Photography (Regression Analysis)

Readings

"Applying Overhead: How to Find the Right Bases and Rates"

This article shows an actual application of regression analysis for determining multiple overhead rates using the spreadsheet software LOTUS 123 (the steps and the results are very similar to EXCEL which has regression under TOOLS/ADD-INS/DATA ANALYSIS in contrast to LOTUS which has regression under DATA). The article explains the interpretation of the R-squared and t-values and provides a good discussion of when regression analysis is useful.

Discussion Questions:

1. What is regression analysis used to accomplish in this article?
2. What are the steps to perform a simple regression analysis?
3. What does Table 7 tell you? Which cost driver would you pick for each cost type—maintenance, packaging, materials handling, storage, and production scheduling?

"Estimation of Production Costs and Labor Hours Using a Free Excel Add-In"

Despite the prominence of learning curves in a few industries such as aerospace, the technical complexities of implementation have hampered their widespread use in other areas. All types of service businesses, construction companies, and light manufacturers can benefit from these tools. They are appropriate for projecting costs, labor times, and quality measures wherever improvement occurs through experience. This article reviews their use through a variety of examples, which are easy to solve using an Excel add-in developed by the author and available free on the Internet.

Discussion Questions: The discussion questions are contained within the article.

Cases

7-1. The High-Low Method and Regression Analysis

The Brenham General Hospital was approached by Health Food, Inc. (HFI) which specializes in the preparation of meals for institutional patients. HFI stated that it would prepare all inpatient meals to provider specifications and deliver them on time for $11.50 per meal. The hospital was facing a steady decline in bed occupancy and was determined to hold the line on costs wherever possible.

Hospital management did not have a clear idea what the present system of providing meals to patients was costing. Hospital staff gathered the information below, which covered expenses for the dietary department for the past year.

The hospital has 120 beds. It is open year-round and has a 33% percent occupancy rate. Patients are served an average of 2.8 meals per occupancy day.

It was determined that the dietitian provided valuable counseling and advising services. Should the hospital eliminate in house meal preparation, it would want to retain her services. Also, the administration wanted to keep and maintain the kitchen and equipment.

REQUIRED:

1. Using the high-low method and regression analysis, determine the variable and fixed costs of the in-house meal service.
2. Which cost estimation method would you choose and why?
3. Should the hospital administration accept the offer of the outside company? Why or why not?

	Dietitian	Other staff	Food Costs	Maintenance	Patient Equipment	Days
January	$2,875	$ 3,122	$ 9,674	$ 1,401	$ 1,649	1,382
February	$2,875	$ 2,908	$ 9,184	$ 1,322	$ 1,415	1,312
March	$2,875	$ 2,655	$ 8,302	$ 1,322	$ 1,313	1,186
April	$2,875	$ 2,600	$ 7,084	$ 1,288	$ 1,105	1,012
May	$2,875	$ 2,433	$ 6,398	$ 1,200	$ 1,089	914
June	$2,875	$ 2,083	$ 4,338	$ 1,133	$ 1,011	604
July	$2,875	$ 1,809	$ 3,612	$ 1,093	$ 900	516
August	$2,875	$ 2,322	$ 6,275	$ 1,122	$ 1,112	896
September	$2,875	$ 1,434	$ 6,734	$ 1,235	$ 1,103	962
October	$2,875	$ 2,700	$ 9,002	$ 1,302	$ 1,300	1,286
November	$2,875	$ 2,798	$ 8,456	$ 1,300	$ 1,442	1,208
December	$2,875	$ 2,600	$ 7,798	$ 1,322	$ 1,396	1,114
TOTAL	$34,500	$29,464	$86,857	$15,040	$14,835	12,392

7-2

7-2. The Pump Division

The Pump Division has one plant dedicated to the design and manufacture of large, highly technical, customized pumps. Typically the contract life (production cycle) is one to three years. Most original equipment (OE) orders are obtained by preparing and submitting a bid proposal from a cost estimate analysis and conducting negotiating sessions with the customer. Sometimes orders are accepted as loss leaders in order to establish a position in the more profitable aftermarket business.

The contracts generally are fixed price. When coupled with the highly technical specifications and the length of the "in process" time, there is a high risk of job cost overruns. Company policy is to record revenue and costs on a completed contract basis, rather than as a percent of completion.

After a major decline in profitability, combined with several unfavorable year-end surprise inventory adjustments, new plant management decided to undertake a review of the operation to identify the key factors that affect inventory control. Management analysis revealed the following:

- The cost estimating function reported to the sales department.
- Final job costs varied significantly from original cost estimates. It was difficult to determine the source of variances until analyses were made upon completion of the jobs.
- The negotiated pricing of a contract was almost always on the basis of "whatever it takes to get the order," particularly when there was excess productive capacity in the industry.
- Progress payments/advanced payments were secured on some contracts, but such payments often were dropped if pricing competition was severe.
- When inflation was at double-digit levels, the company attempted to insert escalation clauses into contracts based on government indexes. However, most often, this resulted in fixed-price contracts with some estimate of inflation included.
- During the audit at the end of each year, a lower-of-cost-or-market analysis was made on major jobs in process. It was this exercise that revealed unfavorable inventory adjustments in recent years. Two examples are shown below:

(In Thousands)	Job 1	Job 2
Original cost Estimate	$2,113	$1,800
Costs Incurred to Date:		
Manufacturing	2,100	—
Engineering	373	100
Estimate to Complete	367	2,500
Total Current Estimate	2,840	2,600
Lower-of-cost-or-market: Contract Sales Price	2,520	2,000
Less 10% Allowance for Normal Profit Margin	(252)	(200)
Inventory Value	2,268	1,800
Inventory Reserve Adjustment (loss)	$ (572)	$ (800)

On job 2, the engineering department determined that the pump would not meet specifications in accordance with the original cost estimate and re-engineered the pump. This led to an increased estimate before the job entered the manufacturing stage.

REQUIRED:

1. What courses of action might be appropriate for the plant manager and his controller relating to (a) estimating costs, and (b) application of the lower of cost or market rule?
2. What is the significance of progress payments/advanced payments and escalation clauses on the performance of the operation?

(IMA, 1986)

7-3. Laurent Products

Laurent Products is a manufacturer of plastic packaging products with plants located throughout Europe and customers worldwide. "There is no doubt that the need to continue to grow sales is an important corporate objective and one which we need to always have in mind," remarked Arnoud Baynard, managing director. "Not only is this important in terms of continuing to increase sales revenue overall but it is an essential part of our commitment for next year's budget. Resisting group pressure and allowing ourselves this time to test the market for other new segments has brought some order into this phase of our development. The segment penetration achieved so far and the opportunity to build on this most successful initiative augers well for the future. Thank you, George, for a comprehensive summary of the market result to date" concluded Arnoud. "It seems as though this initiative is one which will help us meet out short and longer-term objectives." Arnoud Baynard's summary concerned a strategy overview provided by George St. Marc, marketing director of the company.

MARKETING STRATEGY

During the past ten years Laurent Products has successfully developed a line of packaging materials and a unique bagging system which present an important opportunity to increase the productivity of checkout counters in grocery stores. The plastic bags manufactured by Laurent are produced in several sizes, different plastic film colors, and may have attractive multi-color printed designs on one or both sides to meet the specification of a particular grocery store. The company concentrated its efforts in selling to the top twenty grocery market chains in Europe. By limiting its marketing efforts to a relatively few, very large multi-outlet grocery chains (which have centralized purchasing groups), the company achieved low marketing and selling costs but high market penetration. Last year the company reached a market share of 65% in the large grocery chain market and, in turn, relatively large customer order sizes. Two market segments are evident in the large grocery chain market. In the first (called the value added segment) customers buy the company's product primarily because of its advantage in reducing operating costs at checkout counters. The advantages provided by the Laurent bagging system include the lower cost of bags and labor costs of running the checkout counter as well as improved customer service. Frequently, the store operations personnel in this segment are active in making the buying decision. The second segment is referred to as being price sensitive as the customers purchase these products primarily on the basis of price. For these customers, purchasing managers are the key decision-makers in the buying decision.

RECENT COMPETITION

Laurent's success in the grocery chain market has attracted an increasing number of competitors into the market. While the company had been very successful in bringing out a series of new product types with innovative labor-saving features for the grocery stores, the competitors have eventually been able to develop quite similar products. The result has been increased competition with a substantial reduction in Laurent's prices (dropping 26% last year), and a major decline in the firms' profit margin. The size of the price sensitive segment is growing rapidly while the value added market segment is shrinking in size. The company faces an increasingly competitive market situation characterized by significant excess producer capacity.

WHOLESALE MARKET INITIATIVE

As a result of the increased competition in the grocery chain market, George has proposed to begin to a focus on the small independent grocery stores who purchase bags from large wholesale distributors. The potential sales for this wholesaler segment is about the same size as the grocery chain market (20 billion bags per year versus 25 billion bags per year), but includes a much larger number of independent store customers. At this time less than 15% of the bags sold in the wholesaler market are made of plastic. The independent grocery stores differ from the large grocery chains in that they purchase their grocery bags from wholesalers and distributors. Compared to the grocery chains, there are many more independent grocery store outlets widely dispersed over a large geographical area. The pilot marketing studies run last year by Laurent indicate that the customer order sizes for the wholesaler segment tend to be relatively small, and that the number of different product variations (in terms for example of print color, film color, and print type) tend to be relatively large in comparison with the grocery chain market. These studies also indicate that prices (and corresponding profit margins) are much higher than in the price sensitive segment currently served by the company.

MANUFACTURING

To support domestic and export sales, the company has located a number of plants throughout Europe to best support the geographical spread of the supermarket and hypermarket outlets of its various customers. "In the early years," explained Marcel Ray, manufacturing director, "capacity had, by necessity, always chased demand. The rapid growth in sales during the past few years and the need to make major decisions concerning new plant locations and process investments had understandably contributed to this capacity following the demand situation. However, with sales starting to level off this problem of capacity has now corrected itself."

Investments in manufacturing had been to support two principal objectives; to increase capacity and to reduce costs. The cost reduction initiatives principally concerned material costs and reduced processing times. "Current initiatives," explained Marcel "are continuing these themes. Our capacity uplifts will take the form of equipment similar to our existing machines. Over the years we have deliberately chosen to invest in machines which are similar to existing equipment in order to capitalize on the fact that the process is relatively simple and that products can, with relatively few exceptions, be processed on any machine in the plant. The only major restriction is the number of colors which a machine can accommodate on a single pass. Future investment proposals now being considered are based on this rationale."

In order to make best use of total capacity at all sites, customer orders are collated at the head office site in Lyon. They are then allocated to plants to take account of current plant loading, available capacity, customer lead times, and transport distances between the plant and a customer's required delivery location. As a result, forward loading on a plant is only two or, at most three days ahead. Plants then schedule these orders into their production processes in order to meet customer call-offs and individual equipment loading rules.

Once the printing details are agreed with a customer, a plate is produced and checked. In line with a call-off schedule, the plates are allocated to machines. Color changes (where necessary) are also part of the setup details. Table 1 provides an actual schedule of orders for four different bagging lines which is representative of the operations in the Paris Plant (and also for the company's other plants).

CONCLUDING REMARKS

In reviewing the proposed marketing initiatives regarding the wholesaler market, Arnoud Baynard, commented, "Since sales in our traditional markets are leveling off, the new marketing initiative appears to be an important step in giving us a fresh impetus to sales volume growth. We have now reached a point in our company where we do not have to endure capacity shortage problems. In fact, with the drop in sales last year, the company currently has excess capacity with which to pursue the wholesaler market. So, our main concern is to improve the decline in the profit performance that has occurred during the past year, and the new marketing initiatives should help to restore the profit margins and hence to secure this necessary, overall improvement."

REQUIRED

1. Discuss briefly Laurent's competitive position and strategy.
2. What are the implications of the marketing and manufacturing initiatives undertaken by Laurent?
3. How does Laurent's strategy deal effectively with global competition in its business. How should it?
4. Using the data in Table 1 and appropriate methods of analysis such as regression, analyze the effect of order size and product variety on the productivity and cost structure of the Paris plant.

1) competitive position + strategy multi-outlet
   switching from chain market to small
   independent grocery stores who purchase
   from wholesale distributors.
   strategy: low cost, check out efficiency

2)

3) Aligned plants throughout Europe to support
   domestic + international sales.
   Send all orders to central location they
   assign them to different plants according to
   capacity, lead time, geographic location.

4) Analysis: order size affects cost - 33% R-squared
   do

Additional Q: ABC to allocate overhead -
some orders will be more costly than
others. Breaks for larger orders.
Try to coordinate colors or types of bags -
give discounts for using preferred styles.

TABLE 1

Machine Number	Prod. Order Quantity	Print Type Complexity	Per unit Downtime & Setup	Per Unit Runtime	Total Setup & Downtime	Total Runtime	Total Variable Cost/Unit
2	480	1	0.0023	0.0423	1.10	20.30	7.04
2	489	1	0.0001	0.0434	0.07	21.20	6.99
2	480	1	0.0054	0.0419	2.60	20.10	6.99
4	180	1	0.0039	0.0400	0.70	7.20	6.97
4	2160	2	0.0022	0.0355	4.70	76.60	6.94
4	1377	2	0.0023	0.0405	3.10	55.70	6.95
4	120	2	0.0042	0.0400	0.50	4.80	6.97
4	540	2	0.0026	0.0413	1.40	22.30	6.97
4	360	2	0.0142	0.0411	5.10	14.80	6.98
4	1080	2	0.0111	0.0376	12.00	40.60	7.01
4	300	2	0.0037	0.0430	1.10	12.90	7.03
4	2400	2	0.0046	0.0345	11.00	82.90	7.05
4	81	2	0.0457	0.0407	3.70	3.30	7.09
8	360	1	0.0022	0.0425	0.80	15.30	7.82
8	120	1	0.0017	0.0433	0.20	5.20	7.83
8	120	1	0.0067	0.0417	0.80	5.00	8.17
8	60	1	0.0083	0.0417	0.50	2.50	8.83
8	240	1	0.0079	0.0425	1.90	10.20	7.94
8	60	1	0.0050	0.0467	0.30	2.80	7.97
8	240	1	0.0008	0.0583	0.20	14.00	8.2
8	120	1	0.0183	0.0433	2.20	5.20	8.09
8	60	1	0.0183	0.0433	1.10	2.60	7.93
8	480	1	0.0106	0.0435	5.10	20.90	8.23
8	240	2	0.0054	0.0413	1.30	9.90	7.91
8	537	2	0.0047	0.0423	2.50	22.70	7.87
8	420	2	0.0060	0.0421	2.50	17.70	7.89
8	1182	2	0.0150	0.0416	17.70	49.20	7.89
8	60	2	0.0550	0.0483	3.30	2.90	8.83
8	180	2	0.0122	0.0422	2.20	7.60	7.9
8	60	2	0.0417	0.0400	2.50	2.40	7.9
8	240	2	0.0067	0.0429	1.60	10.30	7.86
8	60	2	0.0083	0.0417	0.50	2.50	7.93
8	41	2	0.0293	0.0463	1.20	1.90	7.96
8	60	2	0.0417	0.0467	2.50	2.80	8
8	120	2	0.0117	0.0467	1.40	5.60	8.08
8	60	2	0.0617	0.0417	3.70	2.50	7.9
8	60	2	0.0433	0.0433	2.60	2.60	8
8	360	2	0.0108	0.0428	3.90	15.40	8.01
8	120	2	0.0200	0.0467	2.40	5.60	7.97
8	180	2	0.0144	0.0494	2.60	8.90	8.15
8	60	2	0.0233	0.0433	1.40	2.60	8.27
8	60	2	0.0400	0.0400	2.40	2.40	8.55
8	60	2	0.0417	0.0433	2.50	2.60	8.66
8	60	2	0.0467	0.0467	2.80	2.80	8.17
8	60	4	0.0483	0.0417	2.90	2.50	8.06
8	60	4	0.0150	0.0417	0.90	2.50	8.55
8	60	4	0.0583	0.0417	3.50	2.50	8.11
8	120	4	0.0167	0.0450	2.00	5.40	8.17
8	60	4	0.0567	0.0400	3.40	2.40	8.06
13	120	1	0.0050	0.0392	0.60	4.70	6.98
13	717	1	0.0043	0.0411	3.10	29.50	7
13	1500	1	0.0063	0.0427	9.50	64.10	7.08
13	2475	1	0.0091	0.0335	22.50	83.00	7.2
13	240	1	0.0100	0.0475	2.40	11.40	7.25
13	882	2	0.0178	0.0302	15.70	26.60	6.47
13	1677	2	0.0111	0.0361	18.60	60.50	7.04
13	243	2	0.0021	0.0457	0.50	11.10	7.05

7-4 Regression Analysis

Custom Photography is a small company that provides photography services primarily for medium to large size local businesses. Most of the work is special assignments involving professional models, displays, and sets. At the end of 2001, Janice Glass, the owner of Custom Photography is interested in predicting the average hourly payroll cost of the professional models and others who work in the set-up and design of the photo sessions in 2002. In order to do this, she has taken the payroll costs for each of the prior 20 quarters and the approximate number of hours devoted to these photo sessions during the quarter.

   The independent variable in this application is the number of hours for the sessions and the dependent variable is the payroll expense.

	I	D
QU/YR	Hours	Payroll Expense
1/1997	145	5,122
2	90	3,011
3	25	1,203
4	175	5,188
1/1998	112	3,877
2	267	8,712
3	212	7,355
4	132	4,123
1/1999	289	9,938
2	235	7,327
3	156	5,592
4	277	9,387
1/2000	302	10,993
2	72	2,761
3	88	2,766
4	212	8,246
1/2001	155	5,499
2	222	7,729
3	116	3,892
4	250	8,473
Projected Data for hours:		
1/2002	188	?
2	233	?
3	145	?
4	298	?

REQUIRED:

1. Develop a regression analysis to predict payroll costs, using Excel or equivalent regression software and the first 20 quarters of data. Evaluate the precision and reliability of the regression.
2. Predict payroll expense for each quarter of 2002.

Readings

APPLYING OVERHEAD:
HOW TO FIND THE RIGHT
BASES AND RATES

Determine the relationship between overhead costs and various cost drivers with the help of regression analysis.

By Adel M. Novin

Direct labor no longer may be the most effective base for applying factory overhead costs to various jobs and products. With today's highly automated systems, labor-related costs constitute only a small portion of total manufacturing costs, and overhead costs now correlate more with factors such as machine hours and material quantities. Accordingly, many companies are beginning to identify application bases that better reflect the causes of overhead costs in their unique manufacturing environments.

Selection of proper application bases also has received a boost from the recent growth in activity-based costing (ABC), ABC applies accumulated costs for each activity to products and jobs using a separate base for each activity. Thus, it is crucial to select the right bases (cost drivers) for applying the costs of various activities to products and jobs.

SEARCHING FOR A PROPER BASE

Theoretically, the factory overhead cost application base should be a principal cost driver—an activity (or activities) that causes factory overhead costs to be incurred. In other words, there should be a strong cause-and-effect relationship between the factory overhead costs incurred and the base chosen for their application. Selecting the proper base requires knowledge of the relationships between the overhead costs and various cost drivers such as machine hours, direct labor hours, direct labor costs, space occupied, pounds handled, invoices processed, number of component parts, number of setups, units produced, and material costs or material quantities.

Using an objective technique, regression analysis, rather than experience or observation of activities can be helpful in ascertaining the relationship between the overhead costs and various cost drivers. Regression analysis has not been explored fully in practice, possibly due to its computational complexities coupled with a lack of easily accessible computer software. With the widespread use of spreadsheet programs, however, regression analysis now can be performed rather easily. The regression analysis described below was done using a computer spreadsheet.

Regression analysis is one of the few quantitative techniques available for: (1) determining and analyzing the extent of the relationship between overhead costs and various cost drivers and (2) estimating the linear or curvilinear relationship between overhead costs and cost drivers. One of the values provided by regression analysis, the coefficient of determination or R Squared, measures the extent of the relationship between the two variables. More specifically, the value of R Squared indicates the percentage of variation in the dependent variable (overhead costs in this case) that is explained by variation in the independent variable (the cost driver). The value of R Squared is always between zero and 100%. The closer its value is to 100%, the stronger the relationship between the two variables.

Regression analysis can help us investigate the strength of the relationship between the overhead cost and various cost drivers. In simple terms, the cost driver that receives an R-Squared value closest to 100% will be the most accurate predictor of overhead costs. The following section will illustrate this concept.

To find the proper application base, the first step is to identify the various cost drivers that might explain changes in overhead costs. Suppose that in searching for an application base for overhead costs, we have found three possible cost drivers—direct labor hours, machine hours, and number of production setups.

Regression analysis requires actual data on selected variables for several periods. Suppose we have data from 12 consecutive months (with outliers excluded) on overhead costs, direct labor hours, machine hours, and number of production setups, as shown in Table 1.

With three possible cost drivers, three different regression analyses should be performed. Of course, a different output-range should be selected for each variable.

Table 2 presents the regression output obtained for the three regression analyses. According to the R-Squared values, machine hours explain about 77% of changes in variable overhead costs, while the number of set-ups and direct labor hours explain 39% and 29%, respectively. Thus, it appears that the most proper base for application of overhead costs in our example is machine hours because it has the strongest relationship with overhead costs.

CONSTRUCTION OF A SINGLE OVERHEAD RATE

Referring to the regression results in Table 2, "Constant" represents an estimate of the fixed portion of the overhead cost, while "X Coefficient(s)" represents an estimate of the variable rate of the overhead costs. For example, based on the regression results for machine hours, the estimated linear relationship between monthly overhead costs (OH) and machine hours (MH) can be presented by the following simple regression line: OH = $72,794 + $74.72 MH, where $72,794 is an estimate of total monthly fixed overhead costs and $74.72 is the rate for the application of variable overhead costs (i.e., $74.72 per machine hour).

We then come to the question of how to assign the fixed portion of overhead costs to products and jobs. Often, a separate base that reflects the demands made by products and jobs on a firm's fixed resources is used to apply fixed costs to products and jobs. This base may be determined by engineering methods such as time and motion studies. In this case, there would be two rates based on two different bases for the application of overhead costs, one for fixed overhead and one for variable overhead costs.

TABLE 1
DATA FOR REGRESSION ANALYSIS

	A	B	C	D
1	FOH	DIR LABOR	MACHINE	NO. OF
2	COSTS	HOURS	HOURS	SETUPS
3	155,000	985	1,060	200
4	160,000	1,068	1,080	225
5	170,000	1,095	1,100	250
6	165,000	1,105	1,200	202
7	185,000	1,200	1,600	210
8	135,000	1,160	1,100	150
9	145,000	1,145	1,080	165
10	150,000	1,025	1,090	180
11	180,000	1,115	1,300	204
12	175,000	1,136	1,400	206
13	190,000	1,185	1,500	208
14	200,000	1,220	1,700	212

TABLE 2
REGRESSION OUTPUT

REGRESSION RESULTS FOR OVERHEAD COSTS WITH DL HOURS
Regression Output:

Constant	919.0
Std Err of Y Est	17,267.6
R Squared	0.2
No. of Observations	1
Degrees of Freedom	1
X Coefficient(s)	148.74
Std Err of Coef.	74.35

REGRESSION RESULTS FOR OVERHEAD COSTS WITH MACHINE HOURS
Regression Output:

Constant	72,793.8
Std Err of Y Est	9,799.0
R Squared	0.7
No. of Observations	1
Degrees of Freedom	1
X Coefficient(s)	74.72
Std Err of Coef.	12.91

REGRESSION RESULTS FOR OVERHEAD COSTS WITH NUMBER OF SETUPS
Regression Output:

Constant	74,033.1
Std Err of Y Est	15,909.7
R Squared	0.3
No. of Observations	1
Degrees of Freedom	1
X Coefficient(s)	465.00
Std Err of Coef.	182.47

CONSTRUCTION OF MULTIPLE OVERHEAD RATES

In a complex manufacturing environment, variable overhead costs may be driven by several equally important factors. Under such circumstances, the use of more than one base for the application of variable overhead costs to products and jobs results in a more accurate cost estimate. For example, the cost of one activity, material handling, may be applied to products based upon both the number of material requisitions and the number of parts per material requisition. To accommodate the use of more than one independent variable, we would need to perform a multiple regression. Thus, we can construct more than one overhead rate.

Continuing our prior example, suppose that we want to apply overhead costs based on the two cost drivers with the strongest relationship to overhead cost—machine hours and number of setups. To perform multiple regression analysis, follow the same steps as for performance of simple regression, except that the "X-Range" will consist of the range of observations for both machine hours and number of setups.

Table 3 presents the results for the multiple regression. "Constant" represents an estimate of the fixed overhead cost, while "X Coefficients" represent an estimate of the variable rates of the overhead costs. For example, the estimated relationship between the overhead costs (OH) and the two driving factors, machine hours (MH) and number of setups (NS), can be expressed by the following multiple regression line: $OH = \$19{,}796.43 + \$65.44\ MH + \$322.21\ NS$, where $\$19{,}796.43$ is an estimate of the total monthly fixed overhead costs, and $\$65.44$ and $\$322.21$ are the estimated variable overhead costs per machine hour and per setup, respectively. The value of R Squared for the multiple regression line is 95%, which is greater than that of the simple regression line based solely on machine hours (77%). This fact implies that the application of variable overhead costs based on both machine hours and number of setups would result in more accurate cost estimates.

TABLE 3
MULTIPLE REGRESSION RESULTS FOR OVERHEAD COSTS WITH MACHINE HOURS AND NUMBER OF SETUPS

Regression Output:

Constant		19,796.43
Std Err of Y Est		4,951.11
R Squared		0.95
No. of Observations		12
Degrees of Freedom		9
X Coefficient(s)	65.44	322.21
Std Err of Coef.	6.74	58.66

Here, again, total fixed overhead costs may be applied to jobs and products either using a different base determined by engineering methods such as time and motion studies or using the same base as for variable overhead (machine hours and number of setups). Use of a separate base for the application of fixed costs would result in a total of three overhead rates, one for fixed overhead and two for variable overheads.

It is important to remember that the variable overhead rates computed by regression analysis (the "X Coefficients") are estimates derived from our 12 observations. The reliability of the estimated variable overhead rates can and should be determined by computing the t-test value for each rate. The t-test value equals the "X Coefficients" over the "Std Err of Coef." As a general rule, if the absolute value of the t-test for any variable rate is greater than two, then the estimated overhead rate is considered highly reliable. Referring to Table 3, for example, the value of the t-test for the variable overhead based on machine hours is about 5.8 (74.72/12.91), which tells us that the rate can be relied upon. The overhead sites determined from regression analysis, after adjusting for expected future inflation, would be usable as long as no major change in the cost structure and manufacturing process has occurred.

RATES FOR ACTIVITY-BASED COSTING

For more accurate product costing, firms are beginning to use activity-based costing for computing overhead costs. under this system, accumulated costs for each activity are applied to products and jobs using a separate base for each activity. in a manner similar to that described above, regression analysis can be used to investigate the strength of the relationship between various activities and cost drivers in order to determine the proper base(s) and rate(s) for applying the cost of each activity to products and jobs.

We also may use regression analysis to classify a large number of activities into a few groups (cost pools) based on common bases. Suppose that through use of simple regression analysis, we have computed the R-Squared values for the pairs of activities and cost drivers shown in Table 4. Based on the R-Squared values, we may group the five activities into two cost pools. It appears that the principal cause of the packaging, materials handling and storage activities costs is pounds of materials. a few groups (cost pools) based on common bases. Suppose that through use of simple regression analysis, we have computed the R-Squared values for the pairs of activities and cost drivers shown in Thus, the cost pool consisting of the accumulated costs of these three activities can be applied to products and jobs based on number of pounds of materials used. Similarly, the accumulated costs of maintenance and production scheduling, which have a high correlation with machine hours, can be applied to products and jobs based on machine hours. In this way, all costs included in each cost pool will have the same cause-and-effect relationship with the chosen cost allocation base.

As business becomes increasingly more competitive, decision makers are demanding more accurate cost figures from cost accounting systems. For accurate costing, it is crucial that factory overhead and activity costs be applied to various products and jobs using bases that reflect principal causes of the overhead costs. Regression analysis has proved to be a practical, effective, and objective method for selecting proper cost application bases.

In addition to its usefulness for determining proper application bases, regression analysis is a practical method for developing single or multiple overhead rates for the application of overhead costs to products and jobs. With the widespread use of spreadsheet programs, regression analysis can be performed easily.

Note: The article was edited with the author's permission to remove references to Lotus 1-2-3 and replace them with generic spreadsheet references.

TABLE 4
R-SQUARED VALUES FOR VARIOUS PAIRS OF ACTIVITIES AND COST DRIVERS

	Maintenance	Packaging	Materials Handling	Storage	Production Scheduling
Machine Hours	.85	.46	.68	.45	.82
Pounds of Material	.38	.88	.90	.75	.43
Labor Hours	.30	.28	.38	.22	.43

ESTIMATION OF PRODUCTION COSTS AND LABOR HOURS USING A FREE EXCEL ADD-IN

by C. D. Bailey

Organizations of all sizes and descriptions can benefit from using learning curves—service businesses, small businesses, local governments, and light manufacturers. But one obstacle to widespread use has been the tediousness of the content of available books and resources—users must manipulate logarithms or mysterious tables.[1] I have developed some software that is easy to use (available free from the website, Charles.Bailey@bus.ucf.edu) to handle the tedious calculations.

Large corporations have industrial engineers who are familiar with learning curve techniques. While the software introduced here is entirely appropriate for their use, these experienced users need no examples to demonstrate applicability. The examples below emphasize smaller businesses and nontraditional settings.

BACKGROUND

It is no surprise that as a person or team repeats an activity they become faster at it. Learning occurs through practice, and thus experienced workers should produce more output of a product or service per hour. Cost also should decrease—the cost of the 10th unit should be less than the cost of the first and so on (quality measures also should follow a learning curve). The surprising insight is that the relationship between practice and improvement is rather predictable. By knowing certain data for each of the first few units, one can make useful predictions about the production of future units (cost, time, or quality measures).

A couple of points on learning curves are worth noting. The first is that for a typical production activity, learning occurs fastest during the early stages and then levels off. Although improvement theoretically continues indefinitely, it eventually becomes almost imperceptible—a phenomenon called "plateauing." Thus learning curves are most useful during early phases of production. The second point is that the curve can apply to an individual worker or a team of workers. Furthermore, it may apply even to the entire pool of costs associated with an activity because learning occurs not only in labor skills but also in operating systems, paperwork systems, and so on.

Learning curves can answer many types of questions:

SERVICE BUSINESSES

- A new clerical department of an insurance agency has been processing policy applications for one month. *Will it be able to keep up with anticipated growth?*
- A beginning fast-food cook requires 60 minutes to prepare her first 20 hamburgers, 45 minutes for the second 20, and 36 minutes for the third 20. *What should her production rate be after 24 hours of experience?*
- A new check-encoding clerk in a bank required 60 minutes to encode his first 500 checks, 50 minutes for the second 500, and 45 minutes for the third 500. *When will this employee be able to produce at the standard rate of 1,000 per hour?*

PRODUCTION BUSINESSES

- An electrical contractor has wired two identical homes. *How long should the same team require to wire the third identical home? The 10th?* (Or, as the general contractor, how many labor hours should you expect the electrical contractor to include in a bid?)
- A custom boat builder has produced only a single prototype of a new sailboat. But the producer knows, from accumulated past experience, the learning curve rate for similar boats. *What are the projected labor requirements for the second, third, and so on?*

There is no one "learning curve," although one model seems to be the most popular. A curve is simply an attempt to describe observed learning behavior by a mathematical equation. (I won't get involved in the math here. For those interested, the manual accompanying the free software covers that topic.)

The software package, called Foresee, provides four kinds of learning curves, all of which have exactly the same purpose: to forecast future times (or dollars or quality measures) for each unit of production. Two of the curves use the traditional, well-known logarithmic form. The other two use a form introduced by Bailey and McIntyre[2] that fit better and did a better job predicting the mechanical assembly tasks used in their experiments.

Using either form, you can fit the curve to *average* data or to *marginal (unit)* data. After forecasting either the average or the unit data, conversion to unit times, totals, and so forth is easy. This software produces unit time estimates *from whatever form of curve you use.* Confused? You're not alone. Although I have just stated the distinction between the curves, it is hard to grasp. Academic articles have addressed the topic, but I have yet to find an accounting textbook that distinguishes clearly between the curve forms.

Let's take a look at one learning-curve relationship, the traditional log-linear marginal (unit) curve. It assumes that every time the total number of units produced *doubles*, the *marginal cost decreases by a constant proportion* (called the learning curve percentage). A numerical example appears in Table 1, and Figure 1 shows a graph of the data. These tabular and graphical presentations demonstrate the relationship, but equations are necessary to generate forecasts about units other than the "doubling points."

USING THE SOFTWARE

Foresee is an Excel add-in, written using the spreadsheet's Visual Basic for Applications (VBA) facility. A manual accompanying the software explains the mechanics of entering data and navigating the features of the application. Except for a brief explanation following the first question, the examples below bypass these mechanical steps to show solutions to typical problems.

Foresee can perform learning-curve projections using either of two starting points.

- **An assumed rate of improvement**. This is appropriate for industries, such as aerospace, that have considerable experience with learning curves so that they "know" the learning rate. It also is appropriate for government contracts in which a certain rate is assumed.
- **Raw data from actual experience**. This is appropriate for tasks on which one has little historical experience, such as the nontraditional applications emphasized here.

After navigating the introductory menu in Foresee, you will reach a worksheet like the one shown in Figure 2. The columns at the left of Figure 2, starting with cells A8 and B8, are for entry of unit-cost data from past experience. (Alternatively, you can assume a learning rate by using an "Advanced Forecasting" option.[3]) Forecasts will appear in the columns at the right, starting with D12 and E12. The remaining columns are available for supplemental calculations, which can use all the regular capabilities of Excel.

FORMULATING QUESTIONS

Any question someone might ask can be addressed by using the estimated individual unit (marginal) times (or dollars or quality measures). A future version of the program might provide additional columns with total times and average times, or it might include dialogue boxes to address a variety of questions directly. But in the name of simplicity, the current version provides unit estimates only.

As noted above, the program can base its answers on two sources of information: (1) data reflecting past performance or (2) the initial time and learning rate (percentage) that you can enter directly. Here are several examples that illustrate approaches to formulating and answering typical questions:

Question #1: A worker has performed a mechanical assembly task four times. What is the projected total time for the first 20 units assembled, based on the actual times observed for the first four assemblies?
Figure 3 shows the answer I derived using actual data, in minutes, from a laboratory experiment I conducted. The steps to achieve the output in Figure 3 were as follows:

1. Enter the data in the left-hand columns.
2. Select "Tools; Learning Curve App; Fit Learning Curve."

   This Fit Learning Curve option fits a curve to the data on the current worksheet. If desired, the user can check the "Specify Curve Type" box to select the curve form. Otherwise, the program will choose the curve that best fits the data.[4]

   The New option opens a new worksheet.

   Advanced Forecast allows forecasting with a known learning rate.
3. Enter the numbers 5 through 20 in the forecast column.
4. Select "Tools; Learning Curve App; Forecast."

5. Sum the actual times 1 through 4 and the forecasted times 5 through 20. (I could have produced forecasts for times 1 through 4, but that would make little sense when I have the actual times.)

Question #2: How fast will John (worker from Question #1) be after he has completed 100 units?
An appropriate measure of ability after completing n units would be the projected time for unit n+1, in this case unit #101. To address this question, simply enter the unit number, 101, in cell D12 and perform step 4 from Question #1. The resulting estimate of 2.32 minutes will appear in cell E12.

Question #3: A beginning fast-food cook, working constantly, required 60 minutes to produce her first 20 hamburgers, 45 minutes for the second 20, and 36 minutes to produce her third batch of 20. What is her predicted rate after 24 hours of experience at the task?
The solution lies in forecasting into the future and summing the unit times until they equal 24 hours. The result using hypothetical data appears in Figure 4. I have created the two columns at the far right, labeled "Minutes" and "Hours," to show cumulative times. When the total reaches 24 hours, the estimated marginal time is 6.58 min./batch, or about 9.1 batches/hr. This is the worker's projected speed after that much practice. A physical constraint, such as cooking time or equipment limitations, might prevent the achievement of a 9.1 batches/hr. speed.

Question #4A: A newly hired check-encoding clerk in a bank required 66 minutes to encode his first 500 checks, 59.4 minutes for the second 500, and 51.6 minutes for the third 500. After how much time will this clerk reach the "standard" rate of three batches per hour (20 min./batch)?
The solution appears in Figure 5. Projecting unit times well into the future shows that the clerk will require about 264 batches to reach the standard 20 min./batch. We could, of course, also sum up the batch times to estimate how long this will take. We can monitor his progress against these projections— and refit the curve to revise our projections as more data become available.

Question #4B: Assume that, as in #4A, checks are processed in batches of 500. We know the total number of checks the clerk has processed since starting the job, but we have recorded performance times only for batches 1, 3, and 5. Batches 1 and 3 are as given in Question #4A, but batch 5 turns out to be 43.5 minutes, not the amount forecasted above.

The "gap" in the data does not matter, assuming a unit curve,[5] and the solution is like #4A. Cells A8 to B10 would contain the following:

1 66.0

2 59.4

5 43.5

These data lead to a forecast of 104 batches needed to reach the standard rate versus the 264 batches forecasted in #4A. This difference emphasizes the wide margin of error when relying on only three data points (see the discussion in Question #5 on "goodness of fit").

Question #5: An electrical contractor has wired two identical homes using the same approach and the same team of electricians. The total labor costs were $8,450 for the first job and $6,676 for the second job. For bidding purposes, what should the contractor expect the third, fourth, and fifth units to cost?
Two observations are not much data, and the "goodness of fit" is not meaningful because any curve form can fit two data points perfectly. With two data points, the program defaults to the traditional marginal curve unless you specify the curve form. The following data are inserted in cells A8 to B9:

1 8450

2 6676

The marginal curve produces forecasts as follows:

3 5816.36

4 5274.44

5 4889.11

Even with so few observations, the tool should be useful, although the user needs to exercise judgment.[6]

Question #6A: When starting production of a new circuit board, the Galvanic Board Company at first encounters many rejected boards. The number declines following a learning curve as the operators gain experience and equipment problems are ironed out. What should the company expect given the following data (which are hypothetical, but learning curves are used to track quality improvement)?
Of the first 100 boards, 10 were bad.
Of the second 100, 7 were bad.
Of the third 100, 6 were bad.
Of the fourth 100, 6 were bad.
Of the fifth 100, 5 were bad.
The solution appears in Figure 6, which presents straightforward forecasts after selected numbers of units. The failure rate should be cut in half after about

100 units of production and to less than a third by 1,000 units.

Question #6B: Modify the question in #6A to assume that, because of industry benchmarking information, Galvanic Board Company expects the number of rejects to decline according to an 80% cumulative average curve. Assume also that they have made only 200 boards and thus have only the data on the next page.
Of the first 100 boards, 10 were bad.
Of the second 100, 7 were bad.
What is the benchmark for measuring future improvement?

First, what should we use as a definition of the first batch—100 boards with 10 bad or 200 with 17 bad? Either definition is acceptable. The two results appear in Figure 7, using the "Advanced" option to specify the learning rate. This option requires an initial bit of data, in this case the error rate for an initial batch, the form of curve, and the curve percentage (80%). Note that the spreadsheet contains no data in columns A and B, as no data are used to fit a curve in this example. Only this example follows the approach typically taught in cost accounting textbooks, that is, estimation using a known percentage rate and starting point.

HOW MUCH CONFIDENCE SHOULD YOU PLACE IN THE SOLUTION?

As implied above, learning-curve estimates generally carry a high level of reliability or predictability. This level will vary, however, from application to application. Some factors that affect reliability include:

- Errors in measurement or collection of data;
- Random factors, unrelated to learning, that affect performance for a particular repetition;
- Subtle changes in the production activity itself, such as design changes; and
- The number of data points used to obtain the estimate.

A useful indication of the reliability of the estimate is the "goodness of fit" of the formula used in the estimate. In statistical terminology, this is called r^2, the "coefficient of determination." Stated simply, it is a number between zero and one that indicates the proportion of variation in production time (or cost) that is explained by knowing the number of units produced. For example if $r^2 = .70$, then the experience level, or the number of units produced so far, explains 70% of the fluctuation in production time. The remaining 30% of the overall fluctuation (variance) results from the errors in measurement and so on listed above. For small samples, the curve must fit very well (explain a lot of the variance) to be reliable. While a larger r^2 always is better, the following is a rule of thumb for the absolute minimum to reflect reliability: for two data points it is impossible to evaluate reliability; for three, the minimum acceptable r^2 is 0.98; for four, 0.81; for five, 0.65; for 10, 0.30; and for 40 or more, 0.10.

THE POWER OF LEARNING CURVES

The potential applications of learning curves far outstrip their current usage. Businesses from fast-food restaurants to banks can determine how fast their employees will obtain on-the-job skills. Local governments can improve budgeting processes. Manufacturers can estimate production rates. With software to aid in learning curve use, all the benefits of the technique are within reach. Organizations cannot afford to ignore such a powerful tool.

1 Articles in Management Accounting that have addressed learning curve use include Eugene A. Imhoff, Jr., "The Learning Curve and Its Applications," February 1978, pp. 44-46; and Jackson F. Gillespie, "An Application of Learning Curves to Standard Costing," September 1981, pp. 63-65. A more recent article that illustrates the broad applicability of the learning phenomenon by applying it to the learning of new computer systems is K.M. Boze, "Measuring Learning Costs," August 1994, pp. 48-52.
2 C.D. Bailey and E.V. McIntyre, "Some Evidence on the Nature of Relearning Curves," The Accounting Review, April 1992, pp. 368-378.
3 The "advanced" title is something of a misnomer. The program to fit a curve to new data really is a more "advanced" feature. The name implies a need for caution, though; the user needs advanced knowledge of a learning rate before using this option.
4 The option of selecting the curve form lets advanced users override the program's choice of a best-fit curve. Sometimes a few data points may not reveal the underlying improvement rate.
5 An average curve is not feasible because it requires a cumulative average that would include the missing fourth observation.
6 For example, if the workers showed little or no improvement, the analyst should not blindly extrapolate this trend because temporary setbacks may be followed by large improvements. Workers may have learned without any improvement showing in the most recent performance. One reason may be because of errors committed. See C. D. Bailey and S. Gupta, "Judgement in Learning-Curve Forecasting: A Laboratory Study," Journal of Forecasting, January 1999, pp. 39-57.

Table 1: Traditional Log-Linear Marginal (Unit) Learning Curve		
Cumulative Production (units)	**Marginal Cost**	**Calculation, assuming an 80% curve**
1	$30.00	
2	24.00	.80 x 30 = 24
4	19.20	.80 x 24 = 19.20
8	15.36	.80 x 19.20 = 15.36
16	12.29	.80 x 15.36 = 12.29
32	9.83	.80 x 12.29 = 9.83
64	7.86	.80 x 9.83 = 7.86

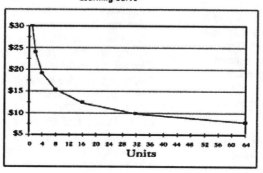

Figure 1: Traditional Log-Linear Marginal (Unit) Learning Curve

Figure 2: Basic Worksheet in Foresee©

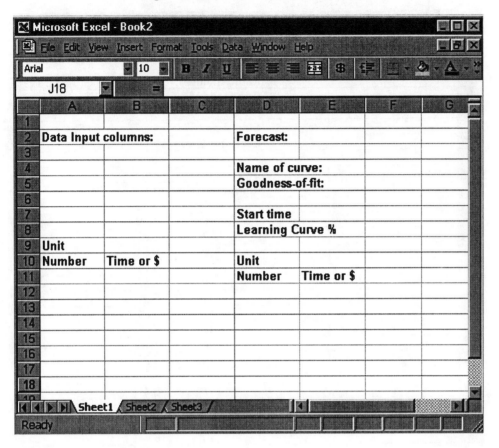

Figure 3: Solution to Question #1

	A	B	C	D	E	F	G
1							
2	Data Input columns:			Forecast:			
3							
4				Name of curve:		Marginal (Unit) Curve	
5				Goodness-of-fit:		88.85%	
6							
7				Start time		60.5	
8				Learning Curve %		72.72%	
9	Unit						
10	Number	Time or $		Unit			
11	1	29.8		Number	Time or $		
12	2	25		5	12.86		
13	3	17.5		6	11.59		
14	4	13.4		7	10.82		
15				8	9.84		
16				9	9.20		
17				10	8.67		
18				11	8.21		
19				12	7.81		
20				13	7.46		
21				14	7.16		
22				15	6.88		
23				16	6.63		
24				17	6.41		
25				18	6.20		
26				19	6.01		
27				20	6.84		
28				Total	217.09	Minutes	

Sheet1 / Sheet2 / Sheet3 /

Figure 4:Solution to Question #3

	A	B	C	D	E	F	G
2	Data Input columns:			Forecast:			
3							
4				Name of curve:		Marginal (Unit) Curve	
5				Goodness-of-fit:		99.48%	
6							
7				Start time		60.5	
8				Learning Curve %		72.72%	
9	Unit						
10	Number	Time or $		Unit			
11	1	60		Number	Time or $	Minutes	Hours
12	2	45		4	31.99	172.99	2.88
13	3	36		5	28.88	201.87	3.36
14				6	26.55	228.42	3.81
15				...	...	...	...
16				...	...	...	...
17				123	6.63	1431.94	23.87
18				124	6.60	1438.54	23.98
19				125	6.58	1445.12	24.09
20				126	6.55	1451.67	24.19
21				127	6.53	1458.20	24.30

Sheet1 / Sheet2 / Sheet3 /

Figure 5: Solution to Question #4a

I23 =

	A	B	C	D	E	F	G
2	Data Input columns:			Forecast:			
3							
4				Name of curve:		Marginal (Unit) Curve	
5				Goodness-of-fit:		94.80%	
6							
7				Start time		66.80	
8				Learning Curve %		86.08%	
9	Unit						
10	Number	Time or $		Unit			
11	1	66		Number	Time or $		
12	2	59.4		4	49.49		
13	3	51.6		5	47.16		
14				...	...		
15				...	...		
16				262	20.03		
17				263	20.02		
18				264	20.00		
19				265	19.89		

Sheet1 / Sheet2 / Sheet3 /

Figure 6: Solution to Question #6a

	A	B	C	D	E	F
1						
2	Data Input columns:			Forecast:		
3						
4				Name of curve:		Average Curve
5				Goodness-of-fit:		98.33%
6						
7				Start time		10.00
8				Learning Curve %		84.81%
9	Unit					
10	Number	Time or $		Unit		
11	1	10		Number	Time or $	
12	2	7		6	5.09	
13	3	6		7	4.89	
14	4	6		8	4.73	
15	5	5		9	4.59	
16				10	4.47	
17				20	3.77	
18				40	3.18	
19				70	2.78	
20				100	2.56	
21				200	2.17	
22				300	1.97	
23				1000	1.48	

Sheet1 / Sheet2 / Sheet3

Figure 7: Alternate Solutions to Question #6b

	A	B	C	D	E	F
1						
2	Data Input columns:			Forecast:		
3						
4				Name of curve:	Average Time Curve	
5				Goodness-of-fit:		
6						
7	Unit			Start time		10.00
8	Number	Time or $		Learning Curve %		80.00%
9						
10			Actual	Unit		
11			Units	Number	Time or $	
12			100	1	10.00	
13			200	2	6.00	
14			300	3	5.06	
15			400	4	4.54	
16			500	5	4.18	
17			600	6	3.92	
18			700	7	3.71	
19			800	8	3.55	
20			900	9	3.41	
21			1000	10	3.29	

Sheet1 / Sheet2 / Sheet3 /

	A	B	C	D	E	F
1						
2	Data Input columns:			Forecast:		
3						
4				Name of curve:	Average Time Curve	
5				Goodness-of-fit:		
6						
7	Unit			Start time		17.00
8	Number	Time or $		Learning Curve %		80.00%
9						
10			Actual	Unit		
11			Units	Number	Time or $	
12			200	1	17.00	
13			400	2	10.20	
14			600	3	8.61	
15			800	4	7.71	
16			1000	5	7.11	
17			1200	6	6.66	
18			1400	7	6.31	
19			1600	8	6.03	
20			1800	9	5.79	
21			2000	10	5.59	

Sheet1 / Sheet2 / Sheet3 /

Chapter 8
Cost-Volume-Profit Analysis

Cases

8-1   Cost-Volume-Profit Analysis and Strategy
8-2   Cost-Volume-Profit Analysis and Cost Estimation
8-3   Cost-Volume-Profit Analysis and Strategy
8-4   Cost-Volume-Profit Analysis and Strategy: The ALLTEL Pavilion
8-5   Sensitivity Analysis; Regression Analysis

Readings

"Tools for Dealing with Uncertainty"

This article explains how to use simulation methods within a spreadsheet program such as Excel to perform sensitivity analysis for a given decision context. The available spreadsheet simulation software systems include the programs Crystal Ball and @Risk, among others. These software systems allow the user to analyze the effect of uncertainty on the potential outcomes of a decision. These tools can be applied directly to CVP analysis. The tools allow the user to see the potential effect on the breakeven level or total profit of potential variations in the key uncertain factors in the analysis. The uncertain factors affecting breakeven might be the unknown level of unit variable cost, price or fixed cost. Also, in determining total profit, the unknown level of demand might be a key uncertain factor.

Exercise: Use a spreadsheet simulation tool such as Crystal Ball or @Risk to analyze the uncertain factors in given case situation. Cases 8-1,2 and 3 could be used or a problem from the text, for example, text problem 8-45, the Omni Graphics Case.

Cases

8-1. Cost-Volume-Profit Analysis and Strategy

Mr. Carter is the manager of Simmons Farm and Seed Company, a wholesaler of fertilizer, seed, and other farm supplies. The company has been successful in recent years primarily because of great customer service—flexible credit terms, customized orders (quantities, seed mix, etc), and on-time delivery, among others. Global Agricultural Products, Inc., Simmons' parent corporation, has informed Mr. Carter that his budgeted net income for 19x7 will be $120,000. The budget was based on data for the prior year and Mr. Carter's belief that there would be no significant changes in revenues and expenses for the coming period.

After the determination of the budget, Carter received notice from Simmons' principal shipping agent that it was about to increase its rates by 10%. This carrier handles 90% of Simmons' total shipping volume. Paying the increased rate will result in failure to meet the budgeted income level, and Mr. Carter is understandably reluctant to allow that to happen. He is considering two alternatives. First, it is possible to use another carrier whose rates are 5% less than the old carrier's original rate. The old carrier, however, is a subsidiary of a major customer; shifting to a new carrier will almost certainly result in loss of that customer and sales amounting to $70,000.

Assume that prior to the recent rate increase, the shipping costs of the principal carrier and the other carriers were the same, and that costs of the other carriers are not expected to change.

As a second alternative, Simmons can purchase its own trucks thereby reducing its shipping costs to 85% of the original rate. The new trucks would have an expected life of 10 years, no salvage value and would be depreciated on a straight line basis. Related fixed costs excluding depreciation would be $2,000. Assume that if Simmons purchases the trucks, Simmons will replace the principal shipper and the other shippers.

Following are data from the prior year:

Sales	$1,500,000
Variable costs (excluding shipping)	1,095,000
Shipping costs	135,000
Fixed costs	150,000

REQUIRED:

1. Using cost-volume-profit analysis and the data provided, determine the maximum amount that Mr. Carter can pay for the trucks and still expect to attain budgeted net income.
2. At what price for the truck would Mr. Carter be indifferent between purchasing the new trucks and using a new carrier?
3. Mr. Carter has decided to use a new carrier, but now is worried its apparent lack of reliability may adversely affect sales volume. Determine the dollar amount of sales that Simmons can lose because of lack of reliability before any benefit from switching carriers is lost completely.
4. Describe what you think is the competitive strategy of Simmons Farm and Seed Company. What should be the strategy? How would the use of a new carrier affect the strategy?
5. Can Mr. Carter use value chain analysis to improve the profits of Simmons Farm and Seed Company? If so, explain how briefly.

8-2. Cost-Volume-Profit Analysis and Cost Estimation

The following requirement is based on information in the Atlantic City Casino case, case 2-33 at the end of Chapter 2. Re-read the case and complete the requirements below.

REQUIRED:

1. Using the data provided in the case, build a cost estimation model to predict net income based on total revenues. Then, use this model to determine an estimate of the industry-wide breakeven point in sales revenue. Evaluate the reliability and precision of the estimation method you have chosen.
2. Develop a cost estimation model to predict casino revenues based on square feet of casino floor space. Use this model to determine the expected full-year revenue for casino number nine. Evaluate the precision and reliability of the method you have chosen.
3. Repeat part (2) above, using number of rooms to predict room revenues, and number of restaurants to predict food and beverage revenues for the full year for casino number nine.

8-3. Cost-Volume-Profit Analysis and Strategy

Melford Hospital operates a general hospital, but rents space and beds to separately-owned entities rendering specialized services such as pediatrics and psychiatric care. Melford charges each separate entity for common services such as patients' meals and laundry, and for administrative services such as billings and collections. Space and bed rentals are fixed charges for the year, based on bed capacity rented to each entity.

Melford charged the following costs to pediatrics for the year ended June 30, 19X2:

	Patient Days (variable)	Bed Capacity (fixed)
Dietary	$ 600,000	—
Janitorial	—	$ 70,000
Laundry	300,000	—
Laboratory	450,000	—
Pharmacy	350,000	—
Repairs and maintenance	—	30,000
General and administrative	—	1,300,000
Rent	—	1,500,000
Billings and collections	300,000	—
Total	$2,000,000	$2,900,000

During the year ended June 30, 19X2, pediatrics charged each patient an average of $300 per day, had a capacity of 60 beds, and had revenue of $6,000,000 for 365 days. In addition, pediatrics directly employed the following personnel:

	Annual Salaries
Supervising nurses	$25,000
Nurses	20,000
Aides	9,000

Melford has the following minimum departmental personnel requirements based on total annual patients days:

Annual Patient Days	Aides	Nurses	Supervising Nurses
Up to 21,900	20	10	4
21,900 to 26,000	26	13	4
26,001 to 29,200	30	15	4

These staffing levels represent full-time equivalents. Pediatrics always employs only the minimum number of required full-time personnel. Salaries of supervising nurses, nurses, and aides are therefor fixed within ranges of annual patient days.

Pediatrics operated at 100% capacity on 90 days during the year ended June 30, 19X2. It is estimated that during these 90 days the demand exceeded 20 patients more than capacity. Melford has an additional 20 beds available for rent for the year ending June 30, 19X3. Such additional rental would increase pediatrics' fixed charges based on bed capacity.

REQUIRED:

1. What is the strategic role of CVP analysis for the pediatrics unit of Melford hospital?
2. Determine the minimum number of patient days required for pediatrics to breakeven for the year ending June 30, 19X3, if the additional 20 beds are not rented. Patient demand is unknown, but assume that revenue per patient day, cost per patient day, cost per bed, and salary rates will remain the same as for the year ended June 30, 19X2.
3. Assume that patient demand, revenue, revenue per patient day, cost per patient day, cost per bed, and salary rates for the year ending June 30, 19X3 remain the same as for the year ended June 30, 19X2. Prepare a schedule of increase in revenue and increase in costs for the year ending June 30, 19X3, in order to determine the net increase or decrease in earnings from the additional 20 beds if pediatrics rents this extra capacity from Melford.

(CMA adapted)

8-4. Cost Volume Profit Analysis and Strategy: The ALLTEL Pavilion[1]

The ALLTEL Pavilion in Raleigh, North Carolina is an outdoor amphitheater that provides live concerts to the public from April – October each year. The seven-month season in 1999-2000 hosts an average of 40 concerts with 12 year-round staff planning and managing each season.

SFX Entertainment Inc., which operates the pavilion, is the largest diversified promoter, producer, and venue operator for live entertainment events in the United States. Upon completion of pending acquisitions, SFX will have 71 venues either directly owned or operated under lease or exclusive booking arrangements in 29 of the top 50 U.S. markets, including 14 amphitheaters in nine of top 10 markets.

HISTORY/DEVELOPMENT

The ALLTEL amphitheater has been operating since 1991. It was originally founded and built by the City of Raleigh and Pace Entertainment Company of Houston, Texas. Cellar Door Inc. of Raleigh, NC (another live entertainment producer/promoter) also had a minority interest in the facility. The facility's original name was Hardee's Walnut Creek Amphitheater to indicate its location (near Raleigh) and sponsor. Hardee's Food Systems Inc. paid an annual fee for the amphitheater to carry the Hardee's name and logo on all signs and ads regarding the amphitheater. In 1999 the title sponsor for the amphitheater became ALLTEL, an information technology company that provides wireless communications.

The idea of building an outdoor facility originally came about because the rapidly growing city of Raleigh needed a major entertainment complex. In the late 1980's and early 1990's, Pace Entertainment and the City of Raleigh came to an agreement to build the facility. The City of Raleigh would own the land while Pace Entertainment would assume sole operations of the facility and Cellar Door would do the booking for all the concerts.

In 1998, SFX Entertainment Inc. acquired Pace Entertainment Inc. The Walnut Creek amphitheater facility and its employees became part of SFX Entertainment Inc. Also, in 1999 SFX Entertainment Inc. acquired Cellar Door Inc. and merged with Clear Channel Communications Inc., the largest owner of radio stations in the country. This move brought together both worlds of the entertainment business. While the company has diverse holding, the philosophy of SFX is *One Company, One Mission.* Many companies that are now owned by SFX were once bitter rivals in the concert promoting business. The companies now maintain good working relationships.

PERSONNEL

The organizational chart (appendix A) shows all the positions present at ALLTEL Pavilion. Teamwork is a key objective for the staff. For example, when the marketing department plans a promotion for an up-coming event, it coordinates with sales to see if there is a conflict in sponsorship. It also coordinates with operations so that operations can plan for security and other event-day operations. Finally, the specific budgets of each department are reviewed by the accounting department and head of finance to provide overall financial management of the project.

---

[1] Prepared by Edward Blocher and Kevin Fox. Used with permission.

BRINGING CONCERTS TO REALITY

A concert becomes reality in many steps. First, a group or performer with an interest in performing at ALLTEL sign a contract with Cellar Door, Inc for an open date at the amphitheater. Appendix B is an example of a confirmation sheet provided for the staff at ALLTEL Pavilion. The sheet shows who will be performing, the date of the event, on sale date, and the first date anyone in the staff can talk about it publicly. The staff plans how they will announce the show and what media sources they will utilize. The marketing department starts advertising the on-sale date, with the heaviest advertising coming 2-3 weeks before the performance. Once the show day comes, operations has an idea of attendance and the marketing department notifies everyone of what radio stations will be on site doing promotions.

Appendix C is an example of the information sheet used on the day of a show. The event-day plans include the scheduling of local and regional contractors to handle the parking and concessions. Also, a time is specified for gate openings, all special promotions are identified, and gate policies regarding chair rentals and other issues are spelled out. The job of the staff during a concert is to make sure every patron of the ALLTEL Pavilion has a pleasant experience and that the mission of the company is clearly seen by everyone that "a concert...*it's better live.*" After a show, a local contractor handles the clean up.

KEY BUSINESS ISSUES

Marketing has an important role in the success of ALLTEL Pavilion, but marketing expenditures are carefully watched. For every show, the marketing budget is limited to $20,000. For some shows it is difficult to stay within the budget, since the Pavilion serves a 5-market region consisting of Raleigh-Durham, Fayetteville, Wilmington, Greensboro, and the Carolina Coast. Most of the marketing budget is spent on advertising with radio and print in the designated regions. While these sources of advertising were viewed initially as cost-based strategic business units (SBUs), SFX now feels it is important to turn these sources of advertising into profit-based SBUs. Different advertising media produce different results, and the effect is not only on the number of tickets sold, but also revenue from parking, merchandise, and concessions. The advertising rates in the Raleigh-Durham region are comparable to the rates in Washington, D.C. The rates have increased two hundred percent over the last five years while the budgets per show are only up fifteen percent over this time span.

As the music industry is growing rapidly, so are the artist costs. The average cost for an artist is approximately $160,000. This number grows annually, so that it is very important for the ALLTEL Pavilion to reduce non-artist costs. There are a number of operating costs at ALLTEL Pavilion, including expenses for parking, security, concessions, and merchandise. Some of the artists are paid on a fixed-fee basis, and others are paid on a per capita basis. The artist paid on fixed base is guaranteed the same fee whether 100 or 15,000 people attend (the capacity of the Pavilion is approximately 20,000 attendance). These shows are normally the shows where the projected attendance is under 10,000. Also, these are the shows that make marketing so important. When ticket sales are low, it becomes harder and harder to stretch $20,000 across a five market region. The entire staff knows that lower ticket sells also mean less money spent on parking, concessions, and merchandise.

The artists paid on a per capita basis pay close attention to ticket sales. The number of "comp" tickets is significantly lower for these shows.[2] It is a little easier to market these shows for the reason that the artists are such big names that they in effect

---

[2] "Comp" tickets are free tickets distributed throughout the community by the management and staff of SFX.

market themselves. Therefore, it is easier to keep marketing costs down for a per capita base show.

The marketing department uses many tools to make the concerts profitable. It uses the parking service to pass out flyers for upcoming events. Also, it trades tickets for online spots in the radio industry and gives local businesses tickets in exchange for advertising on their premises. The marketing staff can completely break down ticket sales geographically over the five-market region. It is important to know the demographics of the five regions and compare them with the demographics of the bands. The more ALLTEL Pavilion can know about the fans, the more they know about where to spend the $20,000.

As an illustration, Appendix D shows the entire marketing budget for the KISS concert for the 2000 season. Notice that the marketing department went over budget. This can be seen in "Net Flash Expenses" at the end of the appendix. Net Flash Expenses represents the actual amount spent to promote the KISS concert, and at $27,611, it is above the $20,000 budget (the "gross" amount is the amount billed to Alltel by the various media, while the "net" is after the standard industry 15% discount). Sections 1, 2, and 3 of Appendix D show the breakdown of total media expense by radio station, TV and print media. The "gross cash" column of these sections refers to the amount billed to ALLTEL by the media, while "trade" and "promo" refer to concert tickets provided to the stations and newspaper in exchange for advertising. Thus "total media" is the total value of advertising, a combination of cash and tickets-in exchange. The reason for the excess over budget in this case is that KISS was guaranteed a large fixed fee, and the Pavilion needed to promote the concert extensively in order to reduce the risk of loss on the concert.

FUNDING AND FLASH REPORT

The main sources of funding for the Pavilion are ticket revenues (62 %), concession revenues (20 %), merchandising revenues (7%), parking revenues (4 %), and sponsorship revenues (3%). Appendix E is a mock flash report for an example show, The KFBS Allstars. A flash report is a projection of what a concert will cost and what revenues will be received. The guaranteed talent costs ($160,635) is the amount the KFBS Allstars are guaranteed for the show. "Attendance" is the number of projected paying ticket holders, while the "drop count" is total attendance, both for paid tickets and comp tickets. The Flash Report then projects total revenues including parking, food, and merchandise. The direct costs for parking, merchandise and concessions are determined based on a contract which includes both a percentage of revenues (10%) and a fixed fee. Operating expenses are an allocation of the total of fixed production, operating, and advertising expenses. These are then added to the direct costs for concessions, merchandise, parking, insurance to determine total operating expenses.

REQUIRED:

1) How would you describe the competitive strategy of the ALLTEL Pavilion at Walnut Creek? marketing Carefully managed budget
2) For the show, The KFBS Allstars, how many tickets must ALLTEL Pavilion sell to break even
3) What ways might the management of ALLTEL Pavilion increase operating income?

1999 — ALLTEL Pavilion at Walnut Creek

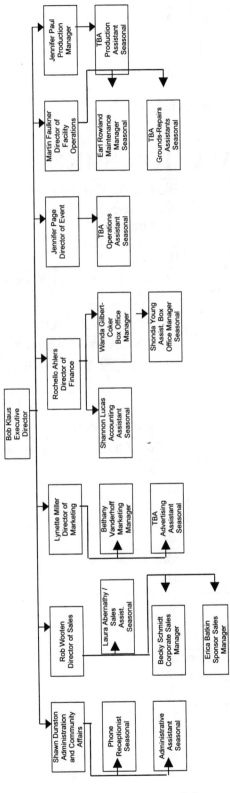

Bob Klaus
Executive Director

Shawn Dunston
Administration and Community Affairs
- Phone Receptionist Seasonal
- Administrative Assistant Seasonal

Rob Wooten
Director of Sales
- Laura Abernathy / Sales Assist. Seasonal
- Becky Schmidt Corporate Sales Manager
- Erica Batkin Sponsor Sales Manager

Lynette Miller
Director of Marketing
- Bethany Vanderhoff Marketing Manager
- TBA Advertising Assistant Seasonal

Rochello Ahlers
Director of Finance
- Shannon Lucas Accounting Assistant Seasonal
- Wanda Gilbert-Coker Box Office Manager
  - Shonda Young Assist. Box Office Manager Seasonal

Jennifer Page
Director of Event
- TBA Operations Assistant Seasonal

Martin Faulkner
Director of Facility Operations
- Earl Rowland Maintenance Manager Seasonal
- TBA Grounds-Repairs Assistants Seasonal

Jennifer Paul
Production Manager
- TBA Production Assistant Seasonal

Appendix A

ALLTEL
PAVILION
at walnut creek

LAST UPDATED: **July 19, 2000 (All changes in bold.)**
IN HOUSE USE ONLY!

SHOW CONFIRMATION SHEET

Event Name	Blue Collar Comedy-PAVILION ONLY
Music	Jeff Foxworthy Bill Engvall Larry The Cable Guy Ron White
Show Date, Show Start Time	Friday August 18, 2000 @ 8:00 pm
Announce Date	Friday June 14, 2000 @ 7:00 am
On-Sale Date	Thursday July 20, 2000 @ 10:00 am
Ticket Prices	$40.00-Covered Reserved $32.50-Uncovered Reserved
On-Sale Promotion and Duration	N/A
Number of Grass Passport Vouchers	Two (Open-Air Reserved Only)
Coupons	$5.00 off all seats
Group Discount Level	$5.00 off all seats for groups of 20+
Comp Policy (None, Limited, NTTD)	Limited
Kids Free?	No
Ticket Limit	N/A
Presented By	N/A
Concert Series	Winn-Dixie Superstar Summer
Tour Sponsor	N/A
Cameras Allowed?	No

Bob Klaus   Marketing   Cellar Door
Cc: Ticketmaster, Teresa Franzen, Debbie Wainwright

Appendix B

YES/Kansas

Event:	YES/Kansas
Venue:	ALLTEL Pavilion at Walnut Creek
Event Date:	7/27/00 Thursday
Parking Opens:	5:30 PM
Venue Gates Open:	5:30 PM
Showtime:	7:30 PM

Estimated Attendance:

Low:	5000	to	High: 10000

Front Gate Inspection: **Medium**

Event Workbook: 7/27/00
Attention: All Departments — Volume Services

Set Times:

	Start		End
Kansas	7:30 PM	to	8:30 PM
Intermission	8:30 PM	to	8:55 PM
YES	8:55 PM	to	10:55 PM
		to	
		to	
		to	
		to	
		to	
		to	
		to	

Gate Policies:

OKAY	PROHIBITED
Backpacks-Bags	Coolers
Blankets	Drugs-Alcohol
Umbrellas	Lawn Chairs
Strollers	Laser Pointers
Water Bottles	Audio Recorders
	Video Recorders
	Cameras

Operations Notes:

Alcohol Cut-off (est.): 9:30 pm
Kids Free - Yes
Lawn Chair Rentals? – Yes
Parking – Front Gate Preferred $15
Parking – Regular Fee $7
Softball Parking – TBD

Operations Checklist:
Mike – FAMILY ZONE!

Humid, mostly sunny, 85 degrees

Production Information

Production Load-in: 9:00 am
Tour Accountant: John Huie
Production Mgr: Ken Kaler

G. Malpass – 3:00pm – TBA
M. Montgomery – load-in to load-out
J. Page - load-in to TBA
B. Klaus – load-in to load-out

Marketing-Sales Activities:	Activity:	Times:	Note:
Broadcast Booth	WRDU		
Camel Casbah	Open	5:30 pm to 10:00 p,	
Corporate Village	N/a		
Fireworks	No		
Flyers	Marketing	Ingress	McLaurin to Hand-out
Inflatables	Mt. Dew, Pepsi		
Kids Free	YES		
Levi's First Stage	State of Consciousness	6:00 pm – 7:00 pm	
Other Marketing Activities	None		
Other Sales Activities	AMEX, Primgles, Pepsi Challenge, Prize Patrol		
Parking Promotions	Park-up-Front		Pay $7 – park in Preferred
Parties	None		
Radio Stations	WRDU		
Set-ups			
VIP Club	Normal Operation	5:30 pm to 11:30 pm	

Appendix C

ALLTEL PAVILION MARKETING GROUP

AS OF:
07/19/00

1. **RADIO**	% BUD 60.7%	GROSS CASH	TRADE	PROMO	TOTAL MEDIA	NET CASH
WRDU	44.4%	$8,750.00	$225.00	$121,250.00	$130,225.00	$7,437.50
WRCQ	6.2%	$1,214.00	$810.00	$22,521.00	$24,545.00	$1,031.90
WBBB	12.2%	$2,400.00	$2,400.00	$11,025.00	$15,825.00	$2,040.00
WRAL	12.2%	$2,400.00	$1,050.00	$8,250.00	$11,700.00	$2,040.00
WRBZ-AM	2.4%	$480.00	$480.00	$9,356.67	$10,316.67	$408.00
WSFM	2.7%	$540.00	$0.00	$8,885.00	$9,425.00	$459.00
WSFL	9.1%	$1,785.00	$720.00	$9,088.33	$11,593.33	$1,517.25
WKRR	9.6%	$1,900.00	$1,140.00	$8,707.50	$11,747.50	$1,615.00
WRQR	0.0%	$0.00	$0.00	$20,150.00	$20,150.00	$0.00
WXQR	0.0%	$0.00	$0.00	$8,080.00	$8,080.00	$0.00
WKQB	0.0%	$0.00	$0.00	$1,075.00	$1,075.00	$0.00
WPXX	0.0%	$0.00	$0.00	$1,405.00	$1,405.00	$0.00
WXRA	0.0%	$0.00	$0.00	$4,140.00	$4,140.00	$0.00
WPTF-AM Calendar	1.3%	$250.00	$0.00	$0.00	$250.00	$212.50
TOTAL RADIO		$19,719.00	$6,825.00	$233,933.50	$260,477.50	$16,761.15

2. **TV**	%BUD 10.2%	GROSS CASH	TRADE	PROMO	TOTAL MEDIA	NET CASH
WRAZ-TV	18.9%	$625.00	$0.00	$0.00	$625.00	$531.25
WLFL-TV	52.3%	$1,730.00	$0.00	$1,375.00	$3,105.00	$1,470.50
WRAL-TV	8.9%	$295.25	$0.00	$0.00	$295.25	$250.96
WCTI-TV	0.0%	$0.00	$0.00	$1,750.00	$1,750.00	$0.00
WXLV-TV	1.7%	$55.15	$0.00	$0.00	$55.15	$46.88
WSFX-TV	0.0%	$0.00	$0.00	$750.00	$750.00	$0.00
TIMEWARNER CABLE	18.2%	$602.49	$0.00	$6,250.00	$6,852.49	$512.12
TOTALTV		$3,307.89	$0.00	$10,125.00	$13,432.89	$2,811.71

3. **PRINT**	%BUD 14.5%	GROSS CASH	TRADE	PROMO	TOTAL MEDIA	NET CASH
NEWS & OBSERVER	28.5%	$1,343.72	$518.91	$0.00	$1,862.63	$1,142.16
INDEPENDENT	13.3%	$629.41	$1,048.80	$1,259.71	$2,937.92	$535.00
HERALD-SUN	4.7%	$220.59	$736.12	$86.68	$1,043.39	$187.50
THE BEAT	0.9%	$41.18	$24.50	$0.00	$65.68	$35.00
TRIAD STYLE	4.7%	$220.59	$613.97	$0.00	$834.56	$187.50
UP & COMING	0.0%	$0.00	$450.00	$0.00	$450.00	$0.00
ENCORE	1.7%	$82.35	$115.00	$0.00	$197.35	$70.00
THIS WEEK	3.7%	$176.47	$498.72	$27.03	$702.22	$150.00
DAILY REFLECTOR	0.0%	$0.00	$412.06	$0.00	$412.06	$0.00
TRIANGLE POINTER	0.9%	$44.12	$75.00	$0.00	$119.12	$37.50
ADDED PRINT	0.0%	$0.00	$84.30	$0.00	$84.30	$0.00
CITYSEARCH.COM	0.0%	$0.00	$250.00	$0.00	$250.00	$0.00
SPECTATOR	1.2%	$58.82	$0.00	$250.00	$308.82	$50.00
FAYETTEVILLE OBSE	38.4%	$1,811.12	$0.00	$0.00	$1,811.12	$1,539.45
COLLEGE ADS	2.0%	$93.21	$0.00	$0.00	$93.21	$79.23
TOTAL PRINT		$4,721.58	$4,827.38	$1,623.42	$11,172.38	$4,013.34

Appendix D

8-12

4.	AD PRODUCTION	NET EXPENSE	6. **PR EXPENSE**	NET EXPENSE
	Radio Production	$847.50	PR Amortization	$500.00
	TV Production (Footage & Spot)	$864.00	Marketing Asst.	$0.00
	Black 4 Copper	$862.82	Staff Photographer	$0.00
	Additional Black + Copper	$0.00	Mass Photo Copying	$25.00

5.	POSTERS/FLYERS	NET EXPENSE	7. **OTHER**	NET EXPENSE
	Calendar Production	$375.00		$0.00
	Banner Production	$0.00	MobilTrak	$100.00
	Flyer Production	$0.00	Fed-Ex/Shipping	$175.00
	Direct Mail Prod. & Postage	$0.00	Comp Tickets	$0.00
	Coming Attractions	$275.90	Misc 1	$0.00

MEDIA RECAP	TOTAL VALUE
RADIO	$260,477.50
TELEVISION	$13,432.89
PRINT	$11,172.38
AD PRODUCTION	$2,574.32
CALENDARS/FLYERS	$650.90
PR EXPENSES	$525.00
OTHER EXPENSES	$275.00
TOTAL VALUE	$289,107.99

NET "FLASH" EXPENSES

			NET	GROSS
1.	RADIO	0.0%	$16,761.15	$19,719.00
2.	TELEVISION	0.0%	$2,811.71	$3,307.89
3.	PRINT	0.0%	$4,013.34	$4,721.58
4.	AD PROD.	0.0%	$2,574.32	$2,574.32
5.	POSTERS/FLYERS	0.0%	$650.90	$650.90
6.	PR EXPENSES	0.0%	$525.00	$525.00
7.	OTHER	0.0%	$275.00	$275.00
		TOTAL	$27,611.42	$31,773.69
			NET FLASH	GROSS

Appendix D (continued)

Generic Amphitheater Model – Show By Show

ARTIST NAME	Input	The KFBS Allstars
ACTIVITY/EVENT NUMBER		0010310001
EVENT MONTH		7
EVENT DATE		7/31/2000
Number of A Seats		2,778
Number of B Seats		2,845
Number of C Seats		1,747
Number of D Seats		881
TOTAL Number of Seats		8,251
Price of A SEATS		$36.29
Price of B SEATS		$22.22
Price of C SEATS		$11.31
Price of D SEATS		$4.92
AVG TIX PRICE NET OF TAX		$22.12
PROJECTED NET ADMISSIONS	40100	$182,479
TAX RATE		3.00%
TALENT %		88.03%
GUARANTEE / TALENT COSTS	50002	$160,635
# OF PERFORMANCES		1
# OF RENTALS		0
ATTENDANCE		8,251
DROP COUNT @	5.00%	10,349
ADMISSIONS (net of tax)		$182,479
Per Capita		$17.63
FACILITY CHARGE	40208	$24,010
Per Capita		$2.91
S/C REBATES	40224	$16,184
Per Capita		$1.96
REVENUE FROM TICKETING		$222,673
Per Capita		$26.99
PARKING	40216	$19,767
Per Capita		$1.91
FOOD	40204	$79,273
Per Capita		$7.66
MERCHANDISE	40214	$36,428
Per Capita		$3.52
RENTALS	40222	$0.00
REV FROM ANCILLARIES		$135,468
Per Capita		$13.09
TOTAL REVENUE		$358,141
Per Capita		$34.61
PARKING CONTRA	40900	$4,448
% of parking revenue		22.0%
CONCESSION CONTRA	40901	$43,356
% of food revenue		58.0%
MERCHANDISE CONTRA	40902	$17,826
% of merchandise revenue		77.0%
TOTAL DIRECT COSTS		$226,264
Per Capita		$21.86
PERCENT		63.2%
GROSS PROFIT		$131,877
Per Capita		$12.74
PERCENT		36.8%
OPERATING EXPENSES:		
TOTAL PRODUCTION EXPENSE		$15,506
TOTAL OPERATIONS EXPENSE		$14,991
TOTAL OTHER VAR. EXPENSE		$14,323
TOTAL ADVERTISING EXPENSE		$20,030
TOTAL OPERATING EXP		$64,850
Per Capita		$6.27
PERCENT		18.1%
OPERATING INCOME		$67,027
Per Capita		$6.48
PERCENT		18.7%

Appendix E

DETAIL OTHER CONCERT
VARIABLE EXPENSE:

			8251		10349
			2	1402.67	1759.33
Insurance Expense per person	50306	$0.17		2887.85	3622.15
COGS - Concession per person	50321	$0.35		9241.12	11590.88
COGS - Merchandise Inventory per person	50322	$1.12			
COGS - Parking per person	50324	$0.08	660.08		827.92
Other Variable Concert Expense per person	50399	$0.02	165.02		206.98
Amphi Show By Show		$0.00			
TOTAL OTHER VAR EXP		$14,323	14356.74		

1.74   18007.26

Appendix E (continued)

total seats 8251 Attendance
Avg. tix price 22.12

3 9.48
- .191
- .766
- .352
- 1.74
unit cm 36.431

FC
15.506
14,991
20,030
160,635
2,471
35,429
14,183
263245

$$\frac{36.431}{39.48} = .92277 \text{ cm}\%.$$

$$Be = \frac{FC}{Cm\%.}$$

$$\frac{263,245}{.92277\,10233} = \$ 285,276.62$$

8-5. Sensitivity Analysis; Regression Analysis

Fast Shop, Inc is a chain of 10 convenience stores located in and around Houston, Texas. Selected operating data for the 10 stores for the most recent month is shown below. All but two of Fast Shop's stores sell gasoline as well as convenience items, primarily food, beverage, and household products. Because of zoning and other restrictions, the other stores sell only convenience items. Jim Sacco, the chief financial officer for Fast Shop, plans to utilize multiple regression analysis to determine which stores are most effective in generating sales, given differences in size (square feet) among the stores, differences in advertising and promotion costs for the stores, and whether or not the store sells gasoline. Jim knows that stores which sell gasoline typically have better than average sales because gasoline sales bring in sales for other convenience items.

Jim also knows that if regression analysis can be used to develop a sensitivity analysis of the effect of advertising and store size on sales. If he prepares a multiple regression analysis in which all the numerical variables are transformed by their natural logarithm, then the coefficients for each independent variable in the resulting regression equation will represent the percentage effect on sales for a given percentage change in the independent variable.

Selected Operating Information for the 10 Locations of Fast Shop Inc

Store	Sales	Advertising	Square Feet	Gas Sales
1	$ 56,034	$ 5,540	2,200	No
2	23,045	3,310	1,200	Yes
3	89,337	8,837	2,800	No
4	66,073	11,200	2,000	No
5	18,993	1,879	1,500	No
6	64,926	6,648	2,300	No
7	28,773	3,756	1,500	No
8	46,294	5,899	1,800	No
9	73,546	6,899	2,400	Yes
10	36,968	5,100	1,600	No
	$ 503,989	$ 59,068		

REQUIRED:

1. Using regression analysis, determine which store(s) seem to be operating below their potential, given advertising expenses, gasoline sales, and size?
2. Using regression analysis and log transforms, determine the sensitivity of sales to advertising and store size.

TOOLS FOR DEALING WITH UNCERTAINTY

Sophisticated spreadsheet software incorporating probability functions can help you forecast more accurately.

BY DAVID R. FORDHAM, CMA, AND S. BROOKS MARSHALL

Aside from the proverbial death and taxes, there is little in life that is certain. As management accountants, we recognize that one of our most crucial uncertainties involves capital investments. Why, then, are so many of us still using analysis tools designed for fixed numbers?

Let's take a simple example. Your company is considering a $1 million capital investment. The project is expected to return 12% per year, with the annual profits reinvested annually. What will be your final compounded return at the end of 20 years?

If you are like most management accountants, you will use the traditional compounding formula (multiplying your initial investment times one plus the rate of return raised to the 20th power). This time-honored analysis approach tells you that your final compounded return should be $9,646,293. But is this the best answer?

Unfortunately, it is not—at least for most capital investment projects. The compounding formula works well for investments in which the annual rate of return

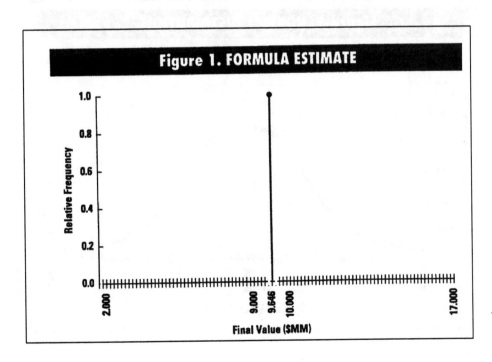

Figure 1. FORMULA ESTIMATE

Relative Frequency

Final Value ($MM)

is fixed. But this is not the situation with most capital investments. While the initial outlay may be a fairly firm number, the annual rate of return most likely will vary from year to year. Thus, this project might yield a 25% (or higher) return in a good year and a 0% return (or even a loss) in another year. Even a relatively safe capital investment (say, a market-rate financial instrument) can involve variable rates of return.

But the compounding formula operates as though the rate of return is exactly 12% for all 20 years, with no variability. Because the formula has no way of recognizing the uncertainty in the annual rates of return, it may not be providing the best answer.

The most popular capital budgeting tools (the compounding formula, the internal rate of return, and net present value calculations) are simple to use and can be handled with little more than a pocket calculator. But they all suffer from a major drawback: They provide a single-number answer by assuming that their input is a set of fixed or known numbers, with no provision for variability.

A POPULAR WAY OF DEALING WITH UNCERTAINTY: SENSITIVITY ANALYSIS

One way of providing for uncertainty is to rerun the calculations several times using different fixed values. Today's computerized spreadsheets make it easy to play "what-if" games. By changing the numbers and re-performing the calculations, we can generate various possible outcomes. Comparing these different outcomes generally provides a better analysis than merely looking at a single point estimate.

Continuing our example above, a modern analyst would use the compounding formula to arrive at the $9,646,293 figure and also to provide alternative possibilities from the what-if analyses, showing the effect of changing the estimated rate of return from 12% to, say, 10% or 14%. By reporting multiple possible final values, the analyst is providing more and better information than by reporting a single point estimate. The name for this technique is "sensitivity analysis."

This approach provides a much more realistic means of analyzing uncertain situations than simply using the compounding formula alone, but it still uses analysis tools that operate on only one set of numbers at a time. The fact remains that no matter how many times we rerun the calculations, the formula still operates as though the rate of return is constant throughout all 20 years of the project's life. Ideally, our analysis should employ a tool that incorporates the possible changes from year to year in the annual rate of return. Even more important, we need to know the probability of earning different amounts from our project, not just a list of some possible amounts.

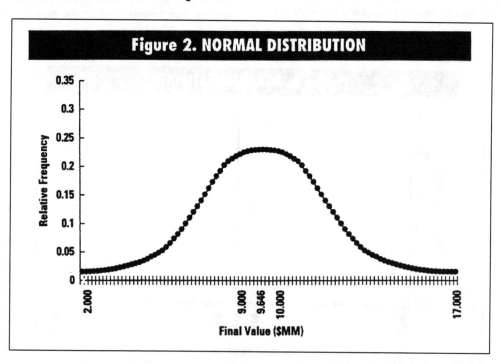

Figure 2. NORMAL DISTRIBUTION

A BETTER WAY: PROBABILITY DISTRIBUTION

Statisticians tell us that the law of large numbers applies to most situations involving uncertainty and that variable numbers tend to cluster around a central value or mean. Financial research has shown that annual rates of return on most modern investments do indeed form a "normal distribution" around a mean. Values close to the mean occur with greater frequency than values farther away from the mean. If you can establish a reasonable estimate of the mean and have some idea of the range of possible realistic values, you generally can get by with handling your uncertainty as a probability distribution.

Traditional analysis tools (the compounding formula in our example) yield a single point estimate of the project's final value (see Figure 1). If we were to use the formula by itself, our analysis would show that the project will return exactly $9,646,293. Most management accountants, however, recognize the uncertainty and report several different possible outcomes, assuming that the most likely final values will center around $9,646,293. Values far away from this figure will be unlikely, while values close to it will be more likely. The analyst even may illustrate the relative likelihood of the different outcomes with such a probability distribution as that in Figure 2.

Figure 2 is superior to Figure 1 in that it shows relative likelihoods of many possible final values ranging from a very unlikely $2 million figure all the way up to an equally unlikely $17 million. The most likely values, however, are close to $9,646,293. And most analysts assume that the probability curve is symmetric, as shown in Figure 2. In other words, they assume the chances of earning slightly less than the projected amount are about the same as the chances of earning slightly more than the projected amount.

But is this the case? Assuming the rate of return does average 12% over the life of the project, are the chances of slightly underperforming the estimate the same as the chances of slightly outperforming it? It might surprise you to learn that Figure 3 is actually a more accurate illustration of the likely final values of our project!

SURPRISES FROM MODERN ANALYSIS TOOLS

Figure 3 reveals some startling new information about our project. First, the most probable final value (represented by the peak of the probability curve) is

---

Some Surprising Statistics

When using analysis models that approximate reality surprising results sometimes emerge. Take the probability distribution of our compound investment's final value. Most people, including many financial analysts, would assume that if the annual rate of return varies in a normal (and symmetric) fashion across the 20-year life of the project, then the possible final values also should vary in a symmetric pattern. This makes intuitive sense. But it isn't what actually happens.

Consider closely the value of the investment at the end of the first year. The exact rate of return during that year is unknown, but it will vary around a 12% expected value. If we expect the rate of return to vary in a normal fashion, at the end of the first year we will have a range of possible final values that will be centered around $1.12 million (for our $1 million original investment). This probability distribution is symmetric because it is the product of a fixed amount (the original investment) multiplied by a normal probability distribution (the rate of return).

Most things change in the second year, though. This time, we are not multiplying a constant by a normal distribution. We are multiplying one normal distribution (the final value at the end of the first year) by another normal distribution. It yields a skewed, asymmetric distribution known in statistical circles as a log-normal distribution.

The skewness of the probability distribution becomes even more pronounced in the third year, and the symmetry continues to degrade as more and more compounding periods are added. By the 20th year, you have the noticeably asymmetric distribution shown in Figure 3. The unusual shape of the distribution curve and the probabilities associated with each of the possible outcomes of the project derive directly from the compounding of the investment. Once the initial investment is made, all future values are unknown figures. Using probability distributions to illustrate these unknown values is a more accurate approach than simply treating them as fixed estimates. Therefore, the asymmetric probability of the project's final value is a better predictor of the project's performance than a perfectly symmetric curve fitted around the traditional financial formula's output.

not the $9,646,293 predicted by the traditional analysis formula! Rather, it is somewhat less. From looking at Figure 3, you see that it is more likely that our project's final value will be approximately $9 million rather than the approximately $9.6 million reported by the traditional analysis approach.

Management accountants and financial analysts who have for years relied on the formulas are astounded to see this increase in the likelihood of underperforming the formula estimate. But even more surprising is the fact that the probability distribution is not symmetric. For example, the chances of the project yielding half a million dollars less than the $9,646,293 are actually much greater (perhaps two or three times as great) than the chances of earning half a million dollars more than that amount. In other words, while the chance of slightly underperforming the formula's prediction has increased, the chance of outperforming the formula's prediction by the same amount has gone down quite dramatically. Also, the probability of "losing one's shirt" has diminished somewhat, while the probability of making much more than the formula estimate has increased.

What causes these surprising results? The answer lies in the fact that the rate of return can vary from year to year. Each year's earnings are dependent not only on that single year's rate of return, but also on all previous years' rates, because the project involves compounding reinvestment. Thus, if you assume that the rate of return averages 12% annually over the course of the 20-year project, and you assume that the changes occur in accordance with the law of large numbers (specifically, in accordance with a normal probability distribution from year to year), you still come up with the skewed probability curve for the final value of the project shown in Figure 3 because of the changing rates of return. (For an explanation of this phenomenon, see the sidebar, "Some Surprising Statistics.")

SOPHISTICATED TOOLS, BUT EASY TO USE

Probability curves such as Figure 3 can give a much more accurate picture of the likely outcome of projects under uncertainty. These analyses can be generated by a little-used analysis tool that is included in most of today's modern spreadsheet software. This tool enables us to create mathematical models that more closely approximate real-life situations involving uncertainty.

As our capital budgeting problem involves an uncertain annual rate of return that varies from year to year, we must develop an analysis model with a rate of return that varies from year to year. In addition, we need to analyze many different combinations of these varying annual rates of return.

Until a few years ago, creating such a model required extensive computer programming, weeks of effort, and significant time on a large mainframe or

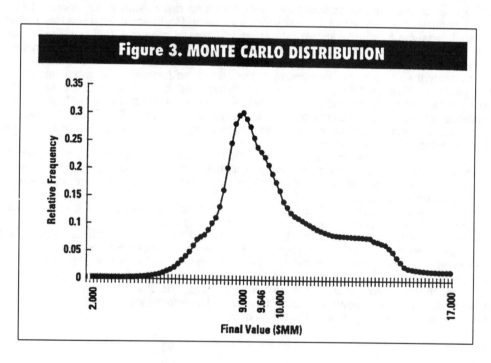

Figure 3. MONTE CARLO DISTRIBUTION

Figure 4		
Year	Rate of Return	Final Value
1	12.00%	$1,120,000
2	12.00%	$1,254,400
3	12.00%	$1,404,928
4	12.00%	$1,573,519
5	12.00%	$1,762,342
6	12.00%	$1,973,823
7	12.00%	$2,210,681
8	12.00%	$2,475,963
9	12.00%	$2,773,079
10	12.00%	$3,105,848
11	12.00%	$3,478,550
12	12.00%	$3,895,976
13	12.00%	$4,363,493
14	12.00%	$4,887,112
15	12.00%	$5,473,566
16	12.00%	$6,130,394
17	12.00%	$6,866,041
18	12.00%	$7,689,966
19	12.00%	$8,612,762
20	12.00%	$9,646,293

Figure 5		
Year	Rate of Return	Final Value
1	11.30%	$1,113,000
2	12.10%	$1,247,673
3	13.30%	$1,413,614
4	14.10%	$1,612,933
5	9.00%	$1,758,097
6	10.00%	$1,933,907
7	13.00%	$2,185,315
8	15.50%	$2,524,038
9	16.50%	$2,940,505
10	14.00%	$3,352,175
11	14.50%	$3,838,241
12	8.00%	$4,145,300
13	11.00%	$4,601,283
14	7.00%	$4,923,373
15	10.30%	$5,430,480
16	13.10%	$6,141,873
17	11.50%	$6,848,188
18	9.50%	$7,498,766
19	14.20%	$8,563,591
20	12.05%	$9,595,504

The tools necessary to construct probability distributions can be found on all of the popular Windows-based spread-sheets—Lotus 1-2-3, Excel, Supercalc, and Quattro-Pro. Specific instructions vary from package to package, but they are contained in the On-Line Help features. Look for Help topics involving random number generators, probability distributions, and statistical tools.

To analyze our sample problem properly, we begin by constructing a spreadsheet showing how the project's returns will be reinvested (Figure 4). But instead of the 12% annual rate of return for all 20 years, we want to substitute a variable rate of return, one that is expected to average 12% over the 20 years.

Because we assume the rates of return will average 12% and might vary between 0% and 25%, we can say that, in any one year, the rate of return will come from a normal distribution with a mean of 12% and a standard deviation of about 6%. We use the computer's random number generator to draw 20 values from a distribution with a mean of 12 and a standard deviation of 6. Then we incorporate these values as the assumed rate of return for each of our 20 years. This approach gives us one possible outcome of our capital project. In other words, if it just so happens that the annual rates of return come out as shown in Figure 5, then our project's final value will be $9,595,504.[1]

The particular combination of annual rates of return shown in Figure 5 is only one of many possible combinations. We also must look at others. In fact, we need to duplicate the scenario many times (a technique known as Monte Carlo analysis) to represent the many different combinations of annual rates of return. By constructing hundreds, or even thousands, of possible combinations and then displaying a histogram of the final outcomes, we begin to get a feel for the likely performance of our project.

There are numerous add-in products on the market that enhance the major spreadsheet packages, making it easy to perform thousands of Monte Carlo scenarios. These software products are surprisingly easy to learn and operate, especially for users already familiar with the Windows point-and-click system. One such package, known as @RISK, is able to perform 1,000 iterations of the above scenario with only a few keystrokes. Therefore, the calculation of 2,000 scenarios of our capital budgeting problem can be performed in less than three minutes on a 486 computer. Furthermore, most of the packages automatically display the histogram upon completion of their calculations, giving you an instant picture of the likely outcomes of your investment.

minicomputer. Today, though, with the recent advances in personal computers, including larger memory capacities, faster and more powerful numerical processors, and advanced software, we now have the ability to build such mathematical models on our desktops in a matter of minutes.

Good News, Bad News: What the Picture Tells Us

Figure 3 is a much more accurate portrayal of our project's expected performance. Most important, it presents some new information that might make a difference in the decision as to whether to accept or reject the project. Let's take a close look at exactly what this new tool is telling us that we didn't know before. To make the comparison, we will use the compounding formula's predicted value ($9,646,293) as a base because it is the figure that most analysts would have presented to management.

First, as mentioned in the text, the probability of the project's value coming in slightly under the base is much higher than the probability of hitting the base or of hitting any other possible value. Some managers may consider it misleading to say that the project likely will return $9,646,293 when, in fact, the most probable return is less than this amount.

More significant, the chance of slightly outperforming the base by a given amount is much less than the probability of slightly underperforming the base by the same amount. Again, managers may consider it misleading to quote the $9,646,293 figure when the chances of making a million less than this figure may be two or three times the likelihood of making a million more than the figure.

The bad news, then, is that the project probably will slightly underperform the base estimate and probably will not slightly overperform the base estimate. But wait! There is some good news, too.

Look at the ends of the curve. The possibility of losing your shirt on the investment has almost disappeared compared with the chance of making a killing. In other words, the possibility of coming out far under the base prediction is extremely low, compared with the chance of outperforming the base by the same large amount. Managers who don't mind the risk of slightly underperforming the base prediction but who want to avoid an extremely low final value—especially if it means a chance at yielding an extremely high final value—might be more inclined to accept the project if they had access to this probability distribution. In short, decision makers find the probability distribution analysis a much richer source of information than the traditional sensitivity analysis using common capital budgeting techniques.

MORE PROBLEM SOLVING

This same technique (drawing numbers from a probability distribution and constructing a histogram of the final outcomes) can be used to simulate the uncertainty of discount rates for net present value analysis. It also can be used to simulate the uncertainty surrounding cash flow amounts, future revenues, and expenses. Yet another use for it might involve modeling possible changes in tax rates or inflation rates—or almost any uncertain figure. All that is needed is some idea (or assumption) about the possible behavior of the uncertain value, such as its expected average and likely variability. Often the assumption can be simply the one that would have been used in the formula analysis, coupled with the estimated rate of variability over time.

By constructing a model that resembles the real situation more closely, you can see that the likely outcome of a capital project may be very different from what you normally would expect, based on the traditional analysis output. The likelihood of doing very poorly, fairly well, or extremely well on a given project may surprise you and other decision makers. A realistic probability distribution requires additional information, which cannot be provided by the traditional analysis tools. This information even may affect management's decision in some situations (see the sidebar, "Good News, Bad News.") Regardless, it always is better to provide management with the best information possible.

THERE IS STILL UNCERTAINTY

Of course, any time we try to predict the future, we are dealing with unknown information. Modem analysis tools are only as good as the input with which they are provided. We will continue to encounter problems trying to estimate future returns' means and their variability. But for a given set of input information, these sophisticated tools can greatly expand the richness of information provided as output.

Remember: The traditional capital budgeting tools may be providing your decision makers with misleading figures regarding the likely performance of your investment projects. A much better tool would be one that enables you to construct a mathematical model that depicts the actual situation more accurately, including year-to-year variations. With the advent of powerful spreadsheet software incorporating statistical probability functions, it now is feasible to perform analyses that portray the real situation more accurately. By using these more sophisticated models, you can do a much better job of forecasting the likelihood of possible outcomes, which can lead to your making better decisions for your company.

David R. Fordham, CMA, CPA, Ph.D, is an assistant professor at James Madison University's School of Accounting. He is a member of the Virginia Skyline Chapter, through which this article was submitted. He can be reached at (540) 568-3024, phone, or e-mail, fordhadr@jmu.edu.

S. Brooks Marshall, CFA. DBA, is an associate professor of finance at James Madison University's College of Business. He can be reached at (540) 568-3075, phone, or e-mail, marshasb@jmu.edu.

---

[i] Note that the annual rates of return in Figure 5 do indeed average 12% across the 20-year life of the project and that the final value is less than the $9,648,293 predicted by the formula. This is in line with the probability curve shown in Figure 3, which predicts that final values slightly less than the $9,646,293 will occur with greater frequency than amounts slightly above it.

Chapter 9
Strategy and the Master Budget

Cases

9-1   Emerson Electric company

Readings

"How to Set Up a Budgeting and Planning System"

This article demonstrates the setting up of a budgeting and planning system for Penn Fuel Gas Inc., a public utility holding company that provides natural gas storage and transportation services. It stresses the need to review the chart of accounts, account classification and the reporting system of the firm. The discussion includes factors to be considered in the budgeting process and moves to update its current accounting information system.

Discussion Questions:
1. What motivates PFG to install a budgeting and planning system?
2. Why is flexibility very important for PFG's budgeting system to be effective?
3. What problems that the budget manager at PFG had to resolve before setting up a budgeting system? Do you find these problems unique to PFG?
4. Why the authors suggest that a thorough review of the firm's chart of accounts, account classifications, and reporting systems is a must before initiating a budgeting and planning system?
5. Describe budgetary games that people play. What are the reasons for PFG to experience minimal budgetary gamesmanship?

"How Challenging Should Profit Budget Targets Be?"

The article argues for using highly achievable budget targets, and explains six key advantages for doing so, including the favorable effect on the managers' commitment and confidence. The article also explains some of the risks of using highly achievable budget targets. The concept of risk is illustrated with probability distributions and with a relatively low-risk environment having a probability distribution with lower variance.

Discussion Questions: 7
1. Explain each of the six advantages of highly achievable budget targets mentioned in the article. Can you think of any in addition?
2. What are the risks of highly achievable budget targets mentioned in the article? Can you think of any in addition?

6. What type of budget target does PFG seem to set?

9-1

7. Why would it be strategically valid for PFG to do so?

Cases

9-1. EMERSON ELECTRIC COMPANY

Emerson Electric Company was founded in 1890 as a manufacturer of motors and fans. In 1993, Emerson marked its thirty-sixth consecutive year of improved earnings per share. On $8.2 billion sales, the diversified St. Louis based company reported a 1993 profit of $708 million. In addition, the company had $2 billion in unconsolidated sales in international joint ventures. It manufactures a broad range of electric, electromechanical, and electronic products for industry and consumers. Brand names include Fisher Control Valves, Skil, Dremel, and Craftsman power tools, In-Sink-Erator waste disposals, Copeland compressors, Rosemount instruments, Automatic Switch valves, and U.S. Electric Motors in the power transmission market. Since 1956, Emerson's annual return to shareholders averaged 18 percent. Sales, earnings per share, and dividends per share grew at a compound rate of 9 percent, 8 percent, and 7 percent, respectively, over the 1983-93 period. Inter-national sales have grown to 40 percent of total sales and present a growth area for the company.

Emerson is a major domestic electrical manufacturer. Its U.S. based competitors include companies such as General Electric, Westinghouse, and Honeywell. Its foreign competitors include companies such as Siemens and Hitachi. Emerson has had the narrowest focus as a broadly diversified manufacturing company among its primary competitors. Other manufacturers, such as GE and Westinghouse, are diversified into financial services, broadcasting, aircraft engines, plastics, furniture, etc. Emerson follows a growth-through-acquisition strategy, but no one acquisition has been very large. There are periodic divestitures as management seeks the appropriate or complementary mix of products.

In 1973, Charles F. Knight was elected Chief Executive Officer, after joining the company the prior year. Under Knight's leadership, Emerson analyzed historical records as well as data on a set of "peer companies" the investment community valued highly over time. From this analysis, top management concluded that Emerson needed to achieve growth and strong financial results on a consistent basis reflecting constant improvements. The company set growth rate targets based on revenue growth above and beyond economy-driven expectations.

During the 1980s, the company maintained a very conservative balance sheet rather than using leverage. Top management felt that this was a competitive weapon because it permitted flexibility to borrow when an attractive business investment became available. In the economic downtown of the 1990s, Emerson, unlike a number of companies, was not burdened by heavy debt and interest payments.

ORGANIZATION

Historically, Emerson was organized into 40 decentralized divisions consisting of separate product lines. A president ran each division. The goal was to be number one or two in the market for each product line. The company resisted forming groups, sectors, or other combinations of divisions as found in other large companies until 1990, when Emerson organized its divisions into eight business segments: fractional horsepower electric motors; industrial motors; tools; industrial machinery and components; components for heating and air conditioning; process control equipment; appliance components; and electronics and computer support products and systems. This new structure exploits common distribution channels, organizational capabilities, and technologies.

This case was written and copyrighted by Joseph G. San Miguel, Naval Postgraduate School.

The Office of the Chief Executive (OCE), which consists of the Chief Executive Officer, the President, two Vice Chairmen, seven business leaders, and three other corporate officers, directs management of the company. The OCE meets 10 to 12 times a year to review division performance; and discuss issues facing individual divisions or the corporation as a whole.

Each division also has a board of directors, which consists of a member of the OCE who serves as chairman, the division president, and the division's key managers. The division boards meet monthly to review and monitor performance.

Corporate staff in 1993 consisted of 311 people, the same number as in 1975, when the company was one-sixth its current size in terms of sales. Staff is kept to a minimum because top management believes that a large staff creates more work for the divisions. To encourage open communication and interaction among all levels of employees, Emerson does not publish an organization chart.

BEST-COST PRODUCER STRATEGY

In the early 1980s, the company was not globally competitive in all of its major product lines, and recognized that its quality levels in some product areas did not match levels available from some non-U.S. competitors, particularly the Japanese. Therefore, top management changed its twenty-year strategy of being the "low cost producer" to being the "best cost producer." There were six elements to this strategy:

1. Commitment to total quality and customer satisfaction.
2. Knowledge of the competition and the basis on which they compete.
3. Focused manufacturing strategy, competing on process as well as product design.
4. Effective employee communications and involvement.
5. Formalized cost-reduction programs, in good times and bad.
6. Commitment to support the strategy through capital expenditures.

Since the 1950s, the low cost producer strategy required the divisions to set cost-reduction goals at every level and required plant personnel to identify specific actions to achieve those goals. Improvements of 6 percent to 7 percent a year, in terms of cost of goods sold, were targeted. With the best-cost producer strategy, Emerson now aims for higher levels of cost reduction through its planning process. For example, machine tools were used to streamline a process to save labor costs, and design changes saved five ounces of aluminum per unit. Sometimes a competitor's products were disassembled and studied for cost improvements. Products and cost structures of competitors were used to assess Emerson's performance. Factors such as regional labor rates and freight costs were also included in the analyses. For example, before investing millions of dollars in a new plant to make circular saws, top management wanted to know what competitors, domestic and global, were planning.

In the period 1983 to 1993, capital investments of $1.8 billion were made to improve process technology, increase productivity, gain product leadership, and achieve critical mass in support of the best-cost producer strategy. Division and plant management report every quarter on progress against detailed cost reduction targets.

Quality was an important factor in Emerson's best-cost producer strategy. Improvements were such that Emerson was counting defects in parts per million. For example, in one electric motor line, employees consistently reached less than 100 rejects per one million motors.

PLANNING PROCESS

CEO Knight made the following comments on Emerson's planning process:

> Once we fix our goals, we do not consider it acceptable to miss them. These targets drive our strategy and determine what we have to do: the kinds of

businesses we are in, how we organize and manage them, and how we pay management. At Emerson this means planning. In the process of planning, we focus on specific opportunities that will meet our criteria for growth and returns and create value for our stockholders. In other words, we "identify business investment opportunities."[1]

Emerson's fiscal year starts October 1. To initiate the planning process, top management sets sales growth and return on total capital targets for the divisions. Each fiscal year, from November to July, the CEO and several corporate officers meet with the management of each division at a one or two day division planning conference. Knight spends 60 percent of his time at these division-planning conferences. The meetings are designed to be confrontational in order to challenge assumptions and conventional thinking. Top management wants the division to stretch to reach its goals. It also wants to review the detailed actions that division management believes will lead to improved results.

Prior to its division planning conference, the division president submits four standard exhibits to top management. Developing these four exhibits requires months of teamwork and discipline among each division's operating managers.

The "Value Measurement Chart" compares the division's actual performance five years ago (1989), the current year's expected results (1994), and the long-range forecast for the fifth year (1999). See Exhibit 1 (Note: the numbers in all exhibits are disguised). The Value Measurement Chart contains the type, amount, and growth rates of capital investment, net operating profit after tax (NOPAT), return on average operating capital, and "economic profit" (NOPAT less a capital charge based on the cost of capital). To create shareholder value, the goal is to determine the extent to which a division's return on total capital (ROTC) exceeds Emerson's cost of capital. Use of the cost of capital rate (Line 3000 on Exhibit 1) is required in all division plans.

The next two exhibits contain sales data. The "Sales Gap Chart" and "Sales Gap Line Chart" show the current year's expected sales (1994) and five-year sales projections (1995-1999). See Exhibits 2 and 3. These are based on an analysis of sources of growth, the market's natural growth rate, market penetration, price changes, new products, product line extensions, and international growth. The "gap" represents the difference between the division's long-range sales forecast and top management's target rate for sales growth (Line 19 in Exhibit 2). Exhibit 2 shows the five-year sources of sales growth in Column H. These are illustrated in the Sales Gap Line Chart in Exhibit 3 for one of the divisions for the 1995-99 periods. The division president must explain what specific steps are being taken to close the gap.

The "5-Back by 5-Forward P&L in Exhibit 4 contrasts detailed division data for the current year (1994) with five prior years of historical data and five years of forecast data (1995-99). This comprises 11 years of profit statements including sales; cost of sales; selling, general and administrative expenses; interest; taxes; and return on total capital (ROTC). This statement is used to detect trends. Division management must be prepared with actions to reverse unfavorable movements or trends.

Beyond the review and discussion of the four required exhibits, the division planning conference belongs to the division president. Top management listens to division management's view of customers, markets, plans for new products, analyses of competition, and reviews of cost reductions, quality, capacity, productivity, inventory levels, and compensation. Any resulting changes in the division plan must be submitted for approval by top management. The logic and underlying assumptions of the plan are challenged so that managers who are confident of their strategies can defend their proposals. CEO Knight views the test of a good planning conference is whether it results in manager actions that significantly impact the business. According to Knight:

---

[1]"Knight, C. F., "Emerson Electric: Consistent Profits, Consistently," *Harvard Business Review,* January-February 1992, p. 59.

Since operating managers carry out the planning, we effectively establish ownership and eliminate the artificial distinction between strategic and operating decisions. Managers on the line do not-and must never-delegate the understanding of the business. To develop a plan, operating managers work together for months. They often tell me that the greatest value of the planning cycle lies in the teamwork and discipline that the preparation phase requires.[2]

Late in the fiscal year, the division president and appropriate division staff meet with top management to present a detailed forecast for the coming year and conduct a financial review of the current year's actual performance versus forecast. The forecast is expected to match the data in the plan resulting from the division planning conference, but top management also requests contingency plans for several lower levels of activity. A thorough set of actions to protect profitability at lower sales levels is presented. These are known as contingency plans. Changes to the division's forecast are not likely unless significant changes occurred in the environment or in the underlying assumptions. Top management must approve changes in the forecast. It is not Emerson's practice to aggregate financial reports for planning and controlling profits between the division and corporation as a whole.

In August, the information generated for and during the division planning conferences and financial reviews is consolidated and reviewed at corporate headquarters by top management. The objective is to examine the total data and prepare for a corporate wide planning conference. In September, before the start of the next fiscal year, top management and top officers of each division attend an annual corporate planning conference. At this meeting, top management presents the corporate and division forecasts for the next year as well as the strategic plan for the next five years. The conference is viewed as a vehicle for communication. There is open and frank discussion of success stories, missed opportunities, and future challenges.

REPORTING

At its meetings the OCE uses the President's Operating Report (POR) to review division performance. Each division president submits the POR (see Exhibit 5), on a monthly basis. This reporting system is different from budget reports found in other companies.

First, the POR contains three columns of data for the "current year." The third column of data (Forecast) reflects the plan agreed to by the division president and top corporate management at the beginning of the fiscal year. The forecast data is not changed during the fiscal year and the division president's performance is measured using the fiscal year's forecast. The first column reports the actual results for completed quarters or expected amounts for the current and future quarters. The division president may update expected quarterly results each month. The second column reports the "prior expected" results so that each month's updated expectations can be compared with data submitted in the prior month's POR. Updated expectations are also compared with the forecast data.

Second, in addition to current year data, the POR lists the prior year's actual results. This permits a comparison with the current year's actual results for completed quarters (or expected results for subsequent quarters) and over (0) or under (U) percentages are reported. Midway through the fiscal year, expected data for the first quarter of the next fiscal year is added to the POR.

Corporate top management meets quarterly with each division president and his or her chief financial officer to review the most recent POR and monitor overall division performance. The meetings are taken very seriously by all concerned and any deviations from forecast get close attention. When a division's reported results and expectations are weak, a shift to contingency plans is sometimes ordered by top management, Emerson does

---

[2]Knight, p. 63.

not allocate corporate overhead to the divisions but does allocate interest and taxes to divisions at the end of the fiscal year.

COMPENSATION

During the year, each division assesses all department heads and higher-level managers against specific performance criteria. Those with high potential are offered a series of assignments to develop their skills. Human resources are identified as part of the strategy implementation. In addition, personnel charts on management team are kept at corporate headquarters. The charts include each manager's photo, function, experience, and career path. About 85 percent of promotions involve internal managers.

Each executive in a division earns a base salary and is eligible for "extra salary," based on division performance according to measurable objectives (primarily sales, profits, and return on capital). An extra salary amount, established at the beginning of the year, is multiplied by "1" if the division hits targeted performance. The multiplier ranges from .35 to 2.0. Doing better than target increases the multiplier. In recent years, sales and profit margin, as identified in the POR forecast column, have had a 50 percent weighting in computing compensation targets. Other factors include inventory turnover, international sales, new product introductions, and an accounts receivable factor. In addition, stock options and a five-year performance share plan are available to top executives.

COMMUNICATION

Top management strongly encourages open communication. Division presidents and plant managers meet regularly with all employees to discuss the specifics of the business and the competition. As a measure of communication, top management feels that each employee should be able to answer four essential questions about his or her job:

1. What cost reduction are you currently working on?
2. Who is the competition?
3. Have you met with your management in the past six months?
4. Do you understand the economics of your job?

The company also conducts opinion surveys of every employee. The analysis uncovers trends. Some plants have survey data for the prior twenty years. The CEO receives a summary of every opinion survey from every plant.

RECENT EVENTS

As a result of a $2 billion investment in technology during the past 10 years, new products as a percent of sales increased from 13 percent in 1983 to 24 percent in 1993. A new product is defined as a product introduced within the past five years. About 87 percent of total U.S. sales are generated from products that are either first or second in domestic position. Still, some in the investment community do not view Emerson as a technology leader, but as a very efficient world-class manufacturer. Although internally generated new products are part of the planning process, Emerson is sometimes a late entrant in the marketplace. For example, in 1989, a competitor introduced a low-cost, hand-held ultra-sonic gauge. Within 72 days, Emerson introduced its own version at 20 percent less cost than its competitor's gauge. Emerson's gauge was also easier to use and more reliable. It was a bestseller within a year.

To some Wall Street observers, it seems that Emerson is attempting to reduce its dependence on supplying commodity-type products, such as motors and valves, to U.S. based appliance and other consumer-durables manufacturers by moving into faster growing global markets, such as process controls. As the economy recovers, Emerson is likely to continue its acquisition strategy, with an emphasis on foreign acquisitions, and international joint ventures.

The impact of the recent business segment organization structure on the planning and control process is not clear. The added layer of management between the division managers and top management might change the previous relationship between them.

QUESTIONS

1. Evaluate Chief Executive Officer Knight's strategy for the Emerson Electric Company. In view of the strategy, evaluate the planning and control system described in the case. What are its strong and weak points?
2. What changes, if any, would you recommend to the CEO?
3. What role should the eight business segment managers have in Emerson's planning and control system?

EXHIBIT 1 The Value Measurement Chart Assesses Value Creation at a Glance*

	Line No.	5th Prior Year Actual FY 1989		Current Year Expected FY 1994		5th Year Forecast FY 1999		5-Year Increment Historical CY vs 5th PY		5-Year Increment Forecast 5th Yr vs. CY		10-Year Increment 5th Yr vs. 5th PY	
		Amt. A	% Sales B	Amt. C	% Sales D	Amt. E	% Sales F	Amt. G	% Sales H	Amt. I	% Sales J	Amt. K	% Sales L
Growth Rate and Capital Requirements													
Working capital operating-Y/E	1127	117.1	29.8%	120.2	21.8%	153.3	18.5%	3.1	1.9%	33.1	12.0%	36.2	8.3%
Net noncurrent assets-Y/E	1128	92.9	23.6%	150.0	27.2%	221.6	26.8%	57.1	35.9%	71.6	26.0%	128.7	29.6%
Total operating capital-Y/E	1129	210.0	53.4%	270.2	48.9%	374.9	45.3%	60.2	37.9%	104.7	38.0%	164.9	37.9%
Average operating capital	1130	201.1	51.1%	267.1	48.4%	370.4	44.7%						
Incremental investment	1584							66.0		103.3		169.3	
Net oper. prof. aft. tax (NOPAT)	1119	33.4		49.5		79.0		16.1		29.5		45.6	
Return on incremental investment								24.4%		28.6%		26.9%	
NOPAT growth rate								8.2%		9.8%		9.0%	
Capital growth rate								5.8%		6.8%		6.3%	
Rate of Return													
Return on total capital = NOPAT / Avg. oper. cap.		16.6%		18.5%		21.3%							
Net sales	0001	393.2		552.2		827.9		159.0		275.7		434.7	
Sales growth rate								7.0%		8.4%		7.7%	
NOPAT margin		8.5%		9.0%		9.5%		10.1%		10.7%		10.5%	
Operating capital turnover (T/O)		1.96		2.07		2.24		2.41		2.67		2.57	
Cost of capital	3000	12.0%		12.0%		12.0%							
Capital charge (L1130 X L3000)	3001	24.1		32.1		44.4		8.0		12.3		20.3	
Economic profit (L1119-L3001)		9.3		17.4		34.6		8.1		17.2		25.3	

*In millions of dollars (all numbers in the exhibit are disguised).

Source: Charles F. Knight, "Emerson Electric: Consistent Profits, Consistently," *Harvard Business Review*, January–February 1992, p. 63. Used with permission of the Emerson Electric Company. All numbers are disguised.

EXHIBIT 2   The Sales Gap Chart Forecasts Five-Year Plans*

	Line No.	Prior Year Actual FY 93 (A)	Current Year Expected FY 94 (B)	Forecast					5-Year Source of Growth (%) (H)	5-Year Company Annual Growth (%) (I)
				FY 95 (C)	FY 96 (D)	FY 97 (E)	FY 98 (F)	FY 99 (G)		
Domestic Excluding Exports										
Current year domestic sales base @ 10/1 prices	1		305.7	305.7	305.7	305.7	305.7	305.7		
Served industry-growth/(decline)	2			3.0	24.6	39.0	49.6	58.3	21.1%	3.6%
Penetration-increase/(decrease) (Including-new line extension/ buyouts)	3			6.3	14.1	21.0	29.8	37.6	13.6	2.0
Price increases-current year through 5th year	4		3.3	7.6	14.7	21.6	29.5	38.0	12.6	1.7
Incremental new products:										
Prior 5 year introduction	5		16.1	16.4	17.7	17.4	17.5	19.0	1.1	
Current year through 5th year	6		1.4	5.6	11.6	18.5	25.9	34.2	11.9	
Other	7		3.1	1.4	1.6	2.3	2.5	2.8	-0.1	
Total Domestic	8	363.7	329.6	346.0	390.0	425.5	460.5	495.6		8.5
International Excluding Sales to U.S.										
Current year international sales base @ 10/1 prices	9		202.9	202.9	202.9	202.9	202.9	202.9		
Served industry-growth/(decline)	10			(0.1)	8.8	17.0	24.8	35.4	12.9	3.3
Penetration-increase/(decrease) (Including-new line extensions/buyouts)	11			(0.5)	18.8	27.2	36.2	45.1	16.4	3.6
Price increases-current year through 5th year	12		2.0	4.9	8.5	12.5	16.9	21.7	7.1	1.4
Incremental new products:										
Prior 5 year introduction	13		6.9	7.1	6.7	7.1	8.0	9.2	0.8	
Current year through 5th year	14		1.1	4.5	6.3	10.1	14.3	16.9	5.7	

EXHIBIT 2 The Sales Gap Chart Forecasts Five-Year Plans* (continued)

	Line No.	Prior Year Actual FY 93 (A)	Current Year Expected FY 94 (B)	Forecast FY 95 (C)	Forecast FY 96 (D)	Forecast FY 97 (E)	Forecast FY 98 (F)	Forecast FY 99 (G)	5-Year Source of Growth (%) (H)	5-Year Company Annual Growth (%) (I)
Currency	15		9.3	-	-	-	-	-	-3.4	
Other	16		0.4	0.8	0.7	0.9	1.0	1.1	0.3	
Total international	17	204.3	222.6	219.6	252.7	277.7	304.1	332.3		8.3
Total consolidated	18	568.0	552.2	565.6	642.7	703.2	764.6	827.9	100.0	8.4
Annual growth %—nominal			-2.8%	2.4%	13.6%	9.4%	8.7%	8.3%		
Gap:										
15% Target—nominal	19			635.0	730.2	839.8	965.7	1,110.6		15.0
Sales gap—over(under)	20			(69.4)	(87.5)	(136.6)	(201.1)	(282.7)		
U.S. exports (excluding to foreign subsidiaries)	21	35.3	31.3	33.7	35.9	39.9	43.9	47.6		8.7
Foreign subsidiaries (excluding sales to U.S.)	22	169.1	191.4	185.8	216.8	237.8	260.3	284.7		8.3

*In millions of dollars (all numbers in the exhibit are disguised).

Source: Charles F. Knight, "Emerson Electric: Consistent Profits, Consistently," *Harvard Business Review*, January–February 1992, p. 64. Used with permission of the Emerson Electric Company.

Exhibit 3

The sales gap line chart projects sales growth against other targets

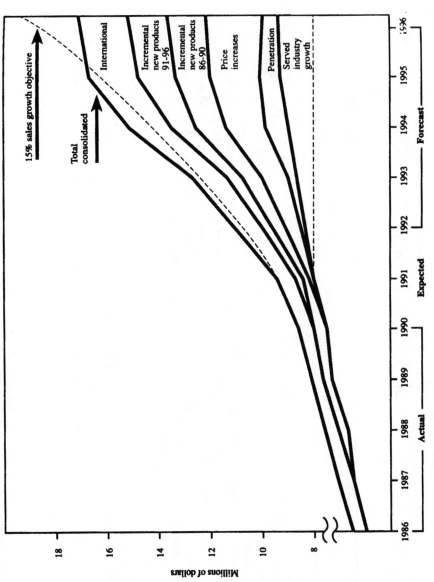

Note: All numbers in the exhibit are disguised.

Source: Charles F. Knight, "Emerson Electric: Consistent Profits, Consistently," *Harvard Business Review*, January–February 19(?), p. 65. Used with permission of the Emerson Electric Company.

1992, p.

Exhibit 4 The 5-Back-by-5-Forward Chart Provides 11 Years of P&L Measures*

	Line No.	Actual/Restated					Current Year	Forecast				
		5th PY FY 89 A	4th PY FY 90 B	3rd PY FY 91 C	2nd PY FY 92 D	Prior Year FY 93 E	Expected FY 94 F	Next Yr FY 95 G	2nd Yr FY 96 H	3rd Yr FY 97 I	4th Yr FY 98 J	5th Yr FY 99 K
Order entries	1143	71,363	77,057	92,716	100,164	126,591	128,247	142,612	157,972	173,743	189,856	207,133
Sales backlog (year end)	1144	13,310	14,051	17,098	16,534	29,334	29,842	31,509	33,082	34,805	36,591	38,363
Net sales	0001	71,163	76,316	89,669	100,728	113,791	127,739	140,945	156,399	172,020	188,070	205,361
Annual growth %-nominal			7.2%	17.5%	12.3%	13.0%	12.3%	10.3%	11.0%	10.0%	9.3%	9.2%
-real						11.3%	7.8%	8.4%	6.7%	6.8%	6.1%
Cost of sales	0009	36,802	39,382	46,487	51,593	60,003	67,651	74,432	82,109	89,966	98,173	106,997
% to sales		51.7%	51.6%	51.8%	51.2%	52.7%	53.0%	52.8%	52.5%	52.3%	52.2%	52.1%
Gross profit	0010	34,361	36,934	43,182	49,135	53,788	60,088	66,513	74,290	82,054	89,897	98,364
% to sales		48.3%	48.4%	48.2%	48.8%	47.3%	47.0%	47.2%	47.5%	47.7%	47.8%	47.9%
SG&A expenses	0011	21,773	22,558	26,246	29,941	32,163	36,150	40,169	44,887	49,714	54,366	59,555
% to sales		30.6%	29.6%	29.3%	29.7%	28.3%	28.3%	28.5%	28.7%	28.9%	28.9%	29.0%
Operating profit	0012	12,588	14,376	16,936	19,194	21,625	23,938	26,344	29,403	32,340	35,531	38,809
% to sales		17.7%	18.8%	18.9%	19.1%	19.0%	18.7%	18.7%	18.8%	18.8%	18.9%	18.9%
Other (inc.)/ded. (excl. int.)	0235	423	1,090	1,395	1,232	1,488	1,764	1,766	1,794	1,530	1,438	1,423
Earnings before interest & taxes	0240	12,165	13,286	15,541	17,962	20,137	22,174	24,578	27,609	30,810	34,093	37,386
% to sales		17.1%	17.4%	17.3%	17.8%	17.7%	17.4%	17.4%	17.7%	17.9%	18.1%	18.2%

EXHIBIT 4 The 5-Back-by-5-Forward Chart Provides 11 Years of P&L Measures* (continued)

	Line No.	Actual/Restated					Current Year	Forecast				
		5th PY FY 89 A	4th PY FY 90 B	3rd PY FY 91 C	2nd PY FY 92 D	Prior Year FY 93 E	Expected FY 94 F	Next Yr FY 95 G	2nd Yr FY 96 H	3rd Yr FY 97 I	4th Yr FY 98 J	5th Yr FY 99 K
Interest (income/ expense, net	0230	(771)	(1,041)	(1,127)	(1,326)	(1,781)	(2,224)	(2,330)	(2,576)	(2,734)	(2,903)	(3,070)
Pretax earnings	0015	12,936	14,327	16,668	19,288	21,918	24,398	26,908	30,185	33,544	36,996	40,456
% to sales		18.2%	18.8%	18.6%	19.1%	19.3%	19.1%	19.1%	19.3%	19.5%	19.7%	19.7%
Income taxes	0016	5,445	6,785	7,788	8,447	9,668	10,551	11,753	13,101	14,497	15,948	17,387
Effective tax rate		42.1%	47.4%	46.7%	43.8%	44.1%	43.2%	43.7%	43.4%	43.2%	43.1%	43.0%
Net earnings	0017	7,491	7,542	8,880	10,841	12,250	13,847	15,155	17,084	19,047	21,048	23,069
% to sales		10.5%	9.9%	9.9%	10.8%	10.8%	10.8%	10.8%	10.9%	11.1%	11.2%	11.2%
Return on total capital	1324	20.4%	19.7%	20.3%	23.6%	23.8%	25.1%	26.1%	28.0%	30.1%	32.0%	33.9%
ROTC excluding goodwill	1323	27.3%	28.0%	27.2%	30.6%	31.5%	32.5%	32.9%	34.7%	36.6%	38.3%	40.2%

*In thousands of dollars (all numbers in the exhibit are disguised).
Source: Charles F. Knight, "Emerson Electric: Consistent Profits, Consistently," *Harvard Business Review*, January–February 1992, p. 66. Used with permission of the Emerson Electric Company.

Exhibit 5 President's Operating Report Division—Fiscal Year by Quarters/Actual and Expected

(Thousands of Dollars)

Line No.		Current Year						Prior Year		% Act/ Exp O/(U) PY
		Actual/ Expected	% Sales	Prior Expected	% Sales	Forecast	% Sales	Actual	% Sales	
1st Quarter Ending December 31										
1	Intercompany Sales	36		36		34		37		-2.7%
2	Net Sales	29,613		29,613		29,463		25,932		14.2%
3	Gross Profit	14,065	47.5%	14,065	47.5%	13,790	46.8%	12,384	47.8%	13.6%
4	SG&A Expenses	8,312	28.1%	8,312	28.1%	8,281	28.1%	7,650	29.5%	8.7%
5	Operating Profit	5,753	19.4%	5,753	19.4%	5,509	18.7%	4,734	18.3%	21.5%
6	Earnings Before Interest & Tax	5,280	17.8%	5,280	17.8%	5,048	17.1%	4,343	16.7%	21.6%
2nd Quarter Ending March 31										
7	Intercompany Sales	5		5		9		56		-91.1%
8	Net Sales	33,324		33,324		31,765		22,661		25.0%
9	Gross Profit	15,283	45.9%	15,283	45.9%	14,812	46.6%	12,518	47.0%	22.1%
10	SG&A Expenses	9,301	27.9%	9,301	27.9%	8,937	28.1%	7,395	27.8%	25.8%
11	Operating Profit	5,982	18.0%	5,982	18.0%	5,875	18.5%	5,123	19.2%	16.8%
12	Earnings Before Interest & Tax	5,785	17.4%	5,785	17.4%	5,612	17.7%	4,918	18.4%	17.6%
3rd Quarter Ending June 30										
13	Intercompany Sales	25		25		39		146		-82.9%
14	Net Sales	32,845		32,845		33,424		30,678		7.1%
15	Gross Profit	15,353	46.7%	15,353	46.7%	15,664	46.9%	14,310	46.6%	7.3%
16	SG&A Expenses	8,916	27.1%	8,916	27.1%	9,399	28.2%	8,424	27.4%	5.8%
17	Operating Profit	6,437	19.6%	6,437	19.6%	6,265	18.7%	5,886	19.2%	9.4%
18	Earnings Before Interest & Tax	6,126	18.7%	6,126	18.7%	5,645	16.9%	5,378	17.5%	13.9%
4th Quarter Ending September 30										
19	Intercompany Sales	94		94		94		25		276.0%
20	Net Sales	36,611		36,611		35,722		30,521		20.0%
21	Gross Profit	17,109	46.7%	17,109	46.7%	16,832	47.1%	14,576	47.8%	17.4%

Exhibit 5 President's Operating Report Division—Fiscal Year by Quarters/Actual and Expected (continued)

(Thousands of Dollars)

Line No.		Current Year						Prior Year		% Act/Exp O/(U) PY
		Actual/Expected	% Sales	Prior Expected	% Sales	Forecast	% Sales	Actual	% Sales	
22	SG&A Expenses	10,537	28.7%	10,537	28.7%	10,029	28.1%	8,695	28.5%	21.2%
23	Operating Profit	6,572	18.0%	6,572	18.0%	6,803	19.0%	5,881	19.3%	11.7%
24	Earnings Before Interest & Tax	6,122	16.7%	6,122	16.7%	8,146	22.8%	5,498	18.0%	11.3%
Fiscal Year Ending September 30										
25	Intercompany Sales	160		160		176		264		–39.4%
26	Net Sales	132,393		132,393		130,374		113,792		16.3%
27	Gross Profit	61,810	46.7%	61,810	46.7%	61,098	46.9%	53,788	47.3%	14.9%
28	SG&A Expenses	37,066	28.0%	37,066	28.0%	36,646	28.1%	32,164	28.3%	15.2%
29	Operating Profit	24,744	18.7%	24,744	18.7%	24,452	18.8%	21,624	19.0%	14.4%
30	Earnings Before Interest & Tax	23,313	17.6%	23,313	17.6%	24,451	18.8%	20,137	17.7%	15.8%
31	Pre-Tax Earnings	25,154	19.0%	25,154	19.0%	24,771	19.0%	21,918	19.3%	14.8%
32	Net Earnings	14,361	10.8%	14,361	10.8%	14,024	10.8%	12,250	10.8%	17.2%
Expected First Quarter Next Fiscal Year										
33	Intercompany Sales	67		65				36		86.1%
34	Net Sales	32,830		32,311				29,613		10.9%
35	Gross Profit	15,142	46.1%	15,143	46.9%			14,065	47.5%	7.7%
36	SG&A Expenses	9,179	27.9%	9,217	28.6%			8,312	28.1%	10.4%
37	Operating Profit	5,963	18.2%	5,925	18.3%			5,753	19.4%	3.7%
38	Earnings Before Interest & Tax	5,628	17.1%	5,619	17.4%			5,280	17.8%	6.6%

HOW TO SET UP A BUDGETING AND PLANNING SYSTEM

BY ROBERT N. WEST, CPA, AND AMY M. SNYDER CPA

Certificate of &Merit

Two years ago, Penn Fuel Gas, Inc. (PFG) initiated its first annual and long-range operating budget process. PFG is a public utility holding company with consolidated revenues of $125 million and 550 employees. In addition to selling natural gas, the company provides natural gas storage and transportation services, provides merchandise services, and has a propane business. PFG's utility operations are split between two subsidiaries, each with a number of locations.

The motivation for budgeting came jointly from PFG's bankers, its board of directors, and its management. The information needs of all three users were fairly similar. All three were interested in cash flow projections and future earnings potential. The board was interested in improving PFG's return on equity (ROE), and it wanted to analyze the prospects of reinstituting a common stock dividend. In addition. management wanted segment P&Ls and improved departmental (cost center) expense and cash flow tracking. PFGs segments are regions, lines of business (utility, propane, and merchandise, and type of customer commercial, industrial, residential).

WHERE TO START?

The first decision was whether to use existing in-house personnel, hire consultants, or hire a full-time budget manager. Consultants or a new hire would offer the benefit of an independent, fresh perspective with no biases. The disadvantage is that they wouldn't know the business as well as an insider. Penn Fuel Gas used consultants to set up its first budget and then hired a full-time, experienced professional to handle its budgeting. PFG wisely gave the position a manager title to assign appropriate status to the position. Once the staffing decision was resolved, the new budget director faced three primary tasks.

Learn the business. PFG hired a self-directed person (co-author Amy Snyder) who could understand the business quickly and get both long-range and operating budget processes up and running. Although the operations of PFGs business are relatively straightforward, the rules and regulations of the public utility industry are complex. PFG did two things to bring the budget manager up to speed. It sent her to a week-long technical program to learn the regulatory side of the business, and it extended her an open invitation to important meetings of operations vice presidents and top management so she could learn the operating side of the business.

Budgeting for natural gas and propane operations is difficult because a significant amount of demand for these products is dependent upon Mother Nature. Penn Fuel experienced two abnormal winters in its first two years of budgeting. In 1994, Pennsylvania had its coldest, iciest winter in history In 1995, it had one of its warmest. But forecasting is difficult for many rapidly growing companies (one group for whom this article is intended). They must be flexible. For example, PFG budgets using the normal weather forecast, but it also provides sensitivity analyses and budget reprojections at least quarterly. Company and budget personnel realize that capital spending is partially a function of the winter season's revenues, which won't be known until the first quarter is over. The first quarter is particularly important in the utility and propane business as it represents 40% of total annual product delivered.

Determine the users' information needs. Different users have different information needs, and users don't always know what information they "need." If managers or board members are not financially oriented, as is the case with many small businesses, they may need a little guidance. PFG's directors included several financially astute individuals who had a clear idea of what information they wanted. Costs were budgeted on both an accrual basis (for P&L reports) and cash basis (for cash flow reports).

Review and update the information system. All accounting information systems (AIS) face the daunting task of trying to provide the appropriate output for multiple sets of users. The reports needed from Penn Fuel's MS included:

1. External financial reports (GAAP),
2. Tax reporting,
3. Internal management segment reports,
4. Cash flow reports, and
5. Reports for regulators.

The budget manager analyzed the AI to determine whether data were classified and summarized in a manner useful for internal business plans and budget reports. Most accounting systems are geared toward external financial reports, and, in the case of regulated industries, for reports to regulators as well. Internal managers usually prefer information provided in a different format, such as results by division, product line, region, or customer group.

DECISIONS TO MAKE

PFG's budget manager faced some interesting information systems setups on which she had to make decisions when she started her work.

Different internal reporting systems. The Northern division, acquired several years ago, reported its results in different formats from the Southern division. Eventually a common reporting system will be attained, but the immediate task was to rearrange the data to assist with the consolidation and make the division data comparable. The underlying information systems differed as well. The two divisions used different accounting software, adding another challenge to the eventual merging of information systems.

Treatment of a different business segment. PFG's propane business segment seems similar to the natural gas business, but it has several key differences. Because it is unregulated. it has direct control over the pricing of its product. The utility's chart of accounts was not a perfect fit. PFG had to decide whether to maintain a uniform chart of accounts or create a separate general ledger account structure for its propane business segment. PFG adapted the propane business unit's account structure to the utility account structure. The tradeoff was ease of corporate reporting versus the individual business unit's desired view of the data. A slight edge was given to corporate reporting.

Management and the board of directors wanted segment information that was difficult to obtain. Total spending and spending by operating unit were

easy to retrieve, but other views of the information had not been developed. For example, segregating operating expenses by business segment was pro-vided partially by existing reports, but aggregation of all segments was tedious to reconcile to the general ledger due to corporate staff allocations. Most corporate personnel, from the president down to the fixed asset accountants, do not keep formal track of their time. Allocations were made to the various business segments on spreadsheets, requiring an audit trail and explanations to reconcile back to the results per the accounting records.

Review expense classifications. As a company grows, its chart of accounts should be reviewed periodically to determine if information is being captured in the most meaningful way. Introducing a budget system is an ideal time to modify the accounting system with a view toward future information needs. PFG's new budget manager reviewed the utility's accounting system with a fresh perspective and came up with a couple of suggestions to improve the precision of the accounting information system.

The first suggestion was to get rid of miscellaneous expense accounts with large balances. Most businesses prefer that almost nothing be recorded in miscellaneous accounts. PFG's state-mandated chart of accounts lent itself to this practice as the chart of accounts included many miscellaneous expense accounts. The challenge here was twofold:

1. Perform an account analysis to reclassify some of the charges to the miscellaneous expense account, and
2. Change the accounting system (add accounts and subaccounts) to ensure that future transactions are put into more descriptive accounts.

Lack of sufficient detail, such as the overuse of miscellaneous expense, is a common small business practice, so many new budget managers will face a housekeeping task similar to PFG's.

The next suggestion was to change the expense classification system. For example, the training & education account included charges for the training course fee, hotel, travel, meals, the salary charge for the time at the training session, and so on. This system actually was an activity-based costing system in which training included all costs driven by the decision to send an employee to a training program. While this classification of costs is perfectly acceptable, some accountants would record these items in separate accounts to maintain more detail. PFG has several hundred active general ledger accounts, so transaction classification is not a trivial task.

Most companies initiating a budgeting and planning

function should review thoroughly the chart of accounts, account classification (particularly expenses), and the reporting system. In many cases, the accounting system will not have kept pace with the changes in the company (for example, expanded product lines or changes in customers and geographical regions served. It is best if the budget manager resolves information classification and reporting issues up front so that future budgets are comparable. It is difficult to change a system once it has been developed, and budget systems are no different from any other information system in that respect.

Difficulty reconciling amounts back to the ledger. Using the example of training costs cited above, some salary costs were included in accounts other than salary expense. Reconciling accounts such as salaries between the ledger and the payroll register can be difficult. Other accounts are difficult to reconcile as well. The budget manager decided to reclassify some data, but verifying the accuracy of reclassified data was, and still is, a challenge.

Information timeliness/availability. Budgeting brought the desire for better and faster information. PFG uses a minicomputer-based accounting package for general ledger, human resources, and payables. Yet portions of the accounting system still are manual, and monthly closings can take up to three weeks. PFG responded to some of its information needs by installing a new billing system that computerizes cash receipts and provides excellent summary information. PFG also is looking into a computerized project tracking system (for its many construction projects) and improving the computerized fixed assets system by adding a budget feature.

DELIVERABLES

Management wanted a one-year business plan prior to year-end as well as monthly updates (for example, budget vs. actual results). In addition, the board of directors wanted a long-range (three-year) plan each year. To meet these needs, the budget manager developed packets for the directors and management. The board wanted the financial and operational data reported by segment—some reports segmented geographically, some by product line, and others by customer type.

The monthly financial packet. The monthly financial packet includes the following schedules:

A. P&L and cash flow (by region and in total)
　1. Current month
　　a. Actual vs. budget
　　b. Actual vs. same month in prior year
　2. Year-to-date (YTD)
　　a. YTD actual vs. YTD budget
　　b. Budget projections for remainder of year
　　c. YTD actual vs. prior YTD actual
　3. Two full-year monthly bar charts
　　a. Actual vs. budgeted cash flow
　　b. Actual vs. budgeted net income
　4. Capital structure and ROE
B. Selected five-year comparative data
　1. Current month and YTD units of product delivered
　　a. Residential
　　b. Commercial
　　c. Industrial
　　d. Resale
　　e. Detail provided for 10 largest customers
　2. Gas and propane stored
　3. Comparative YTD income statements

The annual business plan. The annual business plan contains data similar to the monthly package by region and in total. Full-year budget data are compared with the current year estimated (10 months' actual plus estimates for November and December) results and prior year actual results. These data are shown in tabular and graphical form. The annual plan also contains:

A. Budgeted income statements for all 12 months.
B. Budgeted cash flow statements for all 12 months.
C. Budgeted ROE schedule for all 12 months.
D. Capital expenditures forecasts, including brief written descriptions of the projects, by segment.
　1. New business (line extensions)
　2. Replacements/betterments
　3. Meters
　4. Tools & equipment
F. Personnel data including projected new hiring, replacement hiring, and workforce reductions.

Explanations of significant variances from prior year actual results are provided in both the annual and monthly packages. Second-stage variance analysis (breaking the variance into its price and quantity components) is provided as needed.

Formatting tips. After completing the first budgeting exercises, the budget manager came to the conclusion that some formatting tips might help those persons who were not familiar with the budgeting process. First, she suggests using graphs. Whoever is preparing a budget should consider displaying the information in graphical form rather than tables of numbers so it will appeal to all levels of readers.

Second, she suggests that a company consider the direct method for cash flow reports. PFG uses the direct method for its cash flow statement because it is more informative and is easier for readers to understand. The adjustments to net income with the indirect method are confusing and do not tell the reader where the money is coming from and to whom it is going. Reports for external parties still can use the indirect method if companies prefer. Table 1 contains a sample direct method cash flow statement.

THE BUDGET CALENDAR

What does the budget group do throughout the year? Table 2 shows the other functions performed by the budget manager each month. Notice that the annual budget data collection process begins five months before the packet is due to the board of directors. A four- to six-month lead time is fairly standard.

PFG decided to prepare its three-year forecast before doing the annual budget because the board wanted information on ROE and cash flow to analyze future earnings potential, for financing requirements, and for general business planning purposes. Once the three-year plan was reviewed, the first year's data were used as a guideline for the current year annual budget's operational and segment detail.

ONGOING CHALLENGES

We already highlighted the initial challenges faced by a new budget manager. Now let's look at some ongoing challenges.

Table 1. DIRECT METHOD CASH FLOW STATEMENT						
	Current Month			Year-to-Date		
	Actual	Budget	Variance	Actual	Budget	Variance
Cash Inflows						
Utility						
Propane						
Merchandise						
Total Cash Inflow						
Cash Outflow's						
Gas purchases						
Propane purchases						
Merchandise purchases						
Operating and maintenance expenses						
Labor and benefits						
Insurance						
Outside services						
Leases						
Storage						
Other						
Rate case preparation						
Other taxes						
Income taxes						
Interest on LTD						
Other interest						
Principal payments						
Common dividends						
Preferred dividends						
Total Cash Outflow						
Available funds						
Capital expenditures						
Net Change in Cash						

Table 2. THE BUDGET CALENDAR
PROCEDURES AND REPORTS DUE

December

Annual budget for coming year. Presentation to board of directors. Present current year results; 10 months of actual and projections for remaining two months (November's results would not be available at this point).

January

Issue approved budgets to managers and vice presidents. Set up monthly financial report for the new year.

February

Prepare actual P&Ls and cash flow by month for the prior year.

March

Clean-up work after year-end closing and audit.

April

1st quarter actual vs. budget to board of directors. Nine-month projections. Send out requests for long-range forecast.

May

Prepare long-range forecast.

June

Present long-range forecast to board of directors.

July

Requests for the upcoming year's capital spending, operating revenues, expenses, and cash flows sent to operating units and corporate departments. 2nd quarter actual vs. budget to board of directors. Six-month projections.

August

Follow up on July requests. Help employees unfamiliar with budget requests.

September

July budget requests due. Input, analyze, and summarize the data.

October

Top management reviews budgets. Have meetings, and negotiate final amounts with various vice presidents and managers. 3rd quarter actual vs. budget to board of directors. Three-month projections.

November

Prepare final budget.

Evolving mission. The budget function is formed with planning as its primary mission. In the early stages of its existence, however, it is expected to analyze company and segment performance. Variance analysis can be both interesting and challenging, challenging because no two years are ever the same. One obvious difference in the natural gas and propane business is the weather, which rarely is the same two years in a row. But other changes such as geographical growth, changes in product mix, and restructuring of divisions increase the challenge of reconciling operating results of two consecutive periods.

Gamesmanship. Budgeting also brings behavioral challenges such as lowballing revenues or padding expenses. PFG has experienced minimal budgeting gamesmanship for two reasons that are described next.

1. Budgets are developed with management, arriving at agreed-upon, reasonable expectations.
2. PFG has not used the budget as a "hammer" at year-end for employees or divisions who did not make budget.

Get people up to speed. The behavioral challenge at PFG has been to get people up to speed with budgeting. The budget manager came from a large company where budgeting was part of the culture. At PFG, she sent out schedules and written instructions on completing the budget requests the first time through. But not everyone understood how to complete the budget forms. Her goal the next year was to sit down with people and work through the forms with those who were unaccustomed to the budget process.

When formal budgeting is new to a company, the budget manager may end up doing the bulk of the budget preparation because people are new to the process. One unfortunate byproduct that can occur is that managers then think it's the budget manager's budget. The budget manager has to impress upon them that it is their department and their budget. It is important to determine up front who is responsible and accountable.

Top management support. All new systems require top management's support. To make budgeting effective, management must communicate the importance of well-thought-out input from departments and operating units. If preparing a well-thought-out budget is not included in managers' goals and objectives for the year, employees may not make the time for the process. Resistance may result, not because employees feel threatened by the new budget system, but, rather, because they lack time.

BENEFITS FROM BUDGETING

Budgeting has improved communication throughout Penn Fuel Gas, Inc., and has improved teamwork toward a common goal. It has helped the board of directors to represent shareholders better and has provided support to management on major decisions. PFG expects even better planning in the future to result in operational improvements, improved management of resources, better cost control, earnings growth, and improved responsibility resulting from managers' active participation in the planning process.

Robert N. West, CPA, Ph.D., is an assistant professor at Villanova University. He is the author of several articles and the text, *Microcomputer Accounting Systems*. He is a member of the Valley Forge Chapter, through which this article was submitted, and can be reached at (610) 519-4359.

Amy M. Snyder, CPA, was manager of budgeting and planning at Penn Fuel Gas, Inc., when this article was written. Now she is controller of Espe America, Inc. She is a member of the Valley Forge Chapter and can be reached at (610) 277-3800.

HOW CHALLENGING SHOULD PROFIT BUDGET TARGETS BE?

By Kenneth A. Merchant

Certificate of Merit, 1989-90

It is a basic axiom of management that budget targets should be set to be challenging but achievable. But to establish that target, managers must first determine what "challenging but achievable" really means. Should profits be targeted at some easily obtainable goal, a realistic middle ground, or at a point so high that hope of attainment is slim?

There is no one right answer, given the number of purposes for which budgets are used: planning, coordination, control, motivation, and performance evaluation. Some may argue that planning purposes are served best with a best-guess budget, one that is as likely to be exceeded as missed.[1] Others may propose that, for optimum motivation, budget targets should be highly challenging, with only a 25% to 40% chance of achievement.[2]

There is one target-level choice, however, that serves the combination of purposes for which budgets are used quite well in the vast majority of organizational situations. Therefore, it provides an effective compromise. That choice is to set budget targets with a high probability of achievement—achievable by most managers 80% to 90% of the time—and then to supplement these targets with promises of extra incentives for performance exceeding the target level.[3] This prescription for the optimal budget target level, which is nearest point A in Figure 1, is made assuming that Figure 1 represents the probability distribution of forthcoming profits for an effective management team working at a consistently high level of effort.

These targets with an 80% to 90% probability of achievement are labeled properly "highly achievable" for most managers, but because of the assumption described in the preceding paragraph, the targets are at least somewhat challenging. They are not "easy." Even talented, experienced profit center managers must work hard and effectively to give themselves a good chance of achieving these targets.

THE ADVANTAGES OF USING HIGHLY ACHIEVABLE BUDGET TARGETS

Choosing budget targets with such a high probability of achievement provides many advantages to corporation, including the following:

1. *Managers commitment to achieve the budget targets is increased.* When targets are set to be highly achievable, the corporation can assess profit center managers high penalties for failing to achieve the targets at least many more years than not. These penalties can include loss of reputation, loss of autonomy, inability to get funding proposals approved, and sometimes even loss of job. Corporations can allow managers few or no excuses for not achieving the targets because the high achievability is designed to protect the managers to a considerable circumstances that were unforeseen at the time performance targets were set.

Because profit center managers face the risk of high penalties for performance shortfalls and do not have the safety net of excuses, they become highly committed to achieve their targets. This commitment causes them to prepare their budget forecasts more carefully and to spend more of their time managing rather than inventing excuses to explain their failures.

Firms that switch their budgeting philosophy to using highly achievable targets instead of "stretch" or "best guess" targets note the increase in commitment quite quickly. Comments a profit center manager in a large U.S. chemical corporation which made the switch:

> "Two years ago, our budgets were just best-effort forecasts. Today they are commitments. There is a vast difference. It's better to run this way. We have discipline. People used to make projections, but they forgot about them until they had to make another projection. Nobody ever came back and slapped their hand. Now people are challenged to put the things in place that are required to make the projections happen. The plans have begun to have credibility. Our spending plans are based on realistic projections."

Conversely, when budget targets are set at highly challenging levels, the danger exists that managers will not be committed to try to achieve their targets. For example, in a small publicly held electronics firm, which until recently had used a stretch target budgeting philosophy, profit center managers had started earning bonuses when their division's reported profit exceeded 60% of the budgeted level. But all too often, the profit center and corporate budgets were not achieved. In the words of the chief financial officer: "The system had some fudge in it. The managers were still in bonus territory, so they didn't have to worry about meeting the budget. It was like a wish, too easily blown off."

The corporation now has changed to what is known as "minimum performance standard" budget targets and its managers' commitment to these new targets has increased sharply. Since the change, the profit centers have achieved virtually all their budget targets every quarter.

The danger of lack of commitment to achieve targets is particularly acute if something goes wrong early in the year and loss of commitment leads to lower motivation. In the words of a manager whose entity had not achieved its budget targets for several years, "After the first few months of the year, we began to look at our goals as 'pie in the sky.' [The goals] didn't inspire us to do different things. They were just demoralizing."

2. *Managers' confidence remains high*. Regardless of the level of budget achievability, in the minds of most managers budget achievement defines the line between success and failure. Budget targets are the most specific and tangible goals managers are given, and most people define personal success in terms of their high degree of achievement of predetermined targets. As one manager put it, "If I were to miss my budget, I would feel like a failure. When I exceed my budget, I feel proud."

It is to the corporation's advantage to have its managers feel like winners. Managers who feel good about themselves and their abilities are more likely to work harder and to take prudent risks.

3. *Organizational control costs decrease*. Most corporations use a management-by-exception control philosophy where negative variances from budget signal the need for investigation and perhaps intervention in the affairs of the operating units. If budget targets are set to be highly achievable, negative variances are relatively rare, and top management or staff attention is directed to the few situations where the operating problems are most likely and most serious.

This point is illustrated in Figure 1. The probability distribution of profit outcomes shifts to the left (lower profit) for a lazy or ineffective manager. What was a

highly achievable target for an effective, hardworking manager (point A) is not as highly achievable for an ineffective or lazy manager. Budget misses of two or three years send a strong signal that something is wrong and that top management intervention is necessary. Budget misses also provide objective rationales for relieving poor managers of their jobs.

4. *The risk of managers engaging in harmful earnings management practices is reduced*. Managers who are likely to achieve their budget targets are less likely to engage in costly actions designed to boost

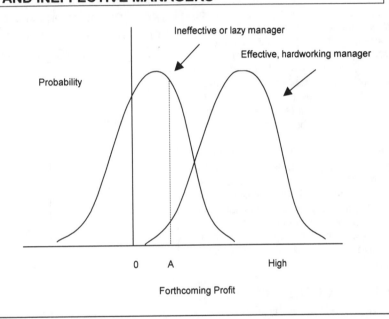

FIGURE 1
PROBABILITY DISTRIBUTIONS OF FORTHCOMING PROFIT FOR EFFECTIVE AND INEFFECTIVE MANAGERS

Ineffective or lazy manager

Effective, hardworking manager

Probability

0   A   High

Forthcoming Profit

earnings in the short term. These actions include making potentially risky operating decisions (such as delaying preventative maintenance) and engaging in deceptive accounting practices (such as altering judgments about reserves).

Highly achievable budget targets also lessen the incentives some managers have to reduce current period income. Those individuals who are facing stretch targets they consider nearly impossible to achieve may "take a bath"; they may take costly actions to position their entities for the subsequent accounting period. For example, they may defer sales and incur as many discretionary expenses as possible in the current period.

5. *Effective managers are allowed greater operating*

flexibility. Highly achievable budget targets allow managers whose entities are performing well to accumulate some slack resources. Most managers will use this slack so that they do not have to respond to unforeseen, unfavorable short-term contingencies in costly ways, such as a suspension of productive long-term investments or a layoff. Some managers also will use the slack in productive, creative ways to fund "skunkworks" that may have high payoffs.

6. *The corporation is somewhat protected against the costs of optimistic revenue projections*. Budgets with optimistic revenue projections often induce managers to acquire resources in anticipation of activity levels that may not be forthcoming. Some of these resources, particularly people, can be difficult to eliminate when reality sets in. As one corporate president expressed it: "I think we ought to have a semiaggressive plan, but one that is achievable. We want to make it every year. It's too hard to adjust on the downside, to slough off commitments of expenses or not launch something you're psychologically committed to."

7. *The predictability of corporate earnings is increased*. When budget targets are likely to be achieved, the consolidated budget provides a highly probably lower bound of forthcoming corporate profits. This earnings predictability is valuable, particularly to managers of publicly held corporations. Earnings are usually less predictable in corporations whose business units face similar business risks, so this earnings-predictability advantage of highly achievable budget targets is higher in undiversified rather than diversified, firms.

A RISK IN USING HIGHLY ACHIEVABLE BUDGET TARGETS

The primary risk in using highly achievable budget targets is that managers may not be challenged to perform at their maximum. They may be satisfied with mediocrity—their levels of aspiration may be too low—and their motivation may slack off after the budgeted profit targets are achieved.

This problem of lack of challenge is potentially more serious when planning uncertainty is relatively high (and the inability to make adjustments for the effects of factors over which the managers had little or no control is relatively low). This is because the distance between

the highly achievable target levels and the best-guess (or even higher) target levels is much greater than when planning uncertainty is low. This is shown in Figure 2. The tall curve shows a profit probability distribution in a relatively low uncertainty environment. The highly achievable budget level (B1) is not far from the most likely performance level (P). The shorter, flatter curve shows a distribution in a relatively uncertain environment. In this case, the highly achievable budget level (B2) is far below the most likely performance level.

Even in environments of high uncertainty, however, this lack-of-challenge problem is not inevitable. Most profit center managers have risen through the ranks because they are good performers with strong internal drives for competition and self-satisfaction. Furthermore, the "winning" feeling generated from budget

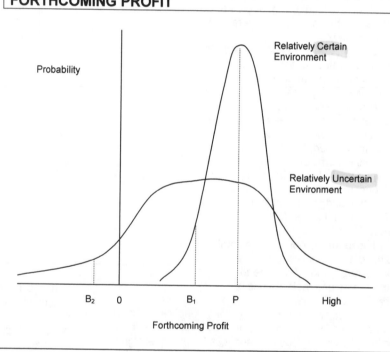

FIGURE 2
EFFECT OF PLANNING UNCERTAINTY ON PROBABILITY DISTRIBUTION OF FORTHCOMING PROFIT

achievement in prior periods is likely to increase, not decrease, the managers' levels of aspiration.

Furthermore, even when the risk of less than optimal challenge does exist, it can be minimized by giving managers incentives to strive for and to produce profits in excess of their budget targets. These incentives can be provided in combinations of many forms of rewards, including extra bonuses, recognition, autonomy, command over resources, and increased prospects for career advancement.

Profit center managers also can be asked to turn in more profit than originally was budgeted. This is a common occurrence in U.S. corporations.[4] These orders, combined with the highly achievable original targets, make the budget somewhat flexible. The highly achievable targets protect the profit center managers from the effects of unfavorable influences not explicitly expounded in the budget forecasts. The requests for profits above budgeted levels can be used to adjust for the effects of unforeseen good fortune on the measures of operating results. They can protect the corporation from the negative effects of excessive easy performance targets, such as managers' lagging ambition and the creation of excessive slack.

Only in a few organizational situations is it not desirable to set highly achievable profit budget targets. One exception is caused by organizational need. A company in grave difficulty may want to set less achievable budget targets as a signal to its managers that a certain higher level of performance is necessary for the corporation to survive or for the profit center to stave off divestment.

A second exception occurs when it is desirable to correct for a profit center's windfall gain. Sometimes when managers have been lucky in a prior period, perhaps earning large and mostly undeserved bonuses, a more challenging budget target can be set as an effective way of making compensation more fair across the multiyear period. Here, though, care must be taken to guard against unwarranted management turnover because current period expected compensation probably will fall below competitive market levels.

In virtually all other situations, it is desirable to set highly achievable profit budget targets while allowing the managers few excuses for not achieving the targets. Setting targets that are highly achievable, but not too easy takes considerable managerial skill. Upper-level managers must know enough about the profit centers capabilities and business prospects to be able to judge the probability of budget success reasonably well in order to make this budget philosophy work properly. But when they implement this combination of mechanisms effectively, they will ensure that all the purposes for which budgets are used—planning, coordination, control, motivation, and performance evaluation—are served well.

Kenneth Merchant is professor of accounting at the University of Southern California.

---

[1] For example, see M. E. Barrett and L. B. Fraser III, "Conflicting Roles in Budgeting for Operations," *Harvard Business Review*, July-August 1977, pp. 137-146.

[2] For example, see R. L. M. Dunbar, "Budgeting for Control," *Administrative Science Quarterly*, March 1971, pp. 88-96.

[3] This finding emerged in a recent intensive study of 12 divisionalized corporations and some related fieldwork. Ten of the 12 corporations participating in the research study had used highly achievable budget targets for some time. One had recently changed its budgeting philosophy. It formerly used "stretch" budget targets but changed to have its targets reflect "minimum performance standards." One firm was still using stretch budget targets, but most of the managers in the firm were recommending that this philosophy of budgeting be changed. (For a detailed report of the findings of this study, see K Merchant, *Rewarding Results: Motivating Profit Center Managers*, Harvard Business School Press, 1989.)

[4] For example, Merchant (1989) found that profit center managers in seven of the 12 firms studied were sometimes given direct orders from upper management to turn in greater profits than were budgeted. In some of these firms, the orders were given virtually every quarter.

Chapter 10
Decision Making with Relevant Costs and Strategic Analysis

Cases

10-1   Decision Making Under Uncertainty
10-2   Profitability Analysis
10-3   Baldwin Bicycle Company
10-4   The Superior Valve Division
10-5   OmniSports Inc.

Readings

"The Leasing Conundrum"

This article looks at some of the complex accounting and tax issues involved in the lease versus buy decision. Both the financial accounting and tax rules are important because they can have a significant effect on the net cost of the lease, and therefore its potential attractiveness in the decision. In fact, as the article makes clear, sometimes the tax and financial reporting concerns are the key drivers in the lease/purchase decision.

Discussion questions:
1. Generally, under what conditions should a lease be treated as a purchase for both accounting and tax purposes?
2. What is usually the effect on income of treating an equipment lease of three to five years as a true lease?
3. What is a leveraged lease?
4. What are 3 or 4 of the key criteria the IRS uses to determine whether a lease is a purchase or true lease?

$$\boxed{\textit{Cases}}$$

10-1. Decision Making Under Uncertainty

Exquisite Foods Incorporated (EFI) sells premium foods. Three independent strategies are being considered to promote a new product, *Soufflés for Microwaves*, to dual-career families. Currently the contribution margin ratio on EFI's foods is 65%, which is expected to apply to the new product. EFI's policy for promoting new products permits only one type of advertising campaign until the product has been established.

STRATEGY ONE

The first strategy concentrates on television and magazine advertising. EFI would hire a marketing consultant to prepare a 30-second video commercial and a magazine advertisement. The commercial would air during the evening to address the working market, while the magazine advertisement would be place in magazines read by career-minded individuals. This advertising campaign would provide EFI $230,000 expected contribution from sales.

STRATEGY TWO

The second strategy promotes the product by offering 25% off coupons in the Sunday newspaper supplements, with a projected 15 percent redemption rate on sales revenue. EFI would hire a marketing consultant for $5,000 to design a one-quarter page, two-color coupon advertisement. The coupon would be distributed in the Sunday newspaper supplements at a cost of $195,000. Based on prior experience, EFI expects the following additional sales from this form of advertisement.

Expected sales	Probability
$500,000	10%
600,000	25
700,000	35
800,000	20
900,000	10

STRATEGY THREE

The third strategy offers a $.50 mail-in rebate coupon attached to each box of *Soufflés for Microwaves*. EFI would hire a marketing consultant for $5,000 to create a one-sixth page, one-color rebate coupon. Printing and attaching costs for the rebate coupon are $.07 per package, and EFI is planning to include the rebate offer on 500,000 packages. Although 500,000 packages may be sold, only a 10 percent redemption rate is expected. EFI expects the following additional sales from this type of promotion:

Expected sales	Probability
$400,000	10%
450,000	30
500,000	35
550,000	20
600,000	5

REQUIRED:

1. Exquisite Foods Incorporated (EFI) wishes to select the most profitable marketing alternative to promote *Soufflés for Microwaves*. Recommend which of the three strategies presented above should be adopted by EFI. Support your recommendation with appropriate calculations and analysis.
2. What selection criteria, other than profitability, should be considered in arriving at a decision on the choice of promotion alternatives?

10-2. Profitability Analysis

Sportway, Inc. is a wholesale distributor supplying a wide range of moderately priced sporting equipment to large chain stores. About 60 percent of Sportway's products are purchased from other companies while the remainder are manufactured by Sportway. The company has a Plastics Department that is currently manufacturing molded fishing tackle boxes. Sportway is able to manufacture and sell 8,000 tackle boxes annually, making full use of its direct labor capacity at available work stations. Presented below are the selling price and costs associated with Sportway's tackle boxes.

Selling price per box		$86.00
Costs per box		
Molded plastic	$ 8.00	
Hinges, latches, handle	9.00	
Direct labor ($15.00/hr.)	18.75	
Manufacturing overhead	12.50	
Selling and administrative cost...	17.00	65.25
Profit per box..............................		$20.75

Because Sportway believes it could sell 12,000 tackle boxes if it had sufficient manufacturing capacity, the company has looked into the possibility of purchasing the tackle boxes for distribution. Maple Products, a steady supplier of quality products, would be able to provide up to 9,000 tackle boxes per year at a price of $68.00 per box delivered to Sportway's facility.

Bart Johnson, Sportway's product manager, has suggested that the company could make better use of its Plastics Department by manufacturing skateboards. To support his position, Johnson has a market study that indicates an expanding market for skateboards and a need for additional suppliers. Johnson believes that Sportway could expect to sell 17,500 skateboards annually at a price of $45.00 per skateboard. Johnson's estimate of the costs to manufacture the skateboards is presented below.

Selling price per skateboard		$45.00
Costs per box		
Molded plastic	$5.50	
Wheels, hardware	7.00	
Direct labor ($15.00/hr.)	7.50	
Manufacturing overhead	5.00	
Selling and administrative cost.....	9.00	34.00
Profit per box..............................		$11.00

In the Plastics Department, Sportway uses direct labor hours as the application base for manufacturing overhead. Included in total manufacturing overhead for the current year is $50,000 of factory-wide, fixed manufacturing overhead that has been allocated to the Plastics Department, and would not change irrespective of the option chosen. For each unit of product that Sportway sells, regardless of whether the product has been purchased or is manufactured by Sportway, there is an allocated $6.00 fixed overhead cost per unit for distribution that is included in the selling and administrative cost for all products. Total selling and administrative costs for the purchased tackle boxes would be $10.00 per unit.

REQUIRED:

1. Prepare an analysis based on the data presented that will show which product or products Sportway Inc. should manufacture and/or purchase to maximize profitability and show the associated financial impact. Support your answer with appropriate calculations.
2. Identify the strategic factors Sportway should consider in its product decisions.

(CMA adapted)

10-3. The Baldwin Bicycle Company[1]

In May 1983, Suzanne Leister, marketing vice president of Baldwin Bicycle Company, was mulling over the discussion she had the previous day with Karl Knott, a buyer from Hi-Valu Stores, Inc. Hi-Valu operated a chain of discount department stores in the Northwest. Hi-Valu's sales volume had grown to the extent that it was beginning to add "house-brand" (also called "private-label") merchandise to the product lines of several of its departments. Mr. Knott, Hi-Valu's buyer for sporting goods, had approached Ms. Leister about the possibility of Baldwin's producing bicycles for Hi-Valu. The bicycles would bear the name "Challenger," which Hi-Valu planned to use for all of its house-brand sporting goods.

Baldwin had been making bicycles for almost 40 years. In 1983, the company's line included 10 models, ranging from a small beginner's model with training wheels to a deluxe 12-speed adult's model. Sales were currently at an annual rate of about $10 million. The company's 1982 financial statements appear in Exhibit 1. Most of Baldwin's sales were through independently owned retailers (toy stores, hardware stores, sporting goods stores) and bicycle shops. Baldwin had never before distributed its products through department store chains of any type. Ms. Leister felt that Baldwin bicycles had the image of being above average in quality and price, but not a "top-of-the-line" product.

Hi-Valu's proposal to Baldwin had features that made it quite different from Baldwin's normal way of doing business. First, it was very important to Hi-Valu to have ready access to a large inventory of bicycles, because Hi-Valu had had great difficulty in predicting bicycle sales, both by store and by month. Hi-Valu wanted to carry these inventories in its regional warehouses, but did not want title on a bicycle to pass form Baldwin to Hi-Valu until the bicycle was shipped from one of its regional warehouses to a specific Hi-Valu store. At that point, Hi-Valu would regard the bicycle as having been purchased from Baldwin, and would pay for it within 30 days. However, Hi-Valu would agree to take title to any bicycle that had been in one of its warehouses for four months, again paying for it within 30 days. Mr. Knott estimated that on average, a bike would remain in a Hi-Valu regional warehouse for two months.

Second, Hi-Valu wanted to sell its Challenger bicycles at lower prices than the name-brand bicycles it carried, and yet still earn approximately the same dollar gross margin on each bicycle sold--the rationale being that Challenger bike sales would take away from the sales of the name-brand bikes. Thus, Hi-Valu wanted to purchase bikes from Baldwin at lower prices than the wholesale prices of comparable bikes sold through Baldwin's usual channels.

Finally, Hi-Valu wanted the Challenger bike to be somewhat different in appearance from Baldwin's other bikes. While the frame and mechanical components could be the same as used on current Baldwin models, the fenders, seats, and handlebars would need to be somewhat different, and the tires would have the name *Challenger* molded into their sidewalls. Also, the bicycles would have to be packed in boxes printed with the Hi-Valu and Challenger names. These requirements were expected by Ms. Leister to increase Baldwin's purchasing, inventorying, and production costs over and above the added costs that would be incurred for a comparable increase in volume for Baldwin's regular products.

On the positive side, Ms. Leister was acutely aware that the bicycle boom had flattened out, and this plus a poor economy had caused Baldwin's sales volume to fall the past two years. As a result, Baldwin currently was operating its plant at about 75 percent of one-shift capacity. Thus, the added volume from Hi-Valu's purchases could possibly be very attractive. If agreement could be reached on prices, Hi-Valu would sign a contract guaranteeing to Baldwin that Hi-Valu would buy its house-brand bicycles only from Baldwin for a three-year period. The contract would then be automatically extended on a year-to-year basis, unless one party gave the other at least three-months' notice that it did not wish to extend the contract.

---

[1] © Robert N. Anthony. Used with permission.

Suzanne Leister realized she needed to do some preliminary financial analysis of this proposal before having any further discussion with Karl Knott. She had written on a pad the information she had gathered to use in her initial analysis; this information is shown in Exhibit 2.

Note: The American bicycle industry had become very volatile in recent years. From 1967 through 1970 sales average about 7 million units a year. By 1973 the total was up to a record 15 million units. By 1975 volume was back down to 7.5 million units. By 1982 volume was back up to 10 million units, still well below the peak years.

REQUIRED:

Should Baldwin accept the High-Value offer? Explain with consideration of both short-term and long-term considerations.

EXHIBIT 1   Financial Statements (thousands of dollars)

BALDWIN BICYCLE COMPANY
Balance Sheet
As of December 31, 1982

Assets		Liabilities and Owners' Equity	
Cash	$ 342	Accounts payable	$ 512
Accounts receivable	1,359	Accrued expenses	340
Inventories	2,756	Short-term bank loans	2,626
Plant and equipment (net)	3,635	Long-term note payable	1,512
		Total Liabilities	4,990
		Owner's equity	3,102
	$8,092		$8,092

Income Statement
For the Year Ended December 31, 1982

Sales revenues	$10,872
Cost of sales	8,045
Gross margin	2,827
Selling and administrative expenses	2,354
Income before taxes	473
Income tax expense	218
Net income	$ 255

EXHIBIT 2   Data Pertinent to Hi-Valu Proposal (*Notes taken by Suzanne Leister*)

1. *Estimated first-year costs of producing Challenger bicycles* (average unit costs, assuming a constant mix of models):

Materials	$39.80*
Labor	19.60
Overhead (@ 125% of labor)	24.50**
	$83.90

2. *Unit price and annual volume:* Hi-Valu estimates it will need 25,000 bikes a year and proposes to pay us (based on the assumed mix of models) an average of $92.29 per bike for the first year. Contract to contain an inflation escalation clause such that price will increase in proportion to inflation-caused increases in costs shown in item 1, above; thus, the $92.29 and $83.90 figures are, in effect, "constant-dollar" amounts. Knott intimated that there was very little, if any, negotiating leeway in the $92.29 proposed initial price.

3. *Asset-related costs* (annual variable costs, as percent of dollar value of assets):

Pretax cost of funds (to finance receivables or inventories)	18.0%
Recordkeeping costs (for receivables or inventories)	1.0
Inventory insurance	0.3
State property tax on inventory	0.7
Inventory-handling labor and equipment	3.0
Pilferage, obsolescence, breakage, etc	0.5

4. *Assumptions for Challenger-related added inventories* (average over the year):
   Materials: two month's supply.
   Work in process: 1,000 bikes, half completed (but all materials for them issued).
   Finished goods: 500 bikes (awaiting next carload lot shipment to a Hi-Valu warehouse).

5. *Impact on our regular sales:* Some customers comparison shop for bikes, and many of them are likely to recognize a Challenger bike as a good value when compared with a similar bike (either ours or a competitor's) at a higher price in a non-chain toy or bicycle store. In 1982, we sold 98,791 bikes. My best guess is that our sales over the next three years will be about 100,000 bikes a year if we forego the Hi-Valu deal. If we accept it, I think we'll lose about 3,000 units of our regular sales volume a year, since our retail distribution is quite strong in Hi-Valu's market regions. These estimates do not include the possibility that a few of our current dealers might drop our line if they find out we're making bikes for Hi-Valu.

Note: The information about overhead in item 1 of case Exhibit 2 can be used to infer that fixed manufacturing overhead is about 1.5 million per year.
*Includes items specific to models for Hi-Valu, not used in standard models.
**Accountant says about 40 percent of total production overhead cost is variable; 125 percent of DL$ rate is based on volume of 100,000 bicycles per year.

10-4. The Superior Valve Division

In 2001, the Superior Valve Division of the Able Corporation found itself in a position typical of fast-growing companies. Although sales revenues were increasing rapidly, capital equipment allocations from Able were less than desired, and profits were variable. Jerry Conrad, the general manager of the division, enrolled that year in a seminar on contribution margin income sponsored by the American Management Association (AMA). According to Conrad, "Before I went to that seminar, my knowledge of contribution margin income was limited to casual comments that I overheard at group general managers' meetings. A large acquisition in the automotive aftermarket industry had always used a contribution margin approach in its accounting systems. All other segments of the Able Corporation used the full costing method, but this company was allowed to keep its contribution margin cost system because a forced change of systems at the time of acquisition would have been too disruptive."

Jerry believed that the full cost reports used in his division were accurate. He and Frances Kardell, the Division Controller, were confident they knew the total manufacturing cost of each of their products. However, Jerry did not have the same confidence in his staff's ability to determine how volume changes would affect profits. He was convinced that better utilization of plant and equipment and a more effective pricing structure would lead to substantially improved earnings. The division was not as profitable as others in the industry or other similar-size divisions in the corporation that had comparable manufacturing processes.

A main point of the AMA seminar was that product lines do not produce profits; they produce contribution margin (sales revenue minus variable costs), which can become profits only after fixed costs are covered. The seminar also underscored not only the importance of cost behavior analysis but also the arbitrariness of many fixed cost allocations. Jerry immediately saw in contribution margin a new approach to solving Superior Valve's problems with both product mix and pricing decisions.

Jerry discussed the subject of contribution margin with Todd Talbott, the Group Controller. After hearing the advantages and disadvantages of the approach, Jerry recommended that his division's product costing system be overhauled for the third time since Able Corporation acquired Superior Valve 20 years ago. Todd agreed to support a change in the management reporting system, but he pointed out that the contribution margin approach was contrary to the reporting philosophy of the corporation and, for external purposes, did not comply with GAAP, S.E.C. reporting requirements, and Internal Revenue Service directives on inventory valuation.

When the decision to proceed was made, Frances and her accounting staff used regression analysis to classify manufacturing costs, other operating costs, and selling and general administration costs as either variable, fixed, or mixed. Mixed costs were separated into their variable and fixed components. Fixed costs then were identified as either discretionary (amounts to be expended based on decisions made annually or at shorter intervals) or committed (usually not subject to change in the short-run). A booklet on contribution margin which Jerry gave to his staff stated that fixed expenses are a function of time, and variable expenses (1) vary directly with changes in volume and (2) are usually expressed as a percentage of sales dollars or direct labor dollars.

SPECIAL ORDER

The Wadsworth Company, which was experimenting with various components of its product line, offered to purchase 6,000 Hydro-Con multi-function control valves from Superior for $160 each. Wadsworth would need 500 units per month with delivery commencing at the start of the new year. The special order would be in addition to the 80,000 units that Ralph Darwin, the division's Marketing Manager, expected to sell at the regular $200 price. Ralph considered the order to represent an excellent opportunity to increase long-term sales volume because it would be a new application for the product. He negotiated a flat $48,000 commission with the selling distributor.

Jerry was concerned that cutting the price of the valve would set an undesirable precedent. He pondered the special deal for several days before going to see Ralph. "The price is below our full cost of $175 per unit," he said. "If we accept the Wadsworth proposal, the firm can always expect favored treatment."

Jerry asked Daria Good, the Manufacturing Manager, and Frances to join this discussion in Darwin's office. When they arrived, he asked, "What is the division's capacity for making Hydro-Con Control?" Good's reply was "One hundred thousand (100,000) units per year, if we don't retool any machines dedicated to another product line."

Frances presented the following standard cost data for Hydro-Con valves:

Raw material	$ 35
Purchased components	30
Direct labor	12
Manufacturing overhead	44
Total standard cost	$121

After distributing copies of the budgeted income statement for the upcoming fiscal year (Table A), Frances revealed the variable overhead for the 80,000 unit Hydro-Con budget was $2,400,000. Of the budgeted fixed manufacturing costs, $400,000 was discretionary, with the remainder committed to basic capacity charges. Variable "other operating expenses" totaled $4 per unit; a 10% distributor commission ($20 per unit) comprised the variable portion of selling and general administration expenses. The Controller further indicated that manufacturing adjustments represented production variances and scrap, which she expected to vary with the number of valves produced. At the budgeted volume level, fixed other operating expenses would add an average of $16 to unit cost. Basic service costs such a production control, engineering administration, and accounting totaling $880,000 were allocated to Hydro-Con; the remaining fixed other operating expenses were directly related to the product line and were discretionary in nature.

As the discussion continued, Ralph reviewed next year's budget. Of the total fixed selling, general, and administrative expense, $160,000 was earmarked for future advertising space in several trade publications and an upcoming trade show. The remainder of the budget related to salaries and other firm commitments.

The Hydro-Con budget was designed to fully recover all costs at the 80,000 unit production level. The other product line budgets also were designed to fully recover costs at budgeted volume levels, and all fixed costs were expected to remain unchanged until the current maximum capacities were surpassed (Table B). Jerry asked his Division Controller what effect the Wadsworth offer would have on profits. But Daria had not yet studied the effects volume changes would have on division operations.

PRODUCT LINE ELIMINATION

Superior Valve's Marketing Department prepared a sales order plan by product line for each new year in both units and dollars. The Production Control Department then used the order plan to develop a sales shipment plan for each of the division's three plants. Ralph Darwin had very little marketing information to use in developing the Made to Order (MTO) Hydraulic Control product line plan. However, he knew that the line's compound growth pattern over the last three years had been quite disappointing, and he saw little prospect for substantial sales growth in the short-term future.

Ralph recommended the division consider eliminating the Made to Order line. Daria had assured him that the MTO-dedicated machinery could be retooled to produce either of the standard lines. Darwin was convinced he could develop a market for the additional standard product in a relatively short time, and he strongly believed the division should concentrate on its two basic product lines. "After all," he commented, "that's where we're most successful." However, until the additional market for the standard product was developed, the elimination of MTO would mean the elimination of 30 manufacturing jobs.

At the last staff meeting of the year, Jerry Conrad told Ralph he would study the product line elimination proposal after he made a decision on the Hydro-Con special order. He assigned the proposal top priority for the new year.

REQUIRED:

1. Assume that inventories will not change during the year. Prepare budgeted contribution approach product line income statements for the year ending 6/30/19X3. Categorize fixed costs as either discretionary or committed.
2. Should Jerry Conrad decide to accept the Wadsworth Company special order? If so, what will be the new Hydro-Con return on sales?
3. Should the Superior Valve Division eliminate the Made to Order product line if there were no alternative uses for its production capacity?
4. If all resulting standard products could be sold, how should the MTO capacity be allocated? (Assume only the capacity currently being used to produce 20,000 MTO units would be used to produce additional standard products.)

(IMA adapted)

TABLE A

Superior Valve Division
Budgeted Income Statement for the Year Ending 6/30/2002
($000)

	Hydro-Con	Pneu-trol	Made to Order	Total Division
Revenue	$16,000	$13,000	$ 5,000	$34,000
Material	5,200	3,900	1,300	10,400
Direct Labor	960	1,235	1,000	3,195
Overhead	3,520	2,990	1,531	8,041
Total Cost of Sales @ Standard	9,680	8,125	3,831	21,636
Gross Margin	6,320	4,875	1,169	12,364
Adjustments	800	520	554	1,874
Net Manufacturing Margin	5,520	4,355	615	10,490
Other Oper. Exp. Expenses	1,600	1,560	750	3,910
Selling & General Administration	1,920	1,560	600	4,080
Operating Income	$ 2,000	$ 1,235	$ (735)	$ 2,500

TABLE B

	Superior Valve Division Product Line Data	
	Pneu-trol	MTO
Unit selling price	$ 50.00	$ 250.00
Variable overhead per unit	$ 6.50	$ 50.55
Total discretionary fixed overhead	$225,000	$100,000
Variable other operating cost per unit	$ 1.50	$ 5.00
Variable selling and general admin. per unit	$ 5.00	$ 25.00
Committed fixed other operating costs	$970,000	$550,000
Committed fixed selling & general admin.	$160,000	$ 75,000

Product Line	Present Max. Capacity in Units	Machine Hrs./Unit
Hydro-Con	100,000	6
Pneu-trol	350,000	2
MTO	50,000	5

10-5. OmniSport Inc.

OmniSport Inc. is a wholesale distributor supplying a wide range of moderately priced sporting equipment to large chain stores. OmniSport has an enviable reputation for quality of its products. In fact, the demand for its products is so great that at times OmniSport cannot satisfy the demand and must delay or refuse some orders, in order to maintain its production quality. Additionally, OmniSport purchases some of its products from outside suppliers in order to meet the demand. These suppliers are carefully chosen so that their products maintain the quality image that OmniSport has attained. About 60 percent of OmniSport's products are purchased from other companies while the remainder of the products are manufactured by OmniSport. The company has a Plastics Department that is currently manufacturing the boot for in-line skates. OmniSport is able to manufacture and sell 5,000 pairs of skates annually, making full use of its machine capacity at available workstations. Presented below are the selling price and costs associated with OmniSport's skates.

Selling price per pair of skates		$98
Costs per pair		
Molded plastic	$8	
Other direct materials	12	
Machine time ($16 per hour)	24	
Manufacturing overhead	18	
Selling and administrative cost	15	77
Profit per pair		$21

Because OmniSport believes it could sell 8,000 pairs of skates annually if it had sufficient manufacturing capacity, the company has looked into the possibility of purchasing the skates for distribution. Colcott Inc., a steady supplier of quality products, would be able to provide 6.000 pairs of skates per year at a price of $75 per pair delivered to OmniSport's facility.

Jack Petrone, OmniSport's product manager, has suggested that the company could make better use of its Plastics Department by manufacturing snowboard bindings. To support his position, Petrone has a market study that indicates an expanding market for snowboards and a need for additional suppliers. Petrone believes that OmniSport could expect to sell 12,000 snowboard bindings annually at a price of $60 per binding. Petrone's estimate of the costs to manufacture the bindings is presented below.

Selling price per snowboard binding		$60
Costs per binding		
Molded plastic	$16	
Other direct materials	4	
Machine time ($16 per hour)	8	
Manufacturing overhead	6	
Selling and administrative cost	14	48
Profit per binding		$12

Other information pertinent to OmniSport's operations is presented below.

An allocated $6 fixed overhead cost per unit is included in the selling and administrative cost for all of the purchased and manufactured products. Total fixed and variable selling and administrative costs for the purchased skates would be $10 per pair.

In the Plastics Department, OmniSport uses machine hours as the application base for manufacturing overhead. Included in the manufacturing overhead for the current year is $30,000 of fixed, factory-wide manufacturing overhead that has been allocated to the Plastics Department.

REQUIRED:

In order to maximize OmniSport Inc.'s profitability, recommend which product or products should be manufactured and/ or purchased. Prepare an analysis based on the data presented that will show the associated financial impact. Support your answer with appropriate calculations and strategic considerations.

(CMA adapted)

THE LEASING CONUNDRUM

William J. Cenker and Robert Bloom: The Leasing Conundrum

Accounting rules, primarily from FASB Statement of Financial Accounting Standards No. 13, "Accounting for Leases," and many Financial Accounting Standards Board Interpretations and Technical Bulletins, offer substantial guidance for treating lease arrangements. Although lease transactions require professional judgment, the rules are clear—they will be accounted for either as a capital or operating lease depending on their parameters. The rules for income tax purposes, however, are less clear-cut. The financial professional must carefully examine the terms of the transaction to determine how it should be treated. In addition, tax criteria often influence the structure of a lease transaction, so accounting professionals need to completely understand both accounting as well as tax rules to be able to aid management in negotiating leases that meet a firm's overall business objectives.

Financial and tax accounting for leases emphasize economic substance over legal form. Although a lease may appear to be a rental agreement, if most of the rewards and risks of ownership are transferred from the lessor (owner) to the lessee (renter), the lease should be accounted for as a capital lease for both accounting and tax purposes. In most cases a capital lease for financial accounting will also be considered a capital lease for tax accounting. But there are other intricate situations in which a lease is treated as a capital lease for financial accounting and an operating lease for tax, and vice versa.

FINANCIAL ACCOUNTING

For financial accounting purposes, eight FASB Standards, 10 Technical Bulletins, six Interpretations, and over 20 Emerging Issues Task Force rulings provide guidance for classifying leases as operating or capital.

Detailed professional guidance is necessary because lease transactions are often complex. There are, however, several basic criteria. In general, leases are classified as capitalized transactions if they meet at least one of the following four SFAS No. 13 criteria:

The TO Test. The lease transfers ownership (TO) of the leased property to the lessee by the end of the lease term.

The BPO Test. The lease contains a bargain purchase option (BPO).

The 75% Rule. The lease term is equal to or greater than 75% of the estimated economic life of the leased asset.

The 90% Rule. The present value of the minimum lease payments (excluding executory costs) is equal to or greater than 90% of the fair value of the leased asset.[1]

Two other criteria also must be met for a lease to be capitalized by the lessor: 1) The lease payments must be relatively predictable, and 2) there must be no important uncertainties concerning nonreimbursable costs not yet incurred.

In practice, most leases are structured so that the terms do not meet any of the above criteria and therefore are not capitalized. Classifying the lease as an operating lease keeps the asset and liability off the lessee's balance sheet and usually results in higher earnings.

Lessees escape the first three criteria all too readily. They also manage to avoid capitalization by circumventing the fourth criterion. Typically, the 90% rule is avoided by structuring the lease so that the lessee does not know the interest rate implicit in the lease and therefore is unable to use the lower of the lessee's incremental borrowing rate versus the interest rate implicit in the lease. Should the lessee's incremental borrowing rate be relatively high, the higher discount rate would produce a lower present value, making it less likely to achieve the fourth criterion.

There is another way that the 90% rule can be avoided. Lessees may be required to insure the residual value of the leased property with a third party. The residual value accrues to the lessor and reduces the required minimum lease payments, making it less likely for the lessee to fulfill the 90% rule. While the lessor would include the present value of the third-party guaranteed residual value in computing the 90%

rule, the lessee disregards this residual value in that computation.

SALE AND LEASEBACK

One means of infusing cash into the business is by using a sale and leaseback financing transaction. In a sale and leaseback, the property is sold and leased back. Substantially all future benefits of the asset are retained by the seller-lessee. The seller-lessee records the transaction as a capital lease if one of the above criteria is met and amortizes any profit in proportion to the amortization of the leased asset.[2]

With real estate, the lease of the land is capitalized if the TO or BPO test is met, but it is not amortized. The land and building are capitalized separately if the TO or BPO test is met. Then only the building is amortized. If TO or BPO is not present, the 75% rule and the 90% rule are applied to the building portion and capitalized. If either the 75% or the 90% rule is met, the lease is also amortized. The portion attributable to land is treated as an operating lease. If land is less than 25% of the fair value of the leased property, the land and building are treated as a single unit, and the unit is capitalized and amortized.

LEVERAGED LEASE

In a leveraged lease, the lender, such as a bank or insurance company, lends a portion, say 80%, of the cash required for acquiring the asset. The lessor puts up the remaining 20% in cash. The loan is usually nonrecourse or, in other words, not secured by the leased asset.

The accounting issues in leveraged leases pertain to the use of debt by the lessor to acquire the leased asset and are complicated from the lessor's perspective primarily for two reasons:

1. The lessor may obtain significant nonrecourse financing of the leased asset. Then generally accepted accounting principles require that the lease receivable be offset by the loan as if it were a single transaction.

2. The income from the transaction must be allocated over the life of the lease based on an initial analysis between net investment recovery and income.[3] The allocation is based on the effective rate that discounts the total earnings to the net investment.

The cash profits accruing to the lessor include the potential differential in interest rates and the residual value. The fact that a lease is leveraged has no impact on the lessee's accounting.

INCOME TAX RULES FOR LEASE TRANSACTIONS

There is substantially less guidance on lease transactions in the U.S. tax law than in the accounting literature. The determination of whether a transaction is a capital or operating lease is quite subjective and based primarily on case law. Because the possibilities for abuse are almost unlimited with leveraged leases, much of the guidance involves such leases.

In most cases, a capital lease for financial accounting should also be treated as a capital lease for tax accounting. It is possible, however, to achieve different results for tax than for accounting purposes.

A lease referred to as an "operating" lease for accounting purposes is often called a "true" lease for tax purposes. Similarly, a "capital" lease in accounting is often termed a conditional "sale" or "purchase" in taxation.

There are no direct provisions in the U.S. Tax Code or Regulations that distinguish true leases from conditional sale and purchases. The long-standing position of the IRS regarding the tax aspects of equipment leasing is stated in Revenue Ruling 55-540.[4] The guidelines set forth in Rev. Proc. 75-21 clarify the circumstances in which an advance ruling recognizing the existence of a true lease will be issued.[5]

REVENUE RULING 55-540

This IRS ruling states the tax aspects of equipment leasing from the perspective of the lessee. Absent compelling factors indicating otherwise, one or more of the following factors would suggest a conditional purchase rather than a true lease:

- Portions of the periodic payment are specifically applicable to an ownership interest to be acquired by the lessee.[6]
- The lessee acquires title upon the payment of a stated amount of rentals.[7] This is similar to the transfer of ownership clause of SFAS No. 13.
- The total of lease payments over a relatively short period of use constitutes an inordinately large portion of the required sum to be paid for securing the title.[8]
- The total of the agreed-upon lease payments materially exceeds the current fair value.[9] This factor, when viewed in conjunction with the preceding factor, is similar to the 90% present value test of SFAS No. 13.
- The property may be acquired at the termination of the lease under a bargain purchase option, defined as nominal in relation to the value of the property or in relation to the total payments to

be made.[10] This is similar to the bargain purchase option clause of SFAS No. 13.

- Some portion of the periodic payments is specifically designated or is readily recognizable as interest.[11]

REV. PROC. 75-21

Rev. Proc. 75-21 sets forth the guidelines that the IRS uses for advanced rulings to determine whether a leveraged lease is actually a true lease for income tax purposes. The IRS emphasizes that such guidelines establish conditions that produce a "distribution of burdens and benefits" whereby it can be assumed that the IRS will not recharacterize a lease under examination.[12] The guidelines pertaining to a true lease reflect the following considerations:

- Minimum unconditional "at-risk" investment.
- Useful life.
- Purchase and sale rights.
- Lessee investments and/or loans.
- Lessor profit requirement.
- Lump-sum payments.

AT-RISK INVESTMENT

The lessor must maintain a minimum "at-risk" equity investment of at least 20% of the cost of the property throughout the lease period. This criterion is particularly important for leveraged leases where the financing is nonrecourse. In addition, the lessor is not entitled to a return of any portion of the minimum investment through any arrangement, directly or indirectly with the lessee, or from any party related to the lessee.

The minimum investment also applies to the residual investment. The fair market value of the residual investment must be at least 20% of the original cost of the property, determined without inflation, after considering removal and redelivery costs.

USEFUL LIFE

In addition to maintaining the minimum investment, the lease term cannot be 100% of the useful life of the property and still be considered a lease. Rev. Proc. 75-21 suggests that the remaining useful life of the asset at the end of the lease term must be the longer of one year or 20% of the originally estimated useful life. The lease term includes all renewal or extension options except renewals or extensions at the option of the lessee at fair rental value.

PURCHASE AND SALE RIGHTS

The lessee or related party cannot be granted an option to purchase the property at a price less than its fair value at the time the right is exercised. Further, when the property is placed into service, the lessor may not hold a contractual right to cause any party to purchase the property. Viewed in conjunction with the required minimum residual investment discussed above, Rev. Proc. 75-21 effectively stipulates a purchase option of more than 20% of the initial fair value of the leased property, reduced by reasonable costs of removal and delivery.

LESSEE INVESTMENT AND/OR LOANS

The lessee or related party cannot contribute toward the cost of the property. More important, the lessee may not improve or make additions to the property unless such improvements or additions are readily removable without causing material damage to the property. Ordinary maintenance and repairs are excluded.

In addition, the lessee or related party cannot enable the lessor to acquire the property by either making a loan to the lessor or guaranteeing his/her indebtedness. Guarantees of maintenance, rent, or insurance are excluded.

LESSOR PROFIT REQUIREMENT

The lessor is required to demonstrate that there is a profit motive in the lease transaction, which is based on two required tests.[13] First, the total lease payments and residual value must exceed the lessor's aggregate disbursements and equity investment. Second, the aggregate lease payments must exceed the lessor's aggregate disbursements by a "substantial" amount. Stated differently, the lease agreement must produce a fair return to the lessor.

The question is: "What is a fair return?" The IRS's Tax Shelters Examination Handbook, IRM 4236-872, advises its examiners to question the lessor's motives for entering into a lease if the present value of the rents plus salvage value does not exceed the present value of the total investment. Further, for transactions arranged for a profit, the rate of return should be at least equal to the risk-free return. The present-value and rate-of-return tests are viewed as providing little more than a preliminary indication of whether a leasing transaction should be closely scrutinized.[14] That the taxpayer uses a figure lower than 20% for reporting the residual value on its financial statements does not necessarily mean that an estimate of 20% or more for advanced ruling purposes is unreasonable. It is not necessary for the taxpayer to realize a profit exclusive of the tax benefits. It is only necessary that the taxpayer engage in the transaction with a reasonable expectation of profit realization.

LUMP-SUM PAYMENTS

The IRS ordinarily does not question leveraged lease arrangements that provide for prepaid or deferred rent if the annual rent does not exceed 10% more than the average rent for the entire lease period, or during the first two-thirds of the lease period such rent is not more than 10% above or below the average for the initial term and the annual rent in the remainder is no greater than the highest rent in the initial period nor lower than one-half the lowest rent in the initial period. If the foregoing guidelines contained in Rev. Proc 75-21 are not satisfied, the IRS will, nonetheless, consider ruling on whether the arrangement is a true lease or conditional sale on the basis of all facts and circumstances.

CASE HISTORY

The U.S. Tax Court looks to the underlying substance of the transaction, often quite apart from its form, to see whether the intent of the parties was to create a rental agreement or a purchase/sale.[15] Short-term agreements covering equipment in which the rent payments have been based on production or mileage have not been viewed as a purchase/sale of property. An agreement to purchase taxicabs, for example, which calls for payments of $50,000 over 10 months, at $5,000 a month with the option to purchase at the end of 10 months for $35,000, was considered a rental agreement. That is, it was a rental for the period prior to exercising the purchase option because the amounts were considered reasonable and the option price was not a bargain purchase.[16] For rental payments of microwave equipment by a television station, the agreement was deemed to be a conditional sales contract. Rental payments equaled the purchase price plus interest.[17]

Under Revenue Ruling 55-540 on "Leases versus Purchases," a deduction for rent depends on whether the taxpayer will receive title or equity as a consequence of rent payments. In almost all cases where rent deduction was disallowed, there was an option to purchase property. However, emphasis has been placed on the primary intent of the parties. Where rentals are excessive, the IRS has disallowed the deduction of rent because of the implicit intent to have the lessee take title.

LEASING PROGRAMS

By permitting the lessor to own the property—and thus receive the depreciation tax shield—the lease may be structured to arrange for reduced lease payment. The lessee would benefit if he/she is unable to take advantage of the tax shield because of limited (or significantly lower) taxable income. It is also possible for one party to the lease to take the depreciation deduction for income tax purposes while the other party takes the depreciation deduction for accounting purposes.

A lease also may be structured to solve other tax problems. For example, the lease might effectively shift income to another country or recharacterize that income by converting business income to portfolio income or utilizing a foreign tax credit.

Another tax problem often created by promoters of lease programs is to rejuvenate an expiring net operating loss. Promoters often structure lease transactions as leveraged and/or sales-leaseback transactions. Equipment leasing programs that are actively marketed usually involve at least one of these structures and are tailored to solve individual tax problems discussed briefly above. Although the possibilities are endless, these programs generally concern short- and medium-term equipment leases involving three or more parties. These programs, however, may create significant tax exposure.

Equipment leases of three to five years are usually structured as true leases.[18] The combination of depreciation and interest resulting from a true lease generally will cause the lessor to show losses in the initial years. The losses may be valuable to offset otherwise highly taxable income. The lessor earns an additional return by re-leasing or selling the equipment for its residual value.

The lease may also be structured for tax purposes using a limited partnership. The lessor sells the equipment to a limited partnership and simultaneously leases it back, usually over a five- to eight-year period.[19] This "paper" transaction usually requires the partnership to finance the purchase through a nonrecourse loan from the lessor. Usually, there will be a "re-marketing" agreement between the lessor and the limited partnership, specifying the amount the lessor will pay the partnership to re-lease the equipment.[20] Under these arrangements, the lessor has a profit equal to the excess of lease income from the operating lease along with the interest income from the partnership "loan" over the interest expense to the lender and the lease payment made to the limited partnership. The limited partnership will have a taxable loss caused by the depreciation and interest expense.

Still other parties could be included in the lease transaction involving limited partnerships. For example, a corporation could serve as the limited partner and the lessor as the general partner. The corporation could sell the receivable to a factoring company and thereby manipulate the timing of income under the arrangement.[21]

Often a "mountain" of paperwork is needed to describe the rights of the various parties.[22] Yet the basic questions remain: Is the transaction a purchase/sale or a true lease? Is tax avoidance the primary purpose of the lease arrangement? Can the transaction be accounted for as a capital lease for accounting purposes and as a true lease for tax purposes? Whether a lease that has been capitalized on the books in accordance with SFAS No. 13 can be treated as an operating lease on the tax return depends on the facts and circumstances of each lease.[23]

For many companies it may be more advantageous to characterize a lease as an operating lease for tax purposes and thereby claim the payments as rent expense. If the lease is capitalized for accounting purposes and treated as an operating lease for tax purposes, then there will be a temporary difference caused by the timing of the deductions. These differences, including interest and depreciation, will appear in the company's federal Form 1120 Schedule M-1.

APPLYING BOTH SETS OF RULES

Now let's look at a leasing transaction in which the issue is whether the lease agreement constitutes an operating lease or capital lease from an accounting perspective and a true lease or conditional sale/purchase from an income tax perspective.

XZY, a medium-sized tool and die maker, supplies JWC, a large manufacturer, with approximately $20 million in parts a year.

To produce a new product line under contract for JWC, XZY must install a new equipment facility costing $3 million. XZY is financially unable to incur additional debt for this acquisition because its revolving bank credit arrangement prohibits it. Accordingly, XZY wants to lease the equipment from JWC.

Various lease options are under consideration. Essentially, the lease terms are as follows:

1. The lease is for six years, and XZY has the option to purchase the facility or renew the lease at fair market value. The estimated economic life of the equipment is at least 40 years.
2. The fair market value of the property upon termination of the lease is assumed to be $800,000. The residual value is not guaranteed by XZY. Substantially all property is recoverable at lease termination. Any property that is not recoverable will be abandoned.

3. The equipment financing by JWC is 20% equity and 80% debt. The debt will be provided by JWC's bank and is expected to be nonrecourse to JWC.
4. XZY has to pay the property taxes, maintenance, and insurance on the equipment.
5. The present value of the minimum lease payments as of the inception of the lease is $2.55 million.[24] The minimum lease payments total $3.7 million over the term of the lease. Total payment on the nonrecourse loan is substantially less than the required minimum lease payments, and the arrangement produces a fair return to JWC.
6. The lease contains a fixed buyout option of $800,000 at the end of the lease term. JWC assumes that the likelihood that XZY will exercise such option is 100%.

FROM AN ACCOUNTING PERSPECTIVE

Analyzing this example lease from an accounting perspective, none of the four criteria for a capital lease (SFAS No. 13) is met:

1. The lease does not transfer ownership of the leased property to the lessee by the end of lease term. Even though JWC assumes that the likelihood of XZY's exercise of the buyout is 100%, the exercise is not guaranteed. Accordingly, until the buyout is exercised, ownership remains with JWC.
2. The lease does not contain a bargain purchase option. The fixed buyout option is not a "bargain" purchase because it reflects the estimated fair value of the equipment.
3. The lease term is not equal to or greater than 75% of the estimated economic life of the leased asset. The economic life of 40 years far exceeds the lease term of six years.
4. The present value of the minimum lease payments (excluding executory costs) is not at least 90% of the fair market value of the leased asset. The present value of the minimum lease payments is $2.55 million, which is 85% of the fair market value of $3 million. Thus, the fourth criterion—the 90% rule—is not fulfilled from an accounting perspective, and, overall, it is an operating lease according to financial accounting.

FROM A TAX PERSPECTIVE

From a tax perspective, the lease terms are analyzed below based on Rev. Ruling 55-540 and Rev. Proc. 75-21. Only one of the IRS criteria for a conditional sale applies to this example (Rev. Ruling 55-540):
- No portion of the periodic payments is specifically applicable to an equity to be acquired by the

lessee. Further, no portion of the payments is specifically or constructively identifiable as interest.

- The lessee does not acquire title upon the payment of a stated amount of rentals.
- The terms do not include a provision whereby property may be acquired under a bargain purchase option defined as nominal in relation to the value of the property or in relation to the total payments to be made.
- The total of the lease payments will not materially exceed the current fair value.
- The amount of the lease payments over a relatively short period of use constitutes an inordinately large portion of the required sum to be paid for securing the title. The life of the asset is 40 years, and the lease terms require payments of $3.7 million over a relatively brief six-year period.[25]

The last criterion is perhaps the most difficult one to overcome with respect to the lease terms. Further, the example meets the criteria for a true (operating) lease from Rev. Proc. 75-21:

1. There is an initial minimum unconditional at-risk investment. This appears valid in this example because JWC is financing the equipment with 20% equity and 80% debt.
2. Maintenance of the minimum investment occurs throughout the lease term. Assuming level annual payments by the lessor and the lessee, this condition appears to be met in this example. Further evidence is provided by the fact that the fixed buyout of $800,000 is 27% of the initial fair value of the equipment.
3. At least 20% of the fair market value of the leased property remains at the end of the lease term. In addition, the fair value of the facility is estimated to be $800,000 at the termination of the lease.
4. At least 20% of the useful life of the leased property remains at the end of the lease term. Again, the lease term is only six out of 40 years of the useful life of the equipment. Therefore, 85% of the estimated useful life remains at the end of the lease term.
5. The property leased is not "limited-use" property. There is no indication of that in the case example. In fact, substantially all property is recoverable at the termination of the lease.

Accordingly, this lease appears to be an operating lease for accounting and a true (operating) lease for tax purposes. If JWC is consistent in its treatment for accounting and tax purposes, there is little to challenge from a tax standpoint.

But the lease terms include several elements that can be negotiated should JWC want to treat the lease as a conditional sale for tax purposes. The lease payments (or lease term) could be increased and the fixed buyout option decreased to an amount less than $600,000. Assuming that the decrease in the buyout option does not render this option a "bargain purchase" for accounting purposes, the lease could be recorded as an operating lease for accounting purposes and a conditional sale for tax purposes.[26] That result could be supported because the 20% residual value test of Rev. Proc. 75-21 would not be met, and, as discussed above, the amount of the payments would be substantially large over a relatively brief time period.

CASE-BY-CASE ANALYSIS

Because leases are common in business, it is important for financial professionals to understand the intricacies of both financial and tax accounting rules.

GAAP on lease accounting is extensive. For tax purposes, the appropriate treatment is less clear. The determination is to be made by reference to the relative distribution of the burdens and benefits of ownership to the parties.[27] Thus, each lease must be evaluated in light of the specific facts and circumstances surrounding the lease.

Because of the lack of specific guidance, lease programs have been marketed to target other tax problems. Management accountants should analyze each proposed lease transaction to gain an understanding of the underlying motivation for the agreements. If the motivation is primarily tax avoidance, if the agreement lacks economic substance, and if the terms are inconsistent with one or more of the tax criteria outlined above, then the transaction may lead to significant tax liability exposure.

ENDNOTES:

1   The 75% economic life and 90% present value criteria tests should not be considered if the lease item begins with the last 25% of total estimated economic life of the leased property.
2   If the lease does not meet any of these criteria, it is treated as an operating lease.
3   For tax purposes, if the lease is treated as a lease rather than as a sale, taxable income is the difference between rents received and the related expenses including depreciation and interest. Accordingly, deferred taxes will also have to be recognized.
4   IRS Rev. Rul. 55-540, 1955-2 C.B. 39.

5 IRS Rev. Proc. 75-21, 1975-1 C.B. 715.
6 Truman Bowen v. Com, 12 TC 446.
7 Hervey v. Rhode Island Locomotive Works, 93 U.S. 664 (1876); Robert A. Taft v. Com, 27 B.T.A. 808; Truman Bowen v. Com, supra.
8 Truman Bowen v. Com, supra.
9 William A. McWaters et al. v. Com, TCM June 15, 1950; Truman Bowan v. Com, supra.
10 Burroughs Adding Machine Co. v. Bogdon, 9 Fed. (2d) 54; Holeproof Hosiery v. Com., 11 B.T.A. 547.
11 Judson Mills v. Com, 11 TC 25., acq., C.B. 1949-1,2.
12 IRS Letter Ruling 8144014.
13 The genuine expectation of profit has been consistently upheld by the courts. See, for example, Newcombe v. Commissioner, 54 T.C. 1298 (1970), or Dupont v. Commissioner, 62 T.C. 36 (1974).
14 This is discussed in TAM 8144014 and IRM 4236-872, Tax Shelters Examination Handbook.
15 Norma Baker Smith (1968), 51TC429.
16 Benton v. Com (1952, CA 5), 42 AFTR229.
17 Int. Mansfield Television, Inc. U.S. (1964, DCVT).
18 These are referred to as "user leases" under typical terminology.
19 These transactions are often referred to as "wrap leases" or "master leases."
20 Funds received after the initial expiration of the lease are termed "remarketing proceeds." Such proceeds allow the lessor to earn a cash profit equal to the value of the equipment after the initial user lease expires. The term "lessor" is used throughout because the "lessor" is a limited partnership, 99% of which is owned by the corporation.
21 Such income is commonly referred to as a "plug" of income.
22 In interviews, an IRS agent who is in charge of large-company audits said the paperwork makes auditing these transactions difficult, and the IRS is hesitant to litigate in this area.
23 Internal Revenue Service, Manual Handbook, HB 4232. (13), 9/20/95, Subsection 463.5, Capital Leases.
24 The present value of the minimum lease payments includes the present value of the residual value. The overall discount rate is approximately 10%.
25 The "required" payments technically would exclude the residual value of $800,000.
26 A bargain purchase option is a lessee's option to purchase the leased property at a sufficiently low price that makes the exercise of the option almost certain (SFAS No. 13, par. 5d). However, there is no specific definition of what constitutes a "bargain."
27 Helvering v. Lazarus & Co., 308 U.S. 252 (1939), 1939-2 C.B. 208; Sun Oil Co. v. Com., 562 F. 2d 258 (3rd Cir. 1977), cert. denied 98 5. ct. 2845 (1978).

Chapter 11
Capital Budgeting

Cases

11-1   The Case of the Almost Identical Twins
11-2   ACE Company (A)
11-3   Ace Company (B)
11-4   Component Technologies, Inc.: Adding Flexconnex Capacity
11-5   General Medical Center

Readings

"How Forest Product Companies Analyze Capital Budgets"
This article presents the result of a survey on the uses of capital budgeting techniques by forest product companies. Capital budgeting for this industry has become more challenging and riskier because of increasing competitiveness and government and environmental pressures.

Discussion Questions:
1. The survey result shows that more firms use one or more discounted cash flow methods in evaluating timber-related capital investments. However, more firms use payback period methods to assess plant and equipment purchases. What are reasons for these differences?
2. List changes in the uses of capital budgeting techniques over the years.
3. List some of the methods for adjusting risks in capital investments.
4. What is post-audit? How do forest product companies conduct post-audits?

"How ABC Was Used in Capital Budgeting"
This article presents a case study on the difference that ABC makes on the investment decision of a new project. A business forecast signaled "Go" to an interactive TV project, but the ABC analysis said, "Stop." The article discusses the utilization and limitations of activity-based costing (ABC) in capital budgeting including capacity to predict operating and capital costs, benchmarking model and steps in using ABC in capital investment project.

Discussion Questions:
1. What is the general business case approach to capital budgeting? *Done at broad level, few details*
2. How does an ABC model approach to capital budgeting differ from the general business case approach?
3. What are the roles of value chain in capital budgeting?
4. List advantages and limitations of ABC approach to capital budgeting.

"Assessing Risk and Uncertainty in New Technology Investments"
This article develops a framework for managers to use in assessing new technology investments, based on both nonquantitative risk factors and quantifiable financial returns and risk factors. The framework extends the conventional two-dimensional risk-return model to a three dimensional approach in which the third dimension is the nonquantifiable, uncertain factors. The analytical hierarchy process (AHP), which is used for assessing nonquantifiable data, is the underlying model of the framework.

Discussion Questions:
1. What approaches are often used in assessing investments in new technology?
2. Why are these approaches inadequate or impractical?
3. How does the proposed model incorporate an assessment of nonquantifiable uncertainties, quantifiable financial returns, and risk parameters in evaluating capital investment projects?
4. How does the method explained in this article differ from previous models that have used the AHP method in investment decision-making?

Cases

Case 11-1. The Case of the Almost Identical Twins[1]

Once upon a time twin boys were born into a typical Ozian family. The boys, named Spender and Saver, were alike in every respect except the one indicated by their names. While they were in high school, both worked at part-time jobs earning the minimum wage of $4.445 per hour for the maximum hours permitted by law, viz., 44 hours per month. There was no income tax in Oz. Spender found many things on which to spend all of his income, while Saver arranged with his parents to add his monthly income to their money market fund which earned 8% per *annum, compounded monthly*.

At the end of four years of high school, each of the boys bought a car costing the amount of Saver's accumulated savings, which he withdrew from his parents' money market account to pay for the car. Spender financed his car on a "no money down," 18% per annum, compounded monthly contract for 48 months. Thus, during four years of university, both boys had cars, both spent the same amounts on other things, but Saver invested each month an amount equal to what Spender was paying on his car, the saving again being at 8% per *annum, compounded monthly*. Both boys financed their expenses while at the university in the same way: partly by working and partly with help from their parents.

When they graduated from the university, the two men continued their identical spending patterns, except that Saver was able to buy a home, using the accumulation of his savings from avoiding car payments in the previous four years as the down payment (20% of the purchase price), financing the remainder on a *10% fixed* rate mortgage, payable monthly over 30 years. Spender rented a similar home, paying (the first year) "net rent" equal to Saver's monthly mortgage payments. Spender's lease also required that he reimburse his landlord for property taxes and insurance on the rental unit- amounts equal to Saver's costs for those items. Thus, Spender continued his pattern of spending all of his income, while Saver paid off his mortgage over 30 years.

Unfortunately for Spender, his "net rent" increased at the rate of 5% per annum, so his housing costs escalated considerably over the 30 years. In the meantime, Saver invested the difference between Spender's escalating "net rent" and his own fixed mortgage payment. Each year he accumulated the monthly saving in his 8% money market fund, then at the end of the year invested in a mortgage bond mutual fund yielding the same rate as he was paying on his own mortgage: 10% perannum, *compounded* monthly. His investments and earnings in that fund continued to compound over the remaining life of his own mortgage.

Upon "burning his mortgage" at the end of 30 years, Saver, now 52 years of age, let his accumulated investment in the mortgage bond mutual fund continue to earn interest for two years but did not add to it. Instead, he departed from his brother's spending pattern by *adding consumption expenditures* equal to what Spender was paying in "net rent." Two years later (age 54) Saver retired to Eve off the income earned on his mortgage bond mutual fund, but kept *the* level of principal unchanged for the rest of his life, leaving it to his heirs. Spender, alas, was in a different position. What does the future hold for him?

---

[1] Adapted from Staubus, George J. 1993. The case of the almost identical twins. *Issues in Accounting Education*. 187-188.

REQUIREMENTS:

1. Specific calculations to be made; please describe any shortcuts or approximations you use:
   a) How much did each lad spend on his car upon graduating from high school?
   b) How much did Saver pay down on his home? What was the total purchase price?
   c) What were Saver's monthly mortgage payments?
      1) Saver invested the difference between his mortgage payments and his brother's rents. What had this investment accumulated to at the mortgage burning date? At age 54? (Note: The calculations involved here may be quite time-consuming; some planning might pay off.)
      2) What annual income did Saver have from age 54 until his death?
2. Describe the differences between Spender's and Saver's consumption expenditures over the several segments of their lives and the positions of their heirs upon their deaths.
3. Which bits of information given, or assumptions made, do you regard as unrealistic on the basis of your own experience? Roughly speaking (or precisely, if you wish), how would the results be affected by substituting your more realistic calculations?

Note: Abbreviated solution: 1(a) $11,021; 1(b) $18,243, $91,213; 1(c) $640; 1(d) $826,621, $1.000.212; 1(e) $100,017. (2) Spender consumed more in high school; same for 34 years; Saver consumed more after age 52. Saver left his mortgage bond mutual fund and his home to his heirs. (3) Income tax, home maintenance, interest rates. etc. Nominal dollar accounting is inherently "unrealistic" during inflation.

Case 11-2. ACE Company[*] (A)

ACE Company is the technology and market leader in the portable electronic games industry. The company is currently enjoying great success with its Model X, which has been on the market for several years. ACE's management believes that because of increased competition from other types of entertainment, the demand for Model X will dry up after three more years. The company has forecast Model X's net cash inflows in the next three years to be $400 million, $300 million, and $200 million, respectively.

NEW PRODUCT DEVELOPMENT

ACE's senior managers are considering the development and introduction of a replacement for Model X, to be called Model Z. According to the engineers, ACE already possesses the technical expertise to develop Model Z. However, the earliest that this product can be introduced into the-market is one year from now, as it will take this long to develop and test the new product, coordinate with suppliers for parts, set up the production process, and arrange for other related logistic activities. The total cost of these development activities is estimated at $550 million.

All of ACE's top managers agree that Model Z's market potential in terms of net cash inflow would be $200 million in year 2, $400 million in year 3, $300 million in year 4, and $100 million in year 5. They also agree that Model Z would maintain ACE's leadership position in the portable electronic games industry.

Management expects that in addition to developing its own customer base, Model Z also would draw some sales away from Model X. The expected amount of this "cannibalization" is $100 million of net cash inflows per year. The following table summarizes ACE's prediction of net cash flows (in millions) for the next five years for Model X by itself and with the introduction of Model Z at the end of year 1 (or, equivalently stated, the beginning of year 2). For simplicity, cash outflows are assumed to occur at the beginning of the year while cash inflows are assumed to occur at year end. Thus, for example, the $550 million development cost in year 1 is assumed to occur at time zero, while the net cash inflow from introducing Model Z at the beginning of year 2 is assumed to occur at the end of that year. Also note that in the table, net cash inflows of $100 million per year are shifted from Model X to Model Z in years 2 and 3.

	Model X	Introduce Model Z After One Year				
Year	Only	Model X	+	Model Z	=	Total
0	$ 0	$ 0	+	$ (550)	=	$ (550)
1	$400	$ 400	+	0	=	$ 400
2	$300	$ 200*	+	300*	=	$ 500
3	$200	$ 100*	+	$ 500*	=	$ 600
4	$ 0	$ 0	+	$ 300	=	$ 300
5	$ 0	$ 0	+	$ 100	=	$ 100

* Reflects $100 cannibalization of Model X by Model Z.

EXTENDING THE DEVELOPMENT PERIOD FOR PRODUCT Z

Several members of top management are concerned about Model Z's erosion of Model X sales. They propose that it would be better to spread the development of Model Z over two years and to introduce it at the beginning of year 3 instead of year 2. They suggest that this plan has two major advantages: (1) it would avoid the $100 million

---

[*] Chow, Chee W., Yuhchang Hwang, and Dennis F. Togo, *Issues in Accounting Education* Vol. 10, No. 2, Fall 1995. 389-391.

erosion in Model X's net cash inflows in year 2; and (2) the engineers have projected that extending the time for the development process will yield substantial savings due to efficiencies in scheduling. They have estimated that the two-year plan would reduce Model Z's total development cost to $300 million. Half of this total would be spent in each of the two years.

The table below summarizes the estimated net cash flows (in millions) for the two-year plan. Compared to the one-year plan, Model X's year 2 net cash inflow is higher by $100 million. This is due to avoiding cannibalization by Model Z in year 2.

	Model X	Introduce Model Z After One Year				
Year	Only	Model X	+	Model Z	=	Total
0	$ 0	$ 0	+	$ (150)	=	$(150)
1	$400	$ 400	+	$(150)	=	$ 250
2	$300	$ 300	+	0	=	$ 300
3	$200	$ 100*	+	$ 500*	=	$ 600
4	$ 0	$0	+	$ 300	=	$ 300
5	$ 0	$0	+	$ 100	=	$ 100

* Reflects $100 cannibalization of Model X by Model Z.

Proponents of the two-year plan acknowledge that delaying Model Z's introduction by one year would require foregoing its year 2 $300 million net cash inflow. But they emphasize that this sacrifice is more than made up by the additional $100 million cash inflow from Model X in year 2 and the $250 million savings in Model Z development costs.

OTHER CONSIDERATIONS

Supporters of the one-year plan argue that proponents of the two-year plan have overlooked a major factor: that the timing of Model Z's introduction could have an impact on competitors' actions. They maintain that if ACE does not introduce Model Z as quickly as possible, ACE's major competitor would most certainly come in with a comparable product. In response to a query from these managers, ACE's engineers have conducted a study of the competitor's current capabilities, They have reported that due to the competitor's less sophisticated technologies, it will require two years to develop a comparable product for market introduction.

The nature of the industry is such that there is a significant first-mover advantage. Similar products that reach the market at the same time tend to get equal shares of the market. But once a product is introduced, it tends to get so entrenched that comparable products introduced subsequently can gain only inconsequential market shares.

ASSIGNMENT

1) Using net present value computations and ignoring income taxes, analyze the one-year and two-year development alternatives. At this time, ignore the potential introduction of a comparable product by ACE's major competitor. Should either alternative be selected? If so, which would you recommend? ACE's cost of capital is 10 percent.[#]

2) How would you modify your analysis in part (1) to address the potential introduction of a competing product by ACE's major competitor?

Source: Balakrishnan, Ramji and Utpal Bhattacharya 1997. Ace Company (B): The Option Value of Waiting and Capital Budgeting. *Issues in Accounting Education.* Vol. 12, No. 2 (Fall) 399-402

[#] Some instructors may feel that tax considerations also should be part of the case. We have omitted tax effects out of a concern that the computation of tax depreciation and depreciation tax shield effects may overly distract student attention from the strategic aspects of the case. Instructors who think otherwise can readily incorporate tax considerations by augmenting the assignment questions and the numerical aspects of the case analysis.

Case 11-3. Ace Company (B)

Upon receiving the analysis of the data provided in Ace Company (A), the firm's managers wanted to better explore the effect of competition on whether and how to introduce Model Z. Diane Callahan, the Marketing Director, believes that the analysis is incomplete. She argues:

> I believe that accelerating the development of Model Z is the right choice if we will not receive any new data. Accelerated development eliminates the possibility of our competitors introducing a product that will significantly erode our market share. Thus, even though accelerated development results in greater cannibalization of our current product (Model X), it is better than spreading the cost out over two years. However, phased development does give us some flexibility that is not available with accelerated development. In particular, if we phase in developmental costs for Model Z over two years, we only commit $150 toward developmental costs in year 1. At the end of that year, we will have a much better idea of total market demand for Model Z. If the demand turns out to be bad, phased development gives us the option of abandoning Model Z without spending too much money. My department has put together some data on expected market conditions (table 1). From that data, I would guess that we may be better off abandoning Model Z unless the market conditions are good. Such an option is not available with accelerated development because it requires us to spend all of the developmental money of $550 in the first year itself. Ignoring the value of the option on further development could have given us an incomplete understanding of the tradeoffs.

Norm Peterson, Director (Product Development), then commented:

> What Diane says make sense to me. In fact, if we defer the decision to introduce Model Z by a year and wait for new market information, there is a third development choice. In particular, we can do all of the development during year 2, *after* we have made the decision to launch or abort. This choice would cost $400. I did not bring this choice up earlier because the phased development strategy of developing Model Z over two years seems to dominate this delayed development strategy.[1] But, Diane's comments indicate that we should consider this alternative as well. After all, if there is a possibility we will abort Model Z at the end of year 1, why waste $150 in year one under the two-year development time table?

Sam Mask, the CEO, summarized as follows before adjourning the meeting.

> I think we have made substantial progress in understanding the tradeoffs in timing the development of Model Z. I suggest we revisit the issue taking Diane's and Norm's comments into account. For simplicity, let us assume a 40 percent chance that a competitor will emerge and a 50-50 chance that the market will have strong demand

---

[1] Case B compares this new strategy (delayed development) with the strategies considered in case A. From case A, notice that phased development (i.e., developing Model Z over two years) costs $300. Also, Model Z would only get introduced at the start of year 3 (t = 2) under both the phased and delayed development strategies. Hence, absent information regarding market conditions, delayed development has no incremental benefit but, even with discounting, has a higher cost relative to phased development. Also, notice that delayed development has lower development costs than accelerated development (i.e., develop Model Z in year I itself and introduce at the start of year 2) even though both choices develop Model Z in one year. The lower cost is expected because the firm would have learned from its experience with other projects and changes in technology.

for Model Z. Finally, let us retain the simplifying assumptions about the timing of cash flows and do the analysis ignoring tax considerations. Why don't we meet early next week to figure out the best strategy?

ASSIGNMENT QUESTIONS

1. For this question only, assume that competition will never emerge and that Ace will obtain no new information regarding market conditions. Notice that expected cash flows, using the CEO's suggested probability estimates, are identical to those given in case A. Compute the expected cash flow for the delayed development strategy. Determine if this alternative is preferred to accelerated or phased development.
2. For this question only, assume that Ace will obtain no new information regarding market conditions. How does the analysis change if there is a 40 percent chance that competition will emerge?
3. Assume that Ace will obtain information regarding realized market conditions at the end of year 1. How does the rank ordering of the development choices change? Why?

COMPUTATIONAL HINTS

1. For all three questions, discount cash flows using a 10 percent rate. Assume that all cash outflows occur at the beginning of the year and all cash inflows occur at the end of the year. It also is helpful to construct a timeline for cash flows. Label the first node (start of year 1) as $t = 0$, the next node (end of year 1 and start of year 2) as $t = 1$, etc.
2. To determine whether or not to proceed with Model Z at time $t = 1$, construct a payoff matrix with 4 cells corresponding to Ace's and the competitor's entry choices. To minimize the potential for errors, look at time $t = 1$ NPV of cash flows at or after time $t = 1$. After you determine optimal choices at $t = 1$, step back to construct a payoff matrix where the rows correspond to Ace's various product development strategies and the columns correspond to the competitor entering and not entering.

TABLE I
Estimated Cash Flows from Model X and Model Z Under Different Scenarios

Panel A: No Development of Model Z

Time (t)	Market Condition: Good				Market Condition: Bad			
	Competitor Enters		Competitor Does Not Enter		Competitor Enters		Competitor Does Not Enter	
	X	Z	X	Z	X	Z	X	Z
0	0		0		0		0	
1	400		400		400		400	
2	300		300		300		300	
3	25		200		175		200	
4	0		0		0		0	
5	0		0		0		0	

Panel B: Accelerated Development of Model Z

Time (t)	Market Condition: Good				Market Condition: Bad			
	Competitor Enters		Competitor Does Not Enter		Competitor Enters		Competitor Does Not Enter	
	X	Z	X	Z	X	Z	X	Z
0	0	-550	0	-550	0	-550	0	-550
1	400	0	400	0	400	0	400	0
2	150	500	150	500	250	100	25	100
3	25	850	25	850	175	150	175	150
4	0	550	0	550	0	50	0	50
5	0	150	0	150	0	50	0	50

Panel C: Phased Development of Model Z

Time (t)	Market Condition: Good				Market Condition: Bad			
	Competitor Enters		Competitor Does Not Enter		Competitor Enters		Competitor Does Not Enter	
	X	Z	X	Z	X	Z	X	Z
0	0	-150	0	-150	0	-150	0	-150
1	400	-150	400	-150	400	-150	400	-150
2	300	0	300	0	300	0	300	0
3	25	425	25	850	175	75	200	150
4	0	275	0	550	0	25	0	50
5	0	100	0	200	0	0	0	0

Panel D: Defer Development Decision on Model Z

Time (t)	Market Condition: Good				Market Condition: Bad			
	Competitor Enters		Competitor Does Not Enter		Competitor Enters		Competitor Does Not Enter	
	X	Z	X	Z	X	Z	X	Z
0	0	0	0	0	0	0	0	0
1	400	-400	400	-400	400	-400	400	-400
2	300	0	300	0	300	0	300	0
3	25	425	200	850	175	75	200	150
4	0	275	0	550	0	25	0	50
5	0	100	0	200	0	0	0	0

1. All cash-flows are assumed to occur at the beginning of the year. Ignore taxes in your analysis. Time $t = 0$ corresponds to the start of the first calendar year and $t = 1$ corresponds to the end of year 1 and the start of year 2.
2. There is a 50% chance that market conditions will be good.
3. There is a 40% chance that the competitor will develop a product that competes with Model Z. The competitor's decision, however, is independent of realized market conditions. The competitor only has the choice of developing the product over 2 years and, thus, makes the launch/abort decision at time $t = 0$ itself.

Case 11-4. Component Technologies, Inc.: Adding FlexConnex Capacity

In 2002, Component Technologies, Inc. (CTI)[1] manufactured components, such as interconnect components, electronic connectors, fiber-optic connectors, flexible interconnects, coaxial cable, cable assemblies, and interconnect systems, used in computers and other electronic equipment. CTI's global marketing strategy produced significant growth; CTI was now one of three major suppliers in its market segments. Major customers included other global companies, such as IBM, HP, Hitachi, and Siemens. These companies, in turn, manufactured and marketed their products worldwide.

FlexConnex, one of CTI's largest selling products, was very profitable (see Exhibit 1). The Santa Clara, California plant that manufactured the FlexConnex component was projected to reach its full capacity of 75 million units in 2003. With sufficient capacity to meet demand, CTI expected its sales of FlexConnex could continue to increase 10 percent per year as applications of computer technology extended into industrial products and consumer products such as automobiles and appliances.

PLANNING MEETING

At a meeting of his staff, Tom Richards, director of manufacturing planning, stated that they needed to plan to bring additional capacity for FlexConnex online in about two years. He suggested that they begin by proposing possible alternatives. The staff quickly identified three promising alternatives:

1. The Santa Clara plant had been designed for future expansion. Additional space was available at the site, and new production capacity could be easily integrated into the existing production processes as long as compatible manufacturing technologies were employed.

2. CTI owned a plant in Waltham, Massachusetts that manufactured a product line that was being phased out. Some existing equipment in the Waltham plant was compatible with the Santa Clara plant's manufacturing technology and could be converted to the production of FlexConnex. Half of the Waltham plant would be available in 2003, and the remainder in 2005.

3. CTI could build a greenfield plant[2] in Ireland, close to its major European customers. To attract such industries, the Irish government would make a site available at low cost. A new technology currently being Beta-tested[3] by an equipment manufacturer could be used to equip this plant.

Source: *Issues in Accounting Education*, by Julie H. Hertenstein, May 2000, Vol. 15 Issue 2, p. 257-261

[1] This case is based on decisions faced by an actual company. Component Technologies, Inc., is a disguised name. Other facts have been changed for instructional purposes.

[2] The term "greenfield plant" is commonly used to refer to a brand new plant built entirely from scratch, as contrasted with the expansion, conversion, refurbishment, or renovation of an existing plant.

[3] A "Beta-test site" refers to equipment being tested using an actual workload at a customer site. Beta-test is often the final testing phase before the equipment is released as commercially available to customers. A customer who consents to be a Beta-test site agrees not only to use equipment that is not fully tested (thus being, in the American vernacular, a "guinea pig"), but also to provide the vendor detailed feedback on operations and problems encountered. In return, the equipment manufacturer often provides incentives such as financial discounts, extra on-site vendor personnel, etc.

Tom believed that these three were promising proposals. To ensure CTI could bring additional, profitable, FlexConnex capacity online in two years, Tom felt that they should begin developing plans for these alternatives. Nonetheless, he wanted the staff to keep an open mind to additional alternatives even as they evaluated these three. As the discussion started to wind down, Gracie Stanton, an engineer, said that she had a suggestion.

Gracie: Before we spend our time developing these three alternatives in detail, I'd like to get a rough feel for the potential profitability of each alternative. We shouldn't waste our time developing detailed plans for an alternative if there is no chance it will ever show a positive NPV.

Tom: Good point, Gracie. Let's break up into three groups, and do back-of-the-envelope calculations based on what we currently know about each alternative. Gracie, would you head up the Santa Clara group, since you were part of the engineering team for that plant? Edward Lodge, how about Waltham? Ian Townsley, could you and your folks take a look at Ireland? To start, what are the facts and assumptions about each facility?

Gracie: Well, there's enough space at the Santa Clara site to produce an additional 30 million units annually. I expect it would cost about $23 million to expand this plant, and bring its total capacity to 105 million units. Of the $23 million, we would spend $5 million to expand the building, and $18 million for additional equipment compatible with Santa Clara's existing manufacturing process. All $23 million would probably be spent in 2003, and the plant would be ready for production in 2004.

I assume that the selling price per unit will remain at its current level; further, since the same manufacturing technology will continue to be used, the variable manufacturing cost will remain the same as we show on the 2002 Santa Clara Cost Analysis Sheet [Exhibit 1]. Expanding the existing plant would allow some fixed manufacturing costs, like the plant manager's salary, to be shared with the existing facility, so I estimate that the additional fixed manufacturing costs, excluding depreciation, will be $2.1 million annually beginning in 2004. In 2006, these fixed costs will rise to $2.4 million and remain at that level for the foreseeable future.

Edward: Well, the Waltham plant is smaller than the space available in Santa Clara, so I think its capacity will be about 25 million units. It will require renovations to adapt the plant to manufacture FlexConnex, say, about $2 million, and approximately $12 million for equipment. Half of this would be spent in 2003, and half in 2005. Initial production would begin in 2004; half of the 25-million-unit capacity should be available in 2004; two-thirds in 2005; the remainder in 2006.

Since the Waltham plant will use the same technology as Santa Clara, we can assume that the variable manufacturing costs will be the same as Santa Clara's. Selling prices will also be the same. However, since Waltham will be a stand-alone faculty, its fixed manufacturing costs, excluding depreciation, would be somewhat higher: $2.4 million annually beginning in 2004. In 2006, however, fixed costs will increase to $2.6 million annually, where I expect them to remain for the foreseeable future.

Ian: I just visited the Beta-test site for the manufacturing equipment using the new technology that I propose we use for the greenfield plant. There I learned that the economic size for a plant using this technology to manufacture a product such as FlexConnex is about 70 million units, so I propose that we prepare our estimates for Ireland based on a 70-million-unit capacity plant. Of course, this will cost more, since it is much larger than other sites. With the help of the Irish government, an appropriate site can be obtained for about $1 million. A building large enough to produce 70 million units can probably be built for about $10 million, and equipping the facility with the new technology equipment will cost about $50 million. Most of this would be spent in 2003, although as much as 10 percent might be spent before the end of 2002 to acquire and prepare the site. The plant would begin production in 2004; some areas of the plant would not be complete, however, and as much as 20-25 percent of the investment would remain to be spent during 2004.

Although FlexConnex's worldwide selling price will be the same as for the other facilities, the new equipment will lower the variable manufacturing cost to $0.195 per unit. The efficiency of this new plant will help keep fixed manufacturing costs down, as well, but since the facility will be so large, fixed manufacturing costs, excluding depreciation, would be higher than the other two facilities: $2.8 million annually beginning in 2004, rising to $2.9 million annually beginning in 2008.

Tom: These assumptions sound like reasonable first cuts to me. Let's just start with a five-year analysis, 2003 through 2007, using the discount rate of 20 percent, which the corporate finance manual states is the hurdle rate for capital investments. For simplicity, let's assume all cash flows occur at the end of the respective year. Discount everything to today's dollars, that is, as of the end of 2002. And, consistent with corporate policy, we'll do a pretax analysis; we'll ask the corporate finance staff to evaluate the tax implications later.

A few minutes later, the buzzing of the small groups died down, and the tapping on the laptop keyboards had ceased.

Tom: Well, what have you learned from this first glance?

Edward: The Waltham site looks promising.

Ian: Not Ireland.

Gracie: This is odd. The Santa Clara plant is right on the margin, and that surprises me since the existing manufacturing facility is one of CTI's most profitable, and we get further economies of scale by expanding that plant. I wonder if the discount rate we are using is too high. At the "Finance for Manufacturing Engineers" seminar I attended recently, we discussed the problems associated with using a discount rate that was too high. The professor stated that there was a sound theoretical basis for using a discount rate that approximated the company's cost of capital, but many companies "added on" estimates for risk, corporate charges, and other factors that were less well grounded. Based on what I learned in that seminar, I tried to estimate CTI's actual cost of capital; it was about 10 percent. I wonder what would happen if we used 10 percent instead?

Tom: With these laptops and spreadsheet programs, that's easy enough; let's check it out.
A few seconds later . . . .

Gracie: Now, that's better!

Edward: Ours too.

Ian: Well, at least we're moving in the right direction. But it doesn't make sense to me that a facility with lower variable cost per unit, and lower average fixed cost per unit at capacity, shows a negative NPV when the others are positive. We checked our calculations; what's the story? Could it be that Ireland would not even be up to capacity production in five years because the plant is so big?

Gracie: Maybe, but our plants are being penalized, too; after all, even though they reach capacity in the first five years, they will presumably continue to produce FlexConnex. Although there is constant technological change in this industry, there is a reasonable probability that demand for FlexConnex will remain strong for at least 10 years.

Ian: Well, then, let's look at each of the three plants over a ten-year period, using Gracie's 10 percent discount rate.
Later . . . .

Edward: Aha! Waltham continues to improve.

Gracie: However, Santa Clara has you beat now!

Ian: I've got bad news for both of you!

QUESTIONS:

1. Prepare the manufacturing staff's calculations for the three alternatives:
    a. In the first set of calculations, the staff used a discount rate of 20 percent, a five-year time horizon, and ignored taxes and terminal value. What is the relative attractiveness of these three alternatives?
    b. In the second set, they used a 10 percent discount rate. What happens to the NPV of each alternative? What happens to their relative attractiveness? Why?
    c. In the third set, they changed the time horizon to ten years, but kept the 10 percent discount rate. Why does Ian say he has "bad news" for the others?
2. In addition to reducing costs, the new technology proposed for the greenfield plant would increase manufacturing flexibility, which would enable CTI to respond more quickly to customers and to provide them more custom features. Should these factors be considered in the analysis? If so, how would you incorporate them?
3. Should other factors be taken into consideration in choosing the location of the FlexConnex plant? If so, what are they?
4. Should Tom Richards continue to develop more detailed plans for these three alternatives? If not, which should be eliminated? Are there other alternatives that his staff should consider? If so, what are they?

EXHIBIT 1 FlexConnex Cost Analysis Sheet
Santa Clara Plant, 2002

Plant Capacity: 75 million units

Selling Price/Unit: $0.85

Variable Cost/Unit: $0.255

Fixed Manufacturing Cost: $9.5 million annually (includes $2.5 million depreciation)

Estimated Plant Profitability at Capacity:

Revenue	$63,750,000
Variable Cost	<19,125,000>
Fixed Manufacturing Cost	<9,500,000>
Plant Profitability [a]	$35,125,000

[a] Excludes interest expenses and corporate selling, general and administrative expenses.

Case 11-5. General Medical Center

The phone rang in the office of Gwen Allbright, a partner in a consulting firm that specializes in health services management. On the line was Dr. George Westford, Chief of Cardiovascular Medicine at General Medical Center (GMC) and Gwen's next-door neighbor. Dr. Westford explained that he needed Gwen's help in understanding an analysis prepared by Brian Alexander, General Medical Center's Chief Financial Officer, of the pending purchase of new imaging equipment for the evaluation of patients with suspected coronary artery disease (CAD). GMC is evaluating two types of imaging equipment—a Thallium scanner and a Positron Emission Technology (PET) scanner. Dr. Westford explained the situation as follows:

> Based on his cost analysis, Brian Alexander has recommended that the hospital purchase the Thallium scanner rather than the PET scanner. The physicians in the cardiovascular medicine department are very upset by this. They want the hospital to purchase the PET scanner because it incorporates the latest imaging technology. In addition, I am not convinced by Brian's analysis that the Thalhum scanner is really the better choice even from a purely financial perspective.

Dr. Westford asked Gwen to evaluate the analysis prepared by Mr. Alexander and to recommend changes to his analysis if she felt that they were warranted. He agreed to bring the analysis to Gwen's house later that evening.

GENERAL MEDICAL CENTER

General Medical Center is a not-for-profit 500-bed community-based hospital. It is located in a metropolitan area with a population of one million people, which has six major hospital systems that provide cardiovascular services. It is the third "busiest" cardiovascular center in the metropolitan area when judged on the number of cardiac catheterizations performed.

GMC recently has become part of an integrated health care delivery system for its metropolitan area. Now that GMC participates in a capitated payment system, its revenue is much more "fixed" than it was under the former fee-for-services arrangement. Capitated payments are per-patient payments to a health care provider (hospital or physician group) for a defined set of benefits for a defined period of time. In a strictly capitated system, a provider receives a predetermined amount for each beneficiary.[1] The

---

[1] While this case assumes strict capitation for all payors, such a system is the exception and not the norm—both in the U.S., generally, and in the particular market served by GMC. A more realistic analysis would recognize that (1) patient care may be reimbursed under various combinations of arrangements—including by capitation, by diagnosis and by fee-for-service or discounted fee-for-service schemes; (2) different payors—which include for-profit and not-for-profit private-sector organizations, government and individual patients—are involved; and (3) the relative amount of reimbursement for Thalhurn and PET may differ across the various payors (in fact, some payors may consider a particular technology "experimental" and provide no reimbursement). Thus, the payor mix is an extremely important consideration in a decision such as that faced by GMC. For pedagogical reasons, however, the case abstracts from this complexity on the revenue dimension in order to focus on the role of costs in this decision setting.

Adapted from Alison Hubbard Ashton, Robert H. Ashton and Laureen A. Maines. 1998. *Issues in Accounting Education.* 13, 4 (November). pp. 985-993. This case is based on a class project prepared by Pamela Jones and John Janes in Duke University's Weekend Executive M.B.A. Program.

actual costs of caring for a beneficiary may be more or less than this predetermined amount. When the actual costs of care are less than the predetermined payment, the provider keeps the "profit." When actual costs exceed the payment, however, the provider is financially responsible and incurs a "loss."

This is in stark contrast to the former fee-for-services system in which the hospital was reimbursed for each imaging procedure performed and for all follow-up procedures (such as cardiac catheterizations) that were triggered by the imaging results. Under the fee-for-services arrangement, the provider's profit increased as a direct function of the number of imaging and follow-up procedures performed, so long as the fee for each exceeded its cost. In effect, the former system rewarded the misdiagnosis of normal individuals as diseased, because of the revenue impact of additional procedures.

Under a capitated system, however, costs that are triggered by misdiagnoses are borne by the hospital. In effect, this payment method merges the insurance function with the provider function in that a portion of the financial risk is borne by the provider. By merging the insurance and provider functions, the capitated payment system encourages the provider to analyze the appropriateness (quality) of care. However, it also provides the short-term financial incentive to reduce costs by undertreating patients. For example, referrals to specialists may be reduced, further testing curtailed, or less costly (but less effective) approaches to treatment prescribed. Future costs of undertreating patients may not be borne by the hospital due to the high mobility level of the working-age patient base.

Dr. Westford and the other physicians in the cardiovascular division realize that in a capitated system the division will be evaluated more on the appropriateness and cost of its care. Since revenues will not increase with the number of procedures performed, they will need to be concerned about performing unnecessary catheterization procedures. The capitation approach strives to lower the cost of care, subject to quality standards, and match the financial risks with the quality of care. Dr. Westford and the other physicians are convinced that the higher accuracy of the PET scanner vis-á-vis the more conventional Thallium scanner will result in more medically appropriate referrals of patients for cardiac catheterization. Dr. Westford is concerned that Mr. Alexander has failed to consider the cost of *inappropriate* referrals in his analysis of the imaging equipment purchase. This is also of concern to the physicians since they typically are directly penalized in their compensation for inappropriate patient referrals.

HEART DISEASE AND CARDIAC IMAGING

Patients undergo diagnostic imaging to provide physicians with information that will be used to verify a diagnosis, order further testing, or prescribe treatment. A patient with suspected heart disease undergoes a tiered diagnostic process to provide a diagnosis in a cost-effective manner. This process can be represented by a type of decision tree that dictates the sequence of diagnostic testing and/or treatment. A simplified version of such a tree appears in exhibit 1.

As the tree demonstrates, the physician uses a combination of clinical judgment and diagnostic testing results to determine which patients will undergo cardiovascular imaging and perhaps further procedures. Once a patient is referred for cardiovascular imaging, the results of that procedure dictate whether the patient will proceed to diagnostic cardiac catheterization. Patients with normal cardiac imaging results have no further evaluation, whereas almost all patients with abnormal imaging results undergo cardiac catheterization. Currently at GMC, this catheterization costs $2,000 and carries a .01 percent mortality rate. The catheterization procedure is used to determine whether the imaging technique has correctly identified the patient as having heart disease. If the imaging technique has correctly identified the patient, the catheterization provides the physician with information that is useful for deciding among medical treatment, coronary angioplasty and coronary artery bypass surgery as the preferred treatment for the disease.

Since the results of the cardiovascular imaging procedure dictate whether the patient will be subjected to cardiac catheterization, it is easy to see why the diagnostic accuracy of the imaging procedure is of paramount importance. An ideal or perfect imaging procedure would correctly differentiate those patients who do and do not have heart disease. A technique that fails to correctly identify patients who actually have heart disease may allow the disease to go undetected for some time, possibly resulting in greater health care risks and costs when the disease later becomes clinically evident. Likewise, a technique that incorrectly diagnoses a healthy patient as having heart disease will result in inappropriate and costly referral for diagnostic cardiac catheterization. The misdiagnosis of a healthy patient as diseased can be a significant factor in the cost analysis of imaging equipment.

GMC is considering two alternative imaging technologies: Thallium and PET. The Thallium scanner has been the standard in cardiovascular medicine for many years. It offers the advantages of lower initial capital outlay, lower annual maintenance costs and a general acceptance by the medical community. The more technologically advanced Positron Emission Technology (PET) scanner was largely restricted to academic medical centers until a few years ago because of its cost. More recently, commercial PET scanners have become available that offer greater clinical accuracy than Thallium scanners. Although the initial costs and maintenance fees of PET have come down in the last few years, they are still substantially higher than those associated with Thallium imaging.

EXHIBIT 1
Decision Tree

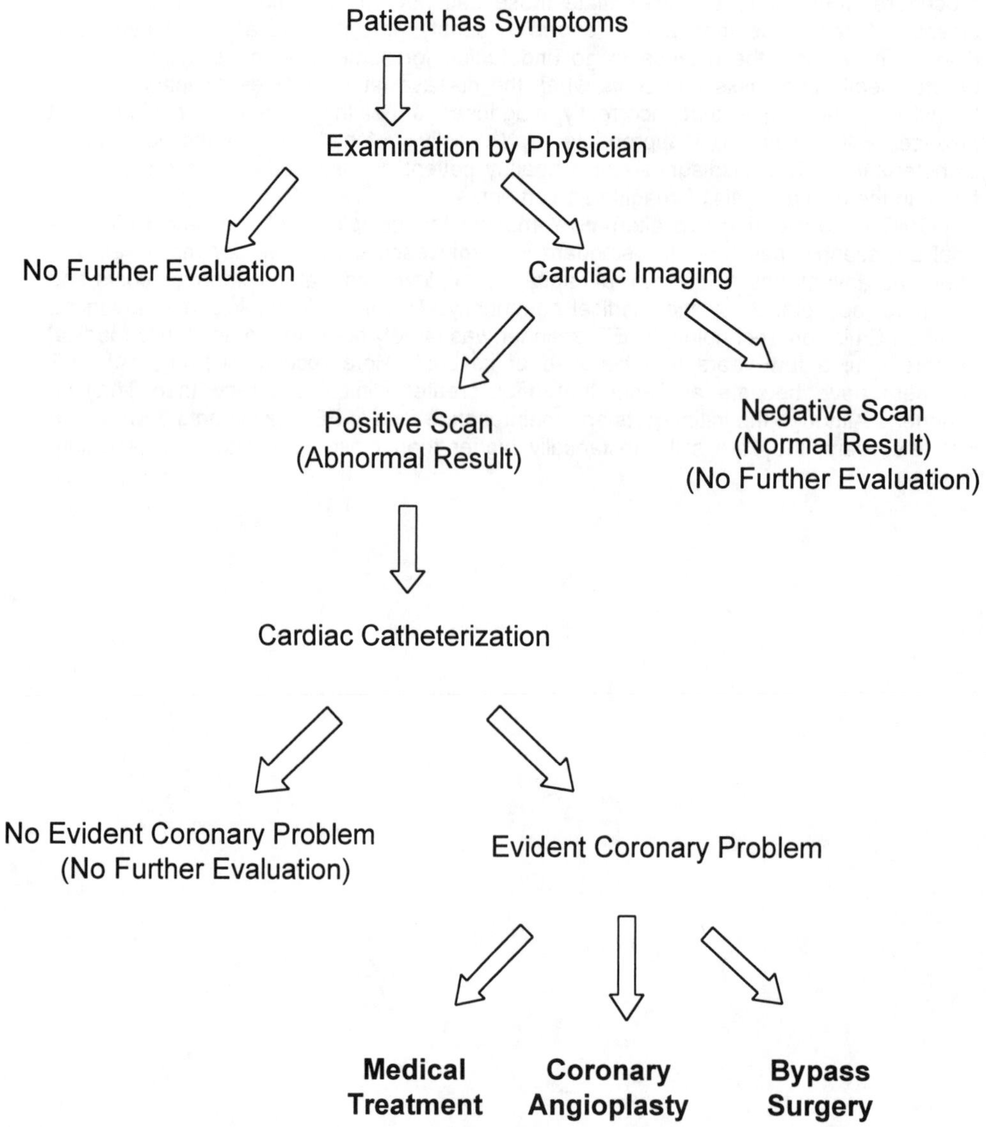

Patient has Symptoms

⇩

Examination by Physician

No Further Evaluation   Cardiac Imaging

Positive Scan   Negative Scan
(Abnormal Result)   (Normal Result)
                                 (No Further Evaluation)

⇩

Cardiac Catheterization

No Evident Coronary Problem   Evident Coronary Problem
(No Further Evaluation)

Medical   **Coronary**   **Bypass**
Treatment   **Angioplasty**   **Surgery**

THE CFO'S ANALYSIS

Brian Alexander, the CFO, analyzed this equipment purchase using an equivalent annual cost (EAC) method. Because the Thallium and PET scanners have different useful lives, EAC appeared to be the best way to determine which type of equipment would be more cost effective for the health care system. Essentially, EAC is the amount of an annuity that has the same life and present value as the investment option being considered. EAC can be viewed as the annual rental payment that would cover both the purchase of the equipment and its operating costs, or the annual amount that GMC would pay if it chose to Outsource the scanning procedure. Thus, Mr. Alexander based the cost comparison on the initial outlay costs of both types of imaging equipment and on the annual maintenance, personnel-related and other costs associated with the two equipment types. His cost estimates are listed and explained in exhibit 2.

Mr. Alexander had to make several assumptions in his analysis. These assumptions, described in exhibit 3, relate to the expected number of cardiac scans in a typical year, the expected useful life of the two scanners, the predicted inflation rate for the various costs associated with scanning and the likely base rate of cardiac disease in the hospital's patient population. Two assumptions are particularly important: the "sensitivity" and "specificity" of the alternative imaging techniques.

Understanding sensitivity and specificity is essential for a comprehensive evaluation of the Thallium and PET scanners. Realizing this, Mr. Alexander included as an addendum to his analysis the definitions of sensitivity and specificity, as well as the definitions of four additional terms on which sensitivity and specificity depend. Mr. Alexander's addendum is summarized in exhibit 4.

Mr. Alexander applied the EAC approach using the relevant data and assumptions from exhibits 2, 3 and 4. The results are presented in exhibit 5. Mr. Alexander determined from this analysis that the EAC for the Thallium scanner is $745,818 and the EAC for the PET scanner is $1,148,004. Based on these calculations, he recommended the purchase of the Thallium scanner because it results in lower cost for the health care system.

SUGGESTED ASSIGNMENT QUESTIONS

1) Evaluate the strengths and weaknesses of the analysis prepared by the CFO.
2) Use the information on sensitivity, specificity and disease prevalence in the population to develop a framework for incorporating the costs of misdiagnoses into the CFO's analysis.
3) Quantify the costs of the expected annual number of cardiac catheterizations that will result from both the Thallium scanner and the PET scanner. After taking these additional costs into account, is the purchase of the Thallium scanner still indicated?
4) How should the costs of the False Negative diagnoses (i.e., classifying diseased patients as normal) be handled?
5) What additional considerations are relevant?

EXHIBIT 2
Cost Information

Cost Classification	Thallium Scanner	PET Scanner
Purchase Price of Equipment	$450,000	$1,600,000
Equipment Maintenance (Per Month)	$3,750	$13,333
Medical Supplies (Per Patient)	$100	$100
Nuclear Isotope (Per Month)	$20,000	$27,000
Lease Space (Per Month)	$2,000	$3,000
Utilities (Per Month)	$500	$1,000
Secretary (Per Month)	$1,667	$1,667
Nuclear Technician (Per Month)	$2,500	$2,500
Nursing Personnel (Per Month)	$2,917	$2,917
Employee Benefits (% of Salary)	28%	28%
Cost of Cardiac Catheterization	$2,000	$2,000

Explanation of Cost Classifications:

Purchase Price: Guaranteed by the manufacturer to be the lowest price offered to any other hospital in the preceding 12-month period.

Equipment Maintenance: First-year maintenance is included in the purchase price. Continuing maintenance is fixed for the life of the equipment at 10 percent of the purchase price.

Supplies: These include patient gowns, EKG electrodes and paper, intravenous kits and pharmacological agents.

Isotope: For the PET technology, a nuclear generator is purchased each month, which supplies the nuclear tracer used in the imaging technique. For the Thallium technology, the nuclear tracer is purchased on a per-dose basis from a nuclear pharmaceutical firm.

Lease Space: The PET equipment requires 50 percent more space than the Thallium equipment.

Utilities: The back-up electrical generators and specialized cooling for the sophisticated computer bank results in twice the utility requirements for the PET scanner as for the Thallium scanner.

Personnel: The two technologies have the same staffing requirements.

EXHIBIT 3
Assumptions

Category	Thallium Scanner	PET Scanner
Sensitivity	85%	95%
Specificity	65%	95%
Useful Life of Equipment	7 years	10 years
Patient Scan Days Per Month	20	20
Patient Scans Per Day	8	8
CAD Rate in Patients	25%	25%
Hospital Cost of Capital	10%	10%
Inflation Factor for Catheterization Procedure	3.2%	3.2%
inflation Factor for Personnel	3.5%	3.5%
Inflation Factor for Other Costs	2.8%	2.8%
Tax Rate for Hospital	0%	0%

Explanation of Assumptions:

Patient Scan Days Per Month: Each manufacturer guarantees equipment "up-time" of approximately 92 percent. The scanners will operate Monday through Friday. Thus, approximately 240 scan days are available each year.

Scans Per Day: This assumes that each scanner will scan the number of patients that currently are referred for imaging. Any potential annual increase in volume is assumed to be offset by the effect of implementing appropriate guidelines for the referral for this type of imaging procedure.

Thallium Specificity: The medical literature provides a range of values. For a community-based patient population, the best studies indicate a specificity of 55 percent to 65 percent. The value of 65 percent was chosen to provide a best-case analysis.

Thallium Sensitivity: The medical literature provides a consensus that this value is 85 percent.

PET Specificity: The medical literature provides a consensus that this value is 95 percent.

PET Sensitivity: The medical literature provides a consensus that this value is 95 percent.

Prevalence of Heart Disease: A review of the hospital's experience, along with reports from the medical literature, reveals that the best estimate of this value is 25 percent.

Useful Life of Imaging Equipment: The manufacturers have provided historical data and engineering projections for these estimates.

Hospital Cost of Capital: The CFO estimates that the hospital's cost of capital in the new integrated health care system will be approximately 10 percent.

Inflation Factors: The CFO has used information from similar integrated health care systems in the region for estimates of inflation rates.

Tax Rate for the Hospital: Since both the hospital and the integrated health care system are not-for-profit, there are no corporate taxes.

EXHIBIT 4
Definitions of Key Terms

True Positive: A test result is positive (abnormal) in a patient with disease. Correct labeling of a diseased patient as having disease.

False Positive: A test result is positive (abnormal) despite the fact that the patient actually does not have disease. Incorrect labeling of a normal patient as having disease.

True Negative: A test result is negative (normal) in a patient who does not have disease. Correct labeling of a normal patient as not having disease.

False Negative: A test result is negative (normal) despite the fact that the patient actually has disease. Incorrect labeling of a diseased patient as not having disease.

Sensitivity: The proportion of diseased patients diagnosed correctly. The ratio of true positives to all patients who have disease (sum of true positives and false negatives above). The ability of a test to correctly identify patients with disease.

Specificity: The proportion of normal patients diagnosed correctly. The ratio of true negatives to all patients without disease (sum of false positives and true negatives above). The ability of a test to correctly identify normal patients.

EXHIBIT 5
The CFO's Analysis

Thallium Scanner Cost Analysis

Year	Initial Cost	Maintenance	Personnel[a]	Other[b]	Total	Present Value
0	$450,000				$450,000	$450,000
1		-0-	$108,810	$462,000	570,810	518,918
2		$45,000	112,619	474,936	632,555	522,772
3		45,000	116,560	488,234	649,794	488,200
4		45,000	120,640	501,905	667,545	455,942
5		45,000	124,862	515,958	685,820	425,840
6		45,000	129,232	530,405	704,637	397,749
7		45,000	133,756	545,256	724,012	371,533
Total						$3,630,954

Equivalent Annual Cost for Thallium Scanner: $745,818 [$3,630,954 / 4.86842 (present value factor for 7-year, 10 percent annuity)].

PET Scanner Cost Analysis

Year	Initial Cost	Maintenance	Personnel[a]	Other[c]	Total	Present Value
0	$1,600,000				$1,600,000	$1,600,000
1		-0-	$108,810	$564,000	672,810	611,646
2		$160,000	112,619	579,792	852,411	704,472
3		160,000	116,560	596,026	872,586	655,587
4		160,000	120,640	612,715	893,355	610,173
5		160,000	124,862	629,871	914,733	567,977
6		160,000	129,232	647,507	936,739	528,765
7		160,000	133,756	665,638	959,394	492,320
8		160,000	138,437	684,275	982,712	458,443
9		160,000	143,282	703,435	1,006,717	426,946
10		160,000	148,297	723,131	1,031,428	397,660
Total						$7,053,989

Equivalent Annual Cost for PET Scanner: $1,148,004 [$7,053,989 / 6.14457 (present Value factor for 10-year, 10 percent annuity)].

[a] [($1,667 + $2,500 + $2,917)1.28] x 12 = $108,810 for year 1, increasing by 3.5% each year.
[b] ($20,000 + $2,000 + $500)12 + $100(1,920) $462,000 for year 1, increasing by 2.8% each year.
[c] ($27,000 + $3,000 + $1,000)12 + $100(1,920) $564,000 for year 1, increasing by 2.8% each year.

HOW FOREST PRODUCT COMPANIES ANALYZE CAPITAL BUDGETS

BY JACK BAILES, JAMES NIELSEN, AND STEPHEN LAWTON

Twenty years ago we conducted a survey of forest products companies to investigate the nature of the capital budget project evaluation techniques, methods of risk analysis, and post audit procedures. Because the forest products industry has changed so much, it is appropriate to once again look at the issue of capital budgeting practices within the industry.

A survey was sent to the chief financial officers of 87 U.S. forest products companies, consisting of all of the independent firms (i.e., separate divisions of a single parent company were not included) currently participating in the Oregon State University Forest Products Industry Monograph Program.[1] The survey questionnaire was completed by 29 firms, representing a response rate of 33%—slightly lower than the 47% response rate received in the 1977 survey. Sixteen of these firms operated in the wood products side of the industry. There were only two firms operating exclusively in the pulp, paper, and packaging side of the industry, and the remaining 11 firms sold both wood and paper-related products. This industry breakdown of firms was similar to the breakdown of firms responding in 1977.

Although there are still a number of smaller forest products companies operating in the U.S., the largest percentage of firms (over 33%) had annual sales and total asset levels exceeding $500 million. Such a finding was not surprising given the consolidation that has taken place within the industry in the past 20 years.

The companies also were asked to report the dollar amount of their annual capital budgets for both timber-related investments and plant and equipment. These results are shown in Table 1. As was the case in 1977, the annual capital budgets were found to be approximately 10% of total assets.

CAPITAL BUDGETING EVALUATION METHODS

The survey provided description of the four major capital budgeting techniques used most often by financial analysts in order to determine the degree to which sophisticated capital budgeting methodologies were being used. These techniques include accounting rate of return, payback period, internal rate of return, and net present value. The company was asked to identify which of these methods were used in the capital budgeting decision-making process and whether or not they were used as a primary evaluation technique, secondary evaluation technique, or only a project screening technique. This was done separately for timber-related investment decisions and plant and equipment investment decisions. In addition, each company was asked to describe other formal evaluation techniques that they employed as well as other factors they considered relevant to the capital budgeting process.

PRIMARY EVALUATION TECHNIQUES

Several interesting results emerge from the data showing the number and percentage of firms using each of the four methodologies as a primary evaluation technique to judge the acceptability of both timberland and plant and equipment purchases. First, a far greater percentage of firms use one of the discounted cash flow techniques in evaluating timber-related investments (76%) than they do in the case of plant and equipment purchases (55%). These results are conceptually reasonable because the long life of timber-related investments makes the time value of money particularly important. By the same token, fewer companies use pay-back period as a primary evaluation technique when making timber investment (15%) than in the case of plant and equipment purchases (33%). The payback period is most useful as a short-term screening technique; therefore, it should be less useful when looking at timber purchases (Table 2).

The most significant finding, however, is the fact that the discounted cash flow techniques of internal rate of return and net present value are much more widely used today as a primary evaluation technique than they were in 1977 when they were used by only 44% of the forest products companies. Furthermore, in 1977, several of the smaller companies reported that they only used subjective judgment in making capital budgeting decisions. Only one of the smaller companies in the current survey relied solely on subjective judgment.

SECONDARY EVALUATION TECHNIQUES

The number and percentage of firms using each of the four methodologies as their secondary evaluation technique has not changed much from the 1977 results (Table 3). The payback period is still the dominant secondary technique although it is more widely used for plant and equipment decisions than

for timber investments. In addition, the accounting rate of return is used substantially more as a secondary evaluation technique than as a primary evaluation technique for all types of investment decisions.

While arguments can be made that neither the accounting rate of return nor payback methods consider the time value of money and the economic impact that this has on the market value of the firm, both of these methodologies have some redeeming features. Both are intuitive and easy to understand. Both are easy to calculate. In the case of the payback period, the focus is on liquidity, which is clearly an important issue for a capital-intensive firm. Moreover, accounting information is almost always available for the project under consideration and for the firm as a whole. Thus, the calculation of accounting rate of return is a normal by-product of the companies' financial accounting information systems.

Table 1. SIZE OF CAPITAL BUDGET

Capital Budget (in millions)	Timber Investments	Other Capital Investments	Total Capital Investments
Less than $5	7 Companies	12 Companies	11 (38%) Companies
$5 to $10	5 Companies	1 Company	2 (7%) Companies
$11 to $50	4 Companies	6 Companies	6 (21%) Companies
Over $50	2 Companies	9 Companies	10 (34%) Companies
Total	18 Companies	28 Companies	29 Companies

Table 2. PRIMARY EVALUATION TECHNIQUES

Capital Budgeting Technique	Timber Investments	Other Capital Investments
Accounting rate of return	3 (9%) Companies	6 (13%) Companies
Payback period	5 (15%) Companies	15 (33%) Companies
Internal rate of return	13 (38%) Companies	15 (33%) Companies
Net present value	13 (38%) Companies	10 (22%) Companies
Total	34 Companies	46 Companies

Table 3. SECONDARY EVALUATION TECHNIQUES

Capital Budgeting Technique	Timber Investments	Other Capital Investments
Accounting rate of return	5 (23%) Companies	6 (22%) Companies
Payback period	8 (36%) Companies	13 (48%) Companies
Internal rate of return	5 (23%) Companies	3 (11%) Companies
Net present value	4 (18%) Companies	5 (19%) Companies
Total	22 Companies	27 Companies

Table 4. PROJECT SCREENING TECHNIQUES

Capital Budgeting Technique	Timber Investments	Other Capital Investments
Accounting rate of return	1 (6%) Company	4 (15%) Companies
Payback period	4 (24%) Companies	11 (42%) Companies
Internal rate of return	6 (35%) Companies	8 (31%) Companies
Net present value	6 (35%) Companies	3 (12%) Companies
Total	17 Companies	26 Companies

PROJECT SCREENING TECHNIQUES

In the 1977 survey we did not ask about the use of any of these four methodologies as screening techniques in the capital budgeting process. These results for 1997 in Table 4 show once again the emphasis forest products firms place on the discounted cash flow methodologies in evaluating timber investments. Seventy percent of the firms find these techniques useful even at the project screening stage. On the other hand, payback is the most commonly used screening technique for investments in plant and equipment.

COMPANY SIZE AND EVALUATION TECHNIQUES

In an analysis of the size of the forest products companies in relationship to the type of evaluation techniques, we see that size is still the dominant factor when it comes to using discounted cash flow analysis in analyzing anything other than timber investments. For timber investments, even the smaller companies favor the discounted cash flow techniques. On the other hand, in plant and equipment decisions, the combined accounting rate of return and payback method responses equaled or exceeded the discounted cash flow responses in all companies whose sales were less than $500 million.

It is also interesting to note that none of the largest forest products firms used either accounting rate of return or payback when evaluating timber purchases, and only two out of the 12 largest firms used accounting rate of return when evaluating plant and equipment. The shares of many of these firms are publicly owned, so it is not surprising that investment decisions tend to be market driven. Because book value and net income do not have much to do with cash flow and market value, accounting rate of return measures do not tell the managers of these publicly owned firms what they really need to know.

OTHER FACTORS RELEVANT TO THE CAPITAL BUDGETING DECISION

When we review the comments that were received from respondents regarding capital budgeting decisions, two conclusions emerged. In the case of timber investments, the most important issue centered on strategic wood supply considerations—namely, current availability, expected acquisition cost, location, age, and class of timber, as well as what was likely to happen to any of these factors in the future. To firms selling wood, pulp, paper, or packaging products, this issue of availability is of prime importance. To remain in business, firms need an ongoing supply of timber. As a result, financial analysis techniques that emphasize the accounting concepts of breakeven analysis and shutdown costs are getting increased attention by forest products firms.

On the plant and equipment side, it was not surprising to learn that one of the most important issues has become the need to comply with the regulatory standards concerning health, safety, and the environment. With more and more of these types of pressures likely in the future and with the dollar cost of failing to satisfy these concerns rising, traditional financial analysis may very well become a secondary criterion used to evaluate investment options. Two companies also mentioned the importance of the custodial role they feel forest products companies have with regard to maintaining the timber resource and the overall welfare of their employees.

RISK ADJUSTMENT METHODOLOGIES

An extended time horizon is implicit in all capital projects. This factor is particularly true in timber acquisition projects and increases the difficulty of accurately forecasting the future costs and returns in these projects. For this reason, risk is an important concern in capital budgeting. Traditionally, there have been three common quantitative methods of adjusting capital projects for risk. The first technique is to raise the cost of capital used as a cutoff rate or used in discounting future cash flows in the net present value methodology. The second technique is to adjust the project life downward. The third approach involves the use of sensitivity analysis where a range of future expectations is considered in the project analysis. In particular, the projected costs can be increased, and/or the projected benefits can be decreased. This approach can determine the extent to which the actual costs and benefits could deviate from the most likely estimate before an acceptable project would become unacceptable.

In 1977 only 44% of the respondent companies reported using one of these three quantitative risk adjustment techniques. Moreover, the majority of the companies used the sensitivity analysis approach. In the 1997 survey, the percentage of companies using formal risk adjustment had risen to 76% (22 of the 29 firms). Only 17% (five firms) reported that they do not adjust for risk at all in evaluating capital budgeting decisions. The remaining 7% (two firms) attempted to consider risk subjectively. These results support the finding noted earlier that forest products companies are becoming more sophisticated in their capital budgeting methodologies.

While sensitivity analysis continues to be the risk adjustment technique of preference for all size categories of firms, and there does not appear to be much difference in the type of risk adjustment technique used in analyzing timber and nontimber investments, some of the larger forest products firms are beginning to use other methods to analyze risk. Some of these techniques include the use of formal probability analysis, in which firms actually attempt to calculate the probability of investments earning a return greater than the cost of capital or earning a positive net present value, and less formal methods such as shortening the payback period and reducing the amount initially invested for projects involving higher risk.

Furthermore, one company reported using a decision tree approach in evaluating plant and equipment purchases. Under this technique, a firm would attempt to lay out several different scenarios, assign probabilities to each scenario, and then calculate expected profitability measures based on either the firm's cash flow or accounting net income. This technique would appear to be particularly relevant in the case of changing regulatory environments or widely fluctuating timber prices noted earlier.

AN INDUSTRY IN TRANSITION

The forest products industry—an industry composed of firms selling wood, pulp, paper, and packaging products—plays a significant role in the global economy, accounting for nearly 3% of the global Gross Domestic Product. A distinguishing feature of this industry is its degree of capital intensity; the assets of firms operating in this industry consist primarily of timber holdings and substantial plant and equipment.

In recent years, the forest products industry has been transformed by external forces that have exerted pressure for new forestry techniques and an overall structural change within the industry. Inflationary pressures alone have caused the cost of timber and timberland to rise to unprecedented levels. Population and economic growth combined with the increased standard of living in many countries has resulted in an increasing demand for forest products. Heightened government regulation and environmental legislation will continue to increase as society places greater emphasis on nontimber benefits that accrue from forests such as bio-diversity, wildlife habitat, water storage, recreation, and aesthetics.

The forest products industry is responding to these forces by implementing capital and technology intensive strategies throughout its operations from the forest to the marketplace. Many forest products firms are shifting their timber supply from natural forests to plantation forests that utilize costly genetics and breeding technologies in their intensive silvicultural practices. These plantation forests are vertically integrated with capital intensive, eco-efficient production facilities. Those firms that have not been able to meet the above challenges either have had to close down operations or they have been acquired by competitors. The net result has been a significant decline in the number of firms in the industry.

POST AUDIT PROCEDURES

It is generally recommended that companies should conduct a post audit to compare the actual results of a capital project with the original forecasts that were used in determining that the project was acceptable. This procedure not only can serve as an evaluation of project implementation but also as an evaluation of the entire capital budget planning process. Companies can use this information to evaluate the accuracy of their forecasts and whether they have been using the appropriate project analysis techniques. In 1977, two thirds of the forest products companies conducted some form of formal post audit of their capital projects. In the 1997 survey, over three quarters of the respondents report that they do post audits of their capital investment projects.

All 12 of the largest companies in the survey do use post audits for their capital projects as do most of the firms in the $50-$100 million and $101-$500 million categories. In fact, post audits seem to be the general practice in all but the smallest companies where only one of the respondent firms has a post audit procedure in place.

Comments about post auditing procedures indicate that post audits typically were conducted between six months to one year after projects were fully operational. Second, in most cases, post audits were mandatory on all large projects (i.e., over $5 million) with the results being reported to the board. Conducting post audits on smaller projects typically was at the discretion of the audit committee, company president, or business unit vice president depending on the size .of the firm involved. Third, most firms conducted post audits on only the first-year results,

with one firm reporting that it audited up to five years' results in the case of very large investments.

The most interesting comment received regarding post audits was:

> "We pick a finance person and a manufacturing person from a different plant/mill to act as a team to perform the audit. They are given a copy of the project and all backup information and are given three to four months to complete the audit, while continuing with all their normal job requirements. They prepare the audit report and then give a presentation to our audit committee. Normally, only larger projects are post audited. All other financially justified projects are reviewed in a less formal process. These reports are completed by the responsible plant/mill and routed around for review."

The fact that this firm used individuals from both finance and manufacturing in addition to requiring that they be from a different operating unit increases the likelihood that the post audit results for the major investments would be unbiased.

MORE COMPANIES USE IRR AND NPV

On the basis of the survey, the following conclusions can be made regarding capital budgeting practices in the forest products industry in the last 20 years. First, there has been a significant increase in the use of the more sophisticated and theoretically preferred discounted cash flow methodologies of internal rate of return and net present value for all capital investment decisions. While firm size continues to be the dominant factor when it comes to the use of these methods in evaluating plant and equipment purchases, even smaller firms use them in the case of timber investments. Moreover, a greater percentage of firms are now applying discounted cash flow techniques in the preliminary or project screening stages of their capital budgeting process.

Second, risk analysis has taken on increased importance. A greater percentage of firms are using quantitative techniques, and those that do not at least attempt to consider risk subjectively.

Third, only smaller firms have failed to implement post audit procedures on a consistent basis as a way to both monitor and control their major capital investments. Post audit procedures in medium-sized and large firms not only are becoming more formal in terms of reporting requirements, they are also more extensive in terms of the actual analysis procedures being employed.

Fourth, other procedures such as breakeven analysis, probability analysis, and decision trees are coming into use as relevant capital budgeting methodologies. In addition, noneconomic issues are taking on a greater degree of importance in the decision-making process. The issue most often cited is the changing regulatory climate in the forest products industry especially as it relates to health, safety, and the environment. Each of these areas relates to the company's custodial role concerning both timber resources and employees.

Jack Bailes is a professor of accounting at Oregon State University. He has a Ph.D. degree in business from the University of Washington. Dr. Bailes has authored several previous articles in MANAGEMENT ACCOUTING and has won several awards for articles published in the management accounting field. He is a former president of Salem Area (Ore.) Chapter, through which this article was submitted.

James Nielsen is a professor of banking and finance at Oregon State University with an MBA and a Ph.D. in Business Administration from the University of Colorado. Dr. Nielsen has authored a number of articles in banking and finance journals.

Stephen Lawton was the coordinator for the MacArthur Foundation Sustainable Forestry Working Group with more than 30 researchers that produced a series of business case studies that illustrated the market opportunities and financial viability of sustainable forestry. Mr. Lawton teaches international business in executive programs in the United States, Europe, and Asia. He is also an associate professor of international business at Oregon State University.

[1] In 1977, there were a total of 241 companies participating in the Oregon State University Forest Products Monograph Program.

HOW ABC WAS USED
IN CAPITAL BUDGETING

By Steve Coburn, CPA; Hugh Grove, CPA; and Tom Cook

How do you estimate cash flows for capital expenditure projects in your company? Many firms use broad strategic approaches for estimating cash flows that are not closely tied to detailed tactical assumptions about future operations. These forecasts may not be very reliable because cash flow projections of new products can have a 30% to 40% margin of error.

A new division of a Fortune 500 company was established to analyze new business opportunities in the electronic (broadband) marketplace of interactive television. The company and data have been disguised here for confidentiality purposes. The initial investment proposal was to develop a "cybermall," similar to the way marketing service organizations bring together sellers and buyers in the traditional television marketplace. At the time, this cybermall proposal was a new idea without any close counterparts in this emerging electronic marketplace.

Senior management of this new division initially had focused upon the marketing strategy of "speed to market" for this cybermall project. Thus, the business case forecast was done at a broad strategic level with few supporting details. A consulting firm provided general forecasts of the electronic market size and market share which it converted into aggregate forecasts of revenue, operating costs, and capital costs. Driven by this "speed-to-market" strategy senior management was willing to commit $50 million to this cybermall project, based upon the business case forecast.

The chief financial officer (CFO) of this new division, however, successfully argued for a tactical translation of the business case's broad strategic view into a detailed analysis of the cybermall's projected business processes and activities. Senior management approved the CFO's proposal because it still had concerns about how the technical development and deployment of the electronic marketplace would impact the cybermall financial forecasts. The CFO's proposal became an activity-based cost (ABC) model (with bench-marking) that created a pro forma process engineering approach for analyzing this business opportunity.

Process analysis typically has been used for reengineering existing—not pro forma—processes.[1] In contrast, this business opportunity related to an emerging industry with new processes. Also, ABC has been advocated for use in annual, not capital, budgeting.[2] Using ABC for capital budgeting analysis of this cybermall project created an example of activity based management (ABM), which has been defined as providing economic information for management decision making.[3]

The ABC model (with benchmarking) forecasted business processes, activities, revenues, operating costs, and capital costs for this cybermall project. This tactical ABC approach generated forecasts that differed significantly from the forecasts of the strategic business case. For example, the ABC model forecasted that an additional $10 million of capital costs would be needed. Also, revenue forecasts were slowed down and startup cost forecasts were increased. Senior management used these ABC results to reverse its initial decision to go ahead with this cybermall project.

Thus, the CFO provided strategic AEM information and became part of the business decision-making process. Senior management also has decided to use this ABC approach for evaluating future business opportunities. Such a strategic role has been advocated as the most important goal for a CFO's mission statement and the future of management accounting.[4]

The ABC analysis provided an understanding of projected business processes and activities that allowed senior management to have more confidence in the detailed tactical ABC forecasts, rather than the initial, broad strategic forecasts. This pro forma ABC approach also is a logical next step for companies currently using ABC and bench-marking to understand existing business processes and activities.

We describe here an overview of the business case and the ABC model approaches; then a description of the ABC approach for analyzing this cybermall project is provided. Finally, the forecasts from both approaches are compared.

BUSINESS CASE VS. ABC MODEL APPROACHES

Figure 1 provides an overview of the business case approach to capital budgeting for this cybermall project. The strategic business case forecasts started with broad market assumptions concerning electronic market size and share provided by a consulting firm.

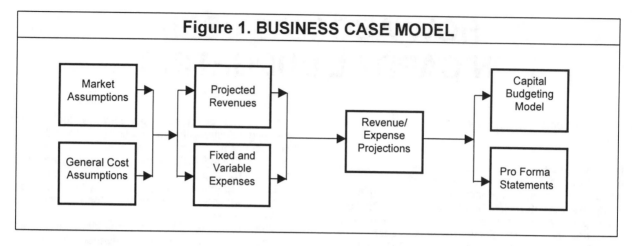

Figure 1. BUSINESS CASE MODEL

These consultants then converted this market data into general projections of revenues with few supporting details. They also used general cost assumptions to project variable and fixed expenses without any detailed cost analyses.

For example, the budget line items of technology development, video production, and network operations were mainly aggregate fixed cost forecasts. The few variable cost forecasts were based upon general revenue projections, such as distribution access as a flat fee per subscriber and order processing as a specified amount per customer. A key capital infrastructure forecast used just one type of client/server technology for all interactive television markets although four different types of client/server technology were being deployed by cable system operators.

The business case provided general revenue and expense projections and pro forma financial statements. Also, the business case provided senior management with capital budgeting information for the decision criteria of net present value (NPV), internal rate of return (IRR), and payback.

Figure 2 provides an overview of the ABC approach to capital budgeting for this cybermall project. The tactical ABC model forecasts were based upon detailed benchmarked data from the cybermall business process analyses provided by the CFO. Using benchmark assumptions, the ABC approach developed a broadband deployment or buildout schedule of the electronic marketplace for potential interactive television subscribers. It also developed a transaction volume schedule for potential cybermall customers. Both schedules were used to help generate the revenue, cost, and capital assumptions and projections of the ABC model.

The ABC model created a broadband network deployment schedule by benchmarking with external parties to obtain detailed data concerning the build-out of the broadband infrastructure for the electronic marketplace. The ten largest cable or multi-system operators (MSOs) were projected to build or deploy broadband infrastructures over five years, starting in 1996, and all other MSOs to deploy over seven years, starting in 1997. This deployment was projected to start in the 50 largest cities or suburbs named as areas of dominant influence (ADI).

Using this deployment schedule as a starting point, the ABC model created a detailed transaction volume schedule by benchmarking shopping participation, purchase frequency, and average spending for this cybermall project. Because no interactive television operators existed for this emerging market, the traditional television marketing operators, Home Shopping Network (HSN) and the QVC system, were used as indirect or "out of market" benchmarks. For example, HSN had about five million active shoppers representing 8.3% of the homes reached, and QVC had four million shoppers representing 8.0% of the homes reached. Also, HSN repeat customers had made purchases between five and seven times a year. Average spending per shopping household for repeat customers was about $300 for HSN and about $500 for QVC.

The tactical ABC model used detailed revenue assumptions and forecasts for this cybermall project, as opposed to the general ones of the strategic business case. The ABC model forecasted slower access to cybermall customers, primarily due to delays in developing and provisioning the broadband network. Accordingly, the revenue forecasts for the early years were lower than in the business case. Concerning the ABC pool costs, the ABC model used a pro forma process engineering approach to construct activity resource consumption profiles and transaction (cost) drivers that were multiplied together to derive the ABC expense projections. A cybermall value chain of workflow or business processes was specified with key activities and cost drivers. This pro forma process engineering approach is described below.

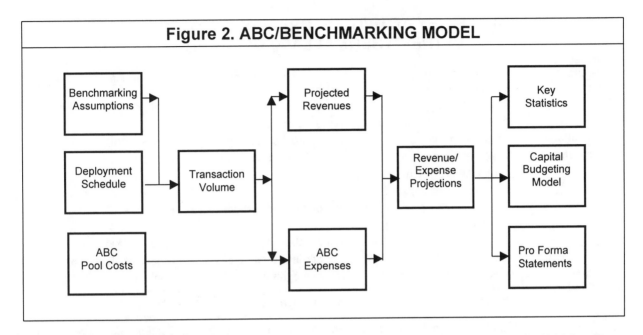

Figure 2. ABC/BENCHMARKING MODEL

PRO FORMA PROCESS ENGINEERING

A pro forma process engineering approach was used by the ABC model to forecast operating and capital costs for the cybermall project. A cybermall value chain was created with six sequential workflows or business processes as shown in Table 1. First, cybermall seller relationships must be developed to provide the goods and services available for purchase on this interactive television system. Second, the system to operate interactive television applications must be developed. Third, content programs must be purchased or produced. Fourth, the ongoing operations of this interactive television system must be performed, especially the processing of cybermall buyers' orders. Fifth, the marketing of the cybermall must be done. Sixth, the network distributors and access fees must be managed.

Major activities were identified for each of these six business processes in the cybermall value chain. Resource consumption profiles and cost drivers were identified for the major activities. Cost pool rates were calculated and multiplied by the number of cost drivers needed at various transaction volumes to project the ABC process expenses as summarized in Table 1.

Detailed capital costs also were forecasted for various levels of activities. The $2 million total capital costs in Table 1 represented four initial broadband deployments. Each deployment used a different type of client/server, and each server type was estimated to require $0.5 million in capital costs. Over the initial 10-year period of this cybermall project, 120 network deployments were estimated for total capital costs of $60 million, which was $10 million or 20% higher than the business case estimate of $50 million, as shown in Table 2.

Also, three types of external parties were identified because they were needed to perform critical activities in various business processes for this cybermall project to become operational. First, cybermall sellers were needed to do core programming in the content production process. They also were needed in the operations process for selling, shipping, billing, and collecting the cybermall goods and revenues. Second, software vendors were needed to develop and test network applications, video content programs, and network operations for the cybermall. Third, distributors were needed to develop, operate, and deploy the interactive broadband network where the cybermall will be located.

Seller relationship process. The seller relationship business process for the cybermall has three major activities. First, for the activity of acquiring cybermall sellers, account managers are needed to obtain and maintain sellers of goods and services. One full-time equivalent (FTE) manager and one secretary are projected for 1995, increasing to a cap of seven FTEs by 1997. Second, for the promotion activity, the cybermall will be publicized with an annual budget for promotional mailings to potential sellers and distributors. Third, a general manager is needed for managing seller relationships. One half-time position is needed in 1995, increasing to a cap of two FTEs by 1997.

Table 1. KEY ACTIVITIES, DRIVERS AND COSTS IN THE CYBERMALL VALUE CHAIN

Business Processes	Major Activities	Cost Drivers	Process Expenses	Capital (000,000)
Seller	Acquire sellers	No. of sellers	Selling	$0
Relationship	Do promotions	No. of direct mailings	Selling	0
	Manage seller relationships	Annual staffing	Selling	0
Application	Product concept	No. of product start-ups	Product R&D	$.4
Development	Design application:	No. of Product Start-ups	Product R&D	
	Asset mgt. system			$.1
	Order process sys.			$.1
	Develop database	No. of product start-ups	Product R&D	
	Technology:			
	Planning	Annual staffing	Product R&D	0
	Deployment	No. of client server types	Product R&D	$.4
Content Production	Brokerage of Program purchases	No. of programs	Content production	0
	Program production	No. of programs	Content production	0
	Post production guidelines	Annual staffing	Content production	0
Operations	Order processing	No. of orders	Operations	$.1
	Customer service	No. of network head-ends	Operations	$.1
	Provision network	No. of fiber loops	Operations	$.5
	Seller interface	Annual staff	Operations	0
Marketing	Buyer acquisition	No. of buyers	Marketing	0
	Advertising	No. of ads	Marketing	0
	Public Relations	Annual staffing	Marketing	0
	Buyer maintenance	Revenue Percent	Marketing	0
Network	Distributor Relationships	Annual staffing	Distribution	0
Distribution	Access Fee	No. of buyers	Distribution	0

Capital Costs in Table 2: 4 types of Deployment * $.5 = $ 2.0

Total Capital Costs in Table 1: 120 Deployments * $.5 = $60.0

Application development process. Application development business process for the cybermall has four major activities. First, product concept will be defined and evaluated with product research, product specifications, and simulated operations. Capital costs of $350,000 are needed for simulation equipment, a client/server, workstations, and personal computers. Second, two key types of design application activities are needed. An asset management system will be developed with a simulated startup for this cybermall. Capital costs of $150,000 are needed for video equipment, software, and production workstations. Also, an automated order processing system for cybermall customers will be developed with $100,000 of capital costs.

Third, for the database activity, a database operations center will be developed. Capital costs of $300,000 are needed for the central hardware to coordinate the workstations. Fourth, two key types of technology activities are needed. For the planning activity, three technical employees and $50,000 for test equipment each year are needed to maintain technical core competency and to update technical strategy continuously. For the deployment activity, this cybermall project will be adapted to four technology types of client/servers and will cost $100,000 for each type of server. Thus, capital costs of $400,000 are needed initially to provision four servers (one for each server type).

Content production process. The content production business process for the cybermall has three major activities. First, for the brokerage of program purchases, rights to use existing programming will be purchased when appropriate for this cybermall. Estimated annual costs are $100,000 in 1995, increasing to a $700,000 cap by 2000. Second, for the program production activity, programs for video content describing the cybermall sellers will be produced in-house or outsourced. It is assumed that the company and the sellers will split these costs equally, which are similar to the brokerage program costs. Third, concerning post-production guidelines, costs to monitor and manage programming and production are estimated as one technical employee in 1995, increasing to cap of four FTEs by 1997.

Operations process. The operations process has four major activities. First, for the order processing activity, there will be two cost structures. Manual processing will be used from 1995 through 1997 until higher cybermall shopper volume is obtained. Thereafter, automated processing will be used with capital costs of $100,000. Second, concerning customer service, employee costs are estimated at one third FTE for each network head-end. Capital costs of $100,000 are estimated for workstations and software.

Third, to provision an interactive (broadband) television network, this cybermall project must be deployed on fiber loops, requiring video server equipment. Each server may feed up to four head-end networks and up to 500,000 interactively passed homes. Capital costs of $500,000 are estimated for the video servers, storage units, and personal computer systems to interface with the fiber loops. Fourth, for cybermall seller interfacing, one manager and three technical employees are needed for the post-production functions of program content and network operations.

Marketing process. The marketing process has four major activities. First, for the buyer acquisition activity, sales persons are needed to obtain cybermall shoppers or buyers. Related selling costs also are included. Such buyer acquisition costs are estimated to decrease over time. Second, advertising primarily via television and radio promotions is necessary. Costs for preparation of such advertisements are budgeted for $200,000 in 1996, increasing up to a $500,000 cap by 1999. Third, public relations activities included marketing management. Personnel are estimated at two FTEs in 1995, four FTEs in 1996, and eight FTEs thereafter. Fourth, concerning buyer maintenance, costs to maintain cybermall shoppers are estimated as a percentage of total revenue.

Network distribution process. The network distribution process has two major activities. First, account managers are needed to manage relationships with the distribution networks used by this cybermall. Personnel are estimated at one half time position in 1995, increasing to a cap of two FTEs by 1998. Second, concerning network access fees from 1995 through 1997, charges are based upon the number of cybermall shoppers making purchases and are paid monthly to the network provider. Thereafter, the charges will be based upon a percentage of total shopping purchases.

In summary, the tactical ABC model engineered pro forma business processes, activities, and cost drivers to calculate detailed revenue and resource consumption patterns, as opposed to the general assumptions of the strategic business case approach. Also, to help senior management make this capital budgeting decision, key operating statistics were compiled by the ABC model. Such statistics were not provided by the business case because it was done without detailed analyses. These statistics were classified by four types of metrics: buyers, sellers, networks, and infrastructure, as shown in Table 3.

If comparisons had been available, the ABC model generally would have provided less optimistic forecasts of operating statistics because its related revenue forecasts were lower and startup cost forecasts higher than the business case. For example, the acquisition cost per buyer would have been higher and the revenue per seller, lower. In the network and infrastructure metrics, the access costs and the cost per minute/content both would have been higher.

If the cost drivers were not already represented in the benchmarked transaction file, they were added to these existing transaction volumes. For example, a new cost driver for the number of client/servers was measured by the interactive television deployment sequence under the cybermall revenue assumptions. From the pro forma engineering analysis, an activity resource consumption profile was established to measure the cost of a client/server. Then, the number and cost of the client/servers were multiplied together to project the ABC expenses at various levels of interactive television deployment.

Thus, detailed resource consumption patterns and transaction (cost) drivers were used to generate the ABC expense and capital forecasts, as opposed to general assumptions in the business case forecasts. For example, the application development and design costs were forecasted using the number of product startups as the cost driver. (A fixed cost was used throughout the business case.) For another example,

Table 2. COMPARISONS OF ABC VS. BUSINESS CASE
(In millions and 10-year totals)

Panel A: Key Projections:

	Business Case	ABC Model	Variances Increase Amount	(Decrease) Percent
Total revenues	$1,650	$1,480	($170)	(10%)
Total cash operations expenses	$1,000	$ 950	($ 50)	(5%)
Total net income aftertax	$ 250	$ 175	($ 75)	(30%)
Total capital expenditures	$ 50	$ 60	$ 10	20%
Total net cash flow (without residual value)	$ 400	$ 320	($ 80)	(20%)

Panel B: Key Decision Criteria:

	Business Case	ABC Model	Increase Amount	(Decrease) Percent
1. Without Residual Value:				
Internal rate of return	43%	33%	(10%)	(23%)
Net present values:				
@20%	$ 60	$ 35	($25)	(42%)
@30%	$ 20	$ 4	($16)	(80%)
@40%	$ 3	($ 8)	($11)	N/A
Discounted payback @20% in yrs.	7	9	2	29%
2. With Residual Value:	61%	50%	(11%)	
Internal rate of return				(18%)
Net present values:				
@20%	$225	$190	($35)	(16%)
@30%	$100	$ 80	($20)	(20%)
@40%	$ 40	$ 25	($15)	(38%)

manual order processing initially was assumed due to low customer volume in the startup phase. Subsequently, automated order processing was assumed. (A variable cost per customer was used throughout the business case.) The ABC model forecasted specific network operating costs using the cost drivers of network head-ends and fiber loops. (Aggregate amounts of fixed costs were used in the business case.) The ABC model forecasted capital costs that represented four types of broadband deployments, one for each of the actual types of client/servers being deployed by cable television operators. (Only one client/server type was used in the business case.)

The ABC model calculated key operating statistics and differences between the ABC and the business case dollar projections and NPV, IRR, and payback results. The operating statistics are described in Table 3. The ABC model also generated pro forma financial statements. All this information was provided to help senior management make its final decision on this cybermall project. The ten different categories of the ABC model in Figure 2 were linked together as a series of related Excel spreadsheets to facilitate risk analysis. The final ABC model used six megabytes of random access memory.

COMPARISONS OF FORECASTS

For this cybermall project, 10-year financial forecasts are summarized in Table 2. Panel A has comparisons of key dollar projections for the business case and the ABC model. Panel B has comparisons of key capital budgeting forecasts for the business case and the ABC model. In Table 2, the residual value for this cybermall project represented the net present value of its sales price in year 10. The ABC spreadsheet

Table 3. KEY OPERATING STATISTICS

Buyers:	Networks:	Infrastructure:	Sellers:
No. of shoppers	Homes passed	Programming shelf life	Items per view hour
Purchases per year	Access cost percent of revenue	Cost per minute/content	Number of sellers
Return percent	ADI coverage percent	Connect time	Revenue per seller
Browse time	Network profitability	Percent automatic fulfillment	Transactions per month
Repeat time	Number of platforms supported	Cost per transaction	Percent ship date target
Acquisition cost per buyer	Number of shopping applications	Transaction response time	Seller renewal rate

model calculated both dollar and percent variances between the two approaches as shown in Table 2.

Key projections of 10-year financial amounts for both approaches were summarized in Panel A of Table 2. For the business case, key dollar projections were (in millions): $1,650 revenues; $1,000 cash operating expenses; $250 net income after taxes; $50 capital expenditures; and $400 net cash flow without residual value. For the ABC model, key dollar projections were (in millions): $1,480 revenues; $950 cash operating expenses; $175 net income after taxes; $60 capital expenditures; and $320 net cash flow without residual value. Concerning the variances, all the business case forecasts were from 5% to 30% higher than the ABC model forecasts, except for capital expenditures, which were 20% ($10 million) lower. Consequently, the ABC dollar projections, especially the 20% reduction in net cash flow, generated lower capital budgeting forecasts than in the business case.

Capital budgeting forecasts for both approaches are summarized in Panel B of Table 2. For the business case, the internal rates of return were 43% without any residual value and 61% with the residual value. The net present values were $60 million, $20 million, and $3 million, using cost-of-capital rates of 20%, 30%, and 40%, respectively, without any residual value. With the residual value, the net present values were much larger at $225 million, $100 million, and $40 million, respectively. The discounted cash flow payback was seven years, using a 20% cost of capital rate.

For the ABC model, the internal rates of return were 33% without any residual value and 50% with the residual value. The net present values were $35 million, $4 million, and negative $8 million, using cost of capital rates of 20%, 30%, and 40%, respectively, without any residual value. With the residual value, the net present values were much larger at $190 million, $80 million, and $25 million, respectively. The discounted cash flow payback was nine years, using a 20% cost-of-capital rate.

The variances for the capital budgeting forecasts showed that the ABC model results were significantly lower than the business case results. The internal rates of return decreased by 23% and 18%, without and with the residual values, respectively The net present values were reduced from 16% to 80%, depending upon which cost of capital rate was used. The discounted cash flow payback was increased by two years or 29%. With higher capital forecasts and lower revenue and cash flow forecasts, the ABC capital budgeting forecasts were less favorable for this cybermall project than the business case forecasts.

From the ABC analysis, the electronic marketplace deployment and resulting market share and revenues were too slow while the startup and investment costs were too big and too early to justify the cybermall project at this time. Also, the operating leverage for profit growth did not become favorable until the mid-life point of this cybermall project, as opposed to an earlier prediction in the business case.

ABC PROVIDES TACTICAL APPROACH

The ABC model provided a methodology to analyze future business opportunities concerning new types of products and services in emerging markets. The additional level of detail was the key difference from the business case approach for this cybermall project. The pro forma analysis of the business processes and activities with linkages to revenue and cost structures provided critical information for the final decision on this cybermall project.

This approach appears to be applicable to all types of capital budgeting decisions and should provide a unique opportunity for senior management to understand how business processes and activities impact revenue and cost forecasts. As in this cybermall project, the business case approach typically analyzes the symptoms of changes using various levels of market shares, revenues, and costs, but no clear analyses of the causes or drivers of these changes are provided. By contrast, such causal analyses *are* provided by this ABC approach which attempts to understand how changes in business processes and activities impact market share, revenues, and costs.

The ABC information provided a better understanding of the cybermall business processes and activities. This additional knowledge allowed senior management to have more confidence in its strategic decision making for this project. Senior management agreed that the additional costs spent on the ABC and benchmarking analyses were justified by the benefits of more detailed operating and financial information.

For example, the following key uses of this ABC model were identified for this cybermall project in the emerging electronic marketplace:

- Establishing linkages between technology (the electronic market deployment and distribution of interactive services) and financial forecasts,
- Using indirect or "out of market" benchmarks for revenue and cost forecasts,
- Creating a dynamic model that showed how unitized ABC costs behaved and changed over time in providing interactive services, and
- Specifying operating leverage more precisely with different step-cost functions at different levels of volume.

These key uses also helped clarify marketing strategies for this emerging industry; i.e., broad market coverage versus narrow or niche market development of interactive services.

As shown by the comparisons in Table 2, the tactical ABC model produced less favorable forecasts for the capital budgeting decision criteria than the strategic business case. Thus, senior management decided not to do this project at this time. Because the ABC model also was a working spreadsheet model, sensitivity and "what-if" risk analyses were performed but the final decision was to reject the project. Senior management decided not to be a first or early entrant into this emerging electronic market.

This ABC model provided a detailed tactical methodology to analyze business opportunities in emerging markets, as opposed to the general strategic view of the business case approach. The initial "speed-to-market" strategy in the business case was tempered by the tactical ABC analysis of the cybermall project's feasibility Forecasts of the ABC model created more confidence in making this cybermall decision; therefore, senior management has decided to use this ABC model for analyzing subsequent business opportunities in the electronic marketplace. Thus, by using this ABC and benchmarking methodology to provide strategic information, the CFO became part of the strategic decision-making process in accordance with the key goal for a CFO's mission statement and the future of management accounting.

Steve Coburn, CPA, is chief financial officer, Teletech Corporation, Denver, Colo.

Hugh Grove, CPA, is professor, School of Accountancy, University of Denver, Denver, Colo., and a member of the Denver Chapter, through which this article was submitted.

Tom Cook is associate professor of finance, Daniels College of Business, University of Denver, Denver, Colo.

[1] Refer to M. Hammer and J. Champy, *Reengineering the Corporation,* Harper Business, New York, 1993.

[2] Refer to J. Schmidt, "Is It Time to Replace Traditional Budgeting?", *Journal of Accountancy,* November 1992, pp.103-107.

[3] Refer to R. Kaplan, "In Defense of Activity-Based Cost Management," MANAGEMENT ACCOUNTING®, November 1992, pp. 58-63.

[4] Refer to A. Pipkin, "The 21st Century Controller," MANAGEMENT ACCOUNTING, February 1989, pp. 21-25; and W. Birkett. "Management Accounting and Knowledge Management," MANAGEMENT ACCOUNTING, November 1995, pp. 44-48.

ASSESSING RISK AND UNCERTAINTY IN NEW TECHNOLOGY INVESTMENTS

By Wilton L. Accola
Wilton L. Accola (deceased) formerly Assistant Professor at University of Memphis.

SYNOPSIS: Recently, much attention has focused on the shortcomings of traditional capital budgeting models in evaluating new technology investments. Critics argue that such models particularly those based on discounted cash flows, lead managers to favor less promising investments over strategic new technology investments because many benefits of the strategic investment are highly uncertain and cannot be quantified. Furthermore, the riskiness of a new technology investment is difficult to assess because outcome probabilities are difficult to estimate. Consequently, several writers have concluded that traditional capital budgeting models are inadequate for evaluating new technology investments.

This paper provides a theory-based framework for evaluating nonquantifiable uncertainties and multiple aspects of risk in capital investments and makes the following contributions:

- The two-dimensional risk-return framework is extended to include a third dimension, nonquantifiable uncertainty. This expanded framework enables managers to formally evaluate all significant nonquantifiable uncertainties relevant to the resource allocation decision.

- The proposed evaluation approach makes a clear distinction between quantifiable returns, quantifiable risks, and nonquantifiable uncertainties. If a clear distinction is not made when evaluating benefits, the quantifiable part of the benefit may be counted twice—once in the quantifiable return and once when nonquantifiable benefits are evaluated. The approach proposed in this paper reduces the possibility of double-counting.

- A composite measure of quantifiable risk is introduced in this paper. By capturing multiple aspects of risk, this composite measure provides managers with more risk information than models which define risk in terms of a single parameter. The composite risk measure also reflects the objectives of the firm.

An important function of a management accounting information system is to provide managers with models that evaluate all relevant information needed for making capital allocation decisions. Ideally, the management accounting information system should provide information and models useful for (1) predicting the future cash flows of prospective investment alternatives, (2) assessing the riskiness of these future cash flows, and (3) assessing the nonquantifiable uncertainties surrounding the estimation of future cash flows.[i]

Recently, much attention has focused on the shortcomings of management accounting information systems in evaluating new technology investments.. The special problems encountered in measuring benefits and risks of computer-integrated-manufacturing (CIM) investments have been of particular concern. Critics argue that quantitative models, particularly discounted cash flow (DCF) models, lead managers to favor less promising investments over strategic new technology investments because many benefits of the strategic investments are highly uncertain and cannot be quantified. Furthermore, the riskiness of a new technology investment is difficult to assess because outcome probabilities are difficult to estimate. Consequently, several writers concluded that traditional quantitative models are inadequate for evaluating new technology investments.

Models enabling managers to evaluate qualitative criteria have been proposed for use in evaluating CIM investments. The Analytical Hierarchy Process (AHP) model, which can be used to assess non-quantifiable data, has received support as a practical aid for evaluating CIM investments. Automan (Weber 1989), a computerized AHP decision aid jointly sponsored by the Institute of Management Accountants and the U.S. Department of Commerce, was developed specifically to evaluate CIM investment decisions (Weber 1989). Expert Choice, developed by Decision Support Software, Inc., is also used for evaluating multiple criteria investment decisions.

Despite the growing interest among managers in AHP and other multiple criteria models, the use of such models may produce undesirable outcomes if these models are applied in inappropriate ways. This paper develops a theory-based framework for evaluating multiple dimensions of risk and uncertainty. Although this paper refers to the AHP model as a means of implementing the proposed framework, other multiattribute weighting techniques also may be used to implement this framework.[ii]

I. PROBLEMS IN EVALUATING NEW TECHNOLOGY INVESTMENTS

Traditional capital budgeting models have been limited to assessing quantifiable financial information and usually disregard nonquantifiable benefits. The ultimate financial productivity of a new technology investment is affected to a considerable extent by non-quantifiable benefits (Kaplan 1986).

Benefits often associated with CIM investments—consistency with business strategy, improved competitive position, improved delivery and service, improved product quality, and reduced product development time—often are difficult to quantify. A survey of American high-technology companies and users of managerial accounting information reveals that more than half of the respondents did not attempt to quantify these benefits (Howell et al. 1987). In Japan, 71 percent of advanced manufacturing companies surveyed justify investments on the basis of difficult-to-quantify benefits (Scarbrough et al. 1991).

Mensah and Miranti (1989) classified CIM benefits into two categories—primary benefits and secondary benefits. Because the primary benefits of automation are based on cost savings, they are reasonably estimable from historical data. These include: (1) direct labor savings, (2) direct material savings, (3) savings from the reduction in set-ups, (4) savings from higher quality products, and (5) savings from reduced materials and in-process inventories.

Secondary benefits are much more difficult to quantify and are often highly uncertain. These benefits include: (1) increased market demand due to improved process control/product reliability, (2) improved product performance, (3) additional manufacturing capabilities/flexibility, (4) rapid learning effects, and (5) improved employee morale.

DIFFICULTIES IN APPLYING DCF TECHNIQUES

Despite these difficulties, several authors attempted to demonstrate how discounted cash flow analysis can be applied to automation projects. Most of these research studies appeared in engineering journals and focus on the economics of specific equipment configurations. Generally, such attempts failed to develop quantitative criteria for evaluating qualitative benefits and/or are based on assumptions which may not hold in practice (Mensah and Miranti 1989).

ARBITRARILY HIGH HURDLE RATES

The use of arbitrarily high hurdle discount rates to account for the high risk inherent in new technologies has often led managers to fund investments which are less desirable strategically than investments in new technology (Kaplan 1986; Sullivan and Reeve 1988). Arbitrarily high hurdle thresholds favor short-term projects over long-term projects with large cash flows in the middle to late part of the project's life. Sullivan and Reeve(1988) pointed out that when high hurdle rates are combined with an incomplete analysis of qualitative benefits, few strategic projects are adopted. They concluded that companies using risk-adjusted hurdle rates to evaluate investments incorporate subjective risk assessments into the analysis twice—once through the use of a high discount rate and again by omitting many of the difficult-to-quantify benefits.

Other authors objected to the use of risk-adjusted discount rates on theoretical grounds (Ronen and Sorter 1972).. A major theoretical weakness involves use of a single measure to reflect both expected cash flows and the riskiness of the expected cash flows. Because there are many different determinants of risk, it is difficult to capture all the aspects of a project's riskiness through a single modification of the discount rate (Ronen and Sorter 1972). In practice, adjustments to the discount rate are affected by managers' attitudes toward risk rather than by an explicit representation of the risks inherent in the investment alternatives (Ronen and Sorter 1972). For these reasons, models used should enable managers to measure and evaluate expected cash flows separately from the risks associated with them. In choice situations involving multiple aspects of risk, models with multiple risk parameters should be used to explicitly represent all significant aspects of risk existing in the choice alternatives.

OTHER RISK MEASUREMENT APPROACHES

Multiple-dimensional risk models represent expected cash flows and their associated risks separately. Two dimensional risk-return models, as typified by Hillier's method (1963) and the Capital Asset Pricing Model, combine a return measure with a single measure of risk.

Many different risk measures have been used as parameters for multiple-dimensional risk models. Two major types of risk measures used as model parameters are *moment-oriented and dimension-oriented measures* (Schoemaker 1979; Aschenbrenner 1984). **Moment-oriented** models assume that data are available to estimate multiple outcomes of alternatives and their related probabilities; **dimension-oriented** models are based on risk "dimensions" and often require less data.

Moment-oriented approaches include Hillier's use of standard deviations to measure the riskiness of cash flows (Hillier 1963; Washburn 1992), variance (Norgaard and Killeen 1990) and confidence limits (Libby and Fishburn 1977). Most sophisticated risky choice capital budgeting models are based on a moment-oriented definition of risk, requiring estimation of the probability distribution of cash flows (Norgaard and Killeen 1990).

Dimension-oriented risk measures are often used when the probability distribution of cash flows is difficult to estimate. These measures are not based on an entire probability of cash flows. Instead, they capture various dimensions of risk present in the choice situation.

An important risk dimension that should often be considered in CIM investment decisions is the possibility of a ruinous loss. The amount of capital investment as a percentage of total assets of the firm may be used to represent the possibility of a ruinous loss. The larger the proportion of resources committed to a capital project, the greater the risk of insolvency. The probability of losses exceeding a certain percentage of total equity also may be used to measure the ruinous loss dimension.

The widespread use of the payback method for evaluating capital projects (Mao 1970; Scapens and Sale 1981; Howell et al. 1987; Pike 1983, 1988), may be attributed to its usefulness as a dimension-oriented risk measure. Payback period often is used as a measure of liquidity risk.

Another risk dimension relevant to capital budgeting decisions is the failure to achieve a target return. Examples of risk measures that capture this dimension include semivariance and the probability of below-target returns. Unlike moment-oriented risk parameters which define risk as an aspect of the entire probability distribution, these measures define risk in terms of only the negative side of a probability distribution. Semivariance, as a measure of downside risk, specifically considers situations where one or more outcomes for an alternative are lower than some critical amount (usually, a target return). Semivariance, unlike variance or standard deviation, does not consider the possibility of a large favorable outcome to be risky. Another measure of downside risk, the probability of below-target returns, associates greater risk with a higher probability of failing to achieve a target return. This measure is an important

risk parameter when it is difficult for managers to estimate a reliable probability distribution of cash flows (Mao 1970).

Although many different quantitative risk measures—both moment- and dimension-oriented—have been used as parameters for risk return tradeoff models, these models primarily use a single measure, such as variance, beta or semivariance, to represent an investment's riskiness (Libby and Fishburn 1977). For some capital budgeting decisions, models with multiple risk parameters may better represent the risk that exists in the situation than simpler models with a single risk parameter.

A restrictive characteristic of both moment- and dimension-oriented risk measures is the requirement that risk must be quantified. The dimension-oriented approach requires quantification of the particular risk dimension being measured. A requirement of the moment-oriented approach is that probability distributions of risky cash flows can be reasonably estimated. In some situations, such as new technology investment decisions, probability distributions are difficult to estimate and quantification of all uncertainties is impossible. In such situations, such as new technology investment decisions, probability distributions are difficult to estimate and quantification of all uncertainties is impossible. In such situations, it may be necessary to use a model that considers nonquantifiable risk and return, to obtain a more complete evaluation of the project's riskiness.

STRATEGIC INVESTMENT

Because traditional capital budgeting models fail to measure qualitative benefits, some authors suggest that certain investments be classified as "strategic" and implemented regardless of financial justification (Haspeslaugh 1982; Logue 1981). These authors define strategic investments as those necessary for the firm's survival. The "best" alternative is not necessarily the optimal alternative as ranked by net present value or internal rate of return, but the one that enables the firm to survive threats from competitors. Because a CIM investment is a strategic investment, these authors argue that it should be adopted regardless of the discounted cash flow projections.

The problem with such an approach is the difficulty firms have in distinguishing between strategic and nonstrategic investments. Not every CIM investment is necessary for the survival of the firm. To properly define and evaluate a strategic investment, criteria must be developed to determine the degree to which an investment opportunity contributes to the firm's survival.

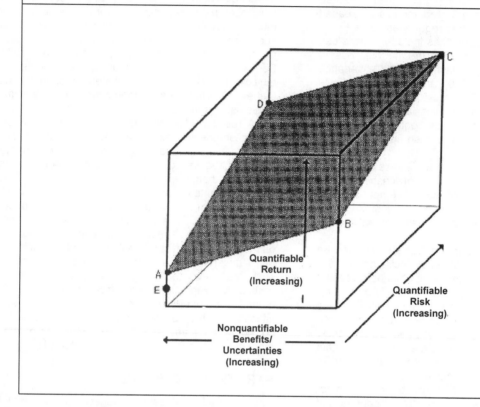

ANALYTICAL FRAMEWORK

Several authors proposed variations of an analytical model, the Analytical Hierarchy Process (AHP), to supplement discounted cash flow techniques in evaluating new technology investments (Arbel and Seidmann 1984; Canada and Sullivan 1989; Neises and Bennett 1989; Stout et al. 1991). Subjective estimates of uncertain benefits for which probabilities cannot be reasonably estimated can be formally incorporated into the analysis through the use of AHP. Rather than requiring decision makers to put a dollar amount on benefits that are by their nature difficult to quantify, AHP enables decision makers to measure the perceived importance of these benefits.

Previous AHP studies focused primarily on use of the AHP model to combine quantitative and qualitative benefits into an overall rating of new technology investments (Canada and Sullivan 1989; Neises and Bennett 1989; Stout et al. 1991). Harper et al. (1992) recommend that AHP users and researchers take care to create hierarchical structures that are grounded in theory. This paper extends previous AHP studies by proposing that AHP can be used to measure non-quantitative benefits. However, previous AHP models can be susceptible to management manipulation because they combine managers' less reliable subjective estimates of qualitative data with quantitative data into a single overall rating.

The framework proposed in this paper requires decision makers to separately evaluate non-quantifiable uncertainties and quantitative measures of financial risk and return. Managers must first estimate the annual cash flows about which they have the greatest confidence: the cost of new process equipment and benefits expected from labor, inventory, floor space, and cost-of-quality savings. The quantitative financial risk and return dimensions of the proposed three-dimensional framework are based on these estimates. After the quantifiable costs and benefits are estimated, the non-quantifiable benefits are subjectively evaluated using AHP and represented as the third dimension of the proposed framework—nonquantifiable uncertainty.

II. A FRAMEWORK FOR EVALUATING MULTIPLE DIMENSIONS OF RISK AND UNCERTAINTY

The appropriateness of any particular risky choice model depends on the nature of the decision and whether the model captures the significant parameters of risk and uncertainty relevant to that particular decision. When available information is insufficient to generate probability distributions of cash flows required for moment-oriented risky choice models, models that capture decision makers' assessments of non-quantifiable uncertainties and other aspects of risk may be more appropriate.

Within the capital budgeting field, one-dimensional discounted cash flow models and two-dimensional risk and return models have dominated. It has become clear, however, that these models are incomplete. In most new technology investment situations, risk is multi-dimensional and cannot be completely represented with a single risk measure.

The approach proposed in this paper extends the two-dimensional risk and return framework to include a third dimension—nonquantifiable uncertainty. In addition, the quantitative risk dimension is a composite measure, incorporating multiple risk parameters. It provides decision makers with more risk information than single-parameter models. Fig. 1 illustrates how non-quantifiable uncertainties and quantifiable financial return and risk dimensions may be evaluated using this approach.

The proposed framework, unlike single-criterion ranking methods such as net present value, does not provide a single optimal alternative. Rather, an "efficient plane"—the shaded region in Fig. 1—provides a set of alternatives that dominate all alternatives below the plane. Alternative A provides many non-quantifiable benefits, has no risk and a small quantifiable return. Alternative B has no uncertain benefits, no risk and a quantifiable return slightly better than Alternative A. Alternative C also has no uncertain benefits, but is very risky, yet provides the highest quantifiable return. Alternative D provides the same amount of uncertain benefits as Alternative A, but is much more risky and provides a higher quantifiable return.

Selection of an alternative from the set of alternatives on the efficient plane depends on the decision maker's preferences for risk and uncertainty. A decision maker averse to risk and uncertainty selects an alternative on the efficient plane located on or near B. A risk- and uncertainty-seeking decision maker selects the alternative on the efficient plane close to D. Alternative E is sub-optimal because E is below the efficient plane. Alternative A, located on the efficient plane, is better than alternative E; both alternatives A and E have the same amount of quantifiable risk and nonquantifiable benefits, but A's quantifiable return is higher than E's.

The efficient plane slopes downward as non-quantifiable uncertainty increases, based on the assumption that the quantifiable returns for investments with large non-quantifiable benefits are less than the quantifiable returns for investments with few nonquantifiable benefits. However, the exact slope of the efficient plane will vary, depending on the set of alternatives being considered by a company.

This framework may be used to evaluate alternatives without non-quantifiable uncertainties. If only quantifiable risk and return are considered, the three-dimensional framework collapses into a two-dimensional risk-return tradeoff framework with all alternatives being represented on the surface on the right side of Fig. 1.

HIERARCHICAL STRUCTURE

The proposed framework requires decision makers to use a hierarchical structure to evaluate a set of alternatives (see panels A, B, and E in Fig. 2.) Each dimension—quantifiable risk, quantifiable return, and on quantifiable benefits (uncertainty)—is represented separately. Managers begin by first estimating quantifiable risk and return for each alternative. After the quantifiable dimensions are computed, AHP is used to subjectively evaluate the non-quantifiable benefits.

In the proposed framework, ratings for each investment alternative are given for each major dimension—quantitative risk; quantitative return, and non-quantifiable uncertainties. Many previously AHP models compute a single, overall rating for each investment alternative rather than rating each investment alternative on each major dimension. The single overall rating approach combines subjective estimates of non-quantifiable factors with quantifiable data. This rating process for three alternatives is illustrated in Fig. 2.

MEASUREMENT OF NON-QUANTIFIABLE BENEFITS (UNCERTAINTY)

Because introduction of non-quantifiable benefits into the decision model is a primary focus of this paper, the use of AHP for this purpose is discussed first. The hierarchy for non-quantifiable benefits in Fig. 2 has only two levels, but AHP can accommodate many levels. At the bottom level of the hierarchy (panel F), managers weigh each investment alternative with respect to each non-quantifiable benefit—product reliability, product performance, flexibility, and employee morale. At the top level, (panel E) managers make pairwise comparisons between each of the non-quantifiable benefits to assign priority weights to each benefit based on its importance in meeting corporate objectives. Because the priority weights for the four non-quantifiable benefits are percentages, they must sum to 1. A rating with respect to non-quantifiable benefits is computed for each alternative based on the bottom level scaled values for each alternative and the priority weights.

FIGURE 2
CALCULATIONS FOR RISK, RETURN, AND UNCERTAINTY DIMENSIONS

Panel A: Quantifiable Return

ROI
(Ratio Scale)

Project 1   = 30%
Project 2   = 35%
Project 3   = 40 %

Panel B: Quantifiable Risk

Quantifiable Risk	Priority Weights
Ruinous Loss (RL) (investment % of assets)	.5
Liquidity Parameter (L) (Payback)	.4
Variability Parameter (V) (Std. Dev.)	.1

Project	Risk	Scaled Values (ratio scale)
1	RL	.50
2	RL	.25
3	RL	.25
1	L	.63
2	L	.25
3	L	.12
1	V	.57
2	V	.29
3	V	.14

(Continued on next page)

Figure 2 (Continued)

Panel C: Calculations for Scaling Quantitative Risk Parameters

Ruinous Loss Parameter:

	Investment as a Percentage of Total Assets (Investment/Total Assets)	Scaled Values
Project 1	40%	.40/80 = .50
Project 2	20%	.20/80 = .25
Project 3	20%	.20/80 = .25
	80%	1.00

Liquidity Risk Parameter:

	Payback Period	Scaled Values
Project 1	5 years	5/8 = .63
Project 2	2 years	2/8 = .25
Project 3	1 year	1/8 = .12
	8 years	1.00

Variability Risk Parameter:

	Standard Deviation of Quantifiable Returns	Scaled Values
Project 1	.2 Std. Dev	.2/.35 = .57
Project 2	.1 Std. Dev	.1/.35 = .29
Project 3	.05 Std. Dev	.05/.35 = .14
	.35 Std Dev.	1.00

Panel D: Calculations for the Composite Quantitative Risk Measure for Each Alternative

Risk Parameter	Bottom-Level Scaled Values		Priority Weights		Adjusted Values
Project 1:					
Ruinous Loss	.5	X	.5	=	.25
Liquidity Risk	.63	X	.4	=	.25
Variability Risk	.57	x	.1	=	.06
			Composite Risk Measure for Project 1		.56
Project 2:					
Ruinous Loss	.25	X	.5	=	.13
Liquidity Risk	.25	X	.4	=	.10
Variability Risk	.29	x	.1	=	.03
			Composite Risk Measure for Project 2		.26
Project 3					
Ruinous Loss	.25	X	.5	=	.13
Liquidity Risk	.12	X	.4	=	.05
Variability Risk	.14	x	.1	=	.01
			Composite Risk Measure for Project 3		.19
			(Continued on next page)		

FIGURE 2 (Continued)

Panel E: Non-quantifiable Benefits (Uncertainties)

Non-quantifiable Benefit	Priority Weights
Product Reliability (PR)	.2
Product Performance (PP)	.2
Flexibility (F)	.4
Employee Morale (M)	.2

Project	Benefit	AHP Scaled Value (Interval Scale)
1	PR	.67
2	PR	.22
3	PR	.11
1	PP	.75
2	PP	.20
3	PP	.05
1	F	.80
2	F	.10
3	F	.10
1	M	.60
2	M	.30
3	M	.10

Panel F: Calculations for the Overall Non-quantifiable Benefits Rating for Each Alternative

Risk Parameter	Bottom-Level Scaled Values		Priority Weights		Adjusted Values
Project 1:					
Product Reliability	.67	X	.2	=	.14
Product Performance	.75	X	.2	=	.15
Flexibility	.80	X	.4	=	.32
Employee Benefits	.60	X	.2	=	.12
Project 1's Overall Rating for Non-quantifiable Benefits					.73
Project 2:					
Product Reliability	.22	X	.2	=	.04
Product Performance	.20	X	.2	=	.04
Flexibility	.10	X	.4	=	.04
Employee Benefits	.30	X	.2	=	.06
Project 2's Overall Rating for Non-quantifiable Benefits					.18
Project 3:					
Product Reliability	.11	X	.2	=	.02
Product Performance	.05	X	.2	=	.01
Flexibility	.10	X	.4	=	.04
Employee Benefits	.10	X	.2	=	.02
Project 3's Overall Rating for Non-quantifiable Benefits					.09

A number of steps must be completed before ratings for each investment alternative can be generated. First, a manager compares each pair of investment alternatives. In each such pair-wise comparison, the manager indicated the strength of his/her preference for one alternative over another by selecting a numeric value ranging from 1 to 9. A description of the degrees of preference associated with the AHP numerical scale values is presented in Table 1.

The results of the manager's pair-wise comparisons of three investment alternatives regarding the non-quantifiable benefits of product reliability are presented in Table 2. The manager judged Project 1 to be moderately preferred over Project 2 with respect to product reliability, assigning a value of 3 to this comparison. In the second comparison, the manager strongly preferred Project 1 over Project 3 with respect to product reliability, assigning a value of 6 to this comparison. Finally, Project 2's product was judged to be slightly more reliable than Project 3's, and a value of 2 was assigned to this comparison.

Only three pair-wise comparisons must be obtained directly from managers, the rest are supplied by the AHP computer program.[iii] Because any alternative is, by definition, equally preferred when compared to itself, the AHP computer program places "1s" along the three diagonal slots in the pairwise comparison matrix, as shown in Table 3. It is not necessary for the manager to fill in the bottom part of the matrix because these three entries are reciprocals of, and therefore can be inferred from, the corresponding entries in the upper part of the matrix which were input by the decision maker.

After all values for the matrix are supplied, the computer program checks the consistency of the manager's input values and generates weights (scaled values) for each project.[iv] The AHP-generated scaled values show that the decision maker believes Project 1, with a scaled value of .67, provides the greatest non-quantifiable product reliability benefits; Project 2 is second with scaled value of .22; and Project 3, with a scaled value of .11, is least preferred. Panel E of Fig. 2, reflects these scaled AHP values for product reliability from the bottom-level of the hierarchy for non-quantifiable benefits.

In this example, the manager's pairwise comparisons were consistent. If comparisons are inconsistent, the AHP program requires the manager to change his input values until his comparisons became consistent.

The same steps are used to generate the AHP scaled values for product performance, flexibility, and employee morale. After generating the bottom-level scaled values for each remaining nonquantifiable attribute, managers use the AHP program to make pairwise comparisons between each non-quantifiable attribute to generate the top-level priority weights. The steps and AHP scale used to generate the priority

TABLE 1
AHP MEASUREMENT SCALE

Description of Degree of Preferences	Numerical Value
Extremely preferred	9
Very strongly preferred	7
Strongly preferred	5
Moderately preferred	3
Equally preferred	1
Note: Intermediate values can be used to provide additional levels of discrimination.	

TABLE 2
PAIRWISE COMPARISON DATA ENTERED INTO THE AHP
COMPUTER PROGRAM BY THE DECISION MAKER

	Non-quantifiable Benefits—Product Reliability			
	Project 1	Project 2	Project 3	Weights
Project 1		3	6	
Project 2			2	
Project 3				

TABLE 3
COMPUTATIONS BY THE AHP COMPUTER PROGRAM
Non-quantifiable Benefits—Product Reliability

	Project 1	Project 2	Project 3	Weights
Project 1	1	3	6	.67
Project 2	1/3	1	2	.22
Project 3	1/6	1/2	1	.11
				1.00

weights are the same as those used to generate the scaled values.

After all scaled values and priority weights in the non-quantifiable benefits hierarchy have been computed for each alternative, as illustrated in panel F of Fig. 2. First, the bottom-level scaled values for each alternative are multiplied by the priority weight for the same benefit. These adjusted values for each alternative are then summed to compute a non-quantifiable benefits rating for each alternative. The ratings represent in relative terms the amount of non-quantifiable benefits of each investment alternative compared to the non-quantifiable benefits of the other alternatives. Project 1, with a rating of .73, is believed to possess the most potential for realizing non-quantifiable revenue uncertainties. Project 3, with an overall rating of .09, has the least potential among the three alternatives. Project 2's non-quantifiable benefit rating of .18 is between Project 1's and Project 3's.

MEASUREMENT OF QUANTIFIABLE RISK

The hierarchy for evaluating quantifiable risk in Fig. 2 consists of two levels. At the bottom level of the hierarchy, scaled values for quantifiable risk parameters—ruinous loss, liquidity, and variability—are estimated for each alternative. The bottom-level scaled values are computed by summing values for the quantitative risk parameters and expressing these values as a percentage of the sum as shown in panel C of Fig. 2.

At the second level of the quantifiable risk hierarchy, management's priority weights establish the relative importance of each risk parameter. In Fig. 2, the priority weight assigned to the ruinous loss parameter (investment as a percentage of total assets) is .5. Compared with the priority weights assigned to the variability parameter, .1, and the liquidity parameter, l4, the ruinous loss parameter is more important in determining an alternative's final rating with respect to quantifiable risk. Because the

priority weights are expressed as percentages, the priority weights for the three risk parameters sum to 1.

Priority weights are management's subjective weights based on the context of the decision and/or differences in corporate policy. Companies with cash flow problems may assign a large priority weight to the liquidity parameter. Small companies may consider the ruinous loss parameter very important, because a single bad investment may result in financial dissolution. Priority weights may be subjectively estimated by managers or computed by an AHP computer program discussed in the section on using AHP to measure nonquantifiable benefits.

After all scaled values and priority weights in the quantifiable risk hierarchy are computed, a composite risk measure can be calculated for each alternative as shown in panel D of Fig. 2. First, the bottom-level scaled values for each alternative are adjusted for the priorities for each risk parameter by multiplying each parameter's bottom-level scaled values by the parameter's priority weight. These adjusted values for each alternative are then summed to compute a composite risk measure for each alternative. Project 1 is the riskiest of the three alternatives with a composite risk measure of .56; projects 2 and 3 are less risky with composite risk measures of .26 and .19 respectively.

MEASUREMENT OF QUANTIFIABLE RETURN

The choice of financial return measure(s) used in the framework depends on company policy and on whether enough reliable information is available to accurately compute a given measure. The quantitative return measure reflects only the costs and revenues which can be reasonably estimated. One such quantitative financial performance measure, return on investment, is illustrated in Fig. 2. Other measures, such as net present value or internal rate of return, can also be used in this framework if enough reliable information is available. This framework does not limit the analysis to only one quantitative financial performance measure or to any particular type of financial performance measure. Just as multiple quantitative risk measures can be combined to measure quantifiable risk, multiple quantitative financial measures can be combined within this framework to measure financial performance.

Return on investment was chosen as the quantitative financial measure for illustration purposes in this paper for three reasons: (1) in many new technology investment situations, not enough reliable information about future cash flows is available to compute discounted cash flow measures, (2) short-term quantitative financial performance measures such as return on investment are complemented in the proposed framework by longer term non-quantifiable factors such as improved quality and increased flexibility, and (3) income-based return measures are widely used in practice by advanced manufacturing firms (Howell et al. 1987). Because only return on investment is used in this paper, the quantitative returns illustrated in the graph in Fig. 3 are the original return on investment percentages for each project. No scaling and adjusting for priority weights is needed when a single measure is used. If multiple quantitative performance measures are used,

---

FIGURE 3
GRAPHICAL PRESENTATION OF EXAMPLE

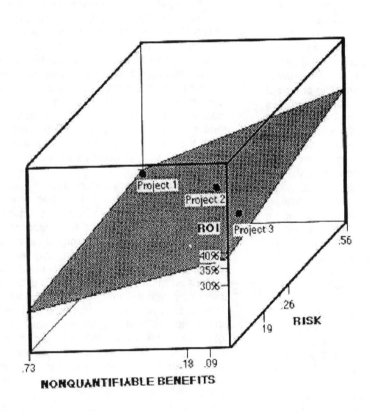

	Composite Quantitative Risk Measure	ROI	Overall Rating For Non-quantifiable Benefits
Project 1	.56	30%	.73
Project 2	.26	35%	.18
Project 3	.19	40%	.09

each measure must be scaled and adjusted for priority weights.

The three alternatives are graphed in the three-dimensional framework in Fig. 3. Because only three alternatives with different levels of quantifiable risk and return and nonquantifiable benefits are compared in the example, all three alternatives lie on the efficient plane. If more alternatives are included in the evaluation, the sub-optimal alternatives will be graphed below the efficient plane. Selection of an alternative from the set of alternatives on the efficient plane is left to the decision maker's trade-off preferences between quantifiable risk, quantifiable return, and non-quantifiable uncertainty.

FRAMEWORK BASED ON DECISION CONTEXT

In figure 2, the quantitative risk parameters—investment as a percentage of total assets, payback period, and standard deviation of returns—all represent different aspects of risk relevant to the projects being evaluated. Managers may use different sets of quantitative risk parameters and uncertainty attributes to evaluate different situations The choice of quantitative risk parameters and uncertainty attributes for inclusion in the framework should be based on two criteria—**representativeness** and **independence**. To fully represent the risks and uncertainties which exist in the actual investment decision, the framework should capture all significant aspects of risk and uncertainty relevant to the project alternatives under consideration. The risk parameters and uncertainty attributes included in the framework must independent of each other so each measures a different aspect of risk and/or uncertainty. For example, variance and standard deviation should not be included as risk parameters in the same framework because they measure the same aspect of risk—variability in cash flows.

Selection of non-quantitative factors for the framework is determined by the decision context. If all factors can be reasonably estimated for a set of alternatives, the evaluation may be based solely on quantifiable risk and return factors. In other investment situations, certain factors may be partially quantifiable and partially non-quantifiable. For example, cost savings from producing more reliable products, such as reductions in rework costs, inspection costs, and warranty costs, may be estimated and included in the quantitative risk and return measures. The effect of producing more reliable products on market demand and revenue, however, may be so uncertain that reasonable estimates cannot be made. This effect would be subjectively evaluated by managers as a non-

quantifiable uncertainty. Similarly, some aspects of employee morale and additional manufacturing capabilities/ flexibility may be quantifiable while other aspects of these factors are highly uncertain and non-quantifiable.

MEASUREMENT SCALES

In this framework, each attribute is measured using the scale that provides the most information about the attribute. The quantitative return dimension is measured on the highest scale, the *ratio scale*. A **ratio scale** provides more information than the other scales—both the difference between values and the ratio of any two values are meaningful, and the value of zero means none. For example, a financial return of 40 percent is twice as much as a 20 percent return, and a zero percent return means no return.

Non-quantifiable uncertainties are measured on the second highest scale, the *interval scale*. On an **interval scale**, the difference between values is meaningful, but the ratio is not meaningful. The AHP scale used to measure non-quantifiable uncertainties is an interval scale; it captures the strength of a decision maker's preference for one alternative over a second alternative. AHP requires that decision makers assign a value of 1 if the two alternatives are equal, and a value of 2 if one alternative is slightly preferred over the other. But an alternative assigned the value of 2 is not twice as good as an alternative assigned a value of 1.[v]

Risk parameters included in the composite risk measure can be either ratio-scaled or interval-scaled measures. For example, variability in cash flows is measured on a ratio scale if standard deviation is used; a cash flow with a standard deviation of 6 is six times as variable as a cash flow with a standard deviation of 1. On the other hand, variability is measured on an interval scale if variance is used; a cash flow with a variance of 6 has greater variability than a cash flow with a variance of 1 but cannot be interpreted as being six times as variable. Regardless of whether risk parameters are ratio- or interval-scale measures, transformations (multiplication, division) or parameters do not change their measurement scales. The quality of the original measurement scale is preserved even though the magnitude of the original measurement is increased by multiplication or decreased by division.

Although ratio-scale measurements of risk parameters are preserved when the parameters are combined into a composite risk measure, an interval-scale interpretation of the composite risk measure is generally appropriate. A composite measure that represents a multidimensional concept, such as risk, is more difficult to interpret than a measure, such as standard deviation, that measures a single observable aspect—cash flow variability—of a multidimensional concept.

Comparing the sizes of two boxes illustrates this problem. A box with a length of 8 feet, height of 6 feet, and width of 4 feet is twice as long, high, and wide as a box that is 4 feet long, 3 feet high and 2 feet wide. Separately, each of these measures—length, height and width—suggest that the first box is only twice as large as the second box. However, when their sizes are compared using a three-dimension measure, volume, the larger box is 8 times as large as the smaller one. Likewise a ratio-scale interpretation of the composite risk measure cannot be inferred from the ratio-scale measures of individual risk parameters. Ratio-scale interpretations of the composite risk measure is further complicated because different risk parameters measure different attributes—time (payback period), variability (standard deviation), dollars (investment as a percentage of total assets).

The nature of the attribute being measured makes ratio-scale interpretations difficult for both single- and multi-dimensional risk measures. Risk is a highly idiosyncratic attribute, based on decision makers' perceptions rather than observable phenomena. Observable phenomena—time, dollars, and variability—can be measured on an absolute measurement scale; different decision-makers using the same measurement method will come to the same conclusions. For example, few people would disagree that a payback period of 8 years is twice as long as a 4-year payback period or that a cash flow with a standard deviation of 6 is six times as variable as a cash flow with a standard deviation of 1. In contrast, the measurement of risk perceptions is based on a relative scale. One decisionmaker may consider a project with a payback of 8 years twice as risky as a project with a 4-year payback, while another believes the project with the 8-year payback is eight times as risky as the one with the 4-year payback. Consequently, both single- and multi-dimensional measures of a perceptually-based attribute can, at best, be interpreted as interval-scale data.

I. SUMMARY AND DISCUSSION

This paper identified the limitations of using traditional models in evaluating new technology investments. A review of risky choice decision models suggests that evaluating an investment based on a single risk parameter may be inadequate in some decision situations. Models used in evaluating new technology investments should consider all risk aspects and non-quantifiable uncertainties relevant to the investment decision. If decision models do not completely capture and represent all factors relevant to the investment

decision, managers may reject alternatives that should be accepted and/or accept those that should be rejected. This paper developed a framework that enables managers to formally include an assessment of nonquantifiable uncertainties, quantifiable financial returns and multiple risk parameters in their evaluation of capital projects, while maintaining a distinction between factors that can be quantified and factors that only can be subjectively assessed. The proposed framework expands the two-dimensional risk-return framework to a three-dimensional framework, including nonquantifiable uncertainty as the third dimension. In addition, a composite measure of quantifiable risk consisting of multiple risk parameters was introduced in this paper. This composite risk measure provides managers with more risk information than singled two-parameter risky choice models.

The framework does not replace discounted cash flow techniques. Rather, it may be used to supplement discounted cash flow techniques when enough information is available to make reliable cash flow projections. For some investment decisions, all revenues, costs, and associated probabilities can be reasonably estimated. In such cases, only quantitative risk and return measures need be evaluated; non-quantifiable uncertainties would not be included in the analysis.

Although this paper illustrates how the proposed framework can be used to evaluate new technology investments, the framework is not limited to new technology investment decisions. It may be used to evaluate more traditional investments involving non-quantifiable legal uncertainties and/or multiple aspects of risk such as mining operations, chemical and nuclear plants, and new product lines for drug companies. The proposed framework is flexible, allowing different risk parameters and uncertainty attributes to be included in the framework depending on the risks and uncertainties present in the investment decision. As new technologies are installed, more information about the benefits and costs of the new technologies becomes known. Consequently, some uncertainties surrounding the new technologies may become reasonably estimable so that traditional quantitative capital budgeting models may adequately capture more of the relevant factors in quantitative terms. Quantification of some non-quantifiable factors does not diminish the need for a framework to evaluate non-quantifiable uncertainties.

[i] A risky alternative may contain two separate components—risk and nonquantifiable uncertainty. Risk is defined as the *known* probability distribution of outcomes (expected cash flows); uncertainty exists when the probability distribution of outcomes (expected cash flows) is unknown and/or potential outcomes cannot be specified (Knight 1948; Luce and Raiffa 1957). Some authors refer to nonquantifiable uncertainty as ambiguity (Einhorn and Horgarth 1986)

[ii] Other methods for obtaining decision makers' weights for multiple attributes include multiattribute stochastic decision models (Bernardo and Upton 1980), conjoint analysis (Wind and Saaty 1980), the Simple Multiattribute Rating Technique (SMART), the Holistic Orthogonal Parameter Estimate (HOPE) procedure, rank weighting techniques, policy capturing techniques, and subjectively dividing 100 points (Adelman et al. 1984; Stillwell et al. 1983). Some of these techniques are less practical than AHP for evaluating nonquantifiable uncertainties because they are inefficient and have restrictive assumptions (Wind and Saaty 1980)

[iii] When only three alternatives are considered as in this example, it is not difficult for individuals to make consistent comparisons. However, when the number of alternatives increases this task becomes more difficult; AHP forces consistency among the pairwise comparisons.

[iv] A manager's input values are consistent if all the columns of the input matrix have the same proportional values. The proportional values for each column of the input matrix in Table 3 are computed by totaling the values in each column and then expressing each value as a percentage of the column total:

	Project 1		Project 2		Project 3	
	Input Values	Propor-tions	Input Values	Propor-tions	Input Values	Propor-tions
Project 1	1	1/1.5 = .67	3	3/4.5 = .67	6	6/9 = .67
Project 2	1/3	.33/1.5 = .22	1	1/4.5 = .22	2	2/9 = .22
Project 3	1/6	.16/1.5 = .11	1/2	.5/4.5 = .11	1	1/9 = .11
	1.5	1.00	4.5	1.00	9	1.00

In this example, the proportional values—.67, .22, and .11—are the same for each column. Consequently, the AHP program generates scaled values (weights) of .67 for Project 1, .22 for Project 2, and .11 for Project 3. If the proportional values for each column are not the same, the AHP program warns the manager that his input values are inconsistent and requires changes in input values until comparisons become consistent.

[v] Transformations of interval-scaled data (multiplication, division) will not convert the original data to a ratio scale. The AHP-generated scaled values for non-quantifiable benefits are based on an interval scale because the values (preferences) that are input into the AHP input matrix are interval-scale data. AHP cannot transform interval-scaled inputs into ratio-scaled output values.

Chapter 12
Job Costing

Cases

12-1   Constructo Inc. (Under or Over-Applied Overhead)
12-2   Standard Soap Corp. (Traditional Job Costing Versus ABC Job Costing)
12-3   East River Manufacturing (A) (Problems of Traditional Job Costing)

Readings

"How I Reengineered a Small Business"

This article describes both the old and new job costing systems at James Street Fashions (also called Latt-Greene), a small textile knitting and converting operation in Vernon, California. The author is the controller of Latt-Greene. He instituted a spreadsheet-based job costing system that helped to reverse a $5 million loss on $65 million in sales revenue to a $3 million profit on just $32 million in sales revenue. He also eliminated unnecessary overtime and increased the overall quality of the company's product line.

Discussion Questions:

1. Briefly describe the company, its products and customers.
2. What problems did the author discover when he conducted his initial interviews with the company in early 1990.
3. Describe the company's old financial costing system, and identify its weaknesses as well as business operating and profit consequences cause by its poor costing system.
4. What are major impacts of the company's new computerized costing system on its business operations, product prices and quality, and company's profit?
5. What are general principles learned by the author for changing or reengineering a company's costing system?

Cases

12-1. Under or Overapplied Overhead

Constructo Inc. is a manufacturer of furnishings for infants and children. The company uses a job cost system and employs a full absorption accounting method for cost accumulation. Constructo's work-in-process inventory at April 30, 2001 consisted of the following jobs.

Job No.	Items	Units	Accumulated Cost
CBS102	Cribs	20,000	$ 900,000
PLP086	Playpens	25,000	420,000
DRS114	Dressers	25,000	250,000
			$1,570,000

The company's finished goods inventory, which Constructo evaluates using the FIFO (First-in, first-out) method, consisted of five items.

Item	Quantity and Unit Cost	Accumulated Cost
Cribs	7,500 units @ $ 64 each	$ 480,000
Strollers	13,000 units @ $ 23 each	299,000
Carriages	11,200 units @ $102 each	1,142,400
Dressers	21,000 units @ $ 55 each	1,155,000
Playpens	19,400 units @ $ 35 each	679,999
		$3,755,400

Constructo applies factory overhead on the basis of direct labor hours. The company's factory overhead budget for the fiscal year ending May 31, 2001, totals $4,500,000, and the company plans to expend 600,000 direct labor hours during this period. Through the first eleven months of the year, a total of 555,000 direct labor hours were worked, and total factory overhead amounted to $4,273,500.

At the end of April, the balance in Constructo's Materials Inventory account, which includes both raw materials and purchased parts, was $668,000. Additions to and requisitions from the materials inventory during the month of May included the following.

	Raw Materials	Purchased Parts
Additions	$242,000	$396,000
Requisitions:		
Job CBS102	51,000	104,000
Job PLP086	3,000	10,800
Job DRS114	124,000	87,000
Job STR077		
(10,000 strollers)	62,000	81,000
Job CRG098		
(5,000 carriages)	65,000	187,000

During the month of May, Constructo's factory payroll consisted of the following.

Account	Hours	Cost
CBS102	12,000	$122,400
PLP086	4,400	43,200
DRS114	19,500	200,500
STR077	3,500	30,000
CRG098	14,000	138,000
Indirect	3,000	29,400
Supervision		57,600
		$621,100

Listed below are the jobs that were completed and the unit sales for the month of May.

Job No.	Items	Quantity Complete
CBS102	Cribs	20,000
PLP086	Playpens	15,000
STR077	Strollers	10,000
CRG098	Carriages	5,000

Items	Quantity Shipped
Cribs	17,500
Playpens	21,000
Strollers	14,000
Dressers	18,000
Carriages	6,000

REQUIRED

1. Describe when it is appropriate for a company to use a job cost system.
2. Calculate the dollar balance in Constructo's work-in-process inventory account as of May 31, 2001.
3. Calculate the dollar amount related to the playpens in Constructo's finished goods inventory as of May 31, 2001.
4. Explain the proper accounting treatment for overapplied or underapplied overhead balances when using a job cost system.

(CMA Adapted)

12-2. Standard Soap Corp.

There are critical times in the growth of a company; times when the way work is defined, managed, measured and evaluated are changed to meet new challenges from the marketplace. The period from 1989-1993 was such a period for Standard Soap Corp. Having reached the growth threshold, this family-owned business has turned to Total Quality Management [TQM] and an Activity-based Cost Management System [ACMS] to smooth its transition from a small job-shop making private label soaps and specialty chemicals to one of the most successful, and innovative, international producers of specialty soaps. The path these implementations have taken has not been without its bumps and dangers as the following "story" suggests.

"WE'RE OUT OF CONTROL"

The gloom of a cold winter morning seemed to penetrate indoors matched by the mood of the four people huddled around the small conference table in the Standard Soap Corp. business office. For the past hour company managers (Joe, Plant Manager; Fran, Treasurer; Bob, Controller) had been describing Standard Soap's history, product line focus, and current status to a professor from a local business school (K.T.). The problem facing the firm was a well-documented one: it had reached the growth threshold, a gap that separated this small "soaper" from the ranks of large, established corporations. The symptoms of the stress the firm was experiencing were everywhere: inventories were growing faster than production volumes, orders were often late, product was being returned at an alarming rate due to defects and other problems, and individual managers were finding it harder and harder to control let alone predict the outcome of operations.

Joe put his feelings in graphic terms, "We're out of control—I simply can't manage the plant anymore. I'm practically living here, but it isn't doing any good at all. We're blowing our schedules, missing ship dates, and turning out bad product. I simply can't handle the system anymore." As this "true confession" was revealed, the room fell silent. Bob looked down, saying little. Fran, a family member just returning to active involvement after a year-long leave, looked puzzled. As with all true confessions, Joe's comments were not greeted with cheers. He had violated a taboo by opening the kimono of this staid firm to an outsider.

BACKGROUND INFORMATION

Standard Soap Corp. is a $30-35 million producer of private label soaps. Owned by the Janssen family since the mid 1960's, the firm has been in continuous operation since its founding in the late 1800's by two immigrants from Warwick, England. The company occupies an old mill building in West Warwick, Rhode Island that abuts a local river used in earlier days for power. It currently employs over 500 people in this plant, operating three shifts a day six days a week.

In any year, Standard Soap produces over 5,000 different varieties of bar soap. Over 40% of these orders represent new business or new products for the firm. The high level of variety and the fact that the source, and characteristics, of future business is always a question mark, makes effective, efficient management of the plant a challenge.

Figure 1 details the process of soap-making at Standard Soap. Raw materials are transformed into natural and synthetic base soap in the kettle room. Still as much of an art as a science, the production of base soap is one of Standard Soap's competitive

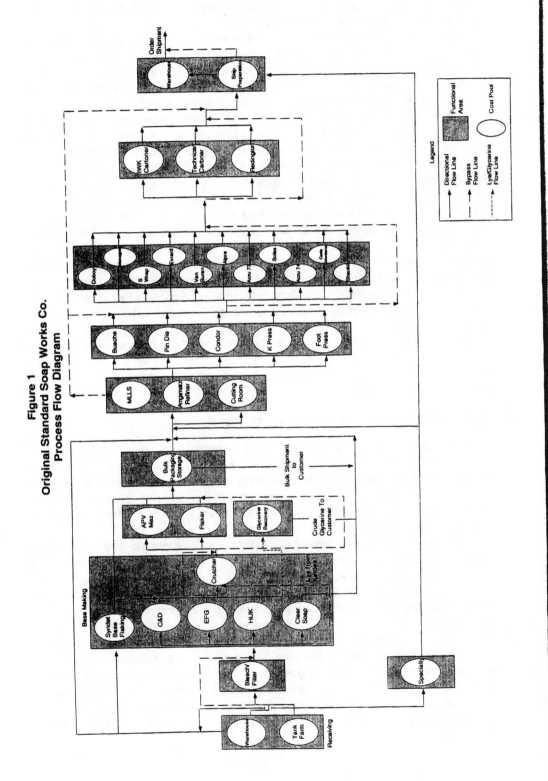

Figure 1
Original Standard Soap Works Co.
Process Flow Diagram

advantages. It can control the supply and quality of the key raw material going into bar soap. In addition, Standard Soap has been able to use its soap-making expertise to develop new soap formulations that competitors cannot match. It is this soap-making expertise that lies at the heart of its recent growth.

Bulk soap is dried and stored for later use in bins and containers on the plant floor. When an order is received, the required bulk soap and additive packages are moved to the amalgamators at the head of the production line. There, a master soap-maker measures the ingredients per the instructions on the product's formulation card, mixes the batch, and then signals the line supervisor that the soap is ready to run.

Soap is extruded as it passes from the amalgamator, forming into a solid block of soap. This unending flow of soap slides down a metal chute to a press where metal dies transform the soap into bars that meet the size and shape requirements set by the customer. After pressing, the bars move down a conveyor belt where visual inspection of each bar takes place. Good bars are allowed to pass on to the packaging machines attached to the end of the line where bars can be wrapped, boxed, and packed in an almost infinite number of ways. Defective bars and scrap from the press are recycled, returning to the amalgamator for remixing and reentry to the soap flow. The apparent simplicity of the process is misleading; there are, in fact, over 5,000 different paths a bar of soap can take through the production facility. Most of this complexity occurs during the packaging stage, where any combination of inner and outer wrappings is possible.

Spanning the entire value chain from base soap production to the completion of a specialty bar of pleat-wrapped soap, Standard Soap Corp. has been able to provide a higher level of service and variety to its customers than its competitors. But, the complexity of the job shop environment at Standard Soap Corp. has created the need for more information to manage operations. In addition to the core variety of the products and services provided by Standard Soap, it has faced major changes in its customer base and product expectations.

NEW CUSTOMERS AND NEW PROBLEMS

Up through the late 1960's, Standard Soap concentrated its sales efforts on specialty chemicals for the New England-based textile industries. As the 60's came to an end, though, so did the presence of the textile industry in the region. Faced with the loss of its key business line, Allen Janssen, CEO and owner of the company, refocused the firm's activities into the fledgling private label bar soap industry. It was a strategic move that has paid off handsomely for the firm and the family.

This shift of focus has resulted in rising sales to the point that available line time has been booked to capacity. And, Standard Soap's soap-making expertise was gaining it a strong reputation in the marketplace as the producer of choice for specialty soaps. In fact, the major growth area for the firm was the skin care and "high end" bar soaps. Standard Soap's willingness to try to make any soap formulation requested by the customer, as well as its well-known concern with safe-guarding its customer's formulations and "secret ingredients," had quickly moved the firm into the top position in this emerging industry.

As can be seen in Figure 2, Standard Soap's sales mix and volume have changed radically since the mid 1960's. Moving from a dominant position in specialty chemicals to private label bar soap, Standard Soap has expanded its customer base. New customers, though, come with new expectations for performance. Acceptable bar quality levels have racheted upward. For instance, high end cosmetic bars, retailing for $15-20 dollars each in department stores, have to be visually perfect. Even the slightest mar on a bar's surface can cause a customer to reject the finished good.

The demand for the "perfect" bar is a new force at Standard Soap. Prior customers, such as hotel bar and novelty soap wholesalers (sea shells, stars, and so on), placed the highest priority on price. A nick on a bar was of little concern. Bulk packing was the norm, with little concern for any but the grossest defects (broken bars). Cosmetic line customers, though, sell hopes and dreams. Hopes and dreams have to be perfect.

Figure 2

Standard Soap Change in Sales Mix

Type of Product	Mid 60's	Early 70's	Time Late 70's	Early 80's	Late 80's	Early 90's
Industrial Soap	50%	30%	17%	15%	13%	5%
Specialty Chemicals	45%	40%	9%	4%	2%	2%
Commodity Bar Soap	5%	17%	23%	22%	6%	2%
Specialty Bar Soap	0%	13%	51%	58%	79%	91%

While bar quality levels have escalated, total bars per order have dropped. Hotel bars are made in massive quantities resulting in price breaks for the customers and simple scheduling of lines at the plant. Cosmetic bars, on the other hand, are made in smaller quantities. That means, in total, the number of setups, inspections, handling operations, and support activities have escalated considerably over the past five years. These forces were coming together in late 1989, creating the "Loss of Control" phenomenon Joe described.

STEPPING INTO THE FUTURE

To better understand the issues at the company, K.T. asked the Standard Soap managers if a student team could come into the firm and map the process flow and document the current types and amount of information available to managers across the firm. Agreement was reached on the boundaries of the project and its timing.

After three months of data dredging and scurrying through the catacombs of the Standard Soap plant, the student team was ready with their report. While many facts about current operations were revealed, the most overwhelming finding was that the firm was drowning in data but had no information. Facts and figures were collected on the plant floor on a daily basis, but these "numbers" did not provide management with the facts necessary to make decisions and manage the plant. So, while it appeared that the company had a sound information system in place, the reality was that it collected a lot of data, but used almost none of it. In addition, the information system had a very short "memory"—data was moved off the mainframe to tape backup, or dumped, once a month. The result? Joe really was managing the plant with intuition and a few hastily calculated performance measures. This management approach even had a name at Standard Soap: gutfact.

Gutfact-based management was occurring everywhere in the organization. Sometimes gutfact was right (managers were very experienced), but many other times it was wrong. The problem was, there was no alternative available, and no real way to separate good gutfact from bad. This was the real challenge facing Standard Soap— it had to design an information system that would support the complexity and uniqueness of its operations, that would be accessible and believed by its managers (it had to replace gutfact), and that could be implemented at minimal cost to the company.

REPLACING GUTFACT WITH INFORMATION

By early 1990, the implementation of the new information system was underway. The implementation time line, shown in Figure 3, reflects the major pressures that were hitting the firm during this period. The "quick fix" database was one outgrowth of these pressures. Consisting of patched numbers and reconstructed data, the quick fix project focused on defining customer profitabilities (see Figure 4). The benefits that came from this pilot project included:

- Definition of key data points needed to construct a the long-term database:

- Recognition that data could not be reconstructed with any level of accuracy:

- Identification of key weaknesses in the existing general ledger package leading to the redesign of the general ledger;

- Introduction of activity-based concepts and approaches to the organization;

- Highlighting of key errors in "gutfact" based on a preliminary analysis of customer and product line profitabilities.

The pilot project laid the groundwork for the development of the current activity-based cost management system [ACMS]. It also nudged along the cultural change needed to help Standard Soap jump the growth threshold by pinpointing areas where gutfact failures were leading to poor operational and financial performance.

The restatement of the general ledger accounts resulted in the structure summarized in Figure 5. As can be seen, the major change made was the recoding of accounts to reflect the underlying structure of the soapmaking process. Indirect expense categories were broken apart and regrouped by activity; general plant overhead was reassigned to machine pools and activities. The general ledger grew by 1/3 as a result of these changes, but it now became possible to physically match the cost information in the general ledger to operations. The system was ready for a test; would the organization really listen to the new information?

Figure 3
ACMS System Timeline

Fall 1998   Opening contact with K.T.
            Joe S., Bob N. Fran G   Joe S. reassigned to HR.

1989   Sequence of proposals   Interviews with management

Spring 1990   MBA Students' Project
            K.T.— facilitator, Process Flow Diagram with cost pools & drivers

Summer 1990   CAT. visit, Quick Fix

Fall/Winter 1990   Realign G/L, restate 1990 G/L, Erin V. hired in 1st quarter 1991

Spring 1991   First Report, patched info
            Training sessions with Supervisors, Crew Leaders renew forms, data
            collection

Spring/Summer 1991 Refine inputs   Politics, Open Kimono
            K.T.'s Report on second round of interviews with Management

Winter 1991   Database development, reports
            Understanding critical elements of price estimating
            Strong, clear data
            2nd half 1991, real clear data

1992   Further development of Reports, understanding of info in Database
            Info used on daily/weekly basis by production, planning managers
            Info used by Sales for pricing & negotiating
            Acceptance of data as accurate
            Estimates tied to G/L twice a year & adjustment slight

Figure 4

Proposed Customer Profitability Analysis Datafile

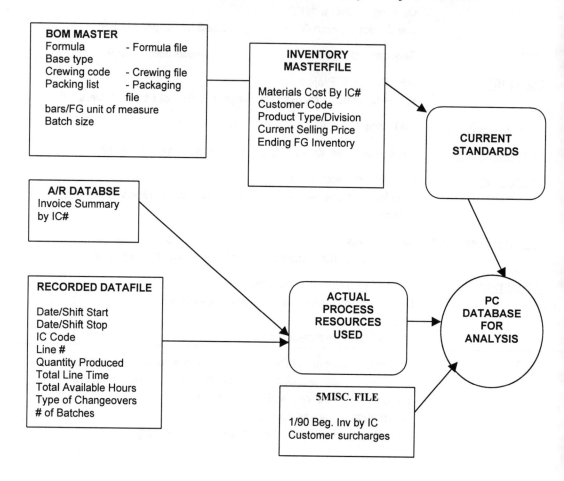

BOM MASTER
Formula   - Formula file
Base type
Crewing code   - Crewing file
Packing list   - Packaging
                 file
bars/FG unit of measure
Batch size

INVENTORY MASTERFILE

Materials Cost By IC#
Customer Code
Product Type/Division
Current Selling Price
Ending FG Inventory

CURRENT STANDARDS

A/R DATABSE
Invoice Summary
by IC#

RECORDED DATAFILE

Date/Shift Start
Date/Shift Stop
IC Code
Line #
Quantity Produced
Total Line Time
Total Available Hours
Type of Changeovers
# of Batches

ACTUAL PROCESS RESOURCES USED

PC DATABASE FOR ANALYSIS

5MISC. FILE

1/90 Beg. Inv by IC
Customer surcharges

THE POLITICS OF CHANGE

Picture a family-run business faced with competitive pressures, operational problems (the control loss issue), and the transfer of power from one generation to the next, and you have an organization under stress. Standard Soap is just such an organization. Two family members, Fran and her brother, John, are both actively involved in the firm. John serves as President, Fran as CFO. The pressures in the business, Allen's gradual withdrawal from daily operations, sibling rivalry, and the natural conflicts accompanying a "changing of the guard" at any firm, combined forces to make the implementation of TQM and ACMS at Standard Soap a highly political process.

Logic serves little purpose when emotions and egos are on the line. The ACMS was built on a logic of activities, costs, and business complexity. Organizations run on personal skills, emotions, and history. While fact can often be used to guide management, it is unusual to see a company use facts to drive the change process. In essence, that is what Standard Soap did. Numbers generated by the ACMS were built from gutfact, enhanced by basic cost and engineering concepts, and molded to fit the information needs of the company's managers. Until profits could be turned around, though, these facts would remain merely interesting tidbits to be used in the political process of managing the organization.

"But a bar isn't a bar...."

The information system at Standard Soap had been built on ongoing input and recommendations from first and second level managers at the company. It would seem that with all of this expert knowledge to draw from, the system should fit the organization, and be accepted by it. Based on this assumption, the ACMS project team began using the information coming out of the system to analyze ongoing business and identify areas for improvement.

Figure 5

Restatement of Income Statement G/L Accounts

Description	old method	new method
Schedule 2 (Square Footage)		
Insurance	Sq Footage	Sq Footage
Workers Comp Insurance	Sq Footage	Labor Cost pools by # of employee's
Bldg. & Land Depreciation	Sq Footage & % of Sales	Sq Footage
Allocation % Changed		
Bar Mfg	49%	57%
Bulk Mfg	34%	37%
Central Services	15%	
Adm	2%	6%

Schedule 3

		Allocated on Use			Based on Studies by Plant Engineer, A. Howland, F. Gammell			
	Bar	Bulk	Cent'l Srv.	Adm.	Bar	Bulk	Cent'l Srv.	Adm.
Electric	50%	42%	5%	3%	75%	25%		
Heat — Steam	50%	42%	5%	3%		75%	25%	
Water	50%	42%	5%	3%	16%	84%		
Sewer Use Fees	50%	42%	5%	3%		80%	20%	
Depreciation-Machinery	50%	42%	5%	3%	70%	30%		
Storage	50%	42%	5%	3%	80%	20%		

Schedule 4

Direct Mfg Expenses	old method	new method
Dies, Supplies	Direct to Bar, Bulk, Centr'l Service	Same as before
Shipping	Arbitarily allocated by Finance	Pounds Shipped
Lab	Arbitarily allocated by Finance	Employee Time & Function Study
Trash	Arbitarily allocated by Finance	to Bulk as well as lbs shipped
Training	Arbitarily allocated by Finance	Labor pools by # of employee's
Machinery Repairs	Direct to Bar, Bulk, Centr'l Service	to Machine Pool G/L #'s by type

Figure 6

Standard Soap Works
Bid Price Estimator Sheet

Customer Name:
Job Description:
Date:
Originator:
Pieces to run:
Bar size legal wt.:
   (enter oz. or grams)

Material Costs:

	%	/bar	# req'd	$/lb	
Base					

$ _____ Total Materials

Packaging Materials:

Description	Bars/unit	Units req'd	$/unit

_____ Total Pckg Mats

Machine Set-up Cost:

Number of pckg machines
Press setup
Total "setups"
X .5 (av. hr./setup)
Total setup hours   X $55.00/set up hr.   Set-up Costs

Life Time Estimate:

Bars Req'd
Est. run rate (bars/hr)
Press hours   X $60.00/press hr.   Line Time Cost

\# laborers/press hour
X Press Hours   X $25.00/lbr hr.
   Total labor hours   Labor Cost

Lab/QC Charge:

Press hours   X $55.00/QC Test
   X .25
Total QC Tests   QC/QA Cost

Line Cleaning Charge: $150.00   Clean Cost

Total Job Cost $ _____

12-13

Figure 7
Job Cost Comparisons

Company/Product	Cost per Traditional System	Cost per Revised System
Ace Soap Company:		

Yellow roses - 5,000 bars
    Run rate: 1,000/hr
    No pckg machines
    1 laborer/press hr.
    Materials ($400.00)
	$88.00	$1,065.00

Hope Novelty:		

Black horses - 1,000 bars
    Run rate: 500/hr
    2 pckg machines
    2 laborers/press hr.
    Materials ($250.00)
	$500.00	$727.00

International Cosmetics:		

Oatmeal Beauty Bar - 500 bars
    Run rate: 500/hr
    3 pckg machines
    1 laborer/press hr.
    Materials ($800.00)
	$1,600.00	$1,157.50

Strand Health & Beauty:		

Louffe Face Bar - 10,000 bars
    Run rate: 2,000/hr
    2 pckg machines
    1 laborer/press hr.
    Materials ($1,500.00)
	$3,000.00	$1,870.00

Norwood Guest Amenities:		

Hotel bars - 10,000 pieces
    Run rate: 2,500/hr
    1pckg machines
    1 laborer/press hr.
    Materials ($500.00)
	$1,000.00	$1,095.00

Figure 8
Case Data Tables

Raw Material Testing		
Customer	# of Raw Tested	Average Test Time
Ace Soap Company	5	30 minutes
Hope Novelty	0	
International Cosmetics	1	15 minutes
Strand Health & Beauty	3	30 minutes
Norwood Guest Amenities	0	

Summary of Cost Information by Activity Pool:

Raw Material Testing	$480,000/yr	12,000 hours
QC—Bar Appearance	$600,000/yr	12,000 hours
Line Cleaning	$960,000/yr	22,000 hours

* High QC bars take about 8 times as much effort as Low QC bars. Low QC orders use about 1 hour of QC per 8 hours of production.

Bar Appearance Level	
Customer	
Ace Soap Company	High
Hope Novelty	Medium
International Cosmetics	High
Strand Health & Beauty	Medium
Norwood Guest Amenities	Low

Cleaning Time	
Color or Additive	time (hours)
White	0.5
Yellow	1.0
Red	2.0
Blue	4.0
Black	4.0
Sparkle	0.5
Oatmeal	3.0
Lanolin	1.0
Louffa	4.0

While there were many ways the information could be used in the company, the job shop environment surrounding the business suggested that focusing on the bid price estimating system would be a logical place to focus the information system. The sales force was interviewed in an attempt to find out exactly how they thought about the business, what factors they used in developing a bid price for a customer, and what type of information system interface would work the best for them in the field. The results of these efforts was a bid price estimator program that used the key cost estimates from the ACMS to bid jobs [see Figure 6].

To test the program a sample of current jobs running in the plant was rebid using the ACMS estimates. The results of this analysis is presented in Figure 7. According to the data many jobs were severely undercosted while others were overcosted. This result was just what the ABC experts had said would happen. So, the results were no surprise to the ACMS project team. A meeting was set up with top management and the sales department to discuss the changes that would need to take place in the bid price procedures based on the new ACMS information.

The meeting was held on a Monday afternoon, the only day all of the salespeople were in the office. Preliminary analysis of the bid price accuracy versus estimated production costs were distributed in advance to everyone to give them time to digest the information and prepare comments. Comments are what the ACMS team got

Steve, Mktg. V.P.: "Where did you get these numbers from? Are you living in la-la land, or what? I've never seen anything so ridiculous! We won't get any business if we price the way you're suggesting!"

Fran: "What's the problem, Steve? You're the one who told us how each of you prices a job. We simply used the information you gave us and put it into the system, used the cost estimates we all agreed upon, and this is what we got. You may not like what you see, but it's reality."

Steve: "I tend to disagree, Fran. You and K.T. may think these numbers look good, but they aren't. The business just isn't this simple...a bar isn't a bar isn't a bar..."

K.T.: "What do you mean, Steve? We've accounted for the weight of the bar, the raw materials, the number of packaging machines and setup times, the pack rates, and machine time. And, we've used ABC charging rates for inspection, quality control, and cleaning. What else could you want? That's the business, isn't it?"

Ed, QA/QC/Development Manager: "What? You treated everything we do in the lab as one big chunk of cost! You must be kidding! Some customers want a lot of testing, some just a little. And, with the new cosmetic bars, the customers won't allow even a small knick in the bar—it has to be visually as well as chemically perfect. How can you compare these bars? They're not the same. We may do the same activities, but how often, and how much, differs a lot."

Rick, Production Manager: "The same goes for the cleaning operation, Fran. You know the business. When we get an order for a black soap, it takes us forever to clean up the machines before we can go back to pastels or white soap. Are you going to charge the same price for clean-ups, no matter what we really do out there? What good is that?"

Fran: "If I'm hearing all of you correctly, it seems we've missed some things in the costing system that are very important to getting an accurate read on the cost of doing business at Standard Soap. I want to know what makes one bar different from another, from each of you, then we'll sit down and find a way to get this information in the system. I don't know how, but between K.T. and I we'll figure something out. So, what are all of these 'differences?'"

The meeting shifted gears and the next hour was spent identifying features of a bar, or a job, that made a big impact on the runnability of the soap or the complexity of the job. After the meeting, K. T. and Fran collected data on the key features of the orders run based on the facts unearthed at the meeting. Several of the summary tables for this information are presented in Figure 8.

The question that remained was, what to do about the lack of fit between the ACMS and the complex business processes that defined Standard Soap? It was possible to keep track of each and every order and the amount of time spent on the various types of tasks in the plant. This data could ultimately be used to create a new set of cost estimates that might be more realistic. But, would that do the trick? In talking about the problem, K.T. and Fran came to a basic conclusion: capturing the static complexity, or "drivers," of cost at Standard Soap simply wasn't good enough. There were differences in orders, and in bars—some that mattered and some that didn't. What to do, though? Abandon the ACMS? Fran's frustration was evident:

"We know this system isn't perfect, but we can't go back to the way we used to do things. We need good information to run this business, or we won't be able to grow profitably. The fact that a bar isn't a bar, that's a problem, but I know we can find a way to include this in the system. But, it can't be by using a ton of detail to get the information—it has to be a quick, easy to understand proxy—we have to capture the dynamic elements of the system in a way we all can understand and agree with. If we don't, we still won't really know if we're doing the best we can do on an order, or where to focus our improvement efforts. No one talks about this problem in any of the articles out there...are we the only ones who don't fit the simple ABC model? I can't imagine that we are, but the fact is, it's our problem now. It has to be solved, or no one will believe the system....."

(IMA Case)

12-3. East River Manufacturing (A)

Power Services Industries has been in business since 1907. PSI's principal business is the design, manufacture, and erection of steam generation equipment for utility and industrial customers. PSI also serves the after-parts market, which includes individual boiler components and loose tubes for repair and replacement. Their primary product, coal-fired boilers, burns fossil fuels to heat water, which turns to steam, and is used either for electrical generation or industrial process. Boilers are highly engineered products which can take anywhere from six months to five years to complete from the design stage through manufacturing and erection phases.

The East River, Illinois plant is one of three manufacturing facilities of the Services Division of the Energy Group. The East River plant has over 503,000 square feet of fabrication area, nine fabrication bays, and a practical capacity load of 1,345,000 manhours. There are over 500 hourly and salaried employees at the East River plant.

MARKET AND COMPETITIVE ENVIRONMENT

Throughout the post-World War II period and up until the mid-1970s, the demand for power-generating capacity increased steadily. PSI was a prime beneficiary of this growth in demand for electricity. They were awash in orders for original equipment. Backlogs of orders for forty or more radiant boilers were common, and when measured in manhours, were equivalent to over five years of work. The typical order for original equipment boilers averaged $30 million. Prior to the eighties, the original-equipment market (OEM) made up more than 60 percent of East River's revenues. Throughout this period, PSI earned a very respectable return on its investment.

As a sideline to the OEM, East River also serviced the replacement-parts (known as loose tubes) market. Tubes wear out in the hostile environment (e.g., coal-fired boilers generate fly ash which is very corrosive when it continually beats against a tube wall) and need to be replaced. However, demand for service work (replacement parts and components or subassemblies) is extremely difficult to project. Replacement-parts business requires short lead times, on-time shipments, and competitive prices. Service work is made more demanding because customers want made-to-order replacement tubes in small quantities. The typical replacement-parts order was $50,000 and usually had to be delivered in less than ten days, although the need to expedite an order overnight was not unusual. Replacement orders made up about 40 percent of revenues. And while the reported gross profit margins on individual loose tubes were high, the absolute size of and total returns on OEM projects made that market more attractive.

In the early eighties, a combination of fuel price increases, high interest rates, and a global recession hit and the bottom fell out of the OEM. In the past, this was normally a temporary setback and orders always picked up once the economy recovered. But this time it was different. The steady growth in electricity consumption, which had been predictable for so long, leveled off and OEM orders plunged. A number of factors led to a permanent drop in demand by the OEM, including the sharp increase in the cost of energy, unsympathetic utility regulatory agencies, uncertainty related to deregulation, environmental concerns about acid-rain, and improved capabilities to transmit excess energy across markets.

This new environment was marked by wide swings in business and fluctuating manning requirements. OEM business picked up again in the mid-eighties, but total OEM business and profits never returned to their former high levels and the total workload at the East River facility continued to drop. The inevitable profit squeeze caused by excess capacity and by ever-rising costs led PSI to look to the replacement-parts business to offset the declining OEM business.

Demand for replacement parts expanded as orders for original equipment declined. The principal reason was that utility and industrial customers wanted to maintain and prolong the useful life of power-generating equipment by replacing worn out parts rather than build new capacity. In addition, PSI engineers worked closely with customers to achieve greater efficiencies and enhance the power output of existing power sources by redesigning components or adding additional parts.

The determinants of successful management of large and complex OEM projects are very different from the key success factors in the replacement-parts market. Critical market drivers in the loose-tube replacement market are:

- Increased flexibility

- Reduced lead time

- Low price

- On-time delivery

- High Quality

Except for high quality, these factors did not carry the same weight in the OEM. As a result, PSI had to quickly adapt. For example, fast turnaround of worn or damaged parts is crucial once a boiler is in operation. Replacement parts availability is critical to a pulp and paper customer like Weyerhaeuser. Customers can suffer losses in the tens of thousands of dollars daily if their boilers are shut down as a result of part failure. East River always tried to accommodate customers' needs for replacement parts. But East River was structured to capitalize on the returns to be made on large-scale OEM projects. Primary considerations on OEM projects were to complete the boiler on time, within budget, and according to contract specifications.

The urgency of meeting contract lead times and completion dates on new equipment was not as critical as it was for replacement parts. But now, replacement parts were the primary source of revenues. And while new boilers were still being sold, replacement parts for existing boilers now made up 70 percent of East River's workload. Since PSI's major competitors (e.g., Asea, Brown, Bovari/Combustion Engineering; Babcock & Wilcox; Riley, Foster, & Wheeler; and Zurn) were suffering from the same drop in OEM orders, they too started to compete aggressively for the growing replacement-parts business. The field was crowded with competitors. But the expanding replacement-parts business was not large enough to offset the lost OEM orders. By the early nineties, total OEM and replacement-parts business was significantly less than it was in the early eighties (Refer to Exhibit 1). There was now a glut of industry-wide capacity. By 1989, the industry was overcapitalized and demand from the OEM and replacement-parts markets was running at a level which utilized only 45-50 percent of East River's capacity. The inevitable outcome was constant pressure on prices, margins, and market share.

MAJOR PRODUCTS

The East River plant manufactures a wide variety of components for boilers including wall panels— a collection of steel tubes (carbon steel, stainless, or composites) which are welded together with membrane bars in between them; loose tubes that have a number of bends in them or studs applied to them for heat transfer capability; burners which can burn coal, oil, or gas; structural members which contain the tubes that make up the walls of the boiler; expansion joints; dampers; economizers; risers and supplies tubes.

The Bay 7 facility was configured and equipped to process straight lengths of loose tubes into various shapes and lengths, suitable for the repair and replacement-parts market or needed as component parts of other assemblies completed at East River. Replacement parts and components are custom-made from unique materials compositions and configurations so that the parts can function reliably in a power-generation environment where steam may be generated by burning any one of hundreds of different kinds of coal or other fossil fuels.

Exhibit 1
East River Plant (A)

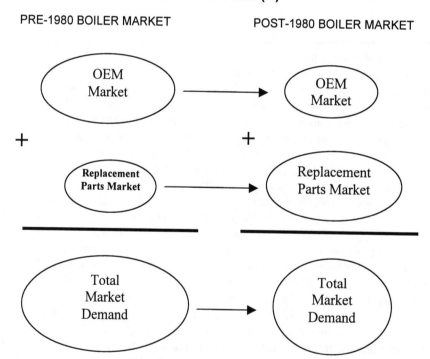

Many of the tubes manufactured have difficult welds and intricate bends in several different planes. All of these bends are engineered to a certain size, dimension, and location on the tube. Quality has to be right the first time. Once parts are in the field, they have to fit exactly. There is no reworking on the line.

ENGINEERING AND PRODUCTION PROCESS

Customer orders for individual boiler components and loose tubes to be fabricated in Bay 7 are initially processed at PSI's Dallas, Texas headquarters. Since there are no off-the-shelf parts, preliminary tube designs are prepared by product design engineers from historical data. Cost estimators use these preliminary tube designs to prepare estimates of the tube's manufacturing and material cost. The base estimating data used by cost estimators was developed from industrial engineering time studies completed in the early seventies. There are enough similarities to previously-fabricated tube variations that customer requested quotes can be developed on a timely basis by querying the parts database. If the proposal is accepted and becomes a contract, the proposal becomes the base-line or "as-sold" estimate (i.e., the budgeted cost) for cost monitoring and measuring actual performance.

Once a proposal is accepted, product design engineers "start from scratch" and prepare detailed part and component designs on computer-aided design (CAD) systems. They also determine the materials composition for all tubes. This product structure and tube geometry, which describes the physical characteristics of the tube, is then transferred to draftsmen who transform the product structure into detailed graphics (blueprints). Draftsmen manually load information on the tube's geometry into three different computer systems: (1) the Bill of Material system; (2) the CAD drawing system; and (3) the Tube Detail file which converts tube geometry along with design, process, machine, and tooling constraints data into process plans. This information is downloaded to East River's mainframe computers.

Purchasing places orders for all stock and non-stock items, many of which have long leadtimes. The process engineering group uses the Tube Detail file to generate the route sheet generation program or RSGP. RSGP creates a routing for each part with specific work centers, operations descriptions, and estimated process times. Customer order information is entered into MAPICS II (Manufacturing Accounting Production Inventory Control System), an IBM MRP II system. MAPICS generates bill of materials, routing sheets, order quantities, and required delivery dates. Manufacturing orders released by MAPICS were hand delivered to their respective work centers. Exhibit 2 shows the sequential flow of a contract from the preliminary proposal through shipment to the customer.

The East River plant has nine manufacturing bays. By 1990, the average age of equipment in Bay 7 was greater than 29 years. Bay 7 has practical capacity of 160,000 manhours. Tubes were received by truck and unloaded by a radio controlled overhead crane with the assistance of two workers. Tubes moved through the shops by a series of overhead cranes, jib cranes hung from building supports, forklifts, and transfer cars.

Tubes were shotblasted, cut to length, and machined as required. Tubes may be welded together prior to moving to the stencil/layout table, where the tubes were paint marked for a variety of studding and bending patterns. Tubes were then moved to a staging area near the stud welders and benders. Tubes were processed through a series of stud welding and bending stations, which were machine-assisted but still highly labor-intensive. Exhibit 3 displays certain tube features. Bending dies were stored outside Bay 7 and, when needed, transported by forklift to the proper bending station. Tube bundles were moved from station to station through Bay 7 by a series of pendant operated overhead cranes. Tubes were then checked, inspected, finished, and cleaned prior to shipment to the customer or transferred to another bay where they were assembled into boiler components. Average throughput time in the bay was approximately 3-4 weeks with high work-in-process. About 40 percent of the manhours in Bay 7 were attributable to material handling at the work stations or movement between work stations. Exhibit 4 shows the process flow for Bay 7, including machine count and headcount.

Exhibit 2
East River Plant (A)
Proposal-to-Shipment Process

SEQUENTIAL FLOW TUBE PROCESS

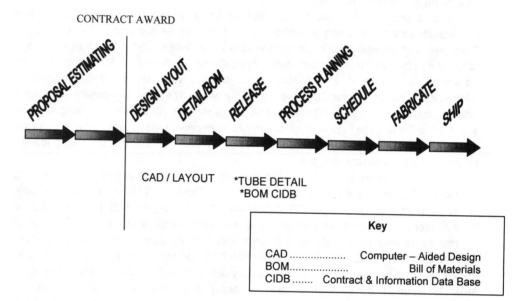

CONTRACT AWARD

PROPOSAL ESTIMATING   DESIGN LAYOUT   DETAIL/BOM   RELEASE   PROCESS PLANNING   SCHEDULE   FABRICATE   SHIP

CAD / LAYOUT   *TUBE DETAIL
                      *BOM CIDB

Key		
CAD	Computer – Aided Design
BOM	Bill of Materials
CIDB	Contract & Information Data Base

It was not unusual for bottlenecks and scheduling difficulties to arise during processing. Work-in-process was stored adjacent to work stations to alleviate any disruptions which might occur in upstream operations. There was approximately $7 million worth of inventory at East River at any given time.

Over the years, maintenance expenditures were kept at levels sufficient to sustain current operations. Competing on cost meant that operations management focused on high levels of equipment utilization. However, machine downtime and costs to repair equipment were now rising rapidly. In addition, depreciation expenditures were not reinvested in new equipment.

Furthermore, the collective bargaining agreement with the union did not allow workers to be cross-trained to run multiple machines and perform a variety of functions. Part of the difficulty was that over the years the collective bargaining unit negotiated fifteen different job levels along with several classes within each level. But now

12-22

competition was placing a premium on flexible work rules and East River was saddled with a labor agreement which made it difficult to respond quickly. With so much to disrupt shop floor control, it was hard to consistently maintain contract work schedules and meet customers' requested shipping dates.

Exhibit 3
East River Plant (A)

TUBE FEATURES

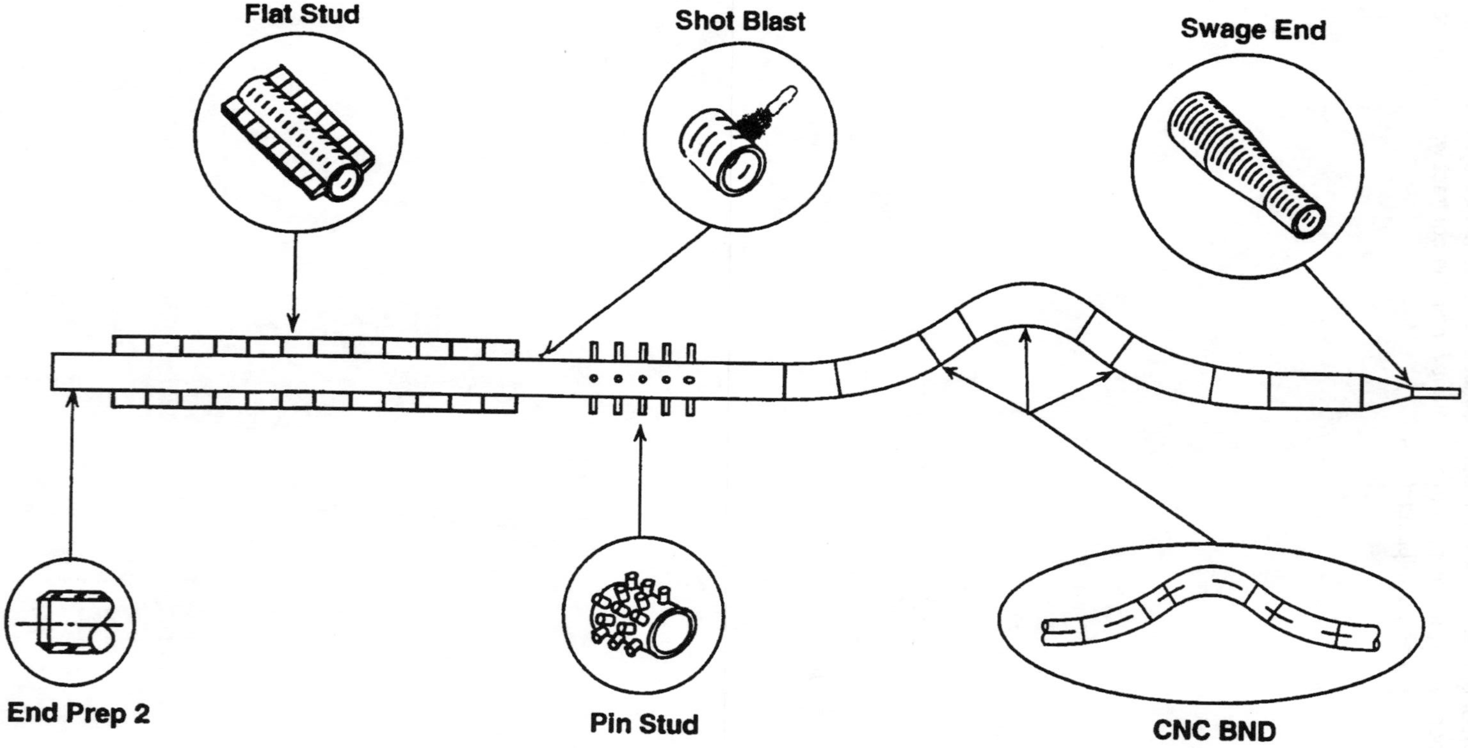

Swage End

CNC BND

Shot Blast

Flat Stud

Pin Stud

End Prep 2

12-24

Exhibit 4
East River Plant (A)
Tube Shop Manual Line

EXISTING PROCESS FLOW/MACHINE COUNT/HEADCOUNT

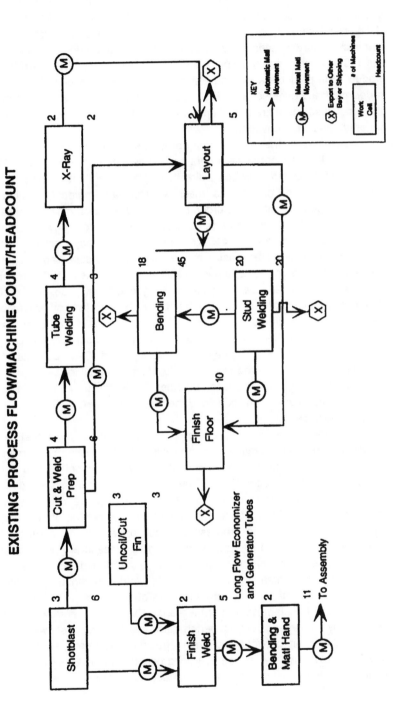

EXISTING COST SYSTEM

Traditionally, throughput in East River's labor-intensive shops was measured by manhours. The East River facility is on a job cost system. The same job cost system was installed in all plants built during the 1950s. In the case of East River, the job cost system was installed in 1951 and remained virtually unchanged until 1992, with two exceptions: (1) practical capacity replaced a three-year average of expected actual capacity for determining burden rates in 1982; and (2) a material burden rate was developed in the late 1980s. A job or contract cost system is necessary since PSI doesn't make a standard product. End products are manufactured to customer's specifications. The entire project is designed and engineered at PSI's Dallas, Texas headquarters. Materials composition and product structure are based upon the type of fossil fuel that will be used by the power generator and other environmental variables.

The contract is the primary cost object. Orders are grouped by contract, and costs are accumulated for purchase orders as well as manufacturing orders. The cost system charges materials and labor costs directly to the contract and to the part. Product design engineering, drafting or graphics, machine setup, and material handling costs are also directly charged to contracts. Burden rates are based upon practical capacity. A material burden rate of 5 percent of material cost covers the cost of purchasing and material control costs. Pressure Shop 415's overhead for three bays includes indirect labor and fringes, equipment-related costs, maintenance and repairs, and supplies. Shop 415 overhead was charged to contracts and other cost objects at 150 percent of direct labor cost. Plant support services, known as works-general costs, consist of production control, plant engineering, quality assurance, payroll, accounting, and other support services and are charged to contracts at the rate of 40 percent of direct labor cost. In addition, operating-all-works (OAW) costs associated with Dallas support services are charged to contracts at the rate of 15 percent of direct labor cost. OAW consists of manufacturing engineering support and the resource allocation group which plans and monitors plant loads, product mix, and production volume. These costing procedures were more than adequate given market conditions and the focus on large OEM projects throughout most of the post-war period.

In addition to costing the contract at practical capacity, the cost system was also capable of providing operating personnel with contract-related performance information. One of the most critical performance indicators was the monthly ratio of Estimated Man Hours to Actual Man Hours (E/A). Given that contracts could easily extend over a period of years, operating management could not wait until the project was completed to determine whether the contract was coming in over budget. It was essential to have some basis for monitoring progress on each project on an on-going Percentage-of-Completion basis. Using information supplied by process engineering, accounting staff estimated time for every task that had to be performed. As tasks were completed, comparisons of estimated manhours with actual manhours resulted in an E/A performance percentage. If performance was at 100 percent or better, the contract was going well and the plant would earn a respectable profit. If performance was below 100 percent, say 75 percent, contract performance was not going very well.

The relationship between equipment age and equipment tolerances is an example of how E/A could gradually worsen over long periods of time even when no changes were made in the tube design. One study of studding machines revealed that time and cost overruns were occurring with increasing frequency. Studding machines spot weld studs to the tubes. These machines were some of the oldest equipment in the Tube Bay. Therefore, controls on the stud welders were old and not as effective as they were when the equipment was newer. The welds did not always achieve the degree of penetration on a weld necessary to pass quality specifications. Studs which were not welded correctly could break off. These studs had to be manually rewelded because the number of studs on the tube precluded it from being rewelded on the studding machine.

Periodic monitoring of actual contract costs against the original bid or as-sold estimate assisted plant management in managing costs on a contract. The contract cost accounting system provides reports which show actual costs incurred for the contract to date, as well as reports which show the actual costs incurred for a contract during a specific period. All reports provide variances between actual costs and as-sold estimated costs and the engineered standards. This information was reviewed informally on a weekly basis and underwent a thorough, formal review each quarter (Exhibit 5).

Exhibit 5
Project / Contract Cost Monitoring

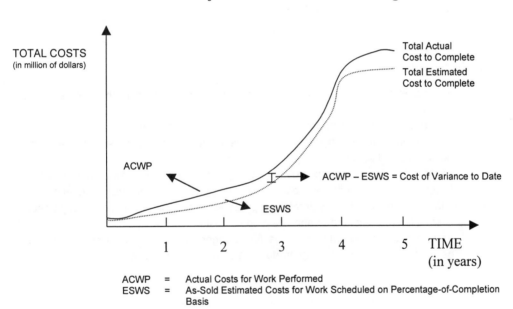

ACWP = Actual Costs for Work Performed
ESWS = As-Sold Estimated Costs for Work Scheduled on Percentage-of-Completion Basis

From a customer's perspective, there are two other critical performance indicators: (I) on-time delivery—meeting the customer-requested delivery schedule; and (2) quality. Often, customers have planned outages and want replacement parts delivered during a certain outage window—a specific date and time. If this window is missed, at the very least, customers lose confidence in suppliers. In some cases, there are substantial liquidating damages associated with a missed delivery date.

Quality Assurance reports defects. If a defect will cost more than $1,000 to repair, a separate sub-account is established for the contract, called a C-order, and all costs of reworking the part(s) is charged to this account. Accounting supplies the cost information to QA, which then identifies what the problem was, where it occurred, what the root cause was, and who had primary responsibility for correcting it. Some defects are due to a design errors, referred to as a D-orders. Design flaws can be identified when parts don't assemble properly. It is important to determine the cause of design errors so that they do not repeat these mistakes on future contracts of a similar nature or, if the error is the result of a flaw in the manufacturing process, the process gets corrected. Guarantee-orders or G-orders accumulate the cost of corrective work on a unit in the field that doesn't meet its warranted performance. Reserves are set up for C-, D-, and G-orders to cover the estimated cost or liability. These costs are built into the base estimating data used for proposals and establish allowances for contract cost.

(IMA Case)

REQUIRED:

1. Briefly summarize and contrast the competitive environment in the pre-1980 era with that of the early nineties.
2. What are the problems that plant management has to resolve?
3. What potential problems may occur between the as-sold cost estimates and the actual contract cost?
4. Diagram the structure of the existing cost system and explain how cost information is used for decision-making, cost control, and performance evaluation purposes.
5. Is the labor-based cost system appropriate for this facility? Should activity-based costing be implemented to analyze product costs?
6. Prepare a set of recommendations for changes in the cost system. Describe a general framework for costing products in an automated facility.

HOW I REENGINEERED A SMALL BUSINESS

BY RICHARD H. SNYDER, CPA

Reengineering is not just for large businesses. It's true that only giant corporations can afford to pay the fees for high-powered consultants to come in and turn the organization upside down. But for those brave souls in small businesses willing to think the unthinkable, reengineering can be managed without huge money outlays.

The major stumbling block in reengineering a small business is the staff who has worked at the business for years and tends to develop an ownership in the current process and, as a result, may be unable or unwilling to consider a revolutionary change in the process. What is required is knowledge of the system that exists and a willingness to consider radical new processes that would dramatically improve the system. In such circumstances an outsider may be necessary in order to produce dramatic change.

Take as an example the case of James Street Fashions dba Latt-Greene, a knitting and converting operation in Vernon, Calif. I became controller of the company on January 2, 1990, at the request of the owner in order to introduce control into the activities of the company. I had a prior knowledge of the textile industry, having been in public accounting for many years and having had some textile companies as clients (not Latt-Greene). I also had controllership, internal auditing, and cost accounting experience and had guided businesses though bankruptcy.

Latt-Greene knits textiles for the women's and children's apparel market, dyes and prints designs on the textiles according to customer instructions, and delivers the product to the customer ready for cutting and sewing into clothing. The customers of the company consist of clothing manufacturers who sell to clothing retailers.

In the initial interviews at this family-owned and operated company, I discovered some of the concerns: severe negative cash flow, a belief that not all sales to customers were being billed or collected, a paper-heavy system that was being crushed by its own weight. In my initial walk-through, I was

Table 1		
YEAR ENDED 05/31	NET SALES	ROI
1985	16.5	11.3%
1986	19.8	(46%)
1987	24.8	(18%)
1988	33.6	33%
1989	39.2	11%
1990	54.8	(6%)
SEVEN MONTHS ENDED 12/31		
1990	31.3	63%
YEAR ENDED 12/31		
1991	54	61%
1992	30	7%
1993	32	41%
1994	38	53%
1995	31	28%
1996	30	30%
1997	36	43%
1998	30	24%

astonished to see that the accountant was still keeping records on a "one-write" system. There wasn't a single computer to be found on the premises. I told the owners that if I were hired I would be making some dramatic changes including introducing data processing.

UNRAVELING THE OLD

The first thing I did upon being hired was to purchase a personal computer. I purchased one without any networking software because at that moment I had no one to network with. But I did look forward to that day in the future and purchased a computer with the capability of being turned into a central server at a future date. The only software that I installed at that time was a powerful spreadsheet, Quattro Pro. In order to gain insight and perspective into the problems of the system, I loaded into a spreadsheet all the invoices billed to customers during the month of November 1989, the most current period available at that time. I then began filling in columns with dyeing and printing costs from the subcontracting companies who did this work for Latt-Greene. I also calculated and added yarn costs and added a knitting cost, a tricky and inaccurate process because such costs had never been accumulated or calculated. The only financial records being prepared at this time were the general ledger, cash receipts journal and customer ledgers, and a cash disbursement journal. As yarn was knitted into unfinished textiles (called greige goods), sheets were manually prepared showing what pieces were assigned to what lot and what the lot weighed. But no attempt was made to cost the greige goods. When the finished goods were delivered to customers, they were billed as per the purchase order, but again no attempt was made to cost the product. The owners believed they knew what their knitting costs should be, and so I used that number as a starting point.

As I developed the cost sheet, several problems began to surface. One, I couldn't locate dyeing and printing invoices that could be matched up against the sales invoices. There was no controlling order number that followed the job through all its steps before the finished product was delivered to the customer. The dye house assigned its own number to the orders, and the print plant did the same. In some cases it was virtually impossible to determine to which order the costs applied. Two, I found purchase orders for which no shipment to the customer could be located. Three, I found many orders being delivered late. The person who placed orders into work kept the orders in an alphabetical file on her desk and each day rummaged through the file, pulled some orders from it, and told her assistant to put them into work. Many orders were delivered very late simply because they didn't get pulled from the file, and there was no control over the orders that were in process.

As I completed input for the month of November, I began seeing that a large number of the orders either had a too low gross margin to generate a profit on the sale, or even incurred a gross loss. I began analyzing these orders, and several problems came to the surface. First, like a conscientious baker who regularly gives his customers a "baker's dozen' Latt-Greene was producing textiles that were heavier than required. If an order called for goods that weighed eight ounces to the running yard, we were filling it with goods that weighed nine ounces. This extra weight made for a nice finished product, but it also often meant the difference between a profit and a loss. Second, in many cases, while the weight was okay, and all other factors in the production were correct, the order didn't produce a profit. We came to the conclusion that in many cases the product was simply being sold for too low a price. No wonder the company's sales increased from $16 million to over $54 million in five short years.

During the time that I was developing this spreadsheet, the solutions to the problems being uncovered were becoming clearer. I developed a manual costing system whereby every new order coming in was costed as it progressed through the stages of production. When it was delivered to the customer we knew immediately whether we made or lost money and the reasons for an unsatisfactory result. But this manual costing system required a tremendous amount of time to maintain and keep current.

KNITTING THE NEW TOGETHER

While searching for computer software that would take the place of the manual system, I looked at several programs, but each had some faults or shortcomings that disqualified them. Finally, I was introduced to a company that had produced a textile conversion system for a business which was smaller than Latt-Greene, and which did no knitting. But I liked what I saw because it had many fine features and controls. Talking with the developer convinced me that the knitting operation could be added to produce a system that met our needs.

In October 1990, we installed a computer system using my old personal computer as the central server and added 10 stations using the Novell system. After installation, I had to train the employees to use the new system. For some who resisted abandoning "the way we had always done it' I had to warn them to either do it my way or I would get someone who would. Over several months they learned to become computer operators, and the old system was forgotten.

As better and better cost data was developed using the new system, we refined our sales prices. In some cases major customers were lost because we raised our prices. But most customers were retained because we improved our service to them in several ways. Delivery schedules were met on a more consistent basis, and product consistency and quality improved as the employees were able to spend more time on those aspects of the product and less time on paperwork and trying to track down product location.

The system developer and I were able to develop a system that works very well for us because we took the time to thoroughly understand the business of Latt-Greene and the problems that occur in the textile industry. I took the time to talk to everyone involved in the process of converting yarn into a dyed and printed textile. I looked at every piece of paper being produced and traced an entire month's orders through to the final invoicing of the finished product. This thorough analysis uncovered the problems. All that was left was the development of the systems necessary to fix the problems. I involved as many of the employees of Latt-Greene as possible in identifying the problems and in suggesting solutions. Then, when the final system was installed, many of the people who would be working with it already felt ownership of the system. The few who felt threatened by it and resisted it subsequently left the company.

How successful were we in turning the company around? The table on page 28 displays sales and return on owners investment (ROI) for the years 1985 to 1998.

The big ROI fluctuations up to the year ended May 31, 1990, represent the agonies the company was experiencing because of its rapid growth without corresponding improvements in the systems. The marked decline in ROI in 1992 was due to the upheavals introduced when the recession hit the clothing industry with a vengeance that year. But the important thing here is that even in the deep recession into which the clothing industry sank that year, Latt-Greene continued to be profitable. The 1998 numbers reflect the fact that tremendous quantities of Asian textiles were "dumped" in the United States at prices that we cannot compete against. Several of our clothing customers closed up because of this situation. Even during this "textile depression" however, Latt-Greene continued to be profitable.

The lesson here is that reengineering can have a dramatic impact upon a business. Huge costs to implement change aren't necessary. The entire cost of our new system was approximately $150,000. Turnaround was swift and dramatic. Downsizing did *not* take place. We have about the same size office staff as we did in 1990 (eight people). The difference is that now we know what our costs are, we bill all our sales, and collect all our receivables. We are able to plan and to develop strategy. While marketing mistakes still occur (for example, when we miss a season because of incorrect designs), the cost of these mistakes is minimized because we can measure them and identify exactly what the nature of the mistake was and make corrections before the mistake becomes a catastrophe.

AN UPDATE

Nine years after inception, the system has changed considerably from the initial setup, but we have never had to do another reengineering. The staff today is still about the same size as it was in 1990. All the personnel that I hired in 1990 to assist in administering the system are still with us. The only office staff to leave were those who refused to work with the new system and had left by the end of 1990.

Some general principles that I learned from this reengineering and which may be helpful to others who would like to upgrade their operation:

- Be open with all employees regarding the process.
- Solicit input from all employees.
- Involve everyone in the implementation of the new system.
- Understand the system yourself because this understanding is more important than bringing in consultants and helps to ensure that costs are kept under control.

Richard H. Snyder, CPA, is controller of Latt-Greene in Vernon, Calif

Chapter 13
Process Costing

Cases

13-1   Kenco Engineering Corp. (A) (A Hybrid Job and Process Costing)
13-2   The Rossford Plant (Two Production Processes with the Traditional
          Volume-Based Costing System)
13-3   The United L/N Plant (Scraps and Defects)

Readings

"How Boeing Tracks Costs, A to Z"

This articles explains the change in Boeing's costing approach, from one based on job -costing to a process costing approach.

Discussion Questions:
1. Explain what Boeing means by process accounting.
2. What are the advantages of the process accounting approach at Boeing?
3. How does the new process accounting approach affect each business unit's incentives and tools to control costs?

Cases

13-1. Kenco Engineering Corporation (A)

History

Ken Lutz, a creative engineer, founded Kenco Engineering Inc. in California. The business is built around proprietary processes and custom designs that extend the wear life of parts on heavy equipment[1]. The key manufacturing process melts steel blade edges and impregnates them with tungsten carbide. Kenco adds value to original equipment manufacturers' (OEMs) products. Such equipment includes road graders and buckets on earth-moving tractors for roadbuilding, mining, and construction.

Also, Kenco outsources the manufacture of foundry castings that it custom designs. An example is hammers in grinding machines. It then wholesales the castings. As with its steel-blade tungsten-impregnating business, Kenco emphasizes castings that wear out. It competes by extending wear cycles with longer lasting products.

The firm is family-owned and small with $4-6 million in sales. It has sought OEM relationships, but primarily bids for jobs with blade or parts end-users. Lot sizes for steel blade impregnating are 1 to 10 units. The norm is single-unit orders.

Kenco was profitable from the beginning. However, in 1988 it suffered a loss of $350,000 (about a third of its equity). From 1984 to 1988 the second generation of family management oversaw a marked change in product mix. The mix of steel-blade impregnating business versus castings-wholesaling moved from $.6 and $1.6 million, respectively, to $3.6 and $1.4 million. Thus, Kenco moved from being primarily a castings wholesaler to predominant activity in tungsten carbide impregnating. Tungsten carbide impregnating is variously termed TCing or steel blade impregnating.

The business' growth unexpectedly resulted in the large, clearly unacceptable loss. With the move to more in-house manufacturing (TCing), profits had suddenly fallen. Inventories for the TCing business had grown to average as much as $80,000. (Average inventories have since been brought down to $6,000.) Ken Lutz's sons understood the need for change.

Responding to the situation, the Lutz brothers created a new position of Controller. They hired Vern Hughes whose background included five years in public accounting and nine years in manufacturing. Hughes had in-depth knowledge of costing systems and significant large-firm experience implementing just-in-time (JIT) production systems. At Kenco he accomplished major changes in operating systems, product costing, and cost control.

PREVIOUS PURCHASING/INVENTORY MANAGEMENT

Each day three or more suppliers bid for TCing's steel requirements. Steel blades are impregnated in job-lots. So steel was purchased in quantity at lowest-bid maximum-discount prices. The de facto operating rule of "sell one ... make 12; somebody will buy the inventory" resulted in increased steel and finished blade inventories. Hughes found that 50% of the finished parts did not turn in 12 months. One part, purchased at a large discount, had a 12 year supply at its current usage rate.

---

[1] Blade edges are like gloves that fit on expensive, larger pieces of equipment. They cover the abrasive parts of equipment that suffer damage in use. The $500 to $2,000 blades are worn out and replaced, rather than the $50,000 to $200,000 equipment parts.

Also, Kenco received bids from three foundries for 95% of its outsourced castings. It bought at the lowest-price quantity discount. Consistent with this rule, the firm contracted with overseas suppliers and received large (one or two container car) deliveries. Resulting problems centered on Kenco's inability to meet delivery dates. This denied customers time to refurbish their equipment. Many customers had seasonal demand, with delivery required in a January to March 1 window. While saving money, late delivery of container cars (due to customs or offshore problems) lost a lot of business.

Kenco's inventory records for castings were less than 25% accurate. For important new orders, clerks had to recount and tag parts. Split lot deliveries were common and added to overhead. Clerks found that they constantly ran out of stock on fast moving seasonal items. Supplier foundries constantly rescheduled and rushed Kenco's orders.

PREVIOUS TCING (PRODUCTION) ENVIRONMENT

Kenco's steel-blade production system had functional work centers, job lots, and high inventory levels. Exhibit 1 shows the shop-floor layout for this traditional job shop. Production was complex with many steps and unique activities. Long cycle times averaged 8 weeks. Cranes and fork-lift trucks moved heavy materials through production.

First, suppliers delivered steel plates weighing tons to the cutting station's incoming inventory rack. An overhead crane moved the huge plates with a lot of physical effort and danger. Workers cut the plates to rough dimensions and placed them in an out-going rack. Fork-lift trucks moved them to beveling's incoming inventory rack. Beveling then placed its output on an out-going rack and so on throughout the production process.

Each work station's use of incoming and out-going inventory racks lengthened set-up times. Combined with the effects of expediting, this caused high in-process inventories and wasted time. The average job used 80% of labor time in setup. Hunt-and-peck was required to sort through incoming inventory and find the next job.

Rework was high with 50% of boltholes out-of-specification. Workers positioned materials by hand at each station, making the work physically demanding and dangerous. Fingers were not just broken, they were crushed. As a result, very high worker compensation rates exceeded $11,000 per month in 1989. (After process redesign, this cost fell to $4,000 per month.)

KEY SUCCESS FACTORS

In order of importance, Kenco's key success factors are quality, on-time delivery, and cost. With quality defined as wear life and custom specifications, Kenco's products have no problems. Its products' lives are several times those of standard replacement parts.

Delivery is a problem. Kenco's markets are very sensitive to leadtime and Kenco had long leadtimes. Sales would increase until leadtime got to eight weeks. Then orders dropped off. When leadtime returned to five weeks, sales again increased. With its previous systems design, Kenco was in a constant cycle of losing and gaining sales as leadtimes stretched and shrunk.

An asphalt plant in Southern California discontinued Kenco's products because Kenco could not deliver on time. The failure to deliver one part idled the customer's entire plant. A part costing $2,000 idled a plant that cost $20 million! Kenco temporarily reduced leadtime by opening a second plant in Georgia. However, when this plant's pipeline filled, the old cycle resumed. Still, Kenco produced and sold 100% of its capacity. There was no alarm until the $350,000 loss in 1988.

Kenco wholesaled castings at minimum bid prices determined by a formula: materials cost times 181%. Thus, a casting with materials that cost $400 was sold for a minimum of $724. Kenco's managers viewed these numbers as implying a large gross profit for the product.

Managers based steel impregnating job bids on their judgment of competitive market conditions. For TCed products, the wholesale markup (181%) was used to estimate gross profits. For example, Kenco sold a steel-impregnated product for $905 at an estimated gross profit of $405.

Management thought, product-by-product, that it was making a lot of money. Market prices often greatly exceeded minimum bid prices and material costs. For example, a product with material costing $75 might sell for $350—far above $75 times 181%. Kenco was making so much money before 1988 that management did not think more accurate product-profitability reporting and a better bidding system were necessary. However, the company's reported net income moved lower in 1988.

NEW PURCHASING/INVENTORY MANAGEMENT

The new Controller, Vern Hughes, developed some key total quality management (TQM) ideas. They focused on value added to the customer and process simplification. Hughes focused quality on designing custom products and emphasizing Kenco's competitive advantage in TCing. Delivery strategies were related to cycle time and the influence of leadtimes on sales demand. Finally, Hughes evaluated bidding effects of product cost accuracy and reported product profitability.

Consistent with a belief in simplicity, Hughes thought many of the firm's practices only obscured the management process. He sought ways to simplify management and better control costs. He also looked for ways to improve purchasing, increase control of inventory, and reduce cycle time. Hughes proposed mutually helpful linkages to Kenco's major suppliers of steel (for manufactured blades) and castings (for wholesaled parts).

The plan was to source specific parts 100% from one supplier and end rush orders. All purchases of a given material were at an annually negotiated price, regardless of individual orders' unit volume. Suppliers gave blanket discounts based on annual purchase volumes and average materials prices dropped 15%. They delivered steel precut to job specifications, eliminating Kenco's cutting operation. All steel deliveries were in a three day window, and foundry castings received four-week delivery.

Most of Kenco's suppliers could not perform according to these arrangements! However, one supplier met them after some arm twisting.

To improve inventory accuracy, Hughes introduced cycle counting. Kenco now counts one-hundred items making up 80% of the wholesaled-castings sales volume every four weeks. It scraps or deeply discounts and sells all inventory not turning in twelve months. Wall-to-wall inventory counts are made every 90 days. Count accuracy improved rapidly. Additionally, Kenco reduced 5,000 castings part numbers to 1,200 stockable items. All other items are purchased only when sold. Hughes successfully rid the company of many of its management headaches, while saving money!

NEW TCING (PRODUCTION) ENVIRONMENT

Aware of cycle time's importance to market demand, the Controller moved to change the manufacturing process. A central objective was to simplify management of Kenco's value-added TCing process. Hughes investigated ways to improve steel impregnating production. Based on JIT and TQM, he guided redesign of the manufacturing process. Kenco moved from a traditional functional layout to what Hughes called an "in-line" (straight-line, single-unit flow) system. With inventories reduced and many part numbers outsourced, manufacturing labor fell 40%. Operating system simplicity, timeliness, and continuous improvement were key elements for success.

To improve process management and costing, Kenco regrouped its many production activities into two activity centers. These are: tungsten crushing and conversion processing. The cutting operation was eliminated by vendors supplying steel precut to specification. Using a proprietary process, tungsten is crushed from scrap parts. Merging tungsten chips with a steel blade occurs in conversion processing.

A single building houses conversion processing, which works as one JIT manufacturing cell. See Exhibit 2 for the factory layout after the change. The conversion processing cell combines five of the previous activities:

(1) beveling, (2) bolthole cutting, (3) tungsten impregnating (TCing), (4) steel blade straightening, and (5) drilling.

This cell focuses on TCing, the critical proprietary process. The other four activities have excess capacity and do not limit conversion processing throughput. Thus, the cell is unbalanced. In many ways it is designed following a Theory of Constraints philosophy.[2] Tungsten impregnating is the constraining process, and the JIT cell serves this process. The TCing machine runs at 80% of maximum capacity. This is average available capacity or maximum capacity net of average downtime for maintenance and repairs.

The conversion processing flow uses conveyors for a single-unit production line through five activities. Achieving this sequential layout required extensive process redesign and added materials-flow equipment. The new design allows the operator at each process to receive and mechanically position each job. There is no more manual raising and lowering of heavy steel plates. This production flow lessens setup time, cuts inventory racks and in-process inventory, and stops the hunt and peck of looking for the next job. Forklifts now bring steel to the beginning of the line and remove finished product at the end.

The savings were dramatic. Three shifts decreased to one. Headcount fell from 40 to 20 people. Cycle time dropped from 8 weeks to 8 days. Manufacturing defects fell from 25% to one per week. Monthly worker compensation savings of $7,000 paid for the additional new production equipment!

REQUIRED QUESTIONS

Construct your answers from the viewpoint of Kenco's environment. Avoid unadapted repetitions of systems from texts or your experience. Tailor your answers to Kenco's requirements for number of cost centers, information system efficiency, and product costing accuracy. Consider those costs associated with tungsten crushing, steel cutting (in the previous manufacturing system), and conversion processing of steel blades. Make any needed assumptions where case facts are not available.

1. For Kenco's previous manufacturing system, develop a product costing design (identify product cost components, pools, and drivers using, for example, traditional or activity-based costs). Then draw a T-account schematic of these costs' flow through a hybrid (job and process) accounting system. Indicate the points in the physical manufacturing flow and the timing for data entry into the accounts.

2. For your requirement 1 product costing system, fully explain
    a. the system's data collection requirements
    b. the system's compatibility with Kenco's new manufacturing systems and external report requirements
    c. the system's product costing accuracy or lack of it
    d. how your system supports or fails to support product pricing and profitability assessment

---

[2] This philosophy is explained in more detail in *The Goal: A Process of Ongoing Improvement* by Eliyahu M. Goldratt and Jeff Cox, (North River Press: 1986).

Exhibit 1

Previous Production Process Layout

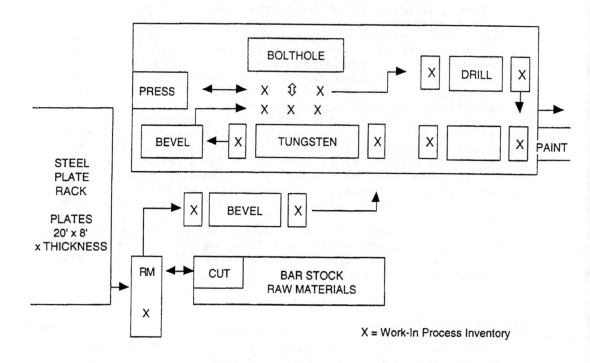

X = Work-In Process Inventory

13-6

Exhibit 2

New Conversion Processing Layout

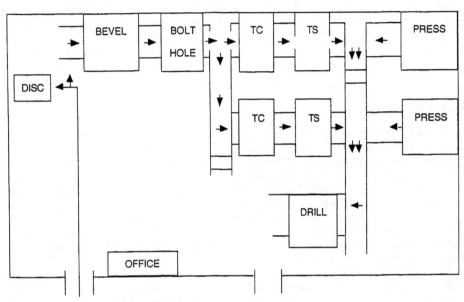

(Precut by Supplier)

TC: Tungsten Carbide Impregnating
TS: Steel Straightening Turnaround Station

CYCLE TIME = 1 Day
SALES LEADTIME ALLOWED = 10 Days
MANUFACTURING LEADTIME ALLOWED = 8 Days

13-2. The Rossford Plant

Having heard Robert Kaplan speak on some of the shortcomings of current cost accounting systems, I decided to undertake a review of the cost accounting system at our Rossford Plant. I was particularly concerned whether the overhead costs were being allocated to products according to the resource demands of the products. Costing our products accurately has become more important for strategic purposes because of pressures to unbundle sets of original equipment windows for the automakers.

Mark MacGuidwin, Corporate Controller
Libbey-Owens-Ford Co.

BACKGROUND

Libbey-Owens-Ford Co. (L-O-F), one of the companies in the Pilkington Group, has been a major producer of glass in the United States since the turn of the century. Its Rossford Plant produces about 12 million "lites" of tempered glass per year. (A lite is a unit such as a rear window, which is called a "back lite," or a side window, which is called a "side lite.") The plant makes front door windows, quarter windows, back windows, and sunroofs. About 96 percent of the lites produced are sold to original equipment (OE) automotive customers; the remaining 4 percent are shipped to replacement depots for later sale to replacement glass wholesalers. Lite sizes range from .73 square feet for certain quarter windows to about 13 square feet for the back lite of a Camaro/Firebird. The average size is approximately four square feet.

The Rossford Plant is comprised of two production processes: float and fabrication ("fab"). The float process produces raw float glass, the raw material for automotive windows. Blocks of float glass are transferred to the fab facility, where lites are cut to size, edged, shaped, and strengthened. The final product is then inspected, packed, and shipped.

Parts of the Rossford Plant date to the founding of the company. Unlike other L-O-F plants, which were designed around the automated Pilkington float-tank process with computer controlled cutting and finishing operations, the Rossford Plant was designed for the older process of polishing plate glass to final products. Pilkington float-tanks were installed in the plant during the 1970s, and the cutting processes were substantially automated during the 1980s. However, the finishing processes have not yet been automated to the extent as at the other plants.

Mark MacGuidwin, Corporate Controller of L-O-F, and Ed Lackner, Rossford's Plant Controller, became concerned during 1987 about the cost allocation process at Rossford for several reasons. First, the process had not been critically evaluated since the automation of the cutting processes. Second, the overhead cost structure at Rossford differed dramatically from that of other L-O-F plants. A larger pool of indirect costs was allocated to equipment centers. Third, they had collected evidence that the cost alloca-tion process at Rossford was not accurately assigning costs to units of product. And fourth, changes in the company's competitive environment were raising strategic issues that demanded accurate product cost information for pricing, product mix, and production scheduling purposes.

RELATIONSHIP OF SIZE TO PROFIT

In his investigation, MacGuidwin discovered what he believed were two key observations made by the Vice Presidents of Engineering and Manufacturing. Historically in the automotive glass business, original equipment customers have purchased a complete set of windows for a car model from a single glass manufacturer. From the glass manufacturer's perspective it was therefore necessary that the markup on cost for the entire set, or bundle, of glass units be adequate for profitability. Despite the buying habits of these OE customers, firms in the industry quoted selling prices for individual units of glass within each set. As easy benchmarks, the selling prices were customarily set in proportion to the size in square feet of the units, with smaller lites priced lower than larger lites.

However, the cost of producing automotive glass is not related proportionately to the size of the unit produced. The production process involves two principal fabricating operations: cutting the unit from a larger block of glass, and then bending it to the necessary shape and strengthening it in a tempering furnace. Neither the cost of cutting nor the cost of tempering is proportional to the size of the unit produced. Only a limited number of units can be fed into either a cutting machine or a tempering furnace regardless of the size of the units, with little or no difference in feed rates or resource consumption related to size.

The joint effect of these two observations is an understanding in the glass industry of the average relationship between unit size and unit profit that is depicted in Figure 1. Margin percentages for passenger car lites are somewhat higher than the industry average.

Recent changes in the competitive structure of the OE automotive glass industry have led to the possibility of "unbundling" sets of windows. Major customers are considering not only allowing different manufacturers to supply units for the same car model (for example, windshields from one and rear windows from another) but also setting target prices based on the manufacturing costs of the units, a process already begun by General Motors. Under these circumstances, the costs reported by the accounting system for individual units of glass have strategic implications that were not relevant in the past.

CURRENT PRODUCT COSTING PROCESS

Figure 2 shows the cost center groupings for the production process. The float and fabricating operations report to the same plant manager and have a common support staff. Raw glass is transferred from float to fab at standard variable plus standard fixed cost. (Profits are measured only at the point of sale of the finished product to the customer.) Direct labor and overhead costs are assigned to units of final product as follows:

      (1)   Direct labor costs are assigned to equipment centers (lines of machines in PC&E and furnaces in Tempering) based on standard crew sizes. Thus, a labor cost per equipment hour is developed for each of the several machines and furnaces based on crew sizes and standard wage and fringe benefit rates.

      (2)   Overhead costs, both variable and fixed, that are directly traceable to a specific equipment center are pooled to develop a rate per equipment hour for that center.

      (3)   A standard feed rate is established for each lite for each applicable cutting machine and furnace, and costs are applied to product based on costs per equipment hour/units fed per hour. (Feed rates to different tempering furnaces differ substantially.)

      (4)   General (indirect) plant overhead costs are allocated in two steps:
           (i)   20 percent of the total is allocated to the float process and 80 percent to fabricating, then
           (ii)   the 80 percent allocated to fabricating is assigned to units of product at a flat rate per square foot (approximately $1.00 per square foot in 1987, adjusted for differing yield rates).

The costs classified as general plant overhead amount to 30 percent of the total indirect costs of the plant. General plant includes approximately 100 salaried employees involved in plant management, engineering, accounting, material control, pollution control, quality control, maintenance management, research and development, production management, and human resources. It also includes depreciation of equipment and buildings not assigned to operating departments, property taxes and insurance, general plant maintenance, and post retirement costs.

MacGuidwin decided to limit his initial analysis to the automotive glass fabricating facility at the Rossford Plant. He and Lackner were confident that the process of assigning costs to units of raw float glass was sufficiently accurate. They also believed that the direct costs of labor and overhead associated with the PC&E and Tempering Furnace equipment centers were being properly attached to units of product based on the units' standard feed rates per hour. The rates had been set with downtime assumptions intended to cover mechanical and electrical problems, stockouts, and part changeovers.

"On the whole, Ed Lackner and I felt pretty good about what we were discovering," commented MacGuidwin. "Over two-thirds of the costs of the plant were being assigned to units of product based on metered usage of our two constraining resources, machine time in the PC&E center and furnace time in the Tempering center."

"On the other hand," Lackner pointed out, "we had a potential problem with our general plant costs. For years we had been assigning them to units produced based on square footage. We knew that this allocation base didn't capture activities that were driving the overhead costs, but we didn't know whether the allocation process was substantially distorting the final product costs. Until recently it didn't matter how these costs were allocated because unit price/cost differentials did not enter into any strategic decisions."

ALTERNATIVE ALLOCATION METHOD

The allocation of general plant overhead costs between float and fab seemed reasonable to the two Controllers. They analyzed a number of factors that could have been driving the allocation, including the number of hourly employees, the space occupied, and the variable costs incurred. They also interviewed managers concerning where time was spent by employees in the overhead base. All indicators pointed to the appropriateness of assigning 20 percent of the general plant costs to float and 80 percent to fab.

"The principal outcome of our analysis was to propose and implement on a test basis an alternative method for re-allocating the 80 percent allocated to fab," explained MacGuidwin. "Under the old method we allocated a flat rate per square foot produced. This might be reasonable if each square foot of glass costs the same to make in the PC&E and Tempering departments. However, we knew from our production engineers and from our own tracking of direct costs in those cost centers that this was just not the case."

To test an alternative allocation method, MacGuidwin and Lackner chose four parts with the following characteristics:

(1) a small, high volume, low profit margin part (Truck Vent);
(2) a small, high volume, moderate profit margin part (Passenger Car Rear Quarter Window);
(3) a large, high volume, moderate profit margin part (Passenger Car Front Door); and
(4) a large, moderate volume, high profit margin part (Passenger Car Back Lite, Heated).

As indicated in the following table, the direct costs of fabricating these parts differ substantially:

Part	Square Feet Per Unit	Cost Per Cutting	Square Foot Furnace
Truck Vent	.77	$2.870	$1.676
Passenger Car Rear Quarter	.73	1.494	3.312
Passenger Car Front Door	5.03	.340	.634
Passenger Car Back Lite	7.07	.206	.682

The input measure selected as the basis for allocating general plant overhead costs to units of product was the most scarce (bottleneck) resource in the facility—time spent in the tempering furnaces. The production plan indicated a furnace capacity of 48,500 hours per year. Dividing the portion of the costs assigned to fab by the furnace capacity resulted in a rate of $503 per furnace hour.

Using the feed rates of the individual pieces, MacGuidwin was able to compute a new standard cost for each of the four products. Figure 3 shows the standard cost per square foot, the cost per lite, and the gross margin percentage of each product under both the old and new methods of allocating general plant overhead. The Corporate Controller was pleased with the results:

"Although the results shown for the four products are not as dramatic as I've seen for some manufacturers, they do indicate a need to rethink and reanalyze our cost allocation system. Basically, the new method of allocating general plant overhead represents more closely what the Engineering and Manufacturing Vice Presidents were telling me about cost incurrence. The old system allocated a large pool of indirect costs equally to output, whereas the new system makes some attempt to associate those costs with the resource demands placed on our productive capacity by individual products. The old method clearly distorted our product costs. The new method should work better as long as we produce at plant capacity."

REQUIRED:

1. What is the cost object before the change in the product costing system? After the change? Why did MacGuidwin and Lackner change the focus of the system?
2. What are the characteristics of a good product costing system?
3. How do the process control and product costing functions of Rossford's cost accounting system interact? What conversion costs are treated as direct product costs in the system?
4. In your opinion, is the new allocation method for general plant costs better than the old method? Why or why not?

FIGURE 1

Unit Size/Profit Relationship

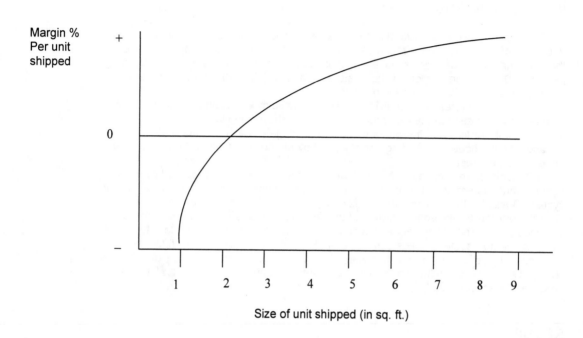

Margin %
Per unit
shipped

Size of unit shipped (in sq. ft.)

FIGURE 2

Production Cost Centers

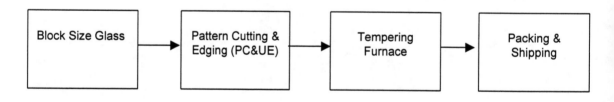

Block Size Glass → Pattern Cutting & Edging (PC&UE) → Tempering Furnace → Packing & Shipping

Figure 3
Unit Data Under Old and New Allocation Methods

Truck Vent

	Old		New	
	Amount	Percent	Amount	Percent
Cutting	$2.870	47	$2.870	42
Furnace	1.676	27	1.676	24
General Plant	1.020	17	1.740	25
All Other Costs	0.566	9	0.566	8
Std. Cost Per Sq. Ft.	$6.132	100	$6.852	100
Sq. Ft. Per Lite	0.770		0.770	
Cost Per Life	$4.722		$5.276	
Selling Price	$2.820		$2.820	
Gross Margin (Percent)	(67)		(87)	

Passenger Car Front Door

	Old		New	
	Amount	Percent	Amount	Percent
Cutting	$0.340	12	$ 0.340	14
Furnace	0.634	23	0.634	25
General Plant	1.036	38	0.800	32
All Other Costs	0.716	26	0.716	29
Std. Cost Per Sq. Ft.	2.726	100	$2.490	100
Sq. Ft. Per Lite	5.030		5.030	
Cost Per Life	$13.712		$12.525	
Selling Price	$16.820		$16.820	
Gross Margin (Percent)	18		26	

Passenger Car Rear Quarter

	Old		New	
	Amount	Percent	Amount	Percent
Cutting	$1.494	21	$1.494	16
Furnace	3.312	47	3.312	36
General Plant	1.022	14	3.020	33
All Other Costs	1.266	18	1.266	14
Std. Cost Per Sq. Ft.	$7.094	100	$9.092	100
Sq. Ft. Per Lite	0.730		0.730	
Cost Per Life	$5.179		$6.637	
Selling Price	$6.680		$6.680	
Gross Margin (Percent)	22		1	

Passenger Car Back Lite

	Old		New	
	Amount	Percent	Amount	Percent
Cutting	$0.206	5	$ 0.206	6
Furnace	0.682	18	0.682	20
General Plant	1.064	28	0.674	20
All Other Costs	1.810	48	1.810	54
Std. Cost Per Sq. Ft.	$3.762	100	$3.372	100
Sq. Ft. Per Lite	7.070		7.070	
Cost Per Life	$26.597		$23.840	
Selling Price	$56.120		$56.120	
Gross Margin (Percent)	53		58	

13-3. The United L/N Plant

We never imagined that we'd ever be looking at the type of costing issues at our United L/N Plant that have now become apparent. The plant design was engineered from the beginning as a state-of-the-art production process that would avoid most of the traditional problems. Now we're in the process of taking a second look.

Ken Marvin
Director, Planning and Control
OE Business Unit
Libbey-Owens-Ford Co.

BACKGROUND

Libbey-Owens-Ford Co. (L-O-F), one of the companies in the Pilkington Group, has been a major producer of glass in the United States since the turn of the century. Its newest plant, United L/N, began producing glass products in November 1987. Located in Kentucky, United L/N is a joint venture between L-O-F and a Japanese company, Nippon Sheet Glass.

Unlike the Rossford Plant, which produces the raw float glass used in its fabrication process, United L/N is a fabrication plant only. The organization of the plant reflects the just-in-time, pull through philosophy. The production process is fully automated, requiring no human intervention from beginning to end. Very high quality and minimal scrap were expected to be the norm.

L-O-F treats the Rossford Plant as a standard cost center, but United L/N is organized as a strategic business unit (SBU). SBUs are evaluated on profit as well as cost control and other goals. The company charges United L/N Rossford's standard manufacturing cost for raw glass transferred between the two plants, whereas transfer prices between SBUs are usually negotiated by their managements.

FABRICATION PROCESS AND PLANT DESIGN

The steps in the fabrication process are essentially the same as at other L-O-F facilities. First, the raw glass goes through pattern cutting where it is trimmed to the basic shape of the lite (window) it will become. Second, the cut pattern is edged. Third, the edged pattern goes through a furnace where it is formed (bent to shape) and tempered. Fourth, the final product is inspected, packed, and shipped.

The principal difference between United L/N's process and the fabrication process of traditional plants lies in the organization of these discrete steps. At the Rossford Plant, for example, pattern cutting and edging, tempering, and packing and shipping are treated as individual cost centers and are physically separated. Each department creates a work-in-process inventory, which is periodically moved to the next stage in the process. The next stage in most cases is located in a different section of the plant. Also, all processes at Rossford require human participation.

By contrast, United L/N's fabrication process is entirely in-line and automated. Raw glass from Rossford plant and other plants arrives packed on special racks that are designed for United L/N's automated loading process. (The racks are also designed to protect the raw glass from damage between the shipping plant and the receiving area.) The glass has been inspected at the shipping plant to determine that each piece meets the specifications of the fabrication process.

A forklift operator loads racks of glass at the beginning of one of United L/N's two production lines. From that point on, the entire process is operated through a numerical control computer system. Human intervention occurs only during planned downtime periods when the line undergoes preventive maintenance, when a problem stops the line's progress, and when finished pieces are inspected prior to packing. Glass is continuously pulled through the process, so that ideally there should be no idle work-in-process inventory.

A small team of operators monitors the process, performs regular preventive maintenance, changes the computer settings for different lites, and makes unscheduled repairs as needed.

PRODUCT COSTING SYSTEM

The product costing system at United L/N is very straightforward compared to those of less automated L-O-F plants. Overhead costs associated with handling, storing, protecting, and accounting for work-in-process inventories are dramatically lower. The major components of cost include short-term fixed operating costs, labor costs of the operating teams, and the transfer prices of raw glass from other plants.

Because the entire process is automated and in-line, the feed rate is constant across all sub-processes for each individual lite being fabricated. The costing system consequently was designed as one large pool, which is assigned to units based on standard input prices and standard feed rates. The system allows for standard levels of downtime and anticipated yields. Products are not charged for either planned downtime or planned scrap, which were expected to be minimal due to the care with which the plant was designed, engineered, and monitored.

PRODUCTION AND COSTING PROBLEMS

"It wasn't long before we began experiencing problems with our yields," commented Ken Marvin, Planning and Control Director of L-O-F's Original Equipment Business Unit. "At first we thought that the problems would be confined to adjusting and learning about the automated process. We thought that as we gained experience with it we could solve our difficulties without introducing more complicated costing mechanisms."

One of the first difficulties encountered was keeping the furnaces on the two lines working efficiently. Each one was designed to work perfectly when a certain number of glass pieces were being fired, a certain number were on the threshold entering the furnace, and a certain number were leaving it.

"In our traditional plants we stockpile pieces in front of the furnaces so that we can keep them filled to their optimal levels when forming and tempering," Marvin explained. "However, the United L/N lines were designed with no accumulators in front of the furnaces to keep them running efficiently at all times. For any number of reasons there might be gaps in the lines as they enter the furnaces. Partly because of these gaps and the resulting imperfect furnace operations, we have had unacceptably high scrap variances. Of course, scrap decreases the plant's yield."

"From the United L/N point of view the problem with scrap is caused by imperfections in the raw glass rather than by problems with the process. The plant's management therefore believes that the scrap variance should be charged to the shipping plants (including Rossford plant.) Shipping plant managers, on the other hand, believe that the charge-back, even if appropriate (which remains an issue), is much too high. United L/N's costing system costs every piece as if it goes through the entire process rather than dropping out at, for example, pattern cutting or edging stages."

Another factor contributing to furnace inefficiency and ineffectiveness is that a line sometimes goes down unexpectedly because of a problem in pattern cutting or edging. The plant then incurs the opportunity costs associated both with having an empty tempering furnace and with having to reset the furnace after it has been empty during periods of time when it was programmed to be full.

"We have been tracking all sorts of variances trying to get some insights into the effects on costs of the kinks in the process," continued Marvin. "We calculate a combined materials usage and spending variance, a downtime variance, a throughput variance, and a scrap (yield) variance. However, all of them are valued on the basis of costs of the entire production process rather than on the value added to the stages of production where problems occur. Now we're reevaluating the design of our costing system at United L/N, especially in light of the ongoing negotiations with Rossford plant and other shipping plants."

REQUIRED:

1. As a member of the Rossford Plant negotiating team, what would be your position regarding the proper treatment of the United L/N scrap variance? As a member of the United L/N team?
2. How could United L/N's management determine the specific causes of defects (for example, bad glass or defective cutting, edging, or tempering operations) in units that are scrapped at the plant? What are the implications for the product costing system?
3. What could be done to solve the problems with furnace inefficiency and ineffectiveness that Ken Marvin discussed? What are the probable effects of your suggestion(s)?

How Boeing Tracks Costs, A to Z

When Boeing's internal customers clamored for better cost information, the company decided to empower its business units by giving them more responsibility for their own costs.

By Robert J. Bowlby

A few years ago, two of Boeing's internal customers, engineering and operations, told the finance department they weren't getting the cost information they needed to manage airplane design and production. They lacked relevant economic information on which to base their decisions.

When we heard that, we knew we had to do something to remedy the situation. Boeing's cost-accounting system worked for tax and financial accounting and could be used to determine product cost and profitability at an airplane model level. But we realized that at an operating level, we were giving our engineering and operations organizations budgets for only a few cost elements.

Further, the cost information we provided individual managers didn't align with their responsibilities or areas they could control or influence. Engineering and operations couldn't use the cost information they routinely received to perform reliable economic design trade studies or to make economically sound investment decisions. They had to generate such information almost exclusively by special analysis.

At Boeing, we've committed ourselves to continuously improving our processes so we can stay ahead of the competition and maintain or increase our long-term market share. We are rethinking and reshaping our corporate strategies, the cornerstone of which is "Customer In," a concept that means we continually seek input from our internal and external customers through internal feedback, customer-satisfaction surveys and market research.

With this type of strategy, finance must be a partner in all aspects of a business, from marketing and product design to production and customer support. One of finance's most important jobs is to help create a systematic framework of financial and nonfinancial information and measures that contribute to making the decisions that ensure the enterprise's success.

Therefore, to improve the cost-management process, Boeing finance, operations and engineering decided to team together to study and rethink our managers' real information needs with respect to unit costs. The team spent some time identifying and reviewing "best practices" by studying industry, academia and our own internal practices. We came up with several key concepts aimed at improving the relevancy of our cost-management information.

FRONT-END ALIGNMENT

First, we decided to align our accounting practices to support the way we manage the enterprise. This includes being flexible and responsive enough so that we can change or redirect the system to enhance continuous process improvement, even in the middle of an accounting period.

Also, we realized we had to routinely provide the financial data that management needs to improve our processes and ultimately our products. We agreed that this data, which includes the costs of such items as materials, labor and energy, should represent the sum of all the resources actually used to build the part or assembly and that the area building that part or assembly must assume the responsibility for generating and tracking the data. From these key concepts, along with others like activity-based analysis, Boeing finance has been progressing toward implementing a modified process cost-accounting system.

Using process accounting means significantly changing cost-management practices and cost-assignment techniques. Part of the problem is that our current system was designed when our primary business was producing military aircraft. Our production methods, the makeup of our costs and the information we need about them have changed a lot since then.

Over time, our traditional job-cost system and cost-accounting practices have caused more and more costs that we'd traditionally categorized as overhead to be unloaded onto an ever-smaller direct-labor base. This evolved to the point where between 70 percent to 80 percent of the costs assigned to the final cost objectives of a manufacturing or engineering line organization were allocations from common overhead pools. Building and equipment maintenance, depreciation costs and the costs of industrial-engineering support activities and other support functions were lumped together in general overhead pools.

In today's factory, it's not uncommon to find that depreciation, technology, energy and nondirect labor expenses are often individually more significant than direct-touch or shop labor. The 20 percent to 30 percent of our costs that were mostly direct-touch labor assigned to the final cost objectives were the only cost elements the manufacturing or engineering line organizations had responsibility for and could directly link to the products they make. This meant that any process-improvement or cost-reduction initiative made by the line organization that didn't involve direct-labor savings wasn't directly reflected, or maybe not reflected at all, in the costs allocated to it. In many cases, the line organization couldn't be sure if total company costs would decrease or increase as a result of its actions.

To better manage the other 70 percent to 80 percent of the costs, traditional cost accounting and cost management separately identified significant chunks of the overhead cost and managed them individually. But, identifying separate cost elements, such as depreciation computing and nondirect labor, and trying to budget and control each one separately, didn't show the ways in which these cost elements interacted with one another.

These old accounting practices meant the overhead the manufacturing or engineering line organization did receive was based on the direct-labor dollars it incurred. Because technology-related costs were buried in overhead, this approach tended to move the dollars from areas with higher technology costs into units with the larger direct-labor elements. What we needed were ways to better align more of our costs directly to what we really do—designing and assembling airplanes and manufacturing parts and assemblies for them.

THAT BILL HAS YOUR NAME ON IT

Aligning costs to operating decisions is an important component of the new management and operating philosophy we're striving to implement. The changes we're going through are substantial. We are moving from a functional enterprise to one organized around product processes, and from a company that allocates its resources by organization to one that aligns them to product processes. And we are replacing part/resource management with product-focused process management.

This new philosophy will allow us to match resources to small, focused product groups. These small business units will then contain one or more product-focused process units. Costs incurred at a broader level in the company will not become the responsibility of the product- or service-producing unit. Rather, these broader-level costs will be the responsibility of the general-purpose processes, such as the sales and marketing organization or the central tax staff. These groups will be accountable from the costs they are adding to the final product shipped to our customers.

By way of comparison, think about a typical activity-based costing model, which you could use to develop the cost drivers for overhead and manufacturing activities. The overhead drivers include the square footage, the headcount, direct-labor hours, and the number of products. Manufacturing's drivers are the unit volume, the number of shifts and the weighted unit volume. With an ABC model, you would use these drivers to link the overhead activities to the manufacturing processes and the manufacturing processes to products.

With process accounting, we trace the overhead costs to product-related manufacturing processes based on the business unit's responsibility for and ability to control and influence the costs that result from operating that process. This is important for several reasons. Under traditional accounting, a business unit can spend less money and thus help the company meet its overall cost-reduction targets. But it's the direct, measurable, cause-and-effect link back to the business unit's products that was missing. Reducing a few direct heads was about the only action the business-unit manager could take to actually see the business unit's costs, or rather the 20 percent to 30 percent of business-unit costs, go down.

Our new process-accounting approach has changed that situation dramatically. Today, the organization can exercise significant influence and control over the costs it incurs. In fact, the basic ground rule for assigning costs is the organization must be able to take some action on that cost element and see a predictable change in the overall costs being charged to it.

The costs the business unit is accountable for and can control now include those for detail and supplier parts, computing, depreciation, support labor and di-

A FRACTION OF THE COSTS

Boeing's new cost-accounting system allows individual business units to portray their planned unit costs in today's environment and how they might compare to the unit costs upper management wants to achieve. The business units calculate their costs with the help of numerator and denominator charts like the ones below. The total dollar cost divided by good parts out equals the cost for good part shipped. Typical elements included under total costs are shown in the numerator chart. The denominator chart shows how we calculate our costs for good parts shipped.

In this example, the expected production, from the denominator table, is 13,439 units of output. The cost to product 13,439 units is estimated at $58.517 million (numerator table). Dividing 13,439 units into $58.517 million yields an expected average unit cost of $4,354.

Boeing's Cost Numerator...

Cost Element	Product Plan Costs (in $ thousands)
Touch Labor	12,150
Support Labor	9,223
Raw Materials	15,113
Equipment Depreciation	2,990
Equipment Maintenance	2,357
Tooling Depreciation	1,983
Tooling Maintenance	1,317
Distributed Material	503
Shop Supplies	915
Computing	6,662
Facilities Cost	3,552
Miscellaneous	1,752
Total	**$58,517**

...and Output Denominator

Part Number	Quantity	Product Weighting Factor	Units of Output
A	158	2.10	332
B	405	3.30	1,337
C	288	13.60	3,917
D	528	5.30	2,798
E	332	13.20	4,382
F	673	1.00	673
	2,384		13,439

rect labor, and other nonlabor costs. The business manager has a much broader sphere of influence in which to exercise control and make improvements within the business unit.

But tracing this bigger bucket of costs to the business units is only part of the solution. The business units now need some tools with which they can manage their costs. Once they identify the resources they consume, they must analyze them and learn to recognize their process and resource cost drivers and the relationship among them by continually asking why a certain item or process costs what it does. Business units need to understand their cost drivers to increase product quality, cut costs, improve customer response time and so on. Our business units will use their unit cost targets and ad-hoc analysis techniques for the data they will track internally (see box on this page).

As you can see from the example shown in the box, our basic approach is to compare and weight the individual parts produced in a product process, based on the differences between the parts or part families. We calculate the relative differences in the resources required to produce the different parts. Then we multiply the result— the product weighting factor for each part or product—by the expected production quantity for each part. The result is the business unit's expected production expressed in equivalent output units.

IT'S ALL RELATIVE

The normal procedure for determining these factors is to first identify the typical or base part or part family. Often that turns out to be the part that is the simplest. We give the base part a value of 1, 10 or 100, depending on the scale we want to use.

Then we review the other parts we produce, compare their features' relative value to the base part and determine their values. Take airplane skin panels, for example. We might assign a simple panel a value of one. A panel with a window could have a value of five, while a panel with an unusual shape could be a nine, and so on. The method also allows us to calculate the relative value of adding to or modifying various features.

Determining the relative value is probably the most complicated part of the whole process, but it's an essential aspect of process accounting. It's important to understand what's driving out current production costs, as well as the relative value of the parts being produced and the impact of process improvements and future production plans.

Individual business units can now project their costs for expected future levels of production. The production-producing business units will now be able to better understand how they fit into the total company production and cost picture.

With this knowledge, Boeing can relate many aspects of the total business to one another in a manner that allows us to take actions at all levels of the company—actions with predictable results and a common focus. For example, we can now begin to trace the hidden costs of capacity to individual business units, and this brings up some different, interesting questions. What is the unit's excess capacity? What's the cost of holding inventory? Who's accountable for excess capacity and why?

Also, process accounting supports other concepts in our continuous process-improvement strategy, including total accountability, responsibility and control: flexibility; and total cost tied to customer value. With our process-accounting tools in hand, we can begin to answer the next round of questions we're asking ourselves in our continuing quest for quality.

Chapter 14
Cost Allocation: Service Departments and Joint Product Costs

Cases
14-1   Southwestern Bell Telephone (Revenue Allocation)
14-2   Brookwood Medical Center (Cost Allocation)

Readings

"Reasonable Joint Cost Allocations in Nonprofits"
This article demonstrates the use of four alternative methods for allocating joint costs in nonprofit organizations. An example is provided of a hypothetical non-profit with two program functions and one fund raising function. The three functions share a joint activity, a joint mailing, with a total cost of $100,000. The four allocation methods are (1) activity-based allocation, (2) equal sharing, (3) allocation based on stand-alone costs, and (4) allocation in proportion to cost savings. Stand-alone costs are the costs each function would incur if it performed the mailing alone.

Discussion Questions:
1. Explain each of the four methods used in the example.
2. Which of the four methods would you prefer, and why?
3. What is the role of stand-alone costs in using each of the methods, and why are stand-alone costs important to consider?

"Managing Shared Services with ABM"
This article outlines the benefits of using shared services (i.e., finance and ac-counting services) in large companies such as Ford Motor Company, Sun Micro-systems and Marriott. There is also a discussion of how activity-based manage-ment (ref: chapter 4) is used to manage the costs of these shared services.

Discussion Question:
How do concepts for cost management of shared services differ from the con-cepts and methods presented in Chapter 14? Who are the customers referred to in the article? What do you think is the best way to manage the costs of shared services such as finance and accounting?

14-1. Southwestern Bell Telephone

In the fall of 1989, the Texas Division of Southwestern Bell Telephone Company (SWBT) was facing considerable earnings uncertainty. Nine months had passed since the Texas Public Utilities Commission (PUC) had initiated an inquiry into SWBT's earnings in Texas. The Company was trying to negotiate a settlement but was having difficulty reaching an agreement with the commission staff and other interested parties. One group was proposing a decrease in SWBT revenues that would result in a 76% reduction in the company's Texas revenues and adversely affect Southwestern Bell Corporation's stock price.

At the same time that the PUC was investigating alleged overearnings related to SWBT's Texas intrastate operations, company officers in Texas were trying to meet budgeted net income objectives. These targets were necessary to keep earnings growing at a conservative yet steady rate. With actual data already available for much of the year, it was apparent that the overall target for 1989 might not be met. One of the main causes of this probable shortfall was the decrease SWBT was experiencing in revenues from long distance telephone calls. This decrease was due largely to increased payments in the form of settlements to other local exchange telephone companies in Texas. SWBT's management was searching for alternatives to the settlement process that would allow the company to retain its fair share of long distance revenues without financially ruining smaller telephone companies operating in the state.

INDUSTRY BACKGROUND

In January 1984, SWBT and six other regional telephone companies were divested from American Telephone and Telegraph Company (AT&T). In addition to retaining ownership of Western Electric (manufacturing), Bell Labs (research and development), and AT&T Information Systems, AT&T was allowed to retain ownership of interstate long distance services and a portion of intrastate long distance. Under the provisions of the Justice Department's Modified Final Judgment decree, each state was divided into Local Access Transport Areas (LATAs). Texas was divided into seventeen LATAs in addition to the standard metropolitan statistical area of San Angelo, which belongs solely to General Telephone (GTE).

Long distance calling between LATAs (interLATA) may be provided only by interexchange carriers (IXCs) such as AT&T, MCI, and Sprint. Local exchange carriers (LECs) such as SWBT and GTE provide basic telephone service and long distance calling within each LATA (intraLATA). In Texas, there are 59 LECs. SWBT is by far the largest, serving approximately 6.6 million telephone lines.

Because IXCs access their customers through LEC facilities, LECs charge IXCs for using their local networks. Theoretically, these per-minute-of-use charges are based on LEC costs. However, state commissions often inflate the rates to subsidize basic telephone rates, thus keeping them priced below cost.

INTERSTATE INTRALATA LONG DISTANCE

When a customer of an LEC makes an intrastate intraLATA long distance (toll) call, completion of the call often requires the use of another LEC's facilities. For example, a call from Dallas to Denton is an intraLATA toll call that originates in a Southwestern Bell area (Dallas) but terminates in a GTE area (Denton). The originator of the call is billed by Southwestern Bell, which must reimburse GTE for costs incurred in assisting in the call. In Texas, this reimbursement is currently handled through a toll revenue pooling agreement among the LECs.

The pooling of intraLATA toll revenues is administered by the Texas Exchange Carrier Association (TECA). Each LEC reports monthly to the TECA administrator not only its billed toll revenues but also its expenses and investment incurred in providing toll service. TECA combines the revenue, expense, and investment information for all 59 LECs and calculates a rate of return equal to billed revenues less expenses (including taxes) divided by investment. Each LEC is allowed to recover its expenses plus the pool rate of return on its investment.

In 1987 the pool rate of return was approximately 19%. Although SWBT billed $555.3 million in toll revenues, it was allowed to retain only the total of its expenses ($285.4 million) and return ($147.9 million). The $122 million difference between what SWBT billed and what it was allowed to keep was paid to the pool administrator for disbursement to those companies whose costs exceeded their billed revenues.

CONCERNS WITH THE POOLING PROCESS

Southwestern Bell's managers have several concerns with the current pooling process. One of their major concerns is that few incentives exist for companies to control costs. IntraLATA toll service is a much larger portion of the total operations of many of the smaller LECs than of SWBT. Consequently, each dollar of additional cost incurred by the smaller companies results in approximately one dollar of additional settlements. On the other hand, Southwestern Bell's retained toll revenues (after settlement with other LECs) decrease by approximately $1 million for each one percent reduction in its costs. This situation is not conducive to the efficient provision of telephone service and therefore is not in the best interest of the public.

The company's managers also are concerned about the manner in which total expenses and investment related to intraLATA toll service are calculated. Each company's accountants computes these amounts using procedures developed by the Federal Communications Commission (FCC). The very complex procedures, referred to in the industry as "separations," allocate monthly journalized expense and investment amounts to various categories of telephone service based on factors developed from studies of call traffic patterns and studies showing how telephone plant resources are utilized. The separations process was developed to provide a means of dividing expenses and investment amounts between state and interstate jurisdictions to facilitate rate setting by regulatory agencies. It never was intended to represent an accurate allocation system.

The first step in separations is to divide expense and investment amounts into traffic-sensitive and non-traffic-sensitive (NTS) categories. Traffic-sensitive expenses are primarily variable and are relatively easy to trace to specific categories of service. NTS expenses are primarily fixed. These amounts (over half the total SWBT reports to the pool) are incurred to provide and service connections between customers' premises and company's central offices. The same investment is required whether a customer makes no calls, a few calls, or hundreds of calls, and also whether those calls are intrastate or interstate.

NTS amounts are separated into three categories: interstate, intrastate toll, and intra-state local. In 1982, the FCC froze at approximately 20% the portion of Southwestern Bell's NTS expenses and investment allocated to intrastate toll operations. Thus, the initial separation of NTS amounts does not represent the current usage of the telephone network's resources. However, the interLATA toll and intraLATA toll components of the 20% factor are determined monthly based on relative actual usage. Therefore, if interLATA toll usage is increasing at a faster rate than intraLATA toll usage, less will be allocated to the intraLATA toll category. IntraLATA toll expenses and related investment could be increasing, but due to the separations process fewer dollars would be assigned to the category and thus recoverable through the pooling process. SWBT's intraLATA toll NTS factor is approximately 8%, whereas the factors of several smaller telephone companies are in the 30% to 50% range.

A third concern of Southwestern Bell managers is that revenues from non-joint-provided toll calls are included in the pooling process. For example, consider that the largest intraLATA toll market in Texas is between Dallas and Ft. Worth. Most toll calls between the two cities use only SWBT facilities, but through the pooling process revenues from the calls are shared with the state's other LECs. Company officials believe both revenues and costs of single-company toll calls should be excluded from the pool, but currently there is no means to isolate those amounts.

A final concern relates to the telecommunications industry goal of providing adequate telephone service to all U. S. citizens at reasonable rates. All telephone companies as well as the entire nation have benefited from the subsidies that higher cost companies have received from lower-cost companies. If local telephone service, especially in rural areas, were priced to cover its costs, the number of residences with service would be substantially lower. The concern at Southwestern Bell is that subsidization of high-cost companies has exceeded its historical intent; publications of the Texas PUC show that many high-cost LECs are earning well over their authorized rates of return.

After reviewing the situation, Southwestern Bell's senior managers realized they had their work cut out for them. They know that the course of action they recommended would have to effectively address both the concerns of SWBT and the financial needs of the other companies.

REQUIRED:

1. Assuming toll revenue sharing will continue to be administered by the TECA, what is the most important modification that could be made to the pooling procedures to produce a more equitable distribution of revenues from the perspective of Southwestern Bell?

2. Should SWBT officials negotiate changes in the subsidization procedures directly with the other Texas LECs or take their concerns to the state Public Utilities Commission and seek mandated changes?

3. What strategy would you recommend to Southwestern Bell managers? How would your recommendation address the four concerns expressed in the case?

(IMA adapted)

14-2. Brookwood Medical Center[1]

"In 1990, a major insurer asked us to bid on performing all of their open-heart surgeries in the Southeast United States. We prepared a bid by pulling charges on all (not just Medicare) patients we had treated in the four diagnostic related groups (DRGs) and applying the hospital-wide cost-to-charge ratio. We did not get the bid and had *no idea* whether to be disappointed or relieved. From talks with third-party payers and major employers, we believed that by the mid-1990s we would be bidding for portions of business, like open-heart surgeries, on a regular basis. We realized that we needed a much better understanding of costs at the DRG and individual patient levels if we're to be able to compete effectively."

—Carolyn Johnson, Vice President of finance

INTRODUCTION

By the end of the 1980s, cost management had become one of the most important issues faced by Brookwood Medical Center (BMC) administrators. BMC faced pressure from managed care providers such as health maintenance organizations (HMOs) and preferred provider organizations (PPOs) to keep medical costs low while continuing to provide high-quality health care services. For the first time, BMC was asked to bid on specific health care services for members of managed care insurance plans. To provide bids that were competitive yet profitable, hospital administrators needed detailed cost information about specific health care procedures. In addition, Medicare and other insurance providers moved to fixed fee reimbursement schedules, paying a defined fixed rate depending on a patient's diagnostic related group (DRG) and severity level. The use of fixed payment rates provided incentives for BMC to identify costs associated with providing health care to specific patients in each DRG. Health care providers realized that reductions in the average length of stay (ALOS) as a result of shorter inpatient hospital stays and increased outpatient services could decrease costs without decreasing the quality of care.

THE NEW COST SYSTEM

As more payers moved to a fixed fee form of reimbursement, BMC administrators determined the existing cost system was not providing sufficiently accurate or detailed cost information. The old methodology provided aggregated cost data by department; but no reliable method existed to trace costs to individual patients or diagnostic groups. The new health care environment required hospitals to compete for managed care contracts and to make strategic decisions based on a solid understanding of costs.

Jan Kelly, Director of cost accounting, identified the following issues to support the need for a new cost management system:

- *Unexplained variation in practice patterns.* Physicians largely drove the health care delivery process through treatment protocols and medical orders that determined patient charges and length of stay. A new cost system could help identify costs associated with specific physician practice patterns.
- *Concern with costs and more appropriate care.* BMC recognized the opportunity to reduce tests and procedures for patients (e.g., ordering a component test rather than a whole profile on blood work). Some inpatient testing and care could be effectively done on an outpatient basis due to advances in medications and

---

[1] Prepared by Thomas L. Albright and Robin Cooper, © Institute of Management Accountants, 1998. Used with permission.

other technology. Many diagnostic tests and longer inpatient stays may not result in better patient outcomes.

- *Questions regarding effectiveness.* Questions concerning the effectiveness of care, especially when evaluating new technology or treatments, were becoming increasingly commonplace. Thus, BMC required more sophisticated cost management tools.

- *Beliefs regarding cost vs. value of care.* Balancing the quality of care with the costs of providing care was a fundamental concern for BMC. For example, if a new surgical procedure allows early discharge or little scarring but costs 10 times more than an old procedure, is it necessary for the hospital to offer the new procedure and incur additional costs? Executives had to identify a strategy for new technology and the existing methodology, management began to explore alternatives to the old cost accounting methodology. They required a cost system that would provide a product-line focus, i.e., open heart surgery, diabetes care, rehabilitation, or respiratory therapy, and that would permit segmentation of the patient population. Details of Mason's oncological study were reviewed, and the results reinforced the belief that costs calculated on a facility-wide basis were not helpful for making decisions that were DRG-specific.

In March 1991, BMC executives hired an Atlanta-based CPA firm to work with Kelly to gain an understanding of departmental operating costs and to build cost standards. They backloaded cost data for 20 months and identified two types of costs, direct and indirect. Meetings were held twice a week with key hospital administrators and clinicians to determine activities that caused costs.

BMC used a computerized information system known as Transition I (TSI) to assist with standard costing, financial modeling, and forecasting. The software allowed cost managers at BMC to identify activities, link activities to costs, and categorize costs based on predetermined or specific allocation bases. The system also generated simultaneous algebraic equations used to allocate indirect costs to revenue-generating departments. TSI allowed the creation of a database with cost and demographic information that could be sorted by both traditional and nontraditional demographic elements. Detailed information allowed BMC to obtain more accurate measurements of costs to provide care and to monitor and improve the quality of care provided to patients. For example, the patient number, length of stay, total charges, direct costs, and indirect costs for all appendectomy patients treated during a specific time period were summarized by the TSI system (see Table 1).

DIRECT COSTS

Direct costs could be traced to a patient or procedure and included resources consumed in providing testing services, supplies, pharmaceuticals, and nursing care. Costs for patient testing and procedures (including X-ray, laboratory services, operating room costs, labor and delivery room costs) were associated with each patient, using the internally calculated direct cost for each test or procedure. Major supplies and pharmaceuticals were individually assigned to the patient based on the actual cost of the supply or drug.

Nursing care costs were driven to the patient level through daily patient classification and room rate charges. These charges were based on the nursing skill level required to care for patients in each specialty area, as well as the average acuity levels in each specialty area. Nursing staff skill levels were divided into three classifications as follows: registered nurse (RN), licensed practical nurse (LPN), and aide. Examples of specialty areas were obstetrics, surgical, psychiatric, and cardiovascular. BMC divided six acuity levels according to the level of clinical attention required by the patient. For example, a direct cost of $123 per day was incurred in the Nursing-MED/SURG department acuity level 1 (see Table 2).

The cost system produced departmental reports identifying the daily rate by acuity level and the underlying assumptions of the allocation routine (see Table 3). Because the number of minutes required to attend patients varied across acuity levels, the estimated (budgeted) volume of patient days was adjusted for daily service levels, expressed in minutes. The department's budgeted cost was allocated to each acuity level as a percentage of total budgeted minutes. Finally, a daily rate for each acuity level was calculated by dividing the allocated costs by the budgeted volume of days within each acuity level.

INDIRECT COSTS

Indirect costs such as depreciation, administrative, and general were allocated to revenue-producing activities using simultaneous algebraic equations. The calculations were performed by BMC's computerized accounting system using allocation percentages based on the amount of services provided to other departments. The system allocated costs among several departments with reciprocal service relationships. For example, assume an organization has two support departments, housekeeping, information systems (IS), and two revenue-producing departments, operating room (OR) and emergency room (ER). The IS department manager estimated the housekeeping department consumed 10% of the IS department's activities, while the ER and OR required 40% and 50%, respectively. Thus, the IS department's direct costs of $100,000 were allocated to housekeeping, OR, and ER consistent with the resources demanded (see Table 4). Next, the housekeeping department's direct ($60,000) and allocated ($10,000) costs of $70,000 were allocated to IS, OR, and ER using 30%, 40%, and 30%, respectively. Though the IS department had allocated all costs total $100,000 in the first step, the housekeeping department transferred costs ($21,000) back into the department that had to be reallocated in the second iteration. Iterations continued until the costs remaining in the support departments were too small to be significant. Thus, after multiple iterations, all support department costs were transferred to the OR and ER (see Table 4).

The cost system used by BMC simultaneously allocated costs associated with all indirect activities to revenue-producing activities based on cost drivers identified by BMC. For example, the education department allocated its costs to various departments including pain management, diabetic services, and emergency room using the percentage of paid hours within each department as the allocation base. Though the process required multiple iterations (see Table 4), the cost management system produced reports after each allocation iteration (see Table 5). When the allocation procedure had completed the final iteration, all costs for support-related departments were contained in the accounts of revenue-producing departments. Thus, education costs were included in the emergency room indirect cost per hour of $142 (see Table 2).

As the health care environment changed, new information demands were placed on the cost reporting system. The Mason study (discussed in the BMC Introduction) added length of stay as well as direct costs within DRG categories to the cost-to-charge ratio. According to Kelly, "TSI represented a significant step toward understanding and managing the costs of delivering health care services at BMC."

REQUIRED:
1. Why didn't the cost data make any sense?
2. What motivated the managers to build a new cost system?
3. How does the TSI system attach costs to a patient or procedure? What are the major design issues?
4. How is the daily rate determined for the Nursing Med/Surg department acuity level 1?
5. How does the reciprocal method allocate indirect costs to revenue-producing departments?
6. Given your understanding of the manner in which TSI allocates costs to patients, would you classify Brookwood's cost system as activity based?

Table 1 Brookwood Medical Center: Appendectomy Patient Listing

Patient Number	Length of Stay	Total Charges	Direct Cost Variable	Direct Cost Fixed	Indirect Cost	Total Cost
1	3	$8,486	751	164	1,187	2,102
2	4	18,394	2,960	566	3,106	6,631
3	2	7,297	926	245	1,280	2,451
4	2	12,350	2,069	258	1,556	3,884
5	2	5,854	765	210	1,152	2,126
6	3	14,574	1,966	395	2,160	4,522
7	2	14,289	2,440	332	1,577	4,349
8	1	5,772	856	102	661	1,619
9	2	11,589	1,404	325	1,553	3,282
10	2	8,398	1,192	365	2,045	3,601
11	2	8,771	1,033	225	901	2,159
12	3	14,920	2,626	295	2,546	5,466
13	3	10,320	1,751	487	2,644	4,882
14	3	8,871	1,097	178	1,460	2,735
15	1	9,103	1,998	221	1,647	3,865
16	2	8,365	1,563	168	1,050	2,781
17	5	13,355	2,195	687	3,237	6,119
18	2	11,235	2,414	258	2,195	4,867
19	1	8,976	1,170	201	1,067	2,438
20	5	18,033	3,123	563	3,457	7,143
21	4	11,756	1,739	229	1,279	3,247
22	1	8,068	1,698	210	1,350	3,258
23	1	8,133	1,669	247	1,257	3,174
24	1	7,396	1,232	160	825	2,217
25	1	6,926	911	147	637	1,695
26	1	7,558	1,268	188	1,141	2,598
27	5	20,140	3,151	468	3,419	7,037
28	2	6,211	718	167	843	1,728
29	2	8,740	1,324	189	1,212	2,724
30	1	6,931	779	140	736	1,656
31	1	8,493	1,345	152	1,013	2,510
32	1	6,580	1,041	153	863	2,056
33	2	8,646	1,328	195	1,200	2,723
34	2	11,319	1,214	247	1,424	2,885
35	1	7,435	1,042	161	817	2,020
36	2	11,765	1,564	267	1,647	3,478
37	1	9,822	1,443	165	1,143	2,752
38	2	10,354	1,929	184	1,669	3,782
39	3	9,117	1,117	126	1,309	2,552
40	1	11,097	1,623	348	1,847	3,818
41	1	9,030	900	141	859	1,901
42	1	7,659	1,558	112	1,045	2,716
43	2	9,943	1,619	174	1,217	3,010
44	2	11,238	1,177	202	1,273	2,651
Total	91	$443,309	67,688	11,017	66,506	145,210

Source: sample of appendectomy patients from TSI data.

Table 2. DRG 470 - Appendectomy Utilization Report

Department Description	Product Description	Direct Cost	Indirect Cost	Quantity	Total Cost
NURSING - MED/SURG	Acuity level 1 -- daily rate	$123.00	$190.00	1	$313.00
	Acuity level 2 -- daily rate	140.00	229.00	2	738.00
OPERATING ROOM	Major surgery -- 1 hour	174.00	170.00	1	344.00
OPERATING ROOM SUPPLIES	Sutures	17.00	7.00	5	120.00
	Basic surgical pack	17.00	6.00	1	23.00
	Additional OR supplies*	118.00	50.00	1	168.00
RECOVERY	Recovery level II -- 1/4 hours	24.00	11.00	3	105.00
CENTRAL STORES	Central store supplies*	25.50	58.00	1	83.50
LABORATORY SERVICES	Blood profile, potassium, renal profile	29.50	11.00	2	81.00
CARDIOLOGY / EKG	EKG 3 channel w/o physician in	13.00	12.00	1	25.00
PHARMACY	Pharmaceuticals*	163.50	133.00	1	296.50
RESPIRATORY THERAPY	Incentive spirometer	4.00	3.00	5	35.00
	New start spirometer & oxygen	6.00	4.00	1	10.00
EMERGENCY ROOM	ER visit level II -- intensive	80.00	142.00	1	222.00
DIETARY	Daily hospital service	24.00	18.00	3	126.00
LAUNDRY / LINEN	Daily hospital service	9.00	6.00	3	45.00
					2,735.00

* Detail of specific items charged collapsed into one line item.

Table 3. Brookwood Medical Center, Department 6103, Nursing MED/SURG

Budget $95,759

Description	Budgeted Volume in Days	Minutes Daily Service	Budgeted Minutes	Percent Allocation	Allocation	Daily Rate
Acuity level 1	18	346	?	?	?	?
Acuity level 2	264	394	?	?	?	?
Acuity level 3	199	464	92,336	0.343	$32,864	$165
Acuity level 4	25	547	13,675	0.051	4,867	195
Observation	165	40	6,600	0.025	2,349	14
Observation	133	30	3,990	0.015	1,420	11
All others	211	200	42,200	0.157	15,020	71
Total			269,045	1.000	95,759	

Table 4. Calculations for Reciprocal Service Department Allocation

	Service Departments		Revenue Departments	
	IS	Housekeeping	OR	ER
Beginning balance	100,000	60,000	0	0
IS allocation (100,000)	10,000[1]	50,000[2]	40,000[3]	
Balance after allocation	*0*	*70,000*	*50,000*	*40,000*
Housekeeping allocation	21,000[4]	(70,000)	28,000[5]	21,000[6]
Balance after allocation	*21,000*	*0*	*78,000*	*61,000*
2nd IS allocation	(21,000)	2,10	10,500	8,400
Balance after allocation	*0*	*2,10*	*88,500*	*69,400*
2nd housekeeping allocation	630	(2,100)	840	630
Balance after allocation	*630*	*0*	*89,340*	*70,030*
3rd IS allocation	(630)	63	315	252
Balance after allocation	*0*	*63*	*89,655*	*70,282*
3rd housekeeping allocation	19	(63)	25	19
Balance after allocation	*19*	*0*	*89,680*	*70,301*
Transfer minimal balances	(19)	0	10	9
Ending balance	*0*	*0*	*89,690*	*70,310*

[1]$100,000 * 10%   [3]$100,000 * 40%   [5]$70,000 * 40%

[2]$100,000 * 50%   [4]$70,000 * 30%   [6]$70,000 * 30%

Table 5. Brookwood Medical Center, Education Allocation to Emergency Room

Allocation base: paid hours
Budget -- $500,000

Department	Paid Hours	Percentage of paid hours by department	Amount allocated
Pain Management	2,083	?	?
Diabetic Services	8,993	?	?
Emergency Room	124,212	?	?
Monitoring Services	40,634	?	?
Quality Assurance	21,314	?	?
Dietary	167,411	?	?
Collections	13,650	0.279320	$1,396.60
Outpatient Registration	19,776	0.404677	$2,023.39
All others	4,488,783	91.854210	$459,271.05
Total	4,886,856	100.00%	$500,000.00

REASONABLE JOINT COST ALLOCATIONS IN NONPROFITS

Questions about the accuracy and reliability of nonprofits' financial statements have led to increased awareness of joint allocation.

By Dennis P. Tishlias

There is growing concern on the part of states' attorneys general that some charitable organizations have been "too liberal" in allocating costs to program expenses (instead of to administration or fund-raising), particularly costs to educate the public. Without objective guidelines, auditors have difficulty determining the reasonableness of nonprofit organizations' joint cost allocations.

Joint cost allocations can have a serious impact on the evaluation of how responsibly a nonprofit social service organization is run. This gave rise to American Institute of CPAs Statement of Position no. 87-2, *Accounting for Joint Costs of Informational Materials and Activities of Not-for-Profit Organizations That Include a Fund-Raising Appeal*, which amended SOP no. 78-10, *Accounting Principles and Reporting Practices for Certain Nonprofit Organizations*, and the AICPA *Audits of Voluntary Health and Welfare Organizations.*

Questions about the accuracy and reliability of data in a nonprofit's financial statement led to increased awareness of joint cost allocation problems. In a notice to members the AICPA said auditors should "carefully review the requirements of SOP no. 87-2 and consider the sufficiency of evidence supporting any allocation of joint costs."

The article's purpose is to explore the bounds of reasonable allocations and offer some equitable solutions to achieve cost sharing within these boundaries.

ALLOCATION ISSUES

Current auditing and accounting standards fail to provide auditors with objectives for evaluating the reasonableness of joint cost allocations. For nonprofits, standards defining reasonableness are based on the relative amounts of money spent on programs versus fund-raising or administration. Reasonableness in cost allocations is crucial; it is directly linked to determining a nonprofit's use of voluntarily contributed funds.

SOP no. 87-2 offers guidance to auditors in deciding when joint cost allocations are appropriate. What is not specified is how allocations should be made. As SOP no. 87-2 says, there are many possible cost allocation methods. These techniques generally are based on the fundamental assumption joint costs should be allocated in a reasonable and fair manner, recognizing the cause-and-effect relationship between the cost incurred and where the cost is allocated. However, the very nature of jointness precludes such an allocation.

When a cause-and-effect allocation is difficult, impractical or impossible to determine, judgment is used to determine the cost assigned to each segment. The principles outlined in the following example help define a range of reasonable allocations.

EXAMPLE OF COST ALLOCATION

One reason nonprofit organizations incur joint costs is the expectation fund-raising, administration and programs can be served simultaneously for less cost than if these goals were pursued separately. The allocation problem arises from the premise that each segment benefiting from a joint action should share in its cost.

Consider an organization with two programs, P1 and P2, and one fund-raising function, FR. Exhibit 1, below, provides data on these activities. The stand-alone cost of P1 is $40,000. The stand-alone costs of P2 and FR are $12,000 and $65,000, respectively, resulting in overall stand-alone costs of $117,000. If P1, P2 and FR act jointly, the total cost is $100,000, saving the organization $17,000.

Participants	Cost
P1	$40,000
P2	12,000
FR	65,000
P1,P2	44,200
P1,FR	88,200
P2,FR	75,000
P1,P2,FR	100,000

While the organization as a whole benefits from incurring joint costs, the managements of the two programs and fund-raising must voluntarily collaborate to obtain cost savings. If a segment's share of joint cost is expected to exceed its stand-alone cost, it has no incentive to act jointly. To motivate sharing or joint action, each segment's allocated share of joint cost must be no more than its stand-alone cost—the upper limit of joint cost a segment could reasonably be expected to absorb.

The lower limit should be no less than the incremental cost it adds to the total joint cost. As demonstrated in Exhibit 1, the incremental cost of having P1 join P2 and FR is $25,000, the difference between the P1, P2, FR cost ($100,000) and the joint cost of P2, FR ($75,000). This is the least amount P1 should absorb. Anything less represents a subsidy from P2, FR to P1.

The range of reasonable cost allocation assignable to P1 is a minimum of $25,000 and a maximum of the stand-alone cost of $40,000, also shown in Exhibit 1. For P2, the lower limit is $11,800, the $100,000 joint cost of P1, P2, FR minus the $88,200 joint cost of P1, FR. The upper limit is P2's stand-alone cost of $12,000. Likewise, the range for FR is $55,800 ($100,000 − $44,200) to FR's stand-alone cost of $65,000.

Finally, the total of joint costs allocated to all segments should not exceed the total joint cost to be allocated. Nor should any joint cost remain unallocated. In this example, the total of each segment's allocated cost must not be greater than or less than $100,000. While many possible allocation schemes can satisfy these constraints, only four are discussed below.

Method 1: Allocate on the basis of activity-based costs. An activity-based allocation is consistent with the cause-and-effect and the benefits-received criteria. It also provides a level of detail that can make the resulting allocations more defensible.

Activity-based accounting focuses on attaching costs to programs and fund-raising based on the activities performed to produce or support them. These costs are attached using cost drivers, which underlie actions or conditions that directly influence or create cost. For example, a joint mailing has at least four components (activities) of the joint cost—postage, printing, envelopes and handling. Each component can be allocated based on the cost driver for the particular activity.

An excellent basis for allocating postage is the incremental weight a program or fund-raising contributes to the mailing's weight. When the mailing's contents are particular to program and fund-raising, specific identification can be used to allocate printing costs. Since the mailing envelopes are shared, each segment is assigned one-third of their cost. Handling

EXECUTIVE SUMMARY

♦ THERE IS SOME CONCERN charitable organizations are too liberal in allocating costs to program expenses instead of to administration or fund-raising. Auditors have difficulty determining the reasonableness of these entities' joint cost allocation.

♦ IDEALLY, A REASONABLE and fair joint cost allocation should recognize the cause-and-effect relationship between the cost incurred and where it is allocated. When such an allocation is not possible, judgment must be used.

♦ MOST ORGANIZATIONS INCUR joint costs with the expectation that cost savings will result. If one segment's share of joint costs exceeds the cost of acting alone, that segment has no incentive to act jointly.

♦ FOUR METHODS of allocating joint costs include activity-based allocations, equal sharing of costs, cost allocated relative to stand-alone cost and cost allocated in proportion to cost savings.

♦ JOINT COST ALLOCATIONS in nonprofit organizations influence perceptions about how well the organizations are run. As a result, auditors must carefully evaluate the chosen cost allocation methods.

is allocated on the basis of the number of pieces put into each envelope.

Exhibit 2 shows an example of this approach. Panel 1 shows the proportions of each activity assignable to the three segments. Panel 2 shows the total assumed cost of each activity. Multiplying the proportions in panel 1 by each activity's cost leads to the allocations shown.

P2's initial allocation of $14,250 exceeds its $12,000 stand-alone cost, violating the upper limit guideline. Assuming this difference is due to handling costs, one solution is to allocate P2's excess stand-alone cost to P1 and FR in a 2-to-1 ratio, the resulting proportions after eliminating P2. This is shown in panel 3.

This new allocation results in P1 and FR absorbing more handling costs than they would have if P2 had not been part of the joint mailing. However, their total costs are still within the reasonable range. In fact, after absorbing the additional handling cost, P1 saves $6,250 ($40,000 − $33,750) from its stand-alone cost;

FR saves $10,750.

Method 2: Allocate equally. Many nonprofits do not have sufficiently sophisticated accounting systems to perform an activity-based allocation. Thus the resources required to gather the necessary data may not seem cost-effective. Under these conditions, management will tend to choose other allocation techniques.

One simple technique is to divide the total joint cost equally among the participants. Dividing the $100,000 total joint cost by three results in each segment receiving a $33,333 share. While P1 and FR's shares are less than their stand-alone costs, P2's share is more, exceeding its upper limit by $21,333. A solution is to charge P2 its $12,000 stand-alone cost and then allocate the $88,000 total cost balance equally to P1 and FR. The resulting allocation is $44,000 to P1, $12,000 to P2 and $44,000 to FR. Now P1's cost share exceeds its stand-alone cost by $4,000. This difference is assigned to FR. The final costs allocated are $40,000 to P1, $12,000 to P2 and

---

EXHIBIT 2
METHOD 1: ACTIVITY-BASED COST ALLOCATIONS

Panel 1

| Activity | Proportions | | | Total |
	P1	P2	FR	
Weight	30.00%	15.00%	55.00%	100%
Specific identification	30.50	9.50	60.00	100
Quantity of envelopes	33.33	33.33	33.33	100
Number of pieces in envelope	50.00	25.00	25.00	100

Panel 2

| Item | Assumed Total | Allocations | | |
		P1	P2	FR
Postage	$ 35,000	$10,500	$5,250	$19,250
Printing	50,000	15,250	4,750	30,000
Envelopes	6,000	2,000	2,000	2,000
Handling	9,000	4,500	2,250	2,250
Total	$100,000	$32,250	$14,250	$53,500

Panel 3

| Item | Assumed Total | Allocations | | |
		P1	P2	FR
Postage	$ 35,000	$10,500	$5,250	$19,250
Printing	50,000	15,250	4,750	30,000
Envelopes	6,000	2,000	2,000	2,000
Handling	9,000	6,000	0	3,000
Total	$100,000	$33,750	$12,000	$54,250

EXHIBIT 3
METHOD 4: ALLOCATION IN PROPORTION TO COST SAVINGS

	P1	P2	FR	Total
Stand-alone cost	$40,000	$12,000	$65,000	$117,000
Incremental cost (a)	25,000	11,800	55,800	92,600
Benefits	$15,000	$ 200	$ 9,200	$ 24,400
Proportion	61.48%	0.82%	37.70%	100%
Allocation (b)	$ 4,550	$ 60	$ 2,790	$ 7,400
Total (a + b)	$29,550	$11,860	$58,590	$100,000

$48,000 to FR.

The effect of this method is least costly segments benefit less, if at all, from participating in a joint effort than larger segments. This may be sufficient for cost measurement but could have at least two unintended effects. First, the method is based on an underlying assumption a segment's size is reflected in its cost and larger segments cause more cost savings than smaller segments. In voluntary nonprofits, cost may not reflect size since many inputs are contributed. Second, P1 and P2 are not motivated to participate with FR because no cost savings accrue to them.

Method 3: Allocate on the basis of standalone cost. This method, which ensures all participants benefit, allocates a joint effort's cost in proportion to the amount of cost that would have been incurred separately. P1's stand-alone cost is 34,188% ($40,000 ÷ $117,000) of the total stand-alone cost. Applying this rate to the $100,000 joint cost results in P1 being assigned $34,188. P2's and FR's stand-alone costs are 10.256% and 55.556%, respectively, resulting in $10,256 being assigned to P2 and $55,256 to FR. As in method 2, implicit in this method is the assumption the segment with the largest cost causes the biggest savings and thus should receive the largest benefit. Unlike method 2, it provides an incentive for all three participants to act jointly.

Method 4: Allocate in proportion to cost savings. An allocation method that reflects benefits received from the group effort is one that allocates joint costs in direct proportion to segment's actual cost savings. Exhibit 3, above, shows the proportionate savings (benefits from participating in the group effort) as the difference between a segment's stand-alone cost and its incremental cost of joining the group.

Exhibit 1 shows the joint cost of P2 and FR acting together is $75,000. Adding P1 to P2, FR changes the total joint cost to $100,000, a $25,000 incremental increase. Comparing P1's incremental cost to its

$40,000 stand-alone cost results in a $15,000 benefit to P1 if it joins P2, FR. Continuing with this logic, if P2 joins P1, FR, the difference between its stand-alone cost and its related incremental cost is $200. If FR joins P1, P2, its benefit is $9,200.

These benefits provide a basis for allocating the cost savings of acting together. That is, given the sum of the incremental costs, $92,600 for all participants, and a joint cost of $100,000, the benefit to be allocated is the difference, $7,400. Allocating this amount based on the proportion of benefit received results in P1 being assigned $4,550 (61.48% × $7,400). The 61.48% is found by dividing $15,000 by $24,400. P2 receives $60 (0.82% × $7,400) and FR receives $2,790 (37.70% × $7,400). Each segment's allocation of benefits plus its incremental cost is the share of the joint cost assigned to it.

REASONABLE AND FAIR ALLOCATION

Joint cost allocations in nonprofit organizations can influence perceptions of organizational stewardship. Because of this, it is incumbent on auditors to evaluate carefully the application of SOP no. 87-2 and the cost-allocation methods chosen, ensuring these allocations are reasonable and fair.

While the above allocations do not cover all circumstances, they provide insight on the effects of different allocation assumptions on measurements of program and fund-raising costs and provide some guidance in evaluating a nonprofit's allocations. Perhaps this will suggest other ways of evaluating reasonableness in cost allocation.

To improve implementation of SOP no. 87-2, the AICPA accounting standards executive committee has authorized the not-for-profit organizations committee to undertake a project to draft guidance in the form of an SOP clarifying or perhaps revising certain aspects of SOP no. 87-2.

MANAGING SHARED SERVICES WITH ABM

By Ann Triplett and Jon Scheumann

Shared service operations combine the efficiency and leverage of centralization (standardization, economies of scale, and a single base for improvement) with the superior customer service usually associated with decentralization.

Companies try to achieve this balance by drawing together activities performed similarly in various locations across the business (often focusing on transaction processes), standardizing on a common process design that emphasizes high quality and customer responsiveness, and putting in place measurement tools to monitor performance and guide improvement efforts.

Companies choose shared services for various reasons, but lower costs are a primary benefit, as are improvements in productivity and customer service. In addition, some companies see shared services as a platform for growing their business without growing administrative costs at the same rate.

Ford has been operating a shared services center (SSC) for finance in Europe since the early 1980s, and DuPont, Digital Equipment, and General Electric established shared services organizations in the United States in the late 1980s. A second wave of companies, including Hewlett-Packard, Dow Chemical, Dun & Bradstreet, IBM, and Allied Signal, followed that lead in the early 1990s, and today many of the top 500 companies in the United States have implemented some form of shared services.

Regardless of the services they provide—Payroll, Payables, Receivables, Fixed Asset Accounting, etc.—all SSCs are faced with the same three cost-related questions:

- What causes costs in our operation, and how can we manage them?
- How do we determine how much to charge each customer for the services we provide?
- How do our costs compare to those of others, in particular the costs of outsourcers who can provide the same services?

SSC managers are discovering that activity-based management (ABM) can be used to create a framework that provides the cost information required to answer these questions. Gunn Partners found that 16% of the service centers in its 1999 Global Shared Services Research project have completed their ABM implementation. But even more interesting is that 30% of the companies are in the process of implementing ABM, and an additional 21% expect to implement within the next three years. This means that by the end of 2002 nearly 70% of the research companies will have implemented ABM. These results clearly show the expected use of ABM as an important management tool.

HOW DO WE MANAGE SSC COSTS?

Critical to the success of any shared service center is a thorough understanding of costs and the ability to impact those costs. After all, most SSCs were founded on the premise of saving money for the corporation. Cost management is key—possibly more so than for any other part of the business. SSC managers must understand what activities are performed and how each activity contributes to total cost. They need to understand the drivers of cost—especially the drivers that are completely under their control. For example, an internal driver might be the number of internal approval levels required for a particular transaction.

A methodology to identify and evaluate the potential of improvement opportunities, on an ongoing basis, also should be in place. In operating shared service centers, managers strive to continually reduce the cost for existing services and to free resources for providing other services that customers may want. This information has to be developed and maintained with minimum complexity and cost.

In recent years, many companies have learned that an activity-based model of operations provides all of the information required to effectively understand and manage costs. Through use of this ABM model on an ongoing basis, they manage the business and answer the first question, "What causes costs in our operation, and how can we manage them?"

The success of an SSC depends on cost management, but the ability to understand how customer requirements, actions, and demands for various types of services drive costs also is critical. It's absolutely necessary for managers to identify which activities are required to provide specific services and understand the external drivers of SSC cost—that is, those factors controlled by customers. The percentage of errors in customer-provided information is an example of an external driver. From this cost information, service prices can be developed, and a center should be able to develop and maintain the information with minimum complexity and cost.

If you need to explain cost information to customers, what language do you use? Answer: The activity-based model of operations can be used and expanded with the information required to determine the cost of providing each service. This process, known as service level costing, involves identifying the activities and costs associated with providing services, using that information to support discussions with customers, and then providing the level of service for which each customer is willing to pay. Customers can relate to this language when you discuss costs in terms of how they are caused by activities.

It's also possible, with additional detail, to establish differential pricing, that is, to charge customers different prices for the same service. These prices can be determined by identifying the specific impact that each customer has on cost, based on behavior as measured by cost drivers. A model to support differential pricing takes more time to develop and is larger and more complex to maintain, but some SSCs feel that it's worth the effort.

For many SSCs, service level costing supports the actual charge-out of appropriate costs to customers based on the types of services they receive. For SSCs whose cost is absorbed at a corporate level, the information is equally valuable and can be used to justify and explain decisions made about the services that will be provided. Approximately 60% of corporations who have implemented shared services charge out shared service costs, according to Gunn Partners research.

Furthermore, the research has shown that charging customers a differential rate based on ease or complexity of the transaction hasn't led to a position of cost or productivity leadership. While charging differential rates in an attempt to influence behaviors is emotionally appealing to the SSC leadership, this isn't yet a leading practice according to the data.

Ideally, a shared service center should regularly compare its cost of providing a service to the cost at which others can provide the service. But this isn't always easily accomplished. In some cases, a center can compare service costs with others in a group benchmarking study. For some services it may be possible to obtain information about how much an outsourcing provider would charge.

Here, again, the activity-based model of operations can provide the required information. The cen-
ter's cost per output of a service is often the piece of information required to benchmark. It's also important to know whether this cost has increased or decreased over time, and a well-maintained model will facilitate this comparison.

One of the challenges is to ensure a valid comparison; the model provides detailed information about which activities are required to provide any given service. Activity costs can be combined in varying ways, if necessary, to arrive at an "apples to apples" comparison for benchmarking.

HOW DO YOU DEVELOP AN ACTIVITY BASED FRAMEWORK?

Companies go through three phases in the development of an activity-based framework to support a shared service center:

- Initial model building effort,
- Customer education and service-level review process, and
- Ongoing maintenance and use of the activity-based framework.

Typically, an ABM modeling software package is used to ensure that the SSC model can be easily sustained over time.

INITIAL MODEL BUILDING

The steps in this phase, illustrated in Figure 1, are those traditionally required to build an activity-based model. Actual implementation of this phase should begin with a much more detailed work plan.

These steps encompass all of the effort required to gather activity and cost information, define the relationships among activities, costs, and services provided, then build the information and relationships into a model. The amount of time it takes to do this will vary according to a number of factors including, but not limited to, resource commitment, size, and scope of center to be modeled, project leadership, and prior experience with ABM.

CUSTOMER EDUCATION AND SERVICE LEVEL REVIEWS

Once the model has been built, the center can begin to use the information to communicate with customers. Typically, the first step in this process is for the center to develop a proposed Service Level Agreement (SLA) for each customer. This document consists of information about which services are being provided, the activity-based cost of each service, and historical information about past service levels. The proposed SLA is the starting point for discussions with your clients.

The client reviews should begin with an introduction to the basic concepts of ABM. Accordingly, initial customer education is critical to the successful, ongoing use of an ABM framework. The rest of the session is spent reviewing the services provided, the level of service provided in the past, the basis for costing, and the actual cost of each service.

The detailed information about the activities required to provide each service should be available but used only if the additional detail is necessary. As each service is reviewed, determine whether or not that service will be provided in the future and, if so, at what level. Remember that the types of services, as described above, will impact these reviews. Some of the services are required for all customers, and others are provided based on customer needs and requirements.

Based on the results from each customer negotiating session, the center can prepare a final SLA for signature. Details about how required information will be gathered and reported over time should be included (for example, number of occurrences). The center should also cover agreements about how billing will be accomplished, whether review is allowed periodically, and so on.

ONGOING MAINTENANCE AND USE

A completed and signed SLA doesn't signify the end of the process, but rather the beginning of an ongoing mutually beneficial relationship between a service center and customer. The three key elements of the ongoing process are:

- Continuous improvement efforts,
- SLA maintenance, and
- Benchmarking.

All of these are linked through the ongoing maintenance of the original ABM model, as illustrated in Figure 2.

Continuous improvement efforts, especially with customer participation, can result in lower costs of services to be incorporated in each ensuing SLA. Information about service cost and customer requirements can support benchmarking efforts. Comparisons can be internal, as in customer to customer, or external comparison can be made to the cost of other service centers or outsourcing service providers. Benchmarking results, in turn, can provide ideas and goals for continuous improvement efforts.

Our work with many clients has demonstrated that a service center goes through three phases during its creation: *installation* (the "birth" of a center), *start-up* (the period of bringing a new center under control), and *steady state* (the ongoing movement into a mode

of continuous improvement). It's in the last of these phases that the benefits of ABM can be realized. In earlier phases, activities aren't necessarily well defined, and processes aren't stable. The priorities of a center, then, should be more basic. Each center's situation is unique, and some may move through the phases more quickly than others. A general rule of thumb for when to consider implementing ABM is the second to fourth year of a center's existence.

And you can achieve impressive results by using an activity-based framework to manage a shared service center. First, it supports a new way of management. The activity-based cost model provides a more effective means of managing service center operations than can traditional cost statements and cost accounting analyses.

Service level costing results in more satisfied customers because they understand and have impacted exactly what services they will receive for their payments.

An improved understanding of costs and drivers by both service center providers and customers can result in a lower total cost to the corporation as a whole. Finally, this effort can provide an improved ability to assess outsourcing, or even insourcing, opportunities. A thorough understanding of processes, activities, and costs results in the information required to make cost-effective and correct decisions.

As a point of reference, the Gunn Partners research data show that the leaders in cost and productivity are more likely to be using ABM as a management tool than their peers. But these leaders almost certainly would tell you it isn't a simple exercise and isn't a "project" to be done once and forgotten. The adoption of an activity-based framework for an SSC requires an ongoing commitment. Your rewards, though, will be great!

FIGURE 1

PROCESS MAPPING AND ACTIVITY IDENTIFICATION

What are the activities performed, and how are they linked together via inputs and outputs?

ACTIVITY AND COST INFORMATION COLLECTION

How much time is spent on various activities? What are the resulting levels of output? Is current cost information readily available?

ACITIVITY COSTING

Which activities caused which costs to occur? What, then, is each activity's cost?

SERVICE INDENTIFICATION

What are the services provided from the customer's viewpoint, and how much differentiation will be required to support fair costing?

SERVICE COSTING

Which services, for which customers, required us to perform which activities? On what basis will each service be charged out?

FIGURE 2

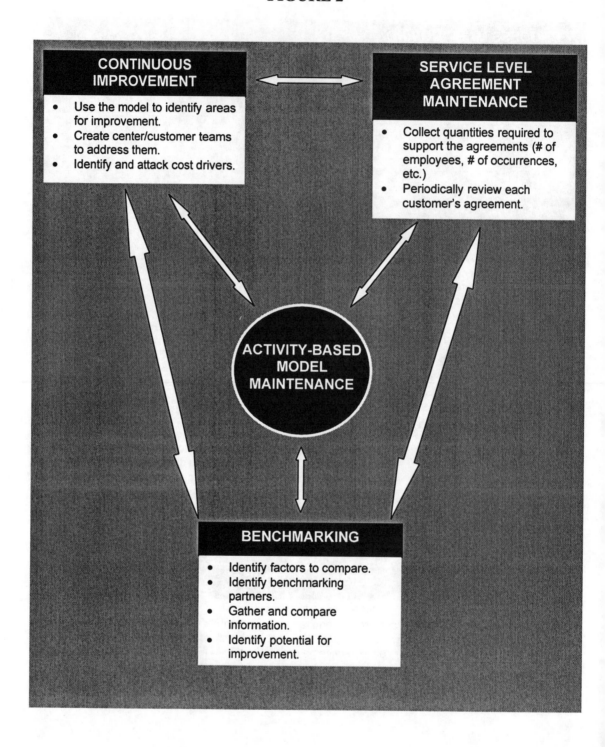

Chapter 15
The Flexible Budget And Standard Costing: Direct Materials And Direct Labor

Cases
15-1   Hoof and Fin Restaurants

Readings

"Standard Costing Is Alive And Well At Parker Brass"
The Brass Products Division of the Parker Hannifin Corporation is a world-class manufacturer of tube and brass fittings, valves, hose, and hose fittings. Despite the introduction of popular new costing systems, the Brass Product Division operates a well-functioning standard costing system.

Discussion Questions:
1. What features in the firm's standard costing that make it a success?
2. In addition to variances seen in the textbook Parker Brass created several new variances. Describe these variances. Why are these variance added at Parker Brass?

"Management Control systems: How SPC enhances Budgeting and Standard Costing"
This article examines some of the effects that statistical process control (SPC) with a standard costing system and standard cost analysis has on management control system. When used properly, SPC can help companies measure how well their processes are working and figure out how to motivate employees to achieve desired targets.

Discussion Questions:
1. What is a statistical process control chart? Why a process must be in statistical control before anyone can attempt process improvement?
2. What is "voice of the customer" and "voice of the process"? Why is that management's action should be guided by the voice of the process, not the voice of the customer?

"Redesigning Cost Systems: Is Standard Costing Obsolete?"
The article shows some new ways to analyze standard cost data, going beyond the traditional emphasis on production costs variances that focus on price and efficiency. Variances for product quality are developed and explained, as well as sales variances based on sales orders received and orders actually shipped. There is also a discussion of how to incorporate activity-based costing, and continuous standard improvement, including benchmarking and target costing.

The main premise of the article is that standard cost systems are the most common cost systems in use, and while there are a number of limitations to these systems, a careful and creative effort can transform them into more useful cost systems.

Discussion Questions:
1. What are the main criticisms of traditional standard cost systems?
2. What is meant by "push through" production? Is it preferred to "pull through" production, and why?
3. What are the best ways to make standard cost systems more dynamic?
4. Considering the suggestions make in this article, in contrast to the chapter presentation of standard costing, which ideas make the most sense to you and why?

15-1. Hoof and Fin Restaurants

David Green is considering his operating report for the most recent year. David is a restaurant manager for one of the 20 restaurants owned and operated by Hoof and Fin, Inc. The first Hoof and Fin restaurant was opened in Austin Texas almost 40 years ago, but has since grown to a 20-location chain throughout the major cities in Texas. The owner, Roger Nisbett, owns most of the stock in the company, which went public 16 years ago to finance the growth of the company. David has been working for Hoof and Fin for 6 years, first as an assistant manager, and currently as the manager for the restaurant located in Waco, Texas. This year is his first year as a manager.

The principal attraction for the restaurant, and the basis for its success, is that diners can select from either a steak menu or a seafood menu, and in each case the prices are very low relative to most restaurants in the area. The menu and restaurant décor is designed to appeal to budget-conscious diners, such as college students. Each of the 20 restaurants is successful, though some more so than others.

Each manager is evaluated on his or her performance relative to a budget set at the beginning of the year. The budget is set by Marv Gregson, chief financial officer for the company, who looks at trends for each of the locations and sets a budget for each location based on past sales and desired future sales and earnings goals for the company. Each manager participates in the budget setting process to a degree, though each manager is quite aware that Marv will have the last say in the determination of the final budget. Each manager is told that a significant bonus is in order for managers whose profit exceeds the budget, and the amount of the bonus will be determined from the amount of the difference from budget. In prior years, managers who have exceeded their budgets by more than 10% have gotten a bonus equal to 20% of the improvement over budget. For some managers this has been a significant monetary reward. For those who do not meet the budget, there is no bonus, but constructive counseling about what can be done to improve performance in the coming year.

David is an ambitious and hard working manager, who has applied himself to the job and has looked for different ways to attract customers and to reduce costs. For example, he has noticed the trend for more customers to prefer the seafood menu, and he has added more selections to that portion of the menu. While the number of steak dinners has fallen slightly, the sales of seafood dinners has increased substantially as a result. Moreover, because of the increased interest in seafood, and because of the increased quality and variety of his seafood offerings, he has been able to increase the average price of his seafood dinners.

Now that the results are in for 2001, it is time for the annual review and bonus determination with Mr. Gregson.

REQUIRED:

You are to play the role of David Green, and develop an analysis and a one-half page memo to Mr. Gregson which explains your performance for the year ended December 31, 2001.

Hoof and Fin Restaurant
Operating Statement

Year Ended Dec. 31, 2001

	Actual	Budget
Gross Sales	$1,811,160	$1,664,000
Net Sales	1,587,560	1,612,000
Less Variable Expenses		
Food	724,350	676,000
Labor	484,688	500,000
Operating Expenses	74,550	83,200
Total Variable Expenses	1,283,588	1,259,200
Net contribution	303,973	352,800
Other Expenses		
Advertising	83,450	83,200
Misc.	3,200	2,000
Depreciation	33,000	33,000
Insurance	7,960	8,800
Taxes	9,220	6,500
Interest	49,000	49,000
Management	84,000	84,000
Total Other Expenses	269,830	266,500
Profit	$34,143	$86,300
Other Data		
Average no. of customers/wk	4,300	4,000
Steak dinners %	40%	50%
Seafood dinners %	60%	50%
Average price for dinner (before discount)		
Steak dinner	$9.00	$9.00
Seafood dinner	$7.50	$7.00
Average discount (both dinners)	$1.00	$0.25
Number of employees	25	25
Hours worked, all employees	2,350	2,500
Wage rate for employees	$8.25	$8.00

Notes about the Operating Statement:

1. Food, labor and operating expenses are considered variable costs, under the control of the restaurant manager.

2. Food costs, the largest element of total costs, are budgeted at $3.50 per meal for steak dinners and $3.00 for seafood dinners. All food items are purchased centrally and delivered to each restaurant daily. Due to David's diligence, he was able to save $.08 per meal by substituting food items of equal value for those of higher cost. As a result, David was able to achieve food usage (at standard prices) of $3.42 and $2.92 for steak and seafood dinners, respectively.

3. Each restaurant manager had control over the hiring, firing and wage rates for their employees, and for the number of hours worked.

4. Operating expenses included maintenance, supplies, bags and boxes for take-aways, and miscellaneous other expenses. These were controllable by each restaurant.

5. Advertising expenses were controlled at the home office and allocated to the 20 restaurants based on a % of actual sales at each location. The budget was based on 5% of gross sales.

6. Miscellaneous expenses were a category for a variety of home office expenses, which were allocated to each restaurant on an equal share basis.

7. Depreciation expense was determined for each store based on a straight-line depreciation of that restaurant's building and equipment costs.

8. Insurance, taxes, licenses, interest, and other corporate costs were allocated to each restaurant based on the net book value of the building and equipment at each restaurant.

9. Management costs consisted of the base salary of the restaurant manager and assistant manager, plus and allocated portion of home office management costs, including legal, accounting, and other corporate management costs.

STANDARD COSTING IS ALIVE AND WELL AT PARKER BRASS

By David Johnsen and Parvez Sopariwala, Ph.D.

Many people have condemned standard costing, saying it is irrelevant to the current just-in-time based, fast-paced business environment. Yet surveys consistently show that most industrial companies in the United States and abroad[1] still use it. Apparently, these companies have successfully adapted their standard costing systems to their particular business environments. In addition, many academics have contributed ideas on how the standard costing system could be and has been made more responsive to the needs of companies operating in this new economy.[2]

The Brass Products Division at Parker Hannifin Corporation (hereafter, Parker Brass), a world-class manufacturer of tube and brass fittings, valves, hose and hose fittings, is one of the standard costing success stories. It operates a well-functioning standard costing system of which we will show you some highlights.

WHAT'S SPECIAL ABOUT THE STANDARD COSTING SYSTEM AT PARKER BRASS?

Parker Brass uses its standard costing system and variance analyses as important business tools to target problem areas so it can develop solutions for continuous improvement. Here are some examples of these standard costing-related tools:

- **Disaggregated product line information.** Parker Brass has been divided into Focus Business Units (FBUs) along product lines. Earnings statements are developed for each FBU, and variances are shown as a percentage of sales. If production variances exceed 5% of sales, the FBU managers are required to provide an explanation for the variances and to put together a plan of action to correct the detected problems. To help the process, a plant accountant has been assigned to each FBU. As a result of these steps,

each unit is able to take a much more proactive approach to variance analysis.

- **Timely product cost information.** In the past, variances were reported only at month-end, but often a particular job already would have been off the shop floor for three or more weeks. Hence, when management questioned the variances, it was too late to review the job. Now exception reports are generated the day after a job is closed (in other words, the day after the last part has been manufactured). Any jobs with variances greater than $1,000 are displayed on this report. These reports are distributed to the managers, planners or schedulers, and plant accountants, which permits people to ask questions while the job is still fresh in everyone's mind.

- **Timely corrective action.** Because each job is costed (in other words, transferred out of Work-in-Process and into Finished Goods) 10 days after the job has closed, there is adequate time for necessary corrective action. For example, investigating a large material quantity variance might reveal that certain defective finished parts were not included in the final tally of finished parts. Such timely information would allow management to decide whether to rework these parts or to increase the size of the next job. This kind of corrective action was not possible when variances were provided at the end of each month.

- **An effective control system.** Summary reports are run weekly, beginning the second week of each month, to show each variance in total dollars as well as each variance by product line and each batch within the product line. In addition, at the end of each month, the database is updated with all variance-related information. As a result, FBU managers can review variances by part number, by job, or by high dollar volume.

- Employee training and empowerment. Meetings are held with the hourly employees to explain variances and earnings statements for their FBU, thereby creating a more positive atmosphere in which the FBU team can work. These meetings help employees understand that management decisions are based on the numbers discussed and that if erroneous data are put into the system, then erroneous decisions may be made. For example, a machine may not be running efficiently. An operator may clock off of the job so that his or her efficiency does not look bad. Because the machine's efficiency is not adversely impacted, no maintenance is done to that machine, and the inefficiency continues. In addition, because the operator is not charging his/her cost to a job, the cost is being included in indirect labor, and manufacturing costs increase. If the operator had reported the hours correctly, management would have questioned the problem, and the machine would have been fixed or replaced based on how severe the problems were.

WHAT NEW VARIANCES HAS PARKER BRASS DESIGNED?

In addition to the aforementioned innovations that Parker Brass has made to adapt its standard costing system to its particular business environment, the company has created the following new variances:

- The standard run quantity variance to explain situations where the size of a lot is less than the optimal batch quantity.
- The material substitution variance to evaluate the feasibility of alternative raw materials.
- The method variance to assess situations where different machines can be used for the same job.

FIGURE 1

PANEL A: THE FACTS

Standard production in 1 hour (units)	50
Standard batch quantity (units)	2,000
Standard hours needed for 2,000 units	40
Standard time needed for 1 setup (hours)	4
Standard labor rate per hour	$10
Actual quantity produced (units)	1,200
Actual setup hours for 1 setup	4
Actual productive labor hours to make 1,200 units	24
Actual labor cost for 28 hours at $10 per hour	$280

PANEL B: WORKINGS

	Setups	Production	Total
Standard time per unit:			
Standard setup time (hours)	4		
Standard production time (hours)		40	
Standard batch size (units)	2,000	2,000	
Hence, standard time per unit (hours)	0.002	0.020	0.022
Standard time charged for 1,200 units:			
Standard time per unit (hours)	0.002	0.020	0.022
# of units actually produced	1,200	1,200	1,200
Standard time charged (hours)	2.40	24.00	26.40

PANEL C: SOLUTION

If SRQV is determined, the journal entry would be:

Work in process [(26.40)($10)]	$264	
SRQV [(4.00 - 2.40)($10)]	$16	
Accrued payroll		$280

If SRQV is not determined, the journal entry would be:

Work in process [(26.40)($10)]	$264	
LEV [{28.00 - (1 .200)(0.022)}{$10}]	$16	
Accrued payroll		$280

FIGURE 2

PANEL A: THE FACTS

Standard price per pound of material MI	$10
Standard price per pound of material M2	$11
Standard material quantity (MI & M2) to make 100 units (lbs.)	2
Actual quantity produced (units)	2,000
Actual pounds of M2 purchased and used	43

PANEL B: WORKINGS

Standard quantity to produce 2,000 units:	
Standard material quantity to make 100 units (lbs.)	2
Actual quantity produced (units)	2.000
Hence, standard quantity to produce 2,000 units	40

PANEL C: SOLUTION

If MSV is determined, the journal entry would be:

Work in process [(40.00)($10)]	$400	
MEV [(43.00 - 40.00)($11)]	$33	
MSV [(40.00)($11 - $10)]	$40	
Material—M2 [(43.00)($11)1		$473

If MSV is not determined, the journal entry might be:

Work in process [(40.00)($11)]	$440	
MEV [(43.00 - 40.00)($11)]	$33	
Material—M2 [(43.00)($11)]		$473

THE STANDARD RUN QUANTITY VARIANCE

The standard run quantity variance (SRQV) represents the amount of setup cost that was not recovered because the batch size was smaller than the earlier determined optimal batch size. Because setup costs are included in the standard labor hours for a batch, producing a smaller quantity per batch than the standard batch quantity is likely to create an unfavorable labor efficiency variance (LEV). Unless, however, the impact of actual production inefficiencies is separated from setup-related inefficiencies, the LEV reflects the combined impact of these two causes of inefficiencies and is not really useful for taking the necessary corrective action.

See Figure 1 for an illustration of this issue. Panel A shows that standard batch quantity is 2,000 units, the standard production during one hour is 50 units, and, hence, 40 standard hours are needed to produce 2,000 units. In addition, it takes four standard and actual hours to set up one batch. Panel B reveals that standard hours for setup and production labor are 0.002 and 0.020 per unit, respectively, for a total of 0.022 per unit. In addition, because actual quantity produced is 1,200 units, the total standard hours chargeable to these 1,200 units is 26.40 [(0.002 + 0.020)(1,200)].

Finally, Panel C shows the recommended journal entry whereby an SRQV is created. This SRQV represents the unrecovered setup costs because 1,200 units were manufactured instead of the standard batch quantity of 2,000 units. Thus, because the company expected to spend $40 [(4 hours)($10 per hour)] on each setup, the setup cost relating to the 800 (2,000 - 1,200) units not produced, or $16 U, is considered an unfavorable SRQV or the cost of producing small lots. On the other hand, using traditional standard costing, this amount of $16 U would most likely have been categorized as an LEV. Yet there really is no LEV,[3] and the variance of $16 U attributed to labor efficiency is merely the unabsorbed portion of the setup cost attributable to the 800 units that were not produced.

The advantages of extracting the standard run quantity variance are many. First, the SRQV ordinarily would be included in the LEV and could provide a misleading impression of labor's efficiency. Second, because just-in-time practices recommend smaller lots and minimal finished goods inventory the SRQV is essentially the cost of adopting JIT Third, to the extent that setup cost and the cost of carrying inventory are competing undesirables, a determination of the cost of small lots could be used in the trade-off analysis against the cost of holding and carrying inventories. Finally, to the extent that this variance can be separated for each customer, it would reveal how much of a loss was suffered by allowing that customer to purchase in small lots. Such information could be used in future bids. If a customer's schedule required a smaller lot, then that customer's job cost could be enhanced appropriately.

THE MATERIAL SUBSTITUTION VARIANCE

The material substitution variance (MSV) assumes perfect or near perfect substitutability of raw materials and measures the loss or gain in material costs when a different raw material is substituted for the material designated in the job sheet. Substitutions may be made for many reasons. For example, the designated material may not be available or may not be available in small-enough quantities, or the company may want to use up material it purchased for a product that it has since discontinued.

The usefulness of MSV is discussed in Figure 2. Panel A shows that both materials, M1 and M2, can be used to manufacture a product, and it is assumed that two pounds is the standard input per unit for both materials. Material M1 is the material designated in the job sheet, but material M2 can be substituted for M1. The standard cost of M2 ($11 per lb.) is higher than that for M1 ($10 per lb.), and M2 is used because M1 is currently not available and a valued customer needs a rush job.[4] Panel B reveals that the standard quantity needed to manufacture 2,000 units is 40 lbs.

For the purposes of this illustration, we assume that material price variance (MPV) is detected when material is purchased (in other words, the material account is maintained at standard cost). Hence, Panel C reveals the recommended journal entry whereby MSV is created. The MSV represents the benefit obtained by substituting a more expensive material (M2) for the less expensive material (M1) and hence represents the loss through substitution. The MSV is $40 U because (1) 40 lbs. is the standard quantity of M1 and M2 needed to manufacture 2,000 units, and (2) M2 costs $1 more per lb. than M1. In addition, the material efficiency variance (MEV) is $33 U because 43 lbs. instead of the standard quantity of 40 lbs. were used to manufacture 2,000 units.

In contrast, the traditional standard costing system might ignore the substitution, and the job might be charged with the standard cost of using 40 lbs. of M2. In that scenario, the job would cost $40 more and could have an impact on customer profitability analysis even though the customer did not request the substitution.

Now Parker Brass is evaluating an extension that would be to relax the simplifying assumption that both materials require the same standard input. See Figure

3. It adopts the facts from Figure 2 except that 1.9 lbs. of material M2 are required for 100 units instead of 2 lbs. for both materials in Figure 2. In this situation, we have two MSVs, one for the price impact called "MSV-Price" and the other for the efficiency impact, called "MSV-Efficiency."

Panel C shows the recommended journal entry whereby two MSV variances are created. First, MSV-Price is unfavorable because M2, a more expensive material, is being substituted for M1. As a result, MSV-Price is $40 U as material M2 costs $1 more per lb. than material M1. On the other hand, as you might expect, the MSV-Efficiency is favorable because only 1.9 lbs. of M2 are required to make 100 units as compared to 2 lbs. required for M1. Thus, MSV-

Effieiency is $22 F because each batch of 100 units requires 38 lbs. of M2 against 40 lbs. of M1. The net result of the MSV variances is $18 U [(38 lbs.)($11)- (40 lbs.)($10)], suggesting that, barring any other complications, the substitution of M2 for M1 is not likely to be profitable under existing circumstances.

Finally, the MEV using material M2 is $55 U, reflecting the fact that 43 lbs. of material M2 actually were used whereas only 38 lbs. of material M2 should have been used. This variance could have been

FIGURE 3

PANEL A: THE FACTS

Standard price per pound of material M1	$10
Standard price per pound of material M2	$11
Standard material quantity of M1 to make 100 units (lbs.)	2
Standard material quantity of M2 to make 100 units (lbs.)	1.9
Actual quantity produced (units)	2,000
Actual pounds of M2 used	43

PANEL B: WORKINGS

	Material M1	Material M2
Standard quantity to produce 2,000 units:		
Standard material quantity for 100 units (lbs.)	2	1.9
Actual quantity produced (units)	2,000	2,000
Hence, standard quantity to produce 2.000 units	40	38

PANEL C: SOLUTION

If MSV is determined, the journal entry would be:

Work in process [(40.00)($10)]	$400	
MEV [(43.00 - 38.00)($11)]	$ 55	
MSV-Price [(40.00)($11 - $10)]	$ 40	
MSV-Efficiency [(40.00 - 38.00)($11)]		$ 22
Material—M2 [(43.00)($11)]		$473

If MSV is not determined, the journal entry might be:

Work in process [(38.00)($11)]	$418	
MEV [(43.00 - 38.00)($11)]	$55	
Material—M2 [(43.00)($11)]		$473

caused because M2 was a new material and required initial learning and other nonrecurring costs. In such a case, the standard quantity of 38 lbs. for 2,000 units may not need to be changed. On the other hand, the MEV variance may have been caused because of the inherent difficulty in working with material M2. In such a case, the standard of 38 lbs. for 2,000 units may need to be amended. In contrast, as was shown in Panel C of Figure 2, the journal entry that is likely to be made using traditional standard costing would completely ignore the impact of material substitution and would likely inflate the cost of this particular job. The advantages of extracting the MSV are as follows. First, determining MSV lets the company assign the MSV cost to a customer whose rush job may have required using a more expensive material like M2. On the other hand, the MSV could be written off if the substitution were made to benefit the company. Also,

FIGURE 4

PANEL A: THE FACTS

Machine A: standard time needed for one unit (minutes)	1.0
Machine B: standard time needed for one unit (minutes)	1.2
Labor rate per hour	$20
Actual quantity produced (units)	1,800
Actual labor hours used to make 1,800 units using machine B	35
Actual labor cost	$700

PANEL B: WORKINGS

	Machine A	Machine B
Standard hours needed for 1.800 units on:		
Standard time needed for one unit (minutes)	1.0	1.2
Actual quantity produced (units)	1,800	1,800
Hence, the standard hours needed	30	36

PANEL C: SOLUTION

If method variance is determined, the journal entry would be:		
Work in process [(30.00)($20)]	$600	
Method variance [(36.00 - 30.00)($20)]	$120	
LEV [(36.00 - 35.00)($20)]		$ 20
Accrued Payroll		$700

If method variance is not determined, the journal entry might be:		
Work in process [(36.00)($20)]	$720	
LEV [(36.00 - 35.00)($20)]		$ 20
Accrued Payroll		$700

creating an MSV and breaking it up into its price and efficiency components allows the company to evaluate whether the substitution of M2 for M1 is a profitable one. While all these calculations can also be performed off the accounting system, creating the MSV makes the process a part of the system so a history of such evaluations is available for future reference.

METHOD VARIANCE

A method variance occurs when more than one machine can be used to manufacture a product.[5] For example, a plant may have newer machines that it normally would expect to use to manufacture a product, so its standards would be based on such new machines. Yet the same plant may also keep, as backups, older and less efficient machines that also could manufacture the same product but would require more inputs in the form of machine and/or labor hours. For this example, we assume that labor hours and machine hours have a 1:1 relationship.[6] As a result, the method variance becomes pertinent because the traditional LEV from operating the older machines could potentially include the following two impacts. First, an older machine may need additional labor hours to perform the same task, and the additional hours would be reflected in the LEV. Second, the LEV would include the workers' efficiency or lack thereof on the older machine.

We evaluate the usefulness of the method variance in Figure 4. Panel A shows that both machines, A and B, can be used to manufacture a product. Machine A is the more efficient machine and the one used for setting the standard time. Machine B is the backup. Panel B shows that the standard machine hours needed to produce 1,800 units are 30 on machine A and 36 on machine B, which can be compared to the 35 hours actually used to manufacture 1,800 units on machine B.

Panel C of Figure 4 reveals the recommended journal entry whereby a method variance is created. This method variance represents the loss incurred by substituting the backup machine B for machine A. Because machine B's standard of 36 labor hours is greater than machine A's standard of 30 hours, there is an unfavorable method variance of $120. On the other hand, because machine B took 35 hours to manufacture 1,800 units instead of its standard of 36 machine hours, there is a favorable LEV of $20. As you can see, while there was a loss incurred by using machine B instead of machine A, the actual usage of machine B was efficient. In contrast, assuming the traditional costing system recognizes that machine B was used, it is likely to charge the job $720 [(36 hours)($20 per hour)] instead of the $600 [(30

hours)($20 per hour)] that would have been charged if machine A had been used.

Here are the advantages of extracting the method variance. First, the impact of the method variance ordi-narily would be included in the LEV and would provide a misleading impression of labor's productivity. Second, the method variance could be used to isolate the additional cost that was incurred during the year by operating machine M2. This could permit a trade-off between purchasing a new machine and continuing to maintain the older machine, especially if tight delivery schedules are not the norm. Finally, the product cost would still be based on the standards for the more efficient new machine, and the job would not be charged a higher cost merely because a less efficient machine was used. That means a job that was completed on the older machine would not be penalized.[7]

RELEVANT, NOT IRRELEVANT

As you can see from the Parker Brass examples, standard costing has not become irrelevant in the new rapid-paced business environment. Parker Brass not only has managed to modify its standard costing system to achieve disaggregated and timely cost information for timely corrective action, but it has also designed additional variances to determine how setup time relating to small batches should be absorbed, whether an alternative raw material is economically feasible, and how a product's cost might reflect the use of alternate production facilities.

David Johnsen is cost accounting supervisor of the Brass Products Division at Parker Hannifin Corporation in Otsego, Mich. You can reach him at (616) 694-9411.

Parvez Sopariwala, Ph.D., is a professor in the Accounting and Taxation Department at Grand Valley State University in Allendale, Mich. You can reach him at (616) 895-2176 or sobariwp@gvsu.edu.

[1]   Studies reporting on the widespread use of standard costing in the U.S., the U.K., Ireland, Japan, and Sweden are summarized by Horngren, Foster, and Datar on page 225 of the 9th edition of their cost accounting text published by Prentice-Hall in 1997.

[2]   C. Cheatham, "Updating Standard Cost Systems," *Journal of Accountancy,* December 1990, pp. 57-60; C. Cheatham, "Reporting the Effects of Excess Inventories," *Journal of Accountancy,* November 1989, pp. 131-140; C. Cheatham and L.R. Cheatham, "Redesigning Cost Systems: Is Standard Costing Obsolete," *Accounting*

Horizons, December 1996, pp. 23-31; H. Harrell, "Materials Variance Analysis and JIT: A New Approach," *Management Accounting,* May 1992, pp. 33-38.

3   The standard production hours needed for 1,200 units were 24 [(1,200)(0.020)], whereas the actual labor hours used have been intentionally set at 24. In addition, the standard and actual labor hours for one setup have been intentionally set at four.

4   An alternative scenario could have the cost per pound of M2 ($9 per lb.) being lower than that for M1 ($10 per lb.) because M2 is used to manufacture other products as well and the company obtains quantity discounts for large purchases of M2.

5   To a limited extent, the rationale behind the method variance is similar to that for the material substitution variance (MSV) discussed earlier.

6   That is, the machine does not work independent of the worker. Hence, the labor hours spent on the machine are the same as the number of hours the machine was operated.

7   A similar reasoning is applied in situations wherein the routing for the manufacture of a product is amended during the year, possibly because the customer wants an additional processing step. In such a case, the resulting process variance could be charged to the customer.

MANAGEMENT CONTROL SYSTEMS: HOW SPC ENHANCES BUDGETING AND STANDARD COSTING

By Harper A. Roehm, CPA, DBA; Lary Weinstein, Ph.D.; and Joseph F. Castellano, Ph.D.

Organizations create processes and systems to achieve their mission and objectives. According to Harvard Professor Robert G. Eccles, control is a large factor in this achievement. He says, "Control is about creating conditions which will improve the probability that desirable outcomes (of the processes and systems) will be achieved." He adds: "A control system is comprised of (1) a set of measures for (2) defined entities, (3) criteria for evaluating these measures, and processes for (4) obtaining these measures and (5) the criteria for evaluating them."[1] Traditional standard costing and budgeting applications are consistent with his definition of a control system. Accounting numbers become the *set of measures* for an organizational unit, and predetermined standards and budgets represent the *criteria for evaluating these measures.*

Typically, management establishes accounting standards and budgets to provide some indication of what they expect from those individuals operating the system and to motivate people. Management compares accounting results to the predetermined standards and budgets and, where significant variances result, either rewards or punishes depending on the direction of the variance. The use of accounting information for this type of control implies that the information will provide an accurate representation of the capability of a process and that the process managers will have the ability and authority to control the components of the process. Consequently, the use of accounting targets makes it possible to motivate these individuals to manage the process more effectively and to measure their contribution and effectiveness.

Dr. W. Edwards Deming viewed businesses and their processes from a different perspective. He believed businesses are integrated systems—including both customers and suppliers—whose purpose is to delight their customers. Management is responsible for the system's components, which define its capability.[2] These components include selecting products, designing products, acquiring resources, designing production processes, hiring employees, managing all processes, and creating a culture in which creativity, innovation, and continuous improvement can flourish. The quality of a system's outputs is the results of the inputs, the components, and their interaction.

Through his association with Walter A. Shewart, a former Bell Telephone employee who developed statistical process control methods and was an originator of the quality movement, Deming came to believe that all processes have a measurable capability.[3] This capability can be predicted only when the process is *in control* or *stable*—when the random pattern of variation remains within the process's control limits. The process will not exhibit results beyond its measured capability without management changing one of its components.

Quality experts believe that it would be inappropriate to use accounting targets to control people and processes and to motivate employee behavior. They say the quality of the components and their interactions determines the process capability—not just the people operating the system. Deming believed that it was impossible to effectively measure an individual's contribution to a system because his or her contribution cannot be separated from the system's on him or her. Furthermore, we believe that neither budgeting nor standard accounting applications consider process capability and process variation.

The purpose of this article is to determine some of the effects that statistical process control (SPC) with a standard cost system and standard cost analysis has on management control systems. We present the following example to illustrate the connection between standard costing and statistical process control. First we will calculate labor efficiency variances using traditional accounting procedures. Next we will prepare an SPC chart from the same data we used to prepare the labor variances. Finally we will analyze the accounting variance data using the information from the chart.

Table 1: Production For 31 Days

	WEEK #1 Shifts		WEEK #2 Shifts		WEEK #3 Shifts		WEEK #4 Shifts		WEEK #5 Shifts	
	#1	#2	#1	#2	#1	#2	#1	#2	#1	#2
Monday	54	58	55	50	51	49	53	63	56	51
Tuesday	52	53	52	61	52	58	55	58	49	53
Wednesday	57	55	53	56	51	62	53	56	56	51
Thursday	59	54	55	49	57	61	49	53		
Friday	60	58	55	62	53	64	57	50		
Saturday	59	52	56	52	59	53	53	52		
Sunday	55	58	58	557	58	60	46	55		
Weekly Hourly Average	56.57	55.43	54.86	55.00	54.43	58.14	52.29	55.29	53.67	51.67

STANDARD COST EXAMPLE

J&J Inc. produces widgets during two shifts seven days a week. The production process was built with the expectations of producing 60 widgets an hour using 40 workers, working two 7 ½ hour shifts per day at a labor rate of $12 per hour. Because the expectation for the department is 60 widgets an hour and there are 40 workers, the expected average production per worker per hour is (60/40), or 1.5. The first 31 days yielded the average hourly results shown in Table 1.

Using the data from Table 1, we compute a labor efficiency variance for Monday of the first week, the first shift:

LABOR EFFICIENCY VARIANCE
Monday, First Week, First Shift

Actual Hours Worked: 7½ x 40 Workers	= 300
Units Produced: 54 x 7½ Hours	= 405
Standard Labor Hours Allowed for 405 Units: 405 Units / 1.5 Units per Worker, per Hour	= 270
Nonproductive Hours	30
Labor Rate	x $12
Unfavorable Labor Efficiency Variance	$360

This variance computation indicates that there were 30 nonproductive hours for the 40 workers, resulting in a $360 unfavorable labor efficiency variance. An examination of the data from Table 1 shows that the first shift was only able to meet expectations on Friday of the first week. The second shift appears to be more effective because it produced an hourly average of 60 widgets or more six times during the 31 days. Neither of the shifts, however, was able to average 60 widgets per hour for any week or for the 31 days. In other words, most accounting efficiency variances were unfavorable.

STATISTICAL PROCESS CONTROL CHART

Now let's look at statistical process control. The 62 data points shown in Figure 1[4] for the 31 days average 55 widgets per hour. The upper control limit (mean + three standard deviations) is 67.8 units; the lower control limit is 42.2.

In order to conclude that the process is in statistical control—that all variation present is due to random causes (often referred to as common cause variation)—the moving range must also be in statistical control. We used data from Table 1 to calculate 61 moving ranges that are plotted in Figure 2. Next, we will calculate control limits for a moving range chart.

Because all points for both the X chart (Figure 1) and the moving range chart fall within their respective upper and lower control limits with no other indications of nonrandom patterns, the process can be declared in statistical control. Processes in control are predictable and will produce parts within the upper and lower control limits of both charts. In this example, the process will produce an average of 55 units per

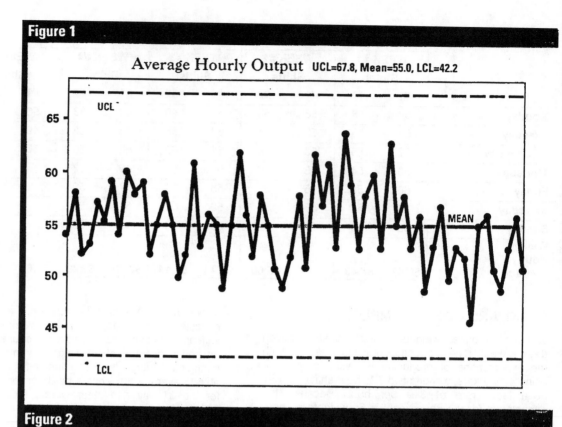

Average Hourly Output UCL=67.8, Mean=55.0, LCL=42.2

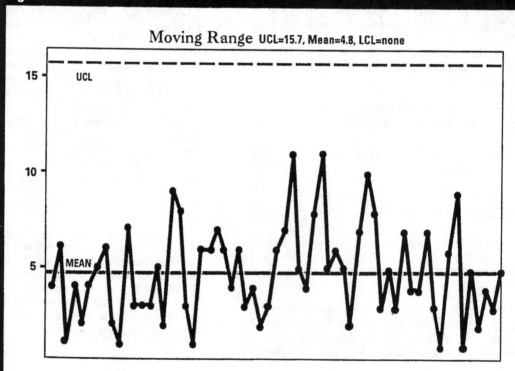

Moving Range UCL=15.7, Mean=4.8, LCL=none

hour, but, for any specific hour, it could produce between 42.2 units (the lower control limit) and 67.8 units (the upper control limit.) With the present system the process is not capable of producing an average of 60 units per hour. As we mentioned earlier, in order for the process to improve its capability, one or more of the process components must be changed. A process must be in statistical control before anyone can attempt process improvement; otherwise, it is not possible to determine if an improvement attempt had yielded positive results. Furthermore, if a process is not in statistical control, it does not have a definable capability and would be unreliable for purposes of making predictions.

ACCOUNTING VARIANCE ANALYSIS USING SPC

SPC analysis indicates that the standard output per hour is 55 units (not 60) and that accounting variances should be based on 55 units as the standard. Those occasions when the process yielded 60 or more units were random occurrences and did not represent process capability. Using an unobtainable standard as a measure of process efficiency can result in incorrect management decisions. Using 55 units as the standard per-hour rate results in the following accounting labor efficiency variance computation.

The expected average production per worker is (55/40), or 1.375:

LABOR EFFICIENCY VARIANCE
Monday, First Week, First Shift

Actual Hours Worked: 7 1/2 x 40 Workers	= 300
Units Produced: 54 x 7 1/z Hours	= 405
Standard Labor Hours Allowed for 405 Units: 405 Units / 1.375 Units per Worker, per Hour	= 295
Nonproductive Hours	6
Labor Rate	x $12
Unfavorable Labor Efficiency Variance	$72

The variance using 55 as the standard is now $72 rather than the $360 unfavorable when 60 units were the standard. Over a period of time the variances will net to zero as long as the process remains in statistical control. Therefore, it would be incorrect to draw any conclusions from a single point analysis (the above variance computation for the first shift on Monday). Any computed accounting variance is a random event and is to be expected. The $360 unfavorable variance is misleading because it is based on an unachievable standard. The $72 variance is correct, but it represents a computation for a single point in time for a process in statistical control. Reacting to individual results in a stable process should be avoided.

For our example, during the time period recorded, the expected range in labor efficiency cost varies from $111.71 unfavorable (55 - 42.2 = 12.8/1.375 = 9.309x$12 = $111.71) to $111.71 favorable (67.8 – 55 = 12.8/1.375 = 9.309 x $12 = $111.71). While the labor efficiency variance remains within this range—$111.71 unfavorable to $111.71 favorable—it is not correct to draw any conclusion about the efficiency of labor. The process is in statistical control, and any variance is random and the result of how the system was designed. Variances that exceed this range should be examined because they are a signal that the process is not in control. The cause of these variances should be identified and corrected, or, if there has been a permanent change in the process, a new average and control limits should be computed.

Attempting to motivate people by assigning arbitrary numbers—accounting or otherwise—as goals for a system and then using these numbers for evaluation is inappropriate. When a process is in statistical control, it is able to produce only its measured capability. When a process is *not* in statistical control, it is impossible to predict future output. In this example the process is only able to produce an average of 55 widgets per hour. Also, employees are only one component of a system. It is impossible to separate the impact of process components on the individuals who operate a system from the contribution these employees make to the process. Process components for which management is responsible include product design, production design, quality of material, quality of machines, physical environment, corporate culture, training of people, and placement of people.

Deming used the following example to illustrate this point: [5]

X = the contribution of the individual to a system
XY = the effect of a system on an individual
XY + X = System Results

Because there are two unknowns in the equation, it is impossible to solve for X, the contribution of the individual. Therefore, Deming concluded that it was impossible to measure an individual's contribution and performance in the short run.

When arbitrary goals that do not represent the capability of a process are assigned to employees as target objectives for evaluation purposes, an organization runs the risk that the employees will either distort the system or the numbers representing the system's output. Employees operating the system may misrepresent the output through inaccurate reporting—indicating the system produced more than it actually did. When this occurs, accounting inventory numbers never march physical inventory. Those operating a system also may "tinker" with it to alter the quality of the output. For example, a local company was adding fruit to one of its products. When too much fruit appeared to be consumed, those operating the system were given a target and a potential bonus to reduce the waste. The target was established without any recognition of the system's capability. The operators reduced the reported accounting waste and earned their bonus by putting less fruit into the product. Later, a study of the process revealed that the original waste was within the process capability and to eliminate this waste required changing several of its components.[6]

"VOICE OF THE CUSTOMER" VS "VOICE OF THE PROCESS"

When accountants arbitrarily establish acceptable variance limits for measuring performance without recognizing the system's capability, they are using the *voice of the customer* rather than the *voice of the process*. The voice of the customer refers to the customer's requirements for the production system. For example, the customer can specify that the average may be 55 items, but the range may not exceed 5%. The output will be acceptable when it falls between 52.25 and 57.75. *The voice of the process* describes the capability of this system: The system will provide an output that varies randomly between 42.2 and 67.8 items each hour. We can determine this capability only through careful statistical analysis of production data. This analysis will determine the range within which the process will produce items 99.7% of the time. We use the upper and lower extreme values of this range as control limits for monitoring the stability of the process.

It is clear that the process described in our example is not capable of meeting the customer's specification. Now it is management's responsibility to reconcile the voice of the process with the voice of the customer—either by changing the specification or by modifying the process. If management used the 5% customer specification for evaluating the process, all variance observations in excess of 57.25 and 52.25 would indicate that there was a problem with the process and that management should take some corrective action. But those observations falling between 42.2 and 52.25 and between 57.75 and 67.8 represent data points where the process is not

exhibiting any unusual or special cause variation. When management modifies a process by interpreting common cause variation as special cause, it might be tampering with a stable process that is behaving exactly as it should. In other words, management's actions should be guided by the voice of the process, not by arbitrary specifications.

A POWERFUL TOOL

Statistical process control is a powerful tool that management accountants need to embrace in order to further their role as business partners. Predetermined accounting standards and budgets are useful tools for planning and overall assessment. All processes are built with some targeted level of performance in mind. In the initial planning stage, standards and budgets are needed as targets for achievement. As processes are designed and developed, their actual capability needs to be determined and compared to the original forecasted standard or budget. Either the original standard and budget will have to be adjusted, or the process will have to be redesigned to meet the planned target. People operating a system can be given targets, but these numerical goals must be determined in the context of a system's capability and with the recognition that individuals are only one component of the process. Use of accounting data to assist in determining the cost of an output is essential, and where a system is in statistical control, these accounting numbers are an indication of future costs. But using accounting or any other numbers to attempt to motivate and evaluate people operating within a process is inappropriate and may lead to dysfunctional behavior and a failure to optimize the process.

Most organizations are analyzing more information today than ever before. Unfortunately, many of these same organizations are frantically trying to explain why outcomes look so good one month and then so poor the next. Before information can be useful, it must be analyzed and interpreted. A simple comparison between results this month and last month, however, cannot fully capture the underlying behavior of the process from which the data were derived. Worse, explanations are usually demanded and blame assessed for any numerical result that misses a target or goal.

To be effective, budgets and standard costing systems must be able to distinguish between common cause variation (noise) and special causes (signals). These or any other measurement system must be able to separate "noise" from "signals" in order to be able to interpret the voice of the process. This important distinction is critical if the measurements derived from any process are to be used to make predictions and provide a basis for process improvement. The primary problem associated with using accounting-based targets designed to control people or processes outside the context of statistical process control is that the variation of every outcome, event, or data point appears to be related to some special event or signal. But many of these data points may be nothing more than common cause variation (noise) caused by how the system or process was designed. Taking action in response to this common cause variation leads to inappropriate adjustments based on the mistaken notion that the results were attributable to some individual or team. Without the use of control charts, management is not able to answer the all-important question: Are the actions we are about to take a response to noise or real signals?

Harper A. Roehm, CPA, DBA, is professor of accounting at the University of Dayton in Dayton, Ohio. He can be reached at (937) 229-2497 or Harper.Roehm@notes.udayton.edu.

Larry Weinstein, Ph.D., is an assistant professor at Wright State University in Dayton.

Joseph F. Castellano, Ph.D., is professor of accounting at the University of Dayton.

1 Robert G. Eccles, "A Note on Control Systems," *Note 9-491-084,* Harvard Business School, Boston, January 1, 1992, pp. 1-3.

2 Harper A. Roehm and Joseph F. Castellano, "The Deming View of a Business," *Quality Progress,* February 1997, pp. 39-45.

3 W. Edwards Deming, *The New Economics For Industry, Government, Education,* Massachusetts Institute of Technology Center for Advanced Engineering Study, Cambridge, Mass. 1993, pp. 176-193.

4 Control charts provide a graphic tool to evaluate process performance data and are used to detect assignable—that is, nonrandom—causes of variation in the process. For most control charts, the control limits are calculated on the basis of process average +/- 3 times the standard deviation of the statistic used. This implies that if random causes of variation alone are present, 99.7% of the charted values would fall within the control limits. Because the probability of falling outside the limits is so low these limits can be used to distinguish between random and assignable causes of variation.

The state of statistical control does not guarantee the process output meets customer requirements. Likewise, a process that is not in a state of control still could produce output that meets customer requirements. The purpose of using the control chart, therefore, is not to determine whether the process meets customer requirements but to determine whether the process is stable. We must determine whether the output of the stable process is capable of meeting the customer requirements separately.

5 Deming, pp. 26-27.

6 Harper A. Roehm and Joseph F Castellano, "The Danger of Relying on Accounting Numbers Alone," *Management Accounting Quarterly,* Fall 1999, pp. 4-9.

REDESIGNING COST SYSTEMS:
IS STANDARD COSTING OBSOLETE?

By Carole B. Cheatham and Leo B. Cheatham,
Professors at Northeast Louisana University.

SYNOPSIS: *Since the early 1980s standard cost systems (SCSs) have been under attack as not providing the information needed for advanced manufacturers. In spite of its critics, SCSs are still the system of choice in some 86 percent of U.S. manufacturing firms.*

This paper discusses the criticisms of SCSs that (1) the variances are obsolete, (2) there is not provision for continuous improvement, and (3) use of the variances for responsibility accounting result in internal conflict rather than cooperation. Updates for SCSs in the form of redesigned variances, suggestions for dynamic standards, and refocused responsibility and reporting systems are presented.

The compatibility of SCSs and its main competitor as a cost system, activity-based costing (ABC), is examined. The authors discuss when it is appropriate to use ABC or SCS or some combination of the two.

Since Eli Goldratt's (1983) charge that cost accounting is the number one enemy of productivity in the early 1980s, traditional cost systems have been under attack. Although Goldratt subsequently softened his stand to say that *cost* rather than accounting was the culprit (Jayson 1987), others were quick to jump on the bandwagon to condemn the cost

systems in use. New systems were proposed of which the most popular was activity-based costing (ABC).

In spite of all the criticism, a 1988 survey shows 86 percent of U.S. manufacturers using standard cost systems (Cornick et al. 1988). A survey by Schiff (1993) indicates that 36 percent of companies use activity-based costing, but only 25 percent of those use it to replace their traditional cost system. It would seem that only about 9 percent (25 percent of the 36 percent) of companies are using ABC as their main system while the vast majority use a standard cost system (SCS).

This is not to say that traditional SCSs could not benefit from being updated. However, accountants in industry (as well as academia) seem unaware that a redesigned SCS can provide the information they need, and that updating their present system is an easier process than adopting a new system. The SCS is one vehicle of articulation among managerial, financial and operations accounting, and it is a *control* system while the candidates for its replacement typically are only cost *accumulation* systems.

In this article the major criticisms of SCSs are examined along with ways that the weaknesses can be remedied or ameliorated. The criticisms relate to the use of specific variances, the lack of provision for continuous improvement, and the fact that administration of the system results in internal competition rather than cooperation. The appropriate use of ABC systems in conjunction with SCSs is also discussed.

Criticisms:
Obsolete
Internal conflict
no continuous improvement
defects/quality
timliness
overhead allocation
ignore customer satisfaction (FG variance, Sales Order Var)
inventory buildup

FIGURE 1
VARIANCES RELATING TO MATERIAL PURCHASING

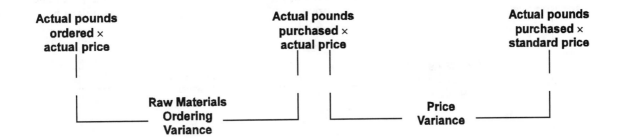

UPDATING THE VARIANCES IN AN SCS

Concerning the variables analyzed in an SCS, most criticisms center on the overemphasis on price and efficiency to the exclusion of quality. Other criticisms center on the use of the volume variance to measure utilization of capacity while ignoring overproduction and unnecessary buildups of inventory. In making such charges, critics fail to realize variance analysis is not "locked-in" to a particular set of variables. Standards are only benchmarks of what performance should be. The particular variables used can be changed as the need arises.

The following discussion focuses on concerns of the new manufacturing environment—raw material ordering and inventory levels, quality, production levels, finished goods inventory levels and completion of sales orders.

VARIANCES PERTAINING TO RAW MATERIALS

The set of variances in Fig. 1 centers on the function of raw material ordering and inventory levels (Harrell 1992). The Raw Material Ordering Variance gives information about the effectiveness of suppliers. It contrasts the raw materials ordered with the raw materials delivered (purchased). Any variation may be considered unfavorable because the goal is to have orders delivered as placed. Too much delivered will result in unnecessary buildups of raw material stocks. Too little delivered is unfavorable because production delays may result.

The Price Variance in Fig. 1 is the traditional price variance computed on materials purchased. This variance has been criticized on the grounds that over-emphasis on price leads purchasing managers to ignore quality. However, price is a legitimate concern that should not be overlooked. This system also uses a Quality Variance (presented in a following section).

If low quality materials are purchased in order to gain a low price, this will result in an unfavorable Quality Variance.

VARIANCES PERTAINING TO MATERIAL INVENTORIES AND EFFICIENT USE

The set of variances in Fig. 2 focuses on raw material inventory levels and quantity or efficiency of material use.

The Raw Materials Inventory Variance (Harrell 1992) shows either more material purchased than used (an inventory buildup) or more material used than purchased (an inventory decrease). With the JIT philosophy, purchasing more than used causes an unfavorable variance, while decreasing previous buildups causes a favorable variance.

The Efficiency Variance in Fig. 2 is based on the difference between the actual pounds of material used and the standard amount for *total* production. The traditional Efficiency or Quantity Variance is the difference between the actual pounds of material used and the standard amount for *good* production. The traditional variance is actually as combination of quality and efficiency factors. As can be seen in the next section, quality is better treated in a separate variance.

VARIANCES PERTAINING TO PRODUCTION LEVELS AND QUALITY

The next set of variances (Fig. 3) turns from input analysis to output analysis and relates to production levels and quality. All cost factors are included in the "standard cost per unit" including labor and overhead.

The Quality Variance is the standard cost of units produced that did not meet specifications (the difference between total units produced and good units produced). In traditional variance analysis, this

15-21

FIGURE 2
VARIANCES RELATED TO MATERIAL USAGE

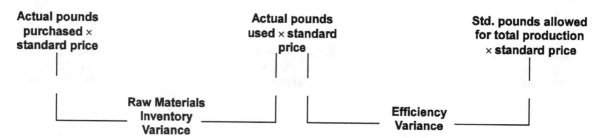

variance is buried in the efficiency variances of the various inputs.

Ignoring labor and overhead, suppose a company used two pounds of material per finished unit at a standard cost of $1.00 per pound. Further assume they used 4,900 pounds in the production of 2,500 total units, of which 100 were defective. Traditional variance analysis would show an unfavorable Efficiency Variance of $100 computed on the difference between the standard cost of the 4,800 pounds that should have been used to produce the 2,400 good units and the 4,900 pounds actually used.

A better breakdown of the traditional variance shows a favorable Efficiency Variance of $100 and an unfavorable Quality Variance of $200. The Production Department did use only 4,800 pounds to produce 2,500 units that should have taken 5,000 pounds. The fact that some of these units were defective should appear as a Quality Variance, as it does in this analysis. The Quality Variance is $200 unfavorable representing $2.00 per unit invested in 100 defective units.

This analysis also yields a Production Variance based on the difference between the standard cost of good units produced and the scheduled amount of production. The goal in advanced manufacturing environments is to produce exactly what is needed for sales orders (scheduled production). A variance from scheduled production either way is unfavorable because too much production results in unnecessary buildups of inventory while too little results in sales orders not filled. As is the case with the Raw Material Inventory variance, the critical factor is the cost of the capital invested in excess inventories. It is desirable to highlight this cost in responsibility reports by applying a cost of capital figure. to the excess (Cheatham 1989).

For simplicity's sake, the above illustrations of input analysis pertain to materials. Labor and volume-related variable overhead can be analyzed in a similar manner. Since there is no difference between labor purchased and labor used in production, the labor

FIGURE 3
VARIANCES RELATED TO QUALITY AND PRODUCTION LEVELS

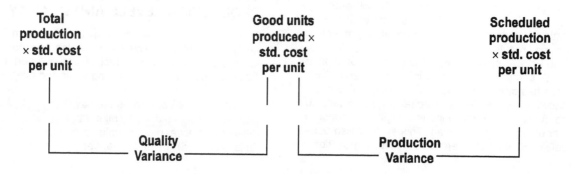

FIGURE 4
VARIANCES RELATED TO SALES

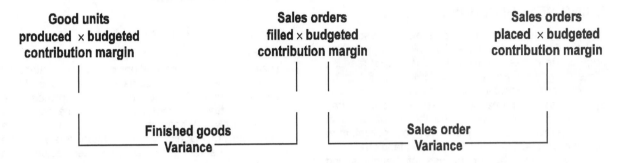

input variances would include the traditional Rate Variance and the updated Efficiency Variance.

Other than showing a budget variance for the various elements of fixed overhead, there is no point in further analysis in terms of a Volume Variance. The updated Production Variance serves the same purpose in a far better fashion.

VARIANCES PERTAINING TO SALES ANALYSIS

There are various ways to analyze sales. One method is to use price, mix and volume variances. A further analysis is to break down the volume variance into market size and market share variances. The analysis in Fig. 4 is presented because it articulates well with the output analysis for production.

The sales variances indicate customer service as well as the cost of lost sales. The variances use budgeted contribution margin as a measure of opportunity cost. The Finished Goods Variance indicates the opportunity cost associated with orders completed but not shipped. A delay in shipment causes a loss because of subsequent delay in receiving payment. The Sales Order Variance represents the opportunity cost associated with sales orders that could not be filled during the time period for whatever reason—lack of capacity, scheduling problems, etc.

The above discussion presents a variety of variances that are not used in a traditional standard cost system. The variances can be used for control purposes alone or can be integrated into the financial accounting records (Cheatham and Cheatham 1993). The system is not intended to be a generic solution for any company's needs. It is intended to demonstrate that, with a little creativity, it is possible to redesign SCSs to measure variables that are important to a particular company in today's manufacturing environment.

UPDATING THE SCS FOR CONTINUOUS IMPROVEMENT

In a manufacturing environment in which continuous improvement is a goal of most companies, the charge has been made that SCSs do not encourage positive change. However, static standards based on engineering studies or historical data are not an essential part of an SCS. Standards can be adjusted to be dynamic, or changing, by any of several methods.

USING PRIOR PERIODS' RESULTS AS STANDARDS

One way to have dynamic standards is to use last period's results as standards. This idea has been advocated in the past as a way for small business to have the benefits of standards without the expense of engineering studies (Lawler and Livingstone 1986; Cheatham 1987). The objection can be made that last period's results may not make very good standards if last period was unrepresentative for whatever reason. If this is the case, last period's results can be modified.

Another variation on using past performances as standards is the use of a base period. Comparisons can be made with the base period and all subsequent periods, if desired. Boer (1991, 40) describes a system of using a base year as a "pseudo flexible budget" from which unit costs are developed. He comments that the system "encourages continuous improvement and never implies that a level of performance is adequate. Instead, it encourages managers to improve continuously."

Still another variation on using prior periods' results as standards is the use of best performance-to-date (BP). BP is a rigorous standard for self-improvement because it motivates workers as well as managers to exceed all past performance.

USING BENCHMARKING

Although past performance costs may be used in a variety of ways to formulate dynamic standards, any such system has an inward focus. Benchmarking looks outside the firm to the performance of industry leaders or competitors. Benchmarking typically is applied to performance measures rather than standard costs. However, using the performance of industry leaders as a standard provides motivation to become world-class in much the same fashion.

The primary barrier to use of benchmarking standards is, of course, lack of information. Edward S. Finein (1990), former vice president and chief engineer of Xerox, lists the following sources of information when using benchmarking for performance measures: (1) external reports and trade publications; (2) professional associations; (3) market research and surveys; (4) industry experts; (5) consultants' studies; (6) company visits; and (7) competitive labs. In the absence of hard information, an approach may be taken to estimate the performance of industry leaders. Trying to meet the supposed standards of industry leaders (or other competitors) can have results that are useful as long as the company is striving toward beneficial goals.

USING MOVING COSTS REDUCTIONS

Still another way to have dynamic standards is through use of predetermined cost reductions. Horngren et al. (1994) describe a system of what they call a "continuous improvement standard cost" or a "moving cost reduction standard cost." This system reduces the standard cost by a predetermined percentage each time period, such as a one percent reduction in standard cost per month computed by setting the new standard at 99 percent of the previous month's standard.

The question that their system raises is how to determine the amount of the cost reduction. One possibility is the use of cost improvement curves. Cost improvement curves are a new variation of the old learning curve idea. Learning curves were based on reduction of direct labor costs due to learning by the workers. With a large percentage of product conversion being brought about by automated equipment rather than laborers, potential cost reductions relate to the experience factor for the organization as a whole which may be measured by cost improvement curves.

Pattison and Teplitz (1989) calculate the new rate of learning for an organization that replaces labor with automated equipment as:

$$Rate_{new} = Rate_{old} + (1 - Rate_{old}) * L * R$$

where $Rate_{old}$ is the rate of learning for the old system, L is the proportion of learning attributed solely to direct labor stated as a percentage, and R is the proportion of direct labor being replaced. The formula actually reduces the learning rate applicable to labor only, the assumption being that workers can learn but not machinery. An updated version of the formula is needed which encompasses factors such as managers', supervisors' and engineers' experience.

The Japanese stress the formula 2V=2/3C, or if volume is doubled, the cost should be two-thirds of what it was originally. This formula equates to a 67 percent learning curve which represents a high degree of learning. However, their attitude is that learning does not just happen—it should be made to happen.

USING TARGET COSTS

Another idea borrowed from the Japanese is the use of target costs based on the market. Target costs are used in Japan primarily for new products that are still in the design stage. The idea is to set a cost that is low enough to permit a selling price that is viable on the market. The price is the starting point for calculating costs, and the various costs are backed out from the price. Typically, the target cost is very low. Hiromoto (1988) describes the use of target costs at the Daihatsu Motor company. First, a product development order is issued. Then an "allowable cost" per car is calculated by taking the difference between the target selling price and the profit margin. Then each department calculates an "accumulated cost" based on the standard cost achievable with current technology. Finally, a target cost is set somewhere between the allowable and accumulated cost. All this takes place before the product is designed. The design stage typically takes three years. When the product is finally in production, the target cost is gradually tightened on a monthly basis. Later the actual cost of the previous period is used to drive costs down further.

Market-based target costs have a strong appeal on a basis for standard costs because they focus on the customer rather than on internal engineering capabilities. However, using target costs is easiest with new products because as much as 90 percent of product costs are set in the design stage (Berliner and Brimson 1988). The way a product is designed determines the way it has to be manufactured and sets the stage for further cost reductions.

Standard costs do not have to be static. Dynamic standards can be formulated using a variety of methods including past performance, industry leader's performance, or target costs based on predetermined reductions or the market. Market-based target costs have the most intuitive appeal because the focus is on the future and on the customer. However, they may work better for new products rather than for established products.

UPDATING MANAGEMENT RESPONSIBILITY AND REPORTING

Besides revamping the SCS to better reflect today's concerns in terms of variables to be measured and continuous improvement, there needs to be improved reporting of variances. Old reporting systems tended to foster internal competition and arguments about whose department was to blame for unfavorable variances. There needs to be an attitude of cooperation among workers, managers and departments.

Revised lines of responsibility used with new plant layouts are improving some of the competitive attitudes that once prevailed in manufacturing organizations. Plants that used to feature "push through" production with large masses of raw materials and semifinished product moving from one process to another are changing to work cells or similar arrangements. The work cell arrangement features equipment that can process a product from start to finish. Workers in the work cell typically can operate all or several types of machinery. This leaner "pull through" approach allows a sales order to be rapidly processed within the work cell which decreases cycle time and holds work in process and finished goods inventories to a minimum.

The work cell arrangement allows a team of workers to be responsible for the entire product and reduces the likelihood that defects will be passed along to the next department. Along with the work cell arrangement many companies are decentralizing functions such as engineering and making these personnel responsible for a particular work area or product line. With the decentralization, there is more

---

FIGURE 5
WORK CELL A
VARIANCE TRADE-OFF REPORT FOR MONTH OF JULY 19X6

Raw Materials:

	Price	Quantity	Total
Material X	100 F	200 U	100 U
Material Y	50 F	100 U	50 U
Material Z	200 F	150 F	350 F
Total	350 F	150 U	200 F

Labor:

	Rate	Efficiency	Total
Type A	400 F	200 F	600 F
Type B	550 U	250 F	300 U
Total	150 U	450 F	300 F

Traceable Overhead Variances:

	Spending	Efficiency	Total
Power	150 F	50 U	100 F
Supplies	100 U	10 U	110 U
Other	50 F	10 F	60 F
Total	100 F	50 U	50 F

Quality Variance on Dept. A Contribution to Product Cost 100 Defective Units @ $7.00	700 U
Total	150 U

15-25

FIGURE 6
PROFITABLE MANUFACTURING COMPANY
EXCESS INVENTORY REPORT FOR MONTH OF JULY 19X6

	Cost	Cost of Capital
Raw Materials		
Excess from previous month	$5,000	$ 50
Current inventory variance	3,000 F	($ 30)
Total	$2,000	$ 20
Work in Process		
Cell A Production variance	$4,000 U	$ 40
Cell B Production variance	$1,000 U	$ 10
Total	$5,000 U	$ 50
Total Excess and Cost of Capital	$7,000 U	$ 70

	Cost	Contribution
Finished Goods:		
Finished goods variance	$ 5,000 F	$(1,500)
Sales order variance	8,000 U	2,400
Total	$ 3,000 U	$ 900
Total Cost of Capital and Lost Contribution Margins		$ 970

---

focused responsibility. Decentralization and a team approach to production eliminates many conflicts that once existed.

In addition to the new attitudes about responsibility, there needs to be improved reporting. The variances outlined in this paper can be reported in two types of management reports. The report illustrated in Fig. 5 shows the trade-offs between price, efficiency and quality. This type of report can be done on a plant level or department level as well as a work cell level. The price variance for work cells or departments should be computed on material used rather than purchased because this gives a better picture of the trade-offs involved. Upper-level management reports should probably show both types of price variances if there are significant differences between purchases and use.

The report illustrated in Fig. 6 shows the effects of variances related to inventories. Raw material excesses at cost, related to both current and past purchases, are listed along with the related cost of capital. In this case it is assumed the excess was held the entire month and the cost of capital was one percent. Work in Process excesses are measured in terms of the Production Variance. This variance measures the difference between scheduled and actual production. Presumably if there were excesses

from the previous month, there was an adjustment made in the scheduled production. Cost of capital figures show the effect of holding these excess inventories.

In the case of Finished Goods, the crucial factor is the opportunity cost of sales orders not filled measured by the lost contribution margins. Therefore, if orders are completed but not shipped or there is an inability to fill a sales order because of lack of capacity, this is indicated by the Finished Goods Variance or the Sales Order Variance. The illustration assumes a favorable Finished Goods Variance because more sales orders were filled than units produced, indicating a decrease in previous finished goods stock.

Although a reporting system such as that illustrated in figures 5 and 6 may not eliminate all conflicts, it is certainly helpful to recognize that trade-offs occur. It is also beneficial for upper-level managers to see the cost of excesses or deficiencies in inventories measured in terms of lost contribution margins and cost of capital.

STANDARD COST SYSTEMS AND ABC

A final consideration in updating SCSs is how an SCS relates to ABC. Although ABC potentially has broader uses, it primarily has been used for manufacturing overhead.

When a company has a significant amount of indirect product cost, ABC results in better product costing because ABC is superior for allocating these costs among products. This permits company managers to more knowledgeably price products. However, ABC is a cost *accumulation* system rather than a cost *control* system. When used with process value analysis (PVA) or activity based management (ABM), ABC can have a cost *management* feature, but there is no day-to-day monitoring system to assure that costs are within certain parameters.

Most companies can benefit from some combination of ABC and an SCS. One possibility is use of ABC for indirect costs and an updated SCS for direct costs. Another possibility is use of an SCS for financial records and ABC for analysis of indirect costs outside the main record-keeping system. A combination of the two systems retains the advantages of the superior control features of an SCS with the benefits of better overhead analysis from ABC.

CONCLUSION

SCSs are not really the dinosaurs of cost systems, but they may benefit from a little evolution. Updated variances along with dynamic standards will vastly improve the usefulness of most SCSs. ABC can coexist with an SCS and bring some order to the general area of indirect costs. Improvements in the reporting of variances can allow managers to assess trade-offs and inventory stocks and their impact on profits.

REFERENCES

Berliner, C., and J. Brimson, eds. 1988. Cost Management for Today's Advanced Manufacturing: The CAM-I Conceptual Design. Boston: Harvard Business School Press.

Boer, G.B. 1991. Making accounting a value-added activity. Management Accounting 73 (August): 36–41.

Cheatham, C. 1987. Profit and productivity analysis revisited. Journal of Accountancy 164 (July): 123–130.

_____. 1989. Reporting the effects of excess inventories. Journal of Accountancy 168 (November): 131–140.

_____, and L. Cheatham. 1993. Updating Standard Cost Systems. Westport, CT: Quorum Books.

Cornick, M., W. Cooper, and S. Wilson. 1988. How do companies analyze overhead? Management Accounting 69 (June): 41–43.

Finein, E.S. 1990. Benchmarking for superior quality and performance. Performance Measurement for Manufacturers Seminar, Institutes for International Research (October).

Goldratt, E.M. 1983. Cost accounting is enemy number one of productivity. International Conference Proceedings, American Production and Inventory Control Society (October).

Harrell, H. 1992. Materials variance analysis and JIT: A new approach. Management Accounting 73 (May): 33–38.

Hiromoto, T. 1988. Another hidden edge—Japanese management accounting. Harvard Business Review 69 (July-August): 22–26.

Horngren, C. et al. 1994. Cost Accounting: A Managerial Approach. 8th ed. Englewood Cliffs, NJ: Prentice Hall: 246.

Jayson, S. 1987. Goldratt & Fox: Revolutionizing the factory floor. Management Accounting 68 (May): 18–22.

Lawler, W., and J. Livingstone. 1986. Profit and productivity analysis for small business. Journal of Accountancy 163 (December): 190–196.

Noreen, E. 1991. Conditions under which activity-based cost systems provide relevant costs. Journal of Management Accounting Research 3 (Fall): 159–168.

Pattison, D., and C. Teplitz 1989. Are learning curves still relevant? Management Accounting 71 (February): 37–40.

Schiff, J. 1993. ABC on the rise. Cost Management Update Issue No. 24 (February). In Cost Accounting: A Managerial Emphasis, 1991, cited by C. Horngren, G. Foster, and S. Datar, 161. Englewood. Cliffs, NJ; Prentice Hall, Inc.

Chapter 16
Standard Costing: Factory Overhead

Cases
16-1   Berkshire Toy Company
16-2   The Mesa Corporation

Readings

"Using Enhanced Cost Models in Variance Analysis for Better Control and Decision Making"

This article points out that oversimplifications of fixed and variable costs can result in the standard costing system not being used or, if used, can lead to bad decisions. For variance reporting to be useful, financial managers need to develop cost models that reflect how costs actually behave.

Discussion Questions:
1. Describe the implications on operating decisions of analyzing a semi-variable cost as either a variable or fixed cost.
2. Describe the implications on operating decisions of analyzing a step-fixed cost as either a variable or fixed cost.
3. Describe the implications on operating decisions of analyzing an operation with mixed costs as either a variable or fixed cost.

"Variance Analysis Refines Overhead Cost Control"

This article attempts to analyze the full costs of selected medical procedures using examples from a healthcare organization. A key feature of the analysis is how the overhead variances are handled, and in particular how to develop an understanding of the volume variance and how it affects profitability. Standard costs are determined for a hypothetical "Procedure 101" and there is an illustration of how variances can be obtained and interpreted, given example actual results for the procedure over a year's time. The analysis shows the effect of volume changes on overhead recovery and on profit contribution.

Discussion Questions:
1. What is the key driver of profitability based on the analysis in this article?
2. Explain how the two variances are developed and interpreted in Exhibit 3.
3. Consider the example in Exhibit 4. Why are expenses improperly matched and the reported income overstated?

"Overhead Control Implications of Activity Costing"
This articles shows limitations of the traditional treatment of standard cost overhead variances. Using a problem from a CMA exam the authors solved the problem both in a traditional format and again using activity-based cost drivers. Regression is used to identify the cost drivers, and a revised solution is derived.

Discussion Questions:
1. What are the limitations of standard cost overhead analysis?
2. How does the activity approach improve upon the standard cost analysis of overhead?

16-1. Berkshire Toy Company[1]

Janet McKinley is employed by the Quality Products Corporation, a publicly traded conglomerate. The corporation manufactures and sells many different kinds of products, including luggage, music synthesizers, breakfast cereals, peanut butter, and children's toys. McKinley is Vice President in charge of the Berkshire Toy Company, a division of Quality Products.

It is late July 2002 and McKinley has just received the preliminary income statement for her division for the year ended June 30, 2002 (see Table 1). The master (static) budget and master budget variances for the same period are included for comparison purposes. McKinley looks at the bottom line, a loss approaching a million dollars, then picks up the phone to call you. You are an accountant in the controller's office at the headquarters of Quality Products Corporation. You worked with McKinley when her company was acquired by Quality Products, and now she has called you for advice.

"I know the bottom line looks pretty bad," she says. "But we made great strides this year. Sales are higher than ever. Customers love our product and respect our quality. There must be a way to make this business work and turn a profit, too. The budget variances should provide some insights. Could you do an analysis of the budget variances?"

BACKGROUND

The Berkshire Toy Company was founded by Franklin Berkshire, Janet McKinley's father, in 1974. Berkshire was an industrial artist who enjoyed making stuffed animals in his spare time. His first creation, a teddy bear that he presented to Janet on her seventh birthday, occupies a place of honor at Berkshire Toy Company's headquarters. In 1974, Frank Berkshire acquired an old pneumatic pump that had been used to fill life-jackets for the Navy during World War II. He modified the machine to mass produce stuffed animals, and the Berkshire Toy Company was born.

The company started small at first, but grew quickly as Berkshire's reputation for quality spread. By 1986, annual sales exceeded a million dollars for the first time. Janet McKinley had learned the business from the bottom up. She had started out with the company in the mailroom as a part-time summer employee. As a college student, she had spent summers and Christmas vacations working on the production floor, in the sales department, and finally in the accounting department. She was named Assistant to the President in 1988 after receiving her M.B.A..

In 1991, at her urging, the company launched an initial public offering (IPO) of common stock and became publicly traded on the NASDAQ. Janet McKinley became CEO of the company on July 1, 1993 when her father retired. On March 17, 1995, Berkshire Toys was acquired by the Quality Products Corporation in a friendly exchange of common stock valued at $23.2 million.[2] The terms of the acquisition included an agreement to employ McKinley for no fewer than five years at an annual salary of $120,000.

---

[1] This case is based on field research at an existing toy company. The essential facts relating to production and sales have been retained. However, all names, dates, actual events, and identifying details have been concealed to protect the privacy and identity of the company. Thus, if any names used in this case are those of actual firms or individuals, then it is purely coincidental.

Source: Dean Crawford and Eleanor G. Henry. Budgeting and Performance Evaluation at the Berkshire Toy Company, *Issues in Accounting Education,* 15 (2) May, 2000, pp. 283-309.

[2] In a friendly acquisition, the terms of the exchange are negotiated by the acquiring company and the incumbent management of the target (acquired) firm. This method of merging two companies is quite different from a "hostile takeover," which is initiated by the acquiring company over the objections of the target's incumbent management.

TABLE 1

Berkshire Toy Company
A Division of Quality Products Corporation

Preliminary Statement of Divisional Operating Income
for the Year Ended June 30, 2002

	Actual	Master (Static) Budget	Master Budget Variance	
Units sold	325,556	280,000	45,556	F
Retail and catalog (174,965 units)	$8,573,285	$11,662,000	$3,088,715	U
Internet (105,429 units)	4,428,018	0	4,428,018	F
Wholesale (45,162 units)	1,445,184	1,344,000	101,184	F
Total revenue	14,446,487	13,006,000	1,440,487	F
Variable production costs:				
Direct materials				
Acrylic pile fabric	256,422	233,324	23,098	U
10-mm acrylic eyes	125,637	106,400	19,237	U
45-mm plastic joints	246,002	196,000	50,002	U
Polyester fiber filling	450,856	365,400	85,456	U
Woven label	16,422	14,000	2,422	U
Designer Box	69,488	67,200	2,288	U
Accessories	66,013	33,600	32,413	U
Total direct materials	1,230,840	1,015,924	214,916	U
Direct labor	3,668,305	2,688,000	980,305	U
Variable overhead	1,725,665	1,046,304	679,361	U
Total variable production costs	6,624,810	4,750,228	1,874,582	U
Variable selling expenses	1,859,594	1,218,280	641,314	U
Total variable expenses	8,484,404	5,968,508	2,515,896	U
Contribution margin	5,962,083	7,037,492	1,075,409	U
Fixed costs:				
Manufacturing overhead	658,897	661,920	3,023	F
Selling expenses	5,023,192	4,463,000	560,192	U
Administrative expenses	1,123,739	1,124,000	261	F
Total fixed costs	6,805,828	6,248,920	556,908	U
Operating income[a]	$(843,745)	$788,572	$1,632,317	U

[a] The actual operating income reported in Table 1 is a preliminary figure that has not been adjusted for fiscal 1998 bonuses, if any.

The Berkshire Toy Company produces the Berkshire Bear, a fifteen-inch teddy bear enjoyed by children and adult toy collectors around the world. The company touts the handcrafted features of the bear and advertises its product as the only teddy bear made in America. The bears are fully jointed, constructed of washable acrylic pile fabric, and stuffed with a polyester fiber filling. The toys are dressed in various accessories, such as bow ties, sports jerseys, or character and occupational costumes. Thus, the product can be personalized for numerous occasions. The Berkshire Bear is sold with an unconditional lifetime guarantee. In communicating with customers, the company refers to its repair center as the "bear hospital." A damaged bear may be returned by the customer and repaired (or replaced, at the company's discretion) free of charge.

The Berkshire Toy Company's 241 employees are organized into three departments: purchasing, production, and marketing. The purchasing department consists of David Hall, the purchasing manager, and a staff of ten. The department is responsible for acquiring and maintaining the supply of production materials. Bill Wilford manages 174 employees in the production department, where the manufacture and assembly of the product takes place. The marketing department is headed by Rita Smith. She is responsible for all aspects of marketing and she supervises the nine sales clerks and 42 sales representatives that make up Berkshire's sales force. The remaining three employees are McKinley, her secretary, and her secretary's assistant.

PRODUCTION

Production begins with a large press that cuts the acrylic pile fabric into the required pattern pieces. The press-cutter machine applies 23,000 pounds per square inch of pressure to a tray of pattern stainless steel dies[3] that are stamped into the fabric. The bolts[4] of fabric are rolled out and layered on the cutting table. The fabric is measured at this time for length and width and inspected for fabric flaws, tears, and soiled areas. Fabric flaws create waste. Shortages in length or width may require a different cutting set-up and increase fabric waste. Additional cutting set-ups increase production time. The press-cutter machine cuts 14 layered bolts at a time, enough for 588 units. The machine produces a clean, crisp, cut edge that will not fray or ravel.

The fabric is also inspected for trueness of color. The Berkshire Bear is advertised as a honey bear. Thus, fabric dye lots are important for matching shades of brown. The toy animal is available also in off-white and dark brown. Off-color fabric must be scrapped or returned to the supplier. Because the toy is designed to be washable, the fabric must be colorfast. Berkshire obtains the most economical price for specified colors by timing its fabric orders with the production runs of its suppliers. Rush orders almost always increase substantially the price of the required fabric.

In the next stage of production, operators of industrial sewing machines construct the six parts of the finished unit: two arms, two legs, the head, and the torso. Each piece is sewn inside-out and then turned right-side-out for assembly. Sewing is the most labor-intensive phase of the production process. Any additional sewing steps, such as appliques[5] or monograms, require additional production time.

In the next step, two optical-grade, acrylic eyes are attached to the head with plastic rivets. If the rivet posts are too short, the eyes may fall off later. If the rivet posts are too

---

[3] Dies are heavy-duty, three-dimensional patterns used to cut the fabric into parts for the bear. Dies function in a manner similar to cookie cutters.

[4] Fabric is shipped from the manufacturer wrapped around a cylindrical core or "bolt." A standard bolt of fabric is ten yards long and 72 inches wide.

[5] Appliques are descriptive or ornamental features made from contrasting materials that are applied to the outside surface of the bear. The alligator emblem used by Izod on sweaters and polo shirts is a common example of an applique. Another example is an identifying patch applied to pockets of uniforms bearing the employer's name and logo.

long, the eyes will stand out from the head, giving a nonstandard appearance. Eye color is also somewhat important. Acrylic eyes are purchased from vendors in "dark brown," but the exact shade may vary from supplier to supplier. Defects are not discovered until the eyes are used in production. At that point, defective eyes are discarded and replaced with ones that meet specifications.

After the cut pieces have been sewn together and eyes attached, the company's unique pneumatic stuffing machine[6] is used to blow the polyester fiber filling into the unassembled parts. Except for two replacements of the electric motor and a new power cord, this is the same machine that Franklin Berkshire acquired from Navy surplus in 1974. Bags of filling are loaded into the machine hopper and mechanically fluffed to the proper loft.[7] An operator places the empty arm, leg, body, or head over a stationary nozzle and uses a foot pedal to control the flow of filling. The machine operator judges whether the part has been filled correctly. Too little filling affects the firmness of the bear; too much filling is unnecessary and expensive. Inferior grade fiber filling is less expensive but can cause clumping and clogging in the hopper. When this happens, production is interrupted and the operator must unclog the vacuum hose and reset the machine.

Next, the arms, legs, and head are attached to the torso using three-part, snap-on, hard plastic disc joints. The disc joints allow the head and limbs to rotate and eliminate the need for sewn attachment. The plastic joints are designed to be foolproof in production and dependable for the life of the product. However, the joints cannot be removed without destroying them. Occasionally, after initial joint insertion, the parts do not fit together properly and they must be removed and replaced.

At the end of the construction process, a woven satin label that states "Made in America by the Berkshire Toy Company" is attached to the back of each bear. More polyester filling is stuffed into the torso and the back seam is hand-stitched, using essentially the same "shoelace" procedure practiced by surgeons. Each seam is brushed by hand to give the bear a seamless look.

The production process is a continuous source of airborne polyester and acrylic fibers that must be controlled, both to protect the health and safety of the employees and to safeguard the production equipment. The company has taken several steps to control the fibers. First, an air filtration system works constantly to remove dust and fibers from the factory. Second, production employees wear dust masks while they are working with fabric or filling. Finally, regular cleaning and maintenance of the sewing, cutting, and stuffing machines is performed to prevent the fibers from building up.

Maintenance is especially important for the sewing machines. Machine oil and static electricity attract pile fabric lint. Lint buildup can cause lines of stitches that are uneven and seams that do not hold. The Berkshire Bear workmanship is guaranteed for life. Burst seams require rework during the production phase and during the lifetime of the product.

All production employees are paid a regular wage for a 40-hour work week. They receive their regular wage plus an overtime premium of one-half the regular wage rate for overtime. The cost of fringe benefits and employer taxes, such as social security, health insurance, and vacation time, adds 20.55 percent to the cost of labor. The employees' regular wages are charged to direct labor. The overtime premium and the fringe benefits are carried as variable overhead costs.

---

[6] Berkshire Toy Company adapted technology used by the Navy. The stuffing machine is not patented.

[7] Fiber filling is a loose material. Two pounds of bagged filling occupy approximately one cubic foot of space. The filling is loaded manually into a metal bin or "hopper." Rotating sets of fork-like tines separate the strands of filling and increase the volume by incorporating air. The proper mixture of air and filling is the "loft."

MARKETING

Marketing of the product takes place at the retail level via catalogue sales and in the company's retail store adjacent to the factory. Retail Internet sales are a new addition to the overall marketing effort. The company also sells wholesale to department stores, toy boutiques, and other specialty retailers. The product can be delivered by two-to-five-day ground service, next-day air, or holiday express. The customer pays the insurance and delivery charges. Berkshire promises same or next-day shipment. Most orders are shipped the same day as received.

When the company receives a customer's order, an employee takes a bear of the requested color and dresses it according to the customer's wishes. Then the bear is packaged with a protective air bag and complimentary piece of chocolate candy, and shipped in a designer box. The designer box contributes to the product image. It is reminiscent of the packaging used for a famous-name cologne and intended to lend an air of status and exclusivity to the product. The box is also important to toy collectors who expect to pay or receive a price premium in the secondary market for items that are in "mint-in-box" condition. Producing the box is a custom job involving a box manufacturer and a printing company. The unit cost of the box decreases with the size of the order that the company places with the manufacturer. Rush orders are more costly than normal orders. In July 1997, the purchasing manager placed an order for enough boxes to cover budgeted sales in the coming year.

Berkshire's policy on sales commissions has remained stable over the past several years. Commissions of 3 percent are paid on retail store sales and sales to wholesale buyers. No commissions are paid on catalog sales. The company-owned retail outlets have proved unprofitable, so all of them, except for the factory store, have been closed in previous years.

THE ACCOUNTING PROBLEM

"I think I know what some of the problems are, but I would like a detailed analysis that provides confirmation from our accounting data," McKinley continues.

"Did inventory change much?" you ask.

"It's pretty negligible. Our peak selling time is from Christmas to Mothers Day, so we don't have much on hand at the June 30 year-end. We started last year with almost nothing and it was all we could do to keep up with demand, so we ended up with almost nothing as well." You jot down a note to ignore changes in raw materials and finished goods inventories and to assume that production volume equals sales volume.

"Didn't you put a new incentive compensation plan in place this year?"

"As a matter of fact, we did. Perhaps it was a factor in what happened this year."

The new incentive compensation plan was adopted effective July 1, 1997. Under this plan, each of the three department heads is rewarded based on the performance of his or her responsibility center. Performance is measured against the company's master budget and its standard cost system. The plan was the result of several meetings with McKinley and her managers who argued and bargained for a plan that rewarded the managers fairly for individual contributions and achievements. McKinley's plan was intended to promote participation and teamwork and the managers accepted the new program enthusiastically. The plan provides for the following:

- David Hall, the purchasing manager, will receive a bonus equal to 20 percent of the net materials price variance, assuming the net variance is favorable. Otherwise, the bonus is zero.
- Rita Smith, the marketing manager, will receive a bonus equal to 10 percent of the excess, if any, of actual net revenues (revenues minus both variable and fixed selling expenses) over master budget net revenues.
- Bill Wilford, the production manager, will receive a bonus equal to 3 percent of the net of several variances: the efficiency (usage or quantity) variances for materials,

labor, and variable overhead; the labor rate variance; and the variable and fixed overhead spending variances. Wilford receives no bonus if his net variance is unfavorable.

INTERNET SALES PROGRAM

"It seems that the incentive plan produced results," continues McKinley. "Smith had a terrific year this year. Unit sales were more than 16 percent above budget (Table 1). She says one of the principal factors was the new Internet sales policy she instituted and the advertising campaign to support it. We've never had that kind of year in sales before."

The Berkshire Toy Company began selling over the Internet in November 1997. At the same time, the company launched a nationwide radio advertising campaign. All radio advertisements are tagged with a reference to the web site that, in turn, provides visual support for the radio advertising and an opportunity for customers to order online. As an additional incentive to attract Internet customers, Rita Smith proposed that Berkshire offer a substantial discount to customers who ordered over the Internet. Because the discounted Internet price ($42.00) was still greater than the price that Berkshire was charging its wholesale customers ($32.00), McKinley approved the price change.

To boost its Internet sales, the company held special holiday sales. The Christmas and Valentine's Day sales featured the Berkshire Bear in special seasonal costumes. Both events were immediate successes not only with Internet customers, but also with retail and wholesale customers who paid the customary prices. The greatest success was the Mother's Day campaign. For this event, the web site displayed an image of "Mama's Boy," a bear sporting sunglasses, jeans and T-shirt, and an appliqued tattoo on its upper arm that said "Mom."

The 15-inch bears produced by the Berkshire Toy Company are identical except for their color and their accessories. Although the bears may be purchased with differing accessories, the unit cost of the accessories per bear has been relatively stable over time. The average historical cost of accessories has been a very small part of the total cost of the bear, and the standard cost of accessories is computed as an average. The price differences in the product reflect the company's discounting practices and not differences in accessories.

The master (static) budget for the year ended June 30, 1998 was prepared before the Internet program and price change were adopted. It called for the sale of 280,000 units, allocated as follows:

Retail and mail order	238,000 units	x	$49.00	=	$11,662,000
Wholesale	42,000 units	x	$32.00	=	1,344,000
Total	280,000				$13,006,000

The expected distribution of 85 percent retail and 15 percent wholesale was based on the company's experience in prior years. Thus, the budgeted average selling price was $46.45. Actual sales for the year were as follows:

Retail and catalog	174,965 units	x	$49.00	=	$8,573,285
Internet	105,429 units		$42.00	=	4,428,018
Wholesale	45,162 units	x	$32.00	=	1,445,184
Total	325,556 units				$14,446,487

16-8

MATERIALS AND PRODUCTION

"Hall had a few triumphs of his own this year," said McKinley. "He managed to get some substantial price discounts on acrylic pile fabric, plastic joints, and polyester fiberfilling. Price discounts of 7 to 10 percent on our three main inputs add up to some real savings." Berkshire Toy Company's schedule of standard manufacturing costs is reproduced in Table 2. The schedule of actual manufacturing costs for the year ended June 30, 2002 is in Table 3.

"So," McKinley continues, "at least on the surface, it looks like marketing and purchasing had a good year, but production is another story. Bill Wilford was not part of the original Berkshire team. Headquarters sent him here from Hercules (the luggage division) to learn the ropes after Jack Johnson left. Jack joined a competitor last July."

"During Bill's first week on the job, we had a freak thunderstorm and the storm drain backed up, ruining a large amount of fiber filling. The loss was uninsured. Since then, I have gotten plenty of feedback from Bill who has been struggling to keep up with production. He has complained about the substandard direct materials, deviations from standard production plans, and the amount of overtime required to meet sales demand. The plant has been operating at near to maximum capacity of 350,000 units. His people are tired. Some of them quit and had to be replaced at higher-than-standard wage rates. Bill also said that extra maintenance was required on the machinery and that, even so, they've experienced frequent breakdowns. He's been vehement about stock-outs of some of the imported accessories. At one point, sales commitments made it necessary to schedule overtime to copy some of the bear outfits and make them in-house. But he tries to be fair and responsible. He admitted that he was the person who moved some of the plastic parts to an empty box marked 'refuse' that was hauled away later by the trash collectors. This is a small place and I hear almost everything that goes on."

"By the way," McKinley winds up, "did you get the information I faxed you?"

"Let's see," you reply. "I have the 2001-02 income statement (prior to bonus calculations), the breakdown of budgeted and actual revenues, and schedules of standard and actual direct production costs. I do need some more detailed information about manufacturing overhead and selling costs. After that, I'll get back to you as soon as I can." McKinley agrees to send you details of actual overhead expenditures for the last five years and actual selling expenses for 2001 and 2002. These are shown in Tables 4 and 5.

REQUIRED

1. a.   Using the information in the case and Tables 1-5, prepare a flexible budget[8] for the Berkshire Toy Company for the year ended June 30, 2002. Analyze the company's total master (static) budget variance for the year. Compare the flexible and master (static) budgets and prepare a schedule showing the sales volume variance. Compare the actual results and the flexible budget, and

---

[8] For the sales revenue categories shown in Table 1, prepare a flexible budget based on actual units sold multiplied by the master (static) budget prices. For Internet sales, use a "revised" budget price of $42. To analyze sales volume effects, also prepare a second flexible budget for the sales revenue categories based on the total of 325,556 units sold, multiplied by the budgeted mix (85 percent for retail, 0 percent for Internet, and 15 percent for wholesale). Multiply these quantities by the respective budgeted sales prices. The difference between the two flexible budget amounts is generally termed a "sales mix variance," which quantifies the effect on income that results because the actual mix of distribution channels deviates from the budgeted mix. A comparison between the master (static) budget and the flexible budget prepared on the basis of the budgeted mix is the "sales volume variance." This variance measures the effect on operating income of selling more or fewer units than planned. The net of the sales mix variance and the sales volume variance equals the "sales activity variance."

prepare a schedule showing the flexible budget variance. Subdivide the flexible budget variances into the appropriate price (rate or spending) and efficiency (usage or quantity) variances for materials, labor, and variable overhead.

    b.   Compute the bonuses earned in fiscal 1998, if any, by David Hall of the purchasing department, Rita Smith of the marketing department, and Bill Wilford of the production department.

2.   a.   You will be assisting in the investigation of certain variances. Using the information provided, formulate some likely explanations for the observed variances.

    b.   Comment on the advantages and disadvantages of the incentive compensation plan as it applies to department heads. What is the appropriate role of the budget in performance evaluation? What modifications to the incentive plan would you recommend? Why?

3.   (Optional) Suppose that Berkshire Toy Company adopts a balanced scorecard (BSC) to measure its performance. What performance dimensions are typically included in a BSC? What specific performance measures (indicators) might be included in the scorecard? For useful background information on BSCs, see Chapter 2 of Cost Management, 2nd edition, by Blocher, Chen, and Lin, Irwin-McGraw Hill, 2002.

TABLE 2
Berkshire Toy Company
A Division of Quality Products Corporation

Schedule of Standard Costs: Fifteen-Inch Berkshire Bear

Normal Capacity: 280,000 units	Quantity Allowed Per Unit	Input Price	Standard Cost Per Unit
Direct materials			
Acrylic pile fabric[a]	0.02381 bolts	$35.00/bolt	0.8333
10-mm acrylic eyes	2 eyes	$0.19/eye	0.3800
45-mm plastic joints	5 joints	$0.14/joint	0.7000
Polyester fiber filling	0.90 lbs.	$1.45/lb.	1.3050
Woven label	1 label	$0.05/each	0.0500
Designer box	1 box	$0.24/each	0.2400
Accessories[b]	various		0.1200
Total direct materials			3.6283
Direct labor			
Sewing	0.50 hours		
Stuffing and cutting[c]	0.30 hours		
Assembly	0.30 hours		
Dressing and packaging	0.10 hours		
Total direct labor	1.20 hours	$8.00/hour	9.6000
Variable manufacturing overhead[d]	1.20 DLH	$3.1140/DLH	3.7368
			16.9651
Fixed manufacturing overhead	1.20 DLH	$1.9700/DLH	2.364
			$19.3291

[a] One bolt of fabric is 10 yards long by 72 inches wide. Fabric for 42 finished units can be cut from one bolt.

[b] The cost of accessories varies from 7 cents per unit for a bow tie to 45 cents per unit for fisherman's gear. The standard of 12 cents per unit reflects the historical assortment of accessories chosen by customers.

[c] Less than 0.01 hour per unit is spent cutting the fabric. Therefore, hours spent in the cutting operation are not separately recorded. They are included with hours spent operating the pneumatic stuffing machine because both operations are usually performed by the same employees.

[d] Variable and fixed overhead are allocated to production on the basis of standard direct labor hours allowed. Standard amounts are computed at normal capacity of 280,000 units. Maximum practical capacity is 350,000 units of production attainable in consideration of planned maintenance and scheduled down time for holidays. Normal capacity is the long-run average productive output that smoothes out seasonal, cyclical, and other variations in customer demand.

TABLE 3
Berkshire Toy Company
A Division of Quality Products Corporation

Schedule of Actual Manufacturing Costs
for the Year Ended June 30, 2002

	Quantity Used	Input Price	Total Cost	
Direct materials				
Acrylic pile fabric	7,910 bolts	$32.4174/bolt	$256,422	
10-mm acrylic eyes	661,248 eyes	$0.l900/eye	125,637	
45-mm plastic joints	1,937,023 joints	$0.1270/joint	246,002	
Polyester fiber filling	344,165 lbs.	$1.3100/lb.	450,856	
Woven label	328,447 labels	$0.0500 each	16,422	
Designer box	315,854 boxes	$0.2200 each	69,488	
Accessories		various	66,013	a
Total direct materials			1,230,840	
Direct labor				
Sewing	189,211 hours			
Stuffing and cutting	104,117 hours			
Assembly	121,054 hours			
Dressing and packaging	34,615 hours			
Total direct labor	448,997 hours	$8.1700/hour	3,668,305	
Overtime premium	103,787 hours	$4.0850/hour	423,970	
Other variable manufacturing overhead			1,301,695	b
Fixed manufacturing overhead			658,897	
			$7,283,707	

a The actual input price for accessories is derived by dividing the actual cost of $66,013 by units sold (325,556), yielding an average accessories cost of $0.20277 per bear.

b The actual input price for variable overhead is obtained by dividing the total variable overhead ($1,301,695 + $423,970) by actual direct labor hours worked, yielding a price or rate of $3.843377 per direct labor hour.

TABLE 4
Berkshire Toy Company
A Division of Quality Products Corporation

Schedule of Actual Manufacturing Overhead Expenditures
for the Years Ended June 30, 1998 through 2002

	2002	2001	2000	1999	1998
Units produced	325,556	271,971	252,114	227,546	201,763
Variable overhead:					
Payroll taxes and fringes	$840,963	$524,846	$467,967	$413,937	$356,150
Overtime premiums	423,970	24,665	2,136	1,874	1,965
Cleaning supplies	4,993	6,842	6,119	5,485	4,996
Maintenance labor	415,224	256,883	232,798	244,037	216,142
Maintenance supplies	27,373	15,944	12,851	15,917	14,323
Miscellaneous	13,142	11,244	9,921	8,906	7,794
Total	$1,725,665	$840,424	$731,792	$690,156	$601,370
Fixed overhead:					
Utilities	$121,417	$119,786	$117,243	$116,554	$113,229
Depreciation-machinery	28,500	28,500	28,500	28,500	28,500
Depreciation-building	88,750	88,750	88,750	88,750	88,750
Insurance	62,976	61,716	57,211	55,544	54,988
Property taxes	70,101	70,101	68,243	68,243	66,114
Supervisory salaries	287,153	274,538	275,198	269,018	254,469
Total	$658,897	$643,391	$635,145	$626,609	$606,050

TABLE 5
Berkshire Toy Company
A Division of Quality Products Corporation

Schedule of Actual Selling Expenses
for the Years Ended June 30, 2002 and 2001

	2002	2001
Units sold:	325,556	271,971
Variable expenses:		
Packing and shipping	$1,580,089	$1,015,913
Commissions	129,080	216,116
Catalogs, brochures, and samples	150,425	65,658
Total	$1,859,594	$1,297,687
Fixed expenses:		
Salaries	$2,734,868	$2,345,121
Advertising and promotion	2,288,324	2,086,021
Total	$5,023,192	$4,431,142

CASE 16-2. THE MESA CORPORATION

The Mesa Corporation, a medium sized manufacturing firm, uses injection molding machines to produce a variety of custom-ordered products for the airline and automotive industries. Recent recessionary pressures in the economy have negatively affected both the airline and the automotive industries. The major airline and auto firms are "squeezing" their suppliers, including Mesa. Consequently, there is a lot of pressure to control costs.

Adrian Bates is the production superintendent for Mesa (see the partial organization chart for Mesa in Figure 1). Her job includes aiding managers in solving production problems, in using management accounting information, and in using techniques to control production costs.

One of Ms. Bates' subordinates, Chris Kenyon, manages the Molding Department of Mesa Corporation. Mr. Kenyon has asked Ms. Bates' opinion about some perceived problems in his department and a potential solution which he is considering. Based on his rudimentary knowledge of cost control and some feedback data from recent production reports, Mr. Kenyon thinks that one of the standards in his department may be outdated. As a proposed solution, he is considering revising the standard usage of plastic which is used as a benchmark to signal an out-of-control machine.

The Molding Department has twelve identical molding machines (Machines A through L) which produces subassemblies for various products. When a machine is properly adjusted, it uses an average of 100 pounds of plastic (with a standard deviation of 3 pounds) to produce a subassembly. When a machine is not properly adjusted, it uses an average of 110 pounds of plastic (with a standard deviation of 5 pounds) to produce a subassembly. Since it is quite costly to adjust the machines, adjustments are made only when variances indicate that a machine might be out-of-control.

Mr. Kenyon's responsibilities include determining which variances should be investigated and whether the existing standard is correct or should be revised. The primary criterion underlying his decisions is to minimize the department's production costs per subassembly and to meet quality expectations. Figure 2 illustrates the situation in Mr. Kenyon's department. The bell-shaped curve on the left represents the distribution of the material usage per unit of output when a machine is in-control. The mean of this distribution, $C_i = 100$, is used as the performance standard. The bell-shaped curve on the right is the distribution of material usage when a machine is out-of-control. The mean of this distribution, C_O, is 110. Since performance is typically subject to a multitude of random factors, actual material usage may be lower (a favorable variance) or higher (an unfavorable variance) than C_i or C_O.

Table I illustrates the two basic types of decision errors which increase the cost of producing the subassemblies. The rows of the table indicate the two alternative actions which Chris may take, while the columns indicate the two alternative states of nature which can occur. A Type I error results in the cost of an unnecessary investigation when a machine is actually in-control and does not need adjustment. A Type II error results in the cost of continuing to use too much plastic by not adjusting a machine which is actually out-of-control. Type I errors are caused by large random unfavorable variances from the in-control distribution. Type II errors are caused by large random favorable variances from the out-of-control distribution.

Recently, Mr. Kenyon received the variance report (shown in Table 2) for the twelve machines in his department. The observations from these twelve machines also are shown in Figure 2. The report shows usage variances, from the standard quantity of 100 pounds, ranging from a favorable 8 pounds to an unfavorable 17 pounds. Because Mr.

Source: Capettini, Robert, C. W. Chow, and J. E. Williamson. 1992. Instructional cases: the proper use of feedback information. *Issues in Accounting Education*. 7, 1 (Spring). 48-56.

Kenyon did not want to incur excessive and unnecessary investigation costs, he decided to have the firm's mechanic inspect and adjust only those machines with unfavorable variances two or more standard deviations from the standard (machines G, H, I, J, K, and Q. From his investigations the mechanic found machines G and H to be in-control while machines L J, K, and L were out-of-control (see Table 3).

Mr. Kenyon feels that knowing the means of both the in-control distribution and the out-of-control distribution is necessary to making sound investigation decisions. Based upon the mechanic's findings, Mr. Kenyon was considering revising the standard quantity allowed for production of the subassemblies from 100 to 108 (the amount used by machine H) pounds of plastic per unit; this is the standard which would have prevented the Type I errors resulting in the unnecessary investigation costs associated with machines G and H. He also was considering revising the expected mean usage of an out-of-control machine from 110 to 113 pounds of plastic per unit (the average usage of the four out-of-control machines).

Adrian Bates is concerned that Chris might be wasting resources by doing unnecessary investigations. However, Ms. Bates also is concerned that if Chris does not do enough investigations, the resultant lower quality may cause the product to be rejected by the airline and automotive firms. This may lead to expensive rework or loss of profitable contracts with these industries.

QUESTIONS

Suppose that you are Adrian Bates who has been asked to evaluate Chris Kenyon.

1. Has Chris Kenyon performed his job well?
2. Which of the twelve machines would you have investigated (i.e., which cost variances do you think were caused by a machine NOT being in proper adjustment)? Why?
3. Why were the means of the two distributions (when a machine is properly adjusted and when a machine is not properly adjusted), based on the variances selected for investigation, higher than what Chris Kenyon thought they were?
4. Re-estimate the means of the two distributions. Is the mean plastic usage of 100 pounds when a machine is in proper adjustment still an appropriate standard or is 108 or some other number a better standard? Is the existing mean plastic usage of 110 pounds when a machine is not in proper adjustment still an appropriate estimate of the mean of that distribution or is 113 or some other number a better estimate?
5. What methods can you suggest to improve Chris Kenyon's ability to update, in the future, the means of the two distributions?
6. Do you agree with Chris is raising the standard to 108 pounds? Why? How often should a standard be reviewed for revisions?

FIGURE I
Mesa Corporation Organization Chart

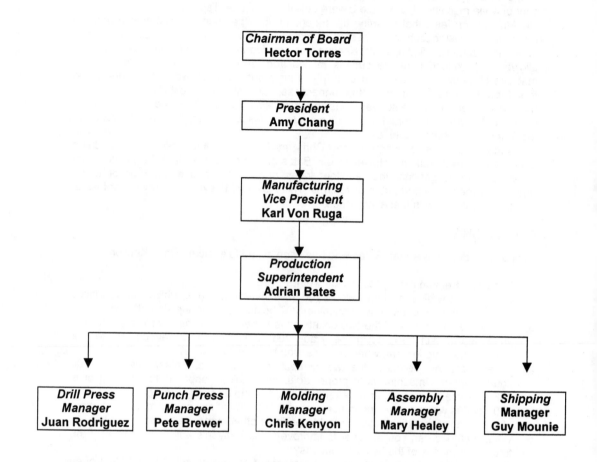

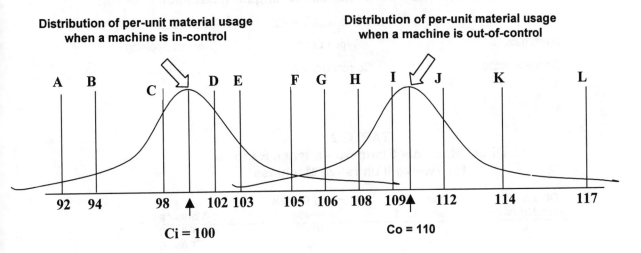

FIGURE 2
Distribution of In-Control and Out-of-Control Costs with the Twelve Machines

Distribution of per-unit material usage
when a machine is in-control

Distribution of per-unit material usage
when a machine is out-of-control

A   B   C   D   E   F   G   H   I   J   K   L

92   94   98   102 103   105 106 108 109   112   114   117

$C_i = 100$ $C_o = 110$

Pounds of Plastic

TABLE 1

Decision Table for Variance Investigation Decision

	Machine Is In-Control	Machine Is Out-of-Control
Investigate	Type I Error	Correct Decision
Do Not Investigate	Correct Decision	Type II Error

TABLE 2
Direct Materials Standard Variance Reports
for Twelve Illustrative Machines

Observation from Machine	Pounds of Plastic Used	Standard Pounds of Plastic	Variance
A	92	100	FAV 8
B	94	100	FAV 6
C	98	100	FAV 2
D	102	100	UNFAV 2
E	103	100	UNFAV 3
F	105	100	UNFAV 5
G	106	100	UNFAV 6
H	108	100	UNFAV 8
I	109	100	UNFAV 9
J	112	100	UNFAV 12
K	114	100	UNFAV 14
L	117	100	UNFAV 17

TABLE 3
Mechanic's Report of the Physical Inspection of Six Machines

In-Control Machines	Lbs. Used		Out-of-control Machines	Lbs. Used
G	106		I	109
H	108		J	112
			K	114
			L	117
Total Useage	214		Total Usage	214
Average Usage	107		Average Usage	113

USING ENHANCED COST MODELS IN VARIANCE ANALYSIS FOR BETTER CONTROL AND DECISION MAKING

By Kennard T. Wing, CMA

The budget and the analysis of variance between budget and actual are two of the most fundamental financial management tools. Yet in many organizations, these tools are "paper tigers" that can encourage or foster a lack of budget discipline. Managers who are called to account for their numbers in these organizations attack the budget variance report rather than going after the problems in their units. Their criticism might go something like this: "That report doesn't take into account the fact that once we pass 100,000 units per month, our preventive maintenance expenses go up. It only looks like we spent too much this month. Following recommended PM schedules is a key to successful financial performance long term." It sounds plausible. The result is that the managers are "off the hook" for their whole variance because no one knows how much of the budget variance for the month the increased maintenance activity should or actually does account for.

The reality is that the typical variance report is not particularly helpful even if managers want to use it to identify meaningful exceptions, which leads to a comment such as: "I can't tell which of those line item variances are just noise in the accounting system and which ones are something I should he doing something about."

Worse still, bad decisions can result when managers do not understand the limitations of the reports. For example, someone might offer: "The report says labor is a variable cost. Volume's down, so people ought to be laid off."

Here's the basic problem. Variance analysis is based on overly simplistic cost models in which every cost has to he treated as either fixed or variable. In the real world, however, many costs do not behave according to those idealized models, which means that managers can always legitimately point to shortcomings in the variance analysis. The reports either do not help them identify cost issues, or managers can use the limitations to reduce their own financial accountability.

Let's take a simple example. XYZ Organization has a cost that is semi-variable. That is, the cost is fixed up to a certain level of volume and variable beyond that point. Suppose the cost is treated as fixed in the variance reporting system. When volume is high and the unit is over budget, the manager can indicate that the variance is from the increased volume (not controllable), the report is no good, and the cost is what it ought to be. Now suppose the cost is treated as variable. When volume is low and the unit is over budget, the manager can say that the variance is due to decreased volume (not controllable), the report is no good, and the cost is what it should be. It does not take too many of these experiences before the budget variance report carries little weight in the organization.

Does every cost need to be treated as fixed or variable? No. We have merely relied on what we were taught in Management Accounting 101 or on whatever capabilities were built into the reporting software we happened to have available. The time has come for financial managers to develop:

- models of cost reflecting how costs actually behave, and
- variance reporting using enhanced cost models.

Calculating a Volume Variance with Semi-Variable Costs in Excel

Let   BVOL be the address of the cell containing budgeted volume.

        AVOL be the address of the cell containing actual volume.

        BKPT be the address of the cell containing the breakpoint between fixed and variable.

        ICU be the address of the cell containing the budgeted (or standard) incremental cost per unit for volumes above the breakpoint.

Then the volume variance is equal to the expression:

= (If(BVOL>BKPT, BVOL, BKPT)
− If(AVOL>BKPT, AVOL, BKPT))
* ICU.

A sample is shown at right. The 50 units above breakpoint should have cost $55 each, implying semi-variable costs should have been $2,750 higher than budgeted. This is our volume variance.

	BUDGET	ACTUAL	VARIANCE
Unit Volume	2,000	2,100	(100)
Total Step-Fixed Costs	$70,000	$78,000	$(8,000)
Budgeted Incremental Unit Cost	$55		
Breakpoint	2,050		
Volume Variance			$(2,750)
Controllable Variance			$(5,250)

I'll explain how to handle variance calculations for semi-variable costs, for step-fixed costs, and for several situations where a shifting mix affects cost behavior. Developing other, more sophisticated cost models and variance reporting is an important direction for the management accounting and financial management profession that will lead to improved control and decision making.

CALCULATING VOLUME VARIANCE WITH SEMI-VARIABLE COSTS

Let's examine how to calculate volume variance with semi-variable costs. Semi-variable costs are fixed below a certain level of volume, called the breakpoint, and are variable above that level. As an example, consider the emergency department of a hospital with which I worked. The largest cost in the department was nursing labor. Because emergency departments must be ready to handle large increases in volume instantaneously, nurses are not sent home or reassigned when volume is low. The department is staffed at a level that is consistent with a wide range of volumes. Still, there is some level of patient volume at which staff must be added. Flexing up above the department's core staffing level in either small or large increments can be handled by overtime, on-call staff and staff pulled from other units. These characteristics

suggested that the semi-variable cost model would be appropriate for nursing labor in this department.

The question was: How much of the budget variance was due to uncontrollable changes in patient volume, and how much was attributable to factors the manager was supposed to control? To provide an answer, we need to decompose the budget variance into a volume variance and a controllable variance.

Because semi-variable costs act like fixed costs over part of the range of volume and like variable costs over the rest of the range of volume, the volume variance associated with semi-variable costs behaves similarly.

- In the fixed cost range, the volume variance is zero.
- In the variable cost range, the volume variance is the same as for a variable cost.

In total, there are four eases financial managers need to be concerned about, depending on how budgeted and actual volume compare to the breakpoint at which semi-variable costs change from fixed to variable:

Calculating a Volume Variance with Step-Fixed Costs

Step-fixed costs are readily handled in Excel using the HLOOKUP function. Let VOL be the address of the cell containing unit volume for which a corresponding step-fixed cost is required. Let ARRAY be the range reference for a two-row section of the spreadsheet, the first row containing the list of unit volumes at which costs step up and the second row containing the amounts to which step-fixed costs are supposed to increase at those points. Then the expression =HLOOKUP(VOL, ARRAY, 2) will return the standard step-fixed cost corresponding to the unit volume at VOL. If AVOL is the address of the cell containing actual volume and BVOL is the address of the cell containing budgeted volume, then the volume variance is equal to the expression: =HLOOKUP(BVOL, ARRAY, 2) – HLOOKUP(AVOL, ARRAY, 2).

A sample is shown below. The additional 50 units above budget should not have led to any increase in cost, so the volume variance is zero.

STEP-FIXED COST FUNCTION

Volume	o	1,000	2,000	3,000
Cost at that Volume	$5,000	$10,000	$15,000	$20,000

	BUDGET	ACTUAL	VARIANCE
Unit Volume	1,900	1,950	(50)
Total Step-Fixed Costs	$10,000	$15,000	$(5,000)
Volume Variance			$ —
Controllable Variance			$(5,000)

Case 1. Budgeted and actual volume are less than breakpoint. In this case, the department was budgeted to operate and actually operated in the fixed cost range. The volume variance is zero.

Case 2. Budgeted volume is less than breakpoint, and actual volume is greater than breakpoint. Cost is fixed between budgeted volume and the breakpoint. This means that the volume variance for this portion of the difference between budgeted and actual volume is zero. Between the breakpoint and actual volume, semi-variable costs act just like variable costs. Therefore, the volume variance for this portion is calculated the same as for a variable cost.

Case 3. Budgeted volume is greater than breakpoint, and actual volume is less than breakpoint. Between budgeted volume and the breakpoint, semi-variable costs behave just like variable costs. The result is that the volume variance for this portion of the difference between budgeted and actual volume is calculated the same way as a traditional volume variance. Cost is fixed between the breakpoint and actual volume, which means that the volume variance for this portion of the difference between budgeted and actual volume is zero.

Case 4. Budgeted and actual volume are greater than breakpoint. In this case, the department was budgeted to operate, and actually did operate, in the variable cost range. Therefore, the volume variance is the same as for a variable cost.

See the sidebar "Calculating a Volume Variance with Semi-Variable Costs in Excel" to learn how to use an Excel spreadsheet for this calculation.

CALCULATING VOLUME VARIANCE WITH STEP-FIXED COSTS

In the step-fixed cost model, costs are fixed tip to a certain level of volume. Then the costs suddenly jump to a higher level of cost that is fixed over a range of volumes until another point is reached at which costs jump suddenly to a higher level, and so on. To calculate the volume variance, we need to know at what points costs jump up and to what levels they jump. The volume variance is merely what the cost is sup-posed to be at budgeted volume minus what the cost is supposed to be at actual volume.

See the sidebar above on "Calculating a Volume Variance with Step-Fixed Costs" for some calculations.

CALCULATING VOLUME VARIANCE FOR COST CENTER WITH MIXED COSTS

Most cost centers contain several kinds of costs, some of which are best modeled as:
- Variable;
- Fixed;
- Semi-variable; and
- Step-fixed.

The volume variance for the entire cost center is simply the sum of the volume variances for each of these four types. Obviously the volume variance associated with fixed costs is zero.

When different semi-variable costs have different breakpoints, variances may need to be calculated by line item and then totaled. If there are different step-fixed costs with different step-up points and amounts, it might be easier to calculate variances by line item and then sum as opposed to creating the aggregate step-fixed cost function required to treat them together.

CALCULATING A MIX VARIANCE

Let's examine the calculation of a mix variance using the same hospital I mentioned before. In that hospital, the radiology department performed a significant variety of procedures that required quite different quantities of labor, materials, and equipment. The mix of procedures was not under the control of the department manager. The idea was to separate the budget variances attributable to procedure volume and procedure mix from those considered under the managers control.

Mix variances have been calculated in other situations. For example, sales mix variances have been used to calculate the effect on a firm's profitability of changes in the mix of products it sold. These variances are not relevant here because revenues are generally not available for individual procedures in hospital billing. Materials mix variances have also been applied in manufacturing to calculate the effect of using a mix of raw materials different from that specified in the

Calculating a Mix Variance

Let each row of the spreadsheet represent data for a different procedure. We'll need columns for actual volume for each procedure, budgeted volumes for each procedure, and budgeted unit variable cost for each procedure. To calculate the mix index, create a column in which each cell is the product of that procedure's actual volume and budgeted variable unit cost. Use the sum function to calculate the sum of all the values in the column you just created. The result is the mix index.

To calculate the flexible budget, create a column in which each cell is the product of that procedure's budgeted volume and budgeted variable unit cost Use the sum function to calculate the sum of all the values in the column you just created. Multiply that sum by total actual vclume and divide by total budgeted volume. The result is the flexible budget.

The volume variance is total budgeted variable costs minus the flexible budget The mix variance is the flexible budget minus the mix index. The unit variable cost variance is the mix index minus actual variable costs.

A sample is shown below.

PROCEDURE	ACTUAL VOLUME	BUDGETED VOLUME	BUDGETED VARIABLE UNIT COST	MIX INDEX	BUDGETED VARIABLE COSTS	FLEXIBLE BUDGET
A	200	150	$100	$20,000	$15,000	
B	1,800	2,000	$35	$63,000	$70,000	
C	2,700	3,000	$25	$67,500	$75,000	
Total	4,700	5,150		$150,500	$160,000	$146,019

	BUDGET	ACTUAL	VARIANCE
Volume	5,150	4,700	450
Variable Costs	$160,000	$155,000	$5,000

Volume Variance		$13,981
Mix Variance		$(4,481)
Unit Cost Variance		$(4,500)

Calculating a Mix Variance with Semi-Variable Costs

Let each row of the spreadsheet represent data for a particular visit type. We'll need columns for actual volume for each visit type, budgeted volume for each visit type, and budgeted incremental cost per visit above the breakpoint for each visit type. Let SV be the address of the cell containing budgeted semi-variable costs below the breakpoint and BKPT be the address of the cell containing breakpoint volume.

First, calculate the mix index. Create a column in which each cell is the product of that visit type's actual volume and budgeted incremental variable unit cost Use the sum function to calculate the total of the column you just created. Call the cell address of that total M. Call the cell address for total actual volume SUMA and the cell address for total budgeted volume SUMB. Then the following Excel expression is equivalent to the mix index: = If (SUMA>BKPT, ((SUMA - BKPT)/SUMA)*M + SV, SV).

Next calculate the flexible budget. Create a column in which each cell is the product of that visit type's budgeted volume and budgeted incremental variable unit cost. Use the sum function to calculate the total of the column you just created. Divide that total by SUMB. Call the cell address of the result F. Then the following Excel expression is equivalent to the flexible budget: = If (SUMA>BKPT, (SUMA – BKPT)*F + SV, SV).

The volume variance is budgeted semi-variable costs minus the flexible budget. The mix variance is the flexible budget minus the mix index. The unit cost variance is the mix index minus actual semi-variable costs.

An example is shown below.

VISIT TYPE	ACTUAL VOLUME	BUDGETED VOLUME	BUDGETED INCREMENTAL VARIABLE UNIT COST	MIX INDEX	BUDGETED VARIABLE COSTS	FLEXIBLE BUDGET
A	200	50	$100	$20,000	$5,000	
B	1,900	1,925	$35	$66,500	$67,375	
C	2,950	2,975	$25	$73,750	$74,375	
Total	5,050	4,950	$30	$160.250	$146,750	$151,482
				$151,587		

Breakpoint Volume	5,000	
Cost at Breakpoint	$150,000	

	BUDGET	ACTUAL	VARIANCE
Volume	4,950	5,050	—100
Step-Fixed Costs	$150,000	$155,000	$(5,000)

Volume Variance	$(1,482)
Mix Variance	$(104)
Unit Cost Variance	$(3,413)

standard. This is also unlike the hospital case, where a mix variance can exist even when every procedure is performed in accordance with standards. In any case. the mix variance developed is analogous to those two. Note that all costs in the radiology department were classified as either fixed or variable.

The total variable cost variance was decomposed into volume variance, mix variance, and unit variable cost variance. See sidebar; "Calculating a Mix Variance."

Creating "what-if" budgets. The basic approach to calculating these variances is to create a pair of "what- if" budgets. Budgeted variable costs are based on budgeted unit volume, budgeted procedure mix, and budgeted unit cost for each procedure. Actual variable costs are based on actual volumes, actual procedure mix and actual but unknown unit costs for each procedure.

The first "what-if" budget is based on budgeted procedure mix, budgeted unit cost per procedure. and actual volume. It is comparable to the flexible budget of traditional variance analysis. Because it uses the same values as total budgeted variable cost for procedure mix and unit costs, differing only in using actual instead of budgeted volume, the difference between budgeted variable cost and the flexible budget is the volume variance—how much variable costs should have differed from budget if the uncontrollable change in volume were the only change from budget that occurred.

The second "what-if" budget is called the mix index. It is based on actual procedure mix and actual volume but budgeted unit costs by procedure. As it differs from the flexible budget only in using actual mix rather than budgeted mix, the flexible budget minus the mix index is the impact of the shift in mix—how much costs should have differed from budget if only the mix had differed from budget.

The mix index differs from actual variable costs only in using budgeted unit costs instead of actual unit costs, so the mix index minus actual variable cost is the impact of departures from budgeted unit cost that usually are held to be controllable by the manager. The first time this mix variance was implemented, a problem developed in which the variances for individual months failed to sum to the variance as calculated on the year-to-date numbers. I investigated the problem to see under what conditions this would be the case. I concluded that as long as the budgeted mix was the same each month, the monthly variances would sum to the variance of the year-to-date. If the budgeted mix changes from month to month, then the monthly variances generally will not sum to the variance of the year- to-date. In that case, variances should he calculated from the individual months and then summed to create variances for aggregate time periods Although I have not investigated this, I suspect that analogous limitations would affect the sales mix and materials mix variances others have developed.

CALCULATING A MIX VARIANCE WITH SEMI-VARIABLE COSTS

The hospital's emergency department also had a mix issue. That department dealt with even-thing from sore throats to cardiac arrests, and it classified all cases into 16 visit types. You would expect some costs to be higher if the visit mix shifted toward more serious cases, even if overall visit volume was flat. The severity of cases was beyond the department manager's control. Unfortunately the mix variance developed above could not he applied directly to the emergency department because it assumed all costs could he classified as either fixed or variable. Thus, what the hospital needed was to extend the mix variance to cases including semi-variable costs.

For an example, see the sidebar on "Calculating a Mix Variance with Semi-Variable Costs." The method is similar to the mix variance created above. We need to calculate two "what-if" budgets that will allow a comparison of numbers that differ in only one respect. As before, the flexible budget is based on actual volume, budgeted mix, and budgeted unit cost. The mix index is based on actual volume actual mix, and budgeted unit cost. Volume variance is budgeted semi-satiable costs minus the flexible budget. Mix variance is the flexible budget minus the mix index. The unit cost variance is the mix index minus actual semi-variable costs.

The situation is more complicated because semi-variable costs force us to deal with multiple cases. Fortunately the calculations for volume variance with a mix are identical to the case with no mix. Two cases are presented as a result of the mix variance, although the first is trivial. When actual volume is less than or equal to the breakpoint, the mix variance is zero. The calculation is as shown in the sidebar when actual volume exceeds the breakpoint.

It may seem counterintuitive that there is no mix variance when actual volume is less than the break-point but budgeted volume is greater than the breakpoint. Here is the explanation: Mix is irrelevant below the breakpoint. For actual volume below the breakpoint, any mix should generate the fixed portion of cost. Therefore, the variance is due solely to the fact that volume is below breakpoint and has nothing to do with possible variations in mix.

The unit cost variance also presents us with two cases, depending on whether actual volume is above breakpoint. See the sidebar for calculations. Given the difficulties with the original mix variance, it seemed appropriate to investigate whether these variances calculated on a monthly basis would sum to the variance on the year-to-date numbers. The answer generally is no. If some periods are above breakpoint but others are below it, the variance calculation on the year-to-date numbers will be erroneous.

When there is a mix variance with semi-variable costs, variances should not be calculated on data for aggregate periods. Rather, variances for the shortest reporting period ought to be aggregated in order to report variances for longer periods.

CALCULATING MIX VARIANCES WITH STEP-FIXED COSTS

Under the standard step-fixed cost model, it is assumed that each unit of output makes a uniform demand on the step-fixed resource. Obviously there is no mix variance under that assumption. A mix variance is possible only when different kinds of output make different demands on a resource.

Calculating Mix Variances with Step-Fixed Costs

Let each row of the spreadsheet represent data for a particular procedure type. We'll need columns for actual volume for each procedure type, budgeted volume for each procedure type, and budgeted or standard unit consumption by each procedure type of the step-fixed resource. Let AC be the address of the cell containing actual consumption of the step-fixed resource. Let ARRAY be the range reference for a two-row section of the spreadsheet the first row containing the level of resource consumption at which costs step up, and the second row containing the amounts to which step-fixed costs are supposed to increase at those points.

First calculate the mix index. Create a column in the spreadsheet in which each cell is the product of that procedure's actual volume and budgeted hours per procedure. Use the sum function to calculate the total of the column you just created. Call the cell address of that total M. Then the mix index is calculated by the following Excel expression: =HLOOKLUP(M, ARRAY, 2).

Next calculate the flexible budget. Create a column in which each cell is the product of that procedure's budgeted volume and budgeted hours per procedure. Use the sum function to total the column you just created. Call the cell address of that total BC. Call the cell address of total actual volume SUMA and of total budgeted volume SUMB. Then the flexible budget is calculated by the following Excel expression: =HLOOKUP(SUMA*BC/SUMB, ARRAY, 2).

Now calculate the consumption index. It is simply the expression =HLOOKUP(AC, ARRAY, 2).

The volume variance is budgeted step-fixed costs minus the flexible budget. The mix variance is the flexible budget minus the mix index. The unit consumption variance is the mix index minus the consumption index. The price variance is the consumption index minus actual step-fixed costs.

An example is shown below.

STEP-FIXED COST FUNCTION

Hours per Month	0	240	480	720
Cost at that Volume	$5,000	$10,000	$15,000	$20,000

PROCEDURE	ACTUAL VOLUME	BUDGETED VOLUME	HOURS PER PROCEDURE	MIX INDEX	FLEXIBLE BUDGET	CONSUMPTION INDEX
A	50	15	1.0	50	15	
B	275	200	0.5	138	100	
C	320	300	0.2	64	60	
Total	645	515		252	175	
				$10,000	$5,000	
Total Hours Used	270					$10,000

	BUDGET	ACTUAL	VARIANCE
Volume	515	645	-130
Step-Fixed Costs	$5,000	$12,000	$(7,000)
Volume Variance			$ —
Mix Variance			$(5,000)
Unit Consumption Variance			$ —
Price Variance			$(2,000)

For example, different diagnostic procedures might require different amounts of hours on a leased machine. Each machine is available for a fixed number of hours but may be augmented by additional leased machines. The method for calculating a mix variance for a step-fixed cost of this sort is shown in the sidebar titled, "Calculating Mix Variances with Step-Fixed Costs."

As before, a flexible budget is created based on actual volume, budgeted mix, and the budgeted step-fixed-cost function. Also created is a mix index based on actual volume, actual mix, and the budgeted step-fixed-cost function. The volume variance is budgeted step-fixed costs minus the flexible budget. The mix variance is the flexible budget minus the mix index.

There is an additional wrinkle for this type of cost. Actual step-fixed costs could differ from the mix index for either of the following reasons:

- Too much of the step-fixed resource was used for the amount of volume, or
- The proper amount was used, but the price was too high.

To separate out these two causes, calculate another "what-if" budget called the consumption index, which is based on actual consumption of the step-fixed resource and the budgeted step-fixed-cost function. The cost of using more of the step-fixed resource than budget or standard would be the mix index less the consumption index. Because these two "what-if" budgets differ only in that the mix index is based on the use of budgeted or standard amounts of the resource per unit of output, while the consumption index is based on the actual amount of the resource used per unit of output, the difference between them isolates the effect of consuming more of the step-fixed resource per unit of output than called for in the budget or standard. Call this the unit consumption variance.

The other element can be called the price variance. It is calculated by taking the consumption index minus actual step-fixed costs. As both are based on actual use of the step-fixed resource, they differ only in how much cost that use generates. Thus, this expression isolates the variance due to the price of the resource.

Again, we investigated whether variances in step-fixed costs can be calculated on data from aggregate time periods or if variances for aggregate time periods must be calculated by summing variances from the shortest reporting periods. Consider this: The cost associated with leasing a single machine month after month is likely to be much different from the cost of leasing multiple machines for a single month. Here is the impact of this difference: When calculating variances where there are both a mix variance and step-fixed costs, it is a mistake to calculate variances directly on data for aggregate time periods. Variances should be calculated on the shortest reporting period and summed to get variances for aggregate time periods.

CALCULATING VARIANCES FOR DEPARTMENTS WITH MIXED COSTS

I limited my analysis to semi-variable costs or step-fixed costs. In reality departments have a mix of costs. As long as all costs in a department are classified as one kind or another, the department's total budget variance will be equal to the sum of the variances of each different kind of cost. In some cases, multiple costs can be lumped together when their cost behavior is similar. When different semi-variable costs have different breakpoints, separate variance analyses will have to be run for different costs. For step-fixed costs, it is probably both easier and more useful to aggregate line-item variances than to create the aggregate cost function needed to calculate variances on aggregated costs. Obviously, the effort and cost involved in developing these analyses must be weighed against the materiality of the costs and the likely benefit of the better information.

APPLYING THE METHODS

I have shown how to decompose budget variances for several cost models more sophisticated than the traditional cases of fixed and variable costs. While the methods I reported grew out of work in the healthcare field, they have wider applicability in other industries.

Calling a cost semi-variable instead of fixed may seem like a small matter. Such is not the case. A large healthcare system, for example, decided to classify all costs as variable. When volume dropped, it laid off more than 1,000 people, and the workload of most of them had no direct relation to patient volume. The result was that morale of the survivors plummeted, and within a year the system was scrambling to replace not only those it had let go, but many others who had quit.

The point is, the accounting systems we design and implement really do affect management decisions in significant ways. A system built on a bad model of the business will either not be used or, if used, will lead to bad decisions. The assumed behavior of a cost— whether fixed, variable, semi-variable, step-fixed, or something else—is a basic assumption affecting any kind of planning, financial analysis, or control. The stakes today are high. We can no longer afford the over-simplification of fixed and variable. Significant costs must be modeled more accurately in order for management accounting systems to better support executive deliberation and decision making. The extensions of variance analysis developed here are merely a first step along that road.

Kennard T Wing, CMA, is a project director at the OMG Center for Collaborative Learning in Philadelphia, Pa., where he heads the practice that helps nonprofit and public sector organizations build their capacity for financial and performance management. Yon can reach him at Ken@omgcenter.org or (215) 732-2200.

Variance Analysis Refines Overhead Cost Control

BY JEAN C. COOPER, PhD, CPA, AND
JAMES D. SUVER, FHFMA, DBA

ACCOUNTING

Many healthcare organizations may not fully realize the benefits of standard cost accounting techniques because they fail to routinely report volume variances in their internal reports. If overhead allocation is routinely reported on internal reports, managers can determine whether billing remains current or lost charges occur. Healthcare organizations' use of standard costing techniques can lead to more realistic performance measurements and information system improvements that alert management to losses from unrecovered overhead in time for corrective action.

Because of current cost reduction pressures from healthcare payers, healthcare decision makers need better cost information for performance measurement, pricing decisions, and management of activities. Like other service organizations, many healthcare facilities have adapted cost accounting systems and techniques developed for the manufacturing sector—such as standard costing and variance analysis—to generate necessary information. But healthcare managers may not realize all potential benefits from variance analysis.

Because of high fixed and indirect costs, estimated at 80 to 85 percent of total costs in most healthcare organizations, overhead control is challenging to healthcare managers.[9] Standard cost systems, such as overhead volume variance, can aid overhead cost control because they are based on predetermined measures of resource consumption. These measures help managers control operations and evaluate performance by giving them standards with which to compare actual results.[10]

---

[9] Overhead costs in this article are defined as all general and administrative expenses. General expenses include indirect patient care costs and all direct patient care costs which are fixed in nature, such as equipment and personnel or salaries.

[10] Adapted from Fundamentals of Management Accounting by Anthony, Weber and Reece, 4th ed. (Richard D. Irwin, 1985), Problem 9-32, pp. 346–347.

PRICING DECISIONS

For effective management of pricing and budgeting decisions, full costs per unit must be determined in advance of providing a service. Determining a service's variable cost component is fairly straightforward because facilities use variable costs directly in the pricing process and can estimate them accordingly.

Most healthcare providers, however, have relatively few true variable costs—costs that vary directly with changes in volume of input or output. Although only fee-for-service and material-related costs such as food and inpatient supplies meet this definition, many healthcare providers treat nursing or other clinical labor costs as variable costs. But unless staff members are paid fee-for-service, their labor is not a true variable cost.

Since most caregivers are salaried, their pay does not change automatically with patient volume. Only their time allocation between patient and nonpatient activities will change as patient volume changes. To change total costs, administrators must decide to increase or decrease staff.

As a result, fixed costs present a more challenging pricing problem. A healthcare organization must estimate the total amount of fixed cost and the volume used as an allocation base. Because most organizations provide several products or services, using a common surrogate, such as labor hours, can be problematic. For example, when the amount of nursing time for a specific diagnosis related group (DRG) already is being recorded, it may be expedient to use nursing hours to allocate direct and indirect overhead costs. If more nursing hours are used than planned, more overhead would be allocated even if total overhead costs were not increased. This apparent change in overhead costs must be recognized in pricing and control decisions.

Estimated per-unit costs are unique, however, to the specific level of estimated fixed costs and the specific volume of estimated output. Whether fixed costs are direct fixed costs in a department or indirect fixed costs of general administration, both must be recovered through pricing.

Exh. 1 presents standard costs for a healthcare

EXHIBIT 1
STANDARDS FOR ABDOMINAL SCAN PROCEDURE 101

Variable costs

Labor (1/2 hour at $12.00)	$ 6.00
Materials (7 scans at $3.00 per scan)	21.00

Fixed costs

Overhead A (direct and indirect)	100.00
Total cost per procedure	$127.00
Profit margin B (10% of total cost)	12.70
Charge for procedure 101 before deductions	$139.70
Deductions from revenue C	$24.65
Charge to be established	$164.35
Estimated number of procedures to be completed	50,000

a. The per-unit overhead costs are determined in the following manner:

Estimated total overhead costs	$5,000,000
Estimated number of labor hours for next accounting period (50,000 procedures x 0.5 hours)	25,000
Overhead rate per labor hour ($5,000,000/25,000 labor hours)	$200
Overhead rate for procedure 101 per labor hour (0.5 x $200)	$100

b. The profit margin in this organization is determined by a 10% markup on full cost.

Note: The flexible budget equation for procedure 101 would be:
Total costs=$5,000,000 + ($27.00 × quantity of procedures)

c. Deductions from revenue for uncompensated care are estimated at 15% of charges.

---

procedure. The per-unit costs ($127) and desired profit margin (10 percent or $12.70) could be used to evaluate offers discounted from the full charge of $164.35. Standard costs also can provide useful planning data for budgeting and control purposes.

A hospital department could develop an income statement to estimate the next month's profit for a certain procedure, assuming a forecast of 50,000 procedures. This income data also would determine the department's budget:

Gross revenues (50,000 × $164.35)	=	$8,217,500
Allowances for uncompensated care (50,000 × $24.65)	=	1,232,500
Net revenues (50,000 × $139.70)	=	6,985,000
Expenses: Standard cost of services (50,000 × $127.00)	=	6,350,000
Projected profit margin (10% of total cost)	=	$ 635,000

Projected profit of Procedure 101 for the next accounting period would be $635,000, assuming that:

50,000 procedures will be completed during the month and capacity in the department is sufficient to accomplish this level without additional costs (such as overtime) being incurred;

- All 50,000 procedures will be billed at the stated charge of $164.35 and allowances will equal 15 percent of charges;
- All cost figures (such as salary costs) occur as planned; and
- The organization achieves all productivity measures (0.5 labor hours per test).

If any assumption is incorrect, a variance from planned profit will occur. Administrators then must determine whether variance was controllable and by whom.

EXHIBIT 2
ACTUAL RESULTS FOR PROCEDURE 101

Standards:

Procedures planned	50,000	
Planned profit (50,000 × $12.70)	$635,000	
Standard charge per procedure		$164.35
Standard costs per procedure		127.00
Standard profit per procedure		12.70
Standard discount from charges		24.65

Actuals:

Procedures completed	49,000	
Gross revenues (49,000 × $164.35)		$8,053,150
Discounts (49,000 × $24.65)		1,207,850
Net revenues (49,000 × $139.70)		6,845,300
Actual labor and material costs (49,000 × $27.00)		1,323,000
Actual overhead		5,000,000
Actual profit		$ 522,300

Variance between planned and actual profit for 49,000 procedures:

Expected profit (49,000 × $12.70)	$522,300
Actual profit	522,300
Variance	$100,000 under-recovery

PERFORMANCE MEASUREMENT

If the results for Procedure 101 were achieved as shown in Exh. 2, the 49,000 procedures actually performed would be expected to provide $622,300 in profits ($12.70×49,000). The actual profit ($522,300), however, is $100,000 less than the expected profit ($622,300) and $112,700 less than the projected profit in the original budget ($635,000).

To evaluate the actual results for Procedure 101, a variance analysis report (Exh. 3) could be constructed from the data in Exh. 1 and 2 to explain the difference in profits. A profit of $12,70 is lost on each of the 1,000 procedures not completed. In addition, the $5,000,000 in overhead is not fully allocated to the 49,000 procedures actually billed. Because the overhead rate of $100 assumes that 50,000 procedures will be performed ($5,000,000 / 50,000), completing only 49,000 procedures results in an under-recovery of $100,000 ($100 × 1000) in overhead never billed to clients.

Failure to achieve the planned volume used in developing the overhead allocation for pricing always will result in an under-recovery of overhead costs. Each examination *not* completed results in a loss of $100 in fixed overhead recovery in addition to the loss of $12.70 in profit margin.

Because the planned and actual overhead totals were the same ($5,000,000), no overhead variance would show on the income statement. The charge for a procedure was established using the planned volume ($5,000,000 / 50,000 or $100), but the actual rate for 49,000 procedures would be $5,000,000 / 49,000 or $102. The difference results in an under-recovery of overhead. Unless a manager is aware of potential under-recovery of overhead, corrective action such as an increase in charges or a reduction in actual overhead expenses will not be taken in time to alleviate the shortfall in profit.

In this example, timely identification of the volume decrease of 1,000 could have led to a recovery of the $100,000 loss through overhead cost reductions or price increases. Managers can always estimate the amount of overhead that will be over- or under-recovered by multiplying the planned overhead rate by the forecasted difference between the planned volume used to establish the rate and the actual volume estimated to be billed.

Effective performance evaluation requires differentiation of costs controllable by managers from those heavily influenced by external events. Most healthcare administrators and managers are not able to control volume of services or even prices set under prospective reimbursement agreements. Physicians admit patients and order services. Only when lost volume is due to capacity constraints can management be held responsible. Assigning responsibility and planning dollar implications *before* a contract is signed are the keys to successful

EXHIBIT 3
VARIANCE ANALYSIS FOR PROCEDURE 101

	Projected budget (50,000 procedures)	(49,000 procedures)	Variances
Gross revenue	$8,217,500	$8,053,150	$164,350 Unfavorable
Discount	1,232,500	1,207,850	24,650 Favorable
Net Revenues	6,985,000	6,845,300	139,700 Unfavorable
Costs[A]	6,350,000	6,323,000	27,000 Favorable
Profit	$ 635,000	$ 522,300	$112,700 Unfavorable
Volume variance[B]		$ 100,000 Unfavorable	=$100,000 Unfavorable
Profit margin variance[C]			=$ 12,700 Unfavorable
Net variance			$112,700 Unfavorable

A. Based on flexible budget costs of $5,000,000 fixed costs + $27 variable costs per procedure.
B. 50,000 procedures were used to determine $100 overhead rate. 1,000 shortfall in procedures × $100 overhead rate per procedure = $100,000 of fixed overhead costs not recovered through billing process.
C. Profit margin lost due to reduced volume. 1,000 reduction in procedures × $12.70 profit per procedure = $12,700 reduction in profit.

contracting. Penalty clauses for not achieving volume and incentives for overachieving need to be negotiated with managed care organizations.

One way to prevent under-recovery of overhead is to stipulate contractually that HMOs will pay the fixed costs per day for each patient day not delivered and only the variable costs per day for each patient day in excess of the agreed on volume. Because variable costs per patient day are lower than fixed costs per patient day, HMOs have an economic incentive to deliver more than the negotiated total, limited, of course, by the provider's current capacity.

Focusing on the bottom line without fully understanding why variances occur can lead to dysfunctional decision making. A flexible budget, as shown in Exh. 3, separates the profit expected under the planned volume from the profit variance caused by under-recovery of fixed overhead. Due to their high fixed costs, healthcare providers are particularly vulnerable to overhead under-recovery.

MANAGEMENT CONTROL

Some managers eliminate overhead volume variances by treating overhead as a period expense and not allocating it to individual outputs as done above. Because direct expensing of overhead eliminates the potential for volume variances, it also eliminates two powerful management tools: identifying impacts of fixed overhead on per unit prices, and monitoring recovery of overhead expenses to

determine if and when fixed expenses should be reduced.

A standard cost system that allocates fixed cost on a per unit basis provides information on the amount of fixed costs over- or under-recovered with volume changes. By monitoring changes between actual and planned (standard) volume, managers can make necessary changes in budgeted fixed costs as required. Volume shortfalls are also critical to other management decisions such as cashflow planning, hiring, and strategic planning. Effective management control requires understanding how volume changes help achieve planned levels of performance and profits.

EXHIBIT 4
STANDARDS FOR ROUTINE PHYSICAL EXAM

Standard charge per exam[A]	$ 80.00
Standard costs for the laboratories:	
Supplies per exam	$ 8.00
Labor per exam	6.00
Variable laboratory overhead	18.00
Fixed laboratory overhead per month[B]	10,000.00
Fixed general administrative expenses per month[C]	2,000.00
Planned volume of exams per month	500
Standard unit cost per exam:	
Supplies	$ 8.00
Labor	6.00
Variable overhead	18.00
Total variable cost per exam	32.00
Lab overhead costs [D]	20.00
Standard full cost per exam	$ 52.00
Standard profit per exam: $80–$52=$28	

A. All patients pay charges for this exam. There are no uncompensated care accounts.
B. Fixed laboratory overhead is considered a product cost and allocated to individual products for control purposes.
C. Fixed administrative costs are treated as a period cost and not allocated to individual exams.
D. The per unit fixed overhead cost is determined in the following manner. $10,000 lab overhead cost divided by the 500 exams estimated to be completed for the month = $20 lab overhead per exam.

HIDDEN INVENTORY

Many healthcare organizations do not report work in process or finished goods inventories in their financial statements, implicitly assuming that all services provided by various cost centers have been entered in the billing system for accounting purposes. However, anecdotal evidence indicates that most clinical departments do not carry interim in-process charges, such as estimating inpatient charges for patients not yet discharged, on year-end financial statements.

The quantity of services provided by various cost centers can differ from the quantity reported in revenue accounts and recognized in accounting statements because of the normal time lag required to complete billing. For example, services (such as radiology, laboratory, and surgical procedures) provided to hospital inpatients usually are not billed until the entire procedure is finished.

Also, work completed at the end of a day typically is not forwarded to the accounting system immediately because patient care has highest priority, while billing comes later. (Time lag does not exist for expense accounts, which usually are recorded promptly.) Lost charges tend to increase when output and billing are not monitored.

Many overhead expenses are incurred as functions of time passing rather than patient volume. For example, most salaried employees insist on being paid without waiting for patient or client billing to be completed or cash received. If revenues and costs are to be monitored by departments, and if a matching of revenues and expenses is to occur, some type of cost system must be implemented to measure output that is in process or completed but not billed.

In manufacturing, unbilled activities are captured in work-in-process and finished goods inventories. As noted above, most healthcare providers do not maintain this type of formal inventory account. As a result, a "hidden inventory" of unbilled output can exist, distorting financial statements and information for management decisions.

For example, Exh. 4 presents data for a healthcare organization providing routine physical examinations including EKG and blood tests. Three hundred and ten examinations are billed on the income statement for the current period:

Revenues		
(310 exams × $80)		$24,800
Expenses: standard cost of service billed		
310 × $52.00	$16,120	
Volume variance	800	
Administrative expenses	$2,000	18,920
Net profit		$ 5,880

The 460 examinations completed in the reporting period are used in calculating the volume variance for the department. The shortfall of 40 exams (500 planned - 460 actual) times the overhead rate of $20 equals the $800 volume variance reported.

Management is concerned because the profit at 310 exams should be $2,880 as determined below:

Revenues 310 × $80		$24,800
Expenses		
Variable 310 × $32.00	$9,920	
Fixed	$12,000	
Total expenses		21,920
Expected profit		$ 2,800

The $800 unfavorable volume variance explains why the reported profit ($5,800) is $3,000 greater than planned ($2,800).

While only 310 examinations were billed, the reported volume variance indicates that 460 were completed. Accordingly, 150 examinations (460 - 310) were *completed by the laboratory but not yet billed.*

Whether the paper work is still in the laboratory or has been lost (intentionally or unintentionally), revenues and expenses are improperly matched and reported income is overstated.

Performance evaluation is difficult to assess if only the bottom line is stressed and actual output measures are not available. A reconciliation can be determined in the following manner:

Expected net profit	$2,880
Actual reported profit	5,880
Unbilled overhead (150 exams × $20 fixed overhead)	$3,000
Actual net profit	$2,880

The difference between examinations completed and examinations billed (460 - 310 = 150) times laboratory overhead costs per examination ($20) equals the $3,000 profit overstatement. If only 310 examinations had been completed, the volume variance would have been $3,800 instead of $800 and profit would have been as planned. Most managers like to report a higher level of productivity for their performance evaluation. Unless performance reports are matched with financial reports, unbilled charges will not be known.

In-process inventories exist in healthcare organizations whenever completed services are not billed. Standard cost accounting allows administrators to monitor both production and billing. Reporting unbilled services on internal financial statements or management reports draws attention to potential problems. Accounts similar to work-in-process and finished goods inventories for external reporting can be used to properly match revenues and expenses and provide more appropriate data for cost management and performance evaluation.

OVERHEAD CONTROL IMPLICATIONS OF ACTIVITY COSTING

By Robert E. Malcom

Robert E. Malcom is Professor of Accounting and MIS at The Pennsylvania State University—University Park Campus.

Management accountants' "overhead control" analysis has historically been a contradiction in terms. We have understood for some time that traditional overhead analysis gave us no really useful control information. Recent research on cost drivers for activity based product cost determination has given us a new perspective on overhead control.[1] In addition to overhead pools being too aggregated and allocation of overhead being based on a single, probably irrelevant base, variance formulas are also being misapplied. As a result, accounting performance reports may signal that no deeper investigation is needed when one is warranted or indicate that consumption is a problem when price changes are to blame, etc.

The objective of this article is to assist in changing accounting practice, management education, and the professional examinations away from traditional overhead analysis and toward cost driver based flexible budgets. At best, any time being spent on the usual meaningless reports is a waste and should be avoided. Additionally, the credibility of other accounting reports may suffer by being tarred with the same brush. At worst, any managers relying on current reports may be misled into costly, incorrect decisions.

THE PROBLEM

Garrison's *Managerial Accounting,* a leading text in the field, contains the following typical treatment. "The variable portion of manufacturing overhead can be analyzed and controlled using the same basic variance formulas that are used in analyzing direct materials and direct labor."[2] As is common, the results are labeled Spending Variance and Efficiency Variance. Garrison then notes, "Most firms consider the overhead spending variance to be highly useful..., feeling that the information it yields is sufficient for overhead cost control."[3] Garrison does warn, as do most other authors, that *"...efficiency variance* is a misnomer" as efficiencies are "...not in the use of

overhead *but rather in the use of the base itself."*[4] The efficiency variance simply tells the overhead effect of the difference between planned labor use and actual labor use. In a similar vein, Horngren and Foster say, "The spending variance is really a composite of price and other factors....For this reason, most practitioners used the term 'spending' variance rather than merely 'price variance.'"[5] As will be demonstrated later with a case problem, faith in the spending variance to provide useful information can be very misplaced. If it can be demonstrated that the traditional spending variance is potentially misleading, and if we can agree that the efficiency variance is really just a reconciling item between absorbed overhead and budgeted overhead, why do we put ourselves through these analyses?

INDUSTRIAL PRACTICE

The traditional overhead analysis method—calculation of spending and efficiency variances—is a common procedure of major American manufacturers. Surveys of overhead accounting practices of *Fortune 500 Industrial Companies* from about a decade ago found that virtually all firms using standard costing computed

---

[1] See, for example, R. Cooper and R. Kaplan, "How Cost Accounting Distorts Product Costs," *Management Accounting* (April 1988), pp. 20-27 or J. Shank, "Strategic Cost Management: New Wine or Just New Bottles?" *Journal of Management Accounting Research* (Fall 1989), pp. 47-65.

[2] R. Garrison, *Managerial Accounting: Concepts for Planing, Control, Decision Making,* 6th ed. (Homewood, IL: Richard D. Irwin, Inc., 1991), p. 371. The views quoted from Garrison are deemed representative of many managerial and cost accounting texts, especially those oriented toward undergraduate majors.

[3] Ibid., p. 416.

[4] Ibid., p. 417.

[5] C. Horngren, and G. Foster, *Cost Accounting:A Managerial Emphasis,* 7th ed. (Englewood Cliffs, NJ: Prentice-Hall, Inc., 1991), p. 255.

summary overhead variances. It was also found that the number of firms using both spending and efficiency variances exceeded those using just a spending variance.[6]

In a broader based survey reported in 1990 at the American Accounting Association annual meeting, Emore and Ness reported, "cost information...has not progressed very far over the past few years, [....despite...] considerable literary attention.... ...[M]ost companies are still using the same labor-focused costing systems that have characterized U.S. industry since the early 1900s.... Even though direct labor accounts for less than 10 percent of production costs for the majority of firms responding, alternative bases for attaching indirect manufacturing costs to products (e.g., machine hours, material value, cycle time, etc.) were being used by fewer than 25 percent of the companies....The majority of firms do not break down overhead into its major component cost elements. Sixty-five percent....maintain five or fewer manufacturing cost elements in their product cost buildups [including materials and labor].... [M]any companies placed greater weight on the computational accuracy of their cost systems than their conceptual integrity."[7]

PROFESSIONAL EXAMINATIONS

As would be expected, standard costing problems have been an important part of the Certified Management Accountant examination since its inception. Problems with an emphasis on overhead spending and efficiency variances have continued through 1990 (the latest available at the time of writing).[8] Such problems occur less often on the Certified Public Accountant examinations, but at least two occurred through the 1980s[9]. Such findings should be expected based on usage in practice.

EDUCATION

Emphasis on overhead variances in the classroom is more difficult to detect. Norvin et al. recently synthesized surveys regarding the cost/managerial accounting curriculum. In all four of the synthesized surveys from the 1980s, standard costing/variance analysis was included in the top ten of the most important topics to be covered. [10]

Textbooks being published in the 90s continue to accommodate this preference. In an ad hoc sampling of numerous basic cost/managerial texts oriented toward the undergraduate accounting major, all incorporated the spending and efficiency overhead variances with their standard costing presentations. It is interesting however that Usry and Hammer, another widely used text (in addition to Garrison and Horngren

and Foster cited above), has additionally an especially rich development of flexible budget detail articulated into its presentation of standard costing processes."

Most interestingly, a survey in final stages by Bayou reveals that less than two percent of AAA academics teaching cost and/or managerial accounting object to these variances. Bayou's survey was focused toward obtaining terminology preferences. The study produced 600 responses, a rather remarkable 40 percent response rate. He found that 23.5 percent preferred "Price Variance," 74.8 percent preferred "Spending Variance," and a mere 1.6 percent objected to the calculation of variable overhead variances (including a few with strong comments).[12]

A CASE DEMONSTRATION

The deficiencies involved in current overhead control techniques are difficult to convey in abstract terms. A case demonstration is therefore provided. As noted earlier, equivalent CMA examination problems on overhead variances have continued through 1990.

---

[6]See J. Chiu and Y. Lee, "A Survey of Current Practice in Overhead Accounting and Analysis," contained in *Proceedings of the Western Regional Meeting, Amen-can Accounting Association* (San Diego, CA: San Diego State University, 1980), p. 240; or, J. Chiu and J. Talbott, Factory Overhead Analysis," *Managerial Planning* (July/August 1978), pp. 36-39.

[7]J. Emore, and J. Ness, "Advanced Cost Management: The Slow Pace of Change," *Collected Abstracts of the American Accounting Association's Annual Meeting* (Sarasota, FL: American Accounting Association, 1990—full papers are available from the presenters), pp. 4, 6, 9, 11, and 14. [Ness is a Cost Management Group partner with Price Waterhouse in St. Louis, which has also published overlapping material from this survey.]

[8]See, for example, the following CMA examinations: December 1990, Part 3, Question 1; December 1989, Part 4, Question 1; and December 1988, Part 4, Questions 17 and 18.

[9]For examples from the CPA examinations, see: November 1987 (Theory Number 1, Question 42 and Practice II, Question 4) and May 1984 (Practice II, Problem Number 5).

[10]A. Norvin, M. Pearson, and S. Senge, "Improving the Curriculum for Aspiring Management Accountants: The Practitioner's Point of View," *Journal of Accounting Education* (Fall 1990), pp. 210-211.

[11]M. Usry, and L. Hammer, *Cost Accounting: Planning and Control,* 10th ed. (Cincinnati, OH: South-Western Publishing Co., 1991), pp. 562-592.

However, a June 1983 CMA problem is unusually rich in detail and was selected for demonstration analysis here.[13] (This problem also appears in Horngren and Foster with the CMA recommended solution.[14]) Relevant data are given in Exhibit 1.

The requirements of the problem include the calculation of variable overhead spending and efficiency variances. Two components make up variable overhead, indirect labor and supplies, but as is typical, only a summary analysis is required. Indeed, in most professional examination and text problems, only the summary data are provided. The published solution is given in Exhibit 2, although in a format to emphasize the generic price and quantity variance formulas and to extend the analysis to the two components.

GENERIC EQUIVALENCES

As shown in Exhibit 2, the spending variance calculation is generically equivalent to the price variance for materials and labor. A difference in prices (standard and actual overhead rates in this case) is multiplied by an implicit "actual" base quantity. Here the analogy to labor and material price variance begins to break down, because the assumed actual is a very arbitrary base. As is common in most traditional systems, the arbitrary base here is direct labor. The actual overhead exceeds the calculated standard overhead and the calculation suggests an unfavorable variable overhead spending variance of $150.

The efficiency variance is calculated as the difference between the actual and expected bases (labor hours in the problem) multiplied by the standard rate. Again, the calculation follows the form for quantity variance for direct materials and labor. Actual direct labor hours are less than standard direct labor hours, and so a favorable overhead variance results. The calculated efficiency variance is $8,850 and the combined spending and efficiency variance for variable overhead is $8,700 favorable.

[12]M. Bayou, Technical Terminology of Management Accounting," research in progress, University of Michigan, Dearborn. Data were provided by personal communication with the author, March 1991.
[13]December 1983 CMA examination, Part 4, Section B, Question 7.
[14]C. Horngren, and G. Foster, op. cit., p. 279.

Exhibit 1
NORTON PRODUCTS' MAY DATA

Variable Overhead	Standard Cost per Unit	Standard per Direct Labor Hour	Planned Costs for May	Actual Costs for May	Standard Costs for May
Indirect Labor	$1.25	$.25	$ 75,000	$ 75,000	$ 82,500
Supplies	1.70	.34	102,000	111,000	112,200
Total	$2.95		$177,000	$186,000	$194,700

Other Activity	Planned Data	Actual Data
Output Units	60,000	66,000
Direct Labor Hours per Output Unit	x 5.000	x 4.772
Total Direct Labor Hours	300,000	315,000

Source: Given or derivable from June 1983 Certificate in Management Accounting Examination, Part 4, Section B, Question 7.

Exhibit 2
PUBLISHED SOLUTION PLUS EXTENDED DETAIL

	Total		Indirect Labor		Supplies	
Spending (or Price) Variance:						
Actual Rate ($ Actual / 315,000 DLH)	$ .590476		$ .238095		$ .352381	
Standard Rate (Given)	− .590000		− .250000		− .340000	
Rate Difference (direction may vary)	.000476	U	.0011905	F	.012381	U
Actual Direct Labor Hours	x 315,000		x 315,000		X 315,000	
Spending Variance	$ 150	U	$ 3,750	F	$ 3,900	U
Efficiency (or Quantity) Variance:						
Actual Base (Direct Labor Hours)	315,000		315,000		315,000	
Standard Base (5 DLH x 66,000#)	− 330,000		− 330,000		− 330,000	
Quantity Difference (always same way, here F)	15,000	F	15,000	F	15,000	F
Standard Rate (Given)	x $ .590000		x $ .250000		x $ .340000	
Favorable Efficiency Variances	$ 8,850	F	$ 3,750	F	$ 5,100	F
Total Variance	$ 8,700	F	$ 7,500	F	$ 1,200	F

Source: Institute of Certified Management Accountants, *Questions and Unofficial Answers for June 1983 CMA Examination* (Montdair, NJ: National Association of Accountants, 1983), p. 62. [Data have been rearranged by the author to emphasize the generic price and quantity aspects of the computations; Spending Variance may be viewed as a flexible budget based on actual direct labor.]

What are the implications of the above analysis? At best there is a signal to management that direct labor; the base, was efficiently used. If that is a fact, that knowledge would be more directly available to management from the direct labor variance analysis. Another message is that since spending is close to budget, activity is probably close to plan and that managers might be criticized lightly because the direction is unfavorable. At worst, managers might incorrectly be commended highly because their overhead usage is reported to be highly favorable. The latter two results might or might not be the case, but it will be demonstrated that the report in Exhibit 2 is not the relevant basis for making this determination.

RESPECIFICATION OF VARIABLES

To know whether overhead is being controlled, in general a more disaggregated report should be used. The data given in the CMA examination are not sufficient for this purpose, so additional data

(consistent with given totals) are provided by the author in Exhibit 3. The new data show prices and quantities for each of the overhead components. For simplicity, supplies are assumed to be barrels of lubricants.

In Exhibit 4 the same generic formulas are used for indirect labor and supplies per se as were used for aggregated overhead in Exhibit 2. Labels have been changed to price and quantity variances as now the calculations truly provide these results, i.e., they are not mixed results (except for the generally inconsequential joint portion).

COMPARISON OF ALTERNATIVES

Where before there was a large favorable overhead quantity variance reported, there are now large unfavorable quantity signals. Where before there was a modest unfavorable spending signal, highly favorable price variances are now indicated.

Exhibit 3

ADDITIONAL DATA FOR ILLUSTRATION

	Indirect Labor	Supplies	Totals
Unit of Measure for Inputs	Hours (hr.)	Barrels (bbl.)	
Actual Input Units	7,500 hr.	1,000 bbl.	
Actual Cost per Input Unit	x $ 10 /hr.	x $ 111/bbl.	
Total Actual Cost (given)	$ 75,000	$111,000	$186,000
Standard Input Units	6,600 hr.	990 bbl.	
Standard Cost per Input Unit	x $ 12.50 /hr.	x $113.333 /bbl.	
Total Standard Cost (given)	$ 82,500	$112,200	$194,700
Total Variance (Total Actual less Standard Cost)	$ 7,500 F	$ 1,200 F	$ 8,700 F

Source: Data assumed by author to be consistent with Exhibit 1; details are needed for a complete solution.

The problem highlighted by this analysis warrants further management attention. The problem is not masked by the offsets of similar favorable and unfavorable variances as was the case in the development of Exhibit 2. A review of Exhibit 4 suggests that the traditional approach to analyzing overhead variances, as exemplified in Exhibit 2, is based on totally false premises.

In this model, actual overhead activity is much different than called for by the original plan. For indirect labor, the indication is that a lower quality or lesser-trained workforce was used, as the hourly rate paid was 20 percent less than standard ($10 versus $12.50). At the same time, much more time had to be spent to accomplish the task. Assuming a review shows that the task was appropriately accomplished, the tradeoff was well worthwhile, with a total favorable indirect labor variance of $7,500. Management should therefore be commended for this action. The variance directions and proportions are the same for supplies as for indirect labor. However, *Exhibit 2 indicates the opposite signal!*

The problems with the traditional approach are several: first, the summary spending variance is too much of an aggregation to provide any useful information for managers. But more importantly, the direct labor hours base for calculating usage (and spending) is at best a gross activity indicator; at worst it is simply irrelevant.

HOMOGENEITY PROBLEM

As noted earlier, a simplifying assumption was made in the case of supplies by deeming the category to be all lubricants of the same type. A common characteristic of overhead is that it is a mixture of many different items, so there is often no applicable price or quantity per se. That is, supplies may be pounds of cleaning agents, gallons of solvents, boxes of computer ribbons, etc.

The price and quantity aspects of analysis are not totally intractable even then. Prices may be sampled for representative items as is done for the Consumer Price Index. Then quantities may be inferred as the remainder; albeit an abstract measure. This could become complex and the cost of developing that data must be weighed against the benefit obtained.

The crucial point is still that the traditional computations for overhead spending and efficiency variances yield meaningless outcomes. Appropriate signals from the traditional variances appear only by coincidence. There is a cost to produce that largely irrelevant, perhaps coincidentally correct data. Why not allocate that effort to the development of more useful information?

THE SOLUTION

An increasingly practical alternative to the traditional analysis is to use flexible budgets

Exhibit 4
SOLUTION PER DETAIL DATA, VOLUME DRIVEN STANDARDS

	Indirect Labor		Supplies		Totals	
Price (Spending) Variance						
Actual Price of Input	$ 10.000	/hr.	$111.000	/bbl.		
Standard Price of Input	−12.500	/hr.	−113.333	/bbl.		
Price Difference (Favorable)	$ 2.500	/hr.	$ 2.333	/bbl.		
Actual Quantity of Input	x 7,500	hr.	x 1,000	bbl.		
Favorable Price Variance	$ 18,750	F	$ 2,333	F	$21,083	F
Quantity (Efficiency) Variance						
Actual Quantity of Input	7,500	hr.	1,000	bbl.		
Standard Quantity of Input	−6,600	hr.	−990	bbl.		
Quantity Difference (Unfavorable)	900	/hr.	10	bbl.		
Standard Price of Input	x $12.500	/hr.	x $113.333	/bbl.		
Unfavorable Quantity Variance	$11,250	U	$1,133	U	$12,383	U
Total Variance	$7,500	F	$1,200	F	$ 8,700	F

Source: Data from Exhibits 1 and 3.

based on appropriate cost drivers for major components of overhead, as is illustrated in Exhibit 5. In this report the large component variances could then well be the basis for further analyses, just as was done earlier in Exhibit 4.

For a number of reasons it is time for us to redirect our standard cost practices and our standard cost teaching. First, overhead itself is a relatively larger cost. American manufacturing cost structures have changed over the years from labor being more than overhead to overhead being more than three times labor (and this is only on the average).[15] Second, the statistical tools necessary to implement the above are much more widely understood by managerial accountants than just a few years ago. Third, and perhaps most importantly, widespread computer processing has made it economical to do both the statistical analyses and maintain more detailed cost data bases. Variable budgeting has been around for a long time, although at best it has been practiced and taught as an adjunct to the traditional standard cost system. I suggest that it is time for us to switch the order of things and give most attention to the development of variable budgeting systems—

[15]J. Miller, and T. Vollmann, The Hidden Factory," *Harvard Business Review* (September-October 1985), Exhibit I, p. 143.

because they have the most potential as control tools—and that we relegate the traditional standard cost overhead analysis to an appendix. That clerical analysis may tell us something about the relationship between our estimated product costs and the actual costs of our production, but it gives us very little information that might be useful for the management of our production activities.

COST DRIVER IDENTIFICATION

Presaging Johnson and Kaplan by many years, B. Goetz wrote in 1949, "Traditional cost data tend to be irrelevant and mischievous" and he proposed that "...the systems should be discontinued to save the clerical costs of operating them." Goetz argued that each overhead account "...should be homogeneous with respect to every significant dimension of managerial problems of planning and control. Some of the major dimensions along which burden may vary are number of units of output, number of orders, number of operations, capacity of plant, number of catalogue items offered, and span of anticipation [life cycle].... These recommendations would tend vastly to increase the number of primary burden accounts...."[16] Such dimensions of variability are today being referred to as cost drivers, i.e., the activity that drives costs.

The identification of cost drivers was an important part of J. Dean's pioneering cost study work of 1936. Indeed, using regression analysis, Dean identified product variety (recently rediscovered) as an important element which influenced cost levels.[17] His nonelectronic computations must have been laborious and a National Association of Accountants research study of 1949-50 implied that the least squares method was little used by industry.[18]

REGRESSION UNDERSTANDING

For accounting students the least squares method was included as a brief appendix by both R. Anthony and C. Horngren in the respective first editions of their managerial accounting texts of 1956 and 1962. Horngren then commented that the method was "cumbersome... [and] not so often used."[19] He did not expand this material until his third edition in 1972. Such coverage is now standard, although often the emphasis is merely on cost separation rather than cost driver selection.

In the meantime, Touche had distributed to academics a case based on practice which focused on using regression analysis to select between product units and pounds as the best cost driver for controlling indirect labor in a shipping department.[20] These foresights notwithstanding, there is very little evidence in practice or academe of an integrated treatment of regression analysis in a flexible budgeting cost control system.

AN ILLUSTRATION

In Exhibit 5 it is assumed that machine hours has been found by regression analysis to be the appropriate cost driver for the supplies (here lubricants). Also it is assumed that while all models of the product have the same direct labor hour standard, the more complex models require many more machine hours than the basic high volume model.

Thus, since Exhibit 5 implies a shift in mix from complex to basic models, less lubricants should be needed than otherwise and the previous positive variance has here been transformed into a large negative variance. The analysis method of Exhibit 4 still applies, but now the standard quantity is 900 rather than 990 barrels. This might indicate that a time-based maintenance schedule should be changed to a use-based schedule for optimum cost control.

Too often, the valuable notion of flexible budgeting has been wasted because we have failed to look diligently for the cost driver. For a useful example, consider forklift operator costs. In general, as output rises, so will direct labor and forklift labor. All appear to be associated. Where the flexible budget is based on direct labor, the resultant spending variance can send a seriously misleading signal. If direct labor usage is inefficient, there is no reason at all to expect more forklift labor, but this is the traditional accounting result. Indeed, if direct labor is inefficient, material may have been used more carefully and less fork lift labor should be needed.

The most likely cost driver for forklift labor is number of pallets moved, with pallet density a secondary consideration. Material usage might be a surrogate for number of pallets. Output volume would not usually be the appropriate driver either, as it would be common for material usage to be above or below expectations due to raw material quality or specification changes or machine malfunctions, etc. The most probable cause for forklift use must be found if the variable budget is to send the correct variance signals.

---

[16]See B. Goetz, *Management Planning and Control: A Managerial Approach to Industrial Accounting,* 1st ed. (New York: McGraw-Hill Book Co., 1949), pp. 162-163, and T. Johnson and R. Kaplan, *Relevance Lost: The Rise and Fall of Management Accounting* (Boston: Harvard Business School Press, 1987).

[17]J. Dean, "The Statistical Determination of Costs with Special Reference to Marginal Costs" in *The Studies of Business Administration,* 7:1 (Chicago: School of Business, University of Chicago, 1936), p. 103 (may possibly be found as a supplement to *Journal of Business);* Dean was not the first to apply the least squares method to the analysis of business costs and he cites an application by R. Livingston, "Control of Operating Expenses," *Mechanical Engineering* (LIV, 1926), p. 18. A Compilation of Dean's cost studies can be found in his *Statistical Cost Estimation* (Bloomington: Indiana University Press, 1976).

[18]National Association of Accountants, *Research Reports 16-18,* "The Analysis of Cost-Volume-Profit Relationships" (New York: National Association of Accountants, 1949-50), p. 16.

[19]See R. Anthony, *Management Accounting: Text and Casts* (Homewood, IL: R. D. Irwin, 1956), pp. 316-19, and C. Horngren, *Cost Accounting: A Managerial Emphasis* (Englewood Cliffs, NJ: Prentice-Hall, 1962), pp. 215-16.

[20]Touche, Ross, Bailey & Smart (now Deloitte & Touche), "Ralston Electric Company," miscellaneous paper, c.1966.

Exhibit 5
NORTON PRODUCTS' ACTIVITY BASED FLEXIBLE BUDGET FOR MAY VARIABLE AND STICKY COSTS

Overhead Item (Activity Base)	(1) Budget Cost Per Activity Unit	(2) Activity Units	(3) Flexible Budget	(4) Actual Cost	(5) Variance
Variable Cost:					
Supplies (Machine Hours)	$17 per Machine Hour	6,000 Machine Hours	$102,000	$ 111,000	$ 9,000 U
Sticky Cost:					
Indirect Labor (Number of Models)	$3,000 per Model	20 Models	$ 60,000	$ 75,000	$15,000 U
Totals			$162,000	$186,000	$24,000 U
	(assumed)	(assumed)	(1) x (2)	Exhibit 1	(3) — (4)

*Implicit Standard supply use is $102,000 + $113.333 = 900 barrels and standard indirect labor hours are $60,000 + $12.50 = 4,800 hours.

STICKINESS OF COSTS

Not only has there been a long run trend for overhead to grow as a proportion of total operating costs, but many of these new costs tend to be somewhat nonvariable in character i.e., lumpy and not strictly proportional to changes in activity. A common example is materials ordering and handling costs. As production grows, additional employees are added to handle the additional load; but, if production decreases, these personnel are not immediately laid off. Thus these lumpy costs stick even if activity declines and such costs have therefore sometimes been labeled "sticky costs."

Sticky costs have sometimes been found to be driven by product variety rather than units of output. Exhibit 5 assumes that in addition to the basic high volume product, two dozen other models have been offered and every model requires roughly $3,000 per month in labor support costs for materials purchasing and handling. For May, twenty models were produced, which should have required only $60,000 in indirect labor. Since $75,000 was actually spent, there is an unfavorable variance now of $15,000.

R. Beyer devoted considerable attention to the problem of such sticky costs in his 1963 book on profitability accounting. He labeled these items "long-range variable costs," seemingly another oxymoron. Beyer's solution was to create two budget figures. The longer-run figure was the responsibility of top management and the shorter-run figure was the responsibility of operational management. He termed the former the "management decision variance" and noted that layoffs from "this 'hard-line' approach... [would]...ultimately result in the most economical operation."[21]

If it is assumed for the Norton Products' case that top management had approved for May operations the $75,000 indirect labor planning budget of Exhibit 1 per longer-run expectations, then top management would be responsible for the difference between the planned $75,000 amount (6,000 hours at $12.50) and the activity based $60,000 budget (4,800 hours) of Exhibit 5, or for 1,200 hours. The rationale for the strategic-operational split is that skilled indirect labor cannot be turned off and on as is usual for materials, but must be maintained with at least an intermediate-run outlook. The staffing level is primarily a higher management level decision.

[21]R. Beyer, *Profitability Accounting for Planning and Control* (New York: Ronald Press Company, 1963), pp. 156-57. Beyer also described in the same book a cost driver index, called the Control Factor Unit, for measuring departmental workloads; see pp. 144-45. Beyer was then managing partner of Touche, Ross, Bailey & Smart.

Exhibit 6
SOLUTION PER DETAIL DATA, ACTIVITY DRIVEN STANDARDS

	Indirect Labor		Supplies		Totals	
Standard Quantity of Input (Exhibit 5)	4,800	hr.	900 bbl			
Longrun Approved Quantity of Input (Exhibits 1 and 3)	− 6,000	hr.				
Difference	1,200	hr.				
Standard Price of Input (Exhibit 3)	x $12.50	hr.				
Strategic Quantity Variance	$15,000	U				
Longrun Approved Quantity of Input	6,000	hr.				
Actual Quantity of Input (Exhibit 3)	− 7,500	hr.	− 1,000	bbl.		
Difference	1,500	hr.	100	bbl.		
Standard Price of Input	x $ 12.50	/hr.	x $113.333	/bbl.		
Operational Quantity Variance	$18,750	U	$ 11,333	U		
Total Quantity Variance	$33,750	U	$11,333	U	$45,083	U
Price Variance (Exhibit 4)	18,750	F	2,333	F	21,083	F
Total Variance (Exhibit 5)	$15,000	U	$ 9,000	U	$24,000	U

Source: Exhibits 1, 3, 4, and 5; adapted from R. Beyer (see text).

Operational management is then responsible for using approved staffing levels as efficiently as possible. Since they were authorized $75,000 and spent $75,000, they have a zero total variance for indirect labor, albeit in a different manner than anticipated ($18,750 U for quantity and $18,750 F for price). Other inputs could be acquired in a similar manner, e.g., take or pay contracts; these would be amenable to the same treatment. Control is a shared responsibility, of course, and various management levels must work together for optimum operations.

Since sticky, lumpy costs may not be strictly variable with activity, the most viable procedure for their determination is likely by an observant "walking around" manager or accountant and/or an engineering study. It is not possible to generalize this process; each company will have to make that determination based on its own cost and production character.

SUMMARY

Accounting for overhead control is an area ripe for improvement. With overhead costs rising as a proportion of manufacturing activity, with better educated business persons, and with computational power readily available to maintain data on a more disaggregated basis and to perform statistical analyses, better reporting is now likely to be cost beneficial and may make the difference between profitable or unprofitable operations.

As demonstrated, at best the continuance of the traditional standard cost approach to overhead analysis in the CMA and CPA examinations, in textbooks and classrooms, and in accounting reports of manufacturers, is a waste of time. It should be abandoned. The traditional labor based, flexible budget approach is almost as dangerous. At worst, the traditional approaches may be counter-productive, resulting in dysfunctional decisions and in a loss of credibility for other accounting reports.

The groundwork for better overhead control through activity based flexible budgets has been in development over the last half-century. Indeed, the professional literature abounds with success stories of leading edge companies in implementing advanced cost techniques. Many of these advances have more to do with production changes, as with materials requirements planning systems, than they do with underlying cost system changes, however.[22]

Mainstream accountants still have quite a long way to go. "Despite major conceptual and technological developments, little of the new thought in the field of cost management has found its way into practical application..."[23] For homogeneous data, regression and other analyses should be used to identify the underlying cost drivers. For less homogeneous data, sampling may be used to establish the underlying causes for differences from cost expectations. Sticky and strictly variable costs should be identified and controlled, respectively, by strategic and tactical techniques. Whenever activity based costing is appropriate for product cost determination, the same drivers should be equally relevant for cost control applications. It is time to set aside our primary occupation with traditional overhead variance analysis and focus our attention on cost-driver based variable budget systems. It is time for us to put our effort where there is more promise of return.

[22]J. Emore, and J. Ness, op. cit., p. 8.
[23]Ibid.

Chapter 17
Managing Marketing Effectiveness
And Productivity
Cases
17-1   Dallas Consulting Group

Readings
"Profit Variance Analysis: A Strategic Focus"
This article uses a fictitious case to demonstrate how variance analysis can be tied explicitly to the strategies of the firm. It expands the Shank and Churchill framework (explained in the article) for variance analysis to include explicitly the strategy and the competitive position of the firm in the analysis and interpretation of results.

Discussion questions:
1. Why is it inadequate and may even be misleading to rely only on the analysis reported in Table 3?
2. Does a favorable variance imply favorable performance?
3. Table 4 shows a rather elaborate and detailed analysis of variances of operating results. The analysis provides us information on the effect of variations of relevant operating factors on the operating result. The analysis includes relevant and important operating factors such as total market size, market share of the firm, sales mix, selling price, and costs. The analysis considers almost all, if not all, the factors that are of interest and important to management. Why is the analysis incomplete?

"Examining the Relationships in Productivity Accounting"
Change in profit of a firm or business unit can be analyzed in terms of a change in productivity and a change in price recovery. Change in product quantities and change in resource quantity drive the change in productivity. Change in product prices and change in resource prices drive the change in price recovery. These relationships can be displayed to provide an instant visual analysis of the causes of profit change. Such visualization can provide a robust method for analyzing strategy and stakeholder relationships.

Discussion questions:
1. What is productivity accounting?
2. How can productivity accounting guide the overall strategy of the firm?
3. Give an example showing that a traditional business performance indicator may give conflicting signals on a firm's performance.

4. What are the elements in using productivity accounting to evaluate changes in profits?
5. What grid diagrams are needed in order to have an overall picture of the business's performance?

"The Role of ABM in Measuring Customer Value"

This is a two-part article. Part I discusses the need for customer lifetime value (CLV) and how it is used to segment customers based on value. Part II explores how to use activity-based management (ABM) to quantify customer lifetime value and how to use CLV information to establish one-to-one customer relationship strategies. Information on CLV can help firm to enhance relationships with value-creating customers, improve customer relationship management (CRM), and select the right blend of customers who will drive value.

Discussion questions:
1. How can activity-based management enhance CRM?
2. Why customer revenue and customer profitability measures are inadequate measures of customer value?
3. What is "value segmentation of customers"? What is the relationship between value segmentation and CLV?
4. What cost dimensions are required for measuring CLV? Why a traditional accounting system is not likely to be able to provide data for these cost dimensions?
5. How can CLV help in developing customer management strategies?

① ABM enhances CRM by enabling the organization to better understand customer profitability + cost structure. ABM provides info that can be used to educate customers on the value of the services or products provided ~~to~~ and the costs involved; ~~ABM also~~ change cust. behavior to reduce costs + provide more benefits to the cust. ABM also Provides info to ~~allow~~s an org. allowing them to set prices based on the services providing to a customer — Instead of ~~not~~ just by product. This allows the org to better match the resources used by a cust w/ the revenue they generate.

② Cust. revenue + profitability are not accurate measures of cust value b/c of CLV. Just looking at revenue alone, does not provide enough info to understand the value of a particular cust. A cust. may bring in a good amount of revenue, but the cost of serving them may be so high that the relationship is really not profitable. ~~Mergers these~~ these are called "demanders." Also, It is quite common for a customer to be profitable in one division, but unprofitable in another. In this case, one must assess the overall CV. ~~profitab~~
Cust. profitability is more accurate than revenue,

but it is still limited in its usefulness, b/c many profitability margins exclude the majority of costs involved in acquiring, retaining, or serving the customer. They focus on direct costs of sales for a specific period of time. Profitability models do not provide a solid understanding CV.

relati-
b/w n vs 3) Value segmentation of customers is
+CLV

17-1. Dallas Consulting Group

"I just don't understand why you're worried about analyzing our profit variance," said Dave Lundberg to his partner, Adam Dixon. Both Lundberg and Dixon were partners in the Dallas Consulting Group (DCG). "Look, we made $800,000 more profit than we expected in 2001 (see Exhibit 1). That's great as far as I am concerned." Continued Lundberg. Adam Dixon agreed to come up with data that would help sort out the causes of DCG's $800,000 profit variance.

DCG is a professional services partnership of three established consultants who specialize in helping firms in cost reduction through time-motion studies, streamling production by optimizing physical layout, and re-engineering operations. For each project DCG consultants spent the bulk of the total project time studying customers' operations.

The three partners each received fixed salaries that represented the largest portion of operating expenses. All three used his or her home office for DCG business. DCG itself had only a post office box. All other DCG employees were also paid fixed salaries. No other significant operating costs were incurred by the partnership.

Revenues consisted solely of professional fees charged to customers for the two different types of services DCG offered. Charges were based on the number of hours actually worked on the job.

Following the conversation with Lundberg, Dixon gathered the data summarized in Exhibit 2. He took the data with him to Lundberg's office and said, "I think I can identify several reasons for our increased profits. First of all, we raised the price for re-engineering studies to $70 per hour. Also, if you remember, we originally estimated that the 10 consulting firms in the Dallas area would probably average about 15,000 hours of work each in 2001, so the total industry volume in Dallas would be 150,000 hours. However, a check with all of the local consulting firms indicates that the actual total coOnsulting market must have been around 112,000 hours."

"This is indeed interesting, Adam," replied Lundberg. "This new data leads me to believe that there are several causes for our increased profits, some of which may have been negative. . . . . Do you think you could quantify the effects of these factors in terms of dollars?"

EXHIBIT 1

2001 BUDGET AND ACTUAL RESULT

	Budget	Actual	Variance
Revenues	$12,600	$13,400	$ 800
Expenses:			
Salaries	9,200	9,200	-----
Income	**$ 3,400**	**$ 4,200**	**$ 800**

EXHIBIT 2

DETAIL OF REVENUE CALCULATIONS

	Hours	Rate	Amount
Budget:			
Re-engineering	6,000	$ .60	$ 360,000
Streamlining production	9,000	1.00	900,000
	15,000		$1,260,000
Actual:			
Re-engineering	2,000	$ .70	$ 140,000
Streamlining production	12,000	1.00	1,200,000
	14,000		$1,340,000

REQUIRED:

Use your knowledge of profit variance analysis to quantify the performance of DCG for 2001 and explain the significance of each variance to Mr. Lundberg.

This case was written and copyrighted by Joseph G. San Miguel, Naval Postgraduate School.

PROFIT VARIANCE ANALYSIS: A STRATEGIC FOCUS

ABSTRACT: This paper uses a disguised case to compare and contrast three different frame works in analyzing profit variances—two that are in common usage today and one that is not but, in our view, should be. The purpose of the paper is to demonstrate how variance analysis needs to be tied explicitly to the strategic context of the firm and its business units.

By Vijay Govindarajan and John K. Shank

Profit variance analysis is the process of summarizing what happened to profits during the period to highlight the salient managerial issues. Variance analysis is the formal step leading to determining what corrective actions are called for by management. Thus it is a key link in the management control process. We believe this element is underutilized in many companies because of the lack of a meaningful analytical framework. It is handled by accountants in a way that is too technical. This paper proposes a different profit variance framework as a "new idea" in management control.

Historically, variance analysis involved a simple methodology where actual results were compared with the budget on a line-by-line basis. We call this Phase I thinking. Phase II thinking was provided by Shank and Churchill [1977] who proposed a management-oriented approach to variance analysis. Their approach was based on the dual ideas of profit impact as a unifying theme and a multilevel analysis in which complexity was added gradually, one level at a time. We believe that the Shank and Churchill approach needs to be modified in important ways to take explicit account of strategic issues. Our framework, which we call Phase III thinking, argues that variance analysis becomes most meaningful when it is tied explicitly to strategic analysis.

John K. Shank is Noble Professor of Managerial Control and Vijay Govindarajan is Associate Professor of Accounting, both at the Amos Tuck School of Business Administration, Dartmouth College.

The authors wish to acknowledge helpful discussions with Ray Stephens.

This paper presents a short disguised case, United Instruments, Inc., to illustrate the three phases or generations of thinking about profit variance analysis. We believe it also demonstrates the superiority of integrating strategic planning and overall financial performance evaluation, which is the essence of Phase III thinking. The purpose of this paper is to emphasize how variance analysis can be, and should be, redirected to consider the strategic issues that have, during the past 15 years, become so widely accepted as a conceptual framework for decision making.[1]

---

[1] During the past 15 years, several books (e.g., Andews [1971], Henderson [1979], and Porter [1980]) as well as articles (e.g., Buzzell et al. [1975] and Govindarajan and Gupta [1985]) have been published in the field of strategic management. In addition, two new journals (*Strategic Management Journal* and *Journal of Business Strategy*) have been introduced in the strategy area during the past ten years. Also, traditional management journals such as *Administrative Science Quarterly, Academy of Management Journal,* and *Academy of Management Review* have, during the past decade, started to publish regularly articles on strategy formulation and implementation.

TABLE 1
UNITED INSTRUMENTS, INC.

		Budget (1,000s)		Actual (1,000s)
Sales		$16,872		$17,061
Cost of goods sold		9,668		9,865
Gross margin		$ 7,204		$ 7,196
Less: Other operating expenses				
Marketing	$1,856		$1,440	
R&D	1,480		932	
Administration	1,340	4,676	1,674	4,046
Profit before taxes		$ 2,528		$ 3,150

UNITED INSTRUMENTS, INC.: AN INSTRUCTIONAL CASE[2]

Steve Park, president and principal stockholder of United Instruments, Inc., sat at his desk reflecting on the 1987 results (T-1). For the second year in succession, the company had exceeded the profit budget. Steve Park was obviously very happy with the 1987 results. All the same, he wanted to get a better feel for the relative contributions of the R&D, manufacturing, and marketing departments in this overall success. With this in mind, he called his assistant, a recent graduate of a well-known business school, into his office.

"Amy," he began, "as you can see from our recent financial results, we have exceeded our profit targets by $622,000. Can you prepare an analysis showing how much R&D, manufacturing, and marketing contributed to this overall favorable profit variance?"

Amy Shultz, with all the fervor of a recent convert to professional management, set to her task immediately. She collected the data in T-2 and was wondering what her next step should be.

United Instruments' products can be grouped into two main lines of business: electric meters (EM) and electronic instruments (EI). Both EM and EI are industrial measuring instruments and perform similar functions. However, these products differ in their manufacturing technology and their end-use characteristics. EM is based on mechanical and electrical technology, whereas EI is based on microchip technology. EM and EI are substitute

products in the same sense that a mechanical watch and a digital watch are substitutes.

United Instruments uses a variable costing system for internal reporting purposes.

PHASE I THINKING: THE "ANNUAL REPORT APPROACH" TO VARIANCE ANALYSIS

A straightforward, simple-minded explanation of the difference between actual profit ($3,150) and the budgeted profit ($2,528) might proceed according to T-3. Incidentally, this type of variance analysis is what one usually sees in published annual reports (where the comparison is typically between last year and this year). If we limit ourselves to this type of analysis, we will draw the following conclusions about United's performance:

1. Good sales performance (slightly above plan).

2. Good manufacturing cost control (margins as per plan).

3. Good control over marketing and R&D costs (costs down as percentage of sales).

4. Administration overspent a bit (slightly up as percentage of sales).

5. Overall Evaluation: Nothing of major significance; profit performance above plan.

How accurately does this summary reflect the actual performance of United? One objective of this paper is to demonstrate that the analysis is misleading. The plan for 1987 has embedded in it certain expectations about the state of the total industry and about United's market share, its selling

---

[2] This case is motivated by a similar case titled "Kinkead Equipment Ltd.," which appears in Shank [1982].

TABLE 2
ADDITIONAL INFORMATION

	Electric Meters (EM)	Electronic Instruments (EI)
Selling prices per unit		
Average standard price	$40.00	$180.00
Average actual prices, 1987	30.00	206.00
Variable product costs per unit		
Average standard manufacturing cost	$20.00	$50.00
Average actual manufacturing cost	21.00	54.00
Volume information		
Units produced and sold–actual	141,770	62,172
Units produced and sold–planned	124,800	66,000
Total industry sales, 1987–actual	$44 million	$76 million
Total industry variable product costs, 1987–actual	$16 million	$32 million
United's share of the market (percent of physical units)		
Planned	10%	15%
Actual	16%	9%
	Planned	**Actual**
Firm-wide fixed expenses (1,000s)		
Fixed manufacturing expenses	$3,872	$3,530
Fixed marketing expenses	1,856	1,440
Fixed administrative expenses	1,340	1,674
Fixed R&D expenses (exclusively for electronic instruments)	1,480	932

prices, and its cost structure. Results from variance computations are more "actionable" if changes in actual results for 1987 are analyzed against each of these expectations. The Phase I analysis simply does not break down the overall favorable variance of $622,000 according to the key underlying causal factors.

PHASE II THINKING: A MANAGEMENT-ORIENTED APPROACH TO VARIANCE ANALYSIS

The analytical framework proposed by Shank and Churchill [1977] to conduct variance analysis incorporates the following key ideas:

1. Identify the key causal factors that affects profit.

2. Break down the overall profit variance by these key causal factors.

3. Focus always on the *profit* impact of variation in each causal factor.

4. Try to calculate the specific, separable impact of each causal factor by varying only that factor while holding all other factors constant ("spinning only one dial at a time").

5. Add complexity sequentially, one layer at a time, beginning at a very basic "common sense" level ("peel the onion").

6. Stop the process when the added complexity at a newly created level is not justified by added useful insights into the causal factors underlying the overall profit variance.

T-4 and 5 contain the explanation for the overall favorable profit variance of $622,000 using the above approach. In the interest of brevity, most of the calculational details are suppressed (detailed calculations are available from the authors).

What can we say about the performance of United if we now consider the variance analysis summarized in T-5? The following insights can be offered organized by functional area:

TABLE 3
THE "ANNUAL REPORT APPROACH" TO VARIANCE ANALYSIS

			Budget (1,000s)					Actual (1,000s)	
Sales			$16,872	(100%)				$17,061	(100%)
Cost of goods sold			9,668	(58%)				9,865	(58%)
Gross margin			$ 7,204	(42%)				$ 7,196	(42%)
Less: Other expenses									
Marketing	$1,856	(11%)			$1,440	(8%)			
R&D	1,480	(9%)			932	(6%)			
Administration	1,340	(8%)	4,676	(28%)	1,674	(10%)	4,046		(24%)
Profit before tax			$ 2,528	(14%)			$ 3,150		(18%)

Marketing

   Comments:
      Market Share (SOM) increase
      benefited the firm $1,443 F

      But, unfortunately, sales mix
      was managed toward the lower
      margin product   921 U

      Control over marketing
      expenditure benefited the firm
      (especially in the face of an
      increase in SOM)   416 F
        Net effect $938 F

      Uncontrollables: Unfortunately,
      the overall market declined and
      cost the firm $680 U
   Overall evaluation: Very good performance

Manufacturing

   Comments:
      Manufacturing cost control cost
      the firm $ 48 U
   Overall evaluation: Satisfactory performance

R&D

   Comments:
      Savings in R& D budget $ 548 F
   Overall evaluation: Good performance

Administration

   Comments:
      Administration budget overspent
         $ 334 U
   Overall evaluation: Poor performance

Thus, the overall evaluation of the general manager under Phase II thinking would probably be "good," though specific areas (such as manufacturing cost control or administrative cost control) need attention. The above summary is quite different—and clearly superior —to the one presented under Phase I thinking. But, can we do better? We believe that Shank and Churchill's framework needs to be modified in important ways to accommodate the following ideas.

Sales volume, share of market, and sales mix variances are calculated on the presumption that United is essentially competing in one industry (i.e., it is a single product firm with two different varieties of the product). That is to say, the target customers for EM and EI are the same and that they view the two products as substitutable. Is United a single product firm with two product offerings, or does the firm compete in two different markets? In other words, does United have a single strategy for EM and EI or does the firm have two different strategies for the two businesses? As we argue later, EM and EI have very different industry characteristics and compete in very different markets, thereby, requiring quite different strategies. It is, therefore, more useful to calculate market size and market share variances separately for EM and EI. Just introducing the concept of a *sales mix* variance implies that the average standard profit contribution across EM and EI together is meaningful.

TABLE 4
VARIANCE CALCULATIONS USING SHANK AND CHURCHILL'S MANAGEMENT-ORIENTED FRAMEWORK

Key Causal Factors:						
Total Market	Expected	Actual	Actual	Actual	Actual	Actual
Market share	Expected	Expected	Actual	Actual	Actual	Actual
Sales mix	Expected	Expected	Expected	Actual	Actual	Actual
Selling price	Expected	Expected	Expected	Expected	Actual	Actual
Costs	Expected	Expected	Expected	Expected	Expected	Actual
Profit Calculation:						
Sales	$16,872	$15,836	$18,034	$16,862	$17,060	$17,060
Variable costs	5,769	5,440	6,195	5,944	5,944	6,334
Contribution	$11,076	$10,396	$11,839	$10,918	$11,116	$10,726
Fixed costs	8,548	8,548	8,548	8,548	8,548	7,576
Profit	$ 2,528	$ 1,848	$ 3,291	$ 2,370	$ 2,568	$ 3,150

Variance Analysis:

Level 1   Overall variance=$622 F

Level 2   Sales volume and mix=$158 U   Sales prices and costs=$780 F

Level 3   Sales volume=$763 F   Sales mix=$921 U   Sales prices=$198 F   Costs=$582 F

Level 4   Market Size=$680 U   Market Share=$1,443F   EM $1,418 U   EI $1,616   Variable costs of manufacturing EM $142 U EI $248 U

Fixed costs
- Manufacturing $342 F
- Marketing $416 F
- Administration $334 U
- R&D $548 F

Note: F indicates a favorable variance and U indicates an unfavorable variance.

17-9

TABLE 5
VARIANCE SUMMARY FOR THE PHASE II APPROACH

Overall market decline	$ 680 U
Share of market increase	1,443 F
Sales mix change	921 U

Sales prices improved
    EM $1,418 U
    EI $1,616 F
	198 F

Manufacturing cost control
    Variable costs $390 U
    Fixed costs $342 F
	48 U

Other
    R&D
    Administration
    Marketing
	548 F
	334 U
	416 F

Total	$ 622 F

For an ice cream manufacturer, for example, it is probably reasonable to assume that the firm operates in a single industry with multiple product offerings, all targeted at the same customer group. It would, therefore, be meaningful to calculate a sales mix variance because vanilla ice cream and strawberry ice cream, for instance, are substitutable and more sales of one implies less sales of the other for the firm (for an elaboration on these ideas, refer to the Midwest Ice Cream Company case [Shank, 1982, pp. 157–173]). On the other hand, for a firm such as General Electric, it is much less clear whether a sales mix variance across jet engines, steam turbines, and light bulbs really makes any sense. This is more nearly the case for United because one unit of EM (which sells for $30) is not really fully substitutable for one unit of EI (which sells for $206).

An important issue in the history of many industries is to determine when product differentiation has progressed sufficiently that what *was* a single business with two varieties *is now* two businesses. Some examples include the growth of the electronic cash register for NCR, the growth of the digital watch for Bulova, or the growth of the industrial robot for General Electric.

Following Phase II thinking, performance evaluation did not relate the variances to the differing strategic contexts facing EM and EI.

PHASE III THINKING: VARIANCE ANALYSIS USING A STRATEGIC FRAMEWORK

We argue that performance evaluation, which is a critical component of the management control process, needs to be tailored to the strategy being followed by a firm or its business units. We offer the following set of arguments in support of our position: (1) different strategies imply different tasks and require different behaviors for effective performance [Andrews, 1971; Gupta and Govindarajan, 1984a; and Govindarajan, 1986a]; (2) different control systems induce different behaviors [Govindarajan, 1986b; Gupta and Govindarajan, 1984b]; (3) thus, superior performance can best be achieved by tailoring control systems to the requirements of particular strategies [Govindarajan, 1988; Gupta and Govindarajan, 1986].[3]

---

[3] Several studies have shown that when an individual's rewards are tied to performance along certain dimensions, his or her behavior would be guided by the desire to optimize performance with respect to those dimensions. Refer to Govindarajan and Gupta [1985] for a review of these studies.

TABLE 6
STRATEGIC CONTEXTS OF THE TWO BUSINESSES

	Electric Meters (EM)	Electronic Instruments (EI)
Overall market (units):		
Plan	1,248,000	440,000
Actual	886,080	690,800
	Declining Market	Growth Market
	(29% Decrease)	(57% Increase)
United's share:		
Plan	10%	15%
Actual	16%	9%
United's prices:		
Plan	$40	$180
Actual	30	206
	We apparntly cut price to build share	We apparently raised price to ration the high demand.
United's margin:		
Plan	$20	$130
Actual	9	152
Industry prices:		
Actual	$50	$110
	We are well below "market."	We are well above "market."
Industry costs:		
Actual	$18	$46
Procuct/market characteristics:	Mature	Evolving
	Lower technology	Higher technology
	Declining market	Growth market
	Lower margins	Higher margins
	Low unit price	High unit price
	Industry prices holding up	Industry prices falling rapidly
United's apparent strategic mission	"Build"	"Skim" or "Harvest"
United's apparent competitive strategy	The low price implies we are trying for low cost position	The high price implies we are trying for a differentiation position.
A more plausible strategy	"Harvest"	"Build"
Key success factors (arising from the plausible strategy)	Hold sales prices vis-à-vis competition.	Competitively price to gain SOM.
	Do not focus on maintaining and improving SOM.	Product R&D top create differentiation
	Aggressive cost control	Lower cost through experience curve effects
	Process R&D to reduce unit costs.	

We will first define and briefly elaborate the concept of strategy before illustrating how to link strategic considerations with variances for management control and evaluation. Strategy has been conceptualized by Andrews [1971], Ansoff [1965], Chandler [1962], Govindarajan [1989], Hofer and Schendel [1978], Miles and Snow [1978], and others as the process by which managers, using a

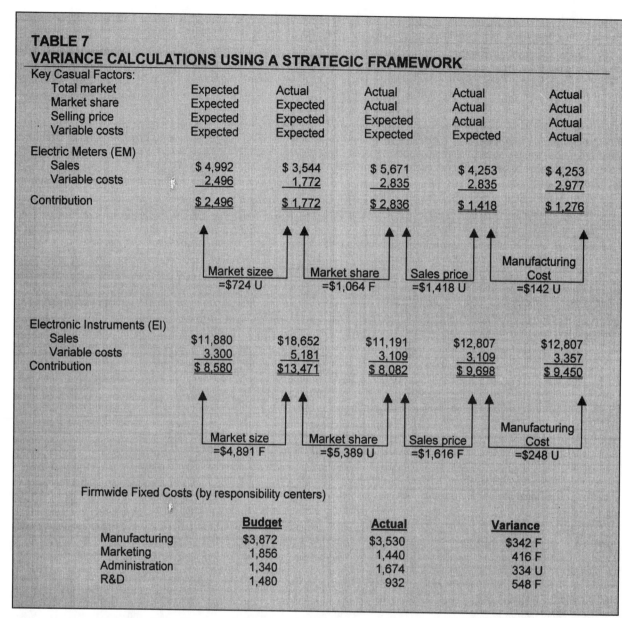

TABLE 7
VARIANCE CALCULATIONS USING A STRATEGIC FRAMEWORK

Key Casual Factors:					
Total market	Expected	Actual	Actual	Actual	Actual
Market share	Expected	Expected	Actual	Actual	Actual
Selling price	Expected	Expected	Expected	Actual	Actual
Variable costs	Expected	Expected	Expected	Expected	Actual

Electric Meters (EM)

Sales	$ 4,992	$ 3,544	$ 5,671	$ 4,253	$ 4,253
Variable costs	2,496	1,772	2,835	2,835	2,977
Contribution	$ 2,496	$ 1,772	$ 2,836	$ 1,418	$ 1,276

Market sizee =$724 U   Market share =$1,064 F   Sales price =$1,418 U   Manufacturing Cost =$142 U

Electronic Instruments (EI)

Sales	$11,880	$18,652	$11,191	$12,807	$12,807
Variable costs	3,300	5,181	3,109	3,109	3,357
Contribution	$ 8,580	$13,471	$ 8,082	$ 9,698	$ 9,450

Market size =$4,891 F   Market share =$5,389 U   Sales price =$1,616 F   Manufacturing Cost =$248 U

Firmwide Fixed Costs (by responsibility centers)

	Budget	Actual	Variance
Manufacturing	$3,872	$3,530	$342 F
Marketing	1,856	1,440	416 F
Administration	1,340	1,674	334 U
R&D	1,480	932	548 F

three- to five-year time horizon, evaluate external environmental opportunities as well as internal strengths and resources in order to decide on *goals* as well as *a set of action plans* to accomplish these goals. Thus, a business unit's (or a firm's) strategy depends upon two interrelated aspects: (1) its strategic mission or goals, and (2) the way the business unit chooses to compete in its industry to accomplish its goals—the business unit's competitive strategy.

Turning first to strategic mission, consulting firms such as Boston Consulting Group [Henderson, 1979],

Arthur D. Little[Wright, 1975], and A. T. Kearney [Hofer and Davoust, 1977], as well as academic researchers such as Hofer and Schendel [1978], Buzzell and Wiersema [1981], and Govindarajan and Shank [1986], have proposed the following three strategic missions that a business unit can adopt:

BUILD:

This mission implies a goal of increased market share, even at the expense of short-term earnings and cash flow. A business unit following this mission is expected to be a net

TABLE 8
VARIANCE SUMMARY FOR THE PHASE III APPROACH

Electric Meters	
Market size	$ 724 U
Market share	1,064 F
Sales price	1,418 U
Variable manufacturing cost	142 U
Electronic Instruments	
Market size	4,891 F
Market share	5,389 U
Sales price	1,616 F
Variable manufacturing cost	248 U
R&D	548 F
Firmwide Fixed Costs	
Manufacturing	342 F
Marketing	416 F
Administration	334 U
TOTAL	$ 622

user of cash in that the cash throw-off from its current operations would usually be insufficient to meet its capital investment needs. Business units with "low market share" in "high growth industries" typically pursue a "build" mission (e.g., Apple Computer's MacIntosh business, Monsanto's Bioechnology business).

HOLD:

This strategic mission is geared to the protection of the business unit's market share and competitive position. The cash outflows for a business unit following this mission would usually be more or less equal to cash inflows. Businesses with "high market share" in "high growth industries" typically pursue a "hold" mission (e.g., IBM in mainframe computers).

HARVEST:

This mission implies a goal of maximizing short-term earnings and cash flow, even at the expense of market share. A business unit following such a mission would be a net supplier of cash. Businesses with "high market share" in "low growth industries" typically pursue a "harvest" mission (e.g., American Brands in tobacco products).

In terms of competitive strategy, Porter [1980] has proposed the following two generic ways in which businesses can develop sustainable competitive advantage:

LOW COST:

The primary focus of this strategy is to achieve low cost relative to competitors. Cost leadership can be achieved through approaches such as economies of scale in production, learning curve effects, tight cost control, and cost minimization in areas such as R&D, service, sales force, or advertising. Examples of firms following this strategy include: Texas Instruments in consumer electronics, Emerson Electric in electric motors, Chevrolet in automobiles, Briggs and Stratton in gasoline engines, Black and Decker in machine tools, and Commodore in business machines.

TABLE 9
PERFORMANCE EVALUATION SUMMARY FOR PHASE III APPROACH

	Electric Meters "Harvest" vs. "Build"	Electronic Instruments "Build" vs. "Skim"
Marketing Comments	If we held prices and share, decline in this mature business would have cost us $724 U But, we were further hurt by price cuts made in order to build our SOM (our prices was $30 vs. the industry price of $50). $1,418 U / 1,064 F Net effect $1,078 U This is a market that declined 29 percent. Why are we sacrificing margins to build market position in this mature, declining lower margin business? We underspent the marketing budget. $416 F But why are we cutting back here in the face of our major marketing problems?	We raised prices to maintain margins and to ration our scarce capacity (our price was $206 vs. The industry price of $110). In the process, we lost significant SOM which cost us (netted against $1,616 F from sales prices). $3,773 U This is a booming market that grew 57 percent during this period. Then why did we decide to improve margins at the expense of SOM in this fast growing, higher margin business? Fortunately, growth in the total market improved our profit picture. $4,891 F We underspent the marketing budget. $416 F But why are we cutting back here in the face of our major marketing problems?
Overall evaluation	Poor performance	Poor performance
Manufacturing Comments	Manufacturing cost control was lousy and cost the firm $142 U If we are trying to be a cost leader, where are the benefits of our cumulative experience or our scale economies? (industry unit costs of $18 vs. our costs of $21)	Variable Manufacturing costs showed an unfavorable variance of $248 U (industry costs of $46 vs. our costs of $54). Does the higher manufacturing cost result in a product perceived as better? Apparently not based on market share data.
Overall evaluation	Poor performance	Poor performance
R&D Comments	Not applicable	Why are we not spending sufficient dollars in product R&D? Could this explain our decline in SOM?
Overall evaluation		Poor performance
Administration Comments	Inadequate control over overhead costs, given the need to become the low cost producer ($334 U).	Administration budget overspent. $334 U How does this relate to cost control?
Overall evaluation	Poor performance	Not satisfactory

DIFFERENTIATION:

The primary focus of this strategy is to differentiate the product offering of the business unit, creating something that is perceived by customers as being unique. Approaches to a product differentiation include brand loyalty (Coca-Cola in soft drinks), superior customer service (IBM in computers), dealer network (Caterpillar Tractors in construction equipment), product design and product features (Hewlett-Packard in electronics), and/or product technology (Coleman in camping equipment).

The above framework allows us to consider explicitly the strategic positioning of the two product groups: electric meters and electronic instruments. Though they both are industrial measuring instruments, they face very different competitive conditions that very probably call for different strategies. T-6 summarizes the differing environments and the resulting strategic issues.

How well did electric meters and electronics instruments perform, given their stratetic contexts? The relevant variance calculations are given in Tables 7 and 8. These calculations differ from Phase II analysis (given in T-4) in one important respect. T-4 treated EM and EI as two varieties of one product, competing as substitutes, with a single strategy. Thus, a sales mix variance was comptued. Tables 7 and 8 treat EM and EI as different products with dissimilar strategies. Therefore, no attempt is made to calculate a sales mix variance. The basic idea is that even though a sales mix variance can always be calculated, the concept is meaningful only when a single business framework is applicable. For the same reason, Tables 7 and 8 report the market size and market share variances for EM and EI separately, and T-4 reported these two variances for the instruments business as a whole. Obviously, a high degree of subjectivity is involved in deciding whether United is in one business or two. The fact that the judgment is to a large extent subjective does not negate its importance. T-9 summarizes the managerial performance evaluation that would result if we were to evaluate EM and EI against their plausible strategies, using the variances reported in T-7 and 8.

The overall performance of United would probably be judged as "unsatisfactory." The firm has not taken appropriate decisions in its functional areas (marketing, manufacturing, R&D, and administration) either for its harvest business (EM) or for its build business (EI). The summary in T-9 indicates a dramatically different picture of United's performance than the one presented under Phase II thinking. This is to be expected because Phase II thinking did not tie variance analysis to strategic objectives. Neither Phase I nor Phase II analysis explicitly focused on ways to improve performance en route to accomplishing strategic goals. This would then imply that management compensation and rewards ought not to be tied to performance assessment undertaken using Phase I or Phase II frameworks.

CONCLUSIONS

Variance analysis represents a key link in the management control process. It involves two steps. First, one needs to break down the overall profit variance by key causal factors. Second, one needs to put the pieces back together most meaningfully with a view to evaluating managerial performance. Putting the bits and pieces together most meaningfully is just as crucial as computing the pieces. This is a managerial function, not a computational one.

Phase I, Phase II, and Phase III thinking yield different implications for this first step. That is, the detailed variance calculations do differ across the three approaches. Their implications differ even more for the second step. The computational aspects identify the variance as either favorable or unfavorable. However, a favorable variance does not necessarily imply favorable performance; similarly, an unfavorable variance does not necessarily imply unfavorable performance. We argue that the link between a favorable or unfavorable variance, on the one hand, and favorable or unfavorable performance, on the other, depends upon the strategic context of the business under evaluation.

No doubt, judgments about managerial performance can be dramatically different under Phase I, Phase II, and Phase III thinking (as the United Instruments case illustrates). In our view, moving toward Phase III thinking (i.e., analyzing profit variances in terms of the strategic issues involved) represents progress in adapting cost analysis to the rise of strategic analysis as a major element in business thinking [Shank and Govindarajan, 1988a, 1988b, and 1988c].

REFERENCES

Andrews, K.R., *The Concept of Corporate Strategy* (Homewood, IL: Dow-Jones Irwin, 1971).

Ansoff, H.I., *Corporate Strategy* (New York: McGraw-Hill, 1965).

Buzzell, R.D., B.T. Gale, and R.G.M. Sultan, "Market Share—A Key to Profitability," *Harvard Business Review* (January-February 1975), pp. 97–106.
_____, and F.D. Wiersema, "Modelling Changes in Market Share: A Cross-Sectional

Analysis," *Strategic Management Journal* (January-March 1981), pp. 27–42.

Chandler, A.D., *Strategy and Structure* (Cambridge, MA: The MIT Press, 1962).

Govindarajan, V., "Implementing Competitive Strategies at the Business Unit Level: Implications of Matching Managers to Strategies," *Strategic Management Journal* (May-June 1989), pp. 251–269.

_____, "Decentralization, Strategy, and Effectiveness of Strategic Business Units in Multi-Business Organizations," *Academy of Management Review* (October 1986a), pp. 844–856.

_____, "Impact of Participation in the Budgetary Process on Managerial Attitudes and Performance: Universalistic and Contingency Perspectives," *Decision Sciences* (1986b), pp. 496–516.

_____, "A Contingency Approach to Strategy Implementation at the Business Unit Level: Integrating Management Systems with Strategy," *Academy of Management Journal* (September 1988).

_____, and A.K. Gupta, "Linking Control Systems to Business Unit Strategy: Impact on Performance," *Accounting, Organizations and Society* (1985), pp. 51–66.

_____, and J.K. Shank, "Cash Sufficiency: The Missing Link in Strategic Planning," *The Journal of Business Strategy* (Summer 1986), pp. 88–95.

Gupta, A.K., and V. Govindarajan, "Business Unit Strategy, Managerial Characteristics, and Business Unit Effectiveness at Strategy Implementation," *Academy of Management Journal* (March 1984a), pp. 25–41.

_____, and _____, "Build, Hold, Harvest: Converting Strategic Intentions into Reality," *Journal of Business Strategy* (Winter 1984b), pp. 34–47.

_____, and _____, "Resource Sharing Among SBUs: Strategic Antecedents and Administrative Implications," *Academy of Management Journal* (December 1986), pp. 695–714.

Henderson, B.D., *Henderson on Corporate Strategy* (Cambridge, MA: Abt Books, 1979).

Hofer, C.W., and M.J. Davoust, *Successful Strategic Management* (Chicago, IL: A.T. Kearney, 1977).

_____, and D.E. Schendel, *Strategy Formulation: Analytical Concepts* (St. Paul, MN: West Publishing, 1978).

"Midwest Ice Cream Company," in J.K. Shank, Ed., *Contemporary Management Accounting: A Casebook* (Englewood Cliffs, NJ: Prentice-Hall, 1982), pp. 157–173.

Miles, R.E., and C.C. Snow, *Organizational Strategy, Structure and Process* (New York: McGraw Hill, 1978).

Porter, M.E., *Competitive Strategy: Techniques for Analyzing Industries and Competitors* (New York: The Free Press, 1980).

Shank, J.K., *Contemporary Management Accounting: A Casebook* (Englewood Cliffs, NJ: Prentice-Hall, 1982).

_____, and N.C. Churchill, "Variance Analysis: A Management-Oriented Approach," *The Accounting Review* (October 1977), pp. 950–957.

_____, and V. Govindarajan, "Making Strategy Explicit in Cost Analysis: A Case Study, " *Sloan Management Review* (Spring 1988a), pp. 19–29.

_____, and _____, "Transaction-Based Costing for the Complex Product Line: A Field Study," *Journal of Cost Management* (Summer 1988b), pp. 31–38.

_____, and _____, "Strategic Cost Analysis—Differentiating Cost Analysis and Control According to the Strategy Being Followed," *Journal of Cost Management* (Fall 1988c).

Wright, R.V.L., *A System for Managing Diversity* (Cambridge, MA: Arthur D. Little, Inc., 1975).

EXAMINING THE RELATIONSHIPS IN PRODUCTIVITY ACCOUNTING

By Anthony J. Hayzen, Ph.D., and James M. Reeeve, CPA, Ph.D.

Productivity measures an organization's ability to convert labor, capital, and material inputs into valued goods and services. This, of course, is not a new concept. The challenge is to turn the concept into useful measures management can use. Peter Drucker put the case for productivity measurement as follows: "Without productivity goals a business has no direction, and without productivity measurement a business has no control." The purpose of productivity measurement, therefore, is control. Linking changes in productivity to resource allocation facilitates control. Therefore, we believe a useful productivity measure will link productivity changes to resources and hence to profitability.

We will demonstrate this link through an analytical technique we term "productivity accounting."[1] This approach measures the change in total resource productivity (that is, the changes in labor productivity. in materials productivity, capital productivity, and energy productivity) and the effects of these changes, taken together or individually, on the corresponding change in business profitability.

With this approach, a business can:

♦ **monitor** historical productivity performance and measure how much, in dollars or percent return on investment (ROL), profits were affected by productivity growth or decline;

♦ **evaluate** business profit plans (budgets) to determine whether the productivity changes implied are overly ambitious, reasonable, or not sufficiently ambitious; and

♦ **measure** the extent to which productivity performance is strengthening or weakening its overall competitive position relative to its competitors.

SOURCES OF PROFIT CHANGE

Productivity accounting seeks to link the change in profit to its underlying causes. Thus, we want to provide a dynamic assessment of the profit-generating ability of a company by focusing on change in profit rather than static profit levels. The drivers of profit

changes will provide much greater directional insight than will descriptions of profit *levels.*

With the same basic accounting information used to calculate revenues and costs, we can gain more insight into the precise drivers of profit. We know that change in product prices and change in product quantities drive the change in revenue. Likewise, change in resource prices and change in resource quantities drive the change in the cost of producing the products. All of this information is available in traditional accounting systems. Thus, the change in profit can be described as the sum of two elements: the change in productivity and change in price recovery.

$$\text{Change in Profit} = \text{Change in Productivity} + \text{Change in Price Recovery}$$

In the equation above, productivity can be expressed in the following familiar way:

$$\text{Productivity} = \frac{\text{Product Quanity (Output Quantity)}}{\text{Resource Quantity (Input Quantity)}}$$

Productivity is a measure of process execution, or the ability to efficiently turn inputs into outputs. A company with superior process execution has very little waste or process leakage. Often this is the only way to successfully compete in hypercompetitive markets, such as consumer electronics.

Similarly, price recovery has the followving relationship:

$$\text{Price Recovery} = \frac{\text{Product Price (Output Price)}}{\text{Resource Price (Input Price)}}$$

Price recovery is a measure of structural position, or the degree to which a firm is able to capture value it creates through pricing power. For example, a firm that has erected barriers to entry or captured markets through patent protection may be able to enjoy pricing

Table 1: CONVENTIONAL PRODUCTIVITY MEASUREMENT

	1998			1999		
	Value	Quantity	Price	Value	Quantity	Price
Sales	$99	11 units	$9	$110	11 units	$10
Rent	$52	26 sq. yards	$2	$78	26 sq. yards	$ 3
1. Profit	$47			$32		
2. Sates per sq. yard	$99/26 sq. yards = 3.8			$110/26 sq. yards = 4.2		
3. Productivity Quantity per sq. yard	11 units /26 sq. yards = 0.42			11 units /26 sq. yards = 0.42		

power that would yield attractive price recovery. Examples of attractive price recovery can be found in firms in the aircraft repair and overhaul parts business, where barriers to entry due to customer-specific design and process knowledge make it difficult for new entrants to compete in the after-market parts sector.

Some firms can compete on the basis of structural position (Microsoft or Coca-Cola), others on process execution (Nucor or Lincoln Electric), and a few others on both (Intel).

Firms without structural position and only average process execution will find it difficult to create and then capture value. More powerful supply chain participants will likely capture any value created. Examples abound in the automotive OEM parts business.

Productivity accounting decomposes these two sources of economic competitiveness—process execution and structural position—to guide the overall strategy of the firm.

TRADITIONAL MEASURES VS. PRODUCTIVITY ACCOUNTING

Traditional business performance indicators, such as sales per square yard, which is used in the retail industry; have the advantage of simplicity and familiarity Their main disadvantage, however, is that they can give conflicting signals because they do not isolate productivity from price recovery effects.

To illustrate this we will use the example of a simple retail business shown in Table 1. This business had revenue of $99 in 1998 from the sale of 11 items priced at $9 each. The revenue increased to $110 in 1999, generated from the sale of 11 items at $10 each. The rent paid for the store was $52 in 1998, which increased to $78 in 1999 for the same floor area of 26 square yards.

The first performance measure in Table 1 compares the profit of the business for the two years. Profitability decreased from $47 in 1998 to $32 in 1999.

The second approach uses the traditional ratio of sales per square yard. This method indicates that the performance of the business improved because the sales per square yard increased from $3.80 to $4.20.

The third method in Table 1 measures the performance of this business using productivity, As the table shows, productivity, and thus performance, has remained constant at 0.42 items per square yard.

We therefore have three conflicting measures of the business's performance. The second approach gives a conflicting signal as it uses revenue in the numerator, which contains both a quantity and a price effect.

The first and third methods (profit and productivity, respectively) give the correct signals. Profits have declined while productivity has remained constant. What would cause this? We must complete the picture by taking into consideration the effect the prices are having on the business. The productivity accounting method takes this into consideration and links both the effect of quantity changes (that is, productivity) and the price changes (that is, price recovery) to the change in profit, thus giving a complete picture of the performance of the business.

We can see from Table 1 what is happening in this business: Product prices have increased by 11% ($9 in 1998 to $10 in 1999) while the rent has increased by 50% ($2 per square yard in 1998 to $3 per square yard in 1999). Thus the decline in profit was due entirely to an inability to recover input price changes and had nothing to do with productivity, which remained constant.

Table2: QUANTITY AND PRICE INFORMATION FOR TWO PERIODS

	January 2000 (Reference Period)			February 2000 (Review Period)		
	Value	Quantity	Price	Value	Quantity	Price
Products						
Shirts	$150.00	10	$15.00	$216.00	12	$18.00
Cost Resources						
Linen (sq. yards)	$ 40.00	10	$4.00	$ 48.00	10	$ 4.80
Labor (staff-hours)	$ 48.00	6	$8.00	$ 60.00	5	$12.00
Total Cost Resources	$ 88.00			$108.00		
Capital Resources						
Machinery	$1,000.00	1	$1,000.00	$1,000.00	1	$1,000.00
% ROI	6.20			10.80		

NINE-BOX DIAGRAM

Profit, by itself, provides little managerial guidance. Rather, the manager needs information that identifies the causes for *change* in profit. Using the productivity accounting approach, one can take the *change in productivity* and the *change in price recovery* and relate them to the *change in profit*. If we now analyze the change in product quantities and change in resource quantities we get the change in productivity. If, in addition, we analyze the change in product prices and change in resource prices we get the change in price recovery. Price indexes may be used in situations where it is difficult to access detailed price and quantity information.

Together the measures give the manager a comprehensive analysis of how the changes in product quantity and resource quantity as well as the change in product price and resource price, are affecting the profitability of the business. Figure 1 shows a "nine-box diagram" summarizing these concepts.

The middle column of the figure explains the change in profit in the conventional way. But changes in revenues and costs include both price and quantity effects. Therefore, the change in profit also can be explained by the middle row, which explains the change in profitability as a function of the change in productivity and change in price recovery. The change in productivity, in turn, is explained by the change in output quantities over input quantities (the left-hand column). The change in price recovery is explained by the change in product prices over the change in resource (input) prices (the right-hand column).

AN EXAMPLE ILLUSTRATING PRODUCTIVITY AND PRICE RECOVERY COMPONENTS

Evaluating changes in profit using productivity accounting requires measures of productivity change and price recovery change over periods of time.

To illustrate changes in productivity and price

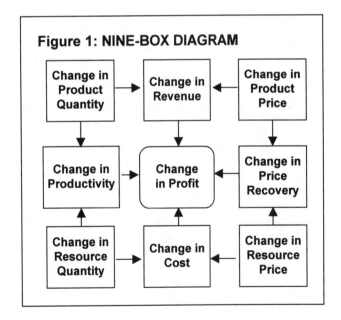

Figure 1: NINE-BOX DIAGRAM

Table 3: CHANGES IN PRODUCTIVITY AND PRICE RECOVERY

| | Profit Variance | Productivity | | Price Recovery | |
		% Change	Variance	% Change	Variance
	A+B	**A**		**B**	
Cost Resources					
Linen (sq. yards)	$ 9.60	20.00%	$ 9.60	0.00%	$ 0.00
Labor (staff-hours)	$ 9.10	44.00%	$26.40	(20.00%)	($17.30)
Total Cost Resources	$18.70	(*) 33.33%	$36.00	(*) 9.09%	($17.30)
Capital Resources					
Machinery	$27.30	20.00%	$12.40	20.0%	$14.90
Total Resources	**$46.00**	**(*) 28.47%**	**$48.40**	**(*) (1.100%)**	**($ 2.40)**

recovery, we will use a simplified example of a business that manufactures shirts as the only product, using linen and labor as the cost resources and machinery as the capital resource. We ignore for the sake of simplicity buttons, cotton, thread, labels, wrapping, premises, and so on, which are also used to produce the shirts.

In our example we compare the performance of February 2000, the review period, with the performance of January 2000, the reference period, to arrive at the change in productivity and change in price recovery The data are shown in Table 2.

Using the basic definition of productivity and the data shown in Table 2, we can measure the change in productivity for each resource contributing to the business operation. Viewed in this context, labor productivity—by far the most commonly quoted productivity statistic—is but one of many aspects of a total resource productivity analysis. For example, the change in linen "productivity" can be measured as the change in the output/input ratio between shirts and square yards of linen across the two periods. The productivity of linen in January was 10 shirts/10 square yards, or 1.0, while it improved to 12 shirts/10 square yards, or 1.2, in February. The productivity change for linen shown in Table 3 is 20%, or (1.2 - 1.0)/1.0. A similar calculation can be performed for productivity change in labor [44% =(2.4 -1.67)/1.67]. Likewise, the productivity change in machinery must be 20% because the same number of machines produced 20% more output (see Table 3 for a summary of these results).

Similarly, there is also a unique price recovery relationship for each resource contributing to a business operation (that is, cost per unit of input). For example, the price recovery for labor can be measured as the change in the output/input ratio for shirt and labor prices across the two periods. The price recovery of labor in January was $15/$8, or 1.875, while it deteriorated to $18/$12, or 1.5, in February The price recovery change for labor shown in Table 3 is -20%, or (1.50- 1.875)/1.875. There was no change in the linen price recovery ($15/$4 = $18/$4.80).

The price recovery for the machine is calculated in the same way. The machine's value remained constant while output prices increased from $15 to $18, thus leading to a positive price recovery of 20% [($18/$1,000) - ($15/$1,000)]/($15/$1,000). This approach intuitively accounts for the opportunity cost of the machine. For example, if the machine's value increased by a hundredfold while the output prices remained steady a strong argument could be made for selling the machine instead of using it. Our approach shows the impact of consuming this opportunity cost.

PRODUCTIVITY ACCOUNTING CONTRIBUTIONS

The percentage changes in productivity and price recovery are in themselves informative to management but do not show the contribution these changes have on profit change, impacts that are far more important to management. The process for converting percentage changes to variances is rather complex as one must eliminate price recovery effects in the productivity variance and productivity effects in the price recovery variance in order to achieve separation of the two effects.

To convert the percentage change in productivity into a dollar measure we take the new resource quantity (five staff—hours of labor) and multiply it by the new price ($12 per hour) and then by the percent change in productivity (44%), that is, 5 x $12 x 44% = $26.40. We have used the new price to show the current effect of the change in productivity. We determine the price recovery variance for labor by first establishing the resource input at assumed constant productivity. For labor, given that output increased by *20%*, the assumed labor (at constant productivity) would also increase by 20%, or from 6 hours to 7.2 hours. Thus, we determine the variance by multiplying the new price by 7.2 hours and then by the percent change in price recovery (-20%), that is, $12 x 7.2 hours x -20% = $17.30. Essentially this calculation holds the productivity effect constant in order to isolate the price effect. The linen variances are calculated in the same way.

For the capital resources (assets) there is an additional step to convert the asset values into a "cost of capital." The asset value must be multiplied by a return on investment (ROI). The ROI could be the ROI achieved in the reference period (January 2000), the ROI in the review period (February 2000), or some other target ROI. In our example we have used the ROI in the reference period (6.2%) and applied it to both the reference and review period assets. For example, the productivity variance for the machinery is 1 x $1,000 x 20% x 6.2% = $12.40. Software developed by one of the authors can be used to facilitate these calculations.[2]

For an illustration of the importance of measuring both productivity and price recovers notice in Table 3 that the financial benefit of the increase in labor productivity was $26.40 but that the unfavorable effect of price recovery of -$17.30 eroded this benefit. Therefore, the overall effect of labor on profit only amounted to a benefit of $9.10 ($26.40 - $17.30).

This simple example clearly illustrates the importance of measuring not only productivity but also price recovery so that the analyst can evaluate the effect of quantity and price changes on the profit of the business. The productivity accounting method of measuring productivity and price recovery shows that you can unambiguously evaluate each and every resource to find its productivity and price recovery impacts (that is, both change in index number and dollar effect) on the products produced. Next we will illustrate how this combined information can be displayed graphically for easier interpretation.

GRAPHICAL INTERPRETATION

In order to easily interpret a productivity accounting analysis for a business, the results should be presented in a visual form that is quick and easy to interpret. We will illustrate a grid format to visually represent the analysis. The "nine-box diagram" illustrated previously represents a large number of interactions, each having different implications for a business. A grid diagram helps to refine this information.

THE PROFIT GRID

The Profit Grid shown in Figure *2* is used to explain profit change in terms of a change in productivity and a change in price recovery. The productivity variance is plotted vertically and the price recovery variance is plotted horizontally. As the variances can be either positive or negative numbers, the grid is segmented into four quadrants with the origin in the center of the grid. The diagonal line connects all points where the productivity variance is offset by an exactly opposite price recovery variance. That is, there is no change in profit along this line. The segments above the diagonal (Segments 1, *2,* and 3) signify an increase in profit while the segments below the diagonal (Segments 4, 5, and 6) signify a decrease in profit.

For example, assume that the business increased its profit by $20. This profit change arose from a $10 improvement in productivity and a $10 improvement in

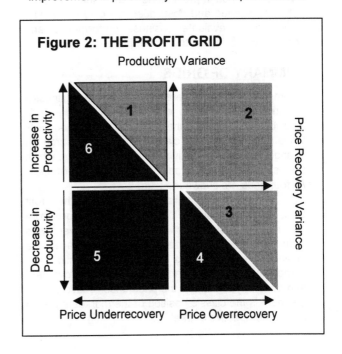

Figure 2: THE PROFIT GRID

Productivity Variance

price recovery. Moving from the origin +10 in the vertical and horizontal directions places us in Segment 2. Segment 2 performance indicates the best of both worlds—the organization is improving productivity and price recovery. But excessive price recovery may create an opportunity for competitors to undercut the business's product prices and thereby reduce market share and profit.

Now assume that the $20 change in profit arose from a $25 productivity improvement, but the business lost $5 from price underrecovery. This is an example of a Segment 1 scenario. In Segment 1 the organization has strong competitive advantages from superior process execution while deterring competitors with price underrecovery (that is, the business has only partially recovered its resource price change through its product price change).

Continuing the example, assume that the $20 change in profit arose from a $10 decline in productivity, but there is a $30 price overrecovery. This places us in Segment 3. Profit in Segment 3 may be very temporary. It occurs primarily from very aggressive pricing relative to resource inputs. An organization will sustain such pricing power only in the face of sustainable competitive position. Without such position, competitors surely will be attracted to the business and erode the margin opportunities, leaving the firm to compete on weak process execution.

In each of these examples the same $20 change in profit had very different strategic interpretations. The favorable change in profit alone (that is, the difference between revenue and cost) does not give the insight necessary to evaluate business performance and competitive position in the marketplace.

SUMMARY OF GRIDS

In order to have an overall picture of the business's performance, one needs to evaluate not only the Profit Grid but also the Quantity, Price, and Productivity Grids. Evaluation will clearly show the source of change in profit, productivity and price recovers, which are essential for understanding business performance. All four grids are shown in Figure 3.

The business appears in Segment 1 of the Profit Grid, indicating that the increase in profit arose from an increase in productivity which, however, was reduced by a price underrecovery. This places the business in a strong competitive position as competitors will require an even greater improvement in productivity to counter the price underrecovery. This segment is the classic position of the market leader in a hypercompetitive market.

The Productivity Grid (Segment 1) shows that the increase in productivity arose from a large gain in capacity utilization, which was eroded by a decline in efficiency. In the short term, if the business improves its efficiency it will be able to increase productivity and thereby profits. The increase in utilization probably was due to increasing market penetration from the business's price leadership position.

We have introduced the concepts of efficiency and capacity utilization here for completeness. These concepts are used to distinguish between fixed and variable resources. Typically cost resources are regarded as variable and capital resources as fixed. In practice these resources fall somewhere between fixed and completely variable.

The Quantity Grid (Segment B) indicates that the business increased its production while discharging resources. In other words, it increased production and reduced resource use, clearly giving an increase in productivity.

The source of the price underrecovery, which placed the business in Segment 1 of the profit grid, is seen on the Price Grid. The decline of product prices exceeded the decline of resource prices, placing the business in Segment F.

Using this framework, it is clear that a business can generate profit growth through productivity growth or price overrecovery. The course that a business chooses, however, has important implications for its long-term competitive position.

STAKEHOLDER ANALYSIS

A simple value chain will link a company from the supplier to the customer. The impact of productivity and price recovery on suppliers and customers also can be evaluated using the grids, as the profit grid in Figure 4 shows.

In the segments to the right of the vertical axis the consumer pays a subsidy to the producer because of increasing product price relative to resource price (that is, product price is increasing faster than resource price). In the segments to the left of the vertical axis the producer is paying a subsidy to the consumer because of decreasing product price relative to resource price (that is, resource price is increasing faster than product price).

In the segments above the horizontal axis the resource supplier is harmed because of decreasing resource content per unit of product (that is, improved productivity). In the segments below the horizontal axis the resource supplier is favored because of increasing

Figure 3: FOUR-GRID FRAMEWORK

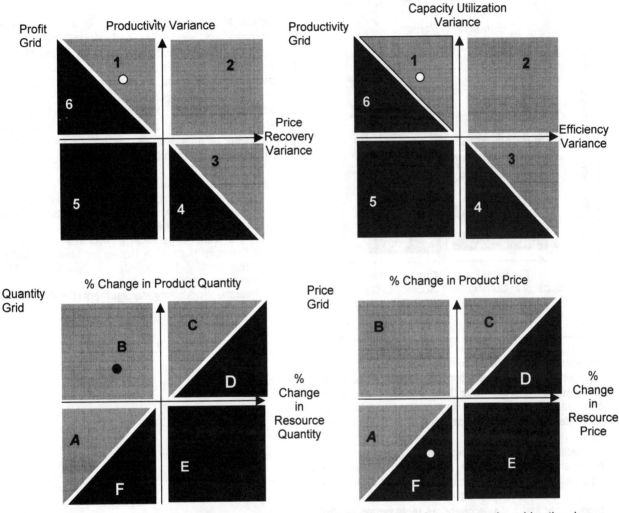

resource content per unit of product (that is, declining productivity).

This type of analysis also can be applied to the productivity, quantity and price grids. The expert analysis report generated by the FPM software automatically gives this analysis.

THE COMPLETE PICTURE

We have seen that a corporation or business unit can *analyze change in profit* in terms of a change in productivity and a change in price recovery. Change in product quantities and change in resource quantity drive the change in productivity. Change in product

prices and change in resource prices drive the change in price recovery.

A corporation or business unit can achieve *productivity improvement* when product quantity increases at a faster rate than resource quantity but will experience *productivity decline* if resource quantity increases at a faster rate than product quantity. If all other factors are held constant, productivity improvement will translate directly into profit improvement.

When product price increases at a faster rate than resource price, the result is *price overrecovery*. If all other factors are held constant, price overrecovery will

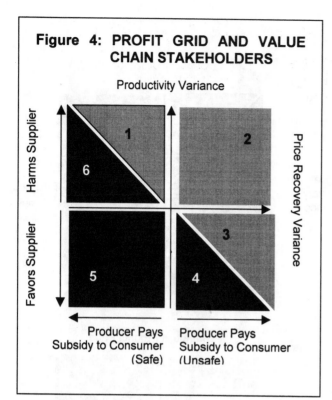

Figure 4: PROFIT GRID AND VALUE CHAIN STAKEHOLDERS

translate directly into increased profits in the short term. *Price underrecovery* occurs when resource price increases at a faster rate than product price. If all other factors are held constant, price underrecovery translates directly into a decrease in profits in the short term.

Instead of the conventional profit analysis represented by the middle column of the "nine-box diagram," many corporations and business units now analyze profit changes as a result of changes in productivity and price recovery, as represented by the middle row

These relationships then can be displayed to provide an instant visual analysis of the caus⁻˙⸱ of profit change. Such visualization can provide a ˙ bust method for analyzing strategy and stake ⸳lder relationships.

Anthony J. Hayzen, Ph.D., is a consultant in Knoxville, Tenn. He has many years of experience in measuring productivity in a variety of businesses and has used this experience to develop the Financial Productivity Management (FPM) software system. This comprehensive software package uses the concept of the grids together with an expert system to report results in a form that easily can be understood by managers at all levels. He can be reached at hayzen@msn.com.

James M. Reeve, CPA, Ph.D., is a Distinguished Professor of Business and Accounting at the University of Tennessee, Knoxville, Tenn. He has published extensively in academic and professional journals including the Journal of Cost Management, Journal of Management Accounting Research, Accounting Review, Management Accounting, *and* Accounting Horizons; *coauthored six textbooks; and consulted or provided training for a wide variety of organizations. He can be reached at* jreeve@utk.edu.

[ ] As descrjbed by
[1] A.J. Hayzen, "Financial Productivity Management— An Overview;" WITS Industrial Engineering Conference, February 1988.
[2] B.J. van Loggerenberg, "Productivity Decoding of Financial Signals: A Primer for Management on Deterministic Productivity Accounting." PMA Monograph, 1988.
[2] Financial Productivity Management (FPM) software.

THE ROLE OF ABM IN MEASURING CUSTOMER VALUE

BY JOSEPH A. NESS, CPA; MICHAEL J. SCHROECK, CMA, CPA; RICK A. LETENDRE, CPA; AND WILLMAR J. DOUGLAS, ACMA

PART ONE

Imagine two customers—let's call them Customer A and B—who on the surface look very similar. Same demographics, about the same revenue levels for or your organization over the past 12 months, they pay their bills on time, and their revenue growth rates are roughly comparable. On the surface you might conclude that these customers were of equal value to your organization. But digging a little deeper, you find that Customer A has been a loyal customer for many years, provides you with 100% of his business, refers friends and associates, orders products and pays invoices electronically, and demands little in the way of extraordinary care and attention. Customer B, on the other hand, has recently been reacquired as a customer for the third time in three years through significant sales and marketing efforts as well as price concessions. In addition, he buys your lowest-margin products, changes orders and delivery terms at the last minute, and requires a considerable degree of time and attention by your customer service group.

Now do you think they're of equivalent value? Probably not. But how would you know whether you were spending enough to keep Customer A loyal or whether you should allow Customer B to take his business to the competition? Enter customer lifetime value (CLV)—a comprehensive, fact-based measure of customer worth over the lifetime of your relationship with your customers.

As organizations in every industry have reached out to grow their business through the use of advanced processes and technology, they have shifted their focus from being "product-centric" to being "customer-centric." Customer relationship management (CRM) is often at the forefront of their efforts. Understanding customer behavior and profitability and leveraging this information to more effectively manage customers in a one-to-one relationship is key to creating a competitive advantage in the new economy. According to AMR Research, the CRM market will be worth more than $16 billion by 2003—phenomenon not to be ignored by anyone who's serious about staying ahead.

Customer relationship management initiatives aren't being employed without reason. The success or failure of corporations and their executives is being determined by their ability to create shareholder value. In a study conducted by PricewaterhouseCoopers and the Conference Board (CEO Conference Board Survey, 1997), leading CFOs said that the two most significant factors in creating shareholder value are revenue growth and margin growth. Clearly, no single constituency has a greater impact on these two measures—and therefore the value of your organization—than your customers.

CRM efforts are targeted at attracting new customers and retaining, up-selling, or cross-selling to existing customers. Incremental revenue is the most frequently used metric in measuring the success of these efforts. Yet companies are increasingly asking the questions: "Are these the right customers? That is, are these profitable customers?" "Are these the customers to whom I should devote my scarce and costly sales and service resources?" "Is revenue alone an adequate measure of customer value?"

Customer lifetime value (CLV) can help you answer those questions. It's a performance measure of long-term customer worth. And activity-based management (ABM) can be key in laying the foundation for quantifying customer lifetime value metrics and integrating the results into customer relationship management.

NOT ALL REVENUE IS GOOD REVENUE!

Customer relationship management is more than growing revenue, getting closer to customers, and anticipating and servicing their needs. It's a business strategy that involves both front-end and back-end business processes. To be fully successful with CRM, corporations must be able to choose the right blend of customers who will drive value. But to understand which of these customers are—and aren't—driving value, it's necessary to understand their margin contribution from the goods and services they buy as well as their consumption of indirect corporate resources. Activity-based management is particularly well suited to enhance your understanding of who's driving value by:

- Making visible the cost of all activities required to create and maintain a relationship with customers.
- Exposing resource consumption patterns that traditional cost accounting practices can't.
- Attributing activity costs to customers based on their consumption of the "drivers" of those activities and their underlying resources.

As companies implement customer-centric business strategies and CRM solutions, it becomes increasingly important for them to understand the value of customer relationships. This takes on added significance in that, for most companies, 20% of customers contribute 80% of profits. Said differently, fully 80% of the typical customer portfolio is either marginally profitable, at break-even, or unprofitable. Unfortunately, few companies can quantify profitability at a customer or household level.

But customer revenue alone is an inadequate measure of customer value. Customer profitability gets closer to the answer. Yet profitability measurements are often highly aggregated to a customer segment level, which limits their effectiveness in one-to-one customer marketing efforts. In addition, few customer profitability models include costs beyond the most obvious and direct costs of sales. They rarely include the cost to acquire the customer or the cost to retain and serve that customer after the sales transaction is complete. In our experience, direct costs of sales rarely exceed 50%.

In addition, customer profitability typically provides only an annual or monthly snapshot of the customer's value. For companies with a high rate of customer turnover, as well as those with long-term customer relationships, periodic measures are usually insufficient. Such periodic measures typically exclude important costs that have been incurred in earlier periods (e.g., customer acquisition) or that may occur across multiple periods (e.g., cost to serve). For customer profitability to help you understand customer value, it should be viewed across more than a single year—ideally over the lifetime of the customer's relationship with your organization. There are a few practical challenges to measuring a customer's lifetime value. One is actually defining a "customer." Is it an individual, an account, or a household or business address? A second challenge is linking customer information into a single customer record when they "churn"—or leave and return—multiple times during their lifetime. In spite of these challenges, we believe the benefits you can gain from an understanding of CLV are compelling enough to take on the challenges.

It's also important that, where applicable, customer lifetime value be evaluated at an enterprise level, rather than solely at a divisional level, particularly when a customer buys goods or services from multiple divisions in an organization. It isn't unusual for a customer to be unprofitable in one division yet highly profitable in another. Obviously a company's CRM strategy has to take this into consideration. Failure to take an enterprise perspective in measuring lifetime value raises the risk that a customer may be treasured in one division while being marginalized in another—hardly a recipe for customer loyalty.

As an enabler of CRM, customer lifetime value isn't a new concept. It's a common yardstick you can use to quantify and evaluate customer relationships over time. Unfortunately, many organizations base CLV only on a customer's revenue contribution rather than their profit contribution. The misconception that revenue alone is king is one of the primary reasons many Internet-based retailers have failed in the past year. It's imperative that companies understand their customers' lifetime costs as well as their lifetime revenue potential. The resulting value, essentially lifetime profitability, is the foundation for calculating customer lifetime value. Yet there hasn't been much practical guidance for calculating customer costs or profitability, and some of the basic tenets of CRM fall short of making this determination.

DEMOGRAPHIC SEGMENTATION ISN'T ENOUGH

One of the basic tenets of successful CRM initiatives is customer segmentation. This segmentation has traditionally been driven by demographic or behavioral characteristics in an attempt to predict how customers in a segment will react to a product or service being offered. An example of customer segmentation for a hypothetical telecommunications company is shown in Table 1.

Though demographic or behavioral segmentation is a good starting point in understanding your customer base, we believe neither goes far enough. They need to be further delineated to reflect the value of customers in that segment—a so-called "value segmentation" CLV provides the "filter" to accomplish such a "value segmentation" as reflected in Figure 1.

Here's an example of value segments that might appear within each of the demographic or behavioral segments:

- "Champions," such as our hypothetical Customer A, are your best customers. Typically they are loyal, regular, high-margin customers who are relatively easy to serve and consume little of your organization's support resources.
- "Demanders" are profitable customers, though they're high-cost customers as well and typically

make heavy uncompensated use of your organization's resources.

- "Acquaintances" are low-profitability customers, yet they demand little in the way of your organization's resources. Though you wouldn't want to base your business on these customers, you would also hate to lose them because they contribute marginal profit and are relatively maintenance free.
- "Losers," such as Customer B, are at the other end of the spectrum from Champions. These are the customers who drain valuable resources from the organization yet provide little in return. "Losers" may include high-churn customers as well.

Clearly, the strategy around each of these customer groups will vary. Champions are to be nurtured and rewarded. The strategy around Demanders and Acquaintances should be to enhance their profit contribution by selling upward into more profitable lines while keeping the cost line flat for Acquaintances and managing it downward for Demanders. Losers must be converted into profitable customers through up-selling and a lower cost of service. If their lifetime

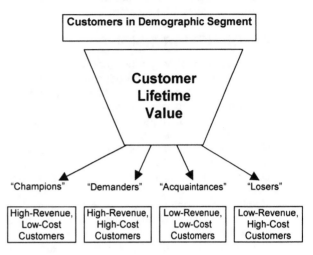

Figure 1: CLV as filter for "value segmentation"

| Customers in Demographic Segment |

Customer Lifetime Value

"Champions"	"Demanders"	"Acquaintances"	"Losers"
High-Revenue, Low-Cost Customers	High-Revenue, High-Cost Customers	Low-Revenue, Low-Cost Customers	Low-Revenue, High-Cost Customers

Table 1: Customer Segmentation by a Hypothetical Telecommunication Company

Market Segments	Demographic Characteristics
SUPER USER	■ Upscale ■ Highest income level, highest communications spending ■ High bandwidth, second line, PC, and wireless ownership
TECHNOLOGY INSTITUTE	■ Higher Income with high communications spending ■ High PC, online, and wireless use ■ Interested in new technologies
FAMILY USER	■ Moderate to high income with high communication spending ■ High PC and moderate online use ■ Some interest In new technology
FREQUENT COMMUNICATOR	■ Moderate income ■ Moderate to high wireless, moderate PC, and limited online usage ■ Little Interest in new technology
BASIC USER	■ Lowest communication spending ■ Low to moderate income and little interest in new technology

value can't eventually be made positive, let these customers defect to your competition, and avoid them in future customer win-back campaigns.

ABM FOR BETTER INSIGHT

Once you've gained insight into the lifetime value of your customers, you'll need to educate them on how their activities drive your cost and their value. Activity-based management can be a useful means of:

- Helping these customers understand the value they receive for the prices they pay.
- Supporting a two-tiered pricing structure in which high-cost services are priced separately from products, particularly for Acquaintances and Losers.
- Modifying their behavior to reduce the "drivers" of cost and complexity that they historically have brought to their dealings with you.

The retail banking industry was an early adopter of this approach. Once these institutions began to better understand their cost structures and customer profitability, they began assessing fees for customers who didn't maintain a minimum level of deposits or buy high-profit services.

CLV isn't the only measure you can use to determine the value of a customer. There are many additional factors, both quantitative and nonquantitative, you must consider when determining the CRM strategy applicable to individual customers. Two of the most important ones are the customer's propensity to spend in the future and the likely duration of your relationship with the customer—the total "lifetime." Another important factor is their likelihood to refer new customers in the future. The ability to accurately forecast customer behavior is important, but it may be just as meaningful, and a good bit easier, to evaluate these factors in conjunction with, yet separate from, historical customer lifetime value.

Up to this point, we've focused on the need for customer lifetime value and how it's used to segment customers based on value. Now we're ready to explore how to use ABM to measure CLV and show how you can use CLV information to establish one-to-one customer relationship strategies. That's the focus of Part 2 in next month's issue.

PART TWO

The measurement of cost—not revenue—to the customer level poses the greatest challenge to customer lifetime value measurement. While revenue can usually be collected by customer from the appropriate billing system, cost information is aggregated into general ledger departments and accounts and requires a good deal of analysis and disaggregation before you can meaningfully attach it to individual customers. Activity-based management gives you the tool set to accomplish this.

In contrast with ABM, traditional cost management techniques are almost exclusively product focused and rarely make visible the cost to acquire customers and, later, to serve and retain them. CLV requires that costs be measurable across four dimensions: Cost to Acquire, Cost to Provide, Cost to Serve, and Cost to Retain. Figure 1 illustrates the components of the CLV calculation.

Before you can develop these cost dimensions, you'll need to understand the activities performed. ABM plays a significant role in measuring CLV since many of these cost dimensions include indirect costs, which are measurable through ABM but aren't readily visible in financial systems.

Here are the cost dimensions of customer lifetime value and a description of how activity-based management is used to quantify them:

Cost to Acquire—consists of all costs related to the customer acquisition process. They are likely to be unique to a specific acquisition channel or even to a specific campaign. Examples are advertising, marketing, direct mail, telesales, proposal or bid development, and direct sales activities. While these are theoretically one-time costs to attract new customers, in practice companies must invest in these areas to reacquire a lost customer as well as to position new products and services with their existing customers.

ABM plays an important role by identifying the cost of all major customer acquisition activities and associating these costs to customers based on their acquisition, and potentially reacquisition, patterns. For example, the cost to acquire an account through a competitive proposal effort would exceed by many times the cost of an unsolicited order received through the company's website.

Acquisition cost includes the cost of successful acquisition efforts and the cost of failed efforts. This gives weight to the adage, "It costs five times more to obtain a new customer than it does to keep an existing customer."

Cost to Provide—comprises all costs related to the products and services provided to customers, such as the cost to build or assemble products or to deliver services. For a manufacturing company, these would consist of materials, labor, and perhaps an appropriately assigned share of indirect manufacturing costs. For a service company, this would likely consist of the human and related support services engaged in providing its core services to that customer. For an asset-intensive company, in an industry like telecommunications or power generation, this would also include an assigned share of asset-related costs such as depreciation or maintenance and could include capital carrying costs as well. Most companies' cost systems typically provide product or service costs, often at a unit level. Even if this is the case in your business, you should take a critical look at the quality of unit cost information because many cost systems are based on antiquated standard cost rules and may yield unreliable product or service unit costs.

For service companies, this is particularly important since a comprehensive service catalog of costs per service may be missing. In this case, ABM techniques can once again be applied to help you understand how the activities of the organization support the services delivered to the customer.

Cost to Serve—refers to all costs related to servicing and maintaining customers. For example, activities related to service provisioning, customer service, billing, warehousing, distribution, and accounts receivable management are derived by way of ABM, based once again on each customer's actual service characteristics.

Through the years, supply chain and pre- and post-sale customer service activities have become large and important expenditures for many companies. In addition, expedited delivery services, customer hotline support, and dedicated account service teams are but a few of the costs to serve that may be consumed by some customers at a different rate from other customers.

In many cases these costs have been considered "below the line" expenses, but they're really significant components of overall customer service cost. As customer services grow more varied and complex, relating these different service levels to customers becomes critical. This is especially true for those services that are differentiators and make up a more significant share of the overall cost structure.

Cost to Retain—includes all costs incurred for the benefit of retaining or enhancing the customer relationship after the initial sale has been made. In concept, these would include the costs of relationship building, cross-sell campaigns, and customer incentives. In practice, many of these costs may be indistinguishable from the costs to serve described above.

Figure 2 illustrates the ability to leverage the ABM architecture, transforming the traditional ledger structure into activities and then associating the

Figure 1: Customer Lifetime Value—Cost Dimensions

Customer Lifetime Value is the sum of customer profitability over the life of the relationship with that customer.

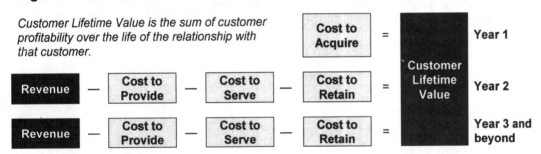

consumption of these activity costs to customers, which results in a fully absorbed cost of the relationship with a customer.

Once you determine the cost of customers and align costs and revenues over the customer's historical lifetime, you can establish the relative value of the customers.

Figure 3 shows how these costs accumulate over the life of the customer relationship and combines the cumulative revenue from the relationship to determine the lifetime value generated from the customer.

Positive customer lifetime value occurs at the point where cumulative revenue exceeds the cumulative costs of customer acquisition, cost to provide, cost to retain, and cost to serve.

At the outset of a relationship, companies may see an initial "loss" of investment in the relationship since acquisition costs have no offsetting revenues. Over time, the cumulative margins generated by that customer will offset the cumulative cost for acquisition, service, and retention, resulting in an eventual positive contribution to profit. Once that occurs, the customer's lifetime value switches from negative to positive. From that point on, the longer a company maintains a productive relationship with that customer, the greater the customer's lifetime value.

It isn't uncommon to hear the argument that many of the costs of acquisition and service are fixed so they aren't relevant to the customer. We disagree. Our experience has shown that the behavior of many so-called "fixed" costs are highly influenced by levels of customer activity, so they tend to be variable based on the methods/approaches used to acquire and service each customer. Unfortunately, once the costs of acquiring and servicing customers are incorporated into a company's cost structure, they rarely disappear, even when the customer leaves.

Further complicating this issue, product pricing all too often doesn't distinguish between the value of product and the value of service the customer is receiving. The two components become blurred in a single price, and, over time, the customer loses sight of what they're paying for. We've found that many organizations can benefit from disassociating their

pricing for product from their pricing for services. This is called menu pricing. Companies who fail to maintain their customers' focus on value for price risk losing their differentiation to an aggressive, no-frills competitor offering a slimmed-down mix of services.

While activity-based management provides a powerful set of tools you can use to measure customer lifetime value, companies who have implemented ABM realize that it requires a greater commitment of resources and management buy-in than traditional cost accounting does. Our experience

has shown that ABM efforts are most successful when ABM doesn't stand on its own but is closely aligned with a "strategic imperative" within the company. Customer relationship management is a good example of a strategic imperative that will benefit from integration with ABM.

TECHNOLOGY ENABLES CLV

The past few years have witnessed major advancements in customer relationship management processes and technology. Companies have moved from implementing single CRM applications such as sales force automation, customer service, marketing automation, and e-channel (B2C) to implementing integrated CRM. Integrated CRM provides a multichannel approach that brings together information from every customer touch point, stores this information within a data warehouse, analyzes this information using sophisticated data mining and customer analytics models, and delivers these results back to each of the customer touch points. Only by combining relevant financial data within the data warehouse and including CLV as an integrated part of customer analytics can companies truly be able to achieve their CRM objectives.

ABM efforts can take advantage of the tremendous strides that have been made in the automation of CRM processes and the new technology that has been developed to help facilitate the collection of financial and statistical information. The implementation of integrated CRM systems has created new opportunities for companies to collect

Figure 2: ABM Cost Management Methodology—Cost Flow

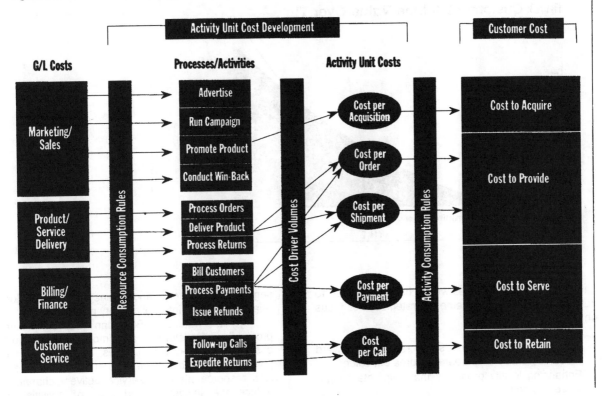

enriched information. This includes resource distribution and cost driver information to produce the outputs required for ABM and CLV. Examples include customer ordering histories and channel usage, customer call frequency and duration, marketing activities, delivery and service requirements, and product volume, mix, and revenue data. As a result of this automation, much of the information needed to produce customer lifetime value measures are a by-product of this customer relationship management automation.

APPLYING CUSTOMER LIFETIME VALUE TO DEVELOP CUSTOMER MANAGEMENT STRATEGIES

As companies shift from a traditional product focus to a customer focus, CRM represents a fundamental change impacting virtually every aspect of an organization. This includes its business strategies and operating processes, application and technology infrastructure, management and organizational structures, and sometimes even its culture. To achieve successful customer relationship management,

organizations must foster behaviors and implement processes and technologies that support coordinated customer interactions throughout every customer touch point. This process often includes new ways of:

- Marketing to and caring for customers;
- Establishing sales channels tailored appropriately to customers;
- Establishing a partner community centered around common customers;
- Fostering innovation and collaboration with the aim of improving customer service and loyalty;
- Investing in the creation, capture, and dissemination of customer knowledge within the organization, among partners, and potentially with customers;
- Leveraging information technology to enable the transformed practices mentioned above.

Customer lifetime value provides a sound basis for decision making regarding investments and strategies for each of these. Through CLV and through the ability to understand and segment customers

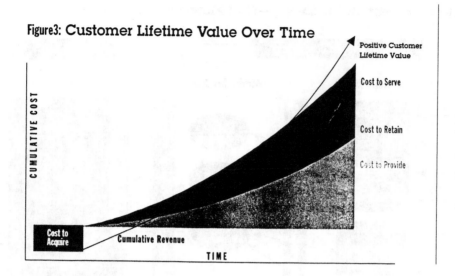

Figure3: Customer Lifetime Value Over Time

(y-axis) CUMULATIVE COST

Positive Customer
Lifetime Value

Cost to Serve

Cost to Retain

Cost to Provide

Cost to Acquire

Cumulative Revenue

(x-axis) TIME

based on value, companies will be better equipped to develop customer management strategies that focus on:

- Directing marketing and sales resources toward those customers that create the greatest value;
- Enhancing loyalty programs that help retain high-value customers;
- Modifying customer service activities for low-value customers;
- Increasing customer service activities for high-value customers;
- Developing service pricing distinct from product pricing (such as menu pricing).

Customer-centric management requires differentiated customer strategies and the ability to match specific customers with "personalized" treatment. CLV measures will segment customers based on their value contribution. Understanding the value customers create will help you develop specific actions, such as those shown in Figure 4, which should result in better and longer relationships with your best customers and increased profitability for your company.

The combination of customer relationship management and activity-based management gives you greater visibility, not only into a customer's relationship with your company, but also regarding how your company invests its own resources to support customers. It lets you establish customer-centric metrics and benchmarking of progress against best practices. It's this visibility that will provide you and other members of management with the information and knowledge you need to effectively

segment customers and manage both customer relationships and internal delivery processes.

By its nature, ABM can deliver accurate profitability of customers and information around the cost of customer-driven activities. This information can guide you in two directions—either move customers to less resource-intensive service delivery channels or reduce the incidence and cost of activities and processes that are delivered for the customer.

Perhaps the most valuable application of CLV is forward looking. By understanding the characteristics of profitable and unprofitable customers, you'll be better able to predict the behavior of future customers and better target your company's business development activities. If you can predict a "Loser" early in the acquisition process, you can avoid costs and resources that you would have spent on negative value creation and invest them instead in providing superior service to "Champion" customers.

MORE VALUE AND CUSTOMER LOYALTY

Customer lifetime value provides an objective approach to identifying a customer's value contribution. Activity-based management serves as the foundation and the tool for measuring CLV. As organizations put this information into motion, they are better able to develop strategies to enhance the value derived from customer relationships.

If your company is contemplating or currently implementing CRM, we invite you to consider the following suggestions:

Assess your CRM Initiative—If your company is implementing CRM, do you have CLV measurements, and are they providing the correct insights?

Figure 4: Customer Strategies by Value and Demographic Segments

Demographic Segments	**"Champions"** Nurture	**"Demanders"** Grow & Reduce Cost	**"Acquaintances"** Grow Revenue	**"Losers"** Improve Profitability
Super User **Technology Astute** **Family User** **Frequent Communicator** **Basic User**	▪ Preferred customer program ▪ Customer loyalty promotions ▪ "Hotline" support ▪ Personalized support for "high-tech" products ▪ Penetration pricing of high retention services ▪ Reward programs for champion referrals ▪ Personal account plans	▪ Focused marketing to increase volume ▪ Align customer service to increase value ▪ Incent to lower cost services (VRU/Internet vs direct customer service) ▪ Direct mail offerings of segment-aligned products ▪ Reduce costs while maintaining customer service	▪ Stimulate volume usage or margins ▪ Direct marketing of cross-sales campaigns through low-cost channels ▪ Bundled product offerings of segment-aligned products ▪ Direct mail offerings of segment-aligned products	▪ No direct customer care ▪ Additional charges for customer services (e.g., charge for calling help center more than 3 times a month) ▪ Reacquire in lower-cost channel ▪ No direct marketing of products ▪ Simplify and reduce billing costs

Value Segments

Determine value of Integrating ABM with CLV—If your organization is implementing CRM, but hasn't implemented ABM, consider the need for ABM in calculating your CLV measurements.

Align current ABM efforts—If your company has implemented ABM and is implementing CRM, there's a powerful opportunity for synergy between these two initiatives.

The result of integrating customer relationship management and activity-based management through the implementation of customer lifetime value will be greater shareholder value and creation of loyalty with customers who create the most value for your company. Organizations that aren't including customer lifetime value in their CRM toolkit, or those basing CLV solely on revenue generation, might find themselves having superior relationships with the wrong customers.

Joseph A. Ness, CPA, is a partner with Management Consulting Services of PricewaterhouseCoopers in St. Louis, Mo. He's responsible for coordinating the firm's Activity Based Management consulting practice throughout the U.S. You can reach him at joe.ness@us.pwcglobal. corn.

Michael I. Schroeck, CMA, CPA, is a partner with Management Consulting Services of PricewaterhouseCoopers in Rosemont, Ill. He is the partner champion for Pricewaterhouse-Coopers' Data Warehousing and Customer Analytics Practices. You can reach him at mike.schroeck@us.pwcglobal.com.

Rick A. Letendre, CPA, is a sales account manager for Management Consulting Services of PricewaterhouseCoopers in Houston, Texas. He's responsible for supporting development of new service offerings and business development in the Financial Management Solutions practice. You can reach him at rick.letendre@us.pwcglobal.com.

Willmar J. Douglas, ACMA, is a principal consultant with Management Consulting Services of PricewaterhouseCoopers in St. Louis. His major experience lies in designing and implementing financial and cost management systems, particularly ABC/M systems. You can reach him at willmar.Douglas@us.pwcglobal. corn.

Chapter 18
Management Control and Strategic Performance Measurement

Cases

18-1   Analysis of the Accounting Function
18-2   Industrial Chemicals Company (Control of Research and Development)
18-3   Absorption Versus Variable Costing and Ethical Issues
18-4   Strategic Performance Measurement
18-5   Strategic Performance Measurement: Employee Benefits
18-6   Strategic Performance Measurement: Regression Analysis

Readings

"Transforming the Balanced Scorecard from Performance Measurement to Strategic Management: Part 1"

This article explains the emerging role of the balanced scorecard—a change from a focus only on performance evaluation to a concern also for strategic management. Through the use of strategy maps, the authors show how the balanced scorecard can be used to inform the development of the firm's strategy and improve shareholder value. This is accomplished through the linking of the scorecard perspectives: from the learning and growth perspective to the internal perspective, then to the customer perspective, and finally to the financial perspective and shareholder value.

Discussion questions:

1. Give an example of a nonprofit or governmental organization that uses the balanced scorecard and explain how it links the scorecard to its overall strategy. *Hospital*

2. What is a Key Performance Indicator (KPI) scorecard and how does it differ from a balanced scorecard?

3. How can the balanced scorecard be used to supplement conventional financial reporting? *Adds non financial areas*

4. Explain the strategy map and how it is used.

Factors that led to development of balanced scorecard

Cases

18-1. Analysis of the Accounting Function

For the past several years, a large U.S. based hotel/restaurant operator has been pursuing a strategy of disposing of its U.S. company-owned properties and focusing instead on property management services. Four years ago, the company owned and operated 106 properties. Today, that number is 40. The number of retained properties is expected to stabilize between 15 and 20 properties.

During this same period, there was a shift in control of property operations. Previously, headquarters operating personnel held control. Now, hotel operations is basically a decentralized organization, with primary responsibility for operating results resting with three regional vice presidents and each hotel's general manager. The three regional vice presidents report directly to the Executive Vice President of U.S. Hotel Operations, and each are responsible for between 10 and 15 properties. Each property's general manager is directly responsible to the regional vice president. Corporate headquarters provides staff support in operations policies, food and beverage, engineering and maintenance, and accounting.

Accounting support has stayed in a relatively unchanged centralized configuration. The staff of the U.S. hotel controller currently numbers approximately sixty-four. However, the ratio of accounting personnel to properties owned has increased. Previously, the ratio was approximately one headcount per property. Today, it is 1.6 headcount per property. Table A describes the department's major functions.

CENTRAL HOTEL ACCOUNTING

In his visits to the properties, the controller would often solicit comments concerning the accounting support being rendered by the headquarters' staff. An all-too-frequent response was that the properties would be better off without such support. The field operators felt that the accounting staff had no idea of the problems the properties had to deal with and demanded information and data without any consideration or knowledge of the situation at the property level.

The controller must now decide how to reduce his staff in order to get the headcount in line with property dispositions. In doing this he has several objectives:

1. To control and, where possible, immediately reduce costs related to accounting functions.

2. To make accounting functions more responsive to the needs of operators.

3. To foster greater familiarity and closer affiliation between accounting staff and field operators.

4. To improve productivity and increase morale among the accounting staff.

18-2

REQUIRED:

1. What organizational alternatives are available to the controller?

2. How can the accounting staff be reduced and still be responsive to the needs of operations?

3. Using this case as an example, comment on the effects of strategic initiatives on the proper scope and functioning of a firm's accounting department.

   (IMA, adapted)

TABLE A
Accounting Functions

Accounts Payable—Most vendors invoice the properties directly. Once approved, invoices are forwarded, at least weekly, to corporate headquarters for payment. Monthly volume over the last 15 months has averaged 21,300 invoices, ranging from 18,000 to 25,800 invoices.

Accounts Receivable—(a) Credit cards represent a significant portion of sales volume. Credit card vouchers are sent daily to corporate headquarters, where they are batched and forwarded to the various credit card companies for payment. In a typical month, 75,000 credit card vouchers will be processed. (b) Direct billing is done at the property. A customer must qualify in order to be billed in this manner. If the direct bill is outstanding for 60 days, it is forwarded to corporate headquarters for further action.

Data Entry—The data processing system requirements mandate three (3) different types of terminals, with three different types of screens, security, and operational procedures. This had led to a separate area of proficiency and dedicated skill.

Field Payroll—Payroll processing is initiated at the property with employees' daily use of time cards. The hours worked are summarized on payroll input sheets, which are sent to corporate headquarters bi-weekly. Payroll information is entered into an automated payroll system that generates paychecks, and maintains the appropriate payroll records. The paychecks are sent to the properties for distribution to employees. Monthly volume averages between 13,000 and 16,500 payroll checks (last year, 14,500 W-2's were prepared).

General Ledger—General ledger processing is by batching process. The general ledger contains about 450 accounts per property. Each property will have about 600 transactions per month. This includes direct feeds from various sub-systems (including accounts payable, payroll, and revenue reporting).

Management Contract Accounting—Management contract accounting makes use of accounts payable, payroll and general ledger functions to prepare daily cash reports and monthly profit and loss statements to be sent to the owners of managed properties.

18-2. Industrial Chemicals Company

In 19X5, events which were thought about and planned for the past several years in the Industrial Chemicals Company (ICC) culminated in the most significant change in the company's 80-plus year history. A major corporate restructuring was announced including the purchase of a large U.S. based pharmaceutical company, for $2.8 billion. ICC is a large multinational manufacturer of industrial chemicals. The parent company is located in Amsterdam, and manufacturing plants and customers are located worldwide.

In February of 19X6, the Chairman of the Board and Chief Executive Officer told a reporter of a major financial magazine: "We felt that if we were to build a strong technology base of biology and biotechnology that would simultaneously serve agriculture, animal nutrition, and health care, we could build a unique powerhouse backing it up in a way that companies in these individual businesses couldn't do; and we've built it." The changes initiated were thus not merely pruning and trimming, but changing the very direction of the company by getting out of commodity chemicals and into more innovative areas.

The magazine article made a key observation in its February 10, issue:

A major problem looms: Can ICC support the level of research needed to make a major impact in biotechnology? Earnings for the first three quarters of 19X5 dropped and the company expects to show a loss for the fourth quarter, even before write-offs on closed chemical plants.

The chairman of the board was well aware of this major concern. In fact, as 19X5 drew to a close, he commissioned a special subgroup of the Executive Management Committee (the EMC is the senior management group dealing with major strategic and operational issues) to review the company's overall R&D spending, its affordability and priorities, and bring back recommendations to the EMC in time for inclusion in the 19X6 budgeting process.

RESEARCH AND DEVELOPMENT

From a total corporate perspective, the R&D effort falls into three classifications:

Class I—Maintain existing businesses—

This effort is associated with managing existing business assets, maintaining competitiveness of products in existing businesses, and supplying technical service.

Class II—Expand existing businesses—

R&D associated with expanding existing business assets, expanding markets of existing products, or substantially lowering costs of existing processes.

Class III—Create new businesses—

R&D associated with creating new business assets.

Organizationally, each of the operating units administers its own R&D efforts which cut across all three categories above. In very simple terms, the operating unit is relatively self-sufficient across all three categories where technology *already exists*. They "purchase" some support services from the corporate R&D group as described later. In terms of performance assessment for incentive compensation, the operating unit R&D groups are tied to the "bottom-line" results achieved by the respective units.

CORPORATE R&D

The corporate R&D group, in addition to providing support services to the operating unit's R&D efforts, is primarily responsible for required *new technology* in creating new businesses. At the point in time in the product invention time line when new-technology-based products reach a level of commercial viability, these programs are "handed-off" to an operating unit R&D group for eventual movement to commercialization. In the past several years, this corporate R&D group has been successful in "inventing" and "handing off" commercial leads despite some operating unit reluctance to fund the research costs. In these instances, funding sometimes remained with corporate R&D after the "hand-off."

A more detailed description of the corporate R&D group follows. The corporate research and development group is headed by a senior vice president reporting to the Chairman of the Board and CEO. The central research laboratory group consists of an information center (20 percent of its costs are charged to operating units on a fee for service basis), an MIS facility, bioprocess development and cell culture groups (which are essentially involved in devising production processes for biotechnology-based products),

```
┌─────────────────────────────────────────────────────────┐
│ SUMMARY OF CORPORATE RESEARCH AND DEVELOPMENT            │
├─────────────────────────────────────────────────────────┤
│ Research Laboratory Group                                │
│   Information Center                                      │
│   MIS Facility                                           │
│   Bioprocess Development and Cell Culture                │
│   Physical Sciences Center                               │
│   Analytical Chemistry Group                             │
│   Chemistry Group                                        │
│                                                          │
│ Biological Sciences Group                                │
│                                                          │
│ Patent Group                                             │
└─────────────────────────────────────────────────────────┘
```

a physical sciences center (a central analytical chemistry group providing very specialized and highly skilled support to many users across the company—65 percent of this group's costs are charged out directly on a fee-for-service basis), a group called controlled delivery which develops vehicles for the transfer of pharmaceutical and animal science products into the living systems within which they must act, and a chemistry group providing very specialized skills in both conventional and biotechnology process chemistry (about 25 percent of this group's costs are charged directly on a fee-for-service basis). In addition to the direct fee-for-service chargeouts described above, a portion of the costs of this central laboratory group (primarily the bioprocess development and cell culture groups) is assigned to the biological sciences segment. The remaining costs, along with overall corporate R&D administrative costs, are allocated as a part of corporate charges.

The biological sciences group has been the major focal point for new technology in the pharmaceutical and animal sciences area. It supports plant sciences for the agricultural unit as well. The costs for the biological sciences group are reported as being for new direction basic research. Also controlled within corporate R&D and reported in this segment are costs of key university relationships supporting basic and applied biomedical, crop chemicals, and animal sciences research efforts.

The patent group has always been decentralized with a patent counsel and staff assigned to each operating unit reporting on a "dotted line" basis to the operating unit and administratively to the general patent counsel. Thus, about 80 percent of patent cost is already directly borne by operating units with the remainder allocated as part of corporate charges.

REQUIRED:

As the controller reflected on the information obtained and the important issues being addressed by the EMC subcommittee, the following questions surfaced in his mind. Develop a response for each question.

1. What is the role of R&D in the firm's overall strategy?

2. Would operating unit control of our key R&D growth programs enhance or mitigate our chances of meeting our goals? That is, should R&D be organized as cost SBUs within each of the operating units? What amount and type of R&D, if any at all, should be done at the corporate level?

3. I know there'll be pressure to level off our R&D spending across the company, including corporate R&D. We've got to make sure we get more for our money in terms of prioritizing those efforts to go after the most promising commercial opportunities if we're going to achieve our goals in biotechnology! How can we be sure we're prioritizing these efforts toward increased commercial success? That is, how do we evaluate the effectiveness of both the R&D cost SBUs in the operating units and corporate-level R&D?

4. How does the fact that ICC operates in several different countries affect the decisions the controller is facing?

(IMA adapted)

18-3. Absorption Versus Variable Costing and Ethical Issues

HeadGear, Inc is a small manufacturer of headphones for use in commercial and personal applications. The HeadGear headphones are known for their outstanding sound quality and light weight, which makes them highly desirable especially in the commercial market for telemarketing firms and similar communication applications, despite the relatively high price. Although demand has grown steadily, profits have grown much more slowly, and John Hurley, the CEO, suspects productivity is falling, and costs are rising out of hand. John is concerned that the decline in profit growth will affect the stock price of the company and inhibit the firm's efforts to raise new investment capital, which will be needed to continue the firm's growth. While the firm is now operating at 68% of available production capacity, John thinks the market growth will soon exceed available capacity.

To improve profitability, John has decided to bring in a new COO with the objective of improving profitability very quickly. The new COO understands that profits must be improved within the coming 10-18 months. A bonus of 10% of profit improvement is promised the new COO if this goal is achieved. The following is the income statement for HeadGear for 2002, from the most recent annual report. Product costs for HeadGear include $25 per unit variable manufacturing costs and $1,920,000 per year fixed manufacturing overhead. Budgeted production was 120,000 units in 2002. Selling and administrative costs include a variable portion of $15 per unit and a fixed portion of $2,400,0000 per year. The same units costs and production level are also applicable for 2001.

HeadGear Inc.		
Income Statement for the Period Ended 12/31/2002		
Sales (125,000 @$75)		$ 9,375,000
Cost of Sales:		
Beginning Inv: 5,000 @ $41	$ 205,000	
Cost of Production: 120,000 @ $41	4,920,000	
Goods Available: 130,000	$5,125,000	
Less Ending Inv: 0 @ $41	-0-	$5,125,000
Gross Margin		$4,250,000
Selling and Administrative		
Variable Costs: 125,000 @ $15	$ 1,875,000	
Fixed Costs	2,400,000	$4,275,000
Net loss		$ <25,000>

The new COO is convinced that the problem is the need to aggressively market the product, and that the apparent decline in productivity is really due to underutilization of capacity. The COO increases variable selling costs to $16 per unit and fixed selling costs to $2,750,000 to help achieve this goal. Budgeted sales and production for 19X3 are set at 175,000 units.

Actual production was 175,000 as planned but sales for 2003 turned out to be only 140,000 units, short of the target. The new COO claims that profits have increased considerably, and is looking forward to the promised bonus.

REQUIRED:

1. Calculate the absorption cost net income for 19X3, assuming the new selling costs, and that manufacturing costs remain the same as 19X2.

2. Calculate the variable cost net income for 19X3 and explain why it is different from the absorption cost net income.

3. Is the new COO due a bonus? Comment on the effectiveness of Hurley's plan to improve profits by hiring the new COO and promising the bonus.

4. Identify and explain any important ethical issues you see in this case.

18-4. Strategic Performance Measurement

Johnson Supply Company is a large retailer of office supplies. It is organized into six regional divisions, five within the United States, and one international division. The firm is
growing steadily, with the greatest growth in the international division. Johnson evaluates
each division as a profit SBU. Revenues and direct costs of the divisions are traced to
each division using a centralized accounting system. The various support departments,
including human resources, information technology, accounting, and marketing, are
treated as cost SBUs and the costs are allocated to the divisions on the basis of sales
revenues. The international division has cash, receivables, payables, and other investments in foreign currencies. As a result, this division experiences occasional significant
losses and gains due to fluctuations in the value of foreign currencies. Based on the idea
that these effects are uncontrollable, the effects of currency changes on the international
division is retained in a single home-office account and is not traced to the division.
Similarly, taxes paid by this division to other countries is pooled in a home office account
and is not traced to it.

Because of rapidly increasing costs in the information technology (IT) department,
Johnson's top management is considering changing this department to a profit SBU. IT
would set prices for its services, and the user divisions could choose to purchase these
services from IT or from a vendor outside the firm. The manager of IT is upset at the idea,
and has told top management that this move would eventually create chaotic and ineffective information services within the firm.

REQUIRED:

1. Should Johnson's six divisions be treated as profit SBUs or some other type of strategic performance measurement system? Explain.

2. Comment on the firm's decision not to trace currency gains and losses and foreign
   tax expense to the international division.

3. Comment on the firm's consideration of changing the IT department from a cost SBU
   to a profit SBU. What are the likely effects on the firm and on the IT department?

18-5. Strategic Performance Measurement: Employee Benefits

In its thirteen year of operations, Mount Drake Software is reviewing the methods it has used to evaluate its profit SBUs. Mount Drake has six product divisions, each of which is a profit SBU, and each markets specialized software products to specific customer groups. For example, one unit markets software systems to dental practices, and another provides software for real estate management firms. A critical factor in Mount Drake's success is the commitment and competence of its systems development and programming staff. While there is a relatively high turnover for these employees, Mount Drake has managed to retain the very best and to attract the very best. In recent months, as their business has grown, and as the software industry generally has grown significantly, it has become more and more difficult for Mount Drake to attract and to retain the best staff. Mount Drake is looking for ways to become more competitive in attracting and retaining these employees. One idea is to increase employee benefits by adding training opportunities, additional paid vacation, stock investment programs, and improved health insurance. The cost of some of these additional benefits could be traced directly to the divisions, while the cost of other benefits (such as improved group health coverage and company-wide training programs) could not be directly traced to the divisions.

REQUIRED:

How should Mount Drake handle employee benefits within its current performance measurement system? Should Mount Drake change the performance measurement system, and if so, how should it be changed?

18-6. Strategic Performance Measurement: Regression Analysis

Maydew Manufacturing Inc. is a large manufacturer of lawn and garden equipment including mowers, edgers, tillers, related equipment and accessories. The firm has been very successful in recent years, and sales have grown more than 10% in each of the last five years. The firm is organized into 15 investment SBUs based on product line groups. Return on investment and residual income calculations have been made for each of the last 4 years and used in management compensation for the last two years. Recently Maydew top management has contracted with MM&PC, a large consulting firm to review the performance measurement process at the firm. One of MM&PC's key recommendations has been to consider the implementation of the balanced scorecard both for performance measurement and for strategic management. As a step in this direction, MM&PC has asked Maydew for some data on ROI and other measures being considered for the balanced scorecard in order to analyze the relationships among these data. It is hoped that the analysis will help MM&PC develop a strategy map for the firm. The following data show the last year's ROI for each SBU and the average for the last three years for: training hours per employee in the SBU, customer retention rate in the SBU (customers are primarily large department store chains and other distributors of lawn and garden equipment), the QSV score, and the defect rate (per thousand products). The QSV score is a measure of the Quality-Service-Value of the SBU made by an analysis of a variety of data including customer complaints, on-site inspection by key operating executives, and other means (the highest score is 10, and the lowest is 0).

Manager	ROI	Training Hours per employee	Customer Retention	QSV Score	Defect Rate
1	21.3	98	99.3	7	3.3
2	15.4	122	98.2	8	4.7
3	9.6	67	86.7	6	11.2
4	12.4	88	84.5	9	13.7
5	18.6	92	91.4	8	2.1
6	4.5	33	90.7	4	28.9
7	8.8	49	88.9	6	1.2
8	22.6	77	93.5	10	12.4
9	11.8	102	95.5	9	8
10	14.6	95	91.1	6	7.4
11	16.5	87	92.7	6	2.8
12	12.1	80	86.4	8	4.9
13	6.2	66	80.2	4	15.3
14	1.3	50	78	4	22.8
15	9.7	78	85.5	7	30.5

REQUIRED:

1. Develop a regression model for predicting ROI using as independent variables: training hours, customer retention, QSV and the defect rate. Use what you think is the best subset of independent variables, and evaluate the regression's reliability and precision.

2. Explain how MM&PC might use these results in implementing the balanced scorecard at Maydew Manufacturing.

Readings

TRANSFORMING THE BALANCED SCORECARD FROM PERFORMANCE MEASUREMENT TO STRATEGIC MANAGEMENT: PART I

Robed S. Kaplan and David P. Norton
Robert S. Kaplan is a Professor at Harvard University and David P. Norton is founder and president of the Balanced Scorecard Collaborative in Lincoln, Massachusetts.[1]

Several years ago we introduced the Balanced Scorecard (Kaplan and Norton 1992). We began with the premise that an exclusive reliance on financial measures in a management system is insufficient. Financial measures are lag indicators that report on the outcomes from past actions. Exclusive reliance on financial indicators could promote behavior that sacrifices long-term value creation for short-term performance (Porter 1992; AICPA 1994). The Balanced Scorecard approach retains measures of financial performance—the lagging outcome indicators—but supplements these with measures on the drivers, the lead indicators, of future financial performance.

THE BALANCED SCORECARD EMERGES

The limitations of managing solely with financial measures, however, have been known for decades.[2] What is different now? Why has the Balanced Scorecard concept been so widely adopted by manufacturing and service companies, nonprofit organizations, and government entities around the world since its introduction in 1992?

First, previous systems that incorporated nonfinancial measurements used *ad hoc* collections of

---

[1] This article is adapted from R. S. Kaplan and D. P. Norton (2001a, 2000). © 2001 American Accounting Association, *Accounting Horizons*, Vol. 15 No.1, March 2001, pp. 87-104

[2] For example, General Electric attempted a system of nonfinancial measurements in the 1950s (Greenwood 1974), and the French developed the Tableaux de Bord decades ago (Lebas 1994; Epstein and Manzoni 1998).

such measures, more like checklists of measures for managers to keep track of and improve than a comprehensive system of linked measurements. The Balanced Scorecard emphasizes the linkage of measurement to strategy (Kaplan and Norton 1993) and the cause-and-effect linkages that describe the hypotheses of the strategy (Kaplan and Norton 1996b). The tighter connection between the measurement system and strategy elevates the role for nonfinancial measures from an operational checklist to a comprehensive system for strategy implementation (Kaplan and Norton 1996a).

Second, the Balanced Scorecard reflects the changing nature of technology and competitive advantage in the latter decades of the 20th century. In the industrial-age competition of the 19th and much of the 20th centuries, companies achieved competitive advantage from their investment in and management of tangible assets such as inventory, property, plant, and equipment (Chandler 1990). In an economy dominated by tangible assets, financial measurements were adequate to record investments on companies' balance sheets. Income statements could also capture the expenses associated with the use of these tangible assets to produce revenues and profits. But by the end of the 20th century, intangible assets became the major source for competitive advantage. In 1982, tangible book values represented 62 percent of industrial organizations' market values; ten years later, the ratio had plummeted to 38 percent (Blair 1995). By the end of the 20th century, the book value of tangible assets accounted for less than 20 percent of companies' market values (Webber 2000, quoting research by Baruch Lev).

Clearly, strategies for creating value shifted from managing tangible assets to knowledge-based strategies that create and deploy an organization's intangible assets. These include customer relationships, innovative products and services, high-quality and responsive operating processes, skills and knowledge of the workforce, the information technology that supports the work force and links the firm to its customers and suppliers, and the organizational climate that encourages innovation, problem-solving, and improvement. But companies were unable to adequately measure their intangible assets (Johnson and Kaplan 1987, 201-202). Anecdotal data from management publications indicated that many companies could not implement their new strategies in this environment (Kiechel 1982; Charan and Colvin 1999). They could not manage what they could not describe or measure.

INTANGIBLE ASSETS: VALUATION VS. VALUE CREATION

Some call for accountants to make an organization's intangible assets more visible to managers and investors by placing them on a company's balance sheet. But several factors prevent valid valuation of intangible assets on balance sheets.

First, the value from intangible assets is indirect. Assets such as knowledge and technology seldom have a direct impact on revenue and profit. Improvements in intangible assets affect financial outcomes through chains of cause-and-effect relationships involving two or three intermediate stages (Huselid 1995; Becker and Huselid 1998). For example, consider the linkages in the service management profit chain (Heskett et al.1994):

- investments in employee training lead to improvements in service quality
- better service quality leads to higher customer satisfaction
- higher customer satisfaction leads to increased customer loyalty
- increased customer loyalty generates increased revenues and margins

Financial outcomes are separated causally and temporally from improving employees' capabilities. The complex linkages make it difficult, if not impossible, to place a financial value on an asset such as workforce capabilities or employee morale, much less to measure period-to-period changes in that financial value.

Second, the value from intangible assets depends on organizational context and strategy. This value cannot be separated from the organizational processes that transform intangibles into customer and financial outcomes. The balance sheet is a linear, additive model. It records each class of asset separately and calculates the total by adding up each asset's recorded value. The value created from investing in individual intangible assets, however, is neither linear nor additive.

Senior investment bankers in a firm such as Goldman Sachs are immensely valuable because of their knowledge about complex financial products and their capabilities for managing relationships and developing trust with sophisticated customers. People with the same knowledge, experience, and capabilities, however, are nearly worthless to a financial services company such as etrade.com that emphasizes operational efficiency, low cost, and technology-based trading. The value of an intangible asset depends critically on the context—the organization, the strategy, and other complementary assets—in which the intangible asset is deployed.

Intangible assets seldom have value by themselves.[3] Generally, they must be bundled with other intangible and tangible assets to create value. For example, a new growth-oriented sales strategy could require new knowledge about customers, new training for sales employees, new databases, new information systems, a new organization structure, and a new incentive compensation program. Investing in just one of these capabilities, or in all of them but one, could cause the new sales strategy to fail. The value does not reside in any individual intangible asset. It arises from creating the entire set of assets along with a strategy that links them together. The value-creation process is multiplicative, not additive.

THE BALANCED SCORECARD SUPPLEMENTS CONVENTIONAL FINANCIAL REPORTING

Companies' balance sheets report separately on tangible assets, such as raw material, land, and equipment, based on their historic cost—the traditional financial accounting method. This was adequate for industrial-age companies, which succeeded by combining and transforming their tangible resources into products whose value exceeded their acquisition and production costs. Financial accounting conventions relating to depreciation and cost of goods sold enabled an income statement to measure how much value was created beyond the costs incurred to acquire and transform tangible assets into finished products and services.

Some argue that companies should follow the same cost-based convention for their intangible assets—capitalize and subsequently amortize the expenditures on training employees, conducting research and development, purchasing and developing databases, and advertising that creates brand awareness. But such costs are poor approximations of the realizable value created by investing in these intangible assets. Intangible assets can create value for or-

---

[3] Brand names, which can be sold, are an exception.

ganizations, but that does not imply that they have separable market values. Many internal and linked organizational processes, such as design, delivery, and service, are required to transform the potential value of intangible assets into products and services that have tangible value.

We introduced the Balanced Scorecard to provide a new framework for describing value-creating strategies that link intangible and tangible assets. The scorecard does not attempt to "value" an organization's intangible assets, but it does measure these assets in units other than currency. The Balanced Scorecard describes how intangible assets get mobilized and combined with intangible and tangible assets to create differentiating customer-value propositions and superior financial outcomes.

STRATEGY MAPS

Since introducing the Balanced Scorecard in 1992, we have helped over 200 executive teams design their scorecard programs. Initially we started with a clean sheet of paper, asking, "what is the strategy," and allowed the strategy and the Balanced Scorecard to emerge from interviews and discussions with the senior executives. The scorecard provided a framework for organizing strategic objectives into the four perspectives displayed in Figure 1:

1. *Financial*—the strategy for growth, profitability, and risk viewed from the perspective of the shareholder.
2. *Customer*—the strategy for creating value and differentiation from the perspective of the customer.
3. *Internal Business Processes*—the strategic priorities for various business processes that create customer and shareholder satisfaction.
4. *Learning and Growth*—the priorities to create a climate that supports organizational change, innovation, and growth.

From this initial base of experience, we subsequently developed a general framework for describing and implementing strategy that we believe can be as useful as the traditional framework of income statement, balance sheet, and statement of cash flows for financial planning and reporting. The new framework, which we call a "Strategy Map," is a logical and comprehensive architecture for describing strategy, as illustrated in Figure 2. A strategy map specifies the critical elements and their linkages for an organization's strategy.

- Objectives for growth and productivity to enhance shareholder value.

- Market and account share, acquisition, and retention of targeted customers where profitable growth will occur.
- Value propositions that would lead customers to do more higher-margin business with the company.
- Innovation and excellence in products, services, and processes that deliver the value proposition to targeted customer segments, promote operational improvements, and meet community expectations and regulatory requirements.
- Investments required in people and systems to generate and sustain growth.

By translating their strategy into the logical architecture of a strategy map and Balanced Scorecard, organizations create a common and understandable point of reference for all organizational units and employees.

Organizations build strategy maps from the top down, starting with the destination and then charting the routes that lead there. Corporate executives first review their mission statement, why their company exists, and core values, what their company believes in. From that information, they develop their strategic vision, what their company wants to become. This vision creates a clear picture of the company's overall goal, which could be to become a top-quartile performer. The strategy identifies the path intended to reach that destination.

FINANCIAL PERSPECTIVE

The typical destination for profit-seeking enterprises is a significant increase in shareholder value (we will discuss the modifications for nonprofit and government organizations later in the paper). Companies increase economic value through two basic approaches—revenue *growth* and *productivity*.[4] A revenue growth strategy generally has two components: build the franchise with revenue from new markets, new products, and new customers; and increase sales to existing customers by deepening relationships with them, including cross-selling multiple products and services, and offering complete solutions. A productivity strategy also generally has two components: improve the cost structure by lowering direct and indirect expenses; and utilize assets more efficiently by

---

[4] Shareholder value can also be increased through managing the right-hand side of the balance sheet, such as by repurchasing shares and choosing the low-cost mix among debt and equity instruments to lower the cost of capital. In this paper, we focus only on improved management of the organization's assets (tangible and intangible).

FIGURE 1
The Balanced Scorecard Defines a Strategy's Cause-and-Effect Relationships

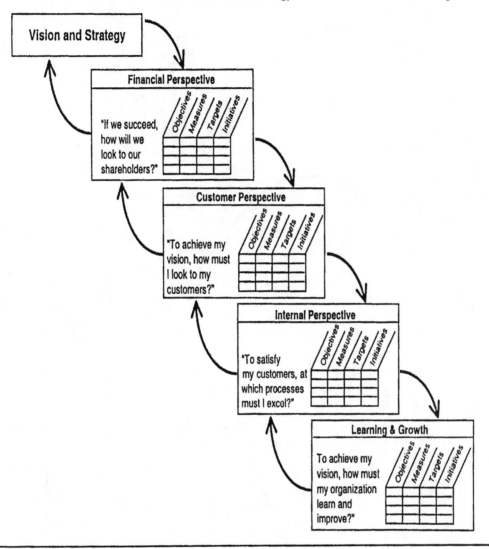

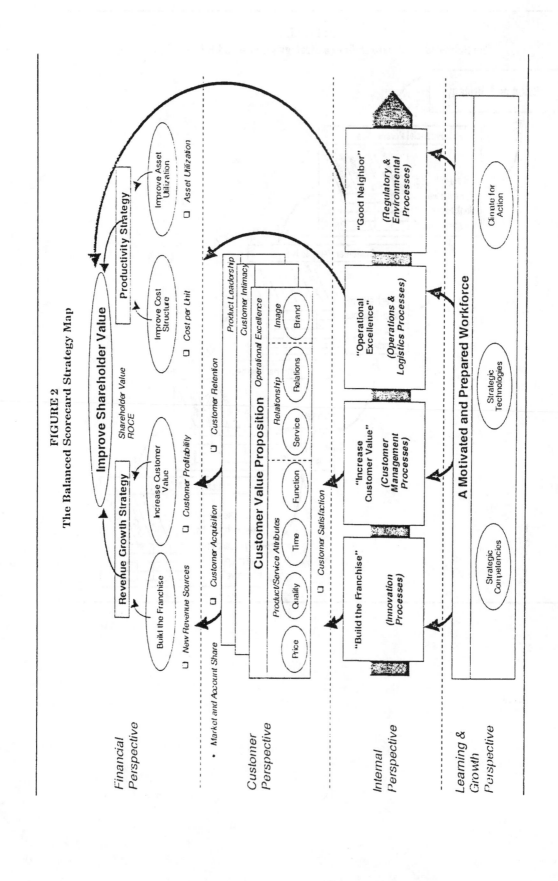

FIGURE 2
The Balanced Scorecard Strategy Map

reducing the working and fixed capital needed to support a given level of business.

CUSTOMER PERSPECTIVE

The core of any business strategy is the *customer-value proposition,* which describes the unique mix of product, price, service, relationship, and image that a company offers. It defines how the organization differentiates itself from competitors to attract, retain, and deepen relationships with targeted customers. The value proposition is crucial because it helps an organization connect its internal processes to improved outcomes with its customers.

Companies differentiate their value proposition by selecting among *operational excellence* (for example, McDonalds and Dell Computer), *customer intimacy* (Home Depot and IBM in the 1960s and 1970s), and *product leadership* (Intel and Sony) (Treacy and Wiersema 1997, 31-45). Sustainable strategies are based on excelling at one of the three while maintaining threshold standards with the other two. After identifying its value proposition, a company knows which classes and types of customers to target.

Specifically, companies that pursue a strategy of operational excellence need to excel at competitive pricing, product quality, product selection, lead time, and on-time delivery. For customer intimacy, an organization must stress the quality of its relationships with customers, including exceptional service, and the completeness and suitability of the solutions it offers individual customers. Companies that pursue a product-leadership strategy must concentrate on the functionality, features, and performance of their products and services.

The customer perspective also identifies the intended outcomes from delivering a differentiated value proposition. These would include market share in targeted customer segments, account share with targeted customers, acquisition and retention of customers in the targeted segments, and customer profitability.[5]

INTERNAL PROCESS PERSPECTIVE

Once an organization has a clear picture of its customer and financial perspectives, it can determine the means by which it will achieve the differentiated value proposition for customers and the productivity improvements for the financial objectives. The internal business perspective captures these critical organiza-

---

[5] Measurement of customer profitability (Kaplan and Cooper 1998, 181-201) provides one of the connections between the Balanced Scorecard and activity-based costing.

tional activities, which fall into four high-level processes:

1. *Build the franchise* by spurring innovation to develop new products and services and to penetrate new markets and customer segments.
2. *Increase customer value* by expanding and deepening relationships with existing customers.
3. *Achieve operational excellence* by improving supply-chain management, internal processes, asset utilization, resource-capacity management, and other processes.
4. *Become a good corporate citizen* by establishing effective relationships with external stakeholders.

Many companies that espouse a strategy calling for innovation or for developing value-adding customer relationships mistakenly choose to measure their internal business processes by focusing only on the cost and quality of their operations. These companies have a complete disconnect between their strategy and how they measure it. Not surprisingly, organizations encounter great difficulty implementing growth strategies when their primary internal measurements emphasize process improvements, not innovation or enhanced customer relationships.

The financial benefits from improvements to the different business processes typically occur in stages. Cost savings from increases in *operational efficiencies* and process improvements deliver short-term benefits. Revenue growth from enhancing *customer relationships* accrues in the intermediate term. Increased *innovation* generally produces long-term revenue and margin improvements. Thus, a complete strategy should generate returns from all three high-level internal processes.

LEARNING AND GROWTH PERSPECTIVE

The final region of a strategy map is the learning and growth perspective, which is the foundation of any strategy. In the learning and growth perspective, managers define the employee capabilities and skills, technology, and corporate climate needed to support a strategy. These objectives enable a company to align its human resources and information technology with the strategic requirements from its critical internal business processes, differentiated value proposition, and customer relationships. After addressing the learning and growth perspective, companies have a complete strategy map with linkages across the four major perspectives.

Strategy maps, beyond providing a common framework for describing and building strategies, also are powerful diagnostic tools, capable of detecting flaws in organizations' Balanced Scorecards. For example, Figure 3 shows the strategy map for the Revenue Growth theme of Mobil North America Marketing & Refining. When senior management compared the scorecards being used by its business units to this template, it found one unit with no objective or measure for dealers, an omission immediately obvious from looking at its strategy map. Had this unit discovered how to bypass dealers and sell gasoline directly to end-use consumers? Were dealer relationships no longer strategic for this unit? The business unit shown in the lower right corner of Figure 3 did not mention quality on its scorecard. Again, had this unit already achieved six sigma quality levels so quality was no longer a strategic priority? Mobil's executive team used its divisional strategy map to identify and remedy gaps in the strategies being implemented at lower levels of the organization.

STAKEHOLDER AND KEY PERFORMANCE INDICATOR SCORECARDS

Many organizations claim to have a Balanced Scorecard because they use a mixture of financial and non-financial measures. Such measurement systems are certainly more "balanced" than ones that use financial measures alone. Yet, the assumptions and philosophies underlying these scorecards are quite different from those underlying the strategy scorecards and maps described above. We observe two other scorecard types frequently used in practice: the *stakeholder scorecard* and the *key performance indicator scorecard.*

STAKEHOLDER SCORECARDS

The *stakeholder scorecard* identifies the major constituents of the organization—shareholders, customers. and employees—and frequently other constituents such as suppliers and the community. The scorecard defines the organization's goals for these different constituents, or stakeholders, and develops an appropriate scorecard of measures and targets for them (Atkinson and Waterhouse 1997). For example, Sears built its initial scorecard around three themes:

- "a compelling place to shop"
- "a compelling place to work"
- "a compelling place to invest"

Citicorp used a similar structure for its initial scorecard—"a good place to work, to bank, and to invest." AT&T developed an elaborate internal measurement system based on financial value-added, customer value-added, and people value-added.

All these companies built their measurements around their three dominant constituents—customers,

shareholders, and employees—emphasizing satisfaction measures for customers and employees, to ensure that these constituents felt well served by the company. In this sense, they were apparently *balanced.* Comparing these scorecards to the strategy map template in Figure 2 we can easily detect what is missing from such scorecards: no objectives or measures for *how* these balanced goals are to be achieved. A vision describes a desired outcome; a strategy, however, must describe *how* the outcome will be achieved, how employees, customers, and shareholders will be satisfied. Thus, a stakeholder scorecard is not adequate to describe the strategy of an organization and, therefore, is not an adequate foundation on which to build a management system.

Missing from the stakeholder card are the drivers to achieve the goals. Such drivers include an explicit value proposition such as innovation that generates new products and services or enhanced customer management processes, the deployment of technology, and the specific skills and competencies of employees required to implement the strategy. In a well-constructed *strategy scorecard,* the value proposition in the customer perspective, all the processes in the internal perspective, and the learning and growth perspective components of the scorecard define the "how" that is as fundamental to strategy as the outcomes that the strategy is expected to achieve.

Stakeholder scorecards are often a first step on the road to a strategy scorecard. But as organizations begin to work with stakeholder cards, they inevitably confront the question of "how." This leads to the next level of strategic thinking and scorecard design. Both Sears and Citicorp quickly moved beyond their stakeholder scorecards, developing an insightful set of internal process objectives to complete the description of their strategy and, ultimately, achieving a strategy Balanced Scorecard. The stakeholder scorecard can also be useful in organizations that do not have internal synergies across business units. Since each business has a different set of internal drivers, this "corporate" scorecard need only focus on the desired outcomes for the corporation's constituencies, including the community and suppliers. Each business unit then defines how it will achieve those goals with its business unit strategy scorecard and strategy map.

KEY PERFORMANCE INDICATOR SCORECARDS

Key Performance Indicator (KPI) scorecards are also common. The total quality management approach and variants such as the Malcolm Baldrige and European Foundation for Quality Management (EFQM) awards generate many measures to monitor internal processes. When migrating to a "Balanced

FIGURE 3
Mobil Uses Reverse Engineering of a Strategy Map as a Strategy Diagnostic

The Template (Strategy Map: Partial)

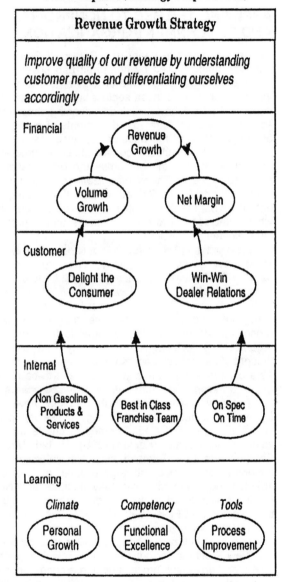

Revenue Growth Strategy

Improve quality of our revenue by understanding customer needs and differentiating ourselves accordingly

Financial

Revenue Growth

Volume Growth

Net Margin

Customer

Delight the Consumer

Win-Win Dealer Relations

Internal

Non Gasoline Products & Services

Best in Class Franchise Team

On Spec On Time

Learning

Climate
Personal Growth

Competency
Functional Excellence

Tools
Process Improvement

SBU A: "Did we eliminate the dealer?"

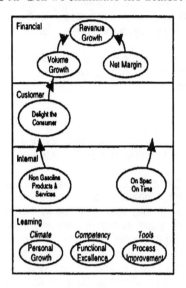

SBU B: "Have we achieved perfection?"

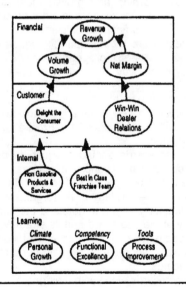

Scorecard," organizations often build on the base already established by classifying their existing measurements into the four BSC categories. KPI scorecards also emerge when the organization's information technology group, which likes to put the company database at the heart of any change program, triggers the scorecard design. Consulting organizations that sell and install large systems, especially so-called executive information systems, also offer KPI scorecards.

As a simple example of a KPI scorecard, a financial service organization articulated the 4Ps for its "balanced scorecard:"

1. Profits
2. Portfolio (size of loan volume)
3. Process (percent processes ISO certified)
4. People (meeting diversity goals in hiring)

Although this scorecard is more balanced than one using financial measures alone, comparing the 4P measures to a strategy map like that in Figure 2 reveals the major gaps in the measurement set. The company has no customer measures and only a single internal-process measure, which focuses on an initiative not an outcome. This KPI scorecard has no role for information technology (strange for a financial service organization), no linkages from the internal measure (ISO process certification) to a customer-value proposition or to a customer outcome, and no linkage from the learning and growth measure (diverse work force) to improving an internal process, a customer outcome, or a financial outcome.

KPI scorecards are most helpful for departments and teams when a strategic program already exists at a higher level. In this way, the diverse indicators enable individuals and teams to define what they must do well to contribute to higher level goals. Unless, however, the link to strategy is clearly established, the KPI scorecard will lead to local but not global or strategic improvements.

Balanced Scorecards should not just be collections of financial and nonfinancial measures, organized into three to five perspectives. The best Balanced Scorecards reflect the strategy of the organization. A good test is whether you can understand the strategy by looking only at the scorecard and its strategy map. Many organizations fail this test, especially those that create stakeholder scorecards or key performance indicator scorecards.

Strategy scorecards along with their graphical representations on strategy maps provide a logical and comprehensive way to describe strategy. They communicate clearly the organization's desired outcomes and its hypotheses about how these outcomes can be achieved. For example, *if* we improve on-time deliv-ery, *then* customer satisfaction will improve; *if* customer satisfaction improves, *then* customers will purchase more. The scorecards enable all organizational units and employees to understand the strategy and identify how they can contribute by becoming aligned to the strategy.

APPLYING THE BSC TO NONPROFITS AND GOVERNMENT ORGANIZATIONS

During the past five years, the Balanced Scorecard has also been applied by non-profit and government organizations (NPGOs). One of the barriers to applying the scorecard to these sectors is the considerable difficulty NPGOs have in clearly defining their strategy. We reviewed "strategy" documents of more than 50 pages. Most of the documents, once the mission and vision are articulated, consist of lists of programs and initiatives, not the outcomes the organization is trying to achieve. These organizations must understand Porter's (1996, 77) admonition that strategy is not only what the organization intends to do, but also what it decides *not* to do, a message that is particularly relevant for NPGOs.

Most of the initial scorecards of NPGOs feature an operational excellence strategy. The organizations take their current mission as a given and try to do their work more efficiently—at lower cost, with fewer defects, and faster. Often the project builds off of a recently introduced quality initiative that emphasizes process improvements. It is unusual to find nonprofit organizations focusing on a strategy that can be thought of as product leadership or customer intimacy. As a consequence, their scorecards tend to be closer to the KPI scorecards than true strategy scorecards.

The City of Charlotte, North Carolina, however, followed a customer-based strategy by selecting an interrelated set of strategic themes to create distinct value for its citizens (Kaplan 199S). United Way of Southeastern New England also articulated a customer (donor) intimacy strategy (Kaplan and Kaplan 1996). Other nonprofits—the May Institute and New Profit Inc.—selected a clear product-leadership position (Kaplan and Elias 1999). The May Institute uses partnerships with universities and researchers to deliver the best behavioral and rehabilitation care delivery. New Profit Inc. introduces a new selection, monitoring, and governing process unique among nonprofit organizations. Montefiore Hospital uses a combination of product leadership in its centers of excellence, and excellent customer relationships—through its new patient-oriented care centers—to build market share in its local area (Kaplan 2001). These examples demonstrate that NPGOs can be strategic and build competitive advantage in ways other than pure operational excellence. But it takes vision and leadership to move from continuous improvement of existing processes to thinking strategically about which processes and activities are most important for fulfilling the organization's mission.

MODIFYING THE ARCHITECTURE OF THE BALANCED SCORECARD

Most NPGOs had difficulty with the original architecture of the Balanced Scorecard that placed the financial perspective at the top of the hierarchy. Given that achieving financial success is not the primary objective for most of these organizations, many rearrange the scorecard to place customers or constituents at the top of the hierarchy.

In a private-sector transaction, the customer plays two distinct roles—paying for the service and receiving the service—that are so complementary most people don't even think about them separately. But in a nonprofit organization, donors provide the financial resources—they pay for the service—while another group, the constituents, receives the service. Who is the customer—the one paying or the one receiving? Rather than have to make such a Solomonic decision, organizations place both the donor perspective and the recipient perspective, in parallel, at the top of their Balanced Scorecards. They develop objectives for both donors and recipients, and then identify the internal processes that deliver desired value propositions for both groups of "customers."

In fact, nonprofit and government agencies should consider placing an over-arching objective at the top of their scorecard that represents their long-term objective such as a reduction in poverty or illiteracy, or improvements in the environment. Then the objectives within the scorecard can be oriented toward improving such a high-level objective. High-level financial measures provide private sector companies with an accountability measure to their owners, the shareholders. For a nonprofit or government agency, however, the financial measures are not the relevant indicators of whether the agency is delivering on its mission. The agency's mission should be featured and measured at the highest level of its scorecard. Placing an over-arching objective on the BSC for a nonprofit or government agency communicates clearly the long-term mission of the organization as portrayed in Figure 4.

Even the financial and customer objectives, however, may need to be re-examined for governmental organizations. Take the case of regulatory and enforcement agencies that monitor and punish violations of environmental, safety, and health regulations. These agencies, which detect transgressions, and fine or arrest those who violate the laws and regulations, cannot look to their "immediate customers" for satisfaction and loyalty measures. Clearly not the true "customers" for such organizations are the citizens at large who benefit from effective but not harsh or idiosyncratic enforcement of laws and regulations. Figure 5 shows a modified framework in which a government agency has three high-level perspectives:

1. *Cost Incurred:* This perspective emphasizes the importance of operational efficiency. The measured cost should include both the expenses of the agency and the social cost it imposes on citizens and other organizations through its operations. For example, an environmental agency imposes remediation costs on private-sector organizations. These are part of the costs of having the agency carry out its mission. The agency should minimize the direct and social costs required to achieve the benefits called for by its mission.
2. *Value Created:* This perspective identifies the benefits being created by the agency to citizens and is the most problematic and difficult to measure. It is usually difficult to financially quantify the benefits from improved education, reduced pollution, better health, less congestion, and safer neighborhoods. But the balanced scorecard still enables organizations to identify the outputs, if not the outcomes, from its activities, and to measure these outputs. Surrogates for value created could include percentage of students acquiring specific skills and knowledge; density of pollutants in water, air, or land; improved morbidity and mortality in targeted populations; crime rates and perception of public safety; and transportation times. In general, public-sector organizations may find they use more output than outcome measures. The citizens and their representatives—elected officials and legislators—will eventually make the judgments about the benefits from these outputs vs. their costs.
3. *Legitimizing Support:* An important "customer" for any government agency will be its "donor," the organization—typically the legislature—that provides the funding for the agency. In order to assure continued funding for its activities, the agency must strive to meet the objectives of its funding source—the legislature and, ultimately, citizens and taxpayers.

FIGURE 4

Adapting the Balanced Scorecard Framework to Nonprofit Organizations

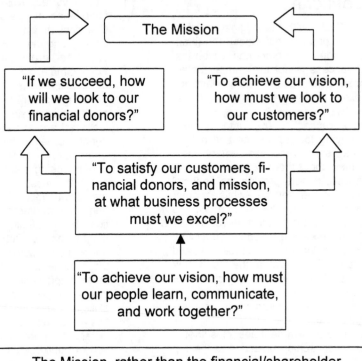

The Mission

"If we succeed, how will we look to our financial donors?"

"To achieve our vision, how must we look to our customers?"

"To satisfy our customers, financial donors, and mission, at what business processes must we excel?"

"To achieve our vision, how must our people learn, communicate, and work together?"

The Mission, rather than the financial/shareholder objectives, drives the organization's strategy.

FIGURE 5
The Financial/Customer Objectives for Public Sector Agencies
May Require Three Different Perspectives

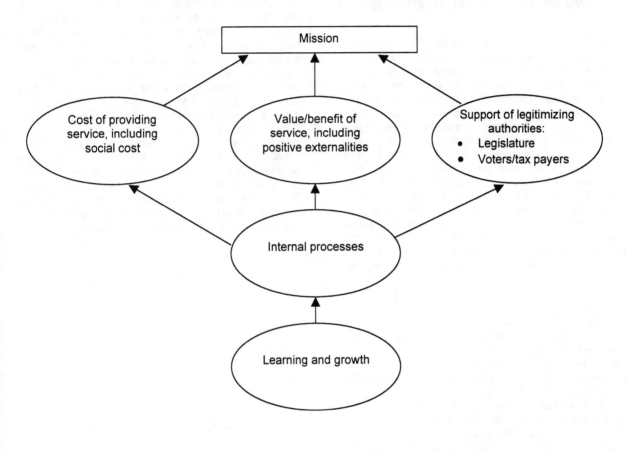

Professor Dutch Leonard, Kennedy School of Government, Harvard University, collaborated to
develop this diagram.

After defining these three high-level perspectives, a public-sector agency can identify its objectives for internal processes, learning, and growth that enable objectives in the three high-level perspectives to be achieved.

BEYOND MEASUREMENT TO MANAGE-MENT

Originally, we thought the Balanced Scorecard was about performance measurement (Kaplan and Norton 1992). Once organizations developed their basic system for measuring strategy, however, we quickly learned that *measurement* has consequences far beyond reporting on the past. Measurement creates focus for the future. The measures chosen by managers communicate important messages to all organizational units and employees. To take full advantage of this power, companies soon integrated their new measures into a *management system.* Thus the Balanced Scorecard concept evolved from a performance measurement system to become the organizing framework, the operating system, for a new strategic management system (Kaplan and Norton 1996c, Part II). The academic literature, rooted in the original performance measurement aspects of the scorecard, focuses on the BSC as a measurement system Ittner et al. 1997; Ittner and Larcker 1998; Banker et al. 2000; Lipe and Salterio 2000) but has yet to examine its role as a management system.

Using this new strategic management system, we observed several organizations achieving performance breakthroughs within two to three years of implementation (Kaplan and Norton 2001a, 4-6, 17-22). The magnitude of the results achieved by the early adopters reveals the power of the Balanced Scorecard management system to focus the entire organization on strategy. The speed with which the new strategies deliver results indicates that the companies' successes are not due to a major new product or service launch, major new capital investments, or even the development of new intangible or "intellectual" assets. The companies, of course, develop new products and services, and invest in both hard, tangible assets, as well as softer, intangible assets. But they cannot benefit much in two years from such investments. To achieve their breakthrough performance, the companies capitalize on capabilities and assets—both tangible and intangible—that already exist within their organizations.[6] The companies' new

strategies and the Balanced Scorecard unleash the capabilities and assets previously hidden (or frozen) within the old organization. In effect, the Balanced Scorecard provides the "recipe" that enables ingredients already existing in the organization to be combined for long-term value creation.

Part II of our commentary on the Balanced Scorecard (Kaplan and Norton 2001b) will describe how organizations use Balanced Scorecards and strategy maps to accomplish comprehensive and integrated transformations. These organizations redefine their relationships with customers, reengineer fundamental business processes, reskill the work force, and deploy new technology infrastructures. A new culture emerges, centered not on traditional functional silos, but on the team effort required to implement the strategy. By clearly defining the strategy, communicating it consistently, and linking it to the drivers of change, a performance-based culture emerges to link everyone and every unit to the unique features of the strategy. The simple act of describing strategy via strategy maps and scorecards makes a major contribution to the success of the transformation program.

---

[6] These observations indicate why attempts to value individual intangible assets almost surely is a quixotic search. The companies achieved breakthrough performance with essentially the same people, services, and technology that previously delivered dismal per-

formance. The value creation came not from any individual asset—tangible or intangible. It came from the coherent combination and alignment of existing organizational resources.

REFERENCES

American Institute of Certified Public Accountants (AICPA), Special Committee on Financial Reporting. 1994. *Improving Business Reporting—A Customer Focus: Meeting the Information Needs of Investors and Creditors.* New York, NY: AICPA.

Atkinson, A. A., and J. H. Waterhouse. 1997. A stakeholder approach to strategic performance measurement. *Sloan Management Review* (Spring).

Banker, R., G. Potter, and D. Srinivasan. 2000. An empirical investigation of an incentive plan that includes nonfinancial performance measures. *The Accounting Review* (January): 65-92.

Becker, B., and M. Huselid. 1998. High performance work systems and firm performance: A synthesis of research and managerial implications. In *Research in Personnel and Human Resources Management,* 53-101. Greenwich, CT: JAI Press.

Blair, M. B. 1995. *Ownership and Control: Rethinking Corporate Governance for the Twenty-First Century.* Washington, D.C.: Brookings Institution.

Chandler, A. D. 1990. *Scale and Scope: The Dynamics of Industrial Capitalism.* Cambridge, MA: Harvard University Press.

Charan, R., and G. Colvin. 1999. Why CEOs fail. *Fortune* (June 21).

Epstein, M., and J. F. Manzoni. 1998. Implementing corporate strategy: From Tableaux de Bord to Balanced Scorecards. *European Management Journal* (April).

Greenwood, R. G. 1974. *Managerial Decentralization: A Study of the General Electric Philosophy.* Lexington, MA: D. C. Heath.

Heskett, J., T. Jones, G. Loveman, E. Sasser, and L. Schlesinger. 1994. Putting the service profit chain to work. *Harvard Business Review* (March-April): 164-174.

Huselid, M. A. 1995. The impact of human resource management practices on turnover, productivity, and corporate financial performance. *Academy of Management Journal:* 635-672.

Ittner, C., D. Larcker, and M. Meyer. 1997. Performance, compensation, and the Balanced Scorecard. Working paper, University of Pennsylvania.

———, D. Larcker, and M. Rajan. 1997. The choice of performance measures in annual bonus contracts. *The Accounting Review* (April): 23 1-255.

———, and D. Larcker. 1998. Innovations in performance measurement: Trends and research implications. *Journal of Management Accounting Research:* 205-238.

Johnson, H. T., and R. S. Kaplan. 1987. *Relevance Lost: The Rise and Fall of Management Accounting.* Boston, MA: Harvard Business School Press.

Kaplan, R. S., and D. P. Norton. 1992. The Balanced Scorecard: Measures that drive performance. *Harvard Business Review* (January-February): 71-79.

———, and ———. 1993. Putting the Balanced Scorecard to work. *Harvard Business Review* (September-October): 134-147.

———, and E. L. Kaplan. 1996. United Way of Southeastern New England. Harvard Business School Case 197-036. Boston, MA.

———, and D. P. Norton.].996a. Using the Balanced Scorecard as a strategic management system. *Harvard Business Review* (January-February): 75-85.

———, and ———. 1996b. Linking the Balanced Scorecard to strategy. *California Management Review* (Fall): 53-79.

———, and ———. 1996c. *The Balanced Scorecard: Translating Strategy Into Action.* Boston, MA: Harvard Business School Publishing.

———. 1998. City of Charlotte (A). Harvard Business School Case 199-036. Boston, MA.

———, and R. Cooper. 1998. *Cost and Effect: Using Integrated Cost Systems to Drive Profitability and Performance.* Boston, MA: Harvard Business School Press.

———, and J. Elias. 1999. New Profit, Inc.: Governing the nonprofit enterprise. Harvard Business School Case 100-052. Boston, MA.

———. 2001. Montefiore Medical Center. Harvard Business School Case 101-067. Boston, MA.

———, and D. P. Norton. 2000. Having trouble with your strategy? Then map it. *Harvard Business Review* (September-October): 167-176.

and . 2001a. *The Strategy-Focused Organization: How Balanced Scorecard companies Thrive in the New Business Environment.* Boston, MA: Harvard Business School Press.

———, and . 200 lb. Transforming the Balanced Scorecard from performance measurement to strategic management. Part II. *Accounting Horizons.* (forthcoming).

Kiechel, W. 1982. Corporate strategists under fire. *Fortune* (December 27): 38.

Lebas, M. 1994. Managerial accounting in France: Overview of past tradition and current practice. *European Accounting Review* 3 (3): 471-487.

Lipe, M., and S. Salterio. 2000. The Balanced Scorecard: Judgmental effects of common and unique performance measures. *The Accounting Review* (July): 283-298.

Porter, M. E. 1992. Capital disadvantage: America's failing capital investment system. *Harvard Business Review* (September-October).

———. 1996. What is strategy? *Harvard Business Review* (November-December).

Treacy, F., and M. Wierserma. 1997. *The Wisdom of Market Leaders.* New York, NY: Perseus Books.

Webber, A. M. 2000. New math for a new economy. *Fast Company* (January-February).

Chapter 19
Strategic Investment Units and Transfer Pricing
Cases
19-1   Investment SBUs; Strategy; International Issues
19-2   Transfer Pricing; Strategy
19-3   Better Life Products, Inc. (Transfer Pricing)
19-4   Transfer Pricing (Foreign Sales Corporations); Use of the Web

Readings
"Setting the Right Transfer Price"
This article uses a case study of a fictitious company, CrysCo, Inc, a manufacturer of crystals used in electronic audio and video equipment, to illustrate the role of international tax issues in transfer pricing. CrysCo has two foreign subsidiaries, one which sells the crystals manufactured in CrysCo's home country, and a second subsidiary which uses the crystals in the manufacture of a high-resolution amplifier. The subsidiaries are assumed to be independent for transfer pricing purposes. The article explains the four methods of setting a transfer price for management purposes: (1) cost-based, (2) market-based, (3) negotiated transfer price, and (4) dictated transfer price. Also, the six transfer pricing methods for tax purposes are explained for both tangible and intangible property. The concept of tangible and intangible property is important here because CrysCo can either transfer the crystals (tangible property) or the license to produce the crystals (an intangible). The tax requirements differ for the two approaches. Tax issues for Japan and for the People's Republic of China are discussed.

Discussion Questions:
1. What is an "advance pricing agreement," and what is its purpose?
2. What are the six tax methods for transfer pricing and how do they differ?
3. Should transfer prices be determined with management or tax purposes in mind?

"Does ROI Apply to Robotic Factories?"
This article provides a useful summary of the limitations of ROI performance evaluation of investment SBUs. Three criteria for appropriate ROI measures are proposed: (1) the ROI measure must include long-term performance, (2) the ROI measure must consider cash flows, and (3) the ROI measure must consider the time value of money. Also, the authors argue that the ROI measure should be consistent with the phases of the project life:
- First: acquisition of the new investment
- Second: use of the new investment
- Third: disposition of the investment

Four methods are developed and illustrated for a hypothetical investment in robotics. The four methods are: (1) annual book ROI, (2) average ROI (over the project's life), (3) discounted book ROI, and (4) discounted cash flow ROI. The authors explain how the different methods are to be used at the different phases of the project's life.

Discussion Questions:
1. Which ROI method(s) should be used at each of the phases of the project's life?
2. What is the profitability index and how is it used?
3. What are the limitations of ROI, and how does the authors' proposed approach deal with these limitations?

Note: This article makes extensive use of the concept of the time value of money, and thus can also be used in Chapter 11: Capital Budgeting.

"Transfer Pricing with ABC"
This article explains how Teva Pharmaceutical Industries Ltd adopted transfer pricing and ABC to enhance profits, to improve coordination between operations and marketing, and to reduce the proliferation of new product lines and small volume orders. The article explains why a marginal cost (based on materials cost only) approach and other traditional approaches to transfer pricing did not work for Teva. Teva introduced ABC costing in its plants, and used this cost information for transfer pricing. The article explains how the ABC based transfer pricing system incorporated batch level costs, product based costs, and plant based costs.

Discussion questions:
1. Why did Teva introduce transfer pricing?
2. What were the goals of the transfer pricing system? How did top management, division managers, and financial staff differ about these goals?
3. Why did traditional approaches for transfer pricing not work at Teva, and why did the ABC approach work instead?
4. How did the ABC transfer pricing system incorporate batch level costs? product level costs? plant level costs?
5. What are some of the benefits of the ABC transfer pricing system at Teva?

Cases

19-1. Investment SBUs; Strategy; International Issues

In 2000, the Polymer Products Company was a multinational company engaged in the manufacture of a widely diverse line of products including chemical and agricultural products, man-made fibers, electronic materials, health care, process controls, fabricated products, and oil and gas. Sales in 2000 were $6.7 billion with the following breakdown as to operating units and major markets:

Operating Unit	Percent	Major Markets	Percent
Agricultural products	18	Agriculture	20
		Construction and home	
Biological sciences	3	furnishings	19
Fibers & intermediates	18		
Industrial chemicals	14	Capital equipment	13
		Pharmaceuticals &	
Polymer products	28	personal products	13
Electronic materials &			
fabricated products	8	Motor vehicles	9
Baker controls	8	Apparel	7
		Chemicals and	
Oil & gas	3	hydrocarbons	7
		Other markets	12

For the past five years the firm has been restructuring its core businesses (industrial chemicals, fibers and intermediates, and polymer products) by withdrawing from those product lines that do not fit with the firm's long-term strategy or which are not expected to produce adequate long-term results.

Polymer's management has carefully examined each of the various business units and is prepared to fully support those that have the potential to compete successfully in selected markets. Businesses which cannot produce returns that exceed the company's cost of capital have been, or will be, disposed of or shut down.

As 2001 ended, the company realigned its financial reporting of operating unit segments to more closely align it with the restructuring and to better reflect the company's operations. These new operating unit segments are:

- Agricultural products
- Crop chemicals
- Animal sciences
- Chemicals
- Electronic materials
- Baker controls
- Pharmaceuticals
- Sweeteners
- Oil and gas (this business was sold during the 4th Quarter of 19X5.)

Fibers and intermediates, industrial chemicals, polymer products, and a portion of fabricated products have been combined to form a new segment—chemicals. Two new segments, pharmaceuticals and sweeteners, include the acquired operations of a pharmaceutical company. The electronics business has been made a separate segment and the separations business, previously part of fabricated products, has been transferred to and combined with Baker controls, serving similar process control equipment markets. The former biological sciences segment has been eliminated and their animal nutrition products are now part of animal sciences. The health care division was merged with the acquired company and is included in the pharmaceuticals segment.

COMPANY PERFORMANCE MEASUREMENT PHILOSOPHY

Up until the start of the decade, Polymer focused on a performance income measure of an operating unit's performance; assigning only the directly controllable elements of sales, cost of goods sold, marketing, administrative, technical expenses, inventory, and receivables to the operating units for internal reporting purposes. Non-directly controllable elements, such as corporate staff support groups, interest expense/interest income and foreign currency gains and losses were pooled corporately and various formulae were used to assign these corporate charges to operating units for determining a pro-forma net income, return on investment, and cash flow. Such overall indicators of performance were thus only directionally representative at the operating unit level.

As some of the company's core businesses matured and declined, an awareness began to emerge of the need to shift business strategies thus requiring tougher decisions as to divestment/investment/acquisition activities. Top management recognized the need for more accurate measurement and understanding of worldwide operating unit results.

For example, currency gains and losses were treated as a component of corporate charges. Thus, if a U.S. produced product were sold to a French customer on 180-day terms, the selling business unit reflected the full sales value at the then current exchange rate; leaving the company exposed to devaluation of the French franc. If devaluation occurred, performance of the operating unit was not affected but the company results were.

As another example, all operating units applied an average worldwide tax rate to compute a pro-forma net income, return on capital, and cash flow. When an operating unit had a choice to source the same product from Belgium or the U.K., a dilemma was created. Although costs were nominally higher in the U.K., lowering a unit's performance income, the company was in a non-tax position there which drastically improved real net income. However, by reporting results using an average worldwide tax rate, all product sourcing from the U.K. appeared disadvantageous. Also, the company was not taking advantage of an entity's tax loss carry-forward situation in various pricing and sourcing decisions.

Top management wanted a reporting and performance measurement system which brought operating unit managements' attention to *all* the financial impacts of a business decision. To accomplish this, it was decided that as many of the income statement and balance sheet items as was practicable would be identified with each operating unit and charged out accordingly. Each operating unit would then be measured by the achievement against goals established for return on investment and cash flow as defined below.

cash flow = net income + depreciation and obsolescence − capital expenditures +/- (change in receivables, inventories, payables, net capitalized interest, deferred taxes, other assets, and other liabilities)

$$\text{return on investment} = \frac{\text{net income} + \text{after tax interest expense}}{\text{investment}}$$

(Where investment is defined as net long-lived investment, working capital, and deferred taxes)

The incentive compensation system employed for upper management positions is essentially based upon the relative success in achieving annual budgets established for the above measures. The total corporate annual incentive award is determined somewhat rigidly, based upon where earnings fall within a budget range determined at the beginning of each year. The award is apportioned to cascade down the organization. Thus a similar quantitative assessment of results is made to reward or penalize managers for their ultimate contribution to results. The incentive awards are then presented 2/3 in cash and 1/3 in restricted stock which is accessible only after 3 years and only if stock prices meet certain appreciation tests. This latter feature was recently employed to add a long-term dimension to the program in addition to near-term annual income/cash flow results.

Prior to the new reporting and measurement scheme (called asset management) the amount of corporately pooled costs allocated as a corporate charge was over 3 percent of worldwide sales. After the asset management program was instituted, along with selected decentralization of certain corporate staff groups, these corporately pooled costs were less than 2 percent of worldwide sales.

REQUIRED:

1. What type of performance measurement system did Polymer Products use prior to the recent change?
2. What type of performance measurement system is Polymer Products using now? Why did Polymer Products move to this new system? How does the change affect the firm's global competitiveness?
3. In the new performance measurement system, should managers be held responsible for foreign currency exchange gains and losses and income taxes.

(IMA adapted)

19-2. Transfer Pricing; Strategy

Robert Products Inc. consists of three decentralized divisions: Bayside Division, Cole Division, and Diamond Division. The president of Robert Products has given the managers of the three divisions authority to decide whether to sell outside the company or among themselves at an internal price determined by the division managers. Market conditions are such that sales made internally or externally will not affect market or transfer prices. Intermediate markets will always be available for Bayside, Cole, and Diamond to purchase their manufacturing needs or sell their product.

The manager of the Cole Division is currently considering the two alternative orders presented below.

- The Diamond Division is in need of 3,000 units of a motor that can be supplied by the Cole Division. To manufacture these motors, Cole would purchase components from the Bayside Division at a price of $600 per unit; Bayside's variable cost for these components is $300 per unit. Cole Division will further process these components at a variable cost of $500 per unit.
- If the Diamond Division cannot obtain the motors from Cole Division, it will purchase the motors from London Company which has offered to supply them to Diamond at a price of $1,500 per unit. London Company would also purchase 3,000 components from Bayside Division at a price of $400 for each of these motors; Bayside's variable cost for these components is $200 per unit.
- The Wales Company wants to place an order with the Cole Division for 3,500 similar motors at a price of $1,250 per unit. Cole would again purchase components from the Bayside Division at a price of $500 per unit; Bayside's variable cost for these components is $250 per unit. Cole Division will further process these components at a variable cost of $400 per unit.

The Cole Division's plant capacity is limited, and the division can accept either the Wales contract or the Diamond order, but not both. The president of Robert Products and the manager of the Cole Division agree that it would not be beneficial in the short or long run to increase capacity.

REQUIRED:

1. Determine whether the Cole Division should sell motors to the Diamond Division at the prevailing market price, or accept the Wales Company contract. Support your answer with appropriate calculations.
2. What strategic factors should Robert Products consider as the Cole and Diamond divisions make their respective decision?

(CMA adapted)

19-3. Better Life Products, Inc.

Better Life Products (BLP), Inc. is a large-size U.S.-based manufacturer of health care products, specializing in cushions, braces and other remedies for a variety of elderly and disabled health problems. BLP knows it is in a competitive industry and is hoping to be competitive through rapid growth, primarily within the U.S., where it has a well-established brand image. Also, because of the competitive conditions in the industry, BLF is focusing on cost and price reductions as a principal means to attract customers. Because of rising domestic production costs, lower production costs in other countries, and due to a modest increase in global demand for its products, BLP manufactures some of these products outside the United States. Much of the foreign manufacturing is such that materials are shipped from the U.S. to the foreign country and then assembled there into the final product, thereby taking advantage of the lower labor costs in the foreign country. For this purpose, three divisions are formed, one in the U.S. to purchase and to perform limited assembly of the raw materials in the U.S., one a foreign division to complete the manufacturing, especially the labor intensive components of manufacturing, and one a marketing and sales division back in the U.S. Approximately 80% of BLP's products are sold in the United States, 10% in Canada and the rest worldwide. The foreign divisions tend to focus only on manufacturing for the U.S. divisions because of the specialized nature of the products and because of BLP's desire to coordinate all sales activities out of the U.S. sales divisions. BLP now has 18 U.S. divisions and 23 foreign divisions operating in this manner.

Shipments back to the United States are subject to customs duties per the U.S. Tariff Code, which adds to BLP's cost of the foreign-based manufacturing. However, the Code allows U.S. companies to pay duty only on the value added outside the United States. For example, a product imported from an Argentine company to BLP would pay customs only on that cost of the product due to the labor costs incurred in Argentina. To illustrate, a product with $10 of materials shipped from the U.S. to Argentina and having $10 of labor costs in Argentina would have tariff charges based on the $10 of Argentina labor costs rather than the $20 of total product cost. Thus, for purposes of paying the tariff, it is an advantage to BLP if the portion of total product cost from the foreign country be as small as possible.

STRATEGIC PERFORMANCE MEASUREMENT

Division managers throughout BLP are evaluated on the basis of profit. This includes the managers of the manufacturing facilities in foreign countries. Jorge Martinez is one such manager, located in the manufacturing plant in Argentina. Jorge's job is to make the manufacturing facility in Argentina as profitable as possible, and his compensation from BLP is based on meeting profit targets.

TRANSFER PRICING

BLP has a transfer pricing approach that is common in the industry, and that is to allow each division within the company to determine the transfer pricing autonomously, in inter-division negotiations.

However, in recent years top management has played a stronger role in such negotiations. In particular, where the transfer price determined by the divisions can lead to increased taxes, foreign exchange exposure, or tariffs, the corporate financial function will get involved. What this has meant is that the transfer prices charged by foreign divisions to U.S. sales divisions have fallen, in order to reduce the "value added" in the foreign country and thereby reduce the tariffs. In order to avoid problems with U.S. and Argentine government agencies, the transfer prices were reduced slowly over time.

One effect of the transfer pricing strategy was the continued decline in profitability of the foreign divisions. Managers such as Jorge were finding it difficult to meet their profit targets and personal compensation goals because of the continually declining transfer prices.

REQUIRED:

1. Assess BLF's manufacturing and marketing strategies. Are they consistent with each other and with what you consider the firm's overall business strategy?
2. Assess BLF's performance measurement system. What changes would you suggest and why?

19-4. Transfer Pricing (Foreign Sales Corporations); Use of the Web

The Foreign Sales Corporation Act, enacted by the U.S. Congress in 1971 provides special tax advantages for U.S. based exporters. The foreign subsidiaries of U.S. corporations are allowed to act as agents for the company, so that the parent firm can exempt up to 15% of the export earnings from federal tax. This apparent subsidy has angered some countries in the European Union. To learn more about Foreign Sales Corporations, search the Web and use whatever other research resources available to you. As a start, you might want to look at web site of the United States Mission to the European Union: http://www.useu.be/ISSUES/FSCdossier.html.

REQUIRED:

1. Explain foreign sales corporations and the nature of the benefits to U.S. exporters. Why have countries in the European Union disputed the existence of these corporations.
2. What role do foreign sales corporations play in transfer pricing, and what is the management accountant's responsibility regarding these types of corporations?

SETTING THE RIGHT TRANSFER PRICE

International managers must consider tax regulations as part of their decision criteria.

By Stephen Crow, CPA, and Eugene Sauls, CPA

When multinational companies transfer products between business segments, the prices they impose on those transfers affect many areas of decision making. An appropriate transfer price satisfies corporate management and strategy requirements and promotes congruency among corporate goals.

The cost of determining an appropriate transfer price depends on the level of harmony inherent among company goals and between those goals and the economic and regulatory environment in which the company operates. Factors affecting harmony include the company's organizational form, its corporate definition (contracts), its information systems, and the diversity of the economic and regulatory climate in which it operates.

When a company's operations are domestic, that is, conducted within a single tax jurisdiction, decision criteria reflect these conditions. When a company goes international, the cost of crossing tax borders increases proportionally with the diversity of the company's operations and the tax environment. Using a fictional company, we'll take you through transfer pricing issues for managers of multinational firms and demonstrate the magnitude of the potential impact of these rules in selected countries of the Asia/Pacific Rim Community (APRC).

CASE STUDY

CrysCo, Inc., is the parent company of a fictitious multinational corporate group that includes two subsidiaries—ManCo, Inc. (ManCo) and SalCo, Inc. (SalCo). CrysCo is domiciled in the United States, and ManCo and SalCo are its foreign subsidiaries. CrysCo produces crystals used in electronic video and audio components and is not the market's sole producer. ManCo buys a custom version of the crystal from CrysCo and uses it in a patented high-resolution amplifier that it sells as a packaged unit. SalCo sells the basic crystal produced by CrysCo to foreign audio and video manufacturers.

If CrysCo sets an inappropriate transfer price, problems could occur on several levels. For example, if the transfer price of the custom CrysCo unit is too high. ManCo may buy from outside the organization even though buying from CrysCo may be better for the organization as a whole. Conversely, if CrysCo sets the transfer price too low, it may not provide the product to ManCo because it could get more money elsewhere. In either case the firm loses because the optimal quantity will not be exchanged.

The multinational corporate group also could be exposed to tax deficiencies, penalties, and audit costs. CrysCo may decide not to comply with foreign tax rule if the U.S. tax rate is lower than the tax rate in ManCo's foreign domicile. Profits can be shifted to CrysCo by setting a high transfer price, but if the transfer price doesn't comply with the tax rules of ManCo's domicile, the benefits gained by the income shift may be lost to tax sanctions including tax assessments and penalties. Less obvious, but just as serious, are the potential costs of double taxation or underutilized tax credits stemming from transfer price revisions based on tax audit findings.

Revenue flight is a problem for national treasuries, stimulating tax legislation and enforcement activity. It has been estimated that as much as $30 billion per year is lost to the United States from transfer pricing problems. This issue will become more significant as countries grow increasingly competitive for the international tax dollar, bringing more pressure on managers and higher costs to firms to maintain appropriate income allocations.

When the transfer price does not satisfy both the corporate management and strategy and tax requirements, the company can resolve the problem in one of three ways. First, it can take no action and accept the status quo, which may be costly and illegal. Second, the firm can redefine its contractual relationships, which may be so expensive as to be impractical and, in some cases, may not be an

TABLE 1
TRANSFER PRICING METHODS FOR TAX PURPOSES: TANGIBLE PROPERTY

Method Description	Comparable Uncontrolled Price	Resale Price	Cost Plus	Comparable Profits	Profits Split	Other
Comparables	Comparable sales between unrelated parties	Price to unrelated party less related gross profit; nonmanufacturing.	Production costs plus gross profit on unrelated sales.	Priced to yield gross profits comparable to those for other firms.	Split of combined operating profits of controlled parties.	Gross profit reasonable for "facts and circumstances."
Comparability and Reliability Standards	Similarity of property; underlying circumstance.	Comparable gross profit relative to comparable unrelated transfer.	Gross profit from same type of goods in unrelated resale.	Gross profit within range of profits for broadly similar product line.	Allocation of combined profits of controlled parties.	As appropriate.
Measures of Comparability	Functional diversity; product category; terms in financing and sales; discounts; and the like.	Functional diversity; product category; terms in financing and sales, intangibles, and the like.	Functional diversity; accounting principles; direct vs. indirect costing, and the like.	Business segment; functional diversity; different product categories acceptable if in same industry	Profits split by unrelated parties or splits from transfers to unrelated parties.	Fair allocation of profits relative to "unrelated" party sales.
Same Geographic Market	Required	Required	Required	Required	Required, but some flexibility.	Required, but some flexibility.
Comments	Deemed the best method for all firms, minor accounting adjustments allowed to quality as "substantially" the same."	The best method for distribution operations, only used where little or no value added and no significant processing.	Internal gross profit ratio is acceptable if there are both purchases from and sales to unrelated parties; if not, GPR based upon comparable firms.	Not if seller has unique technologies or intangibles, because resale price is fixed, adjust the transfer price from seller.	Controlled transaction allocations compared to profits split in uncontrolled transactions.	Least reliable; uncertainty and costs of being wrong are severe.

INTANGIBLE PROPERTY TRANSFER PRICING TAX RULES

Transfer pricing methods for management control and reporting purposes are substantially the same for both intangible and tangible property, but the tax rules are different. The basic "arm's-length" and "best method" tests are common to transfer pricing tax rules for both tangible and intangible property. The specifics of the methods prescribed for each are significantly different.

In Table 2, the methods are compared on four features. "Comparables" are elements that make up the acceptable transfer price, "Comparability and Reliability Standards" are the relative components of a transfer subject to comparison for each method. "Measures of Comparability" are features upon which comparability of the transfer components are assessed. "Same Geographic Market" means comparables must be taken from the same geographic market. This test is necessary but not sufficient.

If CrysCo transfers licenses to ManCo to produce and sell the crystal products rather than produce and transfer the products itself, how would these rules affect the pricing structure of the licensing arrangements between CrysCo and ManCo?

Comparable Uncontrolled Transaction—This method is preferred for pricing intangible property transfers for tax purposes. The method uses comparable transactions between unrelated parties, including contractual terms and economic conditions (such as net present value of potential profit). The rules also state that the intangibles must be used for similar products or similar industries. This method is similar to the comparable uncontrolled price method, but it focuses on the comparability of the whole transaction, not just the product being sold.

Under comparable uncontrolled transactions, the transfer is viewed as a royalty for licenses between CrysCo and ManCo. The amount of the royalty is set by reference to uncontrolled transfers of comparable intangible property under comparable circumstances. This method is preferred when the intangibles compared are the same, but it also is acceptable when they are only similar. In its review of the rules, however, even Congress admitted that it is unlikely that a company such as CrysCo can find uncontrolled companies engaged in similar activities with similar intangibles.

Although the comparable uncontrolled transaction is the preferred method, the comparability and documentation requirements make it extremely difficult, at best, for companies to comply with the criteria.

Comparable Profits Method—Under this method CrysCo sets ManCo's profit ratio at a number that is within a range of the profit ratios of comparable but unrelated competitors. The method is similar to thecomparable price for tangible property because the premise is that similarly situated companies should realize similar returns. In the case of intangibles, however, the new tax rules require that the benchmark companies own similar intangibles. Similarity is based on the similarity of the product and process in which the intangible is used, the industry, contractual terms, and geographic market. Under these compliance and documentation constraints, there is little chance that comparable price can be used to determine a transfer price between CrysCo and ManCo.

Profits Split Method—CrysCo and ManCo also can consider the profits-split method. It is an acceptable method for the transfer of intangible as well as tangible property, but there is a major difference. In addition to the combined profits-split method that CrysCo could use for tangible property transfers, the company can use a residual profits-split approach. Due to the nature of intangible property, the tests of comparability and data reliability are more onerous than with tangible property transfers and seem to preclude the combined approach. In the residual profits-split method, the portion of combined profits attributable to routine business activities may be allocated between CrysCo and ManCo using some other appropriate tax method. The residual profits are attributable to the intangibles and would be allocated between CrysCo and ManCo according to an estimate of the relative value of each entity's contributions of such property. One suggested measure of such relative value is capitalized intangible development expenses.

The practical difficulties inherent in the residual profits-split method include the burden of segregating routine activities, identifying income allocation methods for each, and extracting information for comparable but uncontrolled transfers. If CrysCo and ManCo cannot accomplish these tasks, they cannot use the profits-split method.

"Other" Methods—The final option is some other method that is reasonable under the facts and circumstances. As with the tangible property transfers, there are virtually no objective guidelines under this option, there is little certainty, and there is a very high risk of challenge by tax agencies such as the IRS that could result in high costs of noncompliance

As with tangible property transfer rules, the intangible rules are fraught with comparability and reliability criteria that hamper compliance, which may encourage managers to take conservative positions for tax purposes. It also may encourage taxpayers to seek ex ante agreements with tax agencies for prospective pricing arrangements.

option—such as debt covenants. Third, the company can revise its information systems to support multiple transfer price methods. This approach provides the most practical and generally most economical (but not at zero cost) solution and will be the choice of most companies.

TRANSFER PRICE METHODS FOR MANAGEMENT PURPOSES

Four general types of transfer prices are acceptable for management purposes: cost-based, market-based, negotiated, and dictated.

Cost-based implies a cost-plus model, using full or variable cost. Two major advantages of this method are availability of information from internal records and compatibility with market pricing policies. A major disadvantage is the lack of incentive to control costs because costs are passed on to the buying division.

A *market-based* transfer price is set as a percentage of the market value of the product or service. The transfer price should reflect the cost savings from internal transactions, for example, reduced sales force or credit department, and allocate these cost savings between the purchasing and selling divisions on some acceptable basis. If the transfer price is set at full market value, the purchasing division may transact more business with outsiders than with other divisions. A major advantage of a market-based transfer price is that it is objective—in the sense that it is set by forces outside the organization—but the market price information may not be readily available.

A negotiated transfer price is set by the managements of the buying and selling divisions meeting and agreeing on a price. A major advantage of a negotiated transfer price is that both parties presumably are satisfied with it. A major disadvantage is that divisional profits may be determined more by the negotiating ability of the managers than by their management skills. Further, a great deal of time and effort may be expended in the negotiations.

A *dictated transfer price* is set by top management. If top management has good information concerning the costs and demand characteristics, it could set a price that would optimize profits for the organization as a whole. A disadvantage of a dictated transfer price is that division managers concerned with divisional performance may be suspicious of—and unfavorably disposed toward—the dictated transfer price.

In our case study, CrysCo should choose a cost-based method for pricing its transfers to ManCo because the special production applications it performs are not duplicated in the marketplace. The transfer price to ManCo would be based on CrysCo's cost plus a specified profit margin. CrysCo will price the transfers to SalCo using a market-based transfer price method. CrysCo is not the only crystal producer, so CrysCo can obtain the necessary unrelated sales or market price information from other suppliers.

TRANSFER PRICING FOR TAX PURPOSES

Table 1 describes the six transfer pricing methods that are acceptable for tax purposes. They are compared based on four features. "Comparables" are the elements of a transfer that are examined in the comparability test under each method. "Comparability and Reliability Standards" are the components of the "Comparables" subject to comparison under each method. "Measures of comparability" are the characteristics of the "Comparables" components that are assessed as measures of that comparability. The final characteristic, "Same Geographic Market," means comparables must be taken from the same geographic market. This last item is necessary for acceptability but is not sufficient.

How do these rules affect CrysCo and the other members of the multinational corporate group? (See sidebar, "The Advance Pricing Agreement Program (APA).")

Comparable Uncontrolled Price—For all companies, comparable uncontrolled price using comparable sales transactions between unrelated parties is the preferred method of pricing for tax purposes and market-based corporate management and strategy. CrysCo will find that it cannot use this method for either the ManCo or SalCo transfers. The ManCo crystal is a custom-order product, and there are no sales by CrysCo to unrelated parties, nor are there any purchases by ManCo from unrelated parties.

The SalCo transfers have a related but different problem. While CrysCo has sales to unrelated parties that otherwise would qualify, they are not sales to parties in the same geographic area as ManCo. This problem is common to most multinational corporate groups because the parent generally won't compete with its subsidiary in the subsidiary's own backyard.

Resale Price Method—This method is the best for distribution or market based organizations where little or no value is added and no significant assembly or manufacturing activity takes place. This pricing method is the preferred alternative for SalCo. The transfer price set under this method is the amount received by SalCo on reselling the crystal units to an uncontrolled outsider, reduced for an appropriate markup. CrysCo cannot show sales to unrelated parties in the "same geographic area." Therefore, the markup or gross profit ratio used must be established by reference to information on the profit ratios of unrelated companies distributing products in the "same broad product categories." The companies CrysCo uses as comparable sources also must meet the "same geographic market" requirement. Usually documentation of information on competitors is not readily available or economical to obtain.

The Cost-Plus Method—The cost-plus price is the preferred method of the manufacturing company. ManCo. Under this method CrysCo's cost of production is adjusted for an appropriate gross profit ratio (GPR). CrysCo has no unrelated party sales for com parison, so the appropriate gross profit ratio must

be established from information on the profit ratios of, "comparable companies" that manufacture products "within the same broad product category" or are "within the same industry." Even though CrysCo performs custom-order work for ManCo, the same broad product category criteria should gibe the multinational corporate group sufficient flexibility to find a suitable product line in the same geographic market.

Comparable Profits Method—Failing to meet the requirements for the preferred methods, CrysCo should use the comparable profits method, which is a profit markup method using a markup percentage

TABLE 2
TRANSFER PRICING METHODS FOR TAX PURPOSES: INTANGIBLE PROPERTY

Method Description	Comparable Uncontrolled Transaction	Comparable Profits	Profits Split	Other
Comparables	Comparable transactions between unrelated parties	Priced to yield gross profits comparable to those for other firms.	Combined operating profits of controlled parties.	Gross profit reasonable for "facts and circumstances."
Comparability and Reliability Standards	Similarity of intangible property; underlying circumstance.	Gross profit within range of profits for similar intangibles.	Allocation of combined profits of controlled parties to emulate that of unrelated parties	As appropriate.
Measures of Comparability	Product and process category; terms in financing and sales; discounts; and the like.	Terms of intangible transfer; same industry; terms of contract.	Profits split by unrelated parties or splits from transfers to unrelated parties. Separate out intangible property profits and allocate by relative values added by each division	Fair allocation of profits relative to "unrelated" party sales.
Same Geographic Market	Required	Required	Required, but some flexibility.	Required, but some flexibility.
Comments	Deemed the best method for all firms, minor accounting adjustments allowed to find similarity and comparables.	Not if seller has unique technologies or unique intangibles.	Controlled transaction allocations compared to profit split in uncontrolled transactions.	Least reliable; uncertainty and costs of being wrong are severe.

established by reference to a range of industry averages. The profit ratio should be based on some internal profit indicator, such as rate of return. If the product or process involved is unique in the market, there is little chance that this method can be used for determining a transfer price. It will not be a problem in transfers to SalCo but likely will preclude the use of the comparable profits method for transfers to ManCo because of the custom job order manufacturing services.

Profits-Split Method—The profits-split method relies on an allocation of the combined profits of the controlled entities as calculated after the transfer to customers outside the group. This method can be used by either ManCo or SalCo in its transfers from CrysCo. It requires that the CrysCo group determine combined operating profit on intercompany transfers.

The profit for each member involved in the transfer, hence the transfer price, is comparable to unit profits where uncontrolled entities are engaged in similar activities with comparable products.

The difficulty inherent in this method is isolating reliable detailed data for similar activities and comparable products. While aggregate profit data often are available for product line, the data do not have enough detail to provide for the required analysis and comparison. Therefore, the reliability of this method as the best measure of comparable transfers is compromised.

"Other" Methods— Where none of the five specific methods can "reasonably be applied" to a transfer, the taxpayer may use another method (read as an "other" method) that is reasonable under the facts and circumstances. A major problem with this particular approach is that the method selected is vulnerable to

THE ADVANCE PRICING AGREEMENT PROGRAM (APA)

In March 1991, the IRS set into place the Advance Pricing Agreement Program (APA) in Revenue Procedure 91-22 (soon to be updated) as an alternative to resolving transfer pricing disputes. The following information is taken from a document prepared by the Office of the Associate Chief Counsel (International).

Designed as an alternative dispute resolution process, the APA program supplements the traditional administrative, judicial and treaty mechanisms for resolving intercompany pricing issues.

The APA process depends on coordination, cooperation, and assistance among the various IRS functions and treaty partners involved with the taxpayer. That way, transfer pricing disputes can be resolved in an effective and less labor-intensive manner for all parties. Under this approach, taxpayers can submit a timely filed return to the IRS that is in compliance with the arm's-length standard and section 482 of the Internal Revenue Code.

The general objectives of the APA process are:

- To enable taxpayers to arrive at an understanding with the IRS on three basic issues: the factual nature of the intercompany transactions to which the APA applies; an appropriate transfer pricing method (TPM) applicable to those transactions; And the expected range of results from applying the TPM to the transactions. (A range of results is

not a mandatory element of an APA. The IRS will, in appropriate cases, consider APAs that set forth a TPM without the specification of any range.)

- To do so in an environment that encourages common understanding and cooperation between the taxpayer and the IRS and that harmonizes and incorporates the opinions and views of all the IRS functions involved with the taxpayer.
- To come to an agreement in an expedited fashion, as compared to the traditional method, which entails separate and distinct dealings with the Examination, Appeals, and Competent Authority functions and/or possible subsequent litigation.
- To come to an agreement in a cost effective fashion for both the taxpayer and the IRS.

The IRS team is a multifunctional partnership of personnel from District Office Examination, Appeals, Assistant Commissioner (International), and Associate Chief Counsel (International). Meeting with the IRS team is an important benefit of the program because the taxpayer does not have to deal separately with the various functions of the IRS involved with transfer pricing.

For more information on the advance Pricing Agreement Program, contact: Cindra Rehman, Prefiling Coordinator, APA Program, IRS Reporter's Building, RM 606, 300 7th St. S.W., Washington, D.C. 20024. Phone (202) 260-9825, fax (202) 260-9850.

challenge by a tax agency, so the company risks the costs of noncompliance. More onerous is that the burden of proving why a method was chosen lies with the taxpayer.

TAX METHODS IN JAPAN AND THE PEOPLE'S REPUBLIC OF CHINA

Multinational operations add a dimension to the transfer price decision matrix. For example, assume that ManCo or SalCo is domiciled in either Japan or China. Japanese methods generally are consistent with acceptable tax methods because they were adopted from an agreement of the Organization for Economic Cooperation and Development (OECD), which was modeled after U.S. rules and is the basis for most international transfer price rules. The Japanese version of the comparability standards, however, is different from the standards adopted in the U.S. rules, implying additional substantiation and documentation costs for ManCo or SalCo. Japan is now among the most aggressive countries in the world in enforcing compliance with transfer price rules, which implies a greater likelihood of audit and litigation costs, even in the absence of actual tax adjustments.

The People's Republic of China takes a very different approach. The Chinese income allocation rules do not dictate specific transfer pricing methods. Their approach is to adjust prices to market when they deem the transfer price artificially low or high. Further complicating the problems of CrysCo's managers, China is on the verge of adopting a new tax base, a value-added tax (VAT). It is not clear that any of the methods discussed earlier is acceptable for VAT purposes.

ECONOMIC AND ORGANIZATIONAL IMPLICATIONS

A diverse transfer price environment poses several problems for a company like CrysCo in its efforts to maintain goal congruency and mitigate related cost increases. First, traditional management transfer price methods involve quantitative analysis techniques, such as linear programming, and economic analysis based on marginal revenue and marginal cost. A review of the criteria set forth by tax rules in the United States and most other countries shows that these techniques will satisfy neither the substantiation nor documentation criteria. If CrysCo is intent on using quantitative or economic analysis to set or verify its transfer price based on corporate management strategy, that alone will not satisfy the documentation and verification rules for tax purposes.

Second, there is evidence that managerial performance evaluation autonomy, optimal production decisions, and segment efficiency are the dominant organizational objectives managers use in selecting a transfer price method. They are not tax criteria, and it is not clear from the descriptions that tax and financial criteria are compatible. It is unlikely that CrysCo's transfer price method using tax criteria will meet the corporate management and strategy criteria also.

Third, tax rules require that transfer price methods meet comparability and unrelated or uncontrolled party standards. The implication for CrysCo or any other multinational corporate group is increased information costs incurred to satisfy the more rigorous information and documentation criteria of the tax code. In the international setting, the potential for diversity among countries' tax rules, the range of alternative transfer price methods, and the diversity of compliance requirements exacerbate the problem.

Last, failure to act—that is, accept a status quo— could prove the most economically disadvantageous action of all. The penalties for noncompliance with U.S. rules were changed in January 1993. Japan and a number of other Asia/Pacific and European countries have threatened to make similar changes in their penalty provisions. If, on audit, noncompliance is found, CrysCo could face penalties of up to 40% of the tax deficiency assessed plus $10,000 per month for every month in which CrysCo and the group fail to meet the compliance requirements.

As you can see, an inappropriate transfer price manifests as strategy and control inefficiencies, tax costs, or contracting and information systems costs. A manager must analyze carefully all the potential economic consequences of setting a transfer price to ensure that it is in compliance with corporate management strategy and tax requirements, that it mitigates incremental costs of information and contracting system adjustments, and that it promotes goal congruency throughout the company.

DOES ROI APPLY TO ROBOTIC FACTORIES

By Gerald H. Lander and Mohamed E. Bayou

Return on investment (ROI) has been the most popular method of performance evaluation in most companies for the past 50 to 70 years. Many companies adopted a decentralized management philosophy along with the RO technique. Even though the decentralized structures in large corporations were very complex, the easily understandable ROI ratio offered top management a handy tool for comparing performances of numerous divisions. But ROI has come under increasing criticism, raising the question: Does the growing trend toward automation alter the validity of this criticism? In other words, is the traditional ROI still valid for managerial performance evaluation in the new robotic manufacturing environment?

MAJOR ATTACKS ON ROI

We evaluate various measures of ROI in the context of the three phases of the decision cycle: acquisition, utilization, and disposition of robotic equipment. Then we present an ROI measure that satisfies the other criteria of acceptance.

Several critics have questioned the validity of the ROI method of performance evaluation. Elements targeted by this criticism appear in the ROI model commonly known as the DuPont formula, shown in Table 1. Typically, the variables of earnings, sales, and investments in this formula are all measured annually. Cash flows, time-value of money, and analysis beyond one year are excluded from the ROI measurement. As machinery replaces labor, with the consequent shift to more fixed costs and fewer variable costs, this criticism becomes more cogent. For example, Dearden contends that while ROI is a valid measure of past performance, it is not valid for setting future objectives because the historical costs of assets used in the formula are meaningless in planning future actions.[1]

Another criticism is that ROI creates dysfunctional intercompany goals. For example, an investment project with an ROI higher than the firm's cost of capital may be acceptable, yet the divisional manager may reject it unless it exceeds the currently attained ROI rate. Acceptance would dilute the manager's current ROI level, so many acceptable projects probably never get proposed to top management.

Another dysfunctional type of behavior arises when the investment in the denominator of the ROI formula is evaluated at net book value. Thus, as assets get older, stable earnings augment ROI, which in turn, may lead to management reluctance to replace the old assets with new advanced technology. This criticism of ROI is especially to the point in a robotic factory—robot obsolescence is more significant than obsolescence gnificant than obsolescence in a labor-intensive factory.

Send argues that the use of ROI motivates management to operate near full capacity in order to maximize ROI,[2] Even worse, divisional management may manipulate short-term income, and the asset base to the point of long-term detriment to the earning power of the company.[3] Consider this scenario: An insecure manager would be unlikely to accept projects that generate negative ROI results during the earlier years and large positive ones during later periods. Recognizing this problem, the corporation may be obliged to centralize several strategic discretionary programs such as R&D in order to minimize these ROI manipulations. Such interference by corporate headquarters does not harmonize with the decentralization philosophy.

In spite of these criticisms, ROI still enjoys internal popularity in evaluating managerial performance, for several reasons:

- As a ratio, ROI is simpler to understand than other evaluation methods such as residual income.
- It is a single measure that combines the effects of three critical performance variables—sales, earnings, and investment.
- ROI is popular with financial analysts, investors, creditors, and other external information users, a fact that encourages corporate top management to tie divisional performance to the way the public views the corporation.[4]

So strong are these reasons that ROI gained popularity as attacks on it increased during the '70s.[5] Because the use of ROI as an evaluation method undoubtedly will continue in practice, managers and other business people need to understand the mechanics and limitations of ROI.

CRITERIA FOR AN ACCEPTABLE ROI MEASURE

Given the serious criticisms of ROI and the nature of machine-intensive environments, the following criteria become necessary for an acceptable ROI measure:

- An ROI measure must consider long-term performance. This criterion is particularly relevant to the robotic factory; automation decreases variable labor and variable overhead costs and increases fixed costs over several years.
- An ROI measure must consider cash flows, a corollary of the first criterion. In the long run, cash flows are more relevant than accrual income because most accrued revenues and expenses will be settled in cash. In addition, the use of cash flows instead of accrual income avoids the distortions caused by the latter, namely, discouragement of growth by the use of net book value in ROI computations[6] and the meaningless use of historical costs of assets for planning future actions.[7]
- An ROI measure must consider the time-value of money, a corollary of the first two criteria. Because the ROI measure incorporates cash flows in long-run planning, discounting these flows in the ROI computations becomes natural.

To apply these criteria properly, managers need to understand the role of ROI in the various decision processes for acquisition, utilization, and disposition of robotic assets.

THE DECISION CYCLE FOR ROBOTIC ASSETS

The life cycle of a robotic asset as an investment generally goes through three different phases. First, it is acquired, then used in operations, and finally disposed of by replacement, sale, or discarding. Each phase requires different decisions and information.

Furthermore, each phase has a different impact on the goals of the manager making the investment decision and on the goals of the division as an economic entity.

For fairness and accuracy in performance measurement, the three phases have to be analyzed from the manager's viewpoint separately from that of the division. Dearden argues that the current performance evaluation system fail to distinguish between the financial performance of the manager and that of the organizational unit being managed.[8] The distinction is important because the manager's potential for success and failure often differs from the division's. Moreover, the extent of the manager's controllability of revenues and expenses is irrelevant to measuring a division's performance because the division's performance incorporates both controllable and uncontrollable income determinants.

Fig. 1 shows how ROI and capital budgeting techniques generally are applied in practice to the three phases of the decision cycle.

The acquisition phase includes all activities necessary for the purchase, installation, and preparation for use of a new robotic asset. Capital budgeting models such as the net present value, internal rate of return, profitability index, and payback period commonly are applied in practice for this phase (Box 1 in Fig. 1). ROI usually is not applied in the evaluation of the division's performance during this phase (Box IV in Fig. 1).

The utilization phase involves the actual use of the asset in operations, which normally affects the manager's performance. Hence, ROI is applied frequently (Box V in Fig. 1), and capital budgeting models rarely are applied (Box V in Fig. 1), and capital budgeting models rarely are applied (Box II). This phase has two problems. First, with robotic assets, the manager's controllability decreases because of the large value of the assets, with costs that become sunk as soon as the assets are acquired. In addition, in some companies top management evaluates major investments in robots, reducing the divisional manager's influence over the investment base and

FIGURE 1
ROI AND CAPITAL BUDGETING MODELS APPLIED TO THE THREE PHASES OF THE DECISION CYCLE

	Acquisition	Utilization	Disposition Replacement
Capital Budgeting	I Applied	II N/A	III Applied
ROI	IV N/A	V Applied	VI Applied

TABLE 2
ROI ANALYSIS IN THE SHORT AND LONG RUN

		Year 1	Year 2	Year 3	Year 4	Year 5
Cost of robot and accessories	(a)	90,000	90,000	90,000	90,000	90,000
Installation	(b)	10,000	10,000	10,000	10,000	10,000
Total (a + b)	(c)	100,000	100,000	100,000	100,000	100,000
Annual Costs:						
Depreciation	(d)	20,000	20,000	20,000	20,000	20,000
Maintenance	(e)	1,000	2,000	3,000	4,000	5,000
Operating & program	(f)	3,000	3,000	3,000	3,000	3,000
Insurance	(g)	3,000	3,000	3,000	3,000	3,000
Total (d + e + f + g)	(h)	27,000	28,000	29,000	30,000	31,000
Annual Benefits:						
Quality effect:						
On sales & rework	(i)	20,000	20,000	20,000	20,000	20,000
Materials savings	(j)	12,000	12,000	12,000	12,000	12,000
Labor savings:						
$10/hour	(k_1)	20,000	20,000	20,000	20,000	20,000
$20/hour	(k_2)	30,000	30,000	30,000	30,000	30,000
$30/hour	(k_3)	40,000	40,000	40,000	40,000	40,000
Overhead savings (30% of labor cost):						
$3/hour	(l_1)	6,000	6,000	6,000	6,000	6,000
$6/hour	(l_2)	9,000	9,000	9,000	9,000	9,000
$9/hour	(l_3)	12,000	12,000	12,000	12,000	12,000
Annual Net Benefits $= (l + j + k_l + l_l) - h = m_l$						
Labor = $10/hour	(m_1)	31,000	30,000	29,000	28,000	27,000
Labor = $20/hour	(m_2)	44,000	43,000	42,000	41,000	40,000
Labor = $30/hour	(m_3)	57,000	56,000	55,000	54,000	53,000

1. Annual Book ROI = $\dfrac{\text{Net Annual Benefits}}{\text{Initial Investment}} = \dfrac{m_i}{c}$

The term "net benefits" indicates the use of accrual income rather than cash flows in the computations.

Annual Book ROI:

		Year 2	Year 3	Year 4	Year 5
at $10/hour	31%	30%	29%	28%	27%
at $20/hour	44%	43%	42%	41%	40%
at $30/hour	57%	56%	55%	54%	53%

2. Average ROI = $\dfrac{\text{Average Net Benefits Over 5 Years}}{\text{Initial Investment}} = \dfrac{\Sigma m/5}{c}$

This ROI also is known as the accounting rate of return   Average ROI when labor is $10/hour = 29%
Average ROI when labor is $20/hour = 42%
Average ROI when labor is $30/hour = 55%

3. Discounted Book ROI = $\dfrac{\text{Present Value of Net Benefits}}{\text{Initial Investment}}$

(The discount rate, i.e., cost of capital used = 10%)   Discounted ROI when labor is $10/hour = 111%
Discounted ROI when labor is $20/hour = 160%
Discounted ROI when labor is $30/hour = 209%

4. Discounted-Cash-Flow ROI (DCF ROI) = $\dfrac{\text{Present Value of Net Cash Inflows}}{\text{Initial Investment}}$

Because depreciation expense (d) is not a cash item it is added back:
Net Cash Inflows $= m_i + d - c = n_i$ for year 1
$= m_i + d = n_i$ for each of years 2-5

		Year 1	Year 2	Year 3	Year 4	Year 5
$10/hour	(n_1)	(49,000)	50,000	49,000	48,000	47,000
$20/hour	(n_2)	(36,000)	63,000	62,000	61,000	60,000
$30/hour	(n_3)	(23,000)	76,000	75,000	74,000	73,000

The discount rate, i.e., cost of capital used = 10%: DCF ROI: When labor is $10/hour = 0.86
When labor is $20/hour = 1.36
When labor is $30/hour = 1.85

decreasing the applicability of ROI as a means to evaluate the manager's performance. Yet these limitations do not affect ROI's usefulness in evaluating the investment center's performance. Second, the apparent inconsistency of applying capital budgeting models for the acquisition phase (Box I) and ROI for the utilization phase (Box V) creates confusion and unfair reporting if only one performance report is issued for evaluation.

The disposition phase is, in effect, an acquisition phase if it leads to replacing the old asset with a new one. Thus, capital budgeting models usually are applied (Box III) but only as a secondary justification. That is, a manager rationally would apply ROI first to determine if the replacement improves the currently attained ROI level (Box VI). If it improves the ROI, the manager models to justify the replacement decision to senior management. On the other hand, if the replacement decision negatively affects the current ROI, the replacement issue may be suppressed and never be made known to superiors even if it is acceptable to the corporation.

SCREENING DIFFERENT ROI MODELS

To avoid these conflicts, a modified ROI model should be used in all of the six boxes of Fig. 1. Table 2 illustrates how to accomplish this consistency. A flexible robotic system with an economic life of five years is considered as a replacement for an older labor-intensive system. Flexible manufacturing systems are the new trend in manufacturing. They integrate machines and systems to produce a particular product or a major component from start to finish. A flexible manufacturing system can take different forms. It can be a series of interlocked electronic machining centers, controlled by a computerized robot, which performs a set of prescribed operations or it can be one machine performing a complex series of mechanical tasks. These systems normally provide several benefits: reduced material handling and work-in-process and increased quality, flexibility, and throughput.[9] The example in Table 2 is designed to capture most of these features. In reality, precisely predicting benefits and costs beyond one year is difficult. Probability distributions can be applied to incorporate these uncertainties, but to simplify the analysis, Table 2 does not include probability assessments.

Table 2 shows four different measures of ROI:

1. The Annual Book ROI. This traditional ROI measure, which involves no discounting or averaging and ignores cash flows and the time-value of money, concentrates on a single year of performance. Notice in Table 2 that the ROI ratio increases as automation replaces labor costs. This measure is simple to understand.

2. The Average ROI. This method also is known as the accounting rate of return. The method improves upon the traditional annual ROI because it considers the entire life of the asset. (A moving average ROI may be employed. For example, when the first year of the planning period expires, the sixth year would be added at the end of the period. Thus, a new average for ROI will be calculated every year, giving the manager a continuous five-year planning horizon.) The average ROI method, however, ignores cash flows and the time-value of money.

3. Discounted-Book ROI. This method considers the time-value of money and the long-run performance. Nevertheless, it includes accrual income (which we call net benefits) rather than cash flows in the computations. Accordingly, depreciation expense on line "d" in Table 2, which is not a cash item, is incorporated into the computation. Can the discounted-book ROI be used to evaluate a manager's performance? A manager's performance should be measured over a period longer than one year, a requirement for applying this method, using budgeted and actual data. Therefore, a good performance results when the actual discounted-book ROI ratio equals at least the budgeted ratio.

TABLE 3
THE CAPITAL BUDGETING MODEL OF PROFITABILITY INDEX

Profitability Index	$=$	$\dfrac{\text{Present Value of Total Cash Inflows}}{\text{Initial Investment}}$
Since Net Cash Inflows	$=$	Total Cash Inflows – Initial Investment
Profitability Index	$=$	$\dfrac{\text{P.V. of Net Cash Inflows} + \text{Initial Investment}}{\text{Initial Investment}}$
	$=$	$\dfrac{\text{P.V. of Net Cash Inflows}}{\text{Initial Investment}} + \dfrac{\text{Initial Investment}}{\text{Initial Investment}}$
	$=$	DCF $\quad+\quad$ 1.00
Thus…DCF ROI	$=$	Profitability Index $\quad-\quad$ 1.00

4. Discounted-Cash-Flows ROI (DCF ROI). This method satisfies all three criteria for acceptance, and it considers the time-value of cash flows over the life of the robotic asset. The mathematical format of this model is shown in the first line of section 4, Table 2. The DCF ROI measure relates to the capital budgeting model of the profitability index. This index is defined in the literatures of accounting and finance as shown in Table 3.

Table 2 shows DCF ROI ratios of .86, 1.36, and 1.85 when hourly labor wage rates are $10, $20, and $30, respectively. Thus, larger savings in labor costs increase the DCF ROI ratio. Generally, interpretation of DCF ROI ratios parallels that of the profitability index. For instance, if a project has a DCF ROI ratio of zero, it indicates that the project's internal rate of return (IRR) equals the interest rate (or cost of capital) used in the discounting process. Similarly, a positive DCF ROI ratio indicates an IRR greater than the cost of capital, and a negative DCF ROI means an IRR lower than the cost of capital. In general, the larger the DCF ROI ratio, the more profitable the project. Greater cost of capital used in discontinuing the cash flows also lowers the DCF ROI ratio.

The application of this DCF ROI model to the six cells of the decision cycle depicted in Fig. 1 eliminates the inconsistency problems caused by applying capital budgeting and the traditional ROI models to the decision cycle as discussed above. The DCF ROI model satisfies the three acceptance criteria of: (1) the emphasis on long-run performance, (2) cash flows, and (3) time-value of money. Finally, the DCF ROI can be used in conjunction with the traditional ROI.

Probability distributions can be incorporated into the analysis to account for uncertainties of future cash flows. These computations can be made easily by using available software packages on present value applications.

---

[1] J. Dearden, "The Case Against ROI," *Harvard Business Review*, May-June 1969, pp. 124-135; his arguments on the subject are still valid today.

[2] A. H. Seed, III, "Cost Accounting in the Age of Robotics," MANAGEMENT ACCOUNTING®, October 1984, pp. 39-41.

[3] L. B. Hoshower and R. P. Crum, "Straightening the Tortuous—and Treacherous—ROI Path," MANAGEMENT ACCOUNTING®, December 1986, pp. 41-44.

[4] J. S. Reece and W. R. Cool, "Measuring Investment Center Performance," *Harvard Business Review*, May-June 1978, pp. 28-176.

[5] Ibid.

[6] J. J. Mauriel and R. N. Anthony, "Misevaluation of Investment Center Performance," *Harvard Business Review*, March-April 1966, pp. 98-105.

[7] J. Dearden, "Measuring Profit Center Managers," *Harvard Business Review*, September-October 1987, pp. 84-88.

[8] Ibid.

[9] R. A. Howell and S. R. Soucy, "The New Manufacturing Environment: Major Trends for Management Accounting," MANAGEMENT ACCOUNTING®, July 1987, pp. 21-27.

TRANSFER PRICING WITH ABC

BY ROBERT S. KAPLAN, DAN WEISS, AND EYAL
DESHEH

**Here's the story of how a multinational
pharmaceutical company solved its
transfer pricing problems by using
activity-based costing.**

In the mid-1980s, Teva Pharmaceutical Industries Ltd.
decided to enter the generic drug market. Already a
successful worldwide manufacturer of proprietary
drugs, the Israel-based company wanted to vie
globally in this competitive new market, particularly in
the United States. The move has proved lucrative so
far, as sales have been increasing at an annual rate of
nearly 20%. In 1996, Teva's worldwide sales were
$954 million and its after-tax net income, $73 million.

As part of its new strategy, Teva reorganized its
pharmaceutical operations into decentralized cost and
profit centers consisting of one operations division and
three marketing divisions. The operations division is
made up of four manufacturing plants in Israel, which
are organized as cost centers because plant
managers have no control over product mix or pricing.
The plants produce to the orders placed by the
marketing divisions, and plant managers are
responsible for operational efficiency, quality, cost
performance, and capacity management.

The marketing divisions are organized into the
U.S. market (through Teva's Lemmon subsidiary), the
local market (Israel), and the rest of the world. All
three have substantially different sales characteristics.
The Lemmon USA division handles about 30
products, each sold in large quantities. The Israel
division handles 1,200 products in different packages
and dosage forms, with many being sold in quite small
quantities. The division handling sales to the rest of
the world works on the basis of specific orders and
tenders [a request from a customer for a price/bid to
deliver a specified product or service], some of which
are for relatively small quantities. All three divisions
order and acquire most of their products from the
operations division, although occasionally they turn to
local suppliers. The marketing divisions are
responsible for decisions about sales, product mix,
pricing, and customer relationships.

Until the late 1980s, the marketing divisions were
treated as revenue centers and were evaluated by
sales, not profit, performance. Manufacturing plants in
the operations division were measured by how well
they met expense budgets and delivered the right
orders on time. The company's cost system
emphasized variable costs, principally materials
expenses—ingredients and packaging—and direct
labor. All other manufacturing costs were considered
fixed.

Teva's managers decided to introduce a transfer
pricing system, which they hoped would enhance
profit consciousness and improve coordination
between operations and marketing. They were
concerned with excessive proliferation of the product
line, acceptance of many low-volume orders, and
associated large consumption of production capacity
for changeovers. They proposed a transfer pricing
system based on marginal costs, defined to be just
materials cost. Direct labor would not be included in
the transfer price because the company was not
expecting to hire or fire employees based on short-
term marketing decisions. High costs were associated
with laying off workers in Israel, and, more important,
pharmaceutical workers were highly skilled. With
Teva's rapid growth, managers were reluctant to lay
off workers during short-term volume declines
because if new employees had to be hired later, they
would need up to two years of training before they
acquired the skills of the laid-off workers.

But the proposed transfer pricing system
generated a storm of controversy. First, some
executives observed that the marketing divisions
would report extremely high profits because they were
being charged for the materials costs only. Second,
the operations division would get "credit" only for the
expenses of purchased materials. There would be
little pressure and motivation to control labor
expenses and other so-called fixed expenses or for
improving operational efficiency. Third, if Teva's plants
were less efficient than outside manufacturers of the
pharmaceutical products, the marginal cost transfer
price would give the marketing divisions no incentive
to shift their source of supply. Finally, the executives
concluded that using only a short-run contribution
margin approach would not solve the problems
caused by treating the marketing divisions as revenue
centers. Measuring profits as price less materials cost

would continue to allow marketing and sales decisions to be made without regard to their implications for production capacity and long-run costs. An alternative approach had to be found.

WHAT EVERYONE WANTED

Teva senior management wanted a new transfer pricing system that would satisfy several important characteristics:
1. The system should encourage the marketing divisions to make decisions consistent with long-run profit maximization. The transfer price should not encourage actions that improved the profit or cost performance of a division at the expense of Teva's overall profitability.
2. The system should be transparent enough so that managers could distinguish costs relevant for short-run decisions—such as incremental, occasional bids for orders—from long-term decisions—such as acquiring a new product line, deleting product lines, and adding to existing product lines.
3. The transfer prices could be used to support decisions in both marketing and operating divisions, including:

Marketing	Operations
• Product mix	• Inventory levels
• New product introduction	• Batch sizes
• Product deletion	• Process improvements
• Pricing	• Capacity management
	• Outsourcing: make vs. buy

Division managers wanted a transfer pricing system with the following characteristics:

1. The transfer prices would report the financial performance of their divisions fairly.
2. Managers could influence the reported performance of their divisions by making business decisions within their scope of authority. That is, the reported performance should reflect changes in product mix, improved efficiency, investments in new equipment, and organizational changes.
3. The decisions made by managers of marketing divisions would reflect both sales revenue and associated expenses incurred in the operations division.
4. The system must anticipate that division managers would examine, in depth, the method for calculating transfer prices and would take actions that maximized the reported performance of their divisions.

Finally, the financial staff wanted a transfer pricing system such that:

1. The transfer prices and financial reports derived from them would be credible and could be relied upon for decision making at all levels of the organization without excessive arguments and controversy.
2. The transfer pricing system would be clear, easy to explain, and easy to use. Updating transfer prices should be easy, and the components of the transfer price calculation should promote good understanding of the underlying factors driving costs.
3. The system would be used for internal charging of costs from the operations division to the marketing divisions.

Table 1. PAIN RELIEVER 10 TABLETS, 250 mg.

Annual Sales 1996—$2.1 Million

ABC Cost per Package

Materials use	$1.50
Production costs	2.10
(The traditional production costs per package were only $1.50, 40% difference)	
Total	$3.60

Production Cost Analysis:

Resources

Salaries	$0.86
Energy	0.27
Utilities	0.34
Depreciation	0.41
Administrative	0.22
Total	$2.10

Main Activities

Storage	$0.25
Manufacturing	0.61
Packaging	0.71
Q.A.	0.42
Logistics	0.11
Total	$2.10

Cost Drivers

Number of materials	$0.55
Batches	0.24
Labor hours	0.71
Machine hours	0.47
Samples	0.13
Total	$2.10

TRADITIONAL TRANSFER PRICE APPROACHES WOULDN'T WORK

Teva's managers considered but rejected several traditional methods for establishing a new transfer pricing system: market price, full cost, marginal cost, and negotiated price. Market price for the transferred product was not feasible because no market existed for Teva's manufactured and packaged pharmaceutical products that had not been distributed or marketed to customers. A full cost calculation including materials, labor, and manufacturing overhead was rejected because the traditional methods for allocating overhead (labor or machine hours) did not capture the actual cost structure in Teva's plants. Also, the accumulation of all factory costs into average overhead rates could encourage local optimization by each division that would lower Teva's overall profit. For example, manufacturing plants would be encouraged to overproduce in order to absorb more factory overhead into inventory, while marketing divisions might be discouraged from bidding aggressively for high-volume orders and encouraged to accept more low-volume custom orders. Also, this system would not reveal the incremental costs associated with short-run decisions or the relative use of capacity by different products and different order sizes.

Using short-run marginal cost, covering only ingredients and packaging materials, was the system proposed initially, which the managers already knew was inadequate for their purposes. And, finally, senior executives believed strongly that negotiated transfer prices would lead to endless arguments among managers in the different divisions, which would consume excessive time on nonproductive discussions.

ACTIVITY-BASED COSTING IS THE ANSWER

In December 1989, Teva's senior management attended a presentation on the fundamentals of activity-based costing and decided to implement ABC in its largest production plant. They wanted to investigate the use of ABC for calculating transfer prices between that plant and the marketing divisions. Teva put together a multidisciplinary project team consisting of managers from the production, finance, and marketing divisions. The team worked for about six months to develop an activity dictionary, drive factory costs to activities, identify cost drivers for each activity, collect data, and calculate ABC based product costs. It took the team several more weeks to analyze the results. Table 1 shows a sample calculation (updated to reflect 1996 data) of the costs to produce 10 tablets of a pain reliever. With this information, managers believed they now had a defensible, quantifiable answer to a question about how much it cost to manufacture a special small batch for a customer.

After seeing how ABC worked at the first plant, in subsequent years the project team rolled out the ABC analysis to the remaining production plants. The ABC models were retrospective, calculating the activity costs, activity cost driver rates, and product costs for the prior year. By the end of 1993, senior managers wanted to use ABC prospectively, to calculate transfer prices for the coming year. In November, Teva built its ABC production cost model for 1994 using data from the first three quarters 1993. But managers objected to calculating costs for 1994 based on 1993 historical data. The numbers would not incorporate the impact of new products, new machines, and expected changes in production processes. Also, the historical data contained volume and spending variances that occurred in 1993 but that were not expected to be representative of production operations in 1994.

The project team took this issue to the company's Financial Control Forum where representatives from the operations and marketing divisions and company headquarters met to discuss costing and financial reporting methodologies. After several meetings, the group decided to use the next year's (1994) forecasted costs—based on budgeted expense data, forecasted volume and mix of sales, and projected process utilization and efficiencies—to calculate the transfer prices.

THE ABC TRANSFER PRICE MODEL STRUCTURE

The structure of the early retrospective ABC models and the current prospective model recognizes the ABC hierarchy of unit, batch, product sustaining, and plant-level costs.[1] Unit-level costs represent all the direct expenses associated with producing individual product units such as tablets, capsules, and ampoules. These expenses principally include the cost of raw materials, packaging materials, and direct wages paid to production workers.

Batch-level costs include the expenses of resources used for each production or packaging batch, mainly the costs of preparation, setup, cleaning, quality control, laboratory testing, and computer and production management. The lot sizes for pharmaceutical production usually are predetermined based on the capacity of containers in the production line,[2] but a second batch process, determined by customer orders, occurs for packaging the tablets or syrup. The costs of a production or a packaging batch can vary among different products and, of course, among different plants. For example, a small customer order can trigger the production of a large batch of tablets or syrup of which only a small portion may be packaged for the particular customer order.[3] Thus, the batch costs assigned to a particular order include two components: a pro-rata share of the batch cost of the production setup and the full batch cost of the packaging setup. The calculation of batch-level costs for several different types of customer orders is shown in Table 2.

Product-specific costs include the expenses incurred in registering the products,[4] making changes to a product's production processes, and designing the package. Plant-level costs represent the cost of maintaining the capacity of production lines including depreciation, cost of safety inspections, and insurance, as well as the general expenses of the plant such as security and landscaping. In many ABC applications, machine appreciation would be included in the unit and batch costs associated with producing products and changing from one product to another. Teva decided to treat equipment depreciation as a plant-level cost so the calculated unit and batch costs could be used to estimate more closely the marginal costs associated with producing one more unit or batch of a product.

USING ABC COSTS FOR TRANSFER PRICING

Teva bases its transfer price system on a prospective ABC calculation. Prices are set for the coming year based on budgeted data. The company calculates standard activity cost driver rates for each activity. During the year these costs get charged to products based on the actual quantity of activities demanded during the year. The use of standard activity cost driver rates enables product costs to be calculated in a predictable manner throughout the year. It also eliminates monthly or quarterly fluctuations in product costs caused by variations in actual spending, resource usage, and activity levels.

Transfer prices are calculated in two different procedures. The first one assigns unit and batch-level costs, and the second assigns product-specific and plant-level costs. The marketing divisions are charged for unit-level costs (principally materials and labor) based on the actual quantities of each individual product they acquire. In addition, they are charged batch-level costs based on the actual number of production and packaging batches of each product they order (see examples in Table 2). Now that Teva has the ability to analyze the costs of different presentations, the trend of having a large number of presentations for each product has slowed. For

---

Table 2. BATCH-LEVEL TRANSFER PRICE

The batch-level transfer price has two components: the production setup and the packaging setup. Consider the production and packaging process for a cough syrup. In the production process, the active ingredients, a syrup simplex, and flavors, are mixed together in a 600 liter container to produce the syrup solution. The cost of setup—labor, cleaning, maintenance, and quality control resources—is $300. The setup cost is assigned proportionally to the entire output.

Subsequently, bottles are filled with the syrup solution and packed into cardboard boxes. The entire packaging process is performed on an automatic filling and packing line. The setup of the line costs $500, which includes the cost of a skilled technician, cleaning, maintenance, and quality control. Packing the same syrup into two different presentations, such as different sized bottles (50 ml and 100 ml), or different packaging materials requires two different setups.

The batch-level transfer price consists of the pro-rata share of the production setup and the full cost of the packaging setup. We illustrate the approach with three numerical examples:

Produce a full batch of 6,000 bottles of 100 ml syrup for a large order from a customer in the local market

[$300/6,000] + [$500/6,000] = $.05 + $.083 = $.133/bottle
  mixing   packing

Produce a small order of 1,000 bottles of 100 ml syrup, packed in special boxes, for a special tender in South America

[$300/6,000] + [$500/1,000] = $.05 + $.50 = $.55/bottle
  mixing   packing

Produce a full batch of 12,000 bottles of 50ml syrup for a large order from a customer in the local market

[$300/12,000] + [$500/12,000] = $.025 + $.042 = $.067/bottle
  mixing   packing

---

example, the marketing divisions realized that producing special sample packages of six tablets was very expensive and that it was cheaper to give physicians the regular packages of 20 tablets. In general, the procedure has given marketing managers the flexibility to decide when to accept a small order from a customer or how much of a discount to grant for large orders. Table 3 shows a sample calculation

Table 3. MONTHLY DEBT — MAY 1995

From Plant A to Local Market Division

Product	Quantity Produced	Material (Per Package)	Unit Based Costs (Per Package)	Batch Based Costs (Per Package)	Total Costs [†] (Per Package)	Total Debit [‡]
Pain reliever 20 tablets, 500 mg.	1,000,000	$2.10	$0.22	$0.41	$2.73	$2,730,000
Pain reliever 30 Capsules	1,200,000	1.60	0.20	0.32	2.12	2,544,000
Syrup 200 cc.	200,000	0.81	0.43	0.11	1.35	270,000
• • •						• • •
Total						$15,100,200

[†] Total costs = material + unit based costs = batch based costs
[‡] Total debit = total costs per package x quantity produced

of the monthly unit and batch-level charges from a plant to a marketing division.

The product-specific and plant-level expenses are charged to marketing divisions annually based on budgeted information (see Table 4). The product-specific costs are easy to assign because each marketing division has specific products for its own markets. No individual product is sold to more than one marketing division. The plant-level (capacity-sustaining) expenses are charged to each marketing division based on the budgeted use of the capacity of the four manufacturing facilities.

Activity cost driver rates are calculated based on the practical capacity of each of the four plants. In this way, the rates reflect the underlying efficiency and productivity of the plants without being influenced by fluctuations in forecasted or actual usage. Analysts estimated the practical capacity by noting the maximum production quantities during past peak periods.

What about unused capacity? Unused capacity arises from two sources: (1) declines in demand for products manufactured on an existing line, and (2) partial usage when a new production line is added because existing production lines cannot produce the additional quantities requested by one of the marketing divisions. To foster a sense of responsibility among marketing managers for the cost of supplying capacity resources, Teva charges the marketing division that experienced the decline in demand a lump-sum assignment (see Table 4) for the cost of maintaining the unused production capacity in an existing line. When a marketing division initiates an increment in production capacity or manufacturing technology, it bears the costs of all the additional resources supplied unless or until the increment begins to be used by one of the other marketing divisions. At that point, each marketing division would be charged based on its percentage of practical capacity used.

The assignment of the plant-level costs (still referred to as "fixed costs" at Teva because of its long history with the marginal costing approach) receives much attention, particularly from the managers of the marketing divisions. They want to verify that these costs do indeed stay "fixed" and don't creep upward each period. By separating the unit and batch-level costs from the product-sustaining and plant-level costs, the marketing managers can monitor closely the costs incurred in the manufacturing plants. In particular, the marketing managers make sure that increases in plant-level costs occur only when one or more of them requests a change in production capacity. The responsibility for the fixed cost increment is then clearly assignable to the requesting division.

The integrated budget process lets marketing managers plan their product mix with knowledge of the cost impact of their decisions. When they propose increases in variety and complexity, they know the added costs they will be charged because of their increased demands on manufacturing facilities. Active discussions occur between marketing and operations personnel about the impact of product mix and batch sizes.

19-26

Table 4. ANNUAL DEBIT — 1995

From Plant A to Lemmon Marketing Division (USA)

Product	Annual Budgeted Quantity	Product Based Costs (Per Package)	Plant Based Costs (Per Package)	Total Costs [†] (Per Package)	Total Debit [‡]
Pain reliever 20 tablets, 500 mg.	12,000,000	$0.10	$0.21	$0.31	$3,720,000
Pain reliever 30 Capsules	20,000,000	0.12	0.20	0.32	6,400,000
Syrup 200 cc.	3,500,000	0.14	0.12	0.26	860,000
• • •					• • •
Cost of used capacity					141,900,000
Cost of unused capacity					1,300,000
Total					$143,200,000

[†] Total costs = product based costs + plant based costs
[‡] Total debit = total cost per package x annual budgeted quantity

Marketing managers now distinguish between products that cover all manufacturing costs versus those that cover only the unit and batch-level expenses but not their annual product-sustaining and plant-level expenses. Because of the assignment of unused capacity expenses to the responsible marketing division, the marketing managers incorporate information about available capacity when they make decisions about pricing, product mix, and product introduction.

One example illustrates the value of assigning product-sustaining and plant-level expenses to individual products in the new transfer pricing system. The initial and subsequent ABC analyses revealed that quite a few of Teva's products were unprofitable; that is, the revenues they earned were below the cost of the unit, batch, and product and plant-sustaining expenses associated with these products. But managers were reluctant to drop these products because many of the expenses assigned to them, including direct labor, would remain for some time even if production of the unprofitable products were to cease.

In the early 1990s, however, Teva's growing sales volume led to shortages in capacity. Teva eventually decided to sell 30 low-volume products to another company. These products were not central to Teva's strategy, yet they consumed a great number of resources and managers' attention. By shifting the product mix away from the unprofitable products,

Teva was able to use the freed-up capacity of people, machines, and facilities to handle the production of newly introduced products and the expanded sales of existing profitable products. While the debate about selling off the 30 products lasted three years, the ABC system contributed to the final decision by revealing that the cheapest source of new capacity was the capacity released by reducing the production and sales of currently unprofitable products.

ONGOING BENEFITS FROM ABC TRANSFER PRICING SYSTEM

With Teva's continued growth, requests for investments in new production capacity arise continually. ABC's highlighting of unused capacity often reveals where production can be expanded without spending additional money. A second source is the capacity released by ceasing production of unprofitable products—when feasible without disrupting customer relations. Beyond these two sources, investments in a new production line can be assessed by simulating production costs if the line were to be installed. For example, a new line can reduce batch-level costs because of less need for changeovers on both the existing and the proposed production lines. These cost reductions could provide the justification for the investment decision. In addition, the investment decision for a new production line explicitly incorporates the cost and assignment of responsibility for the unused capacity in the early periods while market demand has not yet built to long-term expected levels. Teva executives say that the discipline of recognizing and assigning unused capacity costs of new production lines provides valuable realism to the demand forecasts provided by the marketing divisions.

The transfer pricing system also motivates cost reduction and production efficiencies in the manufacturing plants. Managers in the different divisions now work together to identify ways to reduce

The activity-based cost information also helps managers determine which manufacturing facility is appropriate for different types of products. For example (see Figure 1), Plant A has a relatively inflexible (high capital-intensive) cost structure with a high percentage of plant-level costs and a low percentage of unit costs. This plant is most appropriate for high-volume production of standard products. Plant B, with a significantly lower percentage of plant-level costs and a relatively high percentage of unit costs, is much more flexible and is

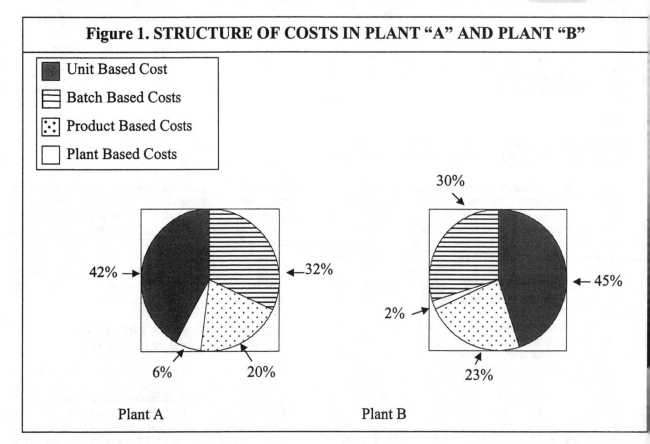

Figure 1. STRUCTURE OF COSTS IN PLANT "A" AND PLANT "B"

■ Unit Based Cost
▤ Batch Based Costs
⦂ Product Based Costs
□ Plant Based Costs

Plant A

Plant B

unit and batch-level expenses. Manufacturing, purchasing, and marketing employees conduct common searches for lower-cost, more reliable, and higher-quality suppliers to reduce variable materials costs. Marketing managers compare Teva's production costs with those of alternative suppliers around the world. They share this information with manufacturing managers who learn where process improvements are required and may concur with a decision to outsource products where the external suppliers' costs are lower than Teva could achieve in the foreseeable future. These actions contribute to increasing Teva's long-term profitability.

appropriate for producing small batch sizes and test runs of newly introduced products. Thus, ABC information also is being used to determine operating strategy.

THE BEST NEWS: HARMONY IS GROWING

An unexpected benefit of the activity-based transfer price system is the ability to measure profit performance under changing organizational structures. Teva, like many other pharmaceutical companies, undergoes periodic organizational changes. By understanding cost behavior at the activity and product level, financial managers can forecast the potential performance of newly created profit centers and reconstruct what the past profit performance history would have been, assuming that the proposed profit center reorganization had existed for the past several years. The ABC system also enables senior executives to measure profit performance across organizational—cost and profit center—boundaries. For example, Table 5 shows the profitability of a significant product family whose individual products are manufactured in different plants and are sold by more than one marketing division.

Jacob Winter, Teva's vice president of pharmaceutical operations, commented on the benefits derived from the ABC transfer price system:

In our changing environment, it is important for us to be able to understand and forecast our cost behavior. Some products remain in certain stages of production for a long time. These stages require resources of professional production and quality assurance staff even when no direct labor is involved. On the other hand, since the supply of these resources is relatively fixed in the short run, we understand that we can use their capabilities for several small batch runs.

He also recognized that activity-based costs are not the primary information used for short-term operational decision making:

The ABC data provide an indication that must be supported by other information and facts One cannot rely only on costing information when making operational decisions. Our short-term operational decisions focus on current bottlenecks and lead-time considerations. ABC provides guidance and insights about where we should be looking, but it is not the primary data for operational decisions.

Perhaps most important, the introduction of ABC-based transfer prices has led to a dramatic reduction in the conflicts among marketing and manufacturing managers. The managers now have confidence in the production cost economics reported by the transfer price system. Manufacturing managers who "sell" the product and marketing managers who "buy" the product concur with the reasonableness of the calculated transfer prices. Teva's senior executives interpret the sharp reduction in intraorganizational conflicts as one of the most important signs that the use of activity-based transfer prices is succeeding.

Table 5. 10 LEADING PRODUCTS (Segment A): 1995

	$ Million
Sales revenue	50
Marketing expenses	
USA Lemmon division	10
Local market division	9
Other export division	-
Total	19
Manufacturing expenses	
Plant A	11
Plant B	-
Plant C	9
Plant D	-
Total	20
Total expenses	39
Profit	11

Robert S. Kaplan is the Marvin Bower Professor of Leadership Development at the Harvard Business School. Dan Weiss is an instructor in the Industrial Engineering and Management Department of the Technion (Israel Institute of Technology) and partner, OIC Technologies Consulting Group. Eyal Desheh, formerly deputy chief financial officer at Teva Pharmaceuticals, is currently vice president and CFO of Scitex Corporation. Comments can be addressed to rkaplan@hbs.edu

[1] R. Cooper, "Cost Classification in Unit-Based and Activity-Based Manufacturing Cost Systems," *Journal of Cost Management,* Fall 1990, pp. 4-14.

[2] Production lot sizes can be expanded, if demand increases to a higher, sustainable level, by making technical changes to the production process and performing a quality control procedure to verify and validate that the product characteristics and quality have not been altered by the larger production batch.

[3] At present, the Teva transfer price system does not charge the customer order for the full cost of setting up the production batch nor for the inventory carrying cost of the unused tablets or syrup. This is a refinement that could be added to the system in future years.

[4] Registration costs include the costs of gaining and maintaining approval from governmental agencies for the right to manufacture each product.

Chapter 20
Management Compensation and Business Valuation

Cases

20-1   Midwest Petro-Chemical Company (Evaluating a Firm)
20-2   Evaluating a Firm
20-3   OutSource, Inc. (Economic Value Added)
20-4   Columbia/HCA Healthcare Corp. (Business Valuation)
20-5   China Huaneng Group

Readings

"Using Shareholder Value to Evaluate Strategic Choices"

The basic principle of the article is that performance evaluation based on accounting measures alone is not sufficient. The evaluation of a business unit or of the unit's manager must also consider the business unit's performance in creating shareholder value. Based on ideas from Alfred Rappaport's book, Creating Shareholder Value, the article develops the measures of cash flow and market risk. An illustration for a hypothetical firm is provided.

Discussion Questions
1. Explain the differences between the two measurement methodologies presented in the article.
2. Why is it important for firms and managers to consider shareholder value?
3. What are the key factors in determining shareholder value?

"Beyond the Numbers"

This article develop a model for business valuation (the authors call it "business assessment"). Six elements of business valuation are identified and explained. Particular attention is given to the element, competitor analysis, in which the author develop a *matrix approach* for analyzing the firm's position relative to competitors, and a *value added approach* for analyzing the firm's operations.

Discussion questions:
1. What does the article say about the role of the management accountant in business valuation?
2. What are the key areas for business valuation? How do these areas compare to the perspectives of the balanced scorecard?
3. What are the key financial performance measures used in the model, and how do these compare to those presented in chapter 19?
4. How does the model differ from the business valuation models presented in chapter 20?

"Structuring Compensation to Achieve Better Financial Results"
This article is based on a survey of 161 executives of U.S. based companies. The objective of the study was to identify the relationship, if any, between executive compensation and corporate performance.

Discussion Questions
1. How has total executive compensation changed in recent years? How has the mix of different types of compensation changed?
2. How do the reported compensation plans differ between high and low performing firms?
3. How is corporate performance measured in this study? What other measures of corporate performance could be used?

Cases

20-1. Midwest Petro-Chemical Company (Evaluating a Firm)[1]

Midwest Petro-Chemical, an industrial chemical distributor, was formed in 1960 by James Fletcher, a chemical engineer who had spent 10 years with the petrochemical division of a major oil company. His oil company experience which included a variety of technical, sales, and management positions, provided valuable business training. His final oil company position was regional marketing manager. He felt hindered by the slow-moving oil company bureaucracy, so he left a corporate career to begin Midwest Petro-Chemical.

The company began operation in Chicago in a rented warehouse with Fletcher as the only full-time employee. First-year sales totaled $113,000 and the company reported a loss of $6,200. Although first-year sales were less than planned and most of his initial capital was lost, Fletcher remained optimistic. Unable to obtain debt capital, he sought equity investors. He approached his college fraternity brothers and oil company colleagues to invest in the new venture. Six accepted, with each providing between $10,000 and $20,000 of much needed capital.

Sales exceeded $300,000 the second year of operations, but the company still reported a small loss of $4,000. The company reported its first profit of $14,000 in year three. Its first bulk distribution facility, capable of handling truck, rail, and barge transportation, was leased the next year.

Over the next 35 years, the company expanded operations beyond Chicago. New offices and plants were opened in five metropolitan cities: St. Louis, Kansas City, Louisville, Cincinnati, and Memphis. Plants were built in industrial areas on sites ranging from two to four acres. Each facility included a warehouse and tank farm with multiple-size tanks with capacities ranging from 1.5 million gallons (barge shipments) to 10,000 gallons (truck shipments). Chemical manufacturers and oil companies were the major supplier of chemicals. Midwest would purchase in bulk (barge, rail, or truck), blend chemicals as necessary, repackage, and ship product in smaller quantities (less than truckload, tote tanks, 55-gallon drums, and other smaller package sizes) to a variety of users.

CURRENT SITUATION

The company prospered and remains a privately held corporation. Annual sales exceeded $95 million in 1995, and a profit of $2,315 million was reported. Fletcher, now in his late 60s, is still CEO and the largest shareholder, owning 314,260 shares or 41.8% of the total shares outstanding. Three of the original investors (Stan Davis, Tom Williams, and Don Stewart) own another 326,216 shares (43.4%), and the company's pension fund owns 78,000 shares. Ron Allen, the company's chief financial officer, is the pension trustee and votes the shares. The remaining 32,524 shares are owned by 37 current or former employees.

There is not an active market for Midwest's stock. Sales or transfers of the stock occur infrequently between a buyer and seller, and Midwest does not participate in the exchange transaction. The sale price of stock is negotiated at arm's length between the buyer and seller. During 1995, approximately 18,000 shares were exchanged in 27 transactions at prices ranging from $21 to $24 per share.

Fletcher, the three remaining original investors (Davis, Williams, and Stewart) and Midwest's local counsel, Frank Armstrong, compose the Board of Directors. Despite

---

[1] Prepared byDavid A. Kunz and Keith A. Russell, © Institute of Management Accountants, 1996. Used with permission.

Midwest's consistent growth and profitability, recent Board meetings have resulted in heated discussions concerning three issues.

1. **Succession plan**. Despite his age, Fletcher remains a more capable leader and has no desire to retire or even plan for retirement. The Board is concerned that no succession plan exists.
2. **Stock value and liquidity**. Stan Davis (age 72) wants to sell his Midwest stock (126,415 shares) but feels the stock is substantially undervalued at its recent trading range of $21 to $24. Like Fletcher, Davis has started his own business—Western Solvents, Inc., a chemical distribution company on the West Coast. With the aid of an investment banking firm, he recently sold Western Solvents at a price that was 16 times earnings. He has been pressuring Fletcher to purchase his Midwest shares.
3. **Offer to purchase the company**. Davis's interest in selling has been heightened due to an unsolicited purchase inquiry from Georgia Chemical, a chemical distributor in Atlanta. The inquiry was made via letter to Fletcher asking if there were any interest in selling Midwest. It is Fletcher's position that Midwest is not for sale, and he does not want to talk about the offer.

At the most recent Board meeting, Fletcher stated he was going to send a letter to Georgia Chemical indicating Midwest is not for sale. Davis objected and argued that it is their fiduciary responsibility as directors to consider all serious offers. Fletcher responded by saying, "Georgia Chemical's inquiry didn't even include a price, so how could it be considered an offer to buy?" Fletcher, Davis, and Allen offered their opinions as to what the stock was worth, but all agreed that their value estimates were not based on systematic or quantifiable processes. They also felt the current stock trading range was low. Stewart felt that without an established valuation of the stock, it would be very difficult, if not impossible, to evaluate objectively any offer to buy the firm. Frank Armstrong agreed with Stewart.

Before a response can be given to the Atlanta inquiry, a reasonable price must be determined. Don Stewart suggested an independent study be undertaken to determine the fair market value of Midwest's common stock. Stan Davis agreed and recommended using the investment banking firm of Warner and David, which recently valued his company. Ron Allen had worked with Warner and David with his previous employer and also thought highly of that firm's ability. Allen also commented that one of the hot new services offered by public accounting firms is business valuation. In fact, a partner in Midwest's auditing firm had mentioned this service in a recent meeting.

Despite his many years in business, Fletcher is unfamiliar with the procedures used to value a business. He is unwilling to bring in any outsider at this point. As a compromise, Tom Williams, a retired banker, suggested that Allen perform an in-house valuation by comparing Midwest's performance with industry norms. Analyses of ratios such as profit margin, return on assets, and return on equity were effective profit measures. Benchmarking Midwest's performance with industry data should be an indication of strength or weakness, which relates to value. Williams also mentioned the price-to-earnings ratio and the price-to-book-value ratio as other possible value indicators. He said that as a banker, he began evaluation of all loan requests with a detailed historic performance analysis using ratios. Sources such as Value Line Investment Survey and Robert Morris Associates Annual Statement Studies provide industry data. Allen agreed that financial analysis was beneficial but was skeptical about it yielding a usable value. Another approach Williams suggested was to perform a valuation using the market values of the firm's assets (appraisals were performed on all properties over the last two years for insurance purposes).

Allen thought a valuation process based on projected future cash flows might be a more accurate measure of the firm's value. Fletcher agreed with Allen because he feels the company is poised for considerable future growth. Davis suggested Allen use the sale of Western Solvents as a reference because the businesses were almost identical except for geographic location.

As the Board members began discussing the various proposals and the advantages and disadvantages of each, Frank Armstrong proposed yet another course of action: giving Ron Allen and his staff the assignment to (1) investigate valuation alternatives, (2) perform an in-house valuation, and (3) prepare a report for review at the next Board meeting (one month away). All Board members agreed, and Allen was given the assignment.

THE ASSIGNMENT

The next day, Ron Allen met with Linda Warren, Midwest's controller, to discuss the task. Warren mentioned that her previous employer used yet another valuation method—capitalization of earnings—to determine its worth. Allen said he planned to use all the methods suggested by the board members plus any other appropriate methods.

Together they reviewed each valuation method and prepared a description of each. They also listed information needed for each technique.

1. *Financial Ratio Analysis*: Allen directed Warren to obtain industry comparative data and suggested starting with Value Line Investment Survey. Other sources of industry comparative data are Robert Morris Associates Annual Statement Studies and Standard and Poor's Industry Surveys.

2. *Asset-Based or Market Value Method*: Although Tom Williams didn't refer specifically to this valuation method, Ron Allen thought he was describing it when he suggested using "market value of the assets." Linda Warren was to gather the most recent appraisals based on replacement values (see Table 1).

3. *Market Comparison Method*: This approach suggested by Stan Davis is based on the assumptions that value of a privately held company can be estimated by comparing it to a similar company whose market values are known. As Davis's company recently sold at 16 times earnings, it can be used as the known market value.

4. *Discounted Cash Flow*: Ron Allen and James Fletcher favor this approach based on expected future cash flows. Linda Warren pointed out that this technique requires forecasting future cash flows. Allen agreed and thought forecasting for five years would be appropriate. In preparing the forecasts, Allen suggested they project revenues to grow at 3.5% per year and forecast operating expenses (including depreciation) as a percentage of sales using an average of actual 1995 and 1994 percentages. As annual depreciation expense has been about $1.4 million the past two years, and no major acquisitions are expected, it was decided to use $800,000 for annual net cash from depreciation (assume $600,000 is reinvestment in existing operations). To keep it simple, Warren suggested forecasting interest expense of $900,000 in 1996 and reducing the amount by $50,000 each subsequent year. She also suggested projecting income tax expense at 30% of income before income taxes. Allen recognized this was an oversimplification, but agreed.

Warren asked how she should handle working capital changes, dividends, and residual values. Allen commented that because the current relationship between revenues, current assets, and current liabilities was close to optimum, they should assume it is maintained. Dividends per share of $.35 should be projected for 1996 with a $.05 per share increase each year thereafter. Book value should be used for residual values.

The rate of return that investors require on equity capital depends on the riskiness of the cash flow stream. The risk premium on equity frequently is regarded at 3% higher than debt capital. Further, the risk and liquidity premium on private small companies without a liquid market indicated an additional premium in the range of 20%.

5. **Capitalization of Earnings**: The capitalization of earnings approach embodies the concept that an investor in a going business has in mind a desired or "target" return on capital. Warren thought it would be another good technique but that they should perform two calculations, one based on past earnings and another using projected earnings. Allen agreed. The target return is expressed as a percentage of after-tax earnings to invested capital or equity and is referred to as return on equity (ROE). Warren thought they should use a capitalization rate based on an average ROE for 1995 and 1994. Allen concurred but told her to use beginning-year equity to calculate ROE.

REQUIRED:

Assume the roles of Ron Allen, Midwest Petro-Chemical's chief financial officer, and Linda Warren, controller, and prepare the required report for the Board. The report should address the following:

1. What is Midwest's strategic competitive advantage, and what type of compensation plan is most consistent with this strategy?

2. Analyze company performance using financial ratio analysis and industry norms as a bench mark. What are the strengths and weaknesses of this evaluation process?

3. Why did financial ratio analysis serve as an effective tool for Tom Williams?

4. Discuss each valuation method. What are the strengths and weaknesses of each? What difficulties are encountered when applying each method?

    a. Asset-based or market value

    b. Market comparison

    c. Discounted cash flow

    d. Capitalization of earnings

        1. Historic earnings

        2. Projected earnings

5. Develop values for Midwest Petro-Chemical's stock using the four valuation methods discussed in requirement 4.

6. Based on your previous answers, develop a fair-market value for Midwest's common stock. Support your value.

7. Recommend a negotiating strategy for dealing with the inquiry from the Atlanta company.

8. Once a price is agreed upon by a buyer and seller, sale terms must be structured.

    a. Will the price be paid in cash at closing? As an initial cash payment plus future payments? As stock or some combination of the aforementioned?

    b. Will stock or assets be sold? Will the sale terms affect price? If so, how? Explain your answer.

(IMA adapted)

TABLE 1

	Acquisition Date	Land	Plant Prop.& Equip	Accumulated Depreciation	Net Book Value
Chicago	1963	$ 634	$ 4,415	$ 3,012	$ 2,037
St. Louis	1967	960	4,602	3,118	2,444
Louisville	1970	1,100	5,809	4,019	2,890
Cincinnati	1980	2,600	6,222	3,216	5,606
Memphis	1982	2,466	7,214	3,037	6,643
		$7,760	$28,262	$16,402	$19,620

	Appraisal Date	Land	Plant. Prop. & Equip	Total
Chicago	1994	$2,010	$2,050	$ 4,060
St. Louis	1991	1,580	1,738	3,318
Louisville	1992	1,720	1,612	3,332
Memphis	1989	2,910	3,702	6,612
Cincinnati	1990	2,700	4,313	7,013
				$24,335

		Shares	%	
James Retcher	CEO/Director	314,260	41.8	
Stan David	Director	126,415	16.8	
Tom Williams	Director	105,060	14.0	
Don Stewart	Director	94,741	12.6	
Pension fund*		78,000	10.4	
Other		32,524	4.4	
	Total	751,000	100.4	
*Shares voted by trustee Ron Allen				

Table 1 (continued)

FINANCIAL STATEMENTS
MIDWEST PETRO-CHEMICAL, INC.
Statement of Income (000s)
For the Years Ending December 31

	1995	1994	1993	1992
Net Sales	$95,652	$92,333	$90,114	$86,414
Costs of Sales and Selling cost				
Cost of sales	77,719	74,882	74,374	70,859
Selling	13,712	13,388	13,049	12,703
Total costs	91,431	88,270	87,423	83,562
Operating income	4,221	4,063	2,691	2,852
Interest expense	914	1,214	1,612	1,728
Income before income	3,307	2,849	1,079	1,124
Income tax expense	992	854	270	259
Net Income	2,315	1,995	809	865
Earnings per share	$3.08	$2.66	$1.08	$1.15
Dividends per share	.30	.25	.22	.20

Statement of Cash Flows (000s)
For the Year Ending December 31, 1995

Operating activities	
Net income	$2,315
Additions (sources of cash)	
Depreciation	1,407
Decrease in inventory	1,153
Increase in accounts payable	2,320
Increase in accrued expense	500
Subtractions	
Increase in accounts receivable	(1,109)
Increase in prepaid assets	(332)
Net Cash provided by operating activities	6,254
Long-term investing activities	
Cash used to acquire fixed assets	(1,030)
Financing activities	
Decrease on long-term debt	(4,701)
Payment of dividends	(225)
Net cash provided by financing activities	(4,926)
Net increase in cash	298
Cash at beginning of year	212
Cash at end of year	$ 510

Table 1 (Continued)

Balance Sheets (000s).
December 31

	1995	1994		1995	1994
Current assets			**Current liabilities**		
Cash	$ 510	$ 212	Accounts payable	$11,264	$8,944
Receivables	13,925	12,816	Accrued expenses	2,245	1,745
Inventories	9,310	10,463	Total current liabilities.	13,509	10,689
Prepaid expenses	745	413			
Total current assets	$24,490	$23,904	Long-term obligations	10,899	15,600
			Total liabilities	24,408	26,289
Property and equipment at cost			**Shareholders' equity**		
			Common stock $1 par value		
Land	7,760	7,760	2,000,000 shares authorized		
Plant, property and equipment	28,262	27,232	751,000 shares outstanding	751	751
Less accumulated depreciation	(16,402)	(14,995)	Paid in capital	2,253	2,253
Total plant and property	19,620	19,997	Retained in earnings	16,198	14,608
			Total shareholders' equity	19,702	17,612
Total assets	$44,110	$43,901	Total liabilities and equity	$44,110	$43,901

20-9

20-2. Evaluating a Firm

REQUIRED:

Consider the financial data below for the Example Company, and assess the value of the Company. Explain your choice(s) of valuation method(s).

Example Company
Selected Financial Data

Account Description	19X8	19X9	19X0	19X1	19X2	19X3
Cash	25,141	25,639	32,977	34,009	49,851	30,943
Accounts Receivable	272,450	312,776	368,267	419,731	477,324	542,751
Prepaids	3,982	4,402	5,037	5,246	5,378	6,648
Inventories	183,722	208,623	222,128	260,492	298,696	399,533
Property & Equipment (net)	47,578	49,931	55,311	61,832	77,173	91,420
Other Assets	18,734	20,738	23,075	26,318	36,248	39,403
Total Assets	551,607	622,109	706,795	807,628	944,670	1,110,698
Accounts Payable	49,831	64,321	70,853	80,861	94,677	78,789
Accrued Expenses	86,087	102,650	113,732	131,899	143,159	164,243
Notes Payable	99,539	118,305	182,132	246,420	237,741	390,034
Long-term Debt	62,622	43,251	35,407	32,301	128,432	126,672
Deferred Taxes Payable	7,551	7,941	8,286	8,518	9,664	11,926
Other Liabilities	5,279	5,521	5,697	5,593	5,252	4,695
Total Liabilities	310,909	341,989	416,107	505,592	618,925	776,359
Capital Stock	73,253	87,851	79,009	71,601	81,238	73,186
Retained Earnings	167,445	192,539	211,679	230,435	244,507	261,153
Total Stockholders Equity	240,698	280,120	290,688	302,036	325,745	334,339
Total Liabilities & Equity	551,607	662,109	706,795	807,628	944,670	1,110,698
Net Sales	982,244	1,095,083	1,214,666	1,259,116	1,378,251	1,648,500
Cost of Goods Sold	669,560	739,459	817,671	843,192	931,237	1,125,261
Depreciation Expense	8,303	8,380	8,972	9,619	10,577	12,004
Interest Expense	11,248	13,146	14,919	18,874	16,562	21,128
Income Tax Expense	26,650	34,000	38,000	32,800	26,500	25,750
Dividends Paid	13,805	17,160	19,280	20,426	20,794	20,807
Net Income	32,563	37,895	41,809	39,577	35,212	37,787
Number of common shares outstanding at year-end	12,817	13,714	13,728	13,684	14,023	13,993
Market price per share	38	43	55	65	43	31

20-3. Economic Value Added; Review of Chapter 19; Strategy[1]

"I've been hearing a lot lately about something called EVA, which stands for Economic Value Added, and I was curious whether it is something we can use at OSI," Keith Martin said as he finished his lunch. Keith is president and CEO of OutSource, Inc. His guest for lunch that day was a computer industry analyst from a local brokerage firm. Keith had invited him to lunch so he could get more information on EVA and its uses.

"Yes," the analyst replied, "I've heard a great deal about EVA. It's a residual income approach in which a firm's net operating profit after taxes—called NOPAT—is reduced by a minimum level of return a firm must earn on the total amount of capital placed at its disposal.

"Have you seen the recent articles on EVA? The after-tax operating profit, NOPAT as you called it, and the amount used for capital don't come directly off the financial statements. You have to analyze the footnotes to determine the adjustments that have to be made to come up with those amounts."

"The article sounds like interesting reading for me, especially at this point," Keith said. "Can you send me a copy?"

"Sure," said the analyst. "But tell me, what is it about EVA that piqued your interest in trying it at OSI?"

"In tracking our industry," Keith replied, "I see the stock prices of some of our key competitors, like Equifax, increasing. Yet, when I compare OSI's recent growth in sales and earnings, our return on equity and earnings per share compare well to those firms, but our stock price doesn't achieve nearly the same rate of increase, and I don't understand why."

The analyst suggested, "Some of those firms might be benefiting from using EVA already, and the market value of their stock probably reflects the results of their efforts. It has been shown that a higher level of correlation exists between EVA and a stock's market value than has been found with the traditional accounting performance measures like ROE or EPS."

"But will EVA work in a small service firm like OSI?"

"I've read about EVA being used at smaller firms," said the analyst. "I'm not an expert on EVA, but I don't see any reason why it wouldn't work at OSI."

"I'd like to find out more about EVA and how we can use it at OSI. For example, we've talked about a new incentive plan-will EVA work in that area? And, if so, will it help us in deciding how we should organize and manage our operations as we expand and grow? What can you do to get more information on these things to me?"

COMPANY INFORMATION

OutSource, Inc. (OSI) is a computer service bureau that provides basic data processing and general business support services to a number of business firms, including several large firms in the immediate local area. Its offices are in a large city in the mid-Atlantic region, and it serves client firms in several Mid-Atlantic States. OSI's revenues have grown rapidly in recent years as businesses have downsized and outsourced many of their basic support services.

---

[1] Prepared by Paul A. Dierks, © Institute of Management Accountants, 1998. Used with permission.

The CorpInfo Data Service (CIDS) classifies OSI as an Information Services firm (SIC 7374). This group is composed, in large part, of smaller, independent entrepreneurs that provide a variety of often disparate services to both corporate and government clients. Market analysts feel a continuously healthy economy translates into strong potential for higher earnings by members of this group. A factor sustaining an extended period of growth is the increased attention of firms to control costs and to outsource their non-core functions, such as personnel placement, payroll, human resources, insurance, and data processing. This trend is expected to continue, probably at an increasing rate. Several firms in this industry have capitalized on their growth and geographic expansion to win lucrative contracts with large clients that previously had been awarded on a market-by-market basis.

Although OSI operates out of its own facilities, which include some computing equipment and furniture, the bulk of its computer processing power is obtained from excess computer capacity in the local area, primarily rented time during third-shift operations at a large local bank. To be successful in the long term, however, OSI management knows it must expand its business considerably, and, to ensure it has full control over its operations, it must set up its own large-scale computing facility in-house. These items are included in OSI's strategic plan.

As OSI's reputation for accurate, reliable, and quick response service has spread, the firm has found new business coming its way in a variety of data processing and support services. The issue has been deciding which services to take on or to stay out of in light of the current limitations on OSI's computing resources and assurance it can continue to provide high-quality service to its customers. Things definitely are looking up for OSI, and industry market analysts recently have begun to look more favorably on its stock.

In 1993, OSI's board decided to pursue additional opportunities in payroll processing and tax filing services, and OSI purchased a medium-sized firm that had an established market providing payroll calculations, processing, and reporting services for several Fortune 500 firms on the East Coast. Now OSI is in the midst of developing a new payroll processing system, called PayNet, to replace the outmoded system that was originally created by the firm it acquired.

Once PayNet is developed, it will give users an integrated payroll solution with a simpler, more familiar graphic user interface. From an administrative perspective, it will allow OSI to reduce its manual data entry hiring, to speed data compilation and analysis, and to simplify administrative tasks and the updating of customer files for adds, moves, and changes. PayNet will serve as the backbone for OSI's service bureau payroll processing operations in the future, but developmental and programming costs have been higher than expected and will delay the roll out of the final version of the new payroll program. Beta testing of the production version of PayNet is being delayed from the second to the third quarter of 1996.

TABLE 1. OUTSOURCE INC.
Balance Sheet
December 31,

	1995	1994
ASSETS		
Current Assets:		
Cash	$144,724	$169,838
Trade and other receivables (net)	217,085	192,645
Inventories	15,829	23,750
Other current assets	61,047	49,239
Total current assets	438,685	435,472
Noncurrent Assets:		
Property, plant, equipment	123,135	109,600
Software and development costs	33,760	14,947
Data processing equipment & furniture	151,357	141,892
Other noncurrent assets	3,650	8,844
	311,902	275,283
Less: Accumulated depreciation	85,108	57,929
Total (net) noncurrent assets	226,884	217,354
Goodwill	88,200	96,600
	$753,769	$749,426

LIABILITIES AND SHAREHOLDERS' EQUITY

	1995	1994
Current liabilities		
Short-term debt & current portion of long-term note	$27,300	$31,438
Accounts payable	67,085	57,483
Deferred income	45,050	32,250
Income taxes payable	19,936	12,100
Employee compensation and benefits accrued	30,155	28,950
Other accrued expenses	28,458	27,553
Other current liabilities	17,192	29,769
Total current liabilities	235,176	219,543
Long-term note, less current portion	98,744	117,155
Deferred income taxes	6,784	4,850
Shareholders' Equity:		
Cumulative Nonconvertible Preferred Stock, $100 par value, authorized 5,000 shares, issued and outstanding 1,000 shares	100,000	100,000
Common stock, $1 par value; 300,000 shares authorized; 219,884 shares issued & outstanding	219,884	219,884
Additional paid-in capital	32,056	32,056
Retained earnings	61,125	55,938
Total shareholders' equity	413,065	407,878
	$753,769	$749,426

OutSource, Inc. - Statement of Income for
The Year Ended December 31, 1995

Operating revenue	$2,604,530
Less: Costs of services	1,466,350
Gross profit	1,138,180
Less: Operating expenses	
Selling, general and administrative	902,388
Research and development	89,089
Other expense (income)	59,288
Write-off of goodwill and other tangibles	13,511
Earnings (Loss) before interest and taxes	73,904
Interest income	1,009
Interest expense	12,427
Earnings (Loss) before income taxes	62,486
Income tax provision	21,870
Earnings (Loss)	$40,616

OutSource, Inc. - Statement of Cash Flows for
The Year Ended December 31, 1995

Cash Flows from Operating Activities

Net Earnings (Loss)	$40,616
Depreciation	21,978
Amortization of software & development	5,111
Decrease (Increase) in trade & other receivables	(24,440)
Decrease (Increase) in inventories	7,921
Decrease (Increase)in other current assets	(11,808)
Increase (Decrease) in deferred income	9,602
Increase (Decrease) in accounts payable	12,800
Increase (Decrease) in income taxes payable	7,836
Increase (Decrease) in employee compensation and benefits	1,205
Increase (Decrease) in other accrued expenses	905
Increase (Decrease) in other current liabilities	(12,577)
Increase (Decrease) in deferred income taxes	1,934
Net cash provided by (used for) operating activities	61,083

Cash Flows from Investing Activities

Expended for capital assets	(36,619)
Goodwill amortized	8,400
Net cash provided by (used for) investing activities	(28,219)

Cash Flows from Financing Activities

Payment of long-term note	(4,138)
Payment of short-term note	(18,411)
Preferred dividends paid	(11,000)
Common stock dividends paid	(24,429)
Net cash provided by (used for) financing activities	(57,978)

Net Cash Flows Provided (Used)	**(25,114)**
Cash at beginning of year	**$169,838**
Cash at end of year	**$144,724**

ADDITIONAL ACCOUNTING INFORMATION

OSI's financial statements for 1995 appear in Table 1. The following list of information is pertinent to calculating a firm's EVA extracted from the footnotes to OSI's annual report for 1995.

A. Inventories are stated principally at cost (last-in, first-out), which is not in excess of market. Replacement cost would be $2,796 greater than the 1994 inventory balance and $3,613 greater than the 1995 inventory balance.

B. On July 1, 1993, the company acquired CompuPay, a payroll processing and reporting service firm. The acquisition was accounted for as a purchase, and the excess cost over the fair value of net assets acquired was $109,200, which is being amortized on a straight-line basis over 13 years. One-half year of goodwill amortization was recorded in 1993.

C. Research and development costs related to software development are expensed as incurred. Software development costs are capitalized from the point in time when the technological feasibility of a piece of software has been determined until it is ready to be put on line to process customer data. The cost of purchased software, which is ready for service, is capitalized on acquisition. Software development costs and purchased software costs are amortized using the straight-line method over periods ranging from three to seven years. A history of the accounting treatment of software development costs and purchased software costs follow:

	Expensed	Capitalized	Amortized
1993	$166,430	$ 9,585	0
1994	211,852	5,362	$ 4,511
1995	89,089	18,813	5,111
	$467,371	$33,760	$ 9,622

ADDITIONAL FINANCIAL INFORMATION

OSI's common stock is currently trading at $2 per share. A preferred dividend of $11 per share was paid in 1995, and the current price of preferred stock is approximately at its par value. Other information pertaining to OSI's debt and stock follows:

Short-term debt	$ 8,889	8.0%
Long-term debt:		
Current portion	$ 18,411	10.0%
Long-term portion	$ 98,744	10.0%
Total long-term debt	$117,155	

Stock market risk-free rate		
(90-day T-bills)	=	5.0%
Expected return on the market	=	12.5%
Expected growth rate of dividends	=	8.0%
Income tax rate	=	35.0%

REQUIRED:

1. The management of OutSource, Inc. has asked you to prepare a report explaining EVA (Economic Value Added), how it is calculated, and how it compares to traditional measures of a firm's financial performance. As part of your answer, calculate EVA from OSI's financial report.

2. What are the advantages and disadvantages of using EVA to evaluate OSI's performance on an on-going basis, as well as in assessing the performance of individual managers throughout its organization? How might EVA help OSI attain its strategic goals?

3. OSI management wants to know if EVA can be used as part of an incentive program for its employees, and if so, how it should be implemented.

(IMA, adapted)

20-4. Columbia/HCA Healthcare Corporation

The names Columbia/HCA Healthcare Corporation and Quorum Health Group, Inc. are familiar ones in the healthcare industry. While Columbia/HCA's affiliates own and operate hospitals and related healthcare entities in 24 states, England and Switzerland, Quorum Healthcare Group, Inc. owns and operates acute care hospitals and healthcare systems in 44 states and the District of Columbia. Columbia/HCA operates general acute care hospitals, outpatient and ancillary health care facilities, and psychiatric hospitals. Quorum's business includes operating acute care hospitals, outpatient services, management services, and operational and strategic consulting services. Below is some selected financial information for both companies:

Columbia/HCA Healthcare Corporation
Consolidated Balance Sheets
December 31, 1999 And 1998
(Dollars In Millions, Except Per Share Amounts)

	1999	1998
ASSETS		
Current assets:		
Cash and cash equivalents	$ 190	$ 297
Accounts receivable, less allowances for doubtful accounts of $1,567 and $1,645	1,873	2,096
Inventories	383	434
Income taxes receivable	178	149
Other	973	887
	3,597	3,863
Property and equipment, at cost:		
Land	813	925
Buildings	6,108	6,708
Equipment	6,721	7,449
Construction in progress	442	562
	14,084	15,644
Accumulated depreciation	(5,594)	(6,195)
	8,490	9,449
Investments of insurance subsidiary	1,457	1,614
Investments in and advances to affiliates	654	1,275
Intangible assets, net of accumulated amortization of $644 and $596	2,319	2,910
Other	368	318
	$16,885	$19,429

Columbia/HCA Healthcare Corporation
Consolidated Balance Sheets (Continued)
December 31, 1999 And 1998
(Dollars In Millions, Except Per Share Amounts)

LIABILITIES AND STOCKHOLDERS' EQUITY

	1999	1998
Current liabilities:		
Accounts payable	$ 657	$ 784
Accrued salaries	403	425
Other accrued expenses	1,112	1,282
Long-term debt due within one year	1,160	1,068
	3,332	3,559
Long-term debt	5,284	5,685
Professional liability risks, deferred taxes and other liabilities	1,889	1,839
Minority interests in equity of consolidated entities	763	765
Stockholders' equity:		
Common stock $.01 par; authorized 1,600,000,000 voting shares and 50,000,000 nonvoting shares; outstanding 543,272,900 voting shares and 21,000,000 nonvoting shares—1999 and 621,578,300 voting shares and 21,000,000 nonvoting shares—1998	6	6
Capital in excess of par value	951	3,498
Other	8	11
Accumulated other comprehensive income	53	80
Retained earnings	4,599	3,986
	5,617	7,581
	$16,885	$19,429

Columbia/HCA Healthcare Corporation
Consolidated Statements Of Operations
For The Years Ended December 31, 1999 And 1998
(Dollars In Millions, Except Per Share Amounts)

	1999	1998
Revenues	$16,657	$18,681
Salaries and benefits	6,749	7,811
Supplies	2,645	2,901
Other operating expenses	3,196	3,771
Provision for doubtful accounts	1,269	1,442
Depreciation and amortization	1,094	1,247
Interest expense	471	561
Equity in earnings of affiliates	(90)	(112)
Gains on sales of facilities	(297)	(744)
Impairment of long-lived assets	20	542
Restructuring of operations and investigation related costs	116	111
	15,373	17,530
Income from continuing operations before minority interests and income taxes	1,284	1,151
Minority interests in earnings of consolidated entities	57	70
Income from continuing operations before income taxes	1,227	1,081
Provision for income taxes	570	549
Income from continuing operations	657	532
Discontinued operations:		
Income (loss) from operations of discontinued businesses, net of income taxes (benefits) of ($26) in 1998 and $18 in 1997		(80)
Losses on disposals of discontinued businesses, net of income tax benefit of $124 in 1997		(73)
Cumulative effect of accounting change, net of income tax benefit of $36	--	--
Net income (loss)	$ 657	$ 379
Basic earnings (loss) per share:		
Income from continuing operations	1.12	0.82
Discontinued operations:		
Income (loss) from operations of discontinued businesses		(0.12)
Losses on disposals of discontinued businesses		(0.11)
Cumulative effect of accounting change		
Net income (loss)	$ 1.12	$ 0.59
Diluted earnings (loss) per share:		
Income from continuing operations	1.11	0.82
Discontinued operations:		
Income (loss) from operations of discontinued businesses		(0.12)
Losses on disposals of discontinued businesses		(0.11)
Cumulative effect of accounting change		
Net income (loss)	1.11	0.59

As of April 28, 2000 the stock price is $28.563 and brokers on biz.yahoo.com vary in their recommendations from rating the stock as a strong buy (15), moderate buy (11), to hold (4).

Quorum Health Group, Inc. And Subsidiaries
Consolidated Balance Sheets
(In Thousands)

	June 30	
	1999	1998
ASSETS		
Current assets:		
Cash	$ 22,258	$ 17,549
Accounts receivable, less allowance for doubtful accounts of		
$83,896 at June 30, 1999 and $65,561 at June 30, 1998	332,312	273,376
Supplies	39,003	29,336
Other	46,838	34,245
Total current assets	440,411	354,506
Property, plant and equipment, at cost:		
Land	88,157	66,424
Buildings and improvements	435,525	291,258
Equipment	584,017	464,577
Construction in progress	24,875	72,676
	1,132,574	894,935
Less accumulated depreciation	297,454	216,229
	835,120	678,706
Cost in excess of net assets acquired, net	226,038	144,315
Investments in unconsolidated entities	259,709	245,551
Other	70,670	67,875
Total assets	$1,831,948	$1,490,953

Quorum Health Group, Inc. And Subsidiaries
Consolidated Balance Sheets (Continued)
(In Thousands, Except Per Share Amounts)

	June 30	
	1999	1998
LIABILITIES AND STOCKHOLDERS' EQUITY		
Current liabilities:		
Accounts payable and accrued expenses	$ 96,904	$ 70,483
Accrued salaries and benefits	72,558	64,196
Other current liabilities	34,841	27,533
Current maturities of long-term debt	913	1,273
Total current liabilities	205,216	163,485
Long-term debt, less current maturities	872,213	617,377
Deferred income taxes	33,422	29,470
Professional liability risks and other liabilities and deferrals	36,456	30,882
Minority interests in consolidated entities	59,975	27,473
Commitments and contingencies		
Stockholders' equity:		
Common stock, $.0l par value; 300,000 shares authorized; 73,166 issued and outstanding at June 30, 1999 and 75,478 at June 30, 1998	732	755
Additional paid-in capital	253,714	290,149
Retained earnings	370,220	331,362
	624,666	622,266
Total liabilities and stockholders' equity	$1,831,948	$1,490,953

Quorum Health Group, Inc. And Subsidiaries
Consolidated Statements Of Income
(In Thousands, Except Per Share Amounts)

| | Year Ended June 30 | |
	1999	1998
Revenue:		
Net patient service revenue	$1,505,027	$1,427,969
Hospital management/professional services	82,698	79,537
Reimbursable expenses	64,859	64,846
Net operating revenue	1,652,584	1,572,352
Salaries and benefits	687,090	628,090
Reimbursable expenses	64,859	64,846
Supplies	231,299	210,056
Fees	156,885	140,859
Other operating expenses	121,948	102,959
Provision for doubtful accounts	126,525	106,733
Equity in earnings of affiliates	(22,348)	(6,993)
Leases and rentals	34,192	26,679
Depreciation and amortization	95,427	87,020
Interest	53,683	40,606
Write-down of assets and investigation and litigation related costs	35,173	22,850
Minority interest	(4,501)	3,118
Income before income taxes and extraordinary item	72,352	145,529
Provision for income taxes	33,494	58,849
Income before extraordinary item	$38,858	$86,680
Extraordinary charges from retirement of debt	—	—
Net income	$38,858	$86,680
Basic earnings per share:		
Income before extraordinary item	$ 0.53	$ 1.16
Extraordinary charges from retirement of debt	—	—
Net income	$ 0.53	$ 1.16
Diluted earnings per share:		
Income before extraordinary item	$ 0.52	$ 1.12
Extraordinary charges from retirement of debt	—	—
Net income	$ 0.52	$ 1.12
Weighted average shares outstanding:		
Basic	73,500	74,733
Common stock equivalents	930	2,434
Diluted	74,430	77,167

As of April 28, 2000 the stock price is $11.00 and according to brokers on biz.yahoo.com their recommendations ranged from moderate buy (7) to hold (10).

REQUIRED:

1. Perform a financial analysis for Columbia/HCA Healthcare Corporation and Quorum Health Group, Inc. based on their respective 1999 financial information.
2. What are issues that the healthcare industry is facing? What are sources of concern for healthcare providers?
3. What is Columbia/HCA Healthcare Corporation's strategy? What is Quorum Health Group, Inc.'s strategy? Support your answer.
4. Go to Columbia/HCA Healthcare Corporation's website at www.columbia-hca.com and Quorum Health Group, Inc.'s homepage at www.quorumhealth.com and determine how the companies are performing now. Would you recommend buying stock in these companies? Explain your reasoning.

20-5. China Huaneng Group[1]

INTRODUCTION

In July of 1999, Ms. Wenxin Jia, Vice Manager of China Huaneng Group's (CHNG) Finance Department, described her company's operating philosophy and systems by the following four principles:

- High quality and scale of projects – new project or subsidiary selection or development must be based on the economy of scale and the adoption of the advanced technology.
- High speeds in construction – to shorten the construction period while guaranteeing the quality standard.
- High level of management – to keep pace with the world's advanced management level.
- High efficiency in operation – the overall evaluation criterion for developments and operations.

According to Jia, CHNG's strategy is "Maintaining to make diversified development, with the power business as CHNG's core industry."

INDUSTRY INFORMATION

In the early 1970s, the long-lasting shortage of electric power in China became an important factor that affected and limited the development of the Chinese economy. During the past 20 years, China has experienced a structure reform in its economy as it began to open up to the outside world. During this time, China's power industry has engaged in developmental twists and turns that eventually led to brilliant achievements attracting worldwide attention.

In 1978, China's total installed generating capacity stood at 57.12 million kwh and the electric power output was 256.6 billion kwh, ranking 8th and 7th in the world, respectively. Over the past 20 years, China's power industry has advanced tremendously with an average annual increase of installed capacity of 10 million kwh. By the end of 1997, China's total installed generating capacity and total power output had reached 250 million kwh and 1,105.4 billion kwh respectively, both ranking second in the world, making China one of the nations with the fastest growing power industries.

With the rapid development of China's power industry, Chinese power enterprises began developing in the directions of industrialization, big company groups, and large-scale plants while speeding up the shifting of operational mechanisms. Especially since 1997, the growth rate of China's power industry has been enormous, with the industry's fixed assets and output value growing steadily. According to China's statistics yearbook, 1997 year-end total assets of the industry was RMB 682.24 billion yuan, 31.82% more than the previous year. (Note: U.S. 1$ = RMB 8.27 Yuan)

In output value, statistics show that the industry gained a total of RMB 203.03 billion yuan in 1997, 19.57% more than the previous year; the industrial added value was

---

[1] Prepared by Thomas W. Lin and Kenneth A. Merchant. Used with permission.

RMB103.89 billion yuan, up 19.26%; and the sales value was RMB197.58 billion yuan, up15.86%.

Overall, the power industry's major economic growths in China have maintained a steadily growing momentum. In the five years from 1993 to 1997, the industry made RMB116.5 billion yuan in total profits and taxes, of which profits were RMB 36.2 billion yuan and taxes were RMB 80.3 billion yuan.

Exhibit 1 presents China power industry's financial data during 1995-1998.

Exhibit 1

Financial Data of China's Power Industry in 1995-1998

	1995	1996	1997	1998
Output (1 billion kwh)	1,007.0	1,081.3	1,105.4	1,125.2
Sales (1 billion kwh)	662.8	716.3	752.5	760.0
Revenues (RMB 1 billion)	154.4	185.9	249.9	258.2
Taxes (RMB 1 billion)	15.3	17.5	22.3	22.7
Net Income (RMB 1 billion)	7.7	8.0	8.2	8.6

COMPANY BACKGROUND

China Huaneng Group (CHNG) was established in August 1988. "Hua" means China, while "neng" means energy. It is a large-scale state-owned enterprise with 20,000 employees and headquarters in Beijing. The company's core business is power generation.

In 1991 CHNG was listed among the first batch of experimental large-size groups in China. In 1996, CHNG merged with the State Power Corporation of China. It is a holding company of many power companies; it also has many peripheral businesses in telecommunications, real estate, finance, cement, and electrical appliances. Most are vertically integrated. CHNG reports to the State Power Corporation of China, which is a part of the government. Consequently, this is a true state-owned enterprise.

At present, CHNG consists of its core enterprise (China Huaneng Group Corporation), nine other member corporations (Huaneng International Power Development Corporation, Huaneng Raw Materials Corporation, China Huaneng Finance Corporation, China Huaneng Technology Development Corporation, Huaneng Comprehensive Utilization Development Corporation, Huaneng Real Estate Development Corporation, Huaneng Industrial Development & Service Corporation, China Huaneng International Trade-Economics Corporation, and Huaneng South Development Corporation) and about 400 subsidiary companies throughout China. In addition, it directly controls about 30 overseas branches and companies.

Only two subsidiaries are publicly held: Huaneng International Power Development Corporation and Shangdong Huaneng Power Development Corporation. Both had their stocks issued on the New York Stock Exchange during the second half of 1994.

CHNG's mission in 1985 was to address the national shortage of power. Now the mission is to increase profits. The government primarily appoints its board of directors. The goal is "slow steady growth in profits." The Chinese government is not very strict; it doesn't look at how much profits have improved each year. Hence, there are no sanctions by the government if no increase in profit is reported.

Exhibit 2 presents CHNG's Annual Power Generation/Production during 1989-1996. Exhibit 3 shows CHNG's financial statement information for 1995 and 1996. Exhibit 4 displays CHNG's major financial data during 1989-1996.

Exhibit 2

CHNG's Annual Power Generation/Production during 1989-1996
(Unit: 1 billion KWH)

	Power Generation	Percentage of the Country
1989	18.30	3.13%
1990	25.60	4.20
1991	39.38	5.81
1992	52.70	6.99
1993	69.77	8.34
1994	81.60	8.80
1995	93.81	9.32
1996	97.70	9.70

Exhibit 3
CHNG's Recent Two Year Financial Statement Information
(Unit: RMB 1,000 yuan)

	1996	1995
Sales Revenues	20,705,540	18,183,350
Cost of Goods Sold	15,740,050	13,591,050
Operation Expenses	130,480	39,960
Administrative Expenses	538,330	488,690
Operating Income	2,293,400	2,028,360
Income Tax	729,470	599,270
Profit before Tax	3,497,700	3,249,850
Total Assets	112,761,330	90,910,650
Current Assets	33,416,340	26,312,540
Accounts Receivable	10,565,720	8,076,000
Inventories	2,932,510	1,865,470
Long-term Investment	5,095,010	5,627,810
Fixed Assets	4,742,330	32,407,040
Projects in Construction	27,974,070	19,044,040
Total Liabilities	82,707,660	63,290,520
Current Liabilities	26,040,720	18,380,360
Long-term Liabilities	56,666,940	44,910,160
Minority Interest	17,269,390	15,761,220
Capital Stock	4,026,810	4,026,810
Stockholders' Equity	30,053,670	27,620,130

Exhibit 4

CHNG's Major Financial Data During 1989-1996
(Unit: RMB 1 billion yuan)

	Total Assets	Stockholders' Equity	Profit before Tax
1989	11.79	1.99	0.27
1990	27.61	2.72	0.35
1991	34.13	3.77	0.66
1992	39.91	4.91	1.03
1993	46.07	6.75	1.83
1994	80.13	24.16	2.17
1995	90.91	27.62	3.24
1996	112.76	30.05	3.49

CONTROL OF SUBSIDIARIES

CHNG has adopted a decentralization philosophy since its establishment. Through its decentralized subsidiary company operations, CHNG enhanced its Performance Evaluation System by continuously adding value to state assets.

CHNG's investments in subsidiary companies are usually in the form of joint ventures with local enterprises. According to the capital structure relationship, CHNG is divided into three levels: core enterprise, member companies, and operating units. Recently, CHNG became the wholly owned subsidiary of State Power Corporation of China, which was established in 1997. The specialized member corporations in different areas are 100% subsidiaries of CHNG. Some of CHNG's core enterprise and member companies also invested in some operating units. The first level of CHNG's core enterprise is its decision-making and management center (i.e., the parent company). Member companies (i.e., one type of subsidiary companies) comprise the second level, and are in charge of the management of operating units as well as making investment decisions. Operating units (i.e., another type of subsidiary companies) constitute the third level. They solely concentrate on business operations instead of making investments.

In periods of a heated economy in the 1980s, CHNG had a fourth level and a fifth level. However, after years of reorganization and improvement, it now has three levels. CHNG uses the equity method to record its investments; it also prepares consolidated financial statements. Member companies manage their investments and have the right to make decisions according to the shareholder's structure. They also implement the management principles of the core enterprise. Previously, the core enterprise considered giving up its close control of its subsidiaries to control through two financial statements (Balance Sheet and Income Statement) and one person (the general manager). Later, they found that this kind of "after the fact" control was highly risky because of the irreversible loss incurred by incorrect decisions. Presently, CHNG maintains both flexibility and necessary control over its subsidiaries.

The parent company and subsidiaries in CHNG are connected by the capital relationship between them. Subsidiary companies are highly autonomous. Meanwhile, the parent company maintains control in three areas:

1. Personnel Control

    - hiring of managers.

    - total annual compensation (salaries plus bonuses).

    - number of positions in each function in each company.

2. Investment Money Control (fixed assets and cash)

    - Investment. Any new investment (> RMB 30 million yuan in large company; > RMB 5 million yuan in small company) must be approved by the parent company.

    - Financing. The government (State Planning Commission) will fund large projects. The parent company also acts as the guarantor of other loans, but sets upper limits. It's difficult to borrow money without the parent company guarantee. China lacks a good credit rating system.

3. Financial Performance Control

    - Each year financial performance targets are set as last year's actual results. Three areas of financial performances are: (a) profit, (b) net worth, and (c) cash flow from operations (after capital charge on capital invested).

    - In general, it is very rare for a company to fail to achieve its financial targets. Typically, a desired ROE is 15%. However, it is lower (10%) for power generation businesses because the Chinese government often sets the price of electricity. Some businesses desired ROE is much higher than 15% (e.g., financial services, trading companies), even as high as 100%.

    - CHNG uses the same planning forms across all of its subsidiary companies. However, some of its accounting systems are different because its subsidiaries are in different businesses.

PERFORMANCE EVALUATION SYSTEM OF CHNG

History of CHNG's Performance Evaluation System

Stage One: Objective System (1989-1991).

In this stage, most of the projects are still in the construction period. Material working units and some other absolute indicators are evaluated under this system. These indicators include Major Product Production Units, Percentage of Completion, Profit, Loans Repayment and Administration Expenses. The major weakness of this system is the rush investment made without evaluating the outcome, and all the subsidiaries were keen on making investments.

Stage Two: Contracting-Based Managerial Responsibility System (1992-1996).

Since 1992, CHNG entered into a contract with the State Finance Department that it would increase the remitted profit 10% every year. The State would compensate CHNG the shortage of profit if not enough, and CHNG could keep part of any extra profit if the actual profit was greater than the contracted profit. CHNG also tied employee compensation to its performance evaluation system. Under this system, CHNG began to focus on profit and divided the authority and responsibility between different units. However, this focus on profit caused harmful battles among units for projects, loans, and scales. Meanwhile, there turned out to be huge differences in the subsidiary companies' increases in assets, debts, or profits. This sparked CHNG's top management to consider how to thoroughly evaluate the efficiency of its management and units instead of only focusing on its short-term profit. As a result, the concept of a Contract-Based Managerial Responsibility System was introduced in 1994. Relative figures reflecting efficiency such as Return on Equity and Increase in Equity were added. In addition, Repayment of Core Enterprise Loans and Profits Remitted were added to the system since they were relevant to the overall profit of CHNG. Later, the top management found the following problems: First, the uniform standards or criteria were not adequate due to the different levels of profitability between different industries. Second, the contracting system did not consider the control and supervision over the process.

Stage Three: Performance Evaluation System (Since 1997).

In order to focus on the efficiency of investments and consider the differences among different industries, CHNG changed the Contracting-Based System to the Performance Evaluation System in 1997. It also adjusted the evaluating indicators to reflect both efficiency and process controls. In this system, Return on Equity, Increase in Equity, and other ratios are used. Meanwhile, in order to reflect the risks of debts and the ability to pay back its debts as well as to change the existing high Debt Ratio in CHNG, it replaced the Increase in Equity with the Return on Total Assets. With the deepening reform, CHNG's power generation subsidiaries became independent and autonomous. The new system also pays attention to the production process. Indicators such as Output, Profit, Loans Repayment, and Securities are used to evaluate the performance in accordance with the character of its operation. For those branches majoring in the management of power corporations, indicators such as Output and Return on Capital are used. In other words, evaluation is conducted separately between power generation subsidiaries, non-power generation subsidiaries, and branches.

In summary, CHNG has three major developing stages of its Control and Performance Evaluation System: First, it transferred from focusing on absolute values to focusing on relative values in order to compare the efficiency levels among subsidiary companies. Second, evaluation standards were changed from the planned figures for each subsidiary company to the average figure of all subsidiary companies in order to minimize the negotiation between both sides of evaluating institutions. Third, it changed the focus from the evaluation of business operations to the evaluation of investors' managerial controls over investments.

Performance evaluation criteria for power generation subsidiary companies (factories):

Starting from 1997, CHNG's parent company has used the following four criteria to evaluate the annual performance of power generation companies: (1) actual vs. planned power production units (in KWH), (2) actual vs. budget profit, (3) actual vs. planned monthly loan repayment and interest payment amount, and (4) factory security.

The power production criterion has a basic score of 40 points. For any 1% deviation between the actual and the planned production, it adds or deducts 1 point up to a maximum of 20 additional or deductible points.

The profit criterion has a basic score of 10 points. For any 1% deviation between the actual and the budget profit, it adds or deducts 0.5 points up to a maximum of 10 additional or deductible points.

The financing criterion has a basic score of 50 points. For any 1% late payment, it deducts 1 point up to a maximum of 20 deductible points.

There are no points assigned to the factory security criterion. However, CHNG will deduct from the subsidiary company's total wages and salaries: (1) RMB 500,000 yuan if an enormous accident occurs; (2) RMB 100,000 yuan if a major accident occurs; and (3) RMB 50,000 yuan for any employee death during working hours.

The maximum, standard, and minimum scores for meeting all four criteria are 150, 100, and 50 points, respectively.

Exhibit 5 shows CHNG's Performance Indicators for its power generation subsidiary companies.

Exhibit 5

Performance Indicators for Power Generation Companies

Company Name: Unit: 1,000RMB

Performance Indicator	1998 Planned	1998 Actual	1999 Forecast	Comments
Profit	xxxxx	xxxx	xxxxx	
Output	xxxxx	xxxxx	xxxxx	
Loan Repayment	xxxx	xxxx	xxxx	
Cost per Unit	xx	xx	xx	

Performance evaluation criteria for non-power generation subsidiary companies:

Since 1997, CHNG's parent company has used the following four criteria to evaluate the annual performance of non-power generation subsidiary companies: (1) actual vs. planned return on stockholders' equity, (2) actual vs. standard return on total assets, (3) actual vs. planned monthly loan repayment and interest payment amount, and (4) actual vs. planned capital charge payment amount.

For the return on stockholders' equity (ROE) criterion, the numerator is the net income after taxes while the denominator is the average stockholders' equity. The basic score of this criterion is 60 points. If the actual ROE is greater than the planned ROE, it adds 1 point for every 0.5% increase up to a maximum of 20 additional points. If the actual ROE is smaller than the planned ROE, it deducts 1.5 points for every 0.5% decrease up to a maximum of 20 deductible points.

For the return on total assets (ROA) criterion, the numerator is the income earnings before interest and taxes (EBIT) while the denominator is the average total assets. The basic score of this criterion is 40 points. The standard ROA considers the bank loan interest rate and CHNG's financial condition. If the actual ROA is greater than the standard ROA, it adds 1 point for every 0.5% increase up to a maximum of 10 addition points. If the actual ROA is smaller than the standard ROA, it deducts 1 point for every 0.5% decrease up to a maximum of 10 deductible points.

The financing criterion has no basic points. Instead, it depends on CHNG's internal loan contracts. For any late payment amount less than 20%, it deducts 5 points; if the late payment amount is greater than 20%, it deducts an additional 1-point for any 20% amount, up to a maximum of 10 deductible points.

For the capital charge payment criterion, every subsidiary company has to pay 8% of the capital amount invested in the parent company by July 1. For any late payment amount less than 20%, it deducts 5 points; if the late payment amount is greater than 20%, it deducts an additional 1-point for any 20% amount, up to a maximum of 10 deductible points.

The maximum, standard, and minimum scores for meeting all four criteria are 130, 100, and 50 points, respectively.

Exhibit 6 presents CHNG's Performance Indicators for its non-power generation subsidiary companies.

———————

Exhibit 6

Performance Indicators for Non-power Companies

Company Name: Unit: 1,000 RMB

Performance Indicator	1998 Planned	1998 Actual	1999 Estimated	Comments
Profit and Taxes				
Net Profit				
Beginning Net Equity				
Ending Net Equity				
Return on Net Equity				
Beginning Total Assets				
Ending Total Assets				
Interest Expense				
Return on Total Assets				
Loan Repayment to core enterprise				
Including: Capital				
Interest				
Balance of Loan				
Profit Remitted				
Including: Last Year Remitted				
This first half year				

Additional Information:

1. Deferred Assets
   Including: Pre-operation costs   RMB
2. Accounts Receivables with more than three years history   RMB
3. Prepaid Expenses   RMB
4. Unrecognized Loss in Assets   RMB
5. Long term investments
   Including those has no return for three consecutive years   RMB
6. Return on Investments   RMB

Notes:

1. Numbers are from the Headquarter's Financial Statement.
2. Unrecognized Losses in Assets include both Current Assets and Fixed Assets.
3. Return from Investments refers to dividend income and the share of earnings recorded under Equity Method.
4. Interest Expense refers to Interest Payable minus Interest Income.

INCENTIVE SYSTEMS

CHNG's total annual subsidiary company bonus amount ties directly to the performance evaluation of the four criteria described in the above section. If a company obtains a performance score of 100 points, the total company bonus amount will be 50% of the total company's wages and salaries. For every performance point over 100 points, it adds 0.5% of the total company's wages and salaries to the bonus amount. On the other hand, for every performance point less than 100 points, it deducts 0.5% of the total company's wages and salaries from the bonus amount. According to the current formula, the maximum bonus amount for a subsidiary company is 65% of the total company's wages and salaries.

The calculation above creates a company-wide bonus pool. The allocation of this bonus pool to individuals depends on the individuals' organization level and their performance ratings. Each organization level is given a number of points. Some examples are 4 points for the high-level managers, 3 points for the middle managers, and 2.3 points for supervisors. Dividing the bonus pool by the points of all the people eligible for bonuses gives a bonus potential per point.

In addition, superiors, peers, and subordinates give performance ratings of their department employees in four performance areas (with weightings shown in parentheses):

Ethics (20%)
Effort (20%)
Capability (20%)
Performance (40%)

The superior's ratings are given the highest weight (50%); peers are given 30% weight; subordinates' ratings are worth 20%.

There is a guideline for calculating each subsidiary company general manager's bonus: (1) For companies doing very well on all four criteria, the general manager's bonus will be 2.5 to 2.8 times greater than the average company employee's bonus amount; (2) For companies meeting all four criteria as planned or in standard amounts, the general manager's bonus will be 2.0 to 2.5 times greater than the average company employee's bonus amount; (3) For companies that have not met the four criteria but still have profit, the general manager's bonus will be 1.5 to 2.0 times of the average company employee's bonus amount; and (4) For companies with no profit, the general manager's bonus should not be greater than the average company employee's bonus amount.

The annual compensation increases for each employee are paid out 65% as increases in monthly salary and 35% as one-time bonus.

The largest bonus paid in 1997 was RMB 30,000 yuan. This is not a large bonus amount, but employees feel comfortable with the bonus system because their jobs are stable while other industries are facing layoffs.

According to Senior Accountant, Huanliang Wang, "The system does not motivate people significantly. The bonus amount is so small. But the performance evaluation system is transparent and fair with the individual employee performance evaluations."

POSITIVE EFFECTS OF THE CHNG'S CONTROL, PERFORMANCE EVALUATION AND INCENTIVE SYSTEM

CHNG's Senior Accountant, Yueguo Liu collected feedback information from top management, and identified the following positive effects of the control system implemented:

1. Performance indicators have influenced the operating behaviors of subsidiary companies. Especially such relative figures as Return on Assets and Return on Equity have helped subsidiary companies to focus more on financial outcome performance and to understand the concept of risk.

2. The objective performance evaluation results showed different performance levels among subsidiary companies. Take the evaluation results of 1997 as an example; four categories exist in non-power generation subsidiary companies. In the first category, the highest score is 106.1. In the last category, the lowest score was only 50. For power generation subsidiary companies, three categories exist with the highest score of 114 and the lowest 99. Performance differences were found although they were not very obvious. For Branches and Offices, the highest score was 121.5 and the lowest, 98.5, in three categories. These numbers help top management to objectively evaluate the performance of different subsidiary companies.

3. The ties between the performance evaluation results and the compensation have encouraged and motivated employees and managers. According to the system, the amount of the total annual bonus pool, which is the resource of the annual bonus of each subsidiary company, is determined by the evaluation criteria. The actual bonus paid to each subsidiary company is decided by the parent company based on the results of each specific company's performance evaluation. At the same time, employees and managers' bonus are also determined by the evaluation results. This incentive system motivates employees and pushes subsidiary companies' business forward. The only constraint is that any increase in the total compensation amount should not exceed any increase in the subsidiary company's profit.

4. The performance evaluation system provides an objective standard to evaluate subsidiary company managers. According to the evaluating system for managers, CHNG has four categories of ratings: Ethics, Effort, Capability, and Performance to evaluate and appoint managers. The Performance criterion has the biggest weighting percentage. The results of a specific subsidiary company's performance evaluation are also an important criterion for assessing the competence of its managers.

5. The overall control, performance evaluation and incentive system improved CHNG's managing style and system for the whole group. CHNG's inner management system is established on the basis of investment capital control. The evaluation results are the basis of exercising the shareholders' rights of making decisions, selecting managers, and enjoying the earnings. The set of evaluating criteria is to standardize the entire companies' behaviors. In order to make evaluating criteria better reflect the subsidiary companies' operating conditions, CHNG's top management also decided to standardize and improve all subsidiary companies' financial management and assets management. For example, Equity Method is used in its long-term investments; interest payable is recorded as Financial Expenses; estimated or unrealized gains or losses should not be included in a subsidiary company's Income Statement as realized profits or losses; and bad debt expenses must be recognized.

REQUIRED:

1. Briefly describe the China Huaneng Group.

2. Describe and evaluate strengths and weaknesses of CHNG's Control of Subsidiaries.

3. Describe and evaluate strengths and weaknesses of CHNG's current Performance Evaluation System.

4. Describe and evaluate strengths and weaknesses of CHNG's current Incentive System.

5. What changes, if any, would you propose with respect to CHNG's existing: (1) Control of Subsidiaries, (2) Performance Evaluation System, and (3) Incentive System? For each change that you propose, explain what problem it is designed to resolve.

USING SHAREHOLDER VALUE TO EVALUATE STRATEGIC CHOICES

Financial metrics is a realistic way for companies to measure value.

By Nick Fera

Creating shareholder wealth or value has become the mantra for most corporate boards, especially in the United States. Yet as recently as the mid-1980s, the idea of "shareholder value" or "shareholder wealth" was not an overwhelmingly accepted principle. But as academics began to teach the principle in business schools around the world, such noted authorities as Professor Alfred Rappaport of Northwestern University's J. L. Kellogg Graduate School of Management, author of *Creating Shareholder Value*,[1] began to apply it to corporate mergers and acquisitions in the 1980s. Shareholder value, or free cash flow analysis, became the measurement standard for the 1980s and into the 1990s. Given today's increased demand for international capital returns, as well as the proliferation of private baby boomer pension funds in the United States, investors have imposed new stringency in their vigil against corporate wealth destruction. Even the brightest stars are not immune to the pressure of pension funds or Wall Street. Witness the pressure that CALPERS (the state of California's teachers' retirement funds) placed on Michael Eisner at Walt Disney Co. despite Eisner's laudable success in Increasing Disney's market value from $5 billion to more than $42 billion during his first 10 years in office. During a 10-year period from January 1986 to December 1996, Disney's stock price grew at a cumulative annual growth rate of more than 21%, while the S&P 500 index has returned approximately 15%. Historical performances are not always enough; investors continue to ask for more.

Measuring performance no longer can be left to the traditional accounting department's calculations of earnings per share (EPS) or return on equity (ROE), as these accrual-based accounting measures aren't always useful indicators of future growth or performance. Thus, it is necessary to understand and adopt measurement techniques that will help make decisions while driving increasing profitability. One of the economic measurement techniques that can be used is free cash flow analysis or Shareholder Value Analysis (SVA).

SHAREHOLDER VALUE ANALYSIS

Because managers began to realize that businesses needed a more realistic means of assessing their value than accrual-based accounting standards offered, such respected academics as Professor Rappaport sought to develop sophisticated economic models for strategic evaluations. As a result, shareholder value analysis was conceived. SVA works by explicitly measuring the economic impact of each strategy on the value of a business. Any strategic decision, regardless of whether it involves internal or external investment, should be evaluated. Examples of such strategic decision-making situations include mergers and acquisitions, joint ventures, divestitures, new product development (R&D), and capital expenditures (major plant and equipment investments).

The actual measurement of shareholder value combines three main factors: 1) cash flow, 2) cash as measured over a given period of time (value growth duration), and 3) risk, otherwise known as the cost of capital. (See Fig. 1.) With a basic understanding of

---

[1] Alfred Rappaport, *Creating Shareholder Value: The New Standard for Business Performance*, New York: The Free Press, 1986.

these three components, you are well on your way to valuing a business or entity. Next, let's discuss the difference between corporate value and shareholder value.

CREATING VALUE

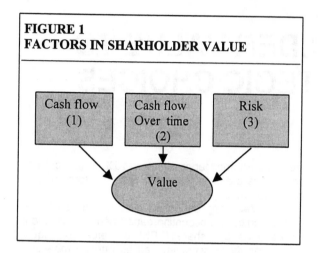

FIGURE 1
FACTORS IN SHARHOLDER VALUE

Corporate value is equal to the net present value of all future cash flows to all investor types, including both debt and equity holders. Shareholder value is the corporate value minus all future claims to cash flow (debt) before equity holders are paid. Future claims typically include both short-and long-term debt, capital lease obligations, underfunded pensions, and other claims such as contingent liabilities—lawsuits brought against the company. (See Fig. 2.) Another way to define shareholder value is to say that it is equal to the net funds a company generates that shareholders could receive in the form of a cash distribution, such as a dividend.

Be careful not to confuse this figure with the actual dividend a company pays. A company's dividend policy has little or nothing to do with the actual cash the company generates. Look at the high growth of businesses such as computer software or biotechnology. Few pay dividends because they have strategic opportunities to reinvest cash flows and earn the higher returns investors desire.

Generally, it's easy to determine the market value of future obligations or debt. In most cases, it's the accumulation of several debt instruments. To obtain the market value of these financial instruments, use the yield to maturity to calculate the *market value* of each debt instrument. Avoid adding the face value of each debt or bond issue. The question to ask is, "If this obligation were to be paid in full today, how much would the lender need to retire it?"

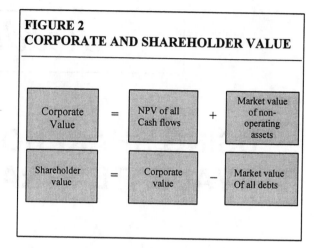

FIGURE 2
CORPORATE AND SHAREHOLDER VALUE

MEASURING CASH FLOW

After determining corporate and shareholder value, the next step is to measure cash flow. The most tangible measurement of cash flow (also referred to as operating cash flow or free cash flow) can be calculated as shown in Table 1.

Notice that the calculation focuses on the relationship between operating cash income and expenses, specifically by using operating cash taxes rather than the provision for income taxes. It accounts for the investments made on the balance sheet. Many companies measure cash flow by looking at net operating profit after taxes (NOPAT), but it tells only part of the story. Investments to grow the business, either by expansion of the plant and facilities or with working capital policies such as extending the receivable period from net 30 to net 60 days, have a significant impact on the capital employed. Remember: Shareholders are looking for returns on their capital invested in business growth, which requires well-planned capital expenditures. Failure to account for the investment makes for a crucial mistake in the evaluation of strategic alternatives.

CALCULATING CASH FLOWS

The calculation of cash flow illustrates a high level of performance in an organization and produces a result that approximates the net cash of a company. In effect, these funds are a potential dividend to shareholders because they reflect optimal use of shareholder monies for ongoing growth. That is why dividend policy and free cash flow are not synonymous. Few companies base their dividend payout on net cash flow, while others are justified in generating free cash flow, without paying dividends.

To forecast cash flow, most companies require a more detailed formula, as presented in Table

TABLE 1
MEASURING CASH FLOW

	Formula	Example	Value Drivers
	Sales	$1,000	Sales growth (Sg)
Less	Operating expenses	–$ 600	Margin (P)
Equals	Pre-tax profit	$ 400	
Less	Cash taxes	–$ 100	Tax rate (T)
Equals	Net operating profit after taxes (NOPAT)	$ 300	
Add	Depreciation expense	$ 75	
Less	Fixed capital investment	–$ 125	Fixed capital investment (F)
Less	Incremental working capital investment	–$ 50	Working capital investment (W)
Equals	Operating cash flow (free cash flow)	$ 250	

1. In most cases, sales growth tells very little about actual sales activity, so companies use metrics such as price, volume, GNP, and other micro or macroeconomic factors to forecast revenues and costs more realistically. This calculation usually is conducted at a strategic business unit level and then consolidated for corporate purposes. The key is to plan accurately at the appropriate level of business activity (business unit, value chain, or some other distinction).

Sales or market growth estimations can be achieved many different ways. Predicting price and volume, for instance, provides for a more manageable metric that can be evaluated readily and used later for compensation purposes. In other words, sales growth is a "*value driver.*" But what *drives* the value drivers? Herein typically lies the metric operational professionals can get their hands on. Planning and forecasting can become a real *operating activity rather than a boardroom exercise.*

CASH FLOW OVER TIME

Once cash flow has been defined, the next step is to determine the length of the forecast period. The definition of cash flow over time or value growth duration is the length of time expected for a company to invest in opportunities that will yield internal rates of return (IRR) above their weighted average cost of capital (WACC). This premise is the core of value creation—performing above expectations for a sustainable period of time.

Management usually plans for cycles of three to five years. If this is the case and if the cash flows are discounted over a period of time, the valuation probably will be inaccurate as it does not allow for fluctuations in cash flow throughout the requisite growth period. To determine the appropriate length of the forecast period (or the value growth duration), consider several factors.

One is Michael Porter's work on the competitive structure and five forces of industries (see Fig. 3). Porter says that management's responsibility is to map the company and its competition according to several factors. Some areas to consider are distribution channels, established brand names, and research and development. Take the pharmaceutical industry, for instance. It has a relatively long value growth duration because of patented products, proven processes, and research and development investment that raise the barriers of entry.

Also, read Alfred Rappaport's discussion of the use of public information to assess the market's expectation for a company's value growth duration.[2] He suggests gathering forecasting information on a particular company as well as identifying competitors. He also advises managers to employ the researched information and forecast the cash flows, as discussed previously. But rather than changing any value driver assumptions, change only the length of the forecast until the present value of the cash flows less debt equals the market value of your company. Surprisingly, most companies in a given industry tend to fall within a certain range; thus, the market is suggesting an implied value growth duration. These "market signals" are helpful for starting an internal analysis and discussion.

[2] Alfred Rappaport, "Stock Market Signals to Managers." Harvard Business Review, November-December 1987, pp. 57-62.

RESIDUAL VALUE

Once you have determined the value growth duration, you must address the value of the cash flows beyond the current period. This determination is called the terminal or residual value. Assume that, after the forecast period, new investments (fixed and working capital) will yield returns equal to the cost of capital. In other words, the internal rate of return is equal to the weighted average cost of capital. Therefore, the net present value of cash flows from new or incremental investments beyond the value growth duration will be equal to zero. The only cash flow left to value in the residual period is the preinvestment cash flow, or NOPAT (see Table 1). Note that depreciation is *not* included because it is viewed as a proxy for reinvestment. Given that the cash flows are valued infinitely, the business probably would not continue to generate the same level of cash flow if the plant, equipment, or other physical assets were allowed to deteriorate fully. In fact, some companies recognize a higher level of "maintenance" spending and will adjust the cash flow in the residual period to reflect higher replacement costs.

TERMINAL VALUE

At this point, it is necessary to discuss some assumptions of terminal value. The net present value of the residual cash flows is equal to an infinite stream of cash flow (as measured by NOPAT) discounted back at the WACC. Mathematically, this is NOPAT at the end of the value growth duration divided by the WACC. Once this calculation is complete, it is necessary to discount the value back to the current period. The formula is presented in Table 2 (assuming a five-year value growth duration and 12% WACC).

DEFINING RISK

The last component of determining the value of an entity is deciding on the overall risk. The risk of a company usually is measured with WACC. The approach assumes there is some mixture of debt and equity that is financing the company. The cost of debt is measured as the after-tax cost, that is, the cost accounting for the tax deductibility of interest payments. The marginal cost of debt is not necessarily the average coupon rate on various debt instruments. Instead, it is the rate for which banks will lend the company an incremental dollar.

The cost of equity is somewhat more complex. If companies use the Capital Asset Pricing Model approach developed by economists Sharpe, Lintner, and Treynor in the mid-1960s, the cost of equity has two basic components: a risk-free return re-

quired by investors and a premium for investing in equities that are of higher risk. The risk-free rate is the treasury rate on 30-year U.S. government bonds. This standard generally is used because these bonds typically are seen as delivering the most risk-free, long-term returns investors can earn. The second compo-

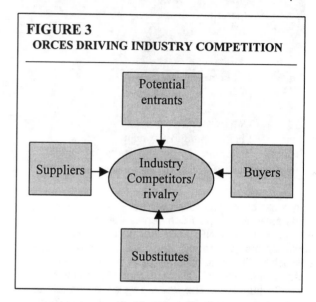

FIGURE 3
ORCES DRIVING INDUSTRY COMPETITION

nent is the premium for investing in something that is of higher risk than the U.S. government. This element is called the market risk premium (MRP itself and a multiplier, called beta, for investments that are more or less risky than the market portfolio.

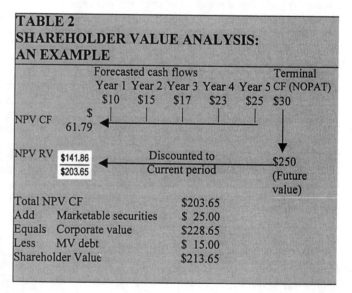

TABLE 2
SHAREHOLDER VALUE ANALYSIS:
AN EXAMPLE

	Forecasted cash flows					Terminal
	Year 1	Year 2	Year 3	Year 4	Year 5	CF (NOPAT)
	$10	$15	$17	$23	$25	$30
NPV CF	$61.79					
NPV RV	$141.86	Discounted to			$250	
	$203.65	Current period			(Future value)	

Total NPV CF		$203.65
Add	Marketable securities	$ 25.00
Equals	Corporate value	$228.65
Less	MV debt	$ 15.00
Shareholder Value		$213.65

MARKET RISK PREMIUM

The market risk premium is calculated and published by sources such as Ibbotson Associates in its annual SBBI (Stocks, Bonds, Bills, and Inflation). Historically, the premium for holding a portfolio of equities, as opposed to investing in a risk-free instrument, is between 6% and 7%, depending on whether you use the arithmetic or geometric average.

Beta is a measure of the relative riskiness of an individual company or portfolio as compared with the market. Thus a beta of 1.0 correlates exactly with market returns. Beta is measured by comparing the returns of an individual security or portfolio with those of the market. Sources of beta estimates include Merrill Lynch, ValueLine, and Alcar.

There is another way to measure the MRP that is consistent with a forecasting approach. This tack uses estimates of the expected return on the market for the next year. Each month Merrill Lynch publishes a 12-month expected return on the market (S&P 500). Using this forecast, you can determine the expected MRP by subtracting the current risk-free rate, as measured by 30-year treasuries, from the current forecast of market returns. As of October 1, 1997, Merrill Lynch's forecast of market returns was 10.9%, while the risk-free rate is currently 6.38%. As a result, the expected market risk premium is 4.52%. Some companies prefer to use the ex-ante approach because it matches the *forecasting* of cash flows with the *forecasting* of expected returns.

Putting all the components of the cost of equity equation together yields the following formula:
Cost of Equity = Risk-free rate + Beta * (Market Risk Premium) or, $K_e = R_f + ß * (MRP)$

Once you have calculated the cost of equity and the cost of debt, you may use the WACC approach to combine both costs (debt and equity). In calculating the WACC, use the market values of debts and equity, not the book values, because the market costs of each source of financing are being measured. The equation is as follows:
WACC (K_c) = % of Debt * [Cost of Debt (K_d)] + % of Equity * [Cost of Equity (K_e)]

Let's look at an example involving a manufacturing company using risk estimation:

A U.S. manufacturing company is publicly traded and has a market capitalization of $550 million. Its outstanding debt totals $250 million at a marginal borrowing rate of 8.5% (assume this is the market value of debt and includes all obligations of the company). The current risk-free rate is 7%, the expected return on the market is 12%, the beta of this company has been published as .90, and its marginal tax rate is 28%. What is the weighted average cost of capital (WACC)?

Measurement Methodologies:
1. Economic Principles
   Shareholder Value Analysis
   (SVA)—also known as Discounted Cash Flow analysis (DCF) or Net Present Value (NPV)

   - Evaluates cash inflows to cash outflows on a risk-adjusted basis

   - Most widely accepted approach to business evaluation

   Economic Value Analysis (EVA)

   - Primarily used as a performance measurement tool to calculate period-by-period performance

   - Helps an organization to focus on value creation or increased cash flow

   - Measuring the change in EVA also may be an effective financial measurement tool

   Cash Flow Return on Investment (CFROI)

   - Derived from market data to determine cash flow growth and the overall discount rate

   - Helps an organization to focus on value creation or increased cash flow

   - Seen as a complex financial measurement device

2. Accounting Principles
   Return on Capital (ROC)
   Return on Invested Capital (ROIC)
   Return on Equity (ROE)
   Earnings per Share (EPS)

MRP	=	12 – 7	= 5%
K_e	=	.07 + .9(.05)	= 11.5%
K_d	=	.085 * (1 – 28)	= 6.12% (after tax)
WACC	=	(250/800) * .0612 +	(550/800) * .115 = 9.8%

FROM THE BOARDROOM
TO THE SHOP FLOOR

Once you have established the methodology, take it out of the boardroom (as a planning exercise), and implement it at all levels, including the shop floor (or any manufacturing or operating activity). The importance of moving the analysis out of the boardroom and into regular practice is that managers and shareholders will have the same economic interests. If managers are compensated on accrual-based accounting measures, they may optimize their own interest when there is a conflict between cash flow and accrual accounting. But if you align the interest and performance measurement of all managers to be the same, both are optimized.

Moving the methodology to the shop floor may pose a challenge. Not only is it more difficult to identify key value drivers on the shop floor (such as production yield, waste, inventory management), but there also is an important educational component. Not all managers have been introduced to the concepts and methodologies of financial metrics. Many still are entrenched with the simpler accrual-based accounting measures. Yet once key drivers are identified and their relative impact on value is measured, managers relate to the results.

ONGOING MAINTENANCE AND
PERFORMANCE MEASUREMENT

Once the methodology is in place, the final challenge is to put it into practice every year. What adds to the complexity of the implementation is the ability to monitor performance in a timely manner due to the multitude of manual and multiple systems currently in place to do the job. Many companies implement and attempt to monitor their performance with the use of disconnected spreadsheet technology. Beyond all the difficulties of performing rigorous economic analysis in a spreadsheet (with factual integrity and documentation leading the pack), the use of spreadsheets can create pockets of information that are disjointed from the rest of the organization. These pockets of information make it difficult to monitor performance, test new scenarios regularly, and make new, informed decisions on a timely basis.

Fortunately, the recent development of new technologies that interface seemlessly with each other is making it easier to gather data quickly and spend the majority of analytical time on planning, testing, and choosing new strategic alternatives. Thus, the planning process is changing from an annual event generally found on the bookshelf to a regularly used strategic exercise that becomes a living document, enabling companies to manage their business by making value-based strategic choices in our ever-evolving environment.

BEYOND THE NUMBERS

By Peter J. Leitner

To help financial managers in this endeavor, we developed a Business Assessment Model, that should improve the quality of management decisions that depend on financial analyses. The model frames financial decisions in the context of the entire business. The foundation of the model includes the core business, market, and competition, which gauge a company's ability to *generate revenue*. The second tier contains the operations and performance elements, which measure a company's ability to *create value* for customers and stockholders, respectively. Finally, there is the management element, which evaluates a company's *leadership quality*.

It is the interrelationships of the elements that strongly influence a business's overall prospects and particularly its resilience during turbulent periods. The model emphasizes the assessment of revenue because it is the least controllable item that an analyst evaluates. Hence, the reasons why the Business Assessment Model improves decision making become clear:

- First, management accountants and financial analysts often are closer to the data source than executive management, so they usually know which information is reliable and which is not.
- Second, it is common for analysts to rely on someone else's work, which, if flawed, can taint the financial analysis that is used for management decisions.
- Third, there is a difference between precision and accuracy, which can be shaded by the robust data and sophisticated quantitative methods that are at the analyst's disposal. An analyst can be quite precise in method yet very wrong in outcome.

The Business Assessment Model intentionally de-emphasizes quantitative methods because most analysts, who already are steeped in data and formulas, need a framework for sifting and sorting through information not another algorithm. Moreover, given that financial statements simply translate decisions and actions into accounting language, analysts must avoid the common pitfall of failing to see beyond the numbers. The Business Assessment Model should enhance the ability of the management accountant or financial analyst to interpret the results of a business assessment accurately.

UNDERSTANDING THE PROCESS

The analyst can gather the data required for the six elements by posing the questions found in Table 1 about a business that is under review.

CORE BUSINESS; "What is their business?" The answer to this question conveys the essence of a company. Indeed, a company that exhibits such clarity of purpose, which is part of a strong mission statement, tends to consistently outperform its competitors because its resources are concentrated on a relatively narrow area for maximum effect. [1]

An often-used illustration involves a company whose business could be defined as either railroads or transportation. Although both are correct, the term transportation conveys what the company actually does, which is moving certain types of cargo from one place to another via steel rails for a particular type of customer. The company's expertise, therefore, is transportation. But this fact does not imply that it should diversify into building cargo ships, which is a different business altogether, nor does it suggest that the company limit itself to steel rails because innovation, like interstate highways and airplanes, eventually will erode too narrow a focus. The nuance here is subtle, but it communicates the focal point of management's attention.

---

[1] James B. Hobbs, *Corporate Staying Power*, D. C. Heath & Co., 1987, p. 22.

TABLE 1
INPUT FOR BUSINESS ASSESSMENT MODEL

Key Elements	Input Requirements
Core Business	"What is their business?"
Market	"Who is the customer?"
	"What customer needs do they satisfy"
	"What are the macro drivers of demand?"
Competition	"What are the key opportunities and risks?
Operations	"How do they make money?"
Performance	"What is the revenue growth rate?"
	"What is the contribution margin?"
	"What is the return on capital?"
Management	"Are they up to the task at hand?"

MARKET: "Who is the customer?" "What customer needs do they satisfy?" "What are the macro drivers of demand?" These questions help the analyst understand how a business generates revenue and from whom. Without this knowledge, any budgeting, financing, or strategic analysis will be of limited value because the analyst cannot be confident that sales will meet expectations. "Who is the customer?" addresses three issues.

1. Who, exactly, is purchasing a company's products or services? The answer to this question should be as specific as possible. Moreover, the analyst should differentiate between actual customers— those who are buying the products or services— and potential customers the company is targeting; they may not be one in the same.

2. What causes the customer to make a purchase? Typical variables to be considered include impulse purchases vs. those that are planned; luxury items vs. necessities; and whether or not the product or service is a complement to another that has a significant influence on demand. An analyst also should consider how price changes influence revenue (price elasticity of demand). Simply knowing that revenue is generated via direct sales, telemarketing, or advertising is insufficient.

3. Are there multiple customer levels to account for in a purchase decision? In other words, who really makes the purchase decision for a given product or service? Consider the average hospital, which has at least three "customers" who are parties to each transaction: the patient who receives the services, the physician who admits the patient and provides the medical care, and the HMO or insurance company that pays the bill. In order to gen-

erate revenue, hospitals must market themselves to everyone who participates in the decision to purchase hospital services.

Asking "*What customer needs do they satisfy?*" is the analyst's attempt to specify the core benefit the product or service provides. The answer to this question gives the solution to the fundamental need that must be satisfied to create demand; as such, it must be broad enough to convey the essence of customers' needs. The management accountant or financial analyst must understand this issue because even subtle changes in customers' needs will affect revenue.

To illustrate the foregoing, we could say that automobile manufacturers do not really sell cars but rather freedom and mobility. To test the validity of this benefit, consider what you don't have when your car's engine won't start. You don't have either freedom or mobility (assuming, of course, that adequate substitutes are unavailable). Therefore, you could conclude that future revenues for the automobile industry are contingent upon satisfying the need for freedom and mobility by producing reliable cars.

Finally, "*What are the macro demand drivers?*" focuses on external forces that could have a material effect on revenue. Examples of such demand drivers include:

*   Government regulations,
*   Interest rates and raw material prices,
*   Weather conditions,
*   Demographics, and
*   General economic conditions.

In looking at these variables, the analyst considers the external factors that create uncertainty in the revenue line as well as how the company can hedge against these risks, if at all.

COMPETITION: "What are the key opportunities and risks?" The model also allows the analyst to expose the strengths and vulnerabilities of a company and its competitors. It is not enough to rank competing firms by sales dollars, market share, geographic coverage, or some other measure. So the model integrates the opportunities and risks of a given competitive environment into a matrix that presents the company vis-à-vis its major competitors in terms of the factors that influence purchase decisions. By identifying the nature of each factor for each company and then arranging the information in the matrix, the analyst can evaluate each one individually and in relation to its peer group.

TABLE 2
COMPETITOR MATRIX: AUTOMOBILE MANUFACTURERS

	Competitor A	Competitor B	Competitor C	ACME
PRODUCT (Reliability; 10 is highest)	10	6	3	7
PRICE (% of mean)	85%	100%	125%	100%
PLACE (Dealerships/1mm population)	35	15	50	20
PROMOTION (Television advertising budget)	**$60 million**	**$85 million**	**$150 million**	**$90 million**
5-Year Growth Rate – Unit Sales	**20%**	**5%**	**2%**	**7%**

In the process of completing the matrix, the analyst should gain two critical insights. First, the company's vulnerabilities become quite obvious (and are, incidentally, synonymous with advantages for the competition). Second, each competitor's weaknesses also become evident, which provides opportunities for the company under review to exploit as competitive advantages. The following hypothetical example illustrates this point.

An automobile manufacturer, ACME Motors, is considering building a new plant that would be funded by cash reserves and the issuance of 30-year bonds. The capital investment analysis indicates that it should proceed, but how confident would you be in the revenue forecast? Demand for automobiles probably will continue, but it is uncertain from whom they will be purchased. To address this problem, measure ACME's prospects in relation to those of its three primary competitors. Assume that all companies produce only one model.

The answer is shown in Table 2, a competitor matrix that highlights ACME's areas of opportunity and risk. Variables that drive consumer decisions in automobile purchases are shown in column 1 and are based on a marketing mix[2] that isolates them. The information in the matrix suggests several things about ACME's revenue prospects. First, market research indicates that the decision to buy a new car is influenced strongly by four factors: reliability, relative price, access to dealerships, and advertising on network television. Second, of ACME's three competitors:

- Competitor A is experiencing the fastest growth because of excellent product reliability, value

---

[2] Robert D. Hisrich and Michael P. Peters, *Marketing Decisions for New and Mature Products: Planning Development, and Control*, Charles E. Merrill Publishing Co, 1984, p. 77.

pricing, broad distribution, and adequate advertising.
- Competitor B resembles ACME Motors most closely, at least from the consumer's perspective. Only marginal differences exist in product reliability, dealership access, ad spending, and unit sales growth.
- Competitor C appears to be surviving because of huge advertising spending and a reputation that once deserved premium pricing, but the stagnant growth rate and horrible product reliability clearly indicate a weakened competitor.

To be confident that the revenue and cash flows will materialize to sustain the new plant, ACME needs to verify that it can attain and sustain sufficient market share. Initiatives that offer such confidence include commitments from management to improve product reliability, maintain or reduce prices, increase the number of dealerships, and maintain media spending on network TV advertising.

If management doesn't commit to these initiatives, the long-term revenue forecast, from which net present value and internal rate of return analyses are derived to justify the new plant, should be reconsidered.

OPERATIONS: "How do they make money?" With this question, the analyst is identifying where in the company's operating cycle value is actually created by delivering to the customer a core benefit or solution to a fundamental need. In this context, value is defined from the customer's perspective. In addition, the analyst can understand any business operation as a system in which resources, such as cash, raw material, information and other assets, are converted and

TABLE 3
VALUE-ADDED OPERATIONS ANALYSIS—ADVERTISING AGENCY

Time	t	t + 1	t + 2	t + 3	t + 4	t + 5	t + 6
Steps in the operating cycle (benefits for clients)	Agency wins competition for a new account	Advertising plan is developed	Market research is planned and conducted	Advertising ideas are created	Ad is filmed and edited	Media time purchased from TV networks for $10,000,000	Submit and collect invoice (15% of media time purchased)
Responsible department*	Account team	Account team	Research department	Creative directors	Production team	Media department	Accounting department
Value created for clients (0 to 5)	0	3	2	5	3	1	0

*For simplicity, the cells in the "Responsible Department" now are limited to one department in each step. But in any company, most of the steps in an operating cycle require input from other departments as well, so the analyst should differentiate between departments having primary or secondary responsibility for each step.

transformed from inputs to outputs.[3] The operations element of the model is important for two reasons:

1. Knowing exactly where value is created (what the customer really pays for) is like knowing which goose, among all others, lays the golden eggs. With this information, it becomes possible to set priorities regarding the allocation of capital and other scarce resources.
2. The vibrancy of the value-creating area indicates a company's future prospects. For example, a high rework rate in a manufacturer or a high turnover rate of creative personnel in an advertising agency may indicate major problems for those companies in the near future.

But classifying each part of a business as either "value added" or "support" does not suggest that support functions (or the people in them) are superfluous. To the contrary, they permit the value-added functions to operate smoothly and efficiently.

Here's one approach to determining where in its operating cycle a company creates value:

- Specify the "...customer needs...they satisfy..." and the benefits they deliver as prescribed in the market assessment.

- Identify the major steps involved in the operation.

- Document the critical resources required for each step in the process, such as labor, raw material, and information. Then,

[3] Roger G. Schroeder, *Operations Management: Decision Making in the Operations Function*, third edition, McGraw-Hill, Inc., 1989, p. 195.

- Assign numerical values to each step to signify the "value added" created for the customer.

Let's use an advertising agency, the classic example of a service firm that relies on "intellectual capital" to create value for its clients, as an illustration. After determining the customer needs that the agency satisfies (defined here as enhancing demand for the client's products or services), we could assemble the information in Table 3.

From this analysis, it is clear that the greatest value added for the client is in developing advertising ideas, such as writing a memorable phase or developing a powerful visual image. Among all of the agency functions, it is what the client pays for. This fact also is reflected in the remuneration paid to senior creative directors, who usually are the best-paid employees in an advertising agency. Therefore, an agency's greatest source of value is in this department.

PERFORMANCE: "What is the revenue growth rate? "What is the contribution (or gross) margin?" "What is the return on capital?" When addressing these questions, the analyst finally has a need to sharpen his or her pencil. But this element of the model is limited to three measures: growth in sales, contribution (or gross) margin, and return on capital. I'm not denying the importance of other ratios and financial measures, especially cash flow analysis, but I'm emphasizing three measures that:

- Are appropriate for assessing any business regardless of its industry or maturity.

- Focus on the economic essence of a company and reveal either fundamental problems or earning power that otherwise may not be obvious; and

- Are not overly complex or time-consuming to calculate.

A caveat: All financial ratios have limitations, especially the ease of manipulation and the reliability of the financial statements on which they are based.

Sales growth: The sales growth ratio is the clearest measure of the demand for a company's products or services especially over a period of years and in comparison to competing firms. Sales growth is calculated as:

Sales Growth
$$\frac{S_t - S_{t-1}}{S_{t-1}}$$

Where: S = Sales
t = Current Period
T − 1 = Previous Period

Adjustments the analyst will find useful include comparing the growth of unit sales to that of dollar sales and factoring out the effects of acquisitions and divestitures on sales. Red flags that warrant closer inspection include:

- Stagnant or falling sales, especially when competitors report growing or stable sales, respectively;

- Divergence in the trend lines of unit sales and dollar sales; and

- Sales growth attributable to acquisitions, especially if the revenue of the base business or acquired companies is actually contracting.

Contribution or gross margin: The contribution or gross margin indicates the franchise power, or brand equity, of a given enterprise. A margin in excess of 50% often suggests the presence of proprietary advantages (such as valuable patents, trademarks, or an extraordinary consumer preference for the goods or services the firm sells). Such advantages usually can support a premium pricing strategy. The formulas for these ratios are:

Contribution or Gross Margin

Contribution Margin:	$\dfrac{S - VC}{S}$	
Gross Margin:	$\dfrac{S - CGS}{S}$	
Where:	S =	Sales
	VC =	Variable Costs
	CGS =	Cost of Goods Sold

Margins that either remain constant or increase (especially when compared in relation to a competitor's) are favorable signs. Moreover, the safety, high contribution or gross margins also can be a quantifiable competitive advantage.

Of these two measures, preference should be given to the contribution margin because it highlights the company's ability to cover fixed charges, which becomes particularly important in turnarounds, startups, and highly-leveraged firms. When variable cost information is not readily available, however, or when a company has few variable costs (as is often the case in information technology enterprises), the gross margin ratio is an excellent substitute.

Red flags indicating a need for further analysis include:

- Income that increases at a slower rate than sales or that decreases at a faster rate than sales:

- Margins that vary more than 5% (+/−) each year over three or more years; and

- Margins that, while at least satisfactory, are the result of relatively few products or services in a company's portfolio (concentration risk). But concentration risk can be mitigated by proprietary advantages such as intellectual property or franchise power.

Return on capital: Return on capital (ROC) conveys a company's overall financial well-being by indicating how efficiently the company uses all of the capital with which management is entrusted to generate a profit, regardless of whether the capital is obtained from stockholders or lenders. Furthermore, as stated in the seminal book, *Graham & Dodd's Security Analysis,* "The most comprehensive gauge of success of an enterprise is the percentage earned on invested capital."[4] It becomes clear that a company must earn an acceptable return on capital, or its prospects will dim quickly. The formula for this ratio is:

Return on Capital

---

[4] Sydney Cottle, Roger F. Murray, and Frank E. Block, Graham & Dodd's Security Analysis, fifth edition, McGraw-Hill, Inc., 1988, p. 351.

$$\frac{EBIT}{Capital}$$

Where EBIT = Earnings Before Interest and Taxes ("operating profit")

Capital = (Equity + LTD + Deferred Taxes)

Equity = (Preferred Stock + Common Stock + Retained Earnings – Treasury Stock)

LTD = (Long-Term Debt + Current Maturities of Long-Term Debt)

Note: Short-term debt, such as commercial paper, should be included in LTD if used to finance long-term assets; any mezzanine securities should also be included in LTD.

Generally speaking, a high ROC minimizes a company's dependence on external capital sources, giving it more financial flexibility. It is essential, however, to compare a company's ROC with that of its competitors in the industry, as well as the industry average ROC with that of other industries, to assess performance fully. The maturity of both the company and its industry, as well as the capital-intensive nature of the industry, are relevant. Of greatest importance for our purposes, however, is that the ROC ratio permits the analyst to determine the real return on capital, or whether or not the company is creating or destroying corporate value. By comparing the firm's ROC with the weighted average cost of capital (WACC), which includes the cost of equity as well as the interest costs of debt, the universal goal of creating shareholder value can be measured unequivocally. This relationship is expressed as:

If ROC > WACC, then value is created.
If ROC < WACC, then value is destroyed.

To quantify the amount of value a company creates or destroys in a given year in dollar terms, consider the financial information about a hypothetical company shown in Table 4. If the ROC had been 4.6% lower than the WACC, then $4,600,000 of value would have been destroyed. A company that consistently earns less than its cost of capital is on a slippery slope that only becomes more so with the passage of time because it cannot sustain such an imbalance indefinitely. At some point, the capital markets, both

TABLE 4
REAL RETURN ON CAPITAL

If:	EBIT	= $15,000,000 and
	Capital	= ($40,000,000$_{Equity}$ + $60,000,000$_{Debt}$) = $100,000,000 and
	WACC*	= 10.4%
And:	ROC	= EBIT/Capital
		= $15,000,000/$100,000,000
		= 15%
		= Return on Capital
Then:	ROC – WACC	= 15.0% – 10.4%
		4.6%
		Real Return on Capital
Therefore:	Value Created	= Real Return X Capital
		= 4.6% × $100,000,000
		= $4,600,000
		= Value Created

*In this example, the WACC is calculated as follows:

	Capital	Weight	Cost	WACC
Equity (market value)	$ 40,000,000	0.4	18.0%	7.2%
Debt (after-tax cost)	$ 60,000,000	0.6	5.4%	3.2%
Total	$100,000,000	1.0		10.4%

public and private, will become less than enthusiastic about investing additional funds. Also, customers will gravitate toward competitors and if the company is publicly owned, hostile suitors will emerge. If not rejuvenated soon, the company is likely to complete its slide into insolvency.

MANAGEMENT: "Are they up to the task at hand?"
Evaluating management is the least precise and most difficult element of any business assessment, yet it is the most critical Professional investors, particularly those who focus on illiquid, high-risk venture capital and leveraged buyout transactions, often agree that management quality is the best predictor of business success or failure. The quality of management and leadership is important because business is fraught with risk. Markets change direction quickly, and these changes often are fueled by new technology and fierce foreign and domestic competition. As such, a company's prospects often are dependent on management's ability to navigate through turbulent and tumultuous times.

To the extent that individual businesses are unique in terms of industry, scale, maturity, historical performance, and specific challenges and opportunities, so, too, are managerial requirements. The skills, abilities, and personalities of the management team must complement the business. True excellence in leadership often can be found in the corporate culture, especially in the manner in which young talent is selected and developed and in the ways management's successors are groomed.

Here are four areas that should be stressed, given the importance of evaluating management.

- "Can the managers demonstrate long-term success during both favorable and unfavorable market conditions?"
- "Do they have the capacity, by means of formal education, intelligence, business acumen, and both physical and emotional well-being, to grow with the business as it grows? If not, do they recruit and empower talented and capable lieutenants?"
- "Are they truly hardworking and appropriately motivated to lead?"
- "Is there any indication that they are less than completely honest and ethical?"

A deficiency in even one of these areas, however minor it may seem, must be considered serious. Although no one is perfect, analysts who discount these particular issues do so at their company's peril. In making these judgments, the analyst must rely on less formal sources of information, especially casual interviews and observations. Above all, he or she should listen carefully to his or her intuition, for often therein lies the answer.

DEVELOPING STRATEGY

Management accountants and financial analysts can use the Business Assessment Model to enhance the value of their work, particularly when they are involved in business combinations, debt or equity funding, capital investments, and new corporate ventures. The model synthesizes data on the core business, the market, competition, operations, historical performance, and management to provide a holistic assessment of a business, regardless of its type industry, or economic sector. Although analysts' contributions traditionally have been limited to accounting and financial issues, it is imprudent to use financial information in a vacuum, particularly in an increasingly competitive business environment. Understanding the elements that drive financial information is crucial. Further, as accounting and finance managers increasingly are called upon to develop and execute corporate strategy, they must go beyond accounting and finance to ensure that strategic business decisions are optimized.

STRUCTURING COMPENSATION TO ACHIEVE BETTER FINANCIAL RESULTS

Stock-based compensation and bonus plans boost relative financial results, according to a new study. In fact, the more incentive pay, the better a company and its employees perform.

By Nancy Thorley Hill, CHA, CPA and Kevin T. Stevens, CPA

Is incentive compensation tied to corporate performance a windfall for executives or an effective pay system that leads to superior financial results? That's essentially what we sought to learn in a research study we completed recently. We analyzed eight years of data covering compensation packages of executives at 161 U.S.-domiciled companies and corresponding financial results of those companies. The companies were all listed on U.S. stock exchanges. They came from every industry except utilities and financial institutions.

Our conclusion? Incentive compensation does work—and works well. Here are some highlights of our study:

- As the amount of compensation pegged to corporate financial performance rises as a percent of overall compensation, the company's return on equity tends to climb in direct proportion—above the average return on equity of its industry.

- Paying a higher percentage of compensation in cash salaries doesn't lead to superior corporate performance.

- There's a direct positive correlation between the amount of unexercised stock options a CEO holds and the corporate performance of his or her firm relative to an industry peer group.

- Increasing the percentage of incentive-based rewards appears to increase relative returns at all levels of compensation.

- Just holding stock options leads to superior employee motivation.

THE STUDY'S PURPOSE

The 1990s saw vast increases in executive compensation because of significant increases in both the number of stock options granted and their value. But critics who complained that executive pay was excessive and that stock options didn't work lamented that stock-based compensation did not incent executives to outperform their competitors. Instead, they claimed that compensation from options was due only to a rising stock market.

We sought to resolve this argument. We wanted to learn exactly what the relationship is between executive compensation and corporate performance. In particular, we sought to understand what elements of compensation lead to superior corporate performance relative to a company's industry peers. Also, we wanted to learn if bonus plans motivate managers to outperform their competitors. And, conversely, what effect do fixed salaries have on corporate performance?

It isn't enough to measure performance absolutely; it must be relative to a company's peer group of firms. Executives may know how their pay compares to counterparts at competitor firms. What they probably don't know—and what we tried to discern—was whether their, or their competitors', compensation packages led to comparable, inferior, or superior results. The study also sought to go beyond compensation benchmarking in terms of job function or industry to find out the relationship of specific elements of compensation to corporate performance by industry.

Until recently, the lack of publicly available compensation data made a comparative analysis of relative managerial compensation and relative corporate performance difficult. But recent reforms requiring more information to be disclosed in annual proxy statements enabled us to compare and analyze components of executive compensation relative to competing firms.

By combining information about the structure of compensation packages with data on corporate stock returns over time, we were able to determine which elements of compensation led to superior corporate performance. The results provided empirical evidence of which compensation components motivated managers to outdo their competitors.

ANALYZING THE RESULTS

In undertaking this study, we examined proxy statements of 161 publicly traded firms from 1991 through 1998 to determine the amount of annual salary, bonus, and current and prior stock option grants for the CEO of each firm. We used a relative measure of corporate performance: the firm's annual stock return minus the industry return. This enabled us to identify those firms which had returns above, below, and similar to their competitors. Because detailed information of the compensation packages of all managers isn't publicly available, we used the CEO's compensation as a proxy for upper management's actual compensation and its structure.

Table 1 reports the average overall total compensation and compensation components of CEOs in the sample and their average compensation components by year. It also shows that the firms had, on average, an annual stock return of 17% from 1991 to 1998. As widely reported in the press, our study showed CEOs were well compensated, with $2.6 million in total compensation on average per year and $1.3 million in average stock option grants per year. Meanwhile, the average CEO held $6.8 million in unexercised stock options.

We take a step beyond Table 1 in Table 2 to show the components of compensation—cash salary, bonus, and stock options—in terms of low-, middle-, and high-performing companies in their respective industries. Table 2 reports that the average relative returns for the low-, middle-, and high-performing groups over the eight-year period are -34%, -1%, and 36%, respectively. Probably the most interesting comparison is between the low- and high-performing firms. Although the sales of these firms are similar, indicating they're somewhat the same size, the ratio of compensation components differs. CEOs of low-performing firms have about 60% of their compensation in fixed salaries and 40% in incentives (bonus and stock option grants), whereas high performers have almost exactly the opposite. Roughly 40% of compensation is fixed salary, and the rest is incentive pay.

Furthermore, Table 2 reports the value of unexercised stock options granted in prior years by firm performance. Notice that CEOs of the highest-performing firms have far more wealth—nearly five times as much—tied up in unexercised stock options than managers of low-performing firms. Thus, the data in Table 2 supports the notion that as annual incentive-based compensation increases, so does relative firm performance.

DESIGNING PAY PACKAGES

Shareholders, directors, and managers can find guidance within the study's outcome on how to design and structure employee pay packages.

The decision on how much and in what form to compensate CEOs and other top managers is crucial to the success of the business. The results of our study support compensation consultants' points of view. They contend that increasing the proportion of compensation based on contingent rewards (i.e., bonuses or stock options) better motivates managers to perform as desired, compared to relying on fixed rewards (i.e., salaries). A key question to resolve is the ratio of incentive compensation.

Essentially, companies can pay managers with fixed salaries, bonuses, or stock options in varying amounts or percentages. Bonus and stock option plans incorporate incentives to improve current (and in the case of options, future) performance, while salaries are fixed awards regardless of current performance.

Bonuses, which are after-the-fact rewards for attaining this year's goals, provide goal-oriented motivation throughout the year. Stock options, unlike bonus plans and salaries, do not result in cash payments in the year they're granted. Still, the executive knows he or she has received an option grant, so the option grant should affect behavior. It should motivate the holder to try to increase share price currently and in the future through his or her individual performance. In contrast, paying a higher percentage of compensation in the form of salaries does not lead to superior corpo-

Table 1:* CEO Pay Packages

	Overall Average	1991	1992	1993	1994	1995	1996	1997	1998
Total Compensation	$2,676,789	$1,640,822	$1,787,551	$1,986,288	$2,326,067	$2,498,329	$3,105,407	$ 4,969,740	$ 3,655,753
Salary [a]	$ 769,358	$ 537,729	$ 578,236	$ 663,740	$ 636,722	$ 661,191	$ 748,658	$1,502,191	$ 967,388
Bonus [b]	$ 588,607	$ 319,338	$ 412,365	$ 461,142	$ 557,557	$ 618,818	$ 764,730	$ 854,454	$ 807,335
Stock Option Grants [c]	$1,299,646	$ 764,724	$ 796,950	$ 861,405	$1,131,781	$1,218,319	$1,476,289	$ 2,585,081	$1,869,137
Unexercised Options [d]	$6,800,832	N.A.	$3,439,270	$2,868,765	$2,917,125	$4,335,428	$7,799,367	$10,864,886	$15,898,607
Sales [e]	$4,537 MM	$4,053 MM	$4,075 MM	$4,042 MM	$4,229 MM	$4,414 MM	$4,834 MM	$ 5,722 MM	$5,166 MM
Annual Return	17%	26%	15%	16%	4%	20%	22%	28%	3%
Relative Return [f]	0%	-18%	-3%	-3%	8%	-3%	6%	11%	5%

* 161 firms analyzed   [a] Salary + Other Cash   [b] Bonus + Long-Term Incentive Plans
[c] Black-Scholes value of stock options + current Restricted Stock Awards (actual shares)
[d] Value of unexercised option granted previously   [e] Sales in millions   [f] Annual firm rate of return minus industry return

Table 2:* When Cash *Isn't* King

Low.performing firms have about a 60:40 ratio of fixed salary to incentive pay; high-performing firms have the opposite.

	Low Performers	Middle Performers	High Performers
Relative Return [a]	-34%	-1%	36%
Annual Return	11%	14%	47%
Salary [b] as a percentage of Total Compensation	58%	43%	41%
Bonus [c] as a percentage of Total Compensation	16%	25%	26%
Stock Option Grants [d] as a percentage of Total Compensation	25%	32%	33%
Unexercised Options	$2,610,000	$4,090,000	$12,800,000
Sales	$3,405,300,000	$5,732,700,000	$4,462,800,000

* 161 firms analyzed; over 400 statistical observations for each performance category

[a] Annual firm rate of return minus industry return

[b] Salary + Other Cash

[c] Bonus + Long-term Incentive Plans

[d] Black-Scholes value of stock options + Restricted Stock Awards (actual shares)

[e] Value of unexercised options granted previously

rate performance.

Moreover, if relative corporate performance is more important than simply firm performance in the aggregate, then compensation plans should also include relative rewards. Firms should consider granting bonuses and stock options that are based on outperforming the competition. For example, instead of setting option prices at the fair market value of the stock at the date of grant (as was typically done in the 1990s), firms can motivate managers to outdo the market or their competitors by tying the option price to future industry growth.

Finally, it appears that just holding stock options motivates superior performance. That means firms should consider granting options with extended vesting periods.